Elementary Physical Education

Growing Through Movement

Fourth Edition

Robert G. Davis, Ph.D.
Virginia Commonwealth University

Larry D. Isaacs, Ph.D.
Wright State University

Hunter Textbooks Inc.

Inquiries should be addressed to:

Hᴛi Hunter Textbooks Inc.

701 Shallowford Street
Winston-Salem, NC 27101

Contents

PREFACE

"Now more than ever" is a quotation which is often heard in politics. It certainly has a nice ring to it, but how does it apply to elementary physical education? The trend that began in the 20th Century continues in the 21st; children's fitness continues to decline. So "now more than ever" is a rallying cry which should be heeded by all educators and not just physical educators. Significant increase in the incidence of childhood obesity; declining levels of flexibility; increased consumption of fatty foods; and declining levels of activity are all signs of the times which have implications to the future health of the Nation. Children represent the largest percent increase in obesity in a nation which leads the world in overweight and obese individuals.

The decline in physical activity along with the reduction in physical education programs were well documented in the 1996 Surgeon General's report, _Physical Activity and Health_. The report reflects the lack of commitment among educators and the population in general for physical education. The consequence of this trend should be obvious. During the 1990s, the central theme in education was "back to basics," and in the eyes of educators, those "basics" do not include physical education. The "mind/body" concept so long valued by philosophers has been replaced with the desire to achieve in the core subjects of language arts, math, science, and social studies/history. Tremendous pressure is being place on teachers to produce results via test scores in these core subject areas. In Virginia, for example, the state's Standards of Accreditation requires that 75% of the school day be devoted to the core subjects. Art, music, health and physical education, and vocational education vie for the remaining 25%. The "back to basics" theme has caused a reduction in physical education programs and a corresponding decreased activity among children.

Another important factor in a child's fitness is their parents. Parental involvement is often cited as the most important factor in a child's education. The 2000 census documents the significant increase in single parent homes and homes where both parents work. Children left to raise themselves tend to watch a great deal of TV while consuming the high fat food which they see advertised. Activity is not part of very many children's lives. Although the politicians as well as the parents want to blame educators for the educational decline, the evidence clearly points to home environment. Think about it, children spend five hours in school and nineteen hours at home. There are no easy answers, and we do not profess to have any magic solution, however, this book does provide numerous activities to get children moving as well as suggestions about how to get them active. Until we get the necessary parental concern and involvement, the health and well being of children will continue to decline.

Another factor which must be considered for this edition is the veritable explosion of the internet or world wide web - web forwshort. The first place many people now go when seeking information is the web. Although it is a convenient source, the information may or may not be accurate. Anyone can post anything they wish on the medium. Who controls it? Who monitors it? The answer to both questions is no one. Will it replace textbooks? Probably not, but textbooks may end up on the web. There are no plans to put this text on the web, but there are references to web sites. The authors recognize the value of the web in providing useful information to those who will work or are currently working with children.

Although the emphasis may change, the goals of elementary physical education rarely do. The purpose of elementary physical education is to develop a healthy, efficiently moving human being who feels good about him/herself. We believe the emphasis should be on the whole child.

No matter what is the emphasis, however, the content and teaching approaches must be sensitive to the child's self-concept development. No other educational area is more important to the child's future success and well-being than self-concept. We believe that physical education's dynamic nature can do more good or more harm to the child's self-concept than any other subject area, and the teacher is the key element.

Self-concept, for example, is affected by the teacher's methods. There are many positive methods which can be used to teach physical education; there are, unfortunately, also many negative methods. There is no one right way to teach, but there are several learning principles which every teacher should practice no matter what teaching style is used. Many of these principles focus on self-concept development. These principles, their implications, and ways to apply them are presented in Chapter 5.

Even though they are so important to self-concept development, those responsible for physical education are often not adequately prepared. Many classroom teachers (who frequently have had only one preparatory course) are responsible for teaching physical education. One course is hardly sufficient to prepare someone to plan and teach this vital subject effectively. Further, the classroom teacher receives tremendous pressure to produce in academic areas such as reading and mathematics, and physical education is seldom a priority area.

Realizing who is often responsible for physical education and what they are looking for in a textbook, we have tried to meet their needs along with those of the specialist. Many new activities, therefore, have been added; the emphasis is on developmental activities and games rather than low participation games such as Duck, Duck, Goose and relays; both the games and activities (each marked accordingly) use the same, easy-to-follow format. The book has also been organized by developmental areas which are further divided into four age levels: four to six years of age, six to eight, eight to ten, and ten to twelve years of age.

In Section One, we deal with basic considerations such as physical education's role in the total school curriculum, growth and development, motor learning, assessment, the teacher, control and discipline, the learning environment, curriculum development, legal liability including playground safety, and fitness and nutrition. These chapters establish a foundation upon which the curriculum can be built. Considerable emphasis is given to the development of a positive, safe learning environment in which the teacher uses child-centered teaching approaches. Since our philosophy emphasizes positive self-concept development, one can legitimately ask why it is not given a separate chapter. Our feeling is that self-concept is so integral to everything in education, there would be too much overlap with a separate chapter. The reader will find self-concept mentioned frequently throughout Section One.

Section Two features curriculum materials and activities. Included is a section on the growth and development characteristics of each of four age groups and their implications for selecting activities. Also included are basic movement competencies, integrated activities, manipulative activities, body awareness, creativity, rhythms and dance, games, fitness activities and programs, activities for children with special needs, and individual and team sports. The overall emphasis is the development of an efficiently moving human being who is healthy and happy. Where appropriate, the chapters are organized by age groups; these groups are suggestions only and many activities can be done successfully across age groups. We feel, however, that curriculum development must be a planned sequence of activities with each activity building on the next. Using the same activity across many age groups, therefore, is only appropriate when it meets the children's needs in each group.

Low organizational games that are featured in Chapter 18 are frequently criticized as being inappropriate for elementary physical education, but we feel that games which have developmental value should be included. Games with low participation level, however, are not recommended. Nearly all the games included in this book are developmental. To be classified as developmental, the game or activity must have all the children moving nearly all the time, and the game must be used to accomplish a physical education objective. Low organizational games can help a child's development as well as provide leisure time activity, but no more than 10% of the curriculum for any grade level should be low organizational games.

The final section, Other Considerations, includes competition, equipment, and cognitive games and activities. Although the chapter entitled "Cognitive Learning Through Movement" is not a part of physical education, we feel it will be helpful to the classroom teacher when dealing with other subject areas. Even though these cognitive activities are not a part of physical education, they do include movement, and the more children move, the better their chances for developing motor ability.

I. Basic Considerations

The Foundations of Elementary Physical Education

1

After completing this chapter, the student should be able to:

1. List at least seven goals of physical education.
2. Draw the triangle in figure 1.2 and describe the importance of each component.
3. Distinguish the difference between the educational domains by describing each and giving examples of physical education goals in each.
4. Describe the importance of the affective domain as it relates to elementary physical education.
5. List at least five ways a teacher can improve a child's self-concept.
6. List and describe at least four trends in elementary physical education.
7. Define the key terms listed below.

Key Terms

Affective domain
Attitudes
Body image
Cognitive domain
Concept
Developmental activity
Educational gymnastics
Games
Goals
Health-related fitness
Integrated activities
Kinesthetic awareness

Liability
Motor fitness
Movement education
Multi-culturalism
Objectives
Perceptual-motor program
Physical education
Principles of learning
Proprioceptive feedback
Psychomotor domain
Self-concept
Self-testing activity

This book is based upon the premise that the goal of elementary physical education is to develop a healthy, efficiently moving child who has a good self-concept, a positive attitude about movement and fitness, and has knowledge about his/her body. To do that, the physical education program must be a *planned* sequence of activities designed to provide each child an equal opportunity to reach his or her full potential physically, socially, emotionally and, to a certain extent, intellectually. The key word in the definition is *planned*. This planning requires a systematic approach to curriculum development: (1) establishing short and long term goals, (2) writing measurable objectives, (3) authentic assessment using the objectives, and (4) selecting appropriate teaching methods and activities to meet the child's needs.

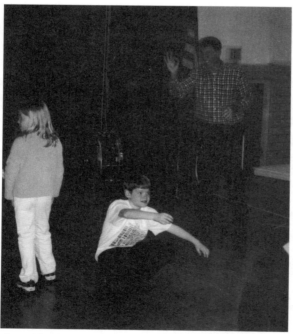

A positive learning environment is important in helping children develop a positive self-concept.

In order to accomplish the goal of physical education, the teacher must use methods which create a positive learning environment. It can safely be said that physical education can do more harm or more good to a child's self-concept than any other subject area. The dynamic and very visible nature of physical education provides an opportunity for this positive or negative development; it is not possible to hide physical performance. The teaching approach often determines which direction self-concept development takes. When considering the fragile nature of a child's self-concept, it makes a positive teaching approach even more important. In quizzing persons about their physical education experiences, physically-skilled individuals usually have a more favorable impression of physical education than the less skilled who often cite experiences in physical education as their most embarrassing.

Physical performance is often embarrassing to the less skilled child.

This chapter is a presentation of several of the factors which serve as a basis for elementary physical education. Included are physical education goals, the three educational domains with particular emphasis on the affective domain, history and trends, and terminology.

GOALS OF PHYSICAL EDUCATION

Goals serve as the foundation for the activities selected as well as the teaching styles used. They are determined, to a great extent, by the teacher's educational philosophy. In physical development, for example, some physical educators emphasize motor learning while others favor health-related fitness. For purposes of this book, the emphasis is on the total development of the child with emphasis on self-concept development as well as those factors important to the child's physical health.

Figure 1.1 is a presentation (in no particular order) of some of the physical education goals which the authors feel are most important.

Figure 1.1. Goals of Physical Education

Psychomotor	*Affective*	*Cognitive*
Physiological Fitness	Self-concept	Creativity
Motor Fitness	Honesty and sportsmanship	Problem-solving
Manipulative skills	Sharing	Body image
Locomotor movement	Respect for authority	Directional terms
Nonlocomotor movement	Respect for self and others	Rules and regulations
Balance	Leadership	Knowledge of
Kinesthetic awareness	Self-discipline	Fitness
Tumbling and gymnastics	Attitudes toward	Health
Rhythmics	Activity	Safety
Relaxation	Fitness	
Sports skills	Health	
Lead-up games to sports	Safety	

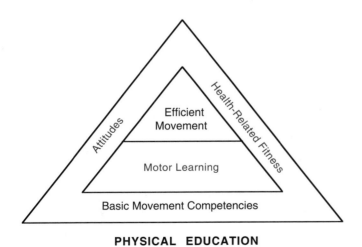

PHYSICAL EDUCATION

Figure 1.2. Purpose of Physical Education

A triangle which reflects the purpose of physical education is shown in Figure 1.2. Basic movement competencies serve as the foundation. The movement goal is an efficiently-moving human being. The other two sides, health-related fitness and attitude development, also serve as foundations. For the movement activities within the triangle to be effective, all three sides must be strong. The movements offered should give the child an opportunity to experience every way his or her body and body parts can move at various speeds, different forces, and at all levels in both individual and common space. The child should also experience all the ways his/her body can manipulate an object. With these experiences, it is then possible to develop more specific skills.

Movement is the foundation of physical education.

Positive attitudes support the triangle's one side. If the values of physical education are to last, a positive attitude towards self, activities, and fitness is absolutely essential. It is possible, for example, to force a child to become physically fit, but if the child hates it, there is little chance he or she will pursue it throughout life. Movement and fitness should not be for a season or a year; they must be a life-style, and attitudes play the biggest role in establishing a lifelong commitment.

The third side is health-related fitness, which is an essential physical education goal. The five health-fitness components are cardiovascular efficiency, muscular strength, muscular endurance, flexibility, and body composition which will be covered under chapter 10.

A positive self-concept is essential to a happy child!

Physical Fitness is a major goal of physical education.

THE EDUCATIONAL DOMAINS

The three educational domains are affective, psychomotor, and cognitive. The following is not intended as an exhaustive review of the subject but instead concentrates on how physical education relates to each domain. The two following examples may help to clarify the domains:

1. An individual is driving a car (the ability to drive falls under the psychomotor domain) when he sees a stop sign (the ability to read and understand the sign is covered by the cognitive domain). The decision to stop is determined by his attitude toward safety and his own health (health and safety practices are attitudes are in the affective domain).

2. During a gymnastics unit, a child is doing a headstand (psychomotor). The child knows (cognitive) that a spotter is necessary prior to doing the headstand. Whether the child makes sure a spotter is present reflects the child's attitude toward safety (affective).

Praise is important!

THE AFFECTIVE DOMAIN

Even though it is potentially the most important, the affective domain has not received the attention it deserves. As a result, such affective areas as ethics, honesty, self-respect, and respect for others have become problems. Values and attitudes can and should be taught.

There are many things a teacher can do which will positively influence affective development. A discussion on honesty and safety can be effective; the teaching technique selected and discipline techniques are important; the teacher's appearance and nonverbal behavior can also play a role; and finally, physical education must be fun. Good teachers who show enthusiasm, have good class preparation, use a positive, humanistic approach to teaching and discipline, and demonstrate dedication, will most likely have a positive influence on a child's affective education.

Although planning is essential, unplanned moments must be anticipated so they can be dealt with effectively. How will the teacher deal with fighting, cheating, booing, and name-calling? The difference between the average teacher and the superior teacher is often how well these unplanned moments are handled. Merely stopping a fight or telling students not to boo is insufficient.

Goals and Objectives

The following broadly-stated affective goals are followed by behaviorally-stated objectives:

1. *Goal:* Students will demonstrate good sportsmanship.
   Objective: Following a game of basketball no student will boo the opposition.
2. *Goal:* Students will have a positive attitude toward physical education.
   Objective: Given an anonymous questionnaire, at least 90 percent of the children will rate the physical education program as good to excellent on a scale of excellent, good, average, fair, and poor.
3. *Goal:* Students will enjoy participating in physical activity.
   Objective: During the year, at least 60 percent of the children will voluntarily participate in an intramural sport.

Physical Education and the Affective Domain

Opportunities for sharing, honesty, self-discipline, and interpersonal relationships occur in nearly every physical education period. Many affective incidents can be sensitive, and how the teacher handles them will determine their positive or negative effect upon a child's self-concept.

Self-Concept Development

Although all affective areas are important, by far the most critical is self-concept development—how a child feels about him/herself. This book is based on the premise that a major educational goal must be for each child to develop a positive self-concept no matter what his or her ability.

As mentioned earlier, physical education can do more good or harm to a child's self-concept than probably any other subject area. The dynamic nature of physical education provides numerous opportunities for interpersonal interaction; unlike cognitive ability, physical performance cannot be hidden. It is also well know that obese and overweight children as well as those with physical deformities are often ridiculed by other children. At the same time, it is also known that those who perform well physically are more readily accepted by their peers. Several factors determine the positive or negative effect of physical education.

Praise and Criticism. One of these factors is the amount of praise and criticism. A good teacher will praise rather than criticize. During the formative years, praise and criticism are critical. Children seek adult approval, and the teacher's response to behavior, both positive and negative, will, therefore, significantly influence the child.

When it is necessary to correct behavior, it can be softened by "sandwiching the correction between two slices of praise." When anyone including a child gives his/her best effort, the first thing one wants to hear is a positive. An example may be seen in a ball-handling skill such as throwing with the wrong foot forward. The teacher might say, "You threw that ball very well. Have you tried doing it while stepping forward with the other foot? Try it that way and keep up the good work."

Respect. Children are human beings and should be treated accordingly. By giving children the same rights and courtesies we expect from them, we will see positive development.

Such things as "please" and "thank you" are expected from children; should they not also be expected from a teacher? Children should listen when the teacher speaks, and vice versa. Further, sarcasm has no place in teaching nor does the act of belittling children.

One way to show respect is to call children by name. There is nothing more beautiful in a language than one's name. Names are not always easy to learn or remember, particularly for a physical educator who may have 800 or more students per week. Photographs can help. Using a 33-mm or digital camera, children can be photographed in two rows of about 10 or 12 children per row. When using the 35-mm camera, a 4 X 6 print works best; names can be written on a strip of paper and taped under or above the faces. If a digital camera is used, the pictures can be put on a computer and names can be electronically placed on the photo prior to printing. This picture technique is quick and inexpensive. More importantly, the teacher will be able to call children by name and communicate more effectively with parents and other teachers.

Discipline. When discipline is necessary, it should be done in a humanistic manner. (See chapter 6.)

Activities. The activity offered can also influence a child's self-concept. Children who are successful at activities are more likely to develop a positive self-concept. The key is to have activities which are challenging but not frustrating. At the same time, they must be activities which allow for a wide ability range so children at various developmental levels can experience success. In using

Using photographs to learn children's names.

this child-centered approach, the teacher must know the growth and development characteristics within any age group as well as the variations within a particular class (see chapter 11).

Communication. Although obviously important to interpersonal relationships and self-concept development, communication skills do not seem to receive sufficient attention in teacher preparation courses. So often teachers talk down to children or focus almost exclusively on verbal communication without regard for the nonverbal messages being transmitted. A great deal is said through facial expressions, posture, and eye contact. There is evidence that up to 70% of the message in communication is determined by nonverbal behavior. Too frequently, a teacher's nonverbal behavior unwittingly transmits negative feelings. (See chapter 5.)

By using videotape, teachers can evaluate their communication ability. The ready availability of taping equipment allows for evaluation of this vital area. Self-evaluation should not threaten a teacher. The good teacher, concerned about the child's self-concept development, must not allow self-doubt to interfere with self-improvement.

Little Things. The expression "little things mean a lot" is important when dealing with children. Things which seem unimportant to adults often are viewed as "big things" to children. Noticing a new dress or new hair style, giving responsibility, or expressing concern following a child's absence are just a few of the things that can make a difference.

Love. Love is an essential item to successful teaching. Love of teaching and love of children go a long way in developing a child's self-concept. Many well-meaning individuals presently teaching elementary school do not like teaching and/or have an obvious disdain for certain children; such feelings are obvious to the children and affect their development. This book is designed for teachers who love the profession and desire to help all children grow and develop through the medium of movement.

THE PSYCHOMOTOR DOMAIN

The psychomotor domain deals with all physical activity such as movement competency, fitness, and sports skills. Many physical education objectives fall into this category. To accomplish physical education goals and objectives, the activities selected should have all the children moving nearly all the time.

Goals and Objectives (Examples)

The following goals are followed by behaviorally-stated objectives:

1. *Goal:* The children will be physically fit.
   Objective: By year's end, at least 80 percent of the students will score above the 50th percentile on all fitness test items.
2. *Goal:* The children will develop rhythmic ability.
   Objective: During a rhythmic activity, all the children will move appropriately to the varying tempos, fast to fast music and slow to slow music.
3. *Goal:* The children will develop manipulative ability.
   Objective: By the end of the class, the child will be able to throw a seven-inch sponge ball higher than his/her head and catch it using two hands at least five times in a row.

Physical Education and the Psychomotor Domain

Although the psychomotor development is not the only aspect of physical education, it is a major factor in activity selection. As indicated under the affective domain discussion, it would be a mistake to view physical education as only the psychomotor domain. As has been indicated throughout this chapter, physical education, as it relates to psychomotor development, is concerned with developing a *healthy, efficiently-moving* human being. *Sports skills* are included in the curriculum for those capable of learning them, and are necessary for those wishing to participate in sports. Such participation can help individuals maintain and, in some cases, improve fitness. It can also help develop a positive self-concept.

THE COGNITIVE DOMAIN

Of the three domains, the cognitive is often the most familiar to readers. It deals with thought processes such as problem-solving and creativity. Bloom and his associates (1956) organized this domain into cognitive ability levels. The lowest level, knowledge, is followed in ascending order by comprehension, application, analysis, synthesis, and the highest level, evaluation. Information such as fitness knowledge, rules and regulations, and safety knowledge are in the cognitive domain.

Goals and Objectives (Examples)

Each of the following goals is followed by a more specifically stated behavioral objective:

1. *Goal:* The children will learn fitness information.
   Objective: By the end of the year, all the children will be able to name one exercise for each of the five health-related fitness components.
2. *Goal:* Students will know the reasons for being physically fit.
   Objective: By the end of the year, every child will be able to give two reasons for being physically fit.
3. *Goal:* Students will develop creativity.
   Objective: By the end of the gymnastics unit, at least 80% of the students will be able to create an original gymnastics routine which includes at least six different stunts.

Physical Education and the Cognitive Domain

There is a body of cognitive physical education knowledge which children should know. *Health fitness,* for example, should be taught along with other information such as *rules and regulations, safety, and sport strategy.* A child should know about his/her *body,* how it functions, and how to care for it. With the obvious need for more attention to children's fitness, this cognitive information should be a significant curriculum component.

Along with knowledge, physical education's dynamic nature provides an excellent laboratory for developing *problem-solving* and *creative ability.* These are important cognitive abilities which should be included in every subject area. It must be cautioned, however, that the problem-solving and creative activities offered in physical education are accomplished through movement.

Movement development must not be sacrificed in order to develop the cognitive domain during physical education time. This is not to say there may not be times when there are health and safety discussions, but whenever possible, the information should be presented while children are actively involved in movement. The teacher, for example, could discuss the importance of certain exercises while the children are actually doing them.

Another area where physical education can make a contribution to cognitive development is through *integrated activities.* The primary purpose of integrated activities is a physical education movement objective. Using integrated activities, it is possible to reinforce information from another subject area such as language arts, math, or science without detracting from the primary objective. These activities are described in more detail in chapter 17.

HISTORICAL PERSPECTIVE AND TRENDS

Over the years, many physical educators have attempted to gain acceptance in the educational community by suggesting that a primary purpose of physical education can and should be cognitive development. Numerous articles have appeared in professional literature touting physical education as medium for teaching or reinforcing language arts, math, science, or social studies concepts. Although movement is an excellent medium for teaching academic subjects, its inclusion in physical education normally takes away from the primary movement goals. Physical educators do not have to justify their existence or importance by including academic subjects in the physical education program.

Understanding the history of physical education can help in curriculum design. Over the years there have been many changes in elementary physical education. Until the 1960s, the primary focus of elementary physical education was low organizational games and team sports. Few elementary schools had professional physical educators, relying instead on the classroom teacher. Where there were physical educators, they tended to be itinerant teachers who traveled among many schools. Serving as classroom teacher advisors, these traveling teachers often served six or more schools and hundreds of students. During the 1970s and 1980s, there was a movement toward more elementary physical education specialists who were trained in a developmental approach which included more activities and fewer games. In practice, however, low organizational games and exercises were still the most prevalent components

Until the 1960s, the physical education curriculum focused on low organizational games.

in elementary physical education programs. During the 1990s there was a growing body of evidence which strongly suggests the need to have more elementary physical education programs which emphasize health-related fitness. With the start of the 21st Century, however, we see a nation concerned almost exclusively with the need to emphasize cognitive development to the exclusion of such subjects as physical education, art, and music. We also see a decline in physical educators at all levels. As in the past, the main responsibility for teaching elementary physical education falls on the ill-prepared and overworked classroom teacher.

The Family Unit

The breakup of the family unit which began in the 1970s has had a profound influence on education. Single family homes, latch key (unsupervised) children, and illegitimate births are just a few of the factors which have influenced both children's and adult's behavior. Within the schools there has been a decline in discipline which can be directly linked to the lack of parental support. There is also less involvement of parents in schools as well as less valuing of education by society in general.

Federal Regulations

Education is a state function, but the Federal Government continues to have a major influence on public education. When thinking about this influence, most people probably focus on the "Title" programs or Public Laws such as 94-142, but with the "Goals 2000" initiative as well as other federal programs, public education is rapidly coming under federal control. There is probably no school system in America which does not receive significant federal money, and with money comes control. It is very likely that public education will become a federal function during the 21st Century. What impact this will have on education as local control and states' rights are diminished is yet to be determined. Suffice to say that many federal programs are and have been of questionable value.

Movement Education

With more specifically prepared physical educators in the 1960s, there was a swing toward a developmental approach focusing on movement competencies. Borrowed from the British infant schools and termed "movement education," the focus was on motor development with the desired outcome being efficiently moving human beings. The curriculum borrowed heavily from the dance discipline, and is still popular in Britain.

Numerous physical educators and others involved in dance began referring to themselves as movement educators. Rejecting the old games approach, they focused almost exclusively on the aesthetics of movement along with its perceived relationship to the cognitive domain. Games and health-related fitness were seldom program objectives. Under the movement education approach, developmental movement activities in which all the

Movement educators focused on the asthetics of movement.

Educational Gymnastics

Another approach begun in the 1970s was educational gymnastics, which allows children to explore movement on apparatus. In educational gymnastics, benches, poles, boxes, and other equipment (often interconnected) are used to explore ways to balance, vault, or travel. An exploratory teaching approach using questions or problems to solve through movement is used. A typical question might be, "How many ways can you travel across or around a piece of equipment?" Unlike gymnastics, there are no spotters or explanations/demonstrations. This approach allows a child to solve the problem at his or her own ability level. Having seen formal gymnastics in other settings, children often tend to be imitative.

It is the similarity between formal and educational gymnastic performance and equipment where legal problems arise. Well-meaning teachers unwittingly put themselves into liability situations by practicing educational gymnastics without establishing appropriate safety guidelines. In court cases involving injuries, some teachers who practice educational gymnastics have been successfully sued. The formal approach, however, has specific rules and guidelines which can be taught, and the teacher, through knowledge, can protect him/herself. The open-ended educational gymnastics approach, however, is more difficult to teach and can be harder to legally defend.

children participated replaced such low participation games as "Duck, Duck, Goose" and "Squirrels In Trees." Developmental activities had all the children moving all the time.

In the 1970s, the emphasis on cognitive development greatly influenced movement educators. It became obvious that many teachers mistakenly felt that a primary physical education objective was to teach academic information from such subject areas as language arts and math. Traditional physical education content, particularly in fitness, was de-emphasized. Researchers have found that over the 20 to 25 years that movement education dominated the curriculum, there was a significant decrease in fitness. (See chapter 10.)

Liability

A growing concern among all teachers, no matter what the approach used, is liability. A slow trend during the 1970s and early 1980s has become a litigation deluge during the "It's Not My Fault" decade of the 1990s. Some people cite the decline in values while others point to the number of lawyers. Whatever the reason, teachers have become a popular target. In the past, teachers

"Running for Life" (appendix C) is a program promoting fitness through running and jogging.

Integrated activities and games, such as "Crows and Cranes," can be used to reinforce another subject.

only had to worry about injuries among the children; liability now focuses as much on affective issues, such as harm to the child's self-concept, as it does on physical injuries. Education it seems is being faulted for all society's ills. Since "knowledge is power," a teacher should know the information presented in chapter 9, Physical Education and the Law.

Movement Themes

Another trend is the "movement themes" approach which promotes the development of fundamental movement and skills as well as learning the concepts underlying both. Fundamental movements include such things as walking, running, skipping, etc.; while skills include throwing, punting, striking, etc. The movement concepts include relationships, quality of movement (force, time, space, and level), and body awareness. Although the term has appeared during the 1990s, it merely reflects what elementary physical educators have been trying to do for years, develop locomotor and nonlocomotor as well as manipulative ability. The concepts underlying skill themes is questionable. The approach suggests that skill development is dependent upon understanding the cognitive concepts associated with them. Since the themes approach is designed for children prior to their ability to understand concepts (nine years of age), it is hard to justify educationally. Children develop basic abilities through movement not cognition. The more cognitive thought during skilled movement, the more awkward the movement.

Fitness

Children's declining fitness levels can be linked directly to decreased activity and increased consumption of high fat foods. Chil-

dren, contrary to popular belief, are not spontaneously active. Many reasons are cited for this inactivity including single parent homes, crime, TV, and video games to name a few. Of these, television is probably the biggest culprit. TV has become the focal point in almost every home, and with the advent of cable and satellite dishes, there is no end to possible programs to watch. Few programs, however, are worth watching, and none require physical activity by the viewer. Also, people on TV tend to eat which can be a stimulus to the viewer. Also, the foods advertised during children's programing are usually high fat and/or high sugar foods.

Although one cause for the declining fitness levels is fairly well known, the solution is extremely difficult. Getting children to be more active and away from fatty food is not easy. With the reduction of physical education programs at all levels, the schools are of little help in reversing the trend. Many school cafeterias have high fat foods such as hamburgers, french fries, and pizza as part of the daily menu.

In those elementary physical education programs which do exist, the emphasis varies with some emphasizing fitness while others focus primarily on motor development. Nationally the trend is toward more focus on developing cardiovascular efficiency through aerobic activities such as running and jumping rope. No matter which philosophy prevails, very few of the physical education activities which are part of the curriculum require vigorous activity. In some cases schools conduct fitness activities or programs outside the normal physical education class. Two national programs, Jump Rope for Heart and Hoops for Heart, have helped focus attention on health-related fitness.

Developmental activities have all the children moving all the time.

Other programs, such as Running for Life which is featured in this text, have promoted fitness through running. The 1996 Surgeon General's report on *Physical Activity and Health*, hopefully, will have a significant influence on the fitness of children well into the 21st Century. Additional information on fitness and nutrition for children is covered in chapter 10.

Developmental Activities

Those recognizing the questionable value of low organizational games and sports have chosen to use developmental activities. These activities are selected for their developmental value. Like any other subject, children's ability is assessed and then activities are chosen to help the child reach their full potential. A developmental activity has all the children moving nearly all the time. Fitness activities as well as rhythmics, self-testing, creativity, movement, story plays, and sports skills would be classified as developmental. Developmental activities should be the primary means by which movement competencies and sports skills are accomplished. In surveying current elementary physical education programs, however, low participation games and sports still play a major role in the curriculum.

Integrated Activities and Games

Integrated activities and games in which both psychomotor as well as cognitive objectives are accomplished have also increased over the years. These developmental physical education activities and games reinforce another subject such as language arts, mathematics, or social studies while accomplishing a movement objective. Integrated activities must have as their primary purpose the accomplishment of a physical education objective with the academic component being secondary. As with any development activity or game, all of the children must be moving nearly all the time. Most story plays (chapter 17), for example, are integrated activities while a game such as "Crows and Cranes" can be adapted to make it integrated (page 254). Integrated activities and games are explained in greater depth in chapter 17.

Games

Although the trend has been toward fewer games, they still play a major role in most physical education programs. Knowledgeable physical educators have moved toward developmental games which, unlike most low organizational games, have all the children moving nearly all the time. A heavy emphasis on sports still dominates the upper elementary physical education program. Competitive games emphasizing winning and losing still appear frequently in most physical education programs.

The Internet

The internet, sometimes referred to as the "World Wide Web," "The Information Highway," or just the "Web" has become a popular communication medium, and has the potential during the 21st century of being the primary communication network. The internet is basically an interconnection of millions of computers all over the world, and when connected to a host computer through a service provider (AOL, Erols, AT&T, etc.), it is possible to communicate with anyone in the world using only a local phone line. With the microphone which comes with most computers, it is also possible to have voice communication with anyone who is on-line and also has a microphone; add a camera, and both voice and picture are possible.

The internet also can be a great source of information, but one must be cautious regarding any information found on this computer network. The internet is not regulated and allows anyone to post anything they wish, right or wrong. In viewing several web sites (sometimes called "pages"), these authors have found mostly low organization and low participation games listed on elementary physical education pages. Seldom have really good developmental activities been listed.

Multi-culturalism

During the 21st Century, it is obvious that the demographics of America will change dramatically. By the year 2020, Hispanic will be a dominate cultural force in the United States. In many parts of the country and in particular areas such as South Florida, Southern Texas, and Southern California, those speaking Spanish equaled or exceed those speaking English. The effect of this change can also be seen in the changing approach of public education.

Teachers must learn to appreciate and accept cultural differences among students. These differences, however, can be problematic when religion becomes a factor. With the separation of church and state in pubic education, meeting the needs of the diverse religious groups can be difficult.

TERMINOLOGY

Each profession has a language which must be understood for effective communication. Education is no different; unfortunately, educational terminology changes frequently, and many educators use the same words to communicate different ideas. The following definitions are provided to aid communication between the authors and the readers.

Body image is the knowledge one has of his or her body and is important to self-concept development.

Concept is a thought or opinion.

Development activity or game has a specific developmental objective and has all the children moving nearly all the time.

Educational gymnastics uses a problem-solving teaching approach and various apparatus to help develop the children's movement as well as problem-solving and creative abilities.

Games are competitive and include winning and losing.

Goals are general statements of purpose, which in education are usually long-term, semester or year.

Health-related or physiological fitness has five components: cardiovascular efficiency, muscular strength, muscular endurance, flexibility, and body composition; all of which are vital to a person's health.

Integrated activities or games have a physical education objective as the primary purpose and, at the same time, reinforce information from another subject area such as language arts, math, science, or social studies.

Internet which is sometimes referred to as the "World Wide Web" or just "Web" is a network of computers which allow for communication throughout the world. Anyone with a personal computer can subscribe to a "provider" which allows the individual to hook into a host computer which then connects him or her to all the other computers in the network.

Kinesthetic awareness is the knowledge of body parts in space and is dependent upon proprioceptive (sensory) feedback from the muscles; it is important in all movement activities.

Learning is a relatively permanent change in observable behavior which is inferred from performance, and can be attributed to practice and experience rather than maturation.

Motor fitness is composed of speed, coordination, balance, reaction time, and agility; all of which are important to motor performance but are not essential to one's physical health.

Movement education is a child-centered teaching approach in which the emphasis is on creativity, problem-solving, and the qualities of movement which include force, time (speed), space (direction), and level.

Objectives are statements of purpose which are expressed in behavioral terms. They are developed from goals and are usually accomplished in a short time period, lesson or unit, but can be used to express long-term behavioral changes such as attitudes.

Perceptual-motor programs are diagnostic and individualized motor development programs developed for children with cognitive learning difficulties. There is little evidence they affect intellectual ability.

Physical education is a planned sequence of activities designed to give each child an opportunity to reach his or her full potential, especially physically, socially, and emotionally.

Principles of learning are fundamental truths about how people learn and should be a part of every teacher's cognitive knowledge.

Proprioceptive feedback is sensory feedback from the muscles, which is important to kinesthetic awareness.

Self-concept is how an individual feels about himself or herself, and is probably the most important factor in education.

13

Self-testing activities are those activities which allow children to evaluate their own performance. Jumping rope, basketball shooting, target activities, and gymnastics are examples of self-testing activities.

Web - see "Internet" above

SUMMARY

This chapter dealt with foundations of elementary physical education with particular attention to goals, the educational domains, history and trends, and terminology. The goals included psychomotor, affective, and cognitive. The goal of physical education is the development of a healthy, efficiently moving child who has a good self-concept, a positive attitude about movement and fitness, and considerable knowledge about his or her body. Each of the three educational domains: psychomotor, affective, and cognitive—were discussed in detail, including their relationship to elementary physical education. In the history and trends section, various factors which have influenced the development of elementary physical education over the years were presented. The chapter ended with a section on the definition of terms.

REFERENCES AND SUGGESTED READINGS

Bloom, B., et al. *Taxonomy of Educational Objectives: Cognitive Domain.* New York: David McKay Co., Inc., 1956.

Boyce, A., and N. Markos. Elementary physical education as a part of a fine arts block. *JOPERD* 68:13-16, 1997.

Bredekamp, S. What is "developmentally appropriate" and why is it important? *JOPERD* 62:31-32, 1992.

Brustad, R. and K. Zehrung. Effects of daily vs. every-other day physical education instruction upon indices of physical fitness, motor skills, and psychological characteristics of third grade children. *Research Quarterly* (65) A-73, 1994.

Butler, L. Fair play: respect for all. *JOPERD*, (71) 32-34, 2000.

Butt, L. and M. Pahnos. Why we need a multi-cultural focus in our schools. *JOPERD* 66:48-53, 1995.

Carleton, B and T Henrich. Strategies for enhancing the performance of low-skilled students. *JOPERD*, 71: 29-31, 2000.

Chad, K, et.al., The effectiveness of the Canadian quality daily physical education program on school physical education. *Research Quarterly* (70) 55-64, 1999.

Chase, M. and G. Dummer. The role of sports as a social status determinant for children. *Research Quarterly* 63:418 - 424, 1992.

Cleland, F. and C. Pearse. Critical thinking in elementary physical education reflections on a year long study. *JOPERD*, 66: 31-38, 1995.

Connor, F. and G. Dummer. Teaching language concepts and labels to preschool children through physical education lessons. *Research Quarterly* (65) A-100,1994.

Faigenbaum, A. Strength training and children's health. *JOPERD*, 72: 24-30, 2001

Gibbons, S., et.al. Fair play for kids: effects on the moral development of children in physical education. *Research Quarterly* 65: 247-255, 1995.

Grineski, S. What is a truly developmentally appropriate physical education program for children? *JOPERD* 62:33-35, 1992.

Hornblower, M. *It takes a school. Time Magazine,* June 3, 1996, pp. 36-38.

Kulinna, P., and S. Silverman. Teachers' attitudes toward teaching physical activity and fitness. *Research Quarterly,* 71: 80-84, 2000.

Martinek, T. Why kids give up: an examination of how teacher and parental expectations influence self-perceptions of children. *Research Quarterly* (65) A-71, 1994.

Morrisey, C. Saving our jobs - making elementary physical education RIF - Resistant. *JOPERD,* 62: 63 - 65, 1992.

Pangrazi, R. and V. Dauer. *Dynamic Physical Education for Elementary Children* (11th ed.). Needham Heights: Allyn and Bacon Publishing Co, 1995.

Portman, P. Is anyone having fun? Students' experience of their physical education classes. *Research Quarterly* (65) 1994.

Sallis, J. et.al. Effects of health-related physical education on academic achievement: project SPARK. *Research Quarterly* 70: 127-134, 1999.

Sallis, J. et.al. The development of self-administered physical activity surveys for 4th grade students. *Research Quarterly* 64: 25-31, 1993.

Sherman, N (Ed.) Tracking the long-term benefits of physical education. *JOPERD,* 72: 5, 2001.

Smith, D. How play influences children's development at home and school. *JOPERD* 65:19-23, 1995.

Smith, T and N. Cestaro. Saving future generations - the role of physical education. *JOPERD* 62:75-79, 1992.

Stevens, D. Movement concepts: stimulating cognitive development in elementary students. *JOPERD* 64: 16-17, 1994.

Thomas, J. Children's control, learning, and performance of motor skills. *Research Quarterly* 71: 1-9, 2000.

Weiller, K. The social-emotional component of physical education for children. *JOPERD* 62:50-53, 1992.

Selective Web Sites

PE Central - Physical Education lesson plans, activities, and games: http://pe.central.vt.edu/

American Alliance for Health, Physical Education, Recreation, and Dance: http://www.aahperd.org/

Center for Disease Control - Health information: http://www.cdc.gov/

Government Services Administration - Free government documents including health information: http://www.pueblo.gsa.gov/

American College of Sports Medicine: http://www.acsm.org/

A great search engine: http://www.google.com/

Chapter

Growth and Development

2

After completing this chapter, the student should be able to:

1. Describe the growth patterns for each of the three areas: physical, social/emotional, and intellectual.

2. Give at least two ways growth patterns affect teaching and/or learning.

3. List at least four factors which account for individual differences and describe the influence each has.

4. Describe each of the conditions discussed under "Children with Special Needs."

5. List at least two characteristics of each area—physical, social/emotional, and intellectual—for each of the age groups discussed in the chapter.

6. Given a growth and development characteristic for a particular age group, be able to give the implication the characteristic has for teaching and/or learning.

7. Define the key terms listed below.

═══**Key Terms**

ADD/ADHD
Cerebral palsy
Development
Down syndrome
Fetal alcohol syndrome
Fine Motor
Gross Motor
Growth

Heredity
Hyperactivity
Nutrition
Ontogenetic
Patterns
Perceptual-motor
Phylogenetic
Readiness

As was so clearly pointed out by the Surgeon General in "Physical Activity and Health," physical activity is essential to the growth and development of the individual. The authors of the report specifically mention the decline in physical education programs as a major reason for adolescents' declining fitness level. The National Association for Sport and Physical Education (NASPE) has produced guidelines for activity among children which includes the need for "An accumulation of more than 60 minutes, and up to several hours per day of age and developmentally appropriate activities . . . ." It is clear that to grow and develop properly, the child must be physically active.

With the rapid changes during the elementary years, a chapter is not sufficient space to deal with all aspects of growth and development. This chapter, therefore, is a brief overview relating growth and development to physical education. The specific areas of focus are: physical, social/emotional, and intellectual.

Growth is an increase in size, while development is a combination of both growth and maturation. There are two types of development, phylogenetic, or in-born behavior, like the sequence of locomotor movement, (i.e., walking), and ontogenetic or learned behavior typical of most sports' skills. Unless there is some genetic problem, humans, given the proper nutrition and exercise, will grow. Development, primarily ontogenetic, is considered to be dependent on environment; a human may grow effectively, but without proper training will not develop fully. Using a poker analogy, heredity deals the cards and environment plays the hand. Few individual ever reach the full potential of the hand they are dealt.

PATTERNS

Although each child is unique, there are certain growth and development patterns in each developmental area, physical, social/emotional, and intellectual. Knowledge of these patterns aids the understanding of human learning and behavior. Such knowledge is used to select developmentally appropriate activities to meet the child's growth and development needs. The patterns discussed in the following section cover several general age groups. Additional information about specific age group characteristics is discussed for each age group, four to six years, six to eight years, eight to ten years, and ten to twelve years of age.

Physical

Much of the child's early physical growth and development are phylogenetic and are not, therefore, dependent upon instruction. One pattern of physical development is from the head to the feet; another pattern is from body's core or center toward the periphery. Children, therefore, will first be able to lift and control the head with other upper body control following. For preschool and early elementary years, these head-to-toe and core-to-extremity patterns suggest that children will be able to perform hand-eye coordination activities better than foot-eye activities. Also, with large muscles being closer to the body core, children will be more successful at gross motor activities before developing fine motor coordination.

Basic Locomotor Movement

A child's locomotor pattern is also inborn and sequential. The child first *crawls* by moving on the belly; this is followed by *creeping* on all fours. Eventually, children pull up, balance and walk. Although some children skip some stages (usually creeping), most children will enter kindergarten with the ability to do the basic locomotor movements including walking, running, leaping, hopping,

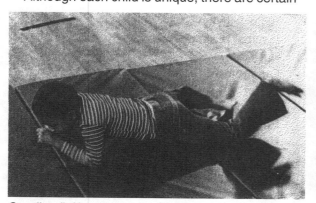 

Crawling (left) and creeping (right) are sequential locomotor movements.

and jumping. They may, however, need to learn the terminology—many adults, for example, do not know the difference between a hop and a jump.

Combined Movements

Combined or learned locomotor skills such as galloping, sliding, and skipping are normally acquired through imitative behavior or instruction. Sliding, a sideward gallop, is fairly simple and will usually develop by imitative behavior. Its use in many sporting activities such as tennis, football, basketball, and soccer make it a fairly common movement and useful to learn. Skipping, a step, hop pattern, is not used in sport activities or for that matter any activities. It is, however, used in some children's games and activities. A child can normally be taught how to skip in less than five minutes.

Body Segments and Growth

It is also important to realize that all body segments do not grow at the same rate. Furthermore, rate and magnitude of segment growth differs between genders. While there is little physical difference between the sexes prior to age ten, substantial differences become evident during adolescence. This two and a half- to three-year rapid growth period generally occurs when the female is around eleven years of age and the male thirteen. During these three years, the female can be expected to gain approximately thirty-five pounds and grow three inches taller each year. Likewise, the male can be expected to gain about forty-five pounds and grow about four inches taller each year during the adolescent growth spurt. These changes can significantly influence motor performance.

Movement and Readiness

There is a continuing effort to link physical patterns and abilities such as skipping and rope jumping with cognitive ability. Tests which include skipping and rope jumping have often been used as indicators of academic readiness. Although there is some relationship between academic readiness and the ability to skip, jump rope, or walk a balance beam, it has no predictive value. In most

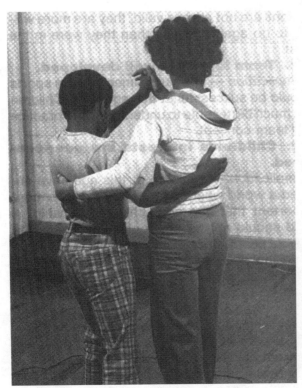

Physical differences between boys and girls are most apparent between ages eleven and thirteen.

The ability to jump rope is not related to intelligence.

cases, children who cannot skip have never had reason to skip or have never been taught how to skip. There seems to be a continued effort to predict cognitive ability, particularly reading readiness, using motor tests; once again, little positive relationship exists between motor ability and academic ability, and even the slight positive relationship found does not seem to be causal.

Physical Education and Physical Growth and Development

The evidence regarding the need and value of physical activity for children is clear, children need to be active. Physical education is one way to aid the child's physical growth and development. Children need to be active for several hours a day, and a daily physical education program can help provide some of this activity while motivating children to be active outside school. Special fitness programs both at school and at home can increase activity time. By learning skills, children will also possess the tools necessary to participate in activities and games outside school.

SOCIAL/EMOTIONAL

Although social and emotional development are often dealt with separately, it is difficult to consider one without the other. The interaction the child has with others influences social development, which has implications to one's emotional well-being. A child, for example, who is ostracized by his peers will frequently exhibit emotional problems.

There are discernible social/emotional patterns which are common to most children. Knowledge of these patterns can help teachers understand behavior as well as select appropriate developmental activities.

Self-Centered Behavior

From birth through about age seven, the focus is almost exclusively on self. This egocentric approach to life often manifests itself in negative ways through temper tantrums, and fighting with siblings, peers, and parents. As would be expected during these early years, however, the focus is on parental attention.

As the child enters school, the egocentric child will seek teacher attention. Depending upon the child, this attention-seeking behavior will be either positive, negative or a combination of the two. The approach taken is often dependent upon how the

Fighting is often a negative way of getting attention.

teacher handles situations. Initially, most children will seek adult approval in a positive manner; receiving none, the approach may take a negative path. During a physical education class, one can often hear, "Watch me, watch me!" as children vie for attention.

To fulfill this need for attention during the early elementary years, the good teacher will select activities which allow for individual attention. Activities such as object manipulation, self-testing activities, target activities, and creative and problem-solving activities all provide opportunities for individual attention. Team-type activities, including relays, do not meet a young child's developmental needs either socially or emotionally, and should not, therefore, be offered until the later elementary years.

Peer-Centered Behavior

Self-centered behavior is followed by a gradual transition toward a peer-centered, group loyalty phase most evident in children ten years of age and up. To these children, the peer group values are more important than those imposed by adults; cliques are common. Although adult acceptance is still important to this age group, peer group status is much more important to self-concept development.

Teachers must be careful, therefore, not to confront children in front of their peers. In order to maintain peer group status, such confrontations will usually produce defiant behavior. If the teacher is able to win such battles, the child is the big loser. By winning, the teacher may also lose class rapport as whole cliques turn against the teacher.

Physical Education and Social/ Emotional Development

The dynamic nature of physical education provides many social contacts which can have either a positive or negative emotional impact. As mentioned in chapter 1, the dynamic nature of physical education can do more good or more harm to a child's social/emotional well-being than any other subject area. Overweight and obese children as well as unskilled children often experience name calling and may be ostracized in physical education.

Conversely, children who perform well physically are more readily accepted by the peer group. Peer acceptance is one of a child's strongest emotional needs.

Cliques are common among older children.

INTELLECTUAL

According to Piaget, a leading cognitive theorist, intelligence develops in four stages: sensori-motor, pre-operational, concrete operational, and formal operational. Piaget's work has been supported by others and is considered to be the most definitive information on intellectual development. For those teaching physical education, probably the two most important aspects of Piaget's work are the emphasis on movement during the early stages of intellectual development, and the ability to think conceptually which comes at about nine years of age.

Movement and Intelligence

The importance of early movement has been used to justify perceptual-motor programs for children with cognitive learning difficulties. In Piaget's work, however, the movement phase is completed during the first two years of life. Some researchers suggest that all intellectual ability is completed during the first three years of life. Early school experiences after age three, therefore, seem to have little effect on the individual's capacity to learn, but should be helpful in enabling children to realize their full potential. Motor programs designed to increase intelligence are, therefore, highly questionable after age three.

Vocabulary

Children enter school with a speaking vocabulary of 2500 to 3000 words which allows the teacher an effective communications channel. Researchers have recently found that some inner city children begin school with only a 500 word vocabulary. Children can understand instructions and simple safety rules and class regulations. Although they are not little adults, teachers can, by using appropriate vocabulary, communicate effectively without talking down to the children.

Physical Education and Intellectual Development

Intelligence is an important consideration in planning physical education. First and most important, consideration must be given to a child's cognitive ability to be successful with a game or activity. Games and activities which have simple rules should be offered during the early years, and team-type games which require conceptual thought should be reserved for children who can think conceptually. Such activities as baseball, basketball, and football which require strategy and have numerous rules should not be played in grades K-4. Some team games such as soccer, however, can be simplified ("That is your goal to kick the ball in" and "Do not let it go in that goal.") and played successfully by children five years of age and older. The general rule is to reserve nearly all team games until the children are nine years of age or older.

When selecting physical education activities, adults must realize that games which seem simple to them can be intellectually complicated for children. In a game like T-baseball, the child can easily be taught to hit the ball and run to first. From

Team games should be reserved for use with older children.

that point on, things become very complicated conceptually. Rules like tag out and force out, infield fly rule, and advancing on a pop fly are difficult even for many adults. Besides the intellectual problems, many team games have self-concept implications as children face situations where they can strike out, miss the pop fly, or drop the touchdown pass. Such pressures should be reserved for later years when the children are better able to handle them.

With regard to the ability of physical education to make contributions to intellectual development, the reader is reminded that intellectual development is complete by three years of age. Some knowledge can be achieved through physical education. Knowledge of games and sports, health and safety knowledge, and problem solving and creative activities, are all enhanced through physical education. There are those, however, who want to teach academic material such as math, and language arts during physical education. It can be assumed that this philosophy is motivated by the perceived need to have physical education join the mainstream of academic acceptance. Although it is well-documented that movement is a viable medium for learning or reinforcing academic information, to use valuable physical education instruction time to teach academic subjects such as reading and math is wrong. Physical education has valuable movement objectives which will obviously have to be compromised when the curriculum is planned around cognitive learning.

INDIVIDUAL DIFFERENCES

Although growth and development patterns are similar among individuals, many factors influence the process leading to individual differences. Sex, heredity, nutrition, family size and birth order, home environment, and culture are several factors accounting for uniqueness among persons.

The Sexes

Sexual differences are apparent at the elementary level; boys tend to develop slower than girls in almost every area. Due to differences in child rearing practices, boys tend to participate in more sports activities than girls, and will, therefore, be better than girls at sports' skills. It should be noted, however, that with comparable training, girls can be as good as if not better than boys at sports. At the elementary level, there is no physiological reason for boys to be athletically superior to girls. In fact, there are few differences in physical body size prior to age ten. Parental attitudes, however, combined with the influence primarily of TV has lead to a male dominance in athletic activities. As a result of the common physiological ability of boys and girls, separating elementary children on the basis of sex during physical education cannot be justified. When separation is necessary, it should be based upon interest, size, and/or ability.

Heredity

Heredity determines many things including eye color, hair density, shape and size of the head, hands and feet, handedness, and, to a certain extent, intelligence. Up to 60% of intelligence, for example, is said to be determined genetically. Numerous researchers using twins as subjects suggest also that body fat is in part a heredity factor. There is no minimizing heredity's influence but environment is still a major developmental factor.

With gene mapping and the discovery of several controlling genes, we have entered an era in which nearly all behavior seems to have a genetic component. This is turn has lead to behavior being blamed on those genes thus negating the need to accept responsibility for one's behavior. It was even suggested that there is a gene for infidelity. Although gene manipulation is the future, it does not negate an individual's responsibility for most behaviors.

Nutrition

Nutrition has always been recognized as a major growth and development factor. With the additional concern about fast foods, dietary fat, and increased childhood obesity, this area has been receiving considerable attention. Previously height and weight were the focus, but now the concern is body composition, or the ratio of lean muscle mass and bone to fat. The increased consumption of fast food and red meat has led to raised blood lipid levels which are closely associated with cardiovascular problems. Medicine has made substantial advances in attempting to solve the problem, but at great health care cost. Fitness and nutrition are the subjects of chapter 10.

Proper nutrition has also been linked to learning. Children with poor dietary habits can be listless and inattentive. Nutritional problems are a constant concern, particularly for teachers working with low socioeconomic children.

Family Size and Birth Order

The family size and birth order can influence a child's personality. Only children, those with older brothers and sisters, the oldest child, the youngest child, and the middle child are just some of the many possible combinations which can affect behavior. Most middle children, for example, tend to exhibit similar personalities even when they have very different socioeconomic backgrounds. Knowing family history can help teachers explain some behavior.

Home Environment

The single most important factor in educational success is home environment. Such factors as discipline, single parent homes, and socioeconomic level all influence a child's behavior. Parents blame the teachers for a child's learning problems and teachers blame the home environment. Who is correct? Although both contribute, the child spends considerable time at home, and most researchers would agree that home life is a key to learning.

Culture

As the United States continues to attract immigrants, both legal and illegal, differing cultures will influence American schools. Bilingual education continues to be an issue. What language should be used or should there be more than one? States such as California, Texas, and Florida have had a significant number of immigrants and have struggled with a number of education issues including bilingual education. It is clear that America has been and will continue to be a multi-cultural nation in which the teacher should know and appreciate a child's cultural background.

CHILDREN WITH SPECIAL NEEDS

Many children in public schools have special needs. The following is a brief discussion of some of these needs. Knowledge of these conditions can help a teacher provide appropriate developmental activities for these children. It is not, however, inclusive and the reader is referred to chapter 20 for information on physical education activities which can help in the development of children with special needs.

Perceptual-Motor Problems

Many children have perceptual-motor problems which are often closely associated with academic difficulties as well as such physical abilities as manipulation, balance, and agility. Other areas often affected include kinesthetic awareness (knowledge of body parts in space), self-concept, laterality, directionality, and body image. Although there is a relationship between perceptual-motor problems and academic difficulties, it is too low to have any predictive value. Nor does the relationship appear to be causal. Intervention programs focusing on improving motor ability in hopes of increasing academic ability are highly questionable. These children, however, have motor problems, and can benefit from motor development programs.

Mentally Challenged Children

Mental problems have many causes and levels; heredity, disease, and trauma all play a part. The results, however, are the same—a child with learning difficulties. The degree of impairment determines the approach. Over the years, there have been attempts to classify children according to learning ability. Many educators, however, avoid labeling, fearing it may restrict educational opportunities. The trend is towards individualized programs. One provision of Public Law 94-142 is the IEP or Individualized Education Program or Plan through which each child's educational experiences are detailed. Specifics of the IEP are covered in chapter 20.

In general, mentally challenged children tend to learn best in a structured environment. For physical education, a teacher-directed approach seems to work best. Order and discipline should be firm. Although group activities can be effective, a more individualized approach is usually necessary. Physical education is one of only two subjects mentioned in the Public Law as being required of all special students. The authors of the law obviously recognize the importance of physical education to overall development. Physical education is often the area where the mentally retarded can have their greatest success.

Although not directly associated with education, the 1990 Americans With Disabilities act is increasing being cited in public school cases. Originally designed to eliminate discrimination in the workplace, court decisions have broadened it to include many conditions and situations never intended by the original designers.

Down Syndrome

Down Syndrome is associated with mental retardation. Most Down children can learn and function within society, albeit at a low level. These children can have success in physical education.

Fetal Alcohol Syndrome

Fetal Alcohol Syndrome like Down Syndrome is associated with reduced mental capacity. The cause is alcohol consumed by the mother during pregnancy. Although most closely associated with alcoholic mothers, this condition can be caused by any pregnant woman who has as few as one heavy drinking bout at the wrong time. Alcohol and pregnancy do not mix.

Cerebral Palsy

Although there are varying palsy conditions, the most visible is spastic palsy characterized by uncontrolled shaking and speech difficulties. This condition may be accompanied by poor academic performance which is often an environmental rather than intellectual factor. Those with cerebral palsy often have a high IQ. In earlier times, these individuals were thought to be possessed and were often institutionalized. Ways are constantly being found to unlock the potential of these individuals.

ADD AND ADHD

Probably the most prevalent conditions in public schools today are Attention Deficit Disorder (ADD) and Attention Deficit Hyperactive Disorder (ADHD). As a result of the inability to stay focused, children with either of these conditions have learning problems. The most common treatment is the drug Ritalin which helps children stay on task. Although the diagnosis of ADD and ADHD increased dramatically during the past few years, some people believe active children are over diagnosed and that many may be taking drugs unnecessarily. ADD and ADHD will continue to be a source of controversy well into the 21st Century.

AGE GROUP CHARACTERISTICS

Although most schools use a grade level approach to grouping students, it seemed more logical to group the children by age group characteristics. We have, therefore, chosen to organize this book where appropriate by age divisions. Due to the similarity of characteristics which cut across various school arrangements, communication using age groups would seem more efficient. The age divisions which we feel best reflect growth and development characteristics are four to six, six to eight, eight to ten, and ten to twelve years of age.

The following is a discussion of characteristics associated with children in these age groups, including physical, social/emotional, and intellectual characteristics and the implications of these characteristics to teaching and learning.

CHARACTERISTICS OF CHILDREN FOUR TO SIX YEARS OF AGE AND IMPLICATIONS FOR INSTRUCTION

Most children enter public school for the first time at age five, but with the trend toward early education, many four-year-old children are commonly found in public education. Those who are covered by Public Law 94-142 may start as young as two years of age. With the tremendous increase in day care, most four- and five-year-old children are use to spending the day away from home. Movement is the most effective way to bridge the gap from day care to public education. Young children want and need movement. It can be the most effective medium of instruction for this age group.

Physical Characteristics

1. By four years of age, the normal child has developed the basic locomotor movements of crawling, creeping, walking, running, jumping, hopping and leaping, plus they are capable of all the non-locomotor movements of bending, stretching, twisting, turning, pulling, and pushing. They may not, however, be able to associate the term with a movement.

   Implication: The children need to be taught to do the locomotor and non-locomotor movements more efficiently by focusing on the qualities of movement— force, time, space, and level. Children need to experience every way their body can move using locomotor and non-locomotor movement. The emphasis must be on exploring movement under the guidance of an individual who can analyze movement and then present appropriate developmental activities. It is also helpful for them to learn to associate a movement with the appropriate term.

Four-to six-year-old children have developed basic locomotor and many non-locomotor movements.

2. Learned tasks such as skipping, rope jumping, catching, and striking with an object can be developed during this period.

Implication: Opportunities should be provided which allow a child to experience every way the body and body parts can manipulate an object. Children should be given the opportunity to manipulative various objects such as balls, and bean-bags. Since children will frequently miss these objects, however, caution must be exercised when selecting them; the objects should be soft so that should they hit the child they will not cause an injury. Scoops can be used to throw and catch beanbags and yarn balls, while hockey sticks can be used to manipulate objects on the floor. Target activities are particularly popular. If the teacher sees the need, skipping can be taught. Rope jumping is a good fitness activity which should be developed during these early years and continued throughout the elementary grades.

3. Girls are more advanced than boys in most areas.

   Implication: Child-rearing practices may provide boys an edge in throwing and catching while girls tend to excel in rope jumping and dance. The physical education curriculum, however, should be the same for both sexes.

4. By age five, most children have developed a dominant body side.

   Implication: When exploring movement, children will favor the dominant side but should be encouraged to use both sides.

5. Manipulative ability is usually poor.

   Implication: The children's ability to catch and propel objects with the hands and feet is usually poor. Manipulative ability should receive constant attention through exploration activities. The objects used should be safe: yarn balls, sponge rubber balls, and beanbags are recommended. A particularly versatile and safe object is the un-coated seven-inch sponge rubber ball; it is large enough to catch, soft enough to be hit, kicked, or thrown anywhere without injury, and it is excellent both indoors and out.

6. Large muscles are better developed than fine muscles.

   Implication: Activities using large muscles will give the child more success than those requiring fine muscle coordination. Most physical education manipulative activities should help to develop large muscle coordination. These children, however,

The ability to catch objects is usually poor; activities should be designed to improve manipulative ability. Note that this ball is too large for the young child, and could cause an injury.

should be given the opportunity to manipulate small, soft objects which promote fine muscle development.

7. Large muscles need to be strengthened.
   Implication: Even though large muscles are better developed than those used for fine motor coordination, they are not necessarily strong. Children must be constantly encouraged to participate in activities which strengthen the upper body.

8. Children are noisy and vigorous, but tire easily.
   Implication: Activities should allow for noise and considerable movement, but should be interspersed with rest periods or less vigorous activities.

9. Large group activities can lead to injuries early in the year.
   Implication: During the summer months, children usually play in small groups, and when school begins, they are not ready to interact safely in large groups. Large group activities can lead to collisions and serious injuries. Children must be taught to share space under controlled conditions. They must be reminded constantly about watching where they are going and about how to avoid collisions.

10. The center of gravity is high.
    Implication: The high center of gravity makes balance difficult and falls frequent. Most activities, therefore, should be done on a soft surface such as grass. Chasing and fleeing activities requiring agility are a particular problem. Large balls such as the thirteen- and sixteen-inch playground balls are heavy, and when carried, further complicate the high center of gravity problem. Backward movement will frequently result in falls particularly in competitive situations. Competitive activities such as games should not be offered for this age group.

11. Bladder control is a problem, particularly under tense situations.
    Implication: Avoid pressure situations and allow the children to use the bathroom upon request. Since children tend to imitate each other and may want to gain attention, teachers must be careful not to have a mass parade to the restroom. Some children may be afraid to ask, however, but will usually show signs of need which a teacher needs to recognize.

Social and Emotional Characteristics

1. Children like to play with others, but are self-centered.
   Implication: Have activities which are individual rather than group oriented. Each child should receive praise each class period.

2. Most children like to test their skills.
   Implication: Self-testing activities which allow for self-evaluation should be used frequently. Most manipulative and target activities can be self-testing. Other self-testing activities include rope jumping,

Most children like to test themselves. Here targets allow for self-testing of skills.

tumbling, and balancing. Children particularly enjoy targets which fall when struck. For years, carnival and fair goers have been lured to self-testing activities such as the baseball throw, dunking the clown, basketball shooting, and many other target activities. The appeal of self-testing activities provides a motivating environment for developing manipulative ability.

3. Children enjoy imitating.
   Implication: Have creative activities which give the children an opportunity to act out different characters and situations. Imitative activities such as story plays, mimicry, and role playing should be a major curriculum component.

4. Children want to please adults.
   Implication: Children will seek adult attention and approval, and teachers must be ready to reinforce positive behavior. Praise can be given either verbally or nonverbally with a wink, pat on the back, or a smile.

5. Children frequently fight among themselves.
   Implication: When everyone is self-centered, fighting is common. Recognizing this as normal, teachers must not over-react to disagreements among the children. Behavior which disrupts the learning environment, however, must be dealt with accordingly.

6. Emotional control is still developing.
   Implication: Most incidents which cause an emotional response such as crying, screaming, and fighting are soon forgotten. By using nonverbal discipline techniques (chapter 6), the teacher is less likely to cause embarrassment which could lead to crying. If verbal reprimands are necessary, the teacher should take the child aside while other children are occupied in activity.

7. The self-concept is fragile.
   Implication: This is a major adjustment period, and the kindergarten experience has self-concept implications which will affect future success. Appropriate teacher-pupil interaction is critical.

8. Children want individual attention.
   Implication: Activities which allow the teacher to give each child attention and praise should be used, and team games should not be played.

Intellectual Characteristics

1. The attention span is short.
   Implication: A young child's on-task time is only about five minutes. The children are not ready, therefore, to listen to long explanations; instructions should be brief. These children learn best by doing, which is fairly obvious in the psychomotor area, but early childhood teachers should use movement frequently to teach all subjects. (See chapter 30.)

2. By age five, children have a speaking vocabulary of 2500-3000 words.
   Implication: Effective communication is possible with this age group as long as appropriate vocabulary is used.

3. Children learn through movement.
   Implication: Although the primary objective must be physical education, integrated activities can be used to help children learn material from other subject areas. Story plays, flash cards, stations, and creative activities can be used to integrate language arts, math, science, and social studies with physical education (chapter 17).

Language arts can be integrated through the use of flashcards.

4. Young children have difficulty with game rules.
   Implication: Although simple games can be played, they are discouraged for this age group. Self-testing, fitness, creative movement, and rhythmic activities should be offered instead of competitive games and sports.

5. Children enjoy problem solving and creative activities.
   Implication: The development process can be enhanced by offering creative movement activities which allow the children to solve problems through movement. Story plays are particularly valuable as are imitation activities. With an indirect teaching approach using open-ended questions (chapter 5), a teacher can help children develop both physically and cognitively.

6. Children are capable of learning some health and fitness facts and safety rules.
   Implication: The curriculum should include health, fitness, and safety information.

7. Conceptual thought is not well developed.
   Implication: Most team games are too complicated conceptually for young children. Activities should be individual or small group. Team games should *not* be played.

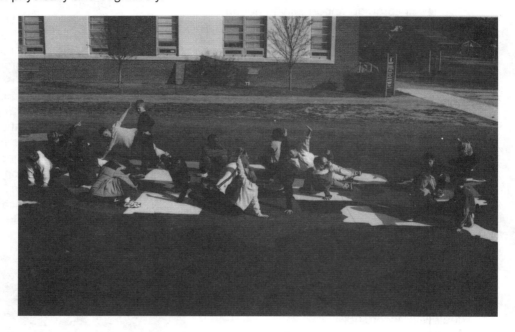

Children enjoy creative activities.

CHARACTERISTICS OF CHILDREN SIX TO EIGHT YEARS OF AGE AND IMPLICATIONS FOR INSTRUCTION

Although six- and seven-year-old children are different in many ways, they have similar characteristics particularly in the psychomotor domain. For purposes of this book, therefore, they are considered together. The academic curriculum for this age group is demanding and usually provides little movement experience. Children are expected to sit at desks for long academic sessions. A seven-year-old is more mature than a six-year-old, but their similar motor ability allow them to share many physical education activities.

Physical Characteristics

1. Posture can be a problem.
   Implication: A teacher has the opportunity to compare children against others, and should, therefore, be able to notice marked postural differences among them. Postural problems identified at this age are frequently functional (correctable with exercise) rather than structural which normally requires bracing or surgery. Suspected problems should be reported to the school nurse or doctor where a professional diagnosis can be made. Teachers must be careful not to suggest to the child or the parent that a postural problem exists; diagnosis and prescription must be left to qualified medical personnel. (See chapter 10.)

Checking posture is important to identify possible problems.

2. Health-related fitness is usually poor.
   Implication: Fitness activities which focus on cardiovascular efficiency, muscular strength, muscular endurance, flexibility and body composition should be a major curriculum component. (See chapter 10.) Although children are energetic, they will tend to fatigue quickly during aerobic activities such as rope jumping and running.

3. Children do not yet possess a firm movement base.
   Implication: As with the younger age group discussed earlier, the emphasis should be on experiencing every locomotor and non-locomotor way their body can move. The curriculum should contain movement experiences which focus on the quality of movement (force, time, space, and level).

4. Sex differences are apparent.
   Implication: The varying background experiences of boys and girls is apparent at this age level. Boys tend to be better at sports skills while girls are superior in dance and gymnastics. There is no physiological reason for these differences, and the curriculum, therefore, should be the same for both sexes. Individualized teaching approaches, however, should be used to account for differences among the children, but they should not be grouped on the basis of sex.

5. Manipulative ability is not well-developed.
   Implication: Children should be given the opportunity to experiment with every way their body can manipulate an object. Soft objects such as 7" sponge rubber balls, yarn balls, and beanbags are safe objects to use for manipulative experimentation.

5. Skills can be developed in first and second grade.
   Implication: Although there is a continued emphasis on exploration particularly for six-year-old children, specific skills such as throwing, catching, and kicking as well as tumbling and gymnastic skills can and should be developed. Poor motor patterns should corrected using the guided discovery and task style teaching approaches.

Social and Emotional Characteristics

1. The child is self-centered.
   Implication: Activities should allow for individual attention and praise. Every child should receive some verbal or nonverbal praise during each class period. Group activities should be minimized and large team games should be avoided altogether.

2. Most children are competitive.
   Implication: Although competition is an inherent part of life, competitive activities should focus on competing with self rather than others. Competition should be low key, particularly during games. Activities and teaching approaches should be selected to challenge children but at the same time allow for success with effort.

3. Children are aware of the opposite sex.
   Implication: Certain activities may cause disruption. Boys, for example, may not wish to have a girl partner in rhythmic activities, and girls should not be allowed to perform tumbling and gymnastics activities without shorts or pants. To establish the pattern for future rhythmic activities, the teacher should insist on boy/girl couples where appropriate. Uniforms are not necessary, but wearing shorts or pants can help minimize disruption and embarrassment.

Certain activities, such as boy-girl partners for rhythmics, may cause disruption.

4. Emotions are more intense but do not last as long as adults.

   Implication: Short emotional outbursts should be ignored whenever possible. Many words and deeds such as striking out at the teacher do not usually reflect a child's true feelings and should, therefore, be treated accordingly.

5. The children desire affection and praise from adults.

   Implication: Since adults and particularly teachers are important to a child, their affection and positive reinforcement can have a positive developmental influence. Each child should receive praise every class period.

6. Children like to play together but are not team oriented.

   Implication: Most children prefer small group activities in which they can receive individual attention. With the tremendous influence professional sports have particularly on boys, however, children will request familiar activities such as soccer, hockey, or football. Even though children seem to desire team games at times, it would appear that the vast majority prefer individual activities.

7. Children will tell on peers.

   Implication: It is considered normal behavior to have children "squeal" on each other. A teacher, however, should not encourage such behavior, but should work to have children accept responsibility for their own actions.

Intellectual Characteristics

1. Attention span is short.

   Implication: Get children into activity quickly. When children come to physical education they are ready for activity, not long explanations. Sitting and listening will not help psychomotor development.

2. Children like to fantasize.

   Implication: At this age, fantasy is important to children; the curriculum, therefore, should include creative activities such as story plays and mimicry.

3. Children have a good imagination.

   Implication: Since the children can be more creative than the teacher, they should be given frequent opportunities for creative movement. They frequently suggest things which the teacher can use.

4. Reasoning is possible.

   Implication: Although the children are not highly sophisticated, it is possible to reason with this age group. Discussing the reasons for rules, actions, and activities can help understanding and develop rapport. Although children are not miniature adults, they do not like to be treated like babies; by involving them in decision making, children will feel valued.

5. Children have a good listening vocabulary.

   Implication: A good vocabulary provides the vehicle to implement number 4 above, and is necessary for effective communication.

A stations arrangement with flash cards can help children increase their vocabulary.

6. A sight vocabulary can be developed.
   Implication: By using a stations arrange-ment or flash cards with various movement terms and body parts, the children can increase their sight vocabulary while still maintaining physical education as the primary class objective, i.e., a teacher can tell the children to walk backward or have the instructions on a flash card. In either case, the children are developing the movement quality while the latter promotes cognitive development along with the movement. Learning can also be accom-plished by using a stations approach (chapter 8).

7. Children are capable of learning facts.
   Implication: Although these children are not capable of understanding most fitness and health concepts, they are able to learn exercise, nutrition, and safety facts.
   Eight- and nine-year-old children are willing to try most anything, love move-ment, and usually will make significant physical gains. This age group is often thought of as the transition years; a tran-sition from a movement base toward more specific skills.

CHARACTERISTICS OF CHILDREN EIGHT TO TEN YEARS OF AGE AND IMPLICATIONS FOR INSTRUCTION

Physical Characteristics

1. Marked differences in skill ability are apparent.
   Implication: Prior to teaching any skill, evaluation should done. Organizational patterns such as stations, learning centers, ability groups, and peer assistants should be used to individualize instruction (chap-ter 8).

2. Fitness levels are low.
   Implication: As at every other grade level, health-related fitness should be a high priority.

3. Children are noisy and active.
   Implication: Physical education was not designed to be a quiet activity and chil-dren, therefore, should be given a space which allows for activity and a reasonable noise level.

4. Children like to do things correctly.
   Implication: Children want to learn skills, especially the ability to control their own body. Self-testing activities such as tum-bling and gymnastics, when done correctly, provide a good feeling about self. It is also possible, of course, to develop high frustration levels during skill development activities. Emphasis on perfection must therefore be avoided. Teaching styles must be used which allow for individual differ-ences in ability levels. Also, Characteris-tics of Children Eight to Ten Years of Age and Implications for Instruction rates must be used. Children should also be able to practice skills without undue attention from others. The common physical education practice of requiring children to perform in front of their peers is educational malprac-tice.

Learning a new skill, such as a lay-up, causes students to feel good about themselves.

31

5. Most children's manipulative ability is fairly well-developed.
   Implication: Most children are capable of manipulating objects. Lead-up games to individual and team sports such as soccer, softball, basketball, and volleyball, therefore, are possible.

Social and Emotional Characteristics

1. Children have developed special friends.
   Implication: Although children should be able to select their own partner, there should be activities which require partners to change.
2. Children like group activities and a sense of team loyalty is developing.
   Implication: The curriculum should include team games and lead-up games to team sports.
3. Behavioral problems are common in this age group, but most like physical education.
   Implication: This is a particularly good age level to teach physical education. Classroom problems, however, can spill into the physical education class. It is also common to have problems with children who have a weak classroom teacher. Cliques are common in this age group, and behavioral problems are on the increase at the elementary level. Given the right (positive) environment, the majority of children seem willing to participate in most physical education activities. Children should experience good improvement in fitness and skills.
4. Children can handle responsibility.
   Implication: In order to improve self-control, children should be given the opportunity to assume responsibility. They should, at times, be allowed to design and conduct their own games under the teacher's supervision but not direction. Choice days on which they can choose activities they wish to play can be helpful in developing leadership and self-control. If space is available, there can be several different activities going on simultaneously.
5. Children are sensitive to criticism and are easily discouraged.
   Implication: A positive learning environment should be established in which there is considerable verbal and nonverbal praise. Since criticism usually leads to discouragement, it should be avoided. The corrections necessary to learning should be "sandwiched between two slices of praise" and should utilize questions; i.e., "What do you think might happen if you step forward with the other foot?" or "Did you tuck your chin to your chest that time?" In order to help children, the teacher must be a critical observer but should not attempt to motivate by being critical. It is unfortunate that sarcasm continues to be a prevalent approach to teaching physical education.

Intellectual Characteristics

1. Attention span is increasing, but is still short.
   Implication: Explanations may be helpful in skill development, but they should be brief. Psychomotor development is best achieved through purposeful movement, not through cognitive input.
2. Children are beginning to understand concepts.

Individual attention with verbal and nonverbal praise helps establish a positive learning environment.

Implication: Communications with this age group can be effective in most matters requiring conceptual thought. Fitness, health, and safety concepts can be discussed along with sports concepts such as offense, defense, and strategy.

3. Children are learning their place in the world.
   Implication: With their conceptual ability, the children are better able to handle discussions regarding the consequences of their actions. In many instances, it is possible to use logic.

4. Self-evaluation is possible.

Implication: Whenever possible, self-evaluation techniques should be used. This can be done by asking probing questions. Children can also help evaluate each other's performance, and self-evaluation is possible using videotape.

5. Children are creative.
   Implication: Although teachers often discourage creativity, many older children are very creative. Teachers should encourage its development and use by allowing children to help plan such activities as demonstrations and shows. Many excellent ideas come from children's minds.

CHARACTERISTICS OF CHILDREN TEN TO TWELVE YEARS OF AGE AND IMPLICATIONS FOR INSTRUCTION

Normally the oldest children in elementary school, this age group can be challenging but rewarding. They are less likely to be cooperative when they disagree with curriculum decisions. The boys tend to dominate, and frequently desire only sports activities. Rhythmics, dance, and creative activities are not always enthusiastically accepted, and teachers, therefore, must work hard to win acceptance of these activities. Properly motivated, these children can make significant gains in fitness and skills as well as contribute useful feedback to the teacher which can be used to improve the physical education program.

Physical Characteristics

1. Posture can be a problem.
   Implication: Posture should be systematically and individually evaluated to determine any deviations. Uncorrected postural problems in this age group can have significant consequences as bones begin to complete the growth process; functional (correctable) problems can become structural (difficult to correct). Physical deformities, particularly among females, adversely affects self-concept. Postural exercises such as sit-ups, push-ups, and pull-ups should be part of a regular home fitness program.

2. Fitness continues to be poor.
   Implication: Children are capable of high fitness levels but must be motivated to

participate; such programs as Running for Life, Jump Rope for Heart, and mile clubs (see appendix A for special fitness programs) can provide that motivation. Extrinsic rewards such as t-shirts and fitness patches, as well as posting records, can help to get and keep children on a fitness program. The focus should be health-related fitness (chapter 10).

3. Physical differences can be significant.
   Implication: Such activities as touch football and hockey tend to have body contact, and care must be exercised when there is a significant difference in size and/or ability. In legal cases, teachers have lost when it was shown that the difference in ability caused the injury (chapter 9). Contact sports should not be a part of an elementary physical education program.

4. Menstruation may begin.
   Implication: Menstruation can be a problem, but unless painful, it does not usually affect the physical as much as it does the emotional. Although many parents believe otherwise, there is little reason girls should be inactive during menstrual flow. The sensitive nature of the issue as well as the increase in sexually related legal cases makes communication around this issue difficult particularly for male teachers. Any subject linked to sex must be handled with extreme caution; teachers, unless specially trained, are discouraged from discussing

sensitive sexual issues. Sex education continues to be a controversial subject.

5. Skills are well developed in some children.
Implication: Instruction should be individualized during skill development. To maintain interest, the teacher must provide for varying ability levels. Many children, and particularly boys, participate in after school activities and may possess higher skill levels. These children should not be forced through a command style to be taught skills they already possess. Evaluation must precede instruction in order to individualize the program. This can be done through organizational structures such as ability grouping, peer assistants, stations, and/or learning centers (chapter 8).

The command style of teaching should be avoided since students may already possess the skill being taught.

Social and Emotional Characteristics

1. Children can see the fallibility of adults.
Implication: Children will not readily accept teacher incompetence. They will normally take advantage of and complain about poor teachers. Although their evaluations are not always valid, they are more willing to go against teachers with whom they disagree. If they want to develop student rapport, teachers must be competent and dedicated.

2. Some girls may be more skilled than boys.
Implication: Although this is a physical characteristic, it has emotional implications. Boys who are "shown up" by girls with more skill than them are often emo-

tionally crushed and will strike back physically. The teacher must be ready to deal with problems between the sexes.

3. Peer group status is extremely important.
Implication: Children at this age have entered a world where peer status is far more important than the adult-child relationship. In determining behavior, researchers have found that the peer group has the most influence. When dealing with problem children, therefore, the teacher should take the child aside to discuss the problem, and never discipline the child in front of the peer group. To "lose face" in the peer group has far reaching self-concept implications, and can often cause the teacher to lose class rapport. Children should also not be pressured to "squeal" on peers. "Squealing" is considered immature behavior at this age level, and may result in physical reprisals from peers. Only in extreme cases such as serious injury should a child be pressured to reveal the guilty party. Even in these serious cases, the identity of those providing information must be protected.

4. Rebellious behavior may occur.
Implication: Rebellious behavior is on the increase in this age group. The oldest children in the school often exhibit superior attitudes ("senioritis"). Common behaviors include questioning the teacher, talking back, boycotts, and general civil disobedience. There is also an increase in teacher assaults by students; it is not uncommon for children to bring weapons including guns into school. The children will often emulate things seen on television, and guns are extremely prevalent on TV. In dealing with any discipline situation, it must be handled carefully. Mishandling a sensitive situation, unfortunately, can have deadly consequences. No matter what the case, however, children must be taught to work for change within the system while following established conduct rules. A basic premise to work from is that no one may infringe upon another's rights.

5. Boy-girl relationships are beginning.
Implication: Problems once only common in middle school are now found at the elementary level. Giggling, passing notes, holding hands, and arguing are common.

More serious situations such as venereal disease and pregnancy may occur at times. Sexual pressures and problems are a constant concern. Any emotional situation, particularly when "love" is involved, can cause disruptive behavior which must be handled cautiously. As with school violence, sexual attitudes and problems can be traced to a great extent to TV and movies. Sexually explicit materials are now common on TV. The proliferation of pornography and children's exposure to it is also an influence. For the physical educators, the situation can be most difficult during partner dances. Teachers who use a random process to determine couples may experience problems. Although couple dances are desirable, dances requiring no partners (the record series *Dances Without Partners* is excellent) are recommended, particularly when introducing a dance unit.

6. Controlled substances may be a problem for some children.
   Implication: Drugs including alcohol are an increasing problem at the elementary level. Although schools are often cited as the cause of increased drug usage, they merely reflect the society in which they operate. Illegal substances can significantly influence learning, and teachers, therefore, must recognize usage. Since some drugs can even cause respiratory and heart failure, teachers should be qualified in first aid with a CPR certification.

7. The unskilled may withdraw or be disruptive.
   Implication: Teachers should establish a program which gives every child a chance to succeed without embarrassment. Even in an individualized program, the unskilled may withdraw or avoid participation while displaying disruptive behavior. Since physical performance is important to peer group acceptance and cannot be hidden, the poorly skilled may develop psychosomatic illnesses or disrupt class in order to avoid participation. Teachers should recognize such behavior and give these children individual attention while avoiding any approach which forces someone to perform in front of peers.

8. Moods change quickly.
   Implication: Rapid mood changes which may affect participation are normal. Teachers, therefore, should not overreact.

9. Unsuccessful children may be discouraged.
   Implication: A positive learning environment in which everyone can achieve success at his or her own speed is essential to developing a positive self-concept. Overemphasizing achievement can discourage the less skilled student.

Intellectual Characteristics

1. The upper elementary child is capable of independent learning.
   Implication: With their ability to read, this age group is capable of individual or small group learning. Instruction can come from many sources other than the teacher. By establishing learning centers, the children can progress at their own speed using audio-video materials and books. There is a continuing myth among teachers in general, and physical educators in particular, that they must use an explanation/demonstration (command) teaching style.

2. Children can think conceptually.
   Implication: These children can learn fitness, health, and safety concepts as well as understand sports concepts. This is the time to teach information from exercise physiology and kinesiology along with sports strategy.

3. It is possible to reason with children.
   Implication: Frank discussions using a questioning approach can be helpful in dealing with this age group. Their intellectual level as well as their ability to think conceptually allows for such discussions. Children will often question the teacher, and he/she must be ready to answer them. Using a reasoning rather than authoritarian approach can help establish or maintain rapport.

4. Children can be very creative.
   Implication: Creative activities should be included in the upper elementary curriculum. Children can work in small groups to create rhythmic routines with ropes, lummi sticks, tinkling poles, and/or the parachute. They also can be involved in the planning

Rhythmic activities such as routines with limmi sticks allow for development of creativity.

and design of PTA shows; some of the best program ideas can come from students.

5. Children can provide useful feedback. *Implication:* By asking questions or using an anonymous questionnaire, a teacher can determine student attitudes. Although not sophisticated evaluators, children have attitudes about the teacher and the program which the teacher should know.

Developing positive attitudes is a major curriculum objective, and the anonymous questionnaire (appendix B) is probably the best instrument to use.

SUMMARY

This chapter dealt with the growth and development of children four to twelve years of age. Growth was described as an increase in size while development was described as being a combination of both growth and maturation. The growth and development patterns for the physical, social/emotional, and intellectual areas were discussed. The two physical growth patterns, head to toe, and core to extremities were also discussed. Socially/emotionally the child was described as moving from a self-centered approach to a peer group orientation. The intellectual stages of development were covered. Some of the conditions and factors which account for individual differences were discussed. There was also a section on children with special needs. The chapter concluded with age group characteristics and the implications each had to teaching and/or learning. The four age groups were: four to six, six to eight, eight to ten, and ten to twelve years of age.

REFERENCES AND SUGGESTED READINGS

Appalachia Educational Laboratory, Inc. *ADHD: instructional strategies that work, The Link,* 14:2 Summer, 1995.

Avery, M. Preschool physical education: a practical approach. *JOPERD,* August, 1994, pp. 37-39.

Brustad, R. Attraction to physical activity in urban schoolchildren; parental socialization and gender influences. *Research Quarterly,* September, 1996, pp. 316-323.

Fisher, S. Developing and implementing a k-12 character education program. *JOPERD,* Vol 69, No. 2, February, 1998, pp. 21-23

Gabbard, C. Windows of opportunity for early brain and motor development. *JOPERD,* Vol 69, No. 8 October, 1998, pp. 54-55 and 61.

Gough, R. A practical strategy for emphasizing character development in sport and physical education. *JOPERD,* Vol 69, No. 2, February, 1998, pp. 18-20 and 23.

Hawks, S. Fetal alcohol syndrome: implications for health education. *Journal of Health Education,* 24:22-25, 1993.

National Association of Governor's Councils on Physical Fitness and Sports. *NASPE releases physical activity guidelines for pre-adolescent children,* Summer, 1996.

Pangrazi, R. and V. Dauer. *Dynamic Physical Education for Elementary Children* (11th ed.). Needham Heights: Allyn and Bacon Publishing Co, 1995.

Payne, V. and L. Isaacs. *Human Motor Development: A Life-span Approach* (6th ed.). Boston, MA: MacGraw-Hill, 2005.

Petray, C. et.al. Understanding students with diabetes: implications for the physical education professional. *JOPERD,* Vol 68, No. 1, January, 1997, pp. 57-63.

Portman, P. Low-skilled students' experiences and behaviors in cooperative learning-based physical education classes. *Research Quarterly,* March 1993 Supplement, p. A-93.

Standards of Learning Objectives. Department of Education, State of Virginia, 1995.

Thompson, L., et.al. Activity patterns of children with movement difficulties in elementary physical education classes. *Research Quarterly,* March 1993 Supplement, p. A-95

Werner, P. Whole physical education. *JOPERD,* August, 1994, pp. 40-44.

White, E., and C. Sheets. If you let them play, they will. *JOPERD* April, 2001, pp. 27-28, 33.

Selective Web Sites

Information on disciplining children with ADD and ADHD http://www.chadd.org/papers/school_discipline1.htm

Child growth and development for education majors: http://www.coe.ilstu.edu/mbgraham/c&i210/home.html

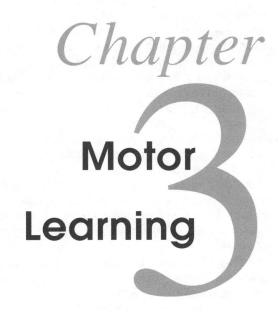

Motor Learning

After completing this chapter, the student should be able to:

1. List and describe each of the four stages of the motor learning process.

2. Describe the differences between the terms "learning" and "performance."

3. Describe the differences between the terms "feedback" and "knowledge of results."

4. Describe the factors which may influence each of the motor learning process stages.

5. Describe the advantages and disadvantages of teacher- versus student-performed demonstrations.

6. Describe a technique for locating student demonstrators.

7. Describe three types of visual aids which can facilitate the presentation of motor skills to children.

8. Describe the instructional implications for each of the motor learning principles.

9. Define the key terms listed below.

―――――――――――――――――――――――――――――――――――― *Key Terms*

Anxiety	Inverted U theory	Precuing
Attention	Kinesthetic	Primacy-regency effect
Background noise	Knowledge of results	Principles of motor learning
Central processing	Length of set	Selective attention
Closed skills	Memory	Sensory systems
Feedback	Motivation	Tactile
Forgetting	Open skills	Task complexity
Input	Output	Task organization

One of the primary goals within the elementary physical education curriculum is to teach new motor skills to children as well as to refine and expand upon existing motor abilities. The first step toward accomplishing these goals requires the teacher to be sympathetic toward the children's feelings of clumsiness which may accompany the initial learning of a new motor task. To refresh one's memory of this sometimes awkward feeling, try several of the following tasks: serve a tennis ball with the non-dominant hand; shoot a basketball with the non-dominant hand; juggle three tennis balls, now four tennis balls; or try the first laboratory activity (3.1) associated with this chapter. Most individuals will experience a feeling of awkwardness, as well as frustration and anxiety, because of their inability to perform as precisely as desired. Now keep in mind that each time a new task is presented to young children, they too may experience some of these same feelings. Obviously, if these frustrations and anxieties are allowed to continue and build during the practicing of new movement tasks, it is highly probable that many youngsters will give up or lose interest. To be a successful teacher, it is imperative at the onset to have an understanding and working knowledge of principles which govern the teaching and learning of motor tasks, and the factors which inhibit skill acquisition and skill performance.

It is also important to realize that the stages which comprise the motor learning model to be discussed hold true, regardless of the teaching method utilized—command, problem-solving, guided discovery, etc. This is because as soon as a motor task is introduced, whether it be to learn a specific skill (dribble a basketball) or just to freely explore the many ways to manipulate a ball, both psychological and physiological factors begin to influence one's performance. The purpose of this chapter is to identify and discuss these intervening factors. Only when these factors are controlled or trained, will the motor skills of students blossom.

LEARNING AND PERFORMANCE

Before describing the motor learning process it is important to first describe the two terms *learning* and *performance*. Learning can be defined as a relatively permanent change in observable behavior which is inferred from performance. Furthermore, this change in behavior must be due to instruction and practice, not maturation. A closer examination of this formal definition of learning reveals that it is composed of three elements: (1) relatively permanent change in performance, (2) is inferred from performance, and (3) is not due to maturation. The term performance can be thought of as the observable behavior.

Because learning is not directly observable, one must be careful in concluding that learning has taken place. Remember, all three elements of the definition must be met before we can conclude that learning has truly taken place. Let an example serve to illustrate the point. Katie, a third grade student in your class, has been trying to learn a cartwheel but has not had much success. However, on test day, for some unexplained reason, Katie performs an excellent cartwheel. But five minutes later Katie is once again unable to perform correctly. Should the teacher conclude that Katie has learned how to perform a cartwheel? The answer is no. Recall that one of the three elements in the definition of learning states that the performance must be "relatively permanent." It appears that during the test Katie was lucky for one performance trial.

THE MOTOR LEARNING PROCESS

The act of learning a new motor skill can indeed be a difficult task for the novice performer. The chain of events leading to skilled motor performance is a complicated one. If one thinks of the learner as a processor of information, the motor learning process can be viewed as consisting of four stages: input, central processing, output, and feedback.

Input

The process of receiving environmental stimulus through one or more of the senses is termed input. For example, someone throws a ball to you; the visual sense of seeing the ball coming initiates the information processing.

Central Processing

The decision-making process involves the central nervous system (brain and spinal cord). Using the example above, once the learner realizes that the ball has been thrown in his or her direction, the learner, on the basis of inputted information, prior experience, and knowledge of the task, must make various decisions about the ball's path in order to catch it. These decisions should include: (1) how fast the ball is traveling, and (2) where the ball will land.

Output

Once a decision has been derived concerning the body adjustments needed to intercept the ball successfully, the brain must direct nerve impulses to the appropriate muscles which then carry out the plotted bodily movements.

Feedback

Both during and following performance the learner will receive feedback as to the correctness of his or her actions. In other words, were the planned actions decided upon during central processing carried out correctly (output)? Furthermore, were these the appropriate actions to successfully accomplish the tasks? If not, then corrections in performance will need to be made.

Thus the simple act of catching a ball requires seeing the ball (input from sensory organ), making a decision as to where the ball will land and how fast the body will have to be adjusted (central processing), and finally, the muscles must be positioned according to plan (output). A breakdown in any part of the process can result in undesirable performance.

Correcting Motor Performance

Obviously, the first time a new motor task is presented to the students, it is not realistic to expect everyone to perform correctly. It then becomes the teacher's duty to analyze why a particular student was not successful, modify instructions and provide additional information to facilitate learning.

Unfortunately, many instructors attempting to correct faulty performance concentrate on requiring the students to make adjustments in their movement patterns (output), when the inability to accomplish the task may be caused by a breakdown in another part of the system (input and/or central processing). When a batter in baseball, for example, consistently swings too late at the pitched ball, he or she is generally instructed to choke up on the bat to accomplish the swing quicker. Such an analysis generally tends to treat the symptom rather that the true cause. It is highly probable that the batter who swings late may not be receiving the appropriate visual information needed to make correct decisions. When analyzing performance, all stages of the motor learning process must be considered.

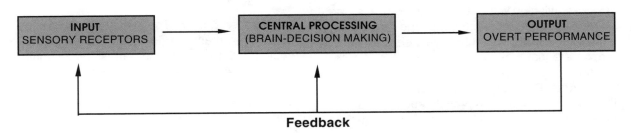

Figure 3.1. The Motor Learning Process

FACTORS AFFECTING INPUT

COMMUNICATING WITH THE LEARNER

To be a good motor skills teacher, it is important to communicate effectively with students. The section to follow explains (1) the role of the perceptual senses in conveying information, (2) how to obtain and maintain student attention, and (3) how to use demonstrations and visual aids as media sources to improve communication skills.

Sensory Systems

The motor learning process is initiated by providing input through one or more of the following sensory receptors:
1. Visual perception—seeing
2. Auditory perception—hearing
3. Tactile perception—touch
4. Kinesthetic perception—feeling (i.e., a muscle sense)
5. Olfactory perception—smell
6. Gustatory perception—taste

The perceptual senses of smell and taste are obviously less important in motor skill learning. The remaining perceptual senses, however, are all used extensively in the learning of motor tasks. The following are simple examples of how one may rely upon the senses in physical performance situations.

Visual Perception. Vision obviously plays an important role in motor skill learning. In physical education, it appears that vision is the primary sense for initiating the motor learning process. The need to observe demonstrations and the need to visually track balls which have been struck or thrown are just two examples illustrating the importance of visual perception.

Auditory Perception. The sound of a ball hitting a bat or racquet can provide auditory clues to indicate how hard a ball has been struck and thus how fast the ball is traveling.

Kinesthetic Perception. An internal "muscle sense" which allows one to determine the body's position in space without utilizing visual cues is referred to as kinesthetic perception. The novice tennis player, for example, must learn to make a preparatory backswing at or below waist level. Since the performer must be looking at the oncoming ball, he or she is unable to look back at his or her arm to affirm its position. Instead, feedback from the muscles must be relied upon to determine its location.

The motor learning process is initiated through input from one or more of the senses.

Tactile Perception. The sense of touch is used extensively in many sports. When dribbling a basketball, for example, the performer must confirm the ball's position in space by utilizing tactile perception—not visual perception. The performer who constantly looks at the ball is not able to spot teammates who may be free to take a shot at the basket. This points out an important concept: instructors of motor skills must be sure to use the correct sensory system when introducing new motor skills.

Demonstrations

Educators have traditionally attempted to teach using the auditory and visual senses. Due to individual differences in students' intellectual abilities (vocabulary), however, the teacher is often faced with the task of "speaking down" to young chil-

Using tactile perception to dribble the basketball.

simply ask the students, for example, to find the best method to dribble a basketball. While the children are participating in this self-discovery process, the teacher should be on the lookout for students who utilize acceptable techniques. After a short period of time, the teacher can point out those who are utilizing the best methods so that other classmates may watch their performance.

A Word of Caution. While demonstrations may be an influential factor in skill development, their use does not guarantee improved rates of learning. For demonstrations to be effective the teacher needs to have the student's attention and, in most instances, would use multiple demonstrations. (For details on multiple demonstrations, see condition #2 below.)

Conditions for Demonstrations and Implications for Instruction

1. **Condition:** The learner must be attentive to the demonstration.
   Implication: Before allowing the demonstrator to perform, care must be taken to ensure student attention. The teacher should eliminate external distractions such as positioning the children so that they are looking into the sun or attempting to do a demonstration in the presence of loud noises which accompany passing trucks. If distractions occur during the demonstration, the teacher should wait until the disturbances have passed.

2. **Condition:** The learner must know in advance the key elements to look for during the demonstration.
   Implication: Since most skills contain more than one key element, the ability to model behavior can be facilitated through multiple demonstrations. During each performance, the teacher can direct the students' attention (precue) to different aspects of the task (one cue at a time). In demonstrating the forward roll, for example, the students' attention should first be directed toward the initial hand position. During the second demonstration, the students should be told to focus their attention as to the position of the chin during performance. Following three to five demonstration trials, students will have been exposed to the key components. Thus multiple demonstrations tend to be more effective than the single demonstration.

dren. Such futile attempts often lead to confusion about the tasks to be performed. To avoid this dilemma, it is suggested that demonstrations accompany verbal explanations. The demonstration presents to the learner an entire picture of the skill to be learned, thus lending the student a sense of direction. The old saying "A picture is worth a thousand words" appears to be especially true when teaching motor skills to young children.

Who Should Demonstrate? Since the primary purpose of utilizing a demonstration is to present to the learner a visual illustration of the task, care must be taken in selecting demonstrators. While many teachers feel an obligation to perform all demonstrations, ideally, the individual who is the most proficient at performing the selected task should be selected to perform. One primary advantage of the teacher demonstration appears to be the earning of students' respect. There are inherent disadvantages, however, to teacher performed demonstrations. Students who experience difficulty in performing the selected tasks generally give up too early and, when reminded of the teacher's demonstration, they will frequently alibi, "Sure you can do it because you are the teacher." Such problems can be avoided by utilizing student demonstrations. The added peer influence from student demonstrations encourages more desire and determination in practice sessions.

Selecting a Student Demonstrator. To find a suitable student demonstrator, the teacher can

Visual Aids

A close examination of many curriculum guides leads one to suspect that instructors tend, for the most part, to teach only skills in which they have expertise and can physically perform. This is truly unfortunate. Teachers should realize that they are not superhuman, and that it would be nearly impossible for one to have expertise in all physical skills. The fact that an instructor does not possess the ability to demonstrate a specific skill and does not have a student who can do the demonstrating does not justify deleting that skill from the curriculum. The dedicated teacher has at his or her disposal other alternatives. Recall that the purpose of a demonstration is to present to the learner a visual representation of expert performance in hopes that the learner will in turn model the behavior. With this in mind it should be clear that any type of visual media may be utilized to present this visual representation of the task. Common sources of visual media which may be effective include the following: (1) filmstrips, (2) videotapes, (3) flow charts, and (4) slides and pictures. Furthermore, researchers support the view that using visual aids (other than live models) is especially beneficial in developing complex motor skills and may be superior to live demonstrations.

For instance, the teacher wants students to view the positioning of the legs and ankles during the execution of a cartwheel-round off. Nature, however, requires that this task be performed at a high rate of speed—a speed so fast that the novice performer is not likely to see clearly the body regions specified by the instructor. In this case, it would be more appropriate to utilize a filmstrip or motion picture showing someone performing this task. These sources of media can then be shown in slow-motion and stop action replay. The utilization of these special projection features will allow the learner to follow the desired regions of observation through the entire range of the activity. For schools with budgets that do not support an extensive film library, a viable alternative is to either make or purchase a series of inexpensive flow charts. Flow charts are actually frame-by-frame pictures or illustrations of someone performing a specific task. Figure 3.2 is an example of a flow chart depicting the cartwheel-round off.

Attention

Attention, or the ability to remain alert, is a concept closely related to information processing. For instance, during task performance we must direct our attention to the most important elements of the task while at the same time ignoring those elements which are of little importance to task performance (background noise). This concept is sometimes referred to as selective attention. As

Figure 3.2: Flow Chart Depicting Cartwheel Round Off

mentioned earlier, precuing, or telling the performer where to focus his or her attention prior to task execution is one technique which can be used to help ensure that the students' attend to the important elements of a specified task. The importance of attending to visual demonstrations has already been addressed.

Why Attention is Lost. Many theories exist which try to explain why we tend to lose attention. One theory suggest that we lose our ability to attend when we are required to perform in monotonous surroundings while another theory suggest that attention is lost when we are required to respond to very infrequent signals. Thus teachers of motor skills should make frequent changes in the physical teaching environment. For example, classes should not always be held at the same location on the field each day, drills and activities should be limited in time to avoid boredom, class routines should be frequently changed, in other words, do not start off each class with formal warm up exercises, and above all, avoid teaching formations which require students to wait in long lines before getting a turn to perform.

FACTORS AFFECTING CENTRAL PROCESSING

DECISION-MAKING

The primary task of the performer during the central processing (decision) phase of the motor learning process is to devise an appropriate plan of action that will suit the task at hand. Following is a brief discussion of several factors which may influence this decision-making process.

Memory

The terms "memory" and "forgetting" go hand-in-hand. Memory can be thought of as information which can be retrieved when needed while forgetting generally is referred to as information which can not be retrieved from memory. For ease of discussion, think of memory as being composed of two structures—short-term memory (STM) and long-term memory (LTM). Unlike LTM, STM is limited in both capacity (the number of items we can recall) and in duration (the length of time we can recall the items). Thus, when teaching motor skills the teacher must be careful not to overload the students' memory capacity by giving them more information or instructions to attend to than is necessary. Furthermore, once information is conveyed to students the teacher must organize the learning environment so that students can practice immediately, lest the students forget what they are suppose to do. Researchers believe that information in STM must be acted upon within twenty to thirty seconds or it will be forgotten.

Levels of Processing

Whenever the teacher presents new information to students, provided that the students are paying attention, this new information will reside in STM. The job of the teacher, however, is to get the students to move this information from STM into LTM. Information can be moved from STM to LTM by acting upon the new information. Let an example serve to illustrate the point. You call the information operator to obtain a telephone number but unfortunately you do not have a pencil to write this number down onto paper. In all likelihood, as soon as you get the number from the operator you start to repeat the number to yourself over and over again until you have successfully dialed the number. This action plan is referred to as a control process known as rehearsal. In other words, you have acted upon the information (new telephone number) in an attempt to move it from STM to LTM. The same idea can be used in the learning of new motor skills. That is why it is so important to let students begin practicing movements within twenty to thirty seconds following demonstrations of skills. Because of this concept, we suggest that students are not asked if they have any questions following demonstrations. If a student does have a question, the twenty to thirty second time frame will expire and you will then be required to repeat the demonstration. Instead, let the children get moving as quickly as possible. It will be evident if they did or did not receive the appropriate information from the demonstration.

Verbal Labels

Memory can also be facilitated if meaningful labels are attached to physical movements. One verbal label which is frequently used in physical education is the clock face. For example, instead of just demonstrating a movement like hitting a tennis ball with a tennis racquet, tell the student to swing the racquet from six o'clock to twelve o'clock. If the student is capable of telling time, then this verbal label will probably help the student establish the vertical swinging technique needed to hit the tennis ball correctly. Above all, the label must be meaningful to the student. For instance, the above example would be of little value to a student who could not tell time.

Primacy-Recency Effect

The primacy-recency effect is a theory which suggests that we remember information which is first presented to us and also the most recent information which is presented. Thus during any class, the student is likely to have the most diffi-culty recalling the middle portion of the lesson. For this reason, it is suggested that the teacher spend the last few minutes of the class period reviewing the day's lesson—paying particular attention to reviewing the middle portion of the lesson.

Past Experience

One reason novice performers tend to experience difficulties in plotting strategies for solving movement problems is their inexperience with the task. The skilled performer, however, needs only to select the appropriate strategy from memory. Students can effectively acquire appropriate strategies by experiencing a wide variety of movement tasks under varying environmental conditions. Through trial and error, the learner will soon realize which strategies work in a given movement situation. This explains, in part, why correct practice generally improves performance.

FACTORS AFFECTING OUTPUT

OVERT PERFORMANCE

A multitude of physical, emotional, social, and cognitive factors can have an influence in accounting for individual differences in children's motor performance. Following is a presentation of some of these selected factors.

Physical

General Development. The sequence of a child's movement patterns is a good indicator of developmental age and provides information on the normalcy of the child. Since development is from the head toward the feet (cephalocaudal), the child will gain control of the head and upper body before the lower portion can be controlled. With development from the center of the body outward (proximodistal), gross motor movements using the large muscles of the arms and legs will develop before fine motor coordination requiring such things as finger dexterity. One can witness this pattern while watching a young child attempt to catch a ball. In the early stages of developing this skill, the child will tend to hug or trap the ball against the body (using large muscles of the shoulder). Not until several years later can the child catch the ball by using the small fine muscles of the hands. Thus maturation is a factor influencing performance.

Body Build. There are basically three body types: ectomorph (thin), mesomorph (muscular-athletic), and endomorph (fat). Body types are not usually well defined at the elementary level but become more obvious after puberty. In general, excess body fat is negatively associated with distance run events and with events which require the body to be projected through space such as high jumping and long jumping. To a great extent, body build is influenced by heredity. Since children will differ greatly in ability according to their body type, individualized instruction is a must.

Weight, Height, and Limb Length. Height and weight charts have been the traditional criteria for determining obesity. Unfortunately, such charts are nearly useless in all but extreme cases. The important factor in determining obesity is a person's percentage of body fat. The determination of body fat is discussed in greater detail in chapter 10. The myth that body fat will go away is just that, a myth. Fat cells developed in early childhood, it is believed, will remain forever, and are a leading cause of obesity in later life. Even those who were fat babies and are now thin find it more difficult to keep their weight down, due, it is thought, to the large number of fat cells which they possess.

Height and weight also affect performance in such things as balance, running, and fitness. Closely linked to height and weight is the center of gravity, which is influenced by the relationship between height and weight. The center of gravity is in the chest area in young children and in the pelvic area at maturity. Young children, therefore, experience difficulty in balance activities and in locomotor tasks which require quick and frequent change in directions.

In addition, closely associated with height and the center of gravity are the differing lengths of body segments. Children with long limbs have an inherited advantage in performing many motor tasks. For example, young children with long legs have a potential for a greater stride length, usually an advantage in running. Children with long arms have an inherited lever advantage which gives them the potential to throw a ball harder and farther than children with shorter arms.

Physical Fitness Factors. Strength, muscular endurance, cardiovascular endurance, and flexibility are all components of physical fitness which can obviously account for individual differences in both motor and physiological performance. Generally children who possess advanced degrees of these fitness components will excel over less fit children in most sports activities. For a complete discussion of these fitness components, refer to chapter 10.

Gender. There are very few physiological differences between boys and girls prior to ten years of age. Interests, however, vary based on background experience and parental attitude toward physical activities. There should be no separation of children based only on gender. Children should be separated according to interests and ability.

Age. Age and performance are directly related, with older children being superior to younger children. Motor learning is progressive and should build upon previous skills. Children who miss a certain stage of learning may have difficulty catching up at a later time.

Social/Emotional

Personality. Most studies on sports participation and personality have been done using college students as subjects. Whether the findings are applicable to elementary children is unknown. Researchers have found that those with aggressive personalities are more likely to participate in collision and contact sports. The researchers believe that the student selects the sport based on his/her own personality rather than the sport creating the personality. It is possible, however, that the personality development of the young child is influenced by participation in certain sports.

Self-Concept. The way a child feels about him/herself will influence performance. Those who have had poor experiences in physical endeavors tend to shy away from physical activity; the physically handicapped often experience problems in this area. Achievement will do much to improve self-concept, so every opportunity should be taken to select activities and present them in a manner that will ensure more success than failure. *The physical educator can do more good or harm to a child's self-concept than perhaps any other teacher.*

Motivation. Performance is dependent somewhat on motivation. The strongest motivation should be the intrinsic reward the student feels from a satisfactory performance. Extrinsic rewards such as stars, trophies, ribbons, etc., can also motivate, particularly in this society which has an extrinsic reward system in almost everything. Threats and punishment will do little to motivate performance or learning.

Anxiety. Stress and anxiety are closely linked to motivation and are important to performance. A certain amount of stress in the form of motivation is required for optimum performance. Figure 3.3 illustrates what is commonly referred to as the "Inverted U Theory." This theory explains the delicate balance between anxiety and performance. For optimum performance to occur just the right amount of stress must be present. Conversely, when anxiety is too low or too high performance will be less than optimum. High levels of anxiety are generally caused when a person's evaluation of a situation results in the person determining that he/she cannot meet the challenge about to be faced. Furthermore, if the outcome (winning or losing) of the event is extremely important to the person, then anxiety is further elevated. With these points in mind, it should be evident that high levels of anxiety can be successfully reduced. The

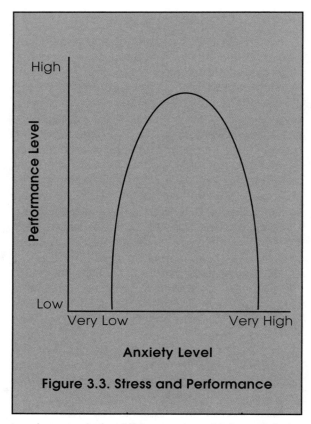

Figure 3.3. Stress and Performance

ent definitions. **Feedback** refers to information that the performer receives through the performer's own senses, while **knowledge of results** refers to information that the performer receives from some external source—generally the teacher. Both feedback and KOR are useful for error correction. KOR tends to be very important during the early stages of learning a new motor skill. This is because, at this stage of learning, novice performers are not capable of knowing what feedback information they should be attending to. As a result, the teacher must point out to the student aspects of performance which need to be corrected. Once the performer is able to establish a "model of correct performance," then feedback becomes more important. A "model of correct performance" is essentially an abstract representation in the performer's mind as to what correct performance should feel like. This abstract representation is compared with actual performance on each attempt and when the two do not match up, then corrections in performance need to be made.

When KOR is conveyed to a performer the teacher must be sure that the information is meaningful. For instance, a first grader can probably understand the direction, "Move a little faster" but would more than likely not be able to derive much useful meaning out of the directions, "You need to move 600 milliseconds faster." Thus for KOR to be useful the information given must be meaningful.

One other point needs to be made regarding KOR. That is, KOR should not be given after every performance trial. This is because the performer needs time to process (think about) the KOR information given to them. Furthermore, recall that the teacher is giving KOR in an attempt to help students develop their own "model of correct performance." When KOR is given after every performance trial students begin to ignore their internal feedback and use KOR as a crutch.

teacher can help children reduce high anxiety by giving them confidence in their ability to perform and meet the demands of the situation they are about to confront. This implies that instruction should emphasize working on skills that will be needed during the contest and that the teacher should make every effort to ensure that children experience success during skill practice. This will help the children to improve their self-confidence regarding their ability to handle the tasks that they will confront during the contest.

Feedback and Knowledge of Results. Sometimes the two terms *feedback* and *knowledge of results (KOR)* are used interchangeably. This is unfortunate because the two terms do have differ-

PRINCIPLES OF MOTOR LEARNING

1. Motor skill learning occurs in three stages.

Implication: When learners begin to acquire a new skill they are generally in a "cognitive stage of learning." Their attention is primarily focused on the cognitive aspects of the skill; for instance, how to hold the racquet, how to toss the ball, how to position the feet, etc. In fact, their minds are so

tied up with cognitive information they experience trouble performing the skill. Characteristics of learners in this beginning stage include large variability in performance, the making of many gross errors, and the inability to detect their own errors. This is why KOR is so important during the early stage of learning a new motor skill. After a lot of practice and experience the learner then enters the "associative stage of learning." In this stage the learner is able to detect some of his/her own errors, fewer gross errors are committed, and variability of performance begins to decrease; in other words, performance is becoming more predictable. The final stage of learning is called the "autonomous stage." At this point on the learning continuum the skill is performed without much conscious thought. As a result, the performer's attention can now be directed toward the opponent's actions instead of being tied up thinking about how to perform the skill. In this stage of learning the performer can detect and correct most all of his/her own errors and performance is very consistent. As should be evident, instruction methods differ depending upon which stage of learning the performer is experiencing.

2. Motor skills can be "closed" or "open."

Implication: Skills which are predictable and are not externally paced are said to be "closed." The key to practicing closed skills is repetition. For example, golf is considered a closed skill. Your goal for the most part is to be able to make a correct swing at the ball each time. Within reason, you are not being rushed by an opponent and the environment is relatively predictable; i.e., the ball will always be stationary when you attempt to strike it. On the other hand, "open" skills are performed in a varying environment and are not as predictable as closed skills. The key to practicing an open skill is variety. Tennis would be an example of an open skill. Your opponent dictates what shot you will hit and when the shot must be hit. Likewise, environmental conditions are always changing. For instance, sometimes your opponent may hit a hard shot, sometimes a soft shot; sometimes the ball is hit high in the air and at other times, close to the net. Because of the unpredictable environmental conditions associated with open skills, closed skills tend to be easier to perform. The teacher, when first introducing a new skill, should determine if the skill is opened or closed. Open skills should be modified during early stages of learning in an attempt to make them closed. For example, hitting a pitched baseball is a difficult open skill. However, the skill of striking a baseball can be simplified by introducing the new skill in the form of T-baseball. As the learner becomes proficient in the correct striking pattern the skill can gradually be made more difficult by making it more open.

Consider the following: The most difficult movement situation is one in which both the performer and the environment (ball) are in motion at the same time (running to hit a moving tennis ball, running to kick a moving ball or running into an already turning jump rope). The easiest movement situation is when a stationary performer is acting upon a stationary object (standing still and kicking a stationary ball). The key is that skills must first be taught in a closed format before proceeding to an open format.

3. Motor learning begins with movement exploration and experimentation.

Implication: The teaching styles used for children four to seven years of age should be free exploration and guided exploration. (See chapter 5 for styles of teaching.) A positive learning environment in which children are free to explore through movement and equipment should be established. The teacher's role is to plan the environment, motivate, and guide the children through a variety of experiences. The primary goal should be the development of the movement qualities and establishing a broad base of physical abilities upon which to build more specific movements and skills.

4. Demonstrations should be minimized during exploration, but are more important in formalized skill learning.

Implication: A command style of explanation/demonstration has limited value in the early childhood curriculum except where individualized instruction is necessary for a child with motor development problems. Most children will progress satisfactorily if the right environment and guidance are provided.

Long relay lines provide children with little movement.

5. There are critical learning periods during which the chances of success will be optimum.

Implication: Motor development progresses in a sequential pattern common to most individuals. Practice before the child has reached a state of readiness will have little positive effect on learning, and there is some evidence to suggest that behaviors not learned at the proper time will be more difficult to learn later. This has given rise to the theory of critical learning periods. Researchers lend support to the importance of a carefully planned movement program to insure optimum growth and development.

6. Motor learning goes from simple to complex.

Implication: A sequential program must be planned to develop prerequisite abilities for later success.

7. Practice does not necessarily make perfect.

Implication: Incorrect practice can lead to poor skill development. Such habits make later skill learning more difficult. Incorrect skill performance, therefore, should be corrected during the initial learning phase. Recall, this is one reason why it is important that the teacher administer knowledge of results regarding task performance.

8. There is a wide variance in skilled performance.

Implication: Although a number of principles of physics are common to sports skills, various forms can be used to apply these principles. One need only watch the different golf swings or tennis strokes to see the variety. The emphasis in teaching, therefore, should be on the application of principles rather than a perfection of form.

9. Success fosters more success.

Implication: Provide a curriculum in which children can achieve success most of the time.

10. Visual cues are more important in the early stages of specific skill learning.

Implication: Correctly administered demonstrations can be very helpful to the performer who is in an early stage of learning a new motor skill.

11. Skills can be practiced as a "whole" or in "parts."

Implication: Children should practice the whole activity whenever possible. It should be broken into parts only when the skill is high in complexity and low in organization. Complexity refers to the number of parts the task requires while organization refers to the relationship of the parts to one another. Thus if the skill is made up of many unrelated parts the "part method" is used. Eventually all the parts must be put together and performed as a whole.

12. Most skills have three parts: preparation, execution, and follow-through.

Implication: If skilled movement is desired, all three phases of the skill must be taught. Do not leave portions of the skill to chance development.

13. Only one cue at a time should be given.

Implication: When teaching, have the child focus on only one aspect of the skill at a time. The cue might be keeping the eyes on the ball or keeping the feet together. Excess cues will cause the learner to freeze (paralysis by analysis). Once the child is out of the "cognitive stage of learning" then it becomes possible to have the child focus attention on more than one aspect of the task at any given time.

14. Motor learning is extremely specific with transfer occurring only when components of the skills are highly interrelated.

Implication: There is no such thing as a natural all-around athlete. Some persons are able to learn different sports more quickly, but they must practice. A good wrestler, for example, may not be a good swimmer and a good swimmer may be a disaster on the basketball court. Even activities which seem highly related, such as badminton and tennis, are actually not. While both are racquet sports, in badminton the performer uses predominantly the wrist while in tennis the stroke is accomplished mainly by swinging from the shoulder. In fact, playing one activity may adversely affect performance in the other activity. This is a concept referred to as "proactive interference." Some general abilities are common to most sports, such as eye-hand coordination, strength, and endurance. Even these factors, however, are skill specific; i.e., strength in wrestling may not aid strength requirements in basketball.

15. Physiologically, warm-up is only necessary prior to all-out muscular endeavors.

Implication: Physiologically, warm-up is not necessary at the beginning of every class period and may sometimes be a waste of instructional time. Many elementary physical education activities do not require a warm-up. Warm-up is of value prior to such activities as sprints or activities which require all-out muscular effort. A warm-up, to be most effective, should raise the internal temperature of the body two degrees Celsius, which will normally produce sweating.

16. Knowledge of the principle behind skills helps children to transfer information to similar skills.

Implication: Skill instruction should be accompanied by an explanation of the principles involved when dealing with upper elementary children capable of understanding such information.

17. Practice of skills should be spaced rather than massed.

Implication: Practice sessions should be interspersed with rest periods to reduce the adverse effects of fatigue on skill performance. Long practice sessions may lead to incorrect performance and injury, as well as boredom or loss of interest in the activity.

SUMMARY

The motor learning process was dealt with in this chapter. The four phases of the process—input, central processing, output, and feedback—were covered in detail. Factors which influence each phase, such as the learner's age, attention span, past experience, and body build, were explained. A primary purpose was to show how complicated the motor learning process is and the need to be aware of the various factors that can affect children's performance and skill learning. In addition, the reader was exposed to selected principles of motor learning.

REFERENCES AND SUGGESTED READINGS

Keogh, J. and D. Sugden. *Movement Skill Development.* New York, NY: Macmillan Publishing Co., 1985.

Magill, R. *Motor Learning and Control: Concepts and Applications* (7th ed.). Boston, MA: McGraw-Hill, 2004.

Payne, V. and L. Isaacs. *Human Motor Development: A Life-span Approach* (6th ed.). Boston, MA: McGraw-Hill, 2005.

Schmidt, R. and Wrisberg. C.A. *Motor Learning and Performance: A Problem-Based Learning Approach (2nd ed.).* Champaign, IL: Human Kinetics Publishers, Inc.,2000.

Shumway-Cook, A. and Woollacott, M.H. *Motor Control: Theory and Practical Applications* (2nd ed.). Baltimore, MD: Lippincott Williams & Wilkins, 2001.

Chapter 4

Motor Assessment

After completing this chapter, the student should be able to:

1. List five important questions that one must ask before beginning the assessment process.

2. Describe five reasons why teachers may want to assess their students.

3. Describe the purpose of the *Mental Measurements Yearbook*.

4. Describe the three characteristics of the "ideal test."

5. Explain why "norms" are population specific.

6. List several physical and psychological needs which may need to be addressed before starting an assessment session.

7. List the three sources of information which must be communicated during a conference designed to share assessment results.

8. Define and then describe the advantages and disadvantages of the "norm-referenced" and "criterion-referenced" assessment instruments.

9. Describe four assessment instruments presented in the chapter.

10. Define the key terms listed below.

Key Terms

Content validity
Criterion-referenced assessment instruments
Norm-referenced assessment instruments
Objectivity

Process-oriented assessments
Product-oriented assessments
Test battery
Test reliability

Time does not often permit much formalized testing, but those who are able or who need to evaluate children with special motor needs should find the information in this chapter helpful. As a result of time constraints, most assessment at the elementary level, unfortunately, must be done through informal observation rather than formal testing. As mentioned several times in this text, however, assessment is extremely important to curriculum planning. So no matter which approach is taken—formal or informal—a teacher should have as much assessment knowledge as possible.

Certain studies suggest that many physical educators fail to properly assess their students' motor behaviors (Safrit & Wood, 1995). In fact, one study that Haubenstricker conducted (1984) found that physical educators devote very little time to motor assessment, and when assessment does occur, it most frequently takes the form of a teacher-made test. Why does this dilemma exist? Many teachers complain that tests are too difficult, too time-consuming, and too expensive to administer, but there are many valid assessment instruments that teachers in school settings can feasibly administer. We believe the primary culprit is a lack of teacher training—many teachers simply do not fully understand the role of assessment and do not know how to select and administer tests. This chapter is designed to help teachers and others overcome this deficiency. It describes why teachers should assess, what they should assess, how to prepare students for assessment, and how to select the assessment instrument that best meets personal needs. Several norm-referenced and process-oriented assessment instruments are also reviewed.

GUIDELINES FOR ASSESSMENT

The assessment process should not be approached haphazardly; it should be planned systematically. Following are five important questions to consider before beginning to assess students:

1. Why do you want to assess your students?
2. What variables do you plan to assess?
3. Which tests purport to assess the important variables that you have identified?
4. How can you prepare your students for assessment?
5. How do you share results?

Why Assess

Many professionals assess student performance as a simple matter of course, probably because when they were in school their instructor periodically assessed their performance. But assessment of student performance should be carried out with a specific purpose in mind, such as one of the following:

1. *Screening.* Screening is a process whereby people are assessed to determine if they should be referred for further testing or whether they need a special program of instruction. Practically speaking, a physical education instructor may want to screen students at the beginning of the school year to identify children who have special needs.

2. *Program content.* Assessment results can be used to help plan the content of your program. By assessing students' incoming ability, you will be able to write program objectives that challenge students.

3. *Student progress.* Assessment can also be used to determine how well students are proceeding toward course objectives.

4. *Program evaluation.* You can assess your students' performance to determine whether a specific program of instruction is fostering their skill development.

5. *Classification.* Through assessment, it is possible to place students in homogeneous or heterogeneous groups. For example, when equating teams for competition, it is best if the two teams competing against each other have similar skills.

What Variables to Assess

Once you have determined why you need to assess, determine which variables to assess. Instructional units that are tied to specific course objectives generally indicate which variables need to be assessed; for example, in a gymnastics unit, you may want to assess balance and upper body strength. In short, assess those variables that are part of your course objectives.

Selecting the Best Test

Now review all available tests that purport to assess the variables in question. Popular physical education measurement textbooks contain descriptions of available tests (Burton & Miller, 1998; Safrit & Wood, 1995), as does the classic *Mental Measurements Yearbook* (Plaket & Impara, 2001).

After consulting these references, you should be able to identify several tests that assess the variables you are interested in. Now you must decide which test instrument best meets your needs. To help you make this decision, consider each of the following questions:

1. Is the test statistically valid, reliable, and objective?
2. If the test is norm-referenced, are the norms established on a population similar to the one you plan to assess?
3. Is the test instrument feasible to administer?
4. Do you have the training and expertise to administer the test as well as interpret the results?

Characteristics of Ideal Tests. Acceptable test instruments should be valid, reliable, and objective. A valid test measures what it claims to measure. One type of validity frequently used in motor development and physical education is *content validity:* the instrument contains tasks that measure specific content of interest. This type of validity is often logically determined by a panel of experts. For example, experts have determined that the 50-yard dash is a valid indicator of running speed because it measures how fast a person runs. Other types of validity are statistically determined; a detailed discussion of them is beyond the scope of this text.

Consistency of test results is another important characteristic of a good test. A test is reliable if student scores do not significantly vary from day to day, assuming that the students have not received additional instruction. Thus test *reliability* is the test score's freedom from error.

The third characteristic of an ideal test is *objectivity* (sometimes called *inter-rater reliability*), which is the degree of accuracy to which a test is scored. Content validity is frequently determined subjectively, but both reliability and objectivity are determined statistically. Statistical determination is possible by computing a *correlation coefficient* for two sets of scores. For example, to determine objectivity, a set of ratings compiled by one scorer is

Assessing kinesthetic awareness.

correlated with the scores obtained by a second scorer. Because the resulting correlation coefficient can never be greater than ±1.00, a correlation of ±.80 or ±.90 is generally deemed acceptable.

Caution: Norms Are Population-Specific. Norms describe how large groups of people score in regard to selected variables. Because one large group can differ from another large group in regard to a variable of interest, norms are population-specific. An example is norms for the variable height. Since American children are generally taller than Japanese children, it would be inappropriate to interchange normative values within these two populations. The same holds true regarding tests of motor proficiency. Therefore, if you decide to use a norm-referenced test, make certain that the norms were established on a population similar to the one you intend to assess.

Test Feasibility. You may find several tests that meet all the selection criteria, so the last step is to determine which of these tests is more feasible to administer. Consider the following points:

1. Which test can be administered in the least amount of time?
2. Must you administer the test individually, or can it be administered to groups?
3. Do you have the training and expertise to administer the test? (Some tests require extensive training.)

4. Do you have all the necessary supplies and equipment needed for test administration? Some tests must be purchased as part of a test kit that may cost several hundred dollars.

5. You must determine if you have the training and expertise to interpret the test results.

Besides referring to the publications mentioned earlier in this section, consult the test manual that accompanies most tests. Generally, the manual describes in detail how the test was developed and how it should be administered.

Preparing Students for Assessment

Without a doubt, requiring children to perform strange motor tasks, in unfamiliar surroundings, in front of strangers, while sometimes using strange-looking equipment, can produce a great deal of test anxiety. However, there are several steps that should help reduce this uneasy feeling that frequently accompanies the administration of an assessment instrument. Horvat and Kalakian (1996) suggested that, before assessing, consideration be given to the test environment and the participants' physical and psychological needs.

Test Environment. The room where the assessment is to be administered should be as comfortable as possible, and the room's temperature and lighting should be ideal. The testing area should be free of unnecessary furniture and free from distractions, such as high noise levels. Above all, the area should be free from potential hazards.

Meeting Physical Needs. Also consider the children's physical needs. For example, thirsty participants or those who must use the restroom will have their attention distracted from the assessment situation. Establish a procedure whereby you ask *before assessment begins* whether or not the child needs to be excused.

Meeting Psychological Needs. The following procedures help reduce test anxiety:

1. When participants arrive, do not rush into the assessment; engage them in informal conversation for a couple of minutes. Introduce yourself, and get the participants to talk about themselves. Ask a question such as, "What are some of your favorite activities?" This technique relaxes the participants by making them focus their attention on themselves instead of the assessment.

2. Tell the participants what they will be doing during the assessment. In other words, reveal the unexpected.

3. When talking with the participants, try not to use the word "test," which can make many people nervous.

4. If equipment is to be used during the assessment, give participants an opportunity to explore it before assessment begins. For example, before requiring participants to catch a ball, first let them informally play with the ball, so they can experience for themselves that the ball is soft and will not harm them.

Sharing Assessment Results

Once test results have been analyzed and interpreted, the information should be shared with the appropriate people. Depending upon the circumstances, these appropriate people are the parents, fellow teachers, the school nurse, and a host of other professionals. This information can be shared through written communication, but face-to-face communication is best for reviewing the written assessment. Realistically, however, individual conferences are not always possible when large groups of people are involved. Nevertheless, whether you convey assessment results individually or through written communication, the goal of the communication is the same: an explanation of why you assessed, what you assessed, and what the assessment revealed. Be careful to use terminology that the lay person will understand; especially avoid using complicated statistical terms. Remember that parents are going to be interested in knowing what they can do to improve their child's motor abilities, so be prepared to offer program suggestions. Also have references available to which you can refer the parents for additional program information.

TYPES OF ASSESSMENT INSTRUMENTS

After realistically considering the questions above, you will be in a better position to choose which type of test will best meet your needs. This section examines the advantages and disadvantages of several assessment tools.

Norm-Referenced

Norm-referenced (NR) assessment instruments are basically *quantitative evaluations* designed to compare a person's skills and abilities with those of others from similar age, sex, and socioeconomic categories. Since the normative scales are derived from statistical procedures, these types of instruments are sometimes referred to as psychometric. Current popular NR tests are the Bruininks-Oseretsky Test of Motor Proficiency (Bruininks, 1978) and the Test of Gross Motor Development-2 (Ulrich, 2000).

Advantages. Norm-referenced tests are popular because most are easy to administer. The examiner needs minimal training to administer the test, and scoring procedures generally are simple. The assessment score provides information as to where a person stands in relation to peers at a given point in time.

Disadvantages. Because NR scales provide information concerning a person's "average" functioning, they are not precise and cannot pinpoint the cause of skill or developmental deficits. They simply supply information as to where a given person stands in comparison to people from similar backgrounds. Scores obtained from NR tests generally offer little insight into programming considerations.

Criterion-Referenced

Criterion-referenced (CR) assessment instruments evaluate the "quality" of a person's performance. Since development proceeds along a predictable sequence of milestones, it is possible to determine where a person lies within this continuum. Thus, one major difference between NR and CR assessments is that the latter compare people to themselves over time, whereas the former compare people to a standardized population at a given point in time. With CR tests, the examiner's primary interest, for example, is not how far a person can throw a ball, but the technique (form) the person uses when projecting the ball. Motor development professionals frequently refer to this type of assessment as "process-oriented" (Gallahue, 1982) as compared to "product-oriented," which is discussed below.

Advantages. Results from CR assessment instruments lend more insight into programming considerations than do results from NR tests. The CR test also provides for true developmental assessment; that is, comparing a person to self-performance along a continuum from immature to mature performance styles.

Disadvantages. CR tests are more complicated to administer than NR tests, so much more training is needed. Frequently, the examiner must learn many functional definitions for intraskill components, which often causes scoring difficulties.

PRODUCT-ORIENTED ASSESSMENT

Motor development researchers in the first half of the century relied heavily upon the use of *product-oriented assessment* techniques. When employing this approach, the examiner is more interested in performance outcomes than the technique used to perform the task, for instance, how far or how fast a person can throw a ball. The form or technique used to throw the ball is generally of little interest to the product-oriented assessment examiner. Thus product-oriented assessments are similar to NR assessments since both measure quantitative performance outcomes. They differ in that with NR assessments, normative data have been established for the quantitative measures. The advantages and disadvantages of product-oriented assessments are similar to those for NR assessments.

Product- vs. Process-Oriented Assessment: A Comparative Example. Pretend that you are to assess the catching ability of a seven-year-old girl. The following examples illustrate major differences between product- and process-oriented assessment.

Product-Oriented Assessment. Without doubt, the simplest product-oriented assessment to evaluate catching performance is the pass-fail system. The girl's performance is assessed by determining the number of thrown balls that she retained versus the number of balls she dropped. To score, one point is awarded for each ball retained; dropped balls are recorded as zero points.

Process-Oriented Assessment. Within the discipline of motor development, the most widely discussed process-oriented assessment techniques are those Roberton and colleagues at the University of Wisconsin-Madison described. Their technique is based on the idea that because development occurs at different times within different body components, assessment of motor behavior should involve a segmental or component approach. This component approach requires "the identification of developmental characteristics of body parts within a task" (Safrit & Wood, 1995, p. 303). Refer to table 4.1 which illustrates the hypothesized developmental sequence for catching. Note that the emphasis in this type of evaluation is how each body component reacts to the oncoming projectile.

Roberton and Halverson (1984, pp. 53-54), both noted for their use of process-oriented assessment, point out several major drawbacks of this approach. They felt that a comprehensive understanding of developmental steps and a prolonged period of study and practice of the techniques are required:

"Pre-observation study of the definitions of each developmental step and the decision rules for identifying that step is always necessary. The ease with which successful coaches and teachers seem to spot the movement characteristics of their athletes and students comes from years of hard work. Fortunately, the satisfaction of being able to help children improve their movement because one could see what they are doing is well worth the effort."

Barrett recognized that learning to correctly observe motor performance for the purpose of assessment is an art that must be practiced. In her textbook *Physical Education for Children: A Focus on the Teaching Process* (Logsdon et al., 1977), Barrett described observational exercises that, if followed, will help you learn the fine art of movement observation.

Table 4.1. Developmental Sequences for Catching: Component Approach

Preparation: Arm Component

Step 1: The arms are outstretched with elbows extended, awaiting the tossed ball.
Step 2: The arms await the ball toss with some shoulder flexion still apparent, but flexion now appears in the elbows.
Step 3: The arms await the ball in a relaxed posture at the sides of the body or slightly ahead of the body. The elbows may be flexed.

Reception: Arm Component

Step 1: The arms remain outstretched and the elbows rigid. There is little to no "give," so the ball bounces off the arms.
Step 2: The elbows flex to carry the hands upward toward the face. Initially, ball contact is primarily with the arms, and the object is trapped against the body.
Step 3: Initial contact is with the hands. If unsuccessful in using the fingers, the child may still trap the ball against the chest. The hands still move upward toward the face.
Step 4: Ball contact is made with the hands. The elbows still flex but the shoulders extend, bringing the ball down and toward the body rather than up toward the face.

Head Component

Step 1: The palms of the hand face upward. (Rolling balls elicit a palms-down, trapping action.)
Step 2: The palms of the hands face each other.
Step 3: The palms of the hands are adjusted to the flight and size of the oncoming object. Thumbs or little fingers are placed close together, depending on the height of the flight path.

Body Component

Step 1: There is no adjustment of the body in response to the flight path of the ball.
Step 2: The arms and trunk begin to move in relation to the ball's flight path.
Step 3: The feet, trunk, and arms all move to adjust to the path of the oncoming ball.

Note: These sequences have not been validated. They were hypothesized by Harper (1979).
Source: Roberton and Halverson (1984)

Example of a Norm-Referenced Instrument

This section briefly describes one popular norm-referenced assessment instrument: the *Bruininks-Oseretsky Test of Motor Proficiency*.

The Bruininks-Oseretsky Test of Motor Proficiency (BOTMP) is a norm-referenced *test battery* of eight subtests comprising forty-six items. A short form, which comprises fourteen items from the complete battery, can be used as a quick screening device. The battery provides both a comprehensive index of motor proficiency and individual measures of fine and gross motor skills for children 4.5 to 14.5 years old. The complete battery can be administered in forty-five to sixty minutes; the short form takes approximately fifteen to twenty minutes.

Test administration does require various pieces of equipment. The required equipment can be made, or it can be bought for about $500 (it comes in a well-designed, well-packaged carrying case). The price includes score sheets, equipment needed to administer the complete battery, and the examiner's manual, which contains all the standardized tables needed to score the text.

The standardization procedures included a sampling of 765 children selected on the basis of age, sex, race, community size, and geographic region in accordance with the 1970 census (Bruininks, 1978). Average test-retest reliability for the complete battery and short form are .87 and .86 respectively. Haubenstricker and associates (1981) found the BTOMP useful for discriminating between "normal" children and those with gross motor dysfunction.

Selected Process-Oriented Assessment Instruments

This section describes four popular process-oriented assessment instruments. Included in the discussion are the Ohio State University Scale of Intra-Gross Motor Assessment (SIGMA), the Developmental Sequence of Motor Skills Inventory, the Fundamental Motor Pattern Assessment Instrument, and the recently developed Test of Gross Motor Development.

SIGMA. The Ohio State University Scale of Intra-Gross Motor Assessment (SIGMA) (Loovis and Ersing, 1979) is a criterion-referenced assessment tool designed to evaluate the motor behavior of normal preschool and elementary school children as well as the young mentally retarded child. Each of the eleven fundamental motor skills examined (walking, stair climbing, running, throwing, catching, jumping, hopping, skipping, striking, kicking, ladder climbing) is presented in four developmental levels. The authors state that SIGMA is unique from other tests in that it can be administered in formal testing situations or in an informal free play setting. Ease of test administration is simplified because of a skill format sheet. Each sheet contains five sources of information to help the examiner: (1) equipment needed to administer the test, (2) directions about the test conditions, (3) criterion test performance, (4) references from which more information about the skill can be obtained, and (5) summative term/phrases that best describe the child's performance.

SIGMA's content validity was determined by a panel of eleven experts who used a 5-point Likert-type scale to rate the test for understandability and usefulness and by documentary analysis of the literature (Sherrill, 1986). Reliability of student performance was not reported. However, thirteen judges were required to rate the performance of twelve children who had been videotaped. The tape was viewed twice, one week apart, and the data were analyzed by Scott's pi statistic. Inter-judge agreement ranged from .50 to 1.00; intrajudge agreement ranged from .67 to 1.00.

One unique aspect of the SIGMA is its accompanying program, the Performance Based Curriculum (PBC). The PBC is essentially an instructional program that states objectives and activities for each developmental level within each skill. The PBC is directly related to the SIGMA in that it provides a critical link between assessment and program intervention.

Developmental Sequence of Motor Skills Inventory. Unlike the segmental analysis Roberton and colleagues used, other professionals prefer to use a more global analysis based on the configuration of the total body during performance of a task. This assessment technique evolved from identification of developmental sequences within selected skills. Each sequence consists of four to five stages stated in terms of observable behaviors. The teacher's task is to observe children performing the skills and to then classify them according to their level of development. Gallahue (1982) called this "total body configuration" approach the Developmental Sequence of Motor Skills Inventory. To date, the developmental sequences that have been studied are running, hopping, skipping, long jumping, throwing, catching, striking, kicking, and punting. Validity and reliability for some of these tasks have been reported elsewhere (Ulrich, 1985).

Fundamental Motor Pattern Assessment Instrument. The Fundamental Motor Pattern Assessment Instrument was developed as an outgrowth of a 1976 doctoral dissertation by McClenaghan and later published by McClenaghan and Gallahue (1978). This observational instrument can be used to assess developmental changes over time for the following fundamental patterns: walking, running, jumping, throwing overhand, catching, and kicking. The performer's quality of movement is scored as being in one of three stages of development: (1) initial stage—first observable attempt at performing the movement pattern; (2) elementary stage—improved coordination and the addition of more mature patterns being integrated into the movement; (3) mature stage—skilled, coordinated, adult-like performance.

Stage descriptions are accompanied by well-illustrated visuals that serve as scoring aids. The authors report test-retest reliability performance of 88.6 percent, with interrater objectivity ranging from 80 to 95 percent (McClenaghan and Gallahue, 1978).

Test of Gross Motor Development - 2. The Test of Gross Motor Development - 2 (TGMD-2) represents a major revision to this assessment instrument, which was first released in 1985 (Ulrich, 2000). This revised instrument can now be used to identify children between 3 and 11 years of age who may be significantly behind their peers in gross motor skill development and therefore eligible for special education services. The test assesses twelve motor skills that are divided into two subtests: locomotor skills and object-control skills. Locomotor skills measured are the run, gallop, hop, skip, horizontal jump, leap, and slide; object-control skills include striking a stationary ball, stationary dribble, catch, kick, overhand throw, and underhand roll. TGMD-2 updates to the first edition include new normative data based on projected 2000 census; normative data stratified by age relative to geography, gender, race, and residence; age norms divided by one-half-year increments; and new reliability and validity studies. Reliability coefficients for the locomotor subtest average .85; for the object-control subtest the average is .88; and for the gross motor composite the average is .91. One recent study found that 88 percent of physical education students and 96

percent of physical education teachers could correctly classify a special education student's level of motor development following only three 50-minute training sessions with the TGMD-1 (Suomi & Suomi, 1997).

ASSESSING THE HANDICAPPED

Comparative studies of handicapped and non-handicapped populations support the contention that although individuals with selected special needs perform behind their "normal" peers, both may follow similar patterns of development (DeRocco, 1979). Unfortunately, many assessment instruments, both norm- and criterion-referenced, are geared toward the so-called normal population and so cannot be appropriately used with special populations. For instance, a child with spina bifida who is confined to a wheelchair may have normal motor ability in the upper extremities, but the inability to use the legs while throwing a ball makes normative performance data comparisons inappropriate (DiRocco, 1979).

Special populations pose other potential problems concerning assessment instruments geared to "normal" populations. Frequently the developmental starting points for special children are so low that their scores are not included in the assessment materials. Clearly, there is a need for the development of more valid test instruments to assess the motor development of those with handicapping conditions. Perhaps the passage of the Education for All Handicapped Children Act (PL 94-142) will ensure more emphasis on the development of such assessment instruments.

AIDS IN ASSESSING MOTOR SKILLS

As mentioned, one disadvantage of many tests is the need for the test examiner to learn many functional definitions describing the criterion behavior associated with each developmental level within a given skill. Checklists or reminder sheets that list key descriptive terms for each developmental level can jog the examiner's memory. Regardless of a person's expertise with the developmental stages of selected tasks, it is still an excellent idea to have such a checklist at hand, to ensure consistent scoring.

Videotaping individual performance is another way to assess motor skills. Certain motor skills must be executed at high rates of speed, so even the experienced examiner may have difficulty denoting exactly what took place within each body segment during the performance of the task. Today's video units are capable of slow-motion playback, thus affording more precise analysis of most motor skills. However, one motor skill that does not totally lend itself to video analysis is the overarm throw for force because the video unit's framing rate is not fast enough to freeze the ballistic movement of the throwing arm. As a result, the throwing arm is likely to be blurred.

Another advantage of videotaping is that it decreases the number of times a child must perform a task so the examiner can evaluate the developmental level of each body segment. Within a given test session, for example, a very young child may become fatigued if required to perform a forward roll twenty times. With videotaping or filming, the child need perform only a few trials. The examiner at a later time can play back the tape or film many times while evaluating each body segment.

SUMMARY

Psychomotor assessment should be systematically, not haphazardly, based on a plan that links assessment with curricular programming.

It is difficult to select an appropriate test instrument. The instrument should be valid, reliable, objective, and feasible to administer and interpret.

However, the most important characteristic is test validity. If the test fails to assess what it purports to assess, the instrument is of no value.

Norm-referenced test instruments are popular because most are easy to administer and usually require minimal examiner training. This type of assessment provides information about a person's average functioning. On the other hand, criterion-referenced assessment instruments evaluate quality of individual performance. The Bruininks-Oseretsky Test of Motor Proficiency is a norm-referenced assessment instrument.

Popular process-oriented assessment instruments include: the Ohio State University Scale of Intra-Gross Motor Assessment (SIGMA), Developmental Sequence of Motor Skills Inventory, the Fundamental Motor Pattern Assessment Instrument, and the Test of Gross Motor Development-2.

Do not use an assessment instrument geared to a "normal" population when assessing handicapped people. At present, there is a need for more assessment instruments to be validated with handicapped populations.

Videotaping individual performance is another way to assess motor skills. Videotaping slows down some movements so they can be analyzed more accurately. Unfortunately, however, if the movements are too fast for the video's framing rate, the images will be blurred.

REFERENCES AND SUGGESTED READINGS

Bruininks, R. H. *Bruininks-Oseretsky Test of Motor Proficiency.* Circle Pines, MN: American Guidance Service, 1978.

Burton, A.W. and D.E. Miller. *Movement skill assessment.* Champaign, IL: Human Kinetics, 1998

DiRocco, P. "Physical Education and the Handicapped: Developmental Approach," *Physical Education,* 36: 127-131, 1979.

Gallahue, D. L. *Understanding Motor Development in Children.* New York: Wiley, 1982.

Huabenstricker, J. *The Assessment of Motor Skills in Grades 4 to 6.* Anaheim, CA: Paper presented at the ARAPCS Measurement and Evaluation Council at the AAHPERD Convention, 1984.

Haubenstricker, J., et al. *The Efficiency of the Briuninks-Osertsky Test of Motor Proficiency in Discriminating Between Normal Children and Those With Gross Motor Dysfunction.* Boston: Paper presented at the Motor Development Academy at the AAHPERD Convention, 1981.

Horvat, M. and L. H. Kalakian. *Assessment in Adapted Physical Education and Therapeutic Recreation* (2nd ed.). Madison, WI: Brown & Benchmark, 1996.

Jasma, P., ed. *The Psychomotor Domain and the Seriously Handicapped.* Washington, D.C.: University Press of America, 1981.

Logsdon, B. J., et al. *Physical Education for Children: A Focus on the Teaching Process.* Philadelphia: Lea & Febiger, 1977.

Loovis, E. M. and W. F. Ersing. *Assessing and Programming Gross Motor Development for Children* (2nd ed.). Loudonville, Ohio: Mohican Textbook Publishing, 1979.

McClenaghan, B., and D. Gallahue. *Fundamental Movement: A Developmental and Remedial Approach.* Philadelphia: Saunders, 1978.

Payne, G.V. and L.D. Isaacs. *Human Motor Development: A Lifespan Approach* (6th ed.). Boston, MA: McGraw-Hill, 2005.

Plake, B.S. and J.C. Impara. *The Fourteenth Mental Measurements Yearbook.* Lincoln, NE: University of Nebraska Press, 2001.

Roberton, M. A. and L. E. Halverson. *Developing Children—Their Changing Movement.* Philadelphia: Lea & Febiger,1984.

Safrit, M. J. and T.M. Wood. *Introduction to Measurement in Physical Education and Exercise Science* (3rd ed.). St. Louis. MO: Times Mirror/Mosby, 1995.

Sherrill, C. *Adapted Physical Education and Recreation: A Multidisciplinary Approach* (3rd ed.). Dubuque, Iowa: Brown,1986.

Suomi, R. and J. Suomi. Effectiveness of a training program with physical education students and experienced physical education teachers in scoring the test of gross motor development. *Perceptual and Motor Skills,* 84, 771-778, 1997.

Ulrich, D.A. *Test of Gross Motor Development - 2.* Austin, TX: Pro-Ed, 2000.

Chapter 5

The Teacher

After completing this chapter, the student should be able to:

1. Give a principle of learning and state its application to a teaching/learning situation.

2. List and describe the importance of at least 80 percent of the measurable teacher behaviors discussed in the chapter.

3. Cite at least four examples of important nonverbal behavior.

4. Discuss why nonverbal behavior is important to the teacher.

5. Describe and give examples of each teaching style.

6. Give one example for each of the four levels of questions.

7. List and describe two ways to evaluate the teaching/learning environment.

8. Define the key terms listed below

Key Terms

Beginning teacher assistance program
Interaction analysis
Measurable teacher behaviors
Nonverbal behavior
Principles of learning

Professionalism
Redundancies
Styles of teaching
Teacher/pupil interaction

In the learning environment, the most important element is the teacher, but what is a good teacher? For years, this question has been the focus of numerous studies, panels, and committees. All this work has generally lead to absolutely no agreement, numerous law suits, and a lot of paper. Many would say teaching is immeasurable. What are behaviors which make one teacher better than another? There is no agreement on a standard set of behaviors. Everyone seems to concur, however, that measuring teaching behaviors is an imperfect science.

Some of the behaviors frequently mentioned as important to good teaching are patience, a sense of humor, effective communication, enthusiasm, knowledge, preparation, character, control and discipline, and professionalism. Although there are obviously many others that could be included, this list is representative. How can enthusiasm be measured? Or character? How about sense of humor? If teaching behaviors are going to be measurable, undefined terms must be clarified.

Behaviorists would suggest that any behavior for which data cannot be obtained cannot be changed. If individuals want to improve their teaching, therefore, they must be able to evaluate their actions. Exhibited behaviors as well as their frequency must be known. One learning principle, for example, specifies that children learn best in a positive learning environment. Since most would agree that a positive environment is fostered by praise rather than criticism, knowing the frequency one praises or criticizes the children would be helpful.

This chapter's focus is on those teaching behaviors which can be measured.

Frequent praise is one teacher behavior that fosters a positive learning environment.

MEASURABLE TEACHER BEHAVIORS

KNOWING AND APPLYING PRINCIPLES OF LEARNING

A teacher's knowledge and use of learning principles is the cornerstone of good teaching. A principle is a fundamental truth about how people learn; it has been researched and, if properly applied, will assist in promoting learning. A violated principle, of course, will have the opposite effect. The importance of the principles of learning cannot be understated. Knowledge of a principle is easy to evaluate, but the practical application of a principle requires additional information. The following is a presentation of some key principles of learning along with information on how they can be practiced in the classroom or gymnasium.

1. **It is more efficient to learn concepts than facts.**

   Application: Although facts are important during early learning, concepts should be emphasized when working with children nine years of age and above. These older children can then begin to apply these concepts in a variety of situations. Several physiological and kinesiological concepts can be generalized to many different tasks. Concepts of balance, propulsion, fitness, giving and receiving force, and trajectory can be applied to movement and sports skills. To improve balance, for example, children can be taught to widen their base of support and lower their center of gravity. Thus the children can apply the concept to activities requiring balance. Attempting to have children younger than nine understand these concepts as suggested by those promoting the "themes" approach is highly questionable.

2. **Learning is facilitated when the child is motivated.**

   Application: Children will be motivated when they achieve success in a program which provides challenging activity; has lots of movement; and is taught by a compassionate teacher that treats them with respect.

3. **Children who help make decisions about their learning will be more motivated to learn.**

   Application: Decision-making can be

Decision-making can be a cooperative group decision.

facilitated at every grade level through use of anonymous attitude questionnaires (see appendix B). Although data obtained from older children are usually more valuable, questionnaires can be used at any grade level. Through open discussion, it is also possible for students to help determine the rules, select activities, and discuss matters affecting them. This is not to suggest that the children design the curriculum or overrule the teacher's decision, but by involving the children, the teacher can determine attitudes which are an important factor in such areas as control, discipline, and enthusiastic participation.

4. **Children who are not afraid to make mistakes learn more rapidly.**

   Application: A child-centered teaching approach such as problem-solving should be used. Approaches which focuses the class' attention on a single child's performance, unless the child volunteers to demonstrate the skill, should be avoided. Anytime a child makes a legitimate effort, he/she should receive praise.

5. **Undue pressure on students may result in negative behavior such as fear, lack of participation, striking out at the teacher either physically or verbally, or psychosomatic illness.**

Application: Obviously, this is not a principle the teacher wants to practice, but many teachers unknowingly place pressure on students through the curriculum and teaching approach. A curriculum heavily oriented toward sports skills and competition, particularly during the early elementary years, can cause undue pressure. Competition should be introduced gradually and should be reserved for grades 3-5, and then at a much reduced level when compared to secondary athletic activities. A child-centered approach should be used at all grade levels.

6. **Any behavior, positive or negative, which receives attention is more likely to recur.**

   Application: Good behavior should be rewarded and negative behavior ignored whenever possible. Children need to be reinforced when they follow the rules and perform correctly. On the other hand, negative behavior is most frequently an attention-getting device, and punishment may actually cause it to be repeated. The correct way to handle negative behavior is discussed in chapter 6. The learning environment is significantly influenced by how effectively the teacher handles both positive and negative behavior.

7. **To be most effective, rewards must be closely connected to the desired behavior.**

Children should not be confronted in front of their peers since their negative behavior may be reinforced.

Application: To reinforce a positive behavior, the teacher must remember to give praise as soon as possible following the behavior.

8. **Threats and punishment have uncertain effects on learning.**

   Application: Although they may be necessary at times, threats and punishment should be avoided in favor of positive consequences for good behavior. Children, however, must know the rules as well as the negative consequences for violations. Prior to making a threat, the feasibility of its implementation must be determined. Consistency of rules and their consequences is one of the biggest difficulties new teachers experience. Punishment can have an immediate effect, but the negative consequences on student attitudes favor a more positive approach.

9. **Children learn best when the task is challenging but not overwhelming.**

   Application: Evaluating the children's ability level and then selecting appropriate activities is essential to accomplishing this principle. As stated in the definition of physical education, the curriculum is a planned *sequence* of activities; this sequence is based upon evaluation. By using problem-solving questions (see "Teaching Approaches" below), the teacher can immediately see how difficult a task is and can direct the children toward greater challenges without causing undue frustration.

10. **Strict discipline may produce anxiety, shyness, and acquiescence in children, while a more relaxed approach is associated with initiative and creativity.**

    Application Discipline is absolutely necessary to successful teaching but how one practices discipline can make a significant difference. For purposes of discussion, one approach is called static control and the other dynamic control. In static control, fear tends to rule, and children are often inhibited. In dynamic control, children feel free to move, explore, and be creative, but when an appropriate signal is given, they immediately stop, look, and listen. In determining how to approach discipline, the problem is determining what is too strict or too permissive. The recommended approach to student control is to use positive reinforcement for correct behavior, and not rewarding bad behavior with attention. Children should be praised individually and as a group when they do the right thing. The children should help to design as well as understand the reason for every rule, and should be required to follow the rules all the time. Negative behavior must be dealt with carefully to avoid giving it too much attention (see chapter 6). Although the positive approach is preferred, children must understand the negative consequences for rule violations.

11. **Criticism, failure, and discouragement will damage a child's self-confidence, level of aspiration, and sense of worth.**

    Application: As pointed out in other principles, the learning environment should be positive. Using a child-centered approach, activities should be offered which challenge the child but provide success with effort. Praise should be liberally used. There is no place in education for physical and mental child abuse. Improving the child's self-concept should be an extremely high priority.

12. **Children learn in different ways and at different rates.**

    Application: No one way of teaching is going to satisfy every learning style. Teachers, therefore, should vary their teaching according to the various learning styles. Children should be evaluated to determine their learning styles, and the learning environment must be individualized as much as possible. An open education classroom will include learning centers for those who learn on their own, leaving the teacher time to work with those requiring more direction.

13. **An intermittent reinforcement schedule will produce behaviors which are difficult to extinguish.**

    Application: This principle has both positive and negative consequences. On the positive side, the intermittent schedule can be used to produce strong positive behaviors. When dealing with negative behavior, teachers must be careful not to give it unnecessary attention, and must be consistent in dealing with problem behavior. When enforcing rules, for example, teachers must not be easy on one occasion and strict the next.

Observable behavior is an indicator of learning

14. **Learning cannot be observed, but can be inferred when there is a relatively permanent change in observable behavior which is not due to maturation.**

    Application: To determine the effectiveness of teaching, one must be able to measure changes in observable behavior. For elementary physical education that normally means seeing changes in physical ability, but can include hearing responses to questions asked. When children's performance improves through teaching, learning can be inferred. By using behavioral objectives, teachers can pre- and post-test the children to determine this improvement.

KNOWLEDGE

A teacher's knowledge is usually evaluated in two areas, *general knowledge* and *subject knowledge.* Obviously, a person must have subject knowledge in order to teach it. There are many, however, that suggest a strong liberal arts background is necessary to properly prepare a classroom teacher. A standardized test which includes a liberal arts section is often required to obtain a state teaching certificate. A commonly used test, *The National Teacher's Exam,* includes sections to evaluate both subject as well as general knowledge. Actions are being taken in some state legislatures to require a liberal arts education at the undergraduate level prior to entering a teacher education curriculum. Thought by many to be an attack against the numerous teaching methods courses, this action also seems to focus on the need to increase a teacher's general knowledge.

COMMUNICATION SKILLS

Without the ability to effectively communicate, little learning would take place in schools. When considering communication: verbal, nonverbal, and written must be considered. Although there are many arguments associated with bilingual education as well as the use of Ebonics, it is generally agreed that effective English language communication, written and oral, is the foundation of good communication within a school. Every teacher, no matter what the subject area, should set an example in the communication's area. Although there is continuous debate among English scholars over such issues as whether "different than" is an acceptable substitute for "different from," there are acceptable English communication standards. Subject/verb agreement, punctuation, spelling, pronunciation, sentence and paragraph construction are just a few areas which must be common teacher behavior.

Along with the use of proper English is the avoidance of any behavior which interferes with the intended message which includes both verbal and non-verbal. Verbal behaviors such as redundances, sarcasm, speaking speed, and volume all play a role in effective communication. Redundancies are those irritating expressions used as fillers when one is unsure of what to say next. "Ah," "OK," "OK, now," "of course," and "ya know" are all examples of fillers that when used frequently are not only unnecessary but adversely affect communication. At best, they suggest the speaker is nervous or unsure and, at worse, they make the speaker appear ignorant and uneducated. In either case, their elimination will enhance communication.

Not only what is said but how it is said will determine what the listener will hear. How many words are spoken per minute and what is the sound level? Too fast or too slow makes a difference; raising or lowering the voice while avoiding a monotone are all teaching considerations.

Sarcasm has no place in teaching, but it appears to be one of the most prevalent forms of communication among physical educators. Sarcasm suggests superiority and is, therefore, demeaning to students. When sarcasm is used, it tends to affect a child's self-concept and will cause negative feeling about physical education.

Besides what and how it is said, another evaluation area is the time a teacher spends talking. There are many ways to learn: some learn best through trial and error, one of the earliest forms of learning; some learn best through the auditory senses; others learn better visually; and some children need an explanation/demonstration. The learning domain also makes a difference; it is generally agreed that in the psychomotor domain, children learn best by doing. Although explanations and demonstrations may be helpful, learning is usually accomplished through movement experience. If the teacher is constantly talking, there is less opportunity for psychomotor learning. When evaluating physical education the amount of teacher talk, therefore, can be critical. A teacher must avoid trying to talk a class through a skill. Seldom does much psychomotor learning take place when the teacher is talking and the children are inactive.

NON-VERBAL BEHAVIOR

In establishing an effective learning environment for elementary children, there is no more important factor than non-verbal behavior; it's importance can not be overemphasized. Since it is estimated as much as 70 percent of the message received is due to nonverbal factors, non-verbal behavior is actually more important than what is said verbally. So much of the atmosphere, attitudes, and communication by both teachers and students within the elementary physical education class is determined by non-verbal behavior. For the teacher, enthusiasm can be expressed with quick movements about the teaching station as well as through posture, gestures, and facial expressions which express excitement and enthusiasm. Even on days when the teacher is not feeling very enthusiastic, they must be a good actor/actress. Teaching is communicating, and more is communicated non-verbally than verbally.

Children also communicate a great deal non-verbally. As with the teacher, facial expressions, movement, and other gestures communicate much

Teacher talk should be minimized.

about how the children are feeling. Teachers who understand and practice the non-verbal information covered earlier will enhance their chances for success with elementary children.

In the teaching/learning situation, important nonverbal considerations include the number of nonverbal praises and criticisms; teacher movement around the room; teacher/pupil interactions; eye contact with the children; room arrangement, and agreement between the teacher's verbal and nonverbal behavior.

Praising gestures are behaviors such as a smile, a pat on the back, clapping the hands, a wink, and the "OK" sign. Such gestures allow for positive feedback even when the teacher is some distance away. During play activities children will usually seek out the teacher's attention. The effective teacher will constantly scan the area to establish eye contact and give positive feedback. Individual nonverbal praise can be given frequently and is usually more effective than group praise.

Control gestures as the name implies are designed to help control children and include a glance or stare, pointing a finger, facial expressions, body gestures, closing the gap between the teacher and the student, or shaking the head. When using nonverbal control gestures, the teacher first makes

eye contact with the deviant child and then shows dissatisfaction. This nonverbal discipline does not call as much attention to the child as a verbal reprimand. Nor does this quiet approach embarrass the child or cause undue attention to the behavior. Since behavior which receives attention is more likely to be repeated, every attempt should be made to control it with the least class disruption.

Message distortion is created when there is disagreement between verbal and nonverbal behavior. A teacher who verbally professes love for children must be willing to be physically close to them. It is also difficult for the students to participate in a fitness and weight control discussion with an overweight, unfit teacher. Similar problems are caused when a teacher smokes, does not follow good health habits, uses incorrect English, or generally does not practice what he/she preaches.

Knowledge is power is a good expression to apply to non-verbal communication. With knowledge of behaviors which can enhance communication a teacher should be more effective. Listed below are some suggestion on how to improve non-verbal communication. The information is unique to American culture; teachers working with ethnic groups should be aware of those nonverbal behaviors appropriate to that particular culture.

1. Eye contact should be maintained for about three seconds before glancing away momentarily. To maintain less than three seconds infers a lack of interest, and constant staring makes the other person uncomfortable.

2. Distance is another factor. Standing too close to a person, less than three feet which is about handshaking distance, can create tension, and more than about four feet away can also hinder communication. Americans have a security zone of about three feet, which only intimate friends may enter. Closer distances, however, can be achieved with children who have not yet built security zones.

3. Sitting posture can be used to indicate interest. Erect posture and leaning or turning toward the speaker indicate interest even when there is none. Posture is particularly important when being interviewed; good interviewers evaluate body language.

4. Objects such as desks and chairs, as well as office and room arrangements, also affect communication. Placing a desk or podium between persons, or between a speaker and the audience, establishes an authoritarian environment which may or may not be desired. The object can also become a speaker's security area and serve as a protective barrier. In the classroom, the teacher's desk should not be a barrier between the teacher and the children.

Every society has a nonverbal language which, if understood, can be used to foster more effective communication. Only a small portion has been discussed here and readers should seek additional information. Nonverbal communication is not a science, but it can be used to put across a strong positive or negative message either intentionally or otherwise. In this time of increased cultural change, a teacher must educate and not offend.

Control and Discipline

Closely associated with both verbal as well as nonverbal behavior is control and discipline. Control is what the teacher does in advance of the children arriving at the teaching station and includes such things as preparing a lesson plan as well as the teaching station. Discipline involves the

Distance is an important factor in communication.

actions taken to bring unruly students back under control. These two items are so important, an entire chapter (chapter 6) is devoted to them.

Praise and Criticism

Every child should receive some praise during a lesson. Although the latter is more effective, this can be done either verbally or non-verbally. A smile, pat on the back, and other non-verbal praises can be given to every child sometime during a lesson. This praising approach not only creates a positive learning environment, it can promote self-concept development.

Greeting the Children

Another communication behavior is how to greet children when they arrive at the teaching station. The children should be met and greeted with a smile and pleasant words such as, "I am happy to see you;" "It looks like everyone is ready;" or "I like the way you walked down the hall." Perhaps a question such as, "Is everyone ready to have fun?" Every lesson should start on a positive note. It should also be noted that children should arrive at and depart from the teaching station in an orderly, quiet fashion — usually a straight line. Any

In the CCA the focus is on the child.

pushing, shoving, hitting, or running should not be permitted. Children who do not follow the rules should be required to practice walking properly in line until they understand the importance of the rules.

APPROACHES TO TEACHING

How one approaches teaching can make a great deal of difference in learning. The approach is determined to a great extent by the audience as well as the lesson objective. For most purposes, children should be taught through a child centered approach which uses problem-solving questions.

A Child Centered Approach

The teaching approach for elementary aged children should be primarily child centered (CCA) rather than a teacher dominated approach. The CCA uses problem-solving questions, and the emphasis is on development through movement exploration and experimentation. The explanation/demonstration followed by practice so common in secondary physical education has only limited application at the elementary level. In many colleges and universities, the physical education method's courses have focus almost exclusively on what is termed "The Command Style" which has the teacher as the primary focus.

Problem-solving questions are the key to the CCA. To be problem-solving, a question must have a multiple of correct responses; properly chosen, these question will allow each child success at his/her ability level and give the opportunity for the child to progress at his/her own speed. Examples of problem-solving question for a manipulative development activity would be:

1. How many ways can you throw and catch the ball?
2. Can you throw the ball up with some back part of the body and catch it with a front part?
3. How about throwing with a lower part and catching with an upper part?
4. How many different body parts can you use to bump the ball to yourself? How about a lower part? An upper part?
5. How many times in a row can you bounce it off a body part without it hitting the floor?
6. Can you throw and catch one ball with a partner?
7. How many different ways can you and your partner throw and catch the ball?

Typical problem-solving questions to get children exploring movement and space are:

1. How many ways can you move across the floor?

Moving across the floor.

The problem-solving style helps children explore all the ways their body can move.

2. How many ways can you move across the floor on three body parts?
3. Can you move just one body part to the music? Two? Three?
4. What can you do with two different pieces of equipment at one time?
5. How many body parts can you use to bounce the ball?

The more open ended the questions, the more creativity possible. Some examples of questions for developing creativity are:

1. What are some things you can do with this equipment?
2. How would you move to this music, and what will you do when it changes?
3. Working with a friend or friends, what game can you can make up using this equipment?
4. Can you set up a target and then make it fall down using two different pieces of equipment?

Using open ended questions, the teacher encourages the children to develop psychomotor ability by solving movement problems. The initial questions should be planned. Additional questions must be developed according to the children's responses to the initial questions. A teacher must do considerable analysis and thinking when using this approach. In any problem-solving situation, there is always a possibility of an incorrect response. By using a problem-solving approach, however, the teacher is free to interact with children having problems while others work on solutions. How different this is when compared with a teacher dominated approach, such as the command teaching style, in which all the attention is on the teacher.

Problem solving can be used at all levels, but has more application during the early learning stages. For young children, four to eight years of age, problem solving can be used to help them explore all the ways their bodies can move in personal and common space as well as all the ways their body can manipulate an object. For older children, problem solving can be the initial teaching style to determine the children's ability level. A question such as, "How many ways can you dribble the basketball?" can be used to see what ball handling experience the children have had.

In developing a lesson around problem-solving questions, the teacher must be careful not to ask questions which are too specific. A question such as, "Can you throw the ball up with your right hand and catch it?", is so narrow as to potentially cause considerable failure among the children. Many people think that as long as a question is asked, it is a child centered approach.

Teacher Dominated Approaches

In a teacher dominated approach (TDA), the focus is on the teacher rather than the child. Everything about the lesson including the objective, the organization, the pace, etc. is determined by the teacher. For the teacher, it is a comfortable way to approach a lesson. Nearly everything can be pre-planned. The TDA can be effective when working with one child or a small groups of children who have been identified as being at about the same point in skill development.

The Command Approach, the most prevalent TDA, is traditionally referred to as the Command Approach (CA) of teaching. This is the most frequently used teaching style in physical education including, unfortunately, the elementary level. It is, for the most part, a really bad way to approach teaching particularly at the elementary level. In a command teaching style, the teacher determines the objective, gives an explanation/demonstration, and then provides practice time. Since it provides considerable control, teachers are comfortable with it. It is frequently the initial or only teaching style used. If used without first evaluating those being taught, it violates many principles of learning; when using it without pre-testing, the teacher assumes that all the children are at the same level, learn in the same way, and learn at the same rate. It can have some application when trying to teach a specific skill, but it is usually a very questionable approach during the early elementary years. To have application at any level, the CA must be preceded by evaluation and ability grouping. Even when the children have been grouped, seldom will they all have the same learning style or progress at the same rate which is an assumption of the CA. When used properly, the CA can be effective in certain situations and with certain groups. It is effective, for example, with children who need a structured learning environment, and it can be used to teach small ability groups or in a one-on-one situation. The CA also works well with mentally challenged children.

Like the command approach, the Task Approach (TA) does allow for some pupil interaction. The children work at their own rate in pairs or small groups to accomplish the lesson's objective. One example of TA is a stations approach in which tasks are posted in writing about the room. Students then move from station to station, working together to accomplish the tasks. Learning centers are another example of TA. Unlike stations, which contain a specific task, a learning center usually contains all the information necessary to accomplish an entire instructional unit containing many tasks. The learning center allows children to begin at different levels and progress at their own rate. Learning centers and the stations approach are covered in more detail in chapter 7. TA can be effective for skill development particularly for upper elementary children.

QUESTION ANALYSIS

As can be seen in the discussion on the CCA to teaching, questions are important, and their type and number can be evaluated objectively. Counting is easy, but determining type requires some additional information. For purposes of this analysis the focus will be only on psychomotor development, and there will be only two types of questions: 1. problem-solving, and 2. command. As discussed previously, to be problem-solving, the question must have a multiple number of correct responses. If there is basically only one correct way to solve the problem as in type 2 below, then the question would be classified as command. *An example question for each type would be*:

Type 1   Problem-Solving, i.e., How many different ways can you throw and catch the ball? Additional problem-solving questions can be seen under "A Child Centered Approach to Teaching" above.

Type 2   Command, i.e., Can you throw and catch the ball with your right hand?

By analyzing the number and type of questions asked by the teacher, the approach to teaching can be determined.

PROFESSIONALISM

A frequently mentioned teacher characteristic is professionalism. The term has various meanings to educators, however, and to evaluate this component objectively it must first be stated in some measurable terms. The following are just a few areas which can be objectively evaluated and seem to indicate professionalism:

1. Be prepared
   a. Have a detailed lesson plan including objectives
   b. Have equipment ready
   c. Have the teaching station set up
   d. Be properly dressed for activity
2. Be sensitive to time
   a. Start class on time
   b. Keep children the full time
   c. Keep children moving as much of the time as possible

3. Follow and enforce school rules
4. Treat colleagues as professionals
5. Participate in all school functions
6. Be an active member of the state and national professional organizations
    a. Attend state conventions as well as national conventions when possible
    b. Participate in in-service training opportunities
    c. Make presentations at conventions or in-service training sessions

PREPARATION

A teacher's preparedness is critical to success and can be objectively evaluated. Such things as unit and lesson plans should include certain elements which can be reviewed, and a teacher's ability to organize a class to maximize learning while minimizing wasted time can also be assessed.

Planning

Although planning was mentioned under professionalism, it is singled out as one of the more important teacher behaviors which can and should be objectively evaluated. In addition to lesson plans, other planning areas which can be objectively evaluated include yearly plans and unit plans. These plans must have goals as well as objectives stated in measurable terms. Although the purpose here is not to present all the evaluation criteria for these plans, it is safe to say that most educators would agree that objective evaluation of plans is possible.

Organizational Ability

A teacher's organizational ability can be determined somewhat by how efficiently a class is conducted. This can be done by doing a time analysis focusing on how much time is spent in teaching and learning compared to the amount of non-learning time such as time to form groups, the time to transition from one activity to the next, and getting equipment.

When designing a lesson, the emphasis must be on learning by doing. Since psychomotor ability is learned best through direct, purposeful movement, children should be moving to learn in physical education. Teachers must use ways to communicate while children are moving. The most prevalent approach to teaching which focuses on a teacher's explanation/demonstration must be abandoned in favor of exploration using problem-solving questions. The focus must be off the teacher and on the children. Learning is not a result of listening but doing. At the elementary level, particularly during the early years of pre-school through second grade, learning is done through trial and error and exploration.

The lesson, therefore, should be designed to maximize movement while minimizing other factors such as transition time (moving from one activity to another) and equipment distribution time; neither of these factors are learning time. For some time physical educators have judged success on their ability to static control children. Handing out equipment is a perfect example of static control. Success is judged when children sit quietly while equipment is distributed individually; what a waste! Equipment should be laid out in such a way that all the children can retrieve an object simultaneously. This time savings technique may seem like a little thing, but it can greatly increase learning time.

When organizing children for activity, again the emphasis must be on maximizing activity while minimizing time wasted arranging children. Most elementary activities should be organized by having them find their own space away from others. Use "free formation" within the play area. If two groups are necessary, have the children choose a partner and then have the partners separate onto two sides of the play area, and the two groups are formed.

If several fairly even groups are needed, designate areas for the number of groups desired, i.e., number the four corners of the room for four groups, or have numbered marker cones or cards on the wall for more groups. Then have the children line up in a straight line. Walk along the line and give each child a number according to the number of desired groups and have them immediately go to the numbered card, cone, etc. that you gave them. Never have children count off and expect them all to remember their number; it gets messed up nearly every time.

When forming lines, it is best to have a line marked on the floor or use markers to designate a line outside. "Please stand side by side on this black line." "Please stand side by side between these two marker cones."

When the composition of the group is not overly important, determine the number of children you want at each location and then tell the children to go to any station they wish but not have more than the number you tell them at the station, i.e., "Go to one of the six numbers you see posted on the wall, but I do not want more than five people at any one station." This technique can be used from kindergarten through fifth grade. There will always be one or two children who will be confused, but it is easy to direct them to a station.

Sometimes a circle is required. This can be a particular problem when there is no circle upon which to stand. A easy way to establish a circle is to have the children gather closely around an object such as a marker cone and then hold hands. Have the children pretend they are slowly blowing up a balloon which is the circle which grows larger. Be sure to have the children drop hands long before they begin pulling each other. Forget to tell them to drop hands, and they will be pulling each other onto the ground as well as falling on the ground themselves. Once the initial circle is established, its size can be increased by asking the children to take one, two, three, etc. giant steps backward.

Getting Children Moving

All the children should be doing purposeful movement within 15 seconds of arriving at the teaching station. This is accomplished by having an activity planned which requires very little explanation and nearly no organization. If equipment is required, it should be spread out along the boundary of the play area so that all the children can retrieve an object at the same time.

Things to Avoid

If the teacher is going to have a successful physical education program, there are certain behaviors which should be avoided. These include:

1. CHOOSING TEAMS
2. Using relay lines in which only one child in each line is participating
3. Formations such as squads, circles, or other arrangements which take time to organize
4. Having children count off
5. Circle games
6. Games which do not have all the children moving nearly all the time
7. Threatening children
8. Administering corporal punishment
9. Using solid objects as bases or turning points
10. Handing out equipment one piece at a time

EVALUATING TEACHER BEHAVIOR

To improve teaching, desirable teacher behaviors must be expressed in behavioral terms. Methods then must be developed to gather data. Numerous subjective instruments are available for evaluating teaching; their subjectivity, however, renders them as basically useless in bringing about change. There are, however, objective ways to obtain data which can be used to assist teachers in making behavioral changes.

AUDIO AND VIDEOTAPING

Audio and/or videotape are excellent for gathering data. Taping can be used to: gather data on the number of times verbal praise and criticism occur; measure the amount of time the teacher spends talking; record the number and type of questions asked; analyze those behaviors important to principles of learning; determine how many individual contacts occurred; record the frequency of fillers (ah, OK, etc.); analyze discipline techniques; and determine the correctness of the grammar used. A small cassette tape recorder can be attached to the teacher's waist and the microphone pinned to his/her shirt. A student can be used to operate a video camera which will help gather both verbal and nonverbal behavior. By using a wireless microphone, verbal data can be obtained in the gym or outside.

TIME ANALYSIS

One of the more effective ways to obtain useful data is to do a time analysis. Using a stopwatch such things as how much time the teacher spends talking, how much time the children spend in meaningful activity, and/or the amount of time spent in transition from one activity to another can help determine the lesson's effectiveness. Time is a critical factor and should not be wasted.

PEER EVALUATION

If they are trained in data-gathering techniques, peer evaluators can be effective, but many teachers do not want to have others watch them teach. Perhaps it is the teacher's poor self-concept or the fact that teachers do not want to burden their peers. Whatever the reason, peers are seldom asked by others to do evaluations. A good arrangement is to have a peer gather the data and then let the teacher do a self-evaluation. Some schools have mandatory peer evaluation processes, but they are not much different from the all-too-frequent subjective principal evaluations; such a process also puts great pressure on teachers, and can lead to morale problems.

SUMMARY

This chapter was a discussion of those teacher behaviors which can be objectively evaluated. The behaviors discussed include: knowledge and application of learning principles, communication skills, approaches to teaching, question analysis, professionalism, planning, and praise and criticism. The chapter concluded with a section on how to evaluate the teaching/learning environment.

REFERENCES AND SUGGESTED READINGS

Cardinal, B. and M. Cardinal. Role modeling in HPERD: do attitudes match behavior. *JOPERD* 72:34-39, 2001.

Darden, G., et.al. The student-teaching experience. *JOPERD.* 72: 50-55, 2001.

Flinchum, B. Early Childhood Movement Programs: Preparing Teachers for Tomorrow, *JOPERD* 59:62-64, 1988.

Gabbei, R. and D. Hamrick. Using physical activity homework to meet the national standards, *JOPERD*, 72:21-26, 2001.

Grineski, S. Teaching and Learning in Physical Education for Young Children, *JOPERD,* 59:91-94, 1988.

Hastie, P. and A. Buchanan. Teaching responsibility through sport education: prospect of a coalition. *Research Quarterly* 71:25-35, 2000.

Hautala, R. The Tape Recorder Teacher: High Tech That We Don't Need, *JOPERD* 60:25-28, 1989.

Loughrey, T. Evaluating Program Effectiveness, *JOPERD* 58:63-64, 1987.

Martinek, T. Confirmation of a Teacher Expectancy Model: Student Perceptions and Causal Attributions of Teaching Behaviors, *Research Quarterly* 59:118-126, 1988.

McBride, R. You, Too, Can Be a Task Master—Using Task Sheets in the Physical Education Program, *JOPERD* 60:62-66, 1989.

McGaha, P. and S. Lynn. Providing leadership and support to the beginning teacher. *JOPERD.* 71:41-43, 2000.

McLaughlin, R. (ed). *Assisting the Beginning Teacher.* Richmond, Virginia Department of Education, 1985.

Morris, G., and J. Stiehl. *Physical Education from Intent to Action.* Columbus: Charles E. Merrill Publishing Co., 1985.

Nichols, B. *Moving and Learning.* (3rd ed.). St Louis: Mosby Publishing Company, 1995.

Pangrazi, R. and V. Dauer. *Dynamic Physical Education for Elementary Children* (11th ed.). Needham Heights: Allyn and Bacon Publishing Co, 1995.

Ritson, R. Psychomotor Skill Teaching: Beyond the Command Style, *JOPERD* 58:36-37, 1987.

Seiss, M., and K. Klint. Show and Tell in the Gymnasium: An Investigation of Developmental Differences in Modeling and Verbal Rehearsal of Motor Skills, *Research Quarterly* 58:234-241, 1987.

Stewart, M. and C. Corbin. Feedback Dependence Among Low Confidence Preadolescent Boys and Girls, *Research Quarterly* 59:160-164, 1988.

Weber, R. Motivating and Teaching Disabled Students, *JOPERD* 60:85-87, 1989.

Treasure, D., and G. Roberts. Students' perceptions of the motivational climate achievement beliefs, and satisfaction in physical education. *Research Quarterly* 72:165-175, 2001.

Weiller, K., and E. Doyle. Teacher-student interaction: an exploration of gender differences in elementary physical education. *JOPERD* 71:43-45, 2000.

Chapter 6

Control and Discipline

After completing this chapter, the student should be able to:

1. Describe the meaning of control by listing and explaining the importance of three control factors.
2. Give a teacher or pupil a rule, explain its importance.
3. Describe the difference between control and discipline.
4. Describe why discipline in necessary.
5. List and describe the steps in group discipline.
6. List and describe the steps in individual discipline.
7. Describe why individual discipline can be more difficult than group discipline.
8. List Felker's two principles of discipline.
9. Indicate a situation where a behavior modification program may be necessary.
10. List and describe the steps in a behavior modification program.
11. Define the key terms below.

––– **Key Terms**

Behavior modification
Control
Discipline

Principles of discipline
Rules

Control and discipline are interrelated but will be dealt with separately. Control, as the word implies, is what the teacher can do in advance as well as during the class to maximize learning and minimize discipline problems. Without control no learning will take place, and within even the best controlled environment, there will be discipline problems. Although control is absolutely essential to learning, it is not an end in itself. Teachers are often evaluated on how well they control a class and not the ability to accomplish program objectives. The program's effectiveness must be judged on measurable accomplishments. Such accomplishments, however, will only be possible when the class is under control and teachers take a positive approach to discipline problems.

Discipline is what the teacher must do to restore control when children disobey the rules. Discipline involves techniques to deal with an individual or group problem. None of these techniques, however, is guaranteed to work. There is no guarantee because a teacher does not have absolute control over any human. What does the teacher do if a child runs away from the class? Leave the others unattended? What can be done about a child who hides on the way to the teaching station? Also, great restraint is placed on teachers as to what they can and cannot legally do with an unruly student.

CONTROL

Some things which the teacher can control include: having a well prepared unit and lesson plan; the preparation of the teaching station; applying learning principles; having a positive program; having rules and enforcing them; and him or herself.

RULES

Of those things which can be controlled, probably the most important is having and enforcing rules. Any learning environment requires rules as well as reasons for those rules. Rules should be developed with student input and focus primarily on safety and learning. The reason for a rule should always be shared with the children. With younger children, ages four to seven, the teacher must take the major responsibility for establishing the rules but should help the children understand reasons for them. During the first class period, the teacher should sit down with the class to discuss rules. The teacher can ask, "Why can there be no pushing or shoving?" "Why should you not slide on the floor?" or "What do you do when the teacher is talking?" With older children, the teacher can use a problem-solving approach by asking, "What are some of the rules we must have in physical education?" or "What should we do if...?"

Student Rules

Listed below are some rules which should be established to insure a safe, effective learning environment. Teachers must analyze their own facilities and determine what additional rules may be required.

1. Stop, look, and listen when the whistle blows. The whistle should be used sparingly and have only one meaning, STOP, LOOK AND LISTEN. As in sports activities, the whistle is an attention-getting device and is, therefore, important to safety. By using the whistle to get the children's attention, the teacher can stop

The whistle should have only one meaning, stop, look, and listen.

inappropriate behavior, give instructions, and generally control the learning environment. The whistle's range also allows the teacher to control children spread over a large area. It also protects one of the most important instruments the teacher has, the voice. Indiscriminate and frequent whistle usage to signal directional changes or to start races can render it ineffective as a safety device.

2. When the whistle is blown, children must put any manipulative equipment on the ground between their feet.

3. Stay inside established boundaries. Outdoors this keeps children away from streets and parking lots. Indoors it can help avoid contact with walls, chairs, tables, door handles, and/or drinking fountains.

and both the tumbler and the spotter can be hurt through incorrect spotting. Formal gymnastics should only be taught by a qualified individual.

7. No talking while the teacher or someone else is talking.

8. No gum chewing or eating of any kind.

9. Each game or sport must have safety rules established before play begins. Prior to conducting any activity, the teacher must think through the injury possibilities and then establish appropriate safety rules.

10. Children will enter and leave the teaching station in an quiet, orderly fashion - usually a line.

Hoops can be used to establish safe personal space.

4. No sliding on the ground or floor. Although this is usually a safe activity for the sliding child, others can be injured by falling over a sliding child. Outside, there is a chance of hitting a stone or glass object as well as ruining good clothes.

5. No pushing or shoving or other horseplay. Tickling during gymnastics, for example, seems to be a favorite activity anytime a child gets in an inverted position. Such behavior endangers the head and neck area.

6. Have a spotter when doing formal gymnastics. Extreme care must be exercised, however, when children are spotting others. Spotters are frequently injured,

Teacher Rules

Just as children must follow rules to enhance learning and safety, so also should the teacher. Listed below are some rules for teachers which make learning safer and more effective.

1. Keep the number of rules short, but follow through with every one.

2. Have a reason for a rule.

3. Objects such as balls and hoops should be placed on the ground when the stop signal is given—children will play with any objects in their hands and will not pay attention or may disrupt others with their play.

4. When talking, keep the sun at the children's back—a teacher's facial

Sun in the children's eyes can block effective communication.

expressions and body movements can communicate a great deal, but children blinded by the sun are unable to see them.

5. Do not wear sunglasses—eye contact is important to communication and is not possible when wearing sunglasses.
6. Keep extra equipment, such as balls, handy during a game. The spare ball can be used to keep the game going while one child retrieves the other.
7. To minimize injuries, teach on grass whenever possible. The next best teaching area is a gymnasium or large cleared indoor area, followed by a blacktop. Classrooms and hallways are the least desirable teaching areas.
8. Never use immovable objects such as walls, poles, or trees as safe bases or turning points in a race. Safe bases should be a marked-off area free of dangerous objects. Turning points in a race should be marker cones or lines. Children running toward an immovable object could easily trip or be pushed resulting in serious head or neck injury.
9. Children's prescription glasses should be removed whenever possible, or should be covered with protectors during any activity which might damage them. Children

should not be allowed to wear sunglasses or other nonprescription eye wear during activity.

10. Require children to dress appropriately for the activity, including shorts and pants for tumbling and gymnastics, and sneakers for most activities. Indoors, children can usually participate in bare feet (stocking feet are dangerous). Sneakers are not always required outside, but loafers, sandals and heavy boots can be dangerous to a child or those playing with him or her.
11. Do not allow children to chew gum.
12. Do not allow children to blow up balloons. There have been cases where children have died when a piece of balloon lodged in their throat.
13. Minimize teacher talk and maximize student activity.
14. Know and practice principles of learning.

SELF-CONTROL

As behavioral problems become more common at the elementary level, a teacher's patience is often tried. It is essential that the teacher maintain his/her self-control at all costs. When stressed, teachers often administer or threaten to administer corporal punishment. Any form of corporal punishment even the threat of same is an assault for which a parent may take criminal action against the teacher. In the past, various forms of corporal punishment, particularly in physical education, were common. Many teachers today do not realize that giving exercises as punishment has been deemed a form of corporal punishment. Such practices as putting a nose in a circle on the board and "time out" have resulted in legal suits. In order to act appropriately in all situations, the teacher must maintain self-control.

PRACTICING PRINCIPLES OF LEARNING

Another means by which control can be maintained is to practice principles of learning. As was pointed out in the discussion of principles (chapter 5), adherence to them will do much to improve the teaching/learning environment. These principles focus primarily on a positive environment including *program content, student input, praise and criticism,* and *student success.*

COMMON COURTESY

Besides using considerable praise, the learning environment is enhanced by practicing common courtesy. A "please" or "thank you" when addressing students will go a long way toward developing the rapport necessary for control. Paying attention to the child when he or she is speaking is also important.

Other Considerations

Other control factors such as preparation of unit and lesson plans, and preparing the teaching station are discussed in chapter 7.

DISCIPLINE

As mentioned earlier, discipline is what the teacher must do to restore control when children disobey the rules. Even when all the control measures are practiced, problems will arise which require disciplinary action to restore control. How a teacher disciplines is very important to a program's success or failure. There are two types of disciplinary situations, individual and group. Both can occur at any time, but new teachers tend to experience more group problems while the experienced teacher will normally encounter problems primarily with individual children. When disciplining an individual child, a teacher must be extremely careful not to harm the child's self-concept or promote more misbehavior. Whenever possible, therefore, discipline should be discreet. Children, for the most part, want a controlled learning environment, and will usually accept discipline when it is viewed as consistent and fair.

A teacher must approach discipline by being firm but fair. The term *firmness* is frequently confused with a negative (punitive) approach; this is not the case. Firmness means to consistently enforce rules in a positive manner. This is done by emphasizing the positive outcomes for good behavior—more activity time, fewer injuries, improving ability, and special activities chosen by the children.

Group Discipline

As a general rule, a new teacher will experience more group discipline problems than the experienced teacher. Children will nearly always test a teacher to see what restrictions will be imposed. The older children may systematically plan a defiant strategy while younger children will merely be themselves and do whatever they can get away with. Teachers who are unable to enforce rules will have a long year.

Group discipline normally requires stopping the class in order to deal with the problem. When is a situation classified as a group problem requiring action? There are no absolutes. In general, the many should not be punished for the crimes of a few. Are the problem children in a small group which can be dealt with easily or are there several isolated problem children? How many children are not following the rules? What is the deviant behavior? These are just a few questions which must be answered prior to taking action.

In order to establish some guidelines, the following is an attempt to answer these discipline questions. A teacher can normally handle up to five discipline problems on an individual basis but beyond that, the teacher will probably have difficulty correcting deviant behavior without losing control of the entire class or at least being unable to do any meaningful instruction. If the children are in a group, as usually happens with older children, it may be possible to deal with the problem even when there are more than five children involved. Behavior which is not disruptive to the entire group may also be handled quietly without the necessity to stop the entire group. Whenever one or more children, however, are endangering themselves or others, the teacher has a legal responsibility to immediately take action.

When it is obvious the teacher is spending more time disciplining than teaching, a group action is necessary. The stop signal (a whistle is recommended) is given and the teacher *waits* for the children to get quiet. Following the whistle, the voice should not be used to shout stop signals such as "freeze," "quiet," or "listen to me." A general rule could be, if the whistle must be blown three times, anyone who has not stopped, looked, and listened will be eliminated from activity. When everyone is listening, the teacher can merely remind them of the rules.

If it is necessary to stop them a second time, the group should be brought together to discuss their behavior. With everyone sitting in a group, the teacher should use a questioning technique to explore the problem: "Why did I bring you together? Do you like the activities we are doing? What are the dangers of not following the rules? What should we do with those unwilling to play safely? Does everyone understand what is expected?" The discussion can end with a reminder that they are only wasting their fun time. It may also be helpful to promise them some special activity if they follow the rules.

The positive approach, however, does not always work, and should it be necessary to stop them a third time, the negative consequences must be emphasized. Bringing them together a third time, the teacher should probably use a more direct approach to the behavior problems. If the group is unwilling to cooperate, or if individual children continue to violate the rules, they should be eliminated from activity. This elimination threat, however, is only valuable when the program is one that children want to participate in; the children must view elimination as a negative rather than positive consequence. Most children, fortunately, normally view elementary physical education very positively.

As a last resort, the class should be eliminated from activity. The teacher should first apologize to those who were following the rules, and then explain the need to stop activity (focus on safety). If

Group discussion

the children are taken back to their classroom, the physical education teacher should remain with them until the normal physical education class time ends. To maintain rapport with the classroom teacher as well as practicing professional behavior, the physical educator must not turn the children over to the classroom teacher even if he or she is in the classroom. The time remaining in the period should be used to discuss future behavior.

Group Discipline Summary

1. Stop the class and remind them of the rules and directions.
2. Stop the class and bring them together for a group discussion using questions. Promise some positive outcome for compliance with rules.
3. Stop the class and bring them together; tell them the negative consequences for continued misbehavior (usually elimination from the activity).
4. Eliminate individuals who do not comply with the rules.
5. If a significant number (usually five or more) continue to misbehave, stop the class and take them back to their classroom and remain with them until the physical education period ends. Be sure to apologize to those who were following directions.

Disciplining Individuals

Fortunately most discipline problems involve only one or two children, but how these children are handled can have a significant effect on the child and the group. For the teacher, the focus must be on preserving the child's self-concept while changing his/her behavior. Children usually misbehave to receive attention, so if the behavior does not endanger the child or others and is not disrupting the learning environment, it should receive little or no attention for the moment. Although no action may initially be taken, a teacher must always keep a mental note of misbehavior which may require further action at a later time. As mentioned under principles of learning, behavior including negative behavior which receives attention is more likely to recur. When disciplining a child, group rapport can be affected when the teacher is judged as unfair to a group member. This group factor is particularly true with children nine years of age and older where peer status is important and cliques are common.

Take the child aside to discuss his or her behavior.

Unsafe or disruptive behaviors must be dealt with immediately. If at all possible, the teacher should use nonverbal techniques; eye contact and an appropriate facial expression may be sufficient, or the teacher can move closer to the deviant child as long as it is not done with the intent to threaten the child. While closing the gap, the teacher can continue to teach or monitor the class activity. Often times just this reduction in distance is enough to stop inappropriate behavior. Nonverbal control techniques should be used, whenever possible, without other children noticing them. Stronger nonverbal behaviors such as finger pointing or head-shaking do not normally go unnoticed by other children. Activities which may result in injury, however, must be stopped immediately without concern for the child receiving attention. The teacher has a legal obligation to protect children.

When nonverbal discipline is not possible (cannot catch the child's eye) or when stronger measures are necessary, the teacher should quietly talk to the child while the others are playing. By first asking "Did you hear the rules which we discussed?" or "Did you hear what I said about staying inside the boundaries?" the teacher is giving the child the benefit of the doubt. These questions can be followed by "Are you going to follow the rules?" The brief discussion should end on a positive note such as "I really care about you and do not want you to get hurt." Unless there is immediate possibility of injury, calling the child by name and reprimanding him/her in front of peers should NOT be done.

Children who persist in dangerous or disruptive behavior should be taken aside while others are in play and reminded of the negative consequences for not following the rules (elimination from activity). This can be followed by the statement, "When you are ready to follow the rules, you may go back into activity." Most children will opt to return immediately, but by doing so have indicated they will follow the rules. When the child returns, the teacher should look for the opportunity to praise the child's good behavior.

The hallway is an inappropriate, unsupervised area.

A child who must be dealt with a third time should be required to stay out until the teacher decides to allow him/her to return. Whenever possible, the child should be allowed to return prior to the class ending. Upon returning, the child, hopefully, will warrant some positive praise thus ending the incident on a positive note.

Some children will not cooperate even when required to sit out; they will try to trip children, grab equipment, make noise, and otherwise continue to seek attention. When this behavior is dangerous, or disrupts others, the child should be removed to a supervised area. Placing the child in the hall is a form of suspension which is legally questionable, and places the child in an unsupervised location which can also lead to legal problems. While in the hall, a child often receives considerable attention which can reinforce the negative behavior. The supervised area most frequently used is the office. This is a legally safe area, but children also receive considerable attention there. Whenever possible, it is best to keep problem children in class.

When all else fails and the teacher finally admits defeat, the child can be sent to the principal. The principal may be helpful, but cannot solve the problem. A principal cannot create discipline for a teacher.

Individual Discipline Summary

1. Unless the behavior is disruptive or dangerous, take no action initially.
2. If the behavior is dangerous, take immediate steps to stop the behavior using whatever techniques will protect the children.
3. If the behavior is disruptive, it should be stopped as quickly as possible.
4. Whenever possible, use nonverbal discipline such as eye contact and closing the gap, but try not to call others' attention to the child.
5. Talk to the child to be sure rules have been understood; keep the discussion positive; look for the opportunity to praise the child's positive behavior.
6. Take the child aside and problem solve a solution allowing the child to determine when he or she is ready to return; warn of consequences for continued misbehavior (elimination from activity).
7. Remove the child; the teacher decides when the child returns. When possible, the child should be returned to activity before the period ends.

8. Children who continue to be disruptive on the sideline should be sent to a supervised area such as the office until the teacher can deal with the problem.
9. When all else fails and the teacher admits defeat, the child can be sent to the principal.

BEHAVIOR MODIFICATION

Children with special behavioral problems may be helped using a behavior modification program. Such a program is time consuming, and should, therefore, be reserved only for chronic behavior problems. Behaviors requiring a modification program could include: (1) self-destructive behavior, (2) behavior dangerous to others, and (3) constant disruptive behavior.

The following are the steps in a behavior modification program:
1. Attempt to change only one behavior at a time.
2. Determine the behavior's frequency.
3. Establish a committee to determine the behavior's cause. The committee should include school and medical personnel along with the parent(s).
4. State program goals and objectives including target dates.
5. Establish the program specifying services which will be used including the reinforcement system. Rewards for good behavior should not be food, but should include something like extra play time, or a chance to pick a favorite classroom game or activity.
6. Conduct the program.
7. Evaluate the program and make necessary changes.

SUMMARY

This chapter was a discussion of control and discipline. Control is what the teacher can do in advance as well as during the class to maximize learning and minimize discipline problems. Discipline is the teacher's behavior in response to misbehaving children. Both group discipline and individual discipline were described in detail. Individual discipline was felt to be a more sensitive issue due to the potential effect it will have on the child's self-concept. The chapter ended with a discussion of behavior modification including the steps necessary for designing and implementing a program.

REFERENCES AND SUGGESTED READINGS

Biehler, R., and J. Snowman. *Psychology Applied to Teaching.* Boston: Houghton Mifflin Co., 1982.

Carter, J. The 'Champions' Program: Behavior Improvement in Physical Education, *JOPERD* 60:66-67, 1989.

Gabbard, C., et.al. *Physical Education for Children.* Englewood Cliffs: Prentice-Hall, Inc., 1987.

Graham, G., et.al. *Children Moving* (2nd ed.). Palo Alto: Mayfield Publishing Co., 1987.

Henkel, S. STP—The Teacher's Edge to Pupil Control, *JOPERD* 60:60-64, 1989.

Keogh, J., and D. Sugden. *Movement Skill Development.* New York: MacMillan Publishing Co., 1985.

Morris, G., and J. Stiehl. *Physical Education from Intent to Action.* Columbus: Charles E. Merrill Publishing Co., 1985.

Pangrazi, R. and V. Dauer. *Dynamic Physical Education for Elementary Children* (11th ed.). Needham Heights: Allyn and Bacon Publishing Co, 1995.

Rimmer, J. Confrontation in the Gym: A Systematic Solution for Behavior Problems, *JOPERD* 60:63-65, 1989.

Selective Web Sites

Information on disciplining children with ADD and ADHD: http://www.chadd.org/papers/school discipline1.htm

School discipline: http://teacherpathfinder.org/Support/discipline.html

School Discipline & Classroom Management: A Bibliography: http://falcon.jmu.edu/~ramseyil/disciplinebib.htm

The legal framework for school discipline: http://www.dfee.gov.uk/circulars/test/discip.htm

Suggested Reading: Developing a School Discipline Code: http://www.ncrel.org/sdrs/areas/issues/envrnmnt/drugfree/sa2deq06.htm

Eric: http://inset.ul.ie/cm/biblio/ed350727.htm

The Google search results on "school discipline:" http://inset.ul.ie/cm/biblio/ed350727.htm

The Teaching Station

After completing this chapter, the student should be able to:

1. Discuss the pros and cons of each teaching station discussed in the chapter.

2. Make a bulletin board which meets the criteria established in the chapter.

3. Describe the difference between recreational and developmental playground equipment.

4. Describe how to analyze the safety of playground equipment.

5. List three ways to increase playground equipment usage.

6. Discuss the problems associated with wooden equipment.

7. List at least six playground rules discussed in the chapter.

8. Define the key terms below.

Key Terms

Blacktop
Bulletin boards
Creative playgounds
Developmental equipment

Learning environment
Recreational equipment
Teaching stations

Many factors influence teaching and learning including where both take place, the teaching station. This chapter's focus will be on the characteristics of the teaching station including ways to enhance it. There is also a section on the playground including playground equipment and safety.

TEACHING STATIONS

OUTDOORS

At many elementary schools, the largest teaching stations are located outdoors. The ideal location has a grass surface which is free of dangerous obstacles. Some schools, particularly those in urban areas, only have hard surface play areas which significantly limit activities that can be offered while greatly increasing the chances for injury. No matter what the surface, the teaching station must be free of holes, stones, glass, and other trash which might cause injuries. Additional concerns include stray animals, strangers, and vehicles—hardtop play areas often double as parking lots. Distance to rest rooms and drinking fountains, as well as the lack of emergency communication, can also be problems. The distance children have to travel to the teaching station could also be a limiting factor; to maximize instruction time, it is usually best for the classroom teacher rather than the physical educator to accompany the children to and from the area.

Grass

Since it can be used safely for most activities, grass is normally a good place to teach. No solid, immovable objects should be inside the playing boundaries nor should dangerous objects such as walls or poles be use as a base or turning point. The teaching area should be large, allowing for lots of movement without the danger of children running into each other. The area should be marked with cones or other visible objects which clearly define the boundaries. Some drawbacks associated with grass include distractions caused by activities around the school such as emergency vehicles, noise, dogs and their waste products, other classes on the playground, and weather including: wind, sun, heat, and cold. With the lack of walls to contain both children and equipment, the teacher must be constantly alert to children's safety as balls go into streets or children wander out of the play area. The lack of walls also allows unauthorized individuals to enter the play area. When outside, children also like to slide on the ground which can lead to damaged clothing; stones and glass can also cause serious injuries to a sliding child.

Hard Surface

Nearly every school has a hard surface (blacktop) play area. This area may be used when the grass is wet, but should, for the most part, be avoided as a physical education teaching station. If a gymnasium or multipurpose room is available, it is preferable to the blacktop. At times, the blacktop could be used for ball-bouncing and rope jumping. If the area doubles as a parking lot, extreme caution must be exercised to be sure a car does not inadvertently drive into the area during class. While children are at play, chains or barricades should be used to seal off where cars can enter.

Grass is usually the safest place for activities.

A blacktop area can be useful and is especially good for ball-handling and jump rope activities.

No chasing and fleeing activities or activities for children four to six years of age should be conducted on blacktop. Even a minor fall will result in a time-consuming injury. A high center of gravity and still-developing movement ability make children four to six years of age more likely to fall; blacktop is not for them.

Game and play activity figures should be painted on the blacktop for use during recess. Geography knowledge, for example, can be improved by painting a state, local, and United States map on the playground; these maps can be used in physical education for creative movement activities. There are companies which sell stencils which make it fairly easy to construct the maps.

INDOORS

Depending upon the teaching space available, indoors can be an excellent place to teach physical education. There is a trend toward adding gymnasiums to elementary schools, and many have a large multipurpose room suitable for movement activities. If the space is designed for physical education, there can be many advantages to teaching indoors: the four walls help to control the children and equipment; it is easier for the teacher to get the children's attention; problems with weather are eliminated; many gymnasiums in hot areas of the country are air conditioned; rest rooms and drinking fountains are readily available; travel time to the facility is short; children can hear better and the teacher does not have to talk as loudly; the danger of cars, people, and animals is not a factor; and use of audiovisual equipment such as tapes, records and compact disks is possible. Other indoor facilities include the stage, hallways, and a converted classroom where limited movement activities can be presented; each, however, poses liability problems.

Hop scotch is a developmental activity.

Gymnasium/Multipurpose Room

The best indoor facility is a gymnasium or multipurpose room which is designed primarily for movement activities. If it is designed properly, it should have a smooth floor which could be carpeted, protective mats on the walls, high ceilings, and protective screens over windows and lights. If the multipurpose room also serves as a cafeteria, it greatly restricts the time it can be used for instruction.

Learning about the world in which we live.

Open Space

When teaching indoors, elementary physical educators are often forced to find any available open space, such as a stage or converted classroom, which greatly limits the activities which can be offered. These spaces restrict movement and increase the chances for injury. If movement activities are to be conducted in limited space, precautions must be taken: all objects such as desks, chairs, and other objects not essential to the environment must be removed; since overhead lights and windows will most likely be factors, only lightweight objects should be used; when teaching on a raised stage, precautions must be taken to insure children will not fall off; children should also not be allowed to jump on or off the stage but be required to use stairs; and because balls may roll too close to the edge, they should not be used on a stage. Very controlled but valuable activities such as creative non-locomotor movement, fitness, and structured rhythmics can be taught in these restricted areas.

A stage can be used for physical education activities, but the teacher must realize that it is a high liability area.

Classroom

The normal classroom is not a viable option for physical education, but classrooms which have been converted to allow for movement may be used for a limited physical education program. When considering conducting physical education in a normal classroom, the liability risks far outweigh the possible benefits. Modern classrooms have too many dangerous objects which cannot be effectively eliminated. Trying to conduct a movement program in an area not designated for movement can create an indefensible position should an injury occur. The converted classroom, on the other hand, can be used to conduct activities requiring limited movement; only soft manipulative objects can be used, and competitive games should not be played. Activities that work well in limited space include structured and creative rhythmics, non-locomotor movement, creativity, manipulative activities, fitness, and tumbling.

A large, cleared space indoors makes a teaching station.

ENHANCING THE TEACHING STATION

Decorating

By decorating the teaching station, the learning environment can be enhanced. The room, for example, should be painted with a color such as light yellow which will brighten. Movement figures can be made and hung about the room or can be painted directly on the walls. Cartoon characters or abstract figures can be used to create a cheerful environment. Along with figures, motivational quotations can also be used. The use of professional athletes' photos and sports scenes are not recommended; using sports as a primary decoration scheme, suggests that physical education is only athletics. It is better to promote the joy of movement as well as fitness. Posters and bulletin boards can also enhance the teaching station.

BULLETIN BOARDS

Bulletin boards can improve the looks of the learning environment as well as provide information and motivation. A motivational board could focus on themes such as fitness, sportsmanship, or movement. Other themes feature movement associated with a season. Other ideas include special events or health themes. No matter what the theme, certain criteria apply to all bulletin boards:

1. Correct English must be used.
2. Neatness counts.
3. The title should be about three to five words.
4. A quick glance should be sufficient to determine the theme.
5. All the letters in one word should be the same color. Words with alternating color letters are extremely difficult to read.
6. The words in the title should all be the same color.
7. Since they are difficult to read, vertically lettered words should not be used.
8. The message should be positive, i.e., a fat person's picture should not be accompanied by the message, "Don't look like this."
9. Since they tend not to be good role models, professional athlete's pictures should not be used.
10. The color contrasts between the background, the words, and the pictures are important considerations.
11. Pictures should be cut neatly from magazines and mounted on construction paper before attaching to the board.
12. The focal point (figure 7.1) is important.

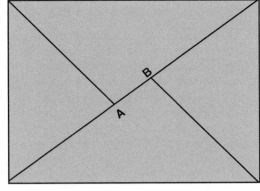

Draw diagonal lines from any corner; then draw a perpendicular line to the diagonal. The intersection of the two lines is the focal point - A and B.

Figure 7.1. Determining Focal Points for Bulletin Boards

13. Unless the purpose is to provide information, the number of words should be kept to a minimum while using pictures to communicate the message.
14. Creativity helps.
15. Use glue to mount pictures.
16. Commercially available figures can be used, or figures can be drawn using an opaque projector or a computer projected image which can be traced. The art teacher may be able to help produce materials for the bulletin board. Most freehand drawings are not of sufficient quality to be useful.
17. A three-dimensional effect using pipe cleaners, string, or other objects should be used whenever possible.

To determine the focal point, draw a diagonal between opposite corners, and then draw a line perpendicular to it. The intersection of the two lines is the focal point.

The opaque or overhead projector can be used to project images for tracing. Little artistic ability is required to produce nice figures. Elementary children relate to cartoon characters.

A bulletin board can both decorate and communicate!

THE PLAYGROUND

The playground is an important movement environment where, unfortunately, most school related injuries occur. Most playgrounds which consist of large open play areas as well as space devoted to playground equipment are an integral part of any elementary school. The open areas usually include grass as well as a hard surface (blacktop) play area. Free play (recess) is an important part of a child's development and should be conducted in a safe environment that includes safe play equipment. Since movement activities including recess are associated with so many injuries, someone must assume responsibility for overseeing the playground, including establishing rules. Traditionally, the physical educator is responsible for the playground and playground equipment.

Playground Rules

The importance of playground rules is underscored when one realizes that most school related injuries occur on the playground. When making a list of rules, some are general and apply to almost any playground while others must be developed based upon the school's location or equipment present. Below are some do's and don'ts for the children using the playground for recess. The list is not inclusive, and responsible persons must analyze their playground to determine additional safety rules which may be necessary.

1. No inverted activities on equipment or on the ground including headstands, handstands, or cartwheels.
2. No tumbling activities such as forward or backward rolls.
3. No tackling games.
4. No "Keep Away" in which all children chase and try to tackle the person with the object.
5. No "Wall Dodge Ball" in which those trying to dodge the ball stand against a wall.
6. When playing softball, only the person at bat may be holding a bat. All other bats must remain on the ground.
7. No sliding when playing softball.
8. Stay away from those on the swings.
9. No going down the sliding board head first.
10. No fighting while on playground equipment.
11. No tickling or other horseplay when using playground equipment.
12. Only one person at a time is allowed on a piece of equipment unless the equipment

Children should not perform inverted activities on playground equipment.

    is designed for simultaneous use by several children.
13. Equipment may only be used for the purpose for which it was designed.
14. No wrestling.
15. No one is allowed in an area which cannot be seen by the teacher supervising the playground.
16. No solid object may be used as a base or a turning point while running or racing.
17. No hard-ball playing.
18. No pushing or shoving.

Playground Rules for Teachers

A teacher who has supervisory responsibility for children at recess must understand they are liable for injuries which might occur. Although supervision is covered in more detail in chapter 9, it is worth noting that supervision is only possible when the children can be seen. It is essential, therefore, that the first playground rule for teachers is, "Be able to see the children." The following is a list of teacher rules for playground supervision:

1. The teacher must be in a position which allows him/her to see all the children for whom he/she is responsible.
2. The playground rules must be enforced.
3. The teacher should know and practice first aid procedures.
4. The teacher should not grade papers or talk with other teachers while supervising.
5. The supervising teacher should not participate in a play activity with children.
6. If the teacher feels there are too many children to fairly supervise, he/she should inform the principal in writing regarding any safety concerns.

PLAYGROUND EQUIPMENT

Play equipment appears on almost every elementary school playground. Although it is not an integral part of a physical education program, some playground equipment can be used as part of a developmental program. There are basically two types of playground equipment, developmental, and recreational. Developmental equipment can help the child improve such areas as balance, upper body strength, and/or creativity. To be developmental, children must be required to be active participants. Developmental equipment includes equipment requiring balance, climbing equipment, hanging equipment such as horizontal ladders or traveling rings, and playgrounds which involve the children's imagination. No matter what the equipment, of course, it is only of value if children use it; too much equipment is selected for its looks without regard for its value, safety, or frequency of use.

Recreational Equipment

Equipment which only requires a passive effort is termed recreational. This equipment includes such things as swings, sliding boards, and sit and ride items which can help satisfy a child's need to relax and have fun but has no other developmental value. Recreational equipment, in particular swings and sliding boards, unfortunately, are also associated with the most number of injuries occurring on playground equipment. One reason for the incidence of injuries is the fact that recreational equipment is on almost every elementary playground, and often is located on a hard surface.

Although fun, recreational equipment can be dangerous.

Developmental Equipment

As the name implies, developmental equipment will assist a child's development and includes such things as jungle gyms, balance beams, horizontal ladders, climbing poles, and equipment specially designed to encourage creativity. Developmental equipment requires the child's active participation through climbing and balancing. As in the case of recreational equipment, safety must be the primary concern.

Developmental equipment requires the child's active participation.

Analyzing Equipment for Safety

Safety evaluation is essential to reducing injuries. How many injuries occur on playgrounds each year, and what can be done to reduce these injuries? The answer to the first part is too many;

and to the second, provide a safe playground. Equipment must be analyzed, and the dangerous equipment removed or modified. Those responsible for manufacturing dangerous equipment, as well as those who knowingly allow its use, should be held liable for injuries. It is interesting to note that there are no federal and few state laws regulating playground equipment. Relating his experience as a child, comedian Bill Cosby jokingly suggests on one of his albums that playgrounds are designed by parents to kill kids. Although Cosby was joking, many dedicated parents, teachers, and administrators often unknowingly allow dangerous equipment to be placed on playgrounds, resulting in many needless injuries. What parent, for example, would knowingly want their child hanging over two stories in the air on a piece of playground equipment? Would they want their child balancing on top of a five-foot high pole which could result in the child being killed or paralyzed? How about hanging by their hands on a merry-go-round while swinging above blacktop? The answers to these questions is obvious, and a partial solution is education; partial because only legislation will significantly reduce the problem.

Knowledge is power, and with knowledge, teachers can reduce playground injuries. How does one determine whether a piece of equipment belongs on an elementary playground? What are the risk factors? Although as previously mentioned, there are few if any laws governing playground equipment, there are legal precedence that suggest two things: **1. equipment should be placed on a soft surface, and 2. equipment should not be over six feet off the ground.** Falls to the surface are the number one reason for playground injuries. The obvious implication is that the higher the equipment, the more serious the injury. When evaluating equipment a key question to ask is: **"If while using equipment correctly, a child momentarily loses the ability to be successful, what is the worst possible injury the child could receive?"** If the answer to this question is death or serious head or neck injuries, the equipment should be modified or removed. Obviously, when equipment is misused serious injuries could occur. What happens, however, when a child loses his/her grip on a high horizontal ladder or falls off a high balancing post? What part of the body could strike the ground first and how hard? Some of the more dangerous equipment which appears frequently on playgrounds include: high balancing poles, some of which are as much as five-feet high;

horizontal ladders eight to ten-feet high; climbing apparatus which causes children to be suspended high above the ground; climbing ropes; wooden equipment with poor hand-holds; and high balancing equipment.

Take balance poles as an evaluation example, suppose a child balancing on a pole five-feet high loses his/her balance; the child could jump off to the side and fall feet first which is a long fall and might lead to a broken arm or leg; or if the feet go one way and the body the other, it would be the same as jumping up five feet into the air and having his/her feet cut out from under him/her. Now the child's head and neck area will most likely strike the ground first. Also, since balancing poles are normally arranged in an ascending/descending order with space between them, there is always the danger of striking a lower pole with the head or neck when jumping down between two poles. Then the question may be raised as to why someone has to balance on a five-foot high pole; what is the value? None!

Selecting Equipment

When determining what equipment to include on the playground, safety is the primary consideration, but other things to consider are usage, material (wood or metal), and location. If children do not use the equipment, it is of little value. It seems children prefer the more passive recreational equipment such as swings and sliding boards as compared with the more developmental. It also appears that children recognize dangerous equipment and tend, except for the more adventuresome children, to stay away from it. The presence of dangerous equipment, however, used or not should not be permitted (see above). To increase participation, the developmental equipment can be used in a fitness program. It can also be part of an obstacle course which children can complete on their own and receive recognition through a fitness club.

Trends

The trend in playground equipment is toward plastic-coated metal equipment which is attractive and has a long life expectancy. It is designed in modules to allow for expansion when money becomes available. The metal provides good hand holds for small children but the selection criteria already discussed must be applied when selecting the individual pieces. Many playgrounds still contain un-coated metal equipment as well as

Metal playground equipment is more durable and safer than wood.

those made of wood. The main problem with uncoated metal is rust, while wooden equipment deteriorates and produces splinters. As a result of its looks, wooden equipment was popular for many years and can be found frequently on playgrounds. Many of these wooden structures use large logs which do not provide the secure hand-holds. When the equipment is wet and slippery, good hand-holds are even more important. Wooden equipment is expensive, does not last as long as metal, and is not, therefore, recommended.

SUMMARY

This chapter was a presentation of some inanimate objects which affect teaching and learning. The various outdoor and indoor teaching areas were discussed. Grass was the favorite outside area and probably the most versatile while indoors the best station is the gymnasium. Hard surface (blacktop) outside areas are to be avoided. Decorations such as bulletin boards can be used to enhance the learning environment. The chapter concluded with a discussion of the playground with an emphasis on playground equipment, its value, and safe usage.

REFERENCES AND SUGGESTED READINGS

Bowers, L. Children Need Playgrounds—But Playgrounds Need Help, *JOPERD* 59:47-51, 1988.

Gabbard, C., et.al. *Physical Education for Children.* Englewood Cliffs: Prentice-Hall, Inc., 1987.

Graham, G., et.al. *Children Moving* (2nd ed.). Palo Alto: Mayfield Publishing Co., 1987.

Jambor, T., and R. Gaggiulo. The Playground—A Social Entity for Mainstreaming, *JOPERD* 58:18-23, 1987.

Keogh, J., and D. Sugden. *Movement Skill Development.* New York: MacMillan Publishing Co., 1985.

Kirn, W. What ever happened to play? Time April 30, 2001. pp. 56-58.

Kraft, R. *Children at Play: Behavior of Children at Recess, *JOPERD* 60:21-24, 1989.

Mitchell, M, and T. Cone. No Gym? No Problem! JOP*ERD* 72:25-29, 2001

Morris, G., and J. Stiehl. *Physical Education from Intent to Action.* Columbus: Charles E. Merrill Publishing Co., 1985.

Sawyer, T., ed. *Nuisance, JOPERD,* 69:7, pp. 9-10, 1998.

———Serious Injuries Are a Serious Problem, *JOPERD,* 69:7, p. 7, 1998.

Selective Web Sites

Playground: http://www.uni.edu/playground/

National Playground Institute: http://www.activeparks.org//education/safety.cfm

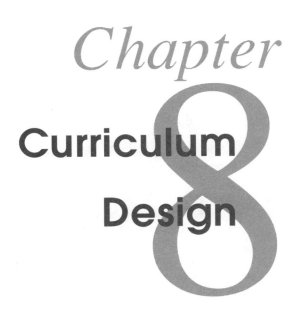

Chapter

Curriculum

Design

After completing this chapter, the student should be able to:

1. List and explain each of the five parts of a systematic approach to curriculum design.

2. Explain how the systematic approach can be used for any planing situation from yearly planning all the way down to an individual lesson.

3. Write one behavioral objective which meets the criteria established in the chapter for each of the three educational domains.

4. Explain the value of using percentages in some of the objectives.

5. Explain how objectives are used to pretest the students.

6. Cite at least three examples in which the stations approach would be an effective class organization.

7. Construct a year plan for each grade level K-6.

8. Write a unit plan for some aspect of elementary physical education.

9. List and explain all the parts of a lesson plan giving at least three characteristics of each of the three phases of the lesson.

10. Write a physical education lesson plan which meets the criteria established in the chapter for an elementary grade of your choice.

11. Define the key terms listed below.

══*Key Terms*

Evaluation	Percentages
Flow	Pretest
Goals	Problem-solving questions
Learning packet	Stations approach
Lesson plan	Timing
Methods	Unit plan
Objectives	Year plan

What is the purpose of curriculum development? It is a planning process to develop an educational program that will give each child an opportunity to reach his or her full potential. If approached systematically, the chances of success are much greater.

A SYSTEMATIC APPROACH

The following process should be a followed in any curriculum development:

1. **Goals,** which are stated in broad terms, are developed to convey the instructional outcome.
2. **Objectives** are developed from the goals, and state in specific (behavioral) terms the purpose of the instruction.
3. **A Pretest** using the objectives is administered to measure the student's present ability or knowledge.
4. **Methods** which are teaching approaches are used by the teacher to achieve the goals and objectives.
5. **Evaluation** using the objectives is conducted by the teaching following the instruction to determine what learning has taken place.

This curriculum development process can be applied to all planning from the yearly plan down to the teaching of an individual skill. A teacher, for example, may wish to help children develop their hand-eye coordination. The goal in this example would be: "The children will develop their manipulative ability;" and the objective could be "Following instruction, at least 80% of the children will be able to toss a 3" yarn ball above their head and catch it three times in a row with both hands." To determine the incoming ability, the children are pretested by asking the question, "How many ways can you throw and catch the yarn ball?" Other problem solving questions would follow to allow children to explore different ways to throw and catch. Near the end of this part of the lesson, the teacher would ask, "How many times can you throw the ball above your head and catch it with two hands?" The teacher would determine success by observing how many balls fell to the floor.

GOALS

Goals are general statements which express instructional outcomes. Following are examples of yearly goals, one for each educational domain:

Evaluating the objective through observation.

Psychomotor -   The children will develop manipulative ability.

Cognitive -   The children will learn fitness concepts.

Affective -   The children will develop sportsmanship.

Goals are used to develop more specifically stated objectives and can help to communicate to others the purpose of your curriculum.

OBJECTIVES

An *objective* must clearly convey what the child should be able to do following the lesson. A well-stated objective must express behavioral expectations. Normally in physical education that behavior will either be something that can be seen or heard. If the objective has been properly stated, anyone viewing the child's performance must be able to determine without further clarification from the teacher whether the objective has been met.

The use of behavioral objectives provides several advantages: (1) the instructional outcome is clear to everyone, (2) accountability is possible, (3) the program can be based on competency rather than time, and (4) individualized instruction is easier. By stating objectives behaviorally, it is also possible to individualize instruction through contracts and learning centers (both discussed later in this chapter) which allow children to progress at their own rate. By using behavioral objectives, data can be collected which can help justify programs.

Educators are often confused as to how specific an objective must be. In determining clarity, it is helpful to think about what would happen if the teacher wrote a behavioral objective and then had someone watch to see if the objective had been accomplished. Could someone determine whether an objective was met without assistance from the teacher who wrote it? A behavioral objective is similar to an objective test question. In most physical education settings, the answer will be some physical performance which can be seen. There are times, however, when cognitive knowledge is an important physical education objective. In a cognitive situation for elementary physical education, the answers most often are given orally. No matter what the case, the objective must be stated in such a way that anyone can determine the purpose of the lesson and whether it has been met.

The child's performance must be observable.

Components of Behavioral Objectives

A behaviorally-stated objective must have three components: (1) the observable behavior, (2) the criteria of acceptable performance or how well the children must perform, and (3) the conditions under which the behavior must be exhibited.

The Behavior. The child's performance must be viewable through one of the five senses. Traditionally, the most frequently used senses are the eyes and ears. In physical education, therefore, we will be able to see or hear the student behav-

ior. In other disciplines, such as home economics and industrial arts, the senses of smell, taste, and feel are frequently employed.

The Criteria of Acceptable Performance. The criteria express how well the child will be able to perform. The child may only have to catch the ball once or may have to catch it four out of five times.

The Conditions. Conditions are those things which must be observed during the performance. If one says the child will be able to shoot the ball in the basket three out of four times from a distance of ten feet, it may seem clear, but what size is the ball and how high is the basket? By not expressing the appropriate conditions, there can be confusion.

The condition must be specific; for example, how high the basket will be.

Examples

The following are examples of behaviorally-stated objectives:

1. Psychomotor domain: Using a junior size basketball and an eight-foot high basket (the condition), the student will be able to make (the behavior) three out of five shots (criteria) from a distance of ten feet (also part of the condition).

2. Cognitive domain: Following a discussion of rules (condition), a child, if asked, will be able to state (behavior) at least two safety rules (criteria).

3. Affective domain: When given an anonymous questionnaire at the end of the year (condition), at least 80 percent (criteria) will rate (behavior) the physical education

program as good to excellent on a scale of excellent, good, average, fair, and poor (also part of the criteria).

It should be noted here that affective domain objectives are written for the teacher and not the children. They are used to determine how effective the teacher has been in the affective domain and, as will be discussed later, they are not shared with the children.

Specificity

How specific must an objective be? As stated earlier, it must clearly convey what must be seen or heard. A hand-eye coordination objective for five-year-old children might be:

The child will be able to throw (behavior) a five-inch plastic ball at least five feet and hit a ten-inch target, three feet off the floor (conditions) three out of four times (criteria).

For a six-year-old a similar task might be:

The child will throw a five-inch plastic ball at least ten feet, stepping forward with the opposite foot while throwing, and hit a ten-inch target three feet off the floor three out of four times.

At times, the specificity can be expressed more easily by referring to the written lesson or to some instructional material provided with the lesson. For example, an objective could be expressed as follows:

The children will be able to do the set shot observing the four points discussed in the lesson and make two out of three shots into an eight-foot basket using a junior basketball from ten feet away.

or

The children will be able to do the forward roll as described on page eight of the curriculum guide.

The Verb

A key to writing behavioral objectives is the verb. figure 8.1 is a list of verbs which can be used when writing behavioral objectives.

Figure 8.1. Verbs for writing behavioral objectives.

Psychomotor Domain

1. bands	11. holds	21. rides
2. bats	12. jumps	22. tosses
3. chases	13. kicks	23. somersaults
4. climbs	14. leaps	24. stretches
5. crawls	15. pitches	25. swims
6. catches	16. pulls	26. swings
7. grabs	17. rolls	27. tosses
8. grips	18. runs	28. twists
9. hits	19. skips	29. walks
10. hops	20. slides	

Affective Domain

1. accepts	15. criticizes	29. permits
2. advocates	16. defends	30. promotes
3. argues	17. disproves	31. proposes
4. asks	18. disputes	32. praises
5. assumes	19. enjoys	33. questions
6. attemps	20. evaluates	34. recommends
7. attends	21. initiates	35. rectifies
8. berates	22. involves	36. rejects
9. bothers	23. joins	37. suggests
10. challenges	24. likes	38. supports
11. chooses	25. loves	39. sustains
12. completes	26. obeys	40. tolerates
13. consoles	27. offers	41. volunteers
14. consults	28. participates	42. watches

Cognitive Domain

Knowledge Level:

1. arranges	7. gives	13. positions
2. checks	8. identifies	14. says
3. circles	9. labels	15. shows
4. copies	10. lists	16. states
5. defines	11. matches	17. tells
6. describes	12. names	18. writes

Understanding level:

1. applies	6. differentiates	11. interprets
2. computes	7. distinguishes	12. plans
3. contrasts	8. evaluates	13. proves
4. defines	9. explains	14. solves
5. demonstrates	10. formulates	15. uses

Processing Level:

Analysis:

1. breaks down	6. extracts
2. disassembles	7. investigates
3. dissects	8. separates
4. divides	9. simplifies
5. examines	10. takes apart

Synthesis:

1. assembles	6. develops
2. builds	7. produces
3. completes	8. puts together
4. constructs	9. reorganizes
5. creates	10. structures

Classify:

1. arranges	6. places
2. chooses	7. regroups
3. grades	8. sequences
4. groups	9. sorts
5. orders	10. tallies

Evaluate:

1. appraises	6. tallies
2. assays	7. ranks
3. assesses	8. rates
4. decides	9. weights
5. grades	10. determines value of

Percentages

Percentages are commonly used in objectives to help the teacher make curriculum decisions; eighty percent (80%) is frequently used. A statement such as "Eighty percent of the children will be able to..." suggests that when 80% can complete the task, it is time to move on to other challenges. The 80% is based upon a philosophy that 80% of the children should be able to achieve 80% of the objectives. At one time, some educators felt 100% of the children should achieve 100% of the objectives; this philosophy was associated with programmed instruction. Currently a more widely accepted figure is 80/80.

An 80/80 philosophy is not an expression of failure for the 20%, but a realization that not all children have to achieve every objective. The physical educator must determine the importance of an objective to future learning. Some sports skill objectives are an end in themselves, and if children are not successful, it is not overly important. If, for example, an overweight child cannot do a headstand, it is not necessary to frustrate the child with additional instruction. This child can live effectively without being able to do a headstand. Perhaps the child would be better off doing an aerobic ac-

Individual attention should be given to children who cannot achieve basic movement competencies.

tivity to help manage his/her weight. The instructional priorities must be appropriate for the child, and the purpose of physical education is not the development of athletes. On the other hand, basic movement competencies are important to all children and serve as the foundation upon which all efficient movement is built. Children who do not accomplish these competencies should receive extra instruction.

Behavioral Objectives and the Educational Domains

In order to have a well-rounded program, goals and objectives should be developed for each of the three educational domains: psychomotor, cognitive, and affective. Most students find it fairly easy to write psychomotor and cognitive objectives but find the affective domain difficult.

Psychomotor Domain. The psychomotor domain objectives deal with the child's physical performance. They can be shared with the students who are old enough to understand them, and are an integral part of some approaches to teaching. They are, for example, essential to the development of a learning center (discussed later in this chapter).

Examples of psychomotor objectives are:

By the end of the lesson (condition), 80% of the children will be able to use either hand to catch (the behavior) a six-inch beanbag thrown underhand from a distance of ten feet (also part of the condition).

Given an eight-foot basket and a junior basketball (condition), 80% of the children will be able to shoot the ball into the basket (behavior) two out of four times (criteria) using the one hand set shot (also part of the behavior) from a distance of ten feet (part of the condition).

During the rhythmic activity (condition), all the children will move (behavior) appropriately, fast to fast music, slow to slow, heavy to loud, and lightly to soft (criteria).

By the end of the year (condition), 80% of the children will be able to perform (behavior) all the skills as specified on the *Test of Gross Motor Development-2* by Ulrich, 2000 (criteria).

The Affective Domain. When writing affective objectives, the rules are the same as those for other domains except affective objectives are written for the teacher rather than the students. When writing affective objectives, the teacher is attempting to determine how effectively he/she has influenced the children's attitudes.

Objectives must be specific; for example, 80% of the children will be able to use either hand to catch a six-inch beanbag thrown underhand from a distance of ten feet.

The teacher must express an observable behavior to be exhibited by a certain percentage of the students. For example, everyone has a preconceived notion about sportsman-like behavior which can be observed. While watching a game, it is possible to see or hear behaviors which suggest an individual or team is demonstrating sportsmanship. Objectives, therefore, can be written which state observable behaviors which the teacher wants students to exhibit or avoid. The teacher then decides how many students must comply by stating a percentage. A reasonable objective, therefore, could be "No child (100% of the children) will argue with the official's call during a twenty-minute game of basketball."

In many cases, the teacher will strive for 100% compliance while in others full compliance may not be realistic. The teacher determines the percentage based upon the importance of compliance and the teaching situation. Safety rules should have 100% compliance, while 60% may be a more realistic expectation for a voluntary intramural program.

Although objectives can be written for any affective area, voluntary participation and ratings on attitude questionnaires are two ways teachers can determine their *affective* effectiveness. Voluntary participation and anonymous ratings both reflect attitude.

Examples of affective domain behavioral objectives are:

Voluntary Participation:

Following a unit in volleyball (the condition), at least 60% of the children (criteria) will voluntarily participate (behavior) in the after-school intramural program.

Anonymous Questionnaire:

Given an anonymous questionnaire at year's end (condition), at least 90% (criteria) of the students will rate (behavior) the physical education program as "good to excellent" (part of criteria) on a scale of "excellent, good, average, fair, and poor" (part of the condition).

Safety:

All the children (criteria) will stop, look and listen (behavior) when the whistle is blown (condition).

During gymnastics (condition), no child (criteria) will disobey (behavior) any (part of the criteria) of the safety rules.

Unlike the other two domains, affective domain objectives are not shared with the students. They are used to guide the teacher's affective instruction. If shared with students, behavioral changes may not really reflect attitudinal changes. For example, if students feel they are being evaluated based upon affective objectives, they may follow safety rules only when the teacher is looking. The teacher must strive to affect attitude changes which will cause students to practice safety all the time. Other students may voluntarily participate in an activity just to help a teacher fulfill an affective objective even when they really do not have a positive attitude toward the activity. If a teacher really wants to determine attitudes, affective objectives should not be shared with students.

Cognitive Domain. Physical education can make contributions to the cognitive domain, particularly in the areas of health, fitness, physiology, and safety knowledge, to name a few. Cognitive objectives, therefore, should be an integral part of the planning process.

Examples of cognitive objectives:

Following a lesson on rules (condition), all the children, if asked, will be able to state (behavior) one safety rule discussed in class (criteria).

After fifteen minutes of instruction and practice (condition), at least 80% of the children will be able to perform (behavior) any structured dance without teacher assistance (criteria).

During a creative movement activity (condition), each child, if asked, will be able to demonstrate (behavior) at least one unique way to move (criteria).

Following a basketball unit (condition), at least 80% of the children will be able to correctly answer (behavior) 80% of the questions on a basketball quiz (criteria).

PRETESTING

The third part of the system is a *pretest* to determine the students' present ability. The behavioral objectives serve as the pretest. It is not necessary nor feasible to evaluate all objectives at the beginning of the year, but no instruction should take place until the present ability level has been determined. Certain areas such as fitness, basic movement competencies, body image, and attitudes should be measured at the beginning of the year. Other more specific skills can be evaluated just prior to the instructional unit.

The pretest can be either formal or informal depending upon the data desired. Formal testing in the psychomotor domain usually requires assessing children individually, as is the case in fitness testing where specific data are required. Anytime the teacher wants to make a comparison of pre-test scores with post-test scores for the purpose of gathering data, formal testing is required. Informal testing is much more efficient, and is done through class observation to get a general assessment of ability. For example, by playing "Simon Says—Body Image" (mentioned earlier) the teacher can evaluate the children's body image. This information can then be used to determine those parts which need work, how much time needs to be spent on this developmental area, and which children need special attention. The teacher must be a keen observer, using the eyes and ears as instruments for observation; behavioral objectives can be used to calibrate these evaluation instruments.

Observational Skills

Observational skills are essential to efficient evaluation. To prepare for observation, the teacher must put the software (knowledge) into the computer (the brain). Behavioral objectives serve as the software, and then the teacher establishes a teaching environment which allows for systematic observation. It may be efficient, for example, to

Observation of the class can provide general assessment of ability.

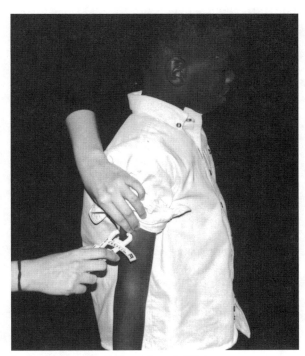

Individual testing is formal evaluation.

have the children moving in a circle to music while evaluating their basic locomotor competencies, or when observing throwing and catching, a key may be the number of balls hitting the floor.

Formal Evaluation

While observation is informal evaluation, individual testing is formal evaluation, and when done properly can provide good data. If formal testing is required, teachers must develop efficient testing procedures which can include the assistance of parents or older students. It is not usually difficult to teach others the testing procedures, and older children enjoy assisting the teacher. A good rapport with parents also will provide a base for parent assistants.

When evaluation is necessary, it is important to ask how precise the information must be. When records are being kept and awards given, it is necessary to be exact, but when making general curriculum decisions, formal testing is probably not necessary. For more detailed information regarding assessment, refer to chapter 4.

METHODS

After the children's incoming ability has been determined, *methods* must be employed to help the children develop. These methods include: learning centers, stations, programmed instruction, etc. When determining a method, the teacher must consider the child's age, intellectual ability, learning rate and style, and the curriculum content. In selecting a method, the focus must be on the goals and objectives as well as individualizing instruction.

Learning Centers

A learning center is a approach which individualizes instruction. A center contains all the information and material necessary for a child to accomplish the specified objectives. The center should include the following parts:
1. A title
2. Instructions on how to use the center
3. Safety information
4. Motivational information (extrinsic rewards)
5. Goals and objectives
6. Self-evaluation materials
7. Instructional information for each task (can be computerized, written, or on film or tape)
8. Equipment necessary to accomplish each task

A center usually deals with an instructional unit such as skills associated with a sport. It is possible, however, to design a learning center for anything which can be presented as self-instruction material. Tasks are presented in a hierarchical arrangement, and children are instructed to determine their present ability level, then enter at the appropriate location and progress at their own speed. Although easier to design for the older child

A learning center is one method of individualizing instruction.

who can read efficiently, younger children can use a computer, and/or video or audiotape to receive information. Figure 8.2 (page 105) is a portion of a gymnastics' learning packet.

The Stations Approach

The stations approach is used to individualize instruction using a series of written instructions placed around the room. The station's focus is usually on one development area such as hand-eye coordination. Each station can deal with a different area. At one station, for example, children could be doing a rhythmic activity while at the next they do gymnastics. Unlike a learning center which contains a whole instructional unit, a

The stations approach uses a series of written instructions placed around the room.

Figure 8.2
A Portion of a Gymnastics Learning Package for Children Age 10-12
Rules and Procedures for Using This Packet

1. Spotters are required for all stunts.
2. Some of the more advanced stunts have special requirements for safety listed beside them. No stunt in Section 3 may be attempted until permission is received from the teacher.
3. No horseplay will be tolerated.
4. Read all instructional information before attempting any stunt.
5. Handle film and tapes carefully.
6. When you are not sure of something, check with your teacher.
   SPOTTERS REQUIRED FOR ALL STUNTS.

The tumbling skills on page 2 of the booklet are arranged from those that are easy to those requiring a good deal of skill. As you can see, a space is provided for your teacher to sign when you have correctly demonstrated the skill. No new skill in any one section should be attempted until the one above has been initialed. Section 1 and 2 must be completed before going on to Section 3.

Beginning on page 4, instructions, including pictures, are provided to help you. Some skill instruction also includes films and/or tapes; if so, a number for the film or tape has been placed in the appropriate column. These materials can be found in the learning centers located around the gymnasium. You are free to use these materials at any time.

SPOTTERS REQUIRED

Section 1. Tumbling Skills Checklist
  1._____Squat forward roll
  2._____Standing forward roll
  3._____Running forward roll
  4._____Dive forward roll
  5._____Fish Flop
  6._____Standing backward roll
  7._____Straddle backward roll
  8._____Straight backward roll
  9._____Backward roll, extension
          and snapdown

Section 2.
  10._____Tripod
  11._____Tip up
  12._____Headstand
  13._____Mule kick

  14._____Handstand
  15._____Walk on hand
  16._____Turn while balancing on hands
  17._____Cartwheel
  18._____Round-Off
  19._____Front walkover
  20._____Kip Up

Section 3.
  21._____Front headspring
  22._____Front handspring
  23._____Back handspring (spotters required)
  24._____Back somersault (belt required)
  25._____Round-off, back handspring (belt required)
  26._____Round-off, back somersault (belt required)
  27._____Front somersault

Instructions

Skill I—Squat forward roll. Get into a squatting position as shown in figure 1, placing arms on outside of knees. Fingers should be pointed straight ahead and should be right next to feet. The chin should be touching the chest. Push off with the feet while holding your weight up on your arms which should be slightly bent. Only the back of your head should touch the mat. Roll forward, reaching the hands out in order to come up on your feet; see Figures 2 and 3.

Skill II—Standing forward roll. Begin in a standing position. Squat and roll forward all in one motion following the rules established in Skill I for chin position, hand placement, etc.
Descriptions for each skill would follow in order.

Performance Standards

Skill I—The forward roll must be done in a continuous motion in a straight line from a squatting position to a squatting position. The hands may touch the mat only at the beginning of the roll. Only the back of the head may touch the mat.

Skill II—Must be done from a stand to a stand observing the criteria of Skill I above except for the squat starting position.

station normally focuses on a problem-solving or self-testing task. In a stations approach, a series of these cards (about six to eight) are placed around the room, and children rotate to each.

When the children enter the room they are told to equally divide themselves among the stations, read the instructions, and complete the task or solve the problems. Self-testing tasks and in particular target activities work well; open-ended questions can be written on the station card to individualize instruction and give children success. When working with older children, specific tasks associated with a sport may be appropriate; younger children, however, would probably benefit more from open-ended questions. It is also possible to combine some open-ended questions with more specific tasks. Figure 8.3 shows examples of stations which use open-ended questions.

Teaching Approaches

The teaching approach used is also an important consideration in determining the method to be employed. (These approaches are discussed in chapter 5.) After evaluating the incoming students' ability, it may be necessary to use a variety of approaches to meet all the students' needs.

EVALUATION

The final component of a systematic approach is *evaluation.* The behavioral objectives discussed earlier are used in this evaluation process. It is also where percentages come into play when making decisions on appropriate curriculum changes. If, for example, all of the children are accomplishing all of the objectives in a relatively short period of time, it may be necessary to establish higher standards. On the other hand, if few are being successful, the criteria may be too high. All children, however, should experience success at their level. Evaluation is used to fine tune the process to insure each child's success.

Figure 8.3. Example of Instruction Stations

First Grade

Station 1: *Hand-eye Coordination*
Can you throw and catch the beanbag?
How many ways can you throw and catch with a friend?
Can you hit the triangle while standing on the square?

Third Grade

Station 4: *Hand-eye Coordination*
How many ways can you throw and catch two beanbags with a friend?
Can you throw the beanbag through the swinging tire while standing behind the line?
How far back can you get and still throw it through the tire?

Fifth Grade

Station 8: *Hand-eye Coordination and Lead-up Skills to Basketball*
Working with a partner, see how many different ways you can get the ball from one person to another.

Station 9:
Play "Monkey in the Middle" with one person on the inside and three people passing the ball. If the middle person touches the ball, someone must take that person's place. Use the passes learned at Station 8.

PLANNING

To be an effective teacher, one must have plans. There should be an overall elementary curriculum which is used to develop the year, unit, and lesson plans in that order.

THE ELEMENTARY CURRICULUM

Most states have standards for each grade level which must be met by all the schools within that state. State standards are then used to develop the curriculum for a particular school system. It is very unusual not to have a curriculum guide for each educational level. This curriculum is then used to develop year plans.

YEAR PLANNING

Year planning can be thought of as the creation of a master schedule. Like any long-range planning instrument, revising and refining of the year plan is a necessary ongoing process. Failure to have a long-range plan within the overall curriculum is a leading cause of an unorganized and often redundant physical education program. How often have you heard students complain that they do the same old thing year after year? A well-organized year plan can help put an end to this unfortunate situation.

If the year plan is to be useful, an overall curriculum for the elementary years must be developed. Listed below are several pre-planning steps which must be accomplished before attempting to construct the actual year plan grid which is introduced in the next section.

1. First, for each grade level that you teach, list by name each unit of instruction that you plan to incorporate during the school year.
2. Now, look over your units of instruction and determine if any can be sub-classified. If so, label as such. For example, in your fifth grade curriculum you may have listed as units of instruction the following: softball skills, volleyball skills, soccer skills, tennis skills. Note that the first three units could be sub-classified as team sport skills while the last one could be sub-classified as individual sport skills.
3. Now determine the percent of time that you plan to devote to each major unit of instruction. For example, you may decide to spend 20% of your instruction time on team sport skills, 10% on individual sport skills, 25% on physical fitness, and so on.
4. Realizing that most public school systems are in session for approximately thirty-six weeks, determine the number of times you will be with any one class during the school year. For example, if you meet only one time per week, then you are scheduled to see each class thirty-six times during the school year; for two class meetings per week, you are scheduled to meet with each class seventy-two times per year.
5. Now determine how many class periods are available for each unit of instruction. For example, if you meet your class one time per week (thirty-six class meetings) and you have devoted 20% of this time to team sport skills, then you can plan on having seven classes devoted to team sport skills. Using the earlier example, recall that you listed three team sports. It will be up to you to decide how you divide these seven class periods among the three team sports.
6. It is usually at this point in time that it will be necessary for you to revise and rethink the information that you generated in steps 1-5.

In all likelihood, especially if you are a beginning teacher, you have overestimated the amount of material that can be effectively covered in one year. Recall step 5 above. How can you effectively introduce new skills in three team sports in only seven class periods? Now that you realize how very little time you have to work with the children in any particular class, it is time to revisit your pre-planning material and attempt to establish a more realistic number of units along with a more realistic percentage of time that you plan to spend on each. To aid you in this process, simply establish a pie graph for each grade level, denoting the grade, unit name, and how many classes are available for each unit of instruction. (See figure 8.4.)

How to Construct the Year Plan

With pre-planning complete, it is now time to further organize this information. Figure 8.5 (page 109) illustrates the general format of the year plan.

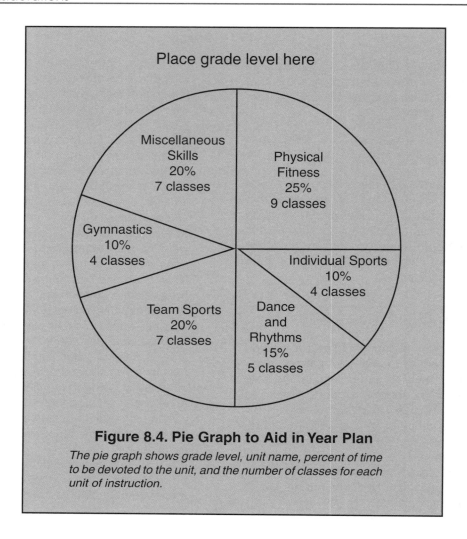

Place grade level here

Miscellaneous
Skills
20%
7 classes

Physical
Fitness
25%
9 classes

Gymnastics
10%
4 classes

Individual Sports
10%
4 classes

Team Sports
20%
7 classes

Dance
and
Rhythms
15%
5 classes

Figure 8.4. Pie Graph to Aid in Year Plan

*The pie graph shows grade level, unit name, percent of time
to be devoted to the unit, and the number of classes for each
unit of instruction.*

The top horizontal aspect of the year plan grid is reserved for recording the dates that school is in session. Rather than numbering (i.e., Week 1-36), it is better to actually incorporate the true dates (for example, September 1-5, etc.). This practice will help you avoid scheduling an activity at an inappropriate time. For example, if you schedule a softball unit of instruction during the nineteenth week of the school year, in many parts of the country it is probable that snow would be on the ground or the outdoor temperature would be too cold.

The outermost portion of the vertical aspect of the grid is reserved for recording grade level, while the inner aspect of the grid is reserved for recording two specific bits of information. First, in the top aspect of each box you should fill in the appropriate name for the given unit of instruction. The remaining area in the box is space where you can briefly list the most important new skills you plan to introduce in this unit of instruction. This step is very important, especially when you have more than one grade level receiving the same instruction. For example, even though both the ten- and eleven-year-old children may be receiving instruction in soccer skills, the skills that each is to learn should be different.

As should be evident, when the entire year plan has been completed the instructor can quickly determine where he or she is in the curriculum and where he or she will be going in the future regarding units of instruction.

As you fill in the year plan, remember to give considerable attention to the placement of each unit within a particular grade level as well as to the flow of units of instruction across different grade levels.

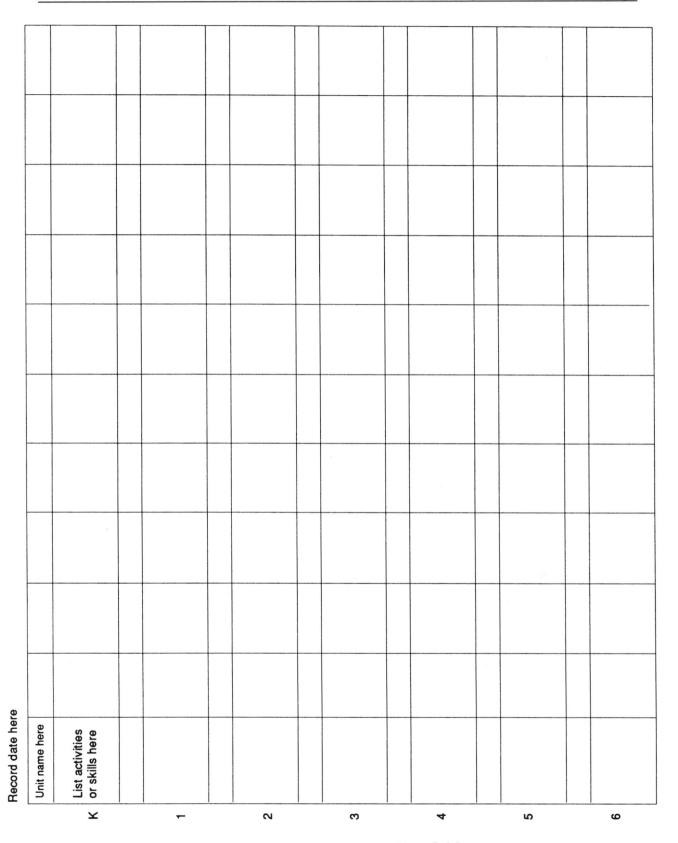

Figure 8.5. Sample Year Plan Grid

UNIT PLANNING

Unit planning is an outgrowth of a systematic approach to curriculum development. Although units may vary in length, each should reflect the careful thinking required in a systematic approach. Although it is difficult to specify a time frame in some cases, almost any aspect of growth and development can be put into a unit format. Sports lend themselves well to unit planning in which time can be specified. Units of four to six weeks are common for upper elementary sports and for rhythmics. Units in basic movement competencies, however, are difficult to specify in terms of time. Even when time cannot be specified, a unit plan is still necessary.

A unit should include each of the following:
1. Goals
2. Objectives
3. Evaluation methods
4. Content
5. Teaching methods
6. Equipment

Figure 8.6 is a Basic Competency Unit for Young Children.

Figure 8.6. A Basic Competency Unit for Young Children

This unit is designed for any child who has not yet developed the basic competencies contained in this unit. It is primarily geared toward four- to six-year old children. Although activities are listed under various categories, any movement activity helps develop the basic competencies which serve as the foundation upon which fitness and other movement skills may be developed. The key is to have all the children moving all the time while participating in activities they enjoy. As with any physical education activity, the emphasis should be on developing a positive self-concept along with movement ability. The developmental activities listed are far from exhaustive, and the reader is referred to other appropriate sections of the book for additional ones.

Goals

Psychomotor Domain
1. To have children experience every way their body and body parts can move both locomotor and non-locomotor at various forces, different speeds, in all directions, and all levels.
2. To have children experience every way their body parts can manipulate an object.
3. To develop kinesthetic awareness.
4. To develop balance.
5. To develop rhythmic ability.
6. To develop the non-dominant side of the body.
7. To develop fitness.

Affective Domain
1. To develop a positive attitude toward movement.
2. To develop a positive self-concept.
3. To follow safety rules.
4. To follow good health habits.

Cognitive Domain
1. To learn the terms for basic locomotor and non-locomotor movements.
2. To learn various body parts.
3. To learn safety rules.
4. To learn good health habits.
5. To develop creativity and problem-solving ability.
6. To learn directional terms.

Objectives

Psychomotor Domain
By the end of the unit, at least 80% of the children will be able to:
1. Do all the basic locomotor movements at varying speeds, in all directions, at various levels, and with varying force without losing his or her balance.
2. Move all body parts capable of non-locomotor movement with varying speed and force while keeping time to a tom-tom or music.
3. Catch a seven-inch sponge ball with two hands thrown underhand from a distance of ten feet at least four out of five times.
4. Throw a seven-inch sponge ball with either hand and hit a four-foot target from a distance of ten feet four out of five times.
5. Kick a stationary eight and a half-inch playground ball with either foot and hit a four-foot target ten feet away four out of five times.
6. Close their eyes and throw a seven-inch sponge ball with either hand to a partner ten feet away. The child may use his/her eyes to make the initial judgement, but must close them before actually throwing the ball.
7. Walk forward, backward, and sideways the length of an eight-foot balance beam which is four inches wide and seven inches high.
8. Score at or above the fiftieth percentile on the health-related fitness test.

Figure 8.6, *continued*

Affective Domain

By the end of the unit, all the children will:

1. Demonstrate a positive attitude toward movement by appropriately responding to statements on an anonymous attitude questionnaire.
2. Have willingly participated in all movement activities.
3. Demonstrate positive health habits through appropriate responses on an anonymous attitude questionnaire.
4. Have followed the safety rules.

Cognitive Domain

By the end of the unit, at least 80% of the children will be able to:

1. Show knowledge of the locomotor and non-locomotor movement terms by demonstrating the movement in response to the teacher's verbal commands.
2. Show knowledge of the body parts covered in the unit by touching the appropriate part in response to the teacher's verbal command.
3. Think of unique ways to move during rhythmic activities.
4. Give the reason for a health habit covered in the unit.
5. Give at least three safety rules.
6. Show knowledge of directional terms by moving appropriately to the teacher's commands.

Assessment

Using the objectives as the guides, the following activities can be used to assess the children's present ability level:

1. Busy Bee: Body image and quality of movement
2. Brothers: Body image and quality of movement
3. Simon Says: Body image
4. Can You?: Any developmental component
5. Moving to music: Rhythmic ability, quality of movement, and creativity
6. Moving to tom-tom: Same as moving to music
7. Walking the balance beam: Balance
8. Sponge balls: Manipulative ability and kinesthetic awareness
9. Hoops: Directional terms
10. Anonymous attitude questionnaire: Attitudes
11. Questions: Cognitive knowledge

Content

The following areas should be included in a basic competency unit:

I. Locomotor and Non-locomotor Movement
 A. Quality of movement
  1. Force — heavy and light
  2. Time (speed) — fast and slow
  3. Space — forward, backward, sideways, personal and common (shared)
  4. Level — high and low
  5. There are numerous activities for developing the quality of movement
   a. Moving to music—particularly creative movement
   b. Moving to a tom-tom
   c. Any activity in which the children can move creatively in all directions, at various speeds, at different levels, and at different forces
   d. Story plays

 B. Basic locomotor movements — Since basic locomotor movements are inborn, all normal children enter kindergarten with the ability to do them. The emphasis, therefore, is on doing them while focusing on the qualities of movement. The children normally do movement straight ahead while interacting with just a few children; in school, they have to share common space with many children. To avoid injuries and help them develop, the basic movements should be done in combination with the four qualities of movement.
  1. Walk — one foot on the ground at all times
  2. Run — take off on one foot and land on the other following a momentary suspension in the air when both feet are off the ground
  3. Leap — similar to a run, but suspension in air is exaggerated
  4. Hop — take off on one foot and land on the same foot
  5. Jump — take off on one or two feet and land on two feet
  6. Rolling — on the side (log roll)

 C. Combination movements — Unlike the basic movements, combination movements must be learned. Some children will learn them through imitation but some, such as skipping, are not frequently done in everyday play or sports. On the other hand, galloping and sliding are used in many activities, such as tennis and basketball. Children, however, should not be expected to know combination movements unless they have been taught. A normal child can be taught the combination movements in a matter of minutes.
  1. Skip — step with one foot and then hop on that foot, and then do the same on the other foot

Figure 8.6, *continued*

2. Gallop — keep the same lead foot at all times
3. Slide — is a side gallop

D. Non-locomotor movements
1. Bend
2. Stretch
3. Twist
4. Turn
5. Swing
6. Bounce
7. Curl
8. Shake
9. Push
10. Pull
11. Activities for developing non-locomotor movements
   a. Moving body parts to music or a tom-tom
   b. Most of the creative activities listed under "V" later in this unit
   c. Mirror Maze

II. Body Parts — Cognitive Domain
A. Parts of the face
B. Neck
C. Shoulders
D. Chest
E. Elbows
F. Abdomen
G. Waist
H. Wrists
I. Hips
J. Thighs
K. Legs
L. Ankles
M. Feet and toes
N. Hands, fingers, and thumbs
O. Some activities for developing body part knowledge:
1. Busy Bee
2. Brothers
3. Simon Says
4. Placing body parts in hoops, on paper, or on a mat, i.e., "Can you put your _____ inside the hoop?"
5. Hokey-Pokey (rhythmic activity)

III. Directional Concepts — Cognitive Domain
A. Front, back
B. Right, left
C. Upper, lower
D. Beside
E. Between
F. Over, under
G. Near, far
H. Around
I. Up, down
J. Away from, toward
K. Next to
L. Through

M. Activities for learning directional terms
1. All the activities listed for "Body Parts" above and, in particular, "Can You?" using hoops
2. Story plays

IV. Rhythmic Development
A. Moving to tom-tom
B. Moving to music
C. Moving to classical music
D. Parachute activities
E. Singing rhythms — Hokey-Pokey, Farmer in the Dell, etc.
F. Lummi Sticks
G. Very simple structured rhythmics, i.e., Chimes of Dunkirk
H. Long and short rope jumping

V. Creativity
A. Moving like . . .
1. Weather — like being in it or being it
2. You were made of... (Examples: rubber, a leaf in the wind)
3. Animals
4. Playing a sport
5. You were a type of food (Jell-O, bacon, etc.)
6. You were a machine
7. A particular person (policeman, fireman, teacher)
8. You were (tired, happy, sad, etc.)
9. You were (a piece of dust, a jet plane, a circus animal, etc.)
10. Any kind of mimicry
11. Statues
B. Story plays

VI. Manipulative
A. Manipulating a balloon with every body part
B. Manipulating a sponge ball with every body part
C. Manipulating a playground ball with every body part in every way possible including using different bases of support — the emphasis should be on dribbling the playground ball with the various body parts including the feet
D. Throwing and catching objects alone
1. Sponge balls
2. Beanbags
3. Plastic softballs
E. Target activities alone
1. Throwing at target
2. Kicking stationary playground ball at target
F. Partner activities
1. Throwing and catching safe objects—beanbags, sponge balls, plastic balls
2. Throwing and catching eight and a half-inch playground balls
G. Games and additional activities for developing manipulative activities:
1. Sponge Ball Soccer
2. Dribble Take Away
3. Snowball Fight
4. Can You?
5. Progressive Tag

Figure 8.6, *continued*

VII. Cognitive Domain — In addition to directional terms and body parts listed earlier, the children learn:
   A. Weather permitting, to play outside at least three hours a day
   B. All the safety rules
   C. The rules of at least five recreational games they can play at home
   D. Fitness concepts and terminology
      1. Location of heart
      2. Increase in heart rate due to exercise
      3. Taking pulse
      4. Terms like strength and flexibility
      5. Drinking lots of water on hot days
VIII. Affective Domain — Attitudes which should be developed
   A. A positive self-concept
   B. Self-respect and respect for others
   C. Respect for authority
   D. Sharing
   E. Following safety rules
   F. Practice good health habits
IX. Safety Rules
   A. Stop, look, and listen when the whistle blows
   B. No pushing or grabbing
   C. No sliding on the floor or grass
   D. Stay inside the boundaries
   E. No gum chewing
   F. No non-prescription glasses
   G. Certain activities or situations may require other safety rules which the children must know
X. Methods
   A. Styles of teaching
      1. Problem solving, guided exploration, and free exploration
      2. The emphasis should be on presenting problems which get the children to explore every way their body can move in locomotor and non-locomotor ways as well as how their body can manipulate an object.
      3. A somewhat more directed approach can be used to learn specific information such as body parts and directional terms.
   B. Where equipment may be minimal, a stations approach can be used to keep everyone active while having the opportunity to use the equipment, i.e., if only five playground balls are available, five children can be at a playground ball station while others are active at other stations using different equipment.
XI. Equipment — Unless otherwise noted, there should be one piece of equipment per child.
   A. Hoops
   B. 7" sponge balls
   C. 8 1/2" playground balls
   D. 6" beanbags
   E. Softball size plastic balls
   F. Tennis balls
   G. Tom-tom
   H. Record player and records
   I. Streamers — two per child
   J. Parachute
   K. Lummi Sticks
   L. Balloons
   M. Plastic containers — antifreeze, milk, soda, etc. (rinse thoroughly)
   N. Long (one for every three children) and short jump ropes
   O. Homemade scoops
   P. Nylon/hanger paddles

LESSON PLANNING

The daily lesson plan which is developed from the unit plan is absolutely necessary to a program's success. Although the lesson plan does not guarantee success, its absence assures failure. A good plan will contain all the information necessary to conduct a class including objectives, activities, time schedule, equipment needs, safety, and administrative data. Although the lesson's purpose must be clearly stated, the lesson plan format can vary significantly.

The lesson plan discussion which follows is based upon research on how children learn as well as the authors' years of experience with children. It also reflects a philosophy associated with the importance of self-concept development, and is based upon principles of learning.

Administrative Data

The administrative data including the number of children, their age, date, time, and duration of the class should be at the top of each lesson. Although it may be possible to write a lesson for a grade level, it is unacceptable to write one lesson which is used for several age groups. When reviewing other elementary texts, it is not uncommon to see suggested lessons for K-3 or 4-6. The difference between kindergarten and third grade is as different as night and day. Even first-graders differ significantly from kindergartners. Although some activities can be used at several grade levels, the way they would be presented and the performance expectations necessitate separate lesson plans. Those who suggest identical lessons for K-3 and 4-6 do not know much about children.

Goal Statement

The goal statement is extremely helpful and is used to develop the lesson objective. By stating the goal, the teacher's focus is on the overall purpose of the lesson. In most lessons, the focus should be on only one or two goals—one psychomotor and one cognitive.

Objectives. The objectives are selected based upon the goal and the children's incoming ability, and specify the lesson's outcome. Following the activities, at least 80% of the children should be able to accomplish the stated objective(s). There can be more than one objective, but seldom can more than two objectives be accomplished in a 30-minute class. It is often possible to accomplish one cognitive objective and one psychomotor objective.

Affective objectives, since they are long-term in nature, should not appear on a lesson plan. Obviously, if children do not have a positive attitude when they enter the classroom, attitudes will not be permanently changed in one 30-minute lesson. The teacher, of course, is always concerned about affective development, and must be ready to handle any situation which arises during a lesson. As indicated earlier, this book is based upon the importance of self-concept development which is a key part of the affective domain. Affective domain objectives should only be included in long-term planning.

Activities

The lesson's activities constitute the heart of the lesson, and the suggestion is that lessons have an opening, a middle, and a closing activity. Not every lesson has to have all three parts but, in general, this three-part organization works well for a 30-minute lesson.

For the **open activity**, the teacher should plan something which can be organized quickly and all the children moving within 15 seconds of the children's arrival at the teaching station. Most children are coming from a non-moving classroom environment and are, therefore, ready to move. Opening activities for early childhood could include story plays, creative movement, or rhythmics. Activities such as relays, circle games, games requiring waiting for a turn, or activities or games which require long explanations and organizational time should *not* be opening activities. In a 30-minute lesson the opening activity should last about five to seven minutes.

Many teachers have a "warm-up" often consisting of calisthenic type exercises at the beginning of each class period. Although daily exercises will promote fitness, one must weigh their value against other important physical education objectives. Just how much class time should be spent on fitness? If children only have a physical education specialist once a week, having exercises at the beginning of each class period seems to be an excessive fitness emphasis. This is not to say fitness is not important, only that there are many other objectives which should be met. It can be a waste of valuable time. If the purpose of the exercises is for warmup rather than fitness, the practice is extremely questionable. Seldom do children need to warm-up prior to participating in physical education activities. Children only need to warm up when a maximum effort such as the physical fitness test is scheduled. Warm-up has been shown to improve test performance in such areas as sprinting and other explosive muscular tasks, but children do not need to warm up at the beginning of every physical education class.

The **middle activity** is most directly related to the objective, and would have all the children moving. Although in an ideal lesson, all activities should focus on the objective, it is not always possible. It is during the middle phase that new information can be presented to challenge the children. This is a time for instruction, but since children learn best by doing, any teacher talk should be limited. Individualized instructional methods—stations, learning centers, etc.—should be used to maximize learning and minimize sitting and listening. In a thirty-minute lesson this activity should last fifteen to twenty minutes.

Whenever possible, **problem-solving questions** should be used, particularly in the lesson's middle phase. To be problem solving, the question must have a multiple number of correct movement responses. Typical problem-solving questions include:

How many ways can you throw and catch the beanbag?

How many different body parts can you use to dribble the ball?

How many different ways can you balance on two body parts without doing a headstand?

Can you throw the object with a lower part of your body and catch it with an upper part?

How many ways can you move to this music?

Can you move just one body part to this music? Now two? Three?

By asking questions, the children are more involved in the learning, and it individualizes instruction by allowing each child an opportunity to solve the problem at his or her ability level. (See chapter 5 for a more detailed discussion about teaching approaches.)

A **closing activity** should be offered which is fun, and whenever possible, closely associated with the middle activity. If, for example, the middle activity was ball handling, the closing activity should include ball handling. Although it is not absolutely necessary, activities and games which have all the children moving all the time should be selected. By having a fun activity with full participation, the class will end on a high note. This phase of a 30-minute lesson should last about five to seven minutes.

Flow

A good lesson should flow from one activity to the next with no distinct breaks. Moving from one activity to another with little wasted time can be accomplished with pre-planning. Formal lines, circles, and military formations requiring organizational time can be replaced with free formations in which children scatter over the play area seeking personal space away from others. Since circles and lines may be necessary at times, efficient ways to assume these patterns should be used.

Transition Time

Flow is enhanced when wasted time, also referred to as transition time, is minimized. Inefficiently handing out equipment is probably the biggest time waster. Too many teachers individually hand out equipment believing it is the only way to control children. How frequently we see a class of twenty-five children sitting on the floor as the teacher walks among them handing out equipment! A much more efficient and just as controllable system is to spread the equipment out and have all the children get it at the same time. Transition time is necessary, but since it is not instructional time, the teacher must seek ways to organize the class to minimize it.

Timing

Three timing factors are important to lesson planning. One is beginning and ending on time; another is to allow time for each activity; and the third is to end an activity at the appropriate time. The first two depend primarily on being sensitive to time. Nearly every school runs on a strict schedule and specialists are expected to respect that schedule. The ability to end an activity at the right time usually requires experience. Knowing when an activity has lasted long enough and needs to be ended cannot be taught in a classroom. With experience, teachers can learn to "read" classes and respond accordingly.

Safety

Maximizing learning in a safe environment is the goal. Throughout the planning process, safety is a constant concern. Such factors as space restrictions, equipment selection, glasses, organizational patterns, and teaching styles are just a few factors which must be analyzed. Accidents can be avoided with careful planning. Giving everyone a playground ball in a restricted space may produce accidents, but substituting sponge balls will accomplish the objective safely.

Special Considerations

As a result of Public Law 94-142, there are more children with special needs in the classroom. Sensitivity in meeting all the children's needs is important. These considerations should be kept in mind throughout the planning process but may necessitate some special notes near the end of the lesson.

Figure 8.7 is a presentation of a lesson plan format. Although it is a format, it is not intended to be a form which is cut out or duplicated and used. Forms restrict lessons; some lessons, for example, may have one objective while others two; one lesson may only require one page while others may take up as much as three or four pages. The administrative data at the top of the page may be useful on a form but the rest of the page should be blank.

Figures 8.8, 8.9, and 8.10 are example lesson plans. There are additional example lesson plans included in chapter 11, Age Group Curricula.

Figure 8.7. Lesson Plan Format

Day_____ Date_____ Time_____

Room Number_____ Teacher's Name_____

Age Level_____ Number of Children_____ Class length_____

Location: [   ] Outside   [   ] Multipurpose room   [   ] Classroom

Equipment Needed:

Goals:

Objectives:

Activities: Formation   Time (minutes)

   I.   Opening   I.   5-7

   II.   Middle   II.   15-20

   III. Closing   III.   5-7

Safety:

Special Considerations (handicapped, restricted area, medical problems, etc.):

Figure 8.8. Example Lesson Plan for 5 Year Olds

Day: Thursday   Date: 9/12/02   Time: 10:00

Room Number: 102   Teacher's Name: Ms. Johnson

Age Level: 5   Number of Children: 24   Class length: 20 min.

Location: [   ] Outside   [X] Multipurpose room   [   ] Classroom

Equipment Needed: Whistle, record player, and music

Goals: To develop creativity

Objectives:

During the creative activities, each child will move appropriately to the music; i.e., fast to lively music and slow to slow music.

At least 80% of the class will think up some original activity during the opening phase of the lesson.

Activities:	Formation	Time (minutes)

I. Statues - using whistle
    A. Animals
    B. Sports
	I. Free	5-7

II. Moving creatively to various musical selections
    Ask children:
        How would you move to this music?
        Can you move backward to this music?
        Can you change your level to the change in the music's volume?
        Can you move just one body part to the music? Two? Three?
        How would an elephant move to this music?
        If you were a tree, how would you move to this?
	II. Free	10

III. Growing like a flower
    Ask:
        What does a flower need to grow?
            Water, sun soil
    Have children become a flower seed and bury themselves in the ground. Then, using music as sunshine, have them grow slowly into different kinds of flowers blowing in the wind. They then can be asked to form a bouquet.
	III. Free	3-5

Safety: Remind children they may not bump into one another during free movement activities.

Figure 8.9. Example Lesson Plan for 7 Year Olds

Day: Wednesday   Date: 9/11/02   Time: 9:00

Room Number: 202   Teacher's Name: Ms. Burnett

Age Level: 7   Number of Children: 23   Class length: 30 min.

Location: [X] Outside   [   ] Multipurpose room   [   ] Classroom

Equipment Needed: Tom-tom, 46 beanbags, 23 sponge balls

Goals: To develop manipulative ability and non-dominant side.

Objectives:

Following individual instruction and practice, at least 80% of the class will be able to throw and catch a beanbag at least four times in a row with the non-preferred hand and will be able to catch two beanbags at one time, one in each hand, at least two out of four times.

Activities:	Formation	Time (minutes)

I. Moving freely to the tom-tom
   A. Different directions
   B. Different levels
   C. Different speeds
   D. Different force
	I. Free	5-7

II. Manipulative activities using beanbags
   Ask:
      How many ways can you throw and catch one beanbag?
      Can you get low and still catch?
      Can you change your level to the change in the music's volume?
      Can you use the hand you do not write with to throw and catch the beanbag?
      Can you move about the area and catch?
      Can you catch the beanbag with a partner?
      How many different ways can you throw with your partner?
      Can you throw and catch two beanbags?
      Can you throw and catch a beanbag in each hand at the same time?
	II. Alone
	One beanbag
	per child
		15-18

III. Progressive Tag - using sponge balls	III. Free	5

Safety: Beanbags may not be thrown hard. Must watch where you are going during Progressive Tag.

Figure 8.10. Example Lesson Plan for 11 Year Olds

Day: Thursday   Date: 9/12/02   Time: 1:00

Room Number: 302   Teacher's Name: Ms. Adams

Age Level: 11   Number of Children: 26   Class length: 30 min.

Location: [   ] Outside   [X] Multipurpose room   [   ] Classroom

Equipment Needed: 26 sponge rubber balls, two volleyball nets and 4 standards

Goal: To develop volleyball skills

Objectives:

By using spongeballs, the children will be able to do an underhand volleyball bump to a partner five consecutive times using the techniques discussed in class.

Activities:	Formation	Time (minutes)

I. Problem-solving exercises
    A. What are some exercises for developing flexibility?
    B. What are ones for developing strength?
    As children show different exercises, the teacher picks one child who is doing an appropriate exercise and allows the child to lead the class in exercise. Several different children may be chosen.
	I. Free	7

II. Volleyball skills
    A. Bump ball to self
        How many different ways can you bump the ball into the air?
        How many times in a row can you do it?
        Can you do it using two hands?
        Can you hold your hands together and do it?
        Can you do it like (Susan) is doing it?
    B. Practice bumping the ball to a partner who throws it to a child.
	II. One ball per child	15

III. Bump Volleyball
    Using 6 to 8 spongeballs simultaneously
    Can you use the bumping skill to get ball back over net?
    At random times, the teacher blows the whistle and the team with the least number of balls on their side gets a point.
	III. 2 games	8-10

Safety: During activity II, children must stay in their own space.

SUMMARY

This chapter was a presentation of a systematic approach to curriculum design, which has five parts: goals, objectives, pretest, methods, and evaluation. Each of the five parts was discussed in detail, including the importance of behavioral objectives as well as how to write them. There was a discussion on how to use objectives to pretest the students in order to obtain data to determine the best strategy (method) for accomplishing the objectives. Some strategies discussed included learning centers and the stations approach. The discussion on planning included year, unit, and lesson planning. The year plan is a long-range planning instrument which should include units of instruction and the time to be allotted to each. The unit plan should include goals, objectives, evaluation methods, content, teaching approaches, and equipment. The lesson plan has administrative data, goals, objectives, and the activities to be offered. It was suggested that most thirty-minute lessons have three activities: an opening, a middle, and a closing activity. The criteria for each of these three activities was also given. The reader was also encouraged to include problem-solving questions in each activity whenever possible. Other lesson plan information included flow, timing, and safety. An example lesson plan format, example lesson plans, and an example unit were included in the chapter.

REFERENCES AND SUGGESTED READINGS

AAHPERD. *Children Need Quality Daily Physical Education Because.* Flyer produced by AAHPERD, Reston, Virginia.

Barrett, K. Two Views—The Subject Matter of Children's Physical Education, *JOPERD* 58:42-46, 1987

Gabbard, C., et.al. *Physical Education for Children.* Englewood Cliffs: Prentice-Hall, Inc., 1987.

Graham, G., et.al. *Children Moving* (2nd ed.). Palo Alto: Mayfield Publishing Co., 1987.

Hensley, L., et.al. Is Evaluation Worth the Effort? *JOPERD* 58:59-62, 1987.

Ignico, A. Elementary Physical Education: Color it Androgynous, *JOPERD* 60:23-24, 1989.

Keogh, J., and D. Sugden. *Movement Skill Development.* New York: MacMillan Publishing Co., 1985.

Loughrey, T. Evaluating Program Effectiveness, *JOPERD* 58:63-64, 1987.

McBride, R. You, Too, Can Be a Task Master—Using Task Sheets in the Physical Education Program, *JOPERD* 60:62-66, 1989.

McLaughlin, R. (ed). *Assisting the Beginning Teacher.* Richmond, Virginia Department of Education, 1985.

Pagano, K, and L. Griffin. Making intentional choices in physical education. *JOPERD* 72:38-40, 2001.

Pemberton, C. and P. McSwegin. Goal Setting and Motivation, *JOPERD* 60:39-41, 1989.

Ulrich, D. A. *Test of Gross Motor Development-2.* Austin, Texas: Pro-Ed, 2000.

Selective Web Sites

Association for Supervision and Curriculum Development: http://www.ascd.org/

Chapter

9

Physical Education and the Law

After completing this chapter, the student should be able to:

1. Discuss the two reasons why one should study legal liability.

2. Define and give an example of at least eighty percent of the legal terms presented in the chapter.

3. Describe potential hazards usually associated with a movement-oriented environment.

4. Describe safeguards for each of the potential hazards.

5. Explain each defense for negligence.

6. Explain the difference between contributory negligence and comparative negligence.

7. List the important information which should be included on an accident report form.

8. Define the key terms listed below.

Key Terms

Attractive nuisance
Comparative negligence
Contributory negligence
Control measures

Negligence
Sudden emergency
Supervision

Few people are aware of legal suits involving teachers and legitimately wonder, therefore, why it is necessary to spend time studying legal liability. Although the percentage of suits is not high, the number is continuing to increase daily in this age of litigation. Reasons for these increases in lawsuits are many. In part, they include the following: more attorneys are willing to work on a contingency basis; many states have switched from contributory to comparative negligence—a concept that will be addressed in more detail later in the chapter; and a more knowledgeable public. A lawsuit, even if won by the teacher, can frequently ruin a career, and losing can mean depletion of one's entire life savings.

Knowledge of legal liability, hopefully, will make a teacher more aware of safety factors which, if adhered to, will protect children. The concerned, knowledgeable teacher will create a safer learning environment. Children, too, must be made safety conscious, but the teacher is mainly responsible for safety. Injuries to children are the leading cause of suits in public schools. It should be evident, therefore, that there are two reasons for studying legal liability: (1) to protect the children and (2) to protect the teacher.

People who teach physical education are no more liable than anyone else, but opportunities for injuries which might lead to suits are greater during physical education than during most other activities. Nearly half of the early childhood injuries during school happen in organized games. This frequency is far too high and can be reduced by reasonable and prudent teacher action.

SELECTED LEGAL TERMS

Ignorance of the law is not a valid excuse for failing to act in accordance with the law. The first step toward improving one's legal I.Q. is to become familiar with legal terms. Hopefully, the definitions and examples to follow will provide a foundation for developing a basic understanding of the law.

Corporal punishment is any type of physical punishment inflicted on the body.

Example: A Washington state physical educator punished rule violators by requiring them to run between two lines of their classmates while being hit by their peers (Appenzeller, 1970).

Assault is intentional force directed toward an individual, such as a threat which could potentially be carried out.

Example: An adult teacher threatens to spank a small child if the child does not follow class rules.

Battery is the actual use of unlawful physical force against another individual.

Example: The adult teacher who threatens to spank the small child actually strikes the child.

In Loco Parentis infers that one is acting in place of a parent or legal guardian.

Example: While on a field trip to another school's athletic field, a child strays from the group and is hit by a car while attempting to cross a street. The teacher is negligent for failing to keep the child in the group.

Negligence is a key word which is defined as not acting as a reasonable and prudent person should have acted under the given circumstances.

Example: During a kick-ball game, the ball is accidently kicked onto the school's roof. The teacher directs one of the children to climb onto the roof to retrieve the ball. The child falls and breaks a leg. The teacher failed to act as a reasonable and prudent person should have acted. The ball should have been allowed to remain on the roof to be retrieved later by the school's janitor.

Attractive nuisance implies that on the school's premises exists an apparatus or piece of equipment which may naturally attract the attention of an individual. In addition, participation on the apparatus is potentially dangerous.

Example: The physical education teacher forgot to fold, lock up, and put away the trampoline following a gymnastics lesson. While passing the gymnasium, several children noticed the trampoline (an attractive nuisance) and proceeded to play on the apparatus. One child fell off and injured his back. The teacher would be charged with negligence because a reasonable and prudent person should have foreseen the danger of leaving the trampoline unlocked and unsupervised. In one case, students broke into a school, found a trampoline set up and were subsequently injured on the apparatus. In this case, the court ruled against the teacher who left the equipment up.

Omission implies that one has failed to act as the law requires.

Example: A student is injured on the playground. An individual arrives who has first aid training, but fails to administer. This person is negligent, since it would have been reasonable for this person to utilize his/her ability to administer the first aid.

LAWSUITS: POTENTIAL CAUSES

Accidents are going to occur; however, the safety-minded teacher can avoid many accidents. The purpous of this section is to identify potential causes for lawsuits and offer suggestions on how to correct these situations. Selected court decisions are presented to emphasize the point.

Unsafe Facilities and Equipment

Teachers should establish a routine for inspecting instructional areas prior to class meeting times. Playground equipment, as well as indoor equipment, should also be inspected periodically. To ensure a safe environment one should follow the guidelines presented below:

A. Playgrounds
   1. Inspect playground for holes, broken glass, and other trash.
   2. Inspect wood structures, such as see-saws, for warpage and splinters.
   3. Inspect jungle gyms and other climbing apparatus for missing bolts and sharp edges.
   4. Determine if protective material should be placed under climbing apparatus.
   5. Inspect ladders and slides for missing or loose rungs.
   6. Inspect swings for worn or rusty chains.

B. Indoor Facilities
   1. Inspect floors for loose or raised boards or missing tiles.
   2. Inspect walls for protrusions such as coat hooks or fire boxes.
   3. Determine if protective mats are needed to help guard against injury.
   4. Inspect the floor surface for slippery spots caused by dust buildup or spilled water.

Court decision. A high court awarded damages to a young boy who was injured while playing football in the school's gymnasium (Appenzeller, 1970). The parents of the boy contended that their son's injury was not the result of being shoved by another student, but instead was the result of several of the boards in the gymnasium floor being elevated above the rest. Damages were awarded because the school district was negligent for failing to provide a safe environment.

Note the hard and uneven surface under this high apparatus.

The same piece of equipment with the horizontal ladder lowered. Note the soft, sandy surface below the apparatus.

Lack of Supervision

Supervision is defined here as the ability to see and control children, and the lack of supervision is the most frequent reason for suits. The frequency is based on the ease of proving that a teacher was or was not present at the time of an injury. Even when one is not present, however, the prosecution must prove that the injury would not have occurred had the teacher been present. To ensure proper supervision teachers should avoid:

1. leaving their class to answer a phone call
2. leaving their class unattended while going to the restroom
3. leaving their class to speak with another teacher
4. allowing the class to go outside for recess while they remain inside to grade papers

Court decision. Aileen and a small group of girls always played a hiding game each day at lunch (Appenzeller, 1970). One day a group of boys were playing in their usual play area so the girls moved to another location. The girls used poor judgement in selecting a glass door as a base. While running toward the base, Aileen pushed her arm through the glass, severing a major artery. Frightened, she ran wildly around the playground before another child caught Aileen and took her to the school nurse. Aileen had lost so much blood that she later died. If a teacher had been present, he or she would have either stopped the game or would have been able to calm the child before so much blood was lost.

Inadequate Control Measures

Rules are essentially limitations imposed on games or general classroom procedures to facilitate both fair play and a safe instructional environment. Failure to adhere to the rules of a game can cause rough play and subsequent injury. In fact, in many instances, innocent bystanders have been injured by individuals failing to follow established classroom procedures. When establishing rules one should keep in mind the age of the students for which the rules are being generated. It is not reasonable to expect young children to be able to remember a long list of rules. Instead, simply establish a few general rules but realize that it may be necessary to add unit-specific rules throughout the school year. You may also want to consider testing your students' knowledge of the rules through a written examination. These written test's results should be kept on file since, if you found yourself in a lawsuit, these documents could possibly be used to establish that each child truly knew class rules. The following guidelines are means of keeping law and order in the gymnasium and in the physical education class. (For more detailed information on rules, refer to chapter 6.)

A. General Rules
   1. Post all rules
   2. Deal with all rule violators
   3. Administer a written test covering all rules
B. Rules Involving Games
   1. Provide instruction on the rules of the game

Court decision. A young girl received injuries during a game of line soccer (Appenzeller, 1970). The activity primarily involved kicking skills. Specific rules had been developed forbidding rough play and uncontrolled, severe kicking. During the conduct of the game, the teacher failed to enforce the rules outlined in the syllabus. The court found the teacher negligent for not adhering to the established rules which cautioned the teacher to penalize rule violators.

Inadequate Instruction

Teachers are required to give adequate instruction before a child is asked to perform. This legal obligation has been interpreted by some as requiring a command style of teaching—explanation and demonstration by the teacher. Instruction, however, can come from any media, including the teacher. These media include films, slides, tape recorders, videotapes, books, computers, and television. No matter what medium is used, children must receive adequate instruction. Teaching styles such as problem-solving and exploration should be used with care, particularly when instruction involves participation in potentially dangerous activities such as gymnastics. For example, a question such as "Can you show me some different ways you can throw the ball?" is relatively safe, while a question such as "Can you show me your tumbling skills?" can lead to some real problems.

To guard against inadequate instruction, it is advisable for the teacher to prepare a checklist of activities for each program area to be included in the curriculum. This checklist should be constructed in a hierarchical fashion, listing activities from simple to complex. This procedure will provide a safeguard against forgetting to teach appropriate lead-up activities before complex skills are attempted. For instance, the "back rocker" (lie on back, hug knees and rock back and forth like a rocking chair) should be taught as a lead-up before introducing the tumbling skill, the backward roll. Within recent years, a guided exploratory approach of teaching tumbling and apparatus skills has become widely known as educational gymnastics. As previously mentioned, instructors should be very careful how they word their guided questions. The practice of instructing students with open-ended questions could prove to be dangerous. For instance, one teacher asked her group of students to find five different ways to roll their bodies. One child attempted to perform a front flip off the school's stage.

It is also worth noting that teachers should file their lesson plans. If a lawsuit were to arise, it would be possible to refer to previous lessons to demonstrate that appropriate lead-up activities and appropriate instruction had been accomplished.

Educational Gymnastics

An indirect approach to teaching gymnastics, termed educational gymnastics, has become very popular at the elementary level. Although this problem-solving, exploratory approach seems sound philosophically, it could prove to be indefensible in court. Many teachers have used this approach to gymnastics for years without serious problems, but should a child ever be injured, the teacher may have no defense. Gymnastics is one of the few activities done at the elementary level that could be truly life-threatening and must, therefore, be preceded by adequate instruction. Asking a child to explore on a set of parallel bars or experiment on the rings can have deadly consequences.

Instruction and Breach of Warranty

When a child attends school there is an implied warranty that the individual will receive the education which is reasonably anticipated. Not receiving an appropriate education may be considered a breach of warranty. This is another reason why teachers should retain lesson plans—to show that they have been accountable in regard to instruction toward meeting stated goals and objectives. In other words, the teacher has not taken a "throw out the ball" approach, but instead has attempted to instruct and provide educational opportunities in order to meet stated goals and objectives.

Failure to Warn

Few elementary physical education activities are such that a special warning is necessary to both students and parents. However, a recent trend at the secondary level, particularly related to football injuries, may apply to gymnastics at the elemen-

tary level. In numerous court cases, judgements have gone against those who, in the court's opinion, failed to warn participants about potential serious injuries as a result of certain sports activities. Whether such a special warning is necessary at the elementary level is dependent upon the extent of the gymnastics program. It would seem, however, that whenever gymnastics equipment such as the high bar or parallel bars are used, the warning would be a prudent act by the teacher. Again, the educational gymnastics approach to the use of gymnastics equipment is extremely dangerous, and should be avoided.

Court decision. In the case LaValley vs. Stanford, the court ruled that the teacher was negligent for allowing two boys to take part in a potentially dangerous activity in which the teacher failed to warn the boys of the danger involved and also failed to provide instruction in the art of the activity (Appenzeller, 1970).

DEFENSES

No matter how knowledgeable or careful a teacher is, accidents will occur. To prove an injury was a result of teacher negligence, the prosecution must show that the teacher's actions led directly to the student injury. If it is possible to show that something occurred between the teacher's actions and the injury, negligence cannot be proven (with the exception of comparative negligence—a concept to be discussed later in this chapter). These intervening actions are termed defenses against negligence and include (1) act of God, (2) contributory negligence, (3) assumption of risk, and (4) sudden emergency.

Act of God

Injuries due to uncontrollable forces are termed "acts of God." An example would be a child hit by lightning. A gymnasium roof falling could also be classified under this defense category. None of the above examples, however, is a sure defense since each may have additional circumstances associated with it. Suppose, for example, children were allowed to continue practicing golf while a thunderstorm was approaching and a child was hit by lightning. A reasonable and prudent person would have gotten the clubs out of hand and sought appropriate shelter. Lightning has killed more people in this country than all other storms combined. It is a killer and must be respected.

Contributory Negligence

If it can be shown that the actions of the injured child rather than the teacher's actions caused the injury, the defense is called contributory negligence. For example, suppose the teacher instructs all the children on trampoline usage and forbids flips. The child, in defiance of the teacher, does a flip and is injured. The teacher may not be liable because the child failed to follow established directions. If the teacher had talked only with the injured child about not doing flips and had not given the rule to the rest of the class, then they could not have come forward in the teacher's defense. Within recent years, however, most states have taken the position that minors under seven years of age are incapable of contributory negligence. Furthermore, most states have laws in which standards of ordinary conduct are defined differently for minors (7-18 years of age) and adults (Baley & Matthes, 1984). Be sure to check state statutes as well as local, municipal, city, or county ordinances that may apply to your school district.

Also be aware that some states have now opted to enact what is commonly referred to as **comparative negligence**. Comparative negligence allows a judge or jury to award proportionate damages. For example, the defendant may only be 50% guilty.

Assumption of Risk

Injury is more likely to occur in certain activities than in others. Any collision or contact sport, of course, is inherently more dangerous than a non-contact activity. Many activities which are classified as non-contact, however, do cause their share of injuries. To participate in any collision or contact activity requires a certain assumption of risk, and parental permission is absolutely essential. Since collision sports should not be part of an elementary curriculum, teachers need not be concerned with this aspect of participation. For other activities, though, proper precautions should be taken. Accidents will happen, and as long as negligence cannot be proven, assumption of risk could apply.

Sudden Emergency

In a life or death situation, a teacher can be relieved of normal supervisory duties. However, the situation must be truly life-threatening. Example: A child falls and badly cuts her chin. Direct pressure is immediately applied by the teacher, who then leaves 29 children unsupervised to take the child to the nurse. Horseplay among the children left unsupervised results in serious injury to a child and his parents sue. The judgement goes against the teacher. The teacher should not have left the class; a child, teacher's aid, or another teacher should have gone for the nurse. The bleeding child was in no immediate danger, and the teacher's actions, therefore, could not be covered by "sudden emergency." Had the injured child stopped breathing for some reason, the situation would be different because this medical emergency would be considered life-threatening.

PRECAUTIONS

Listed below are several precautions a teacher should take for self-protection as well as for child protection.

Insurance

Low-cost liability insurance is available to members of the National Education Association (NEA), the American Alliance for Health, Physical Education, Recreation, and Dance (AAHPERD) and some state professional associations. Furthermore, most insurance companies will allow their

Organized games such as Paul Revere Relay have a high possibility of injury, particularly if played on a hard surface.

clients to purchase a rider which can be attached to a homeowner's policy. In brief, a prudent individual should carry supplemental liability insurance. A person without insurance who loses a judgement can be wiped out financially.

Know the Health of Students

Classroom teachers should be able to keep up with their students' health status, but a physical educator with larger teacher/pupil loads has more difficulty. A classroom teacher can be extremely helpful by keeping the physical education teacher informed of the children's health problems. Anyone teaching physical education must know a child's limitations and restrictions.

Administer First Aid Only

The American Red Cross is considered the first aid authority and all teachers who want to act reasonably and prudently should have a valid Red Cross First Aid certification, including CPR. It is important to understand that first aid is the "immediate and temporary help given to an injured individual." Unfortunately, many physical educators and classroom teachers go beyond their first aid responsibility and are frequently guilty of practicing medicine, diagnosing injuries, prescribing treatment and, in some cases, prescribing drugs. This is a hazardous practice and one need only see how much liability insurance costs a doctor to realize it. "It's just a sprain;" "Soak it in hot water;" "Walk it off;" "Take an aspirin tonight for the pain." These frequently heard expressions could lead directly to a suit if a child is seriously injured as a result. Know what to do when an accident occurs, follow proper procedures when treating the victim, and leave the medical practice to those properly trained. Above all, remember that first aid is only the immediate and temporary help given an injured individual.

Keep Accident Records

Records can be a valuable aid in a court case. Such things as time, place, circumstances, witnesses, and actions taken should all be recorded as soon after an accident as possible. Do not rely on someone else to fill out the report, such as the school nurse. Figure 9.1 illustrates a sample accident report form.

Permission Slips and Liability Disclaimers

Teachers who conduct special activities, such as field trips and trips to athletic participation after school, should obtain a permission slip or waiver from a parent. Some teachers believe such slips make them immune to lawsuits. Parents also believe such documents restrict their rights and will not, therefore, sign them. The only value of such slips is the parents' acknowledgement that their child is allowed to participate. In no way does a permission slip relieve the teacher's legal obligations. Parents may not sign away their child's rights. In fact, no person may sign away another individual's rights, except through court action. A permission slip or waiver, therefore, is worth nothing if negligence can be proved. Likewise, disclaimers will not hold up in court if negligence can be proven. In short, disclaimers are simply an attempt to release one from a negligent act which may occur in the future. To allow such behavior would only encourage an atmosphere of carelessness.

Handling Parental and Medical Excuses

Teachers frequently receive a written excuse from a parent requesting that their child not take

---

Figure 9.1: Sample Accident Report Form

Name:_____Date:_____

Place of accident:_____

Time of accident: _____

Nature of injuries sustained:_____

_____

Circumstances surrounding injury:_____

_____

Was first aid administered?_____

If yes, explain actions taken.

_____

Witness:_____

Witness:_____

Instructor:_____

part in physical education because of some specific health problem. By all means, this excuse must be honored even if you question the validity of the excuse. However, if a child misses more than two weeks of class the teacher should request that the parent submit a written doctor's excuse.

Also be aware that on some occasions you may receive a parental excuse requesting that their child not take part in a particular unit of instruction on the grounds of religious beliefs. For example, some religions do not endorse dancing. Like written medical excuses, you must also honor excuses based on religious beliefs.

SUMMARY

In this chapter, you have been exposed to the liability associated with teaching in general and physical education specifically. Various legal terms were discussed with the most important being negligence, which is not acting in a reasonable and prudent manner under the given set of circumstances. Also discussed were the most frequent reasons for being sued with the lack of supervision leading the list, along with using unsafe equipment, having poor control, not providing adequate instruction, and failure to warn children or parents of potential danger. The four main defenses: act of God, contributory negligence, assumption of risk, and sudden emergency were also covered. Finally, a list of precautions every teacher should take to avoid lawsuits was included.

REFERENCES AND SUGGESTED READINGS

Appenzeller, H. *From the Gym to the Jury*. Charlottesville, VA: The Michie Company, 1970.

Lumpkin, A. *Introduction to Physical Education, Exercise Science, and Sport Studies* (5th ed.). Boston: McGraw Hill Publishing Co. 1998.

Pangrazi, R. and V. Dauer. *Dynamic Physical Education* (11th ed.). Boston: Allyn and Bacon, Inc. 1995.

Sawyer, T. (ed.). Battery or Discipline, *JOHPERD* 73:3, March 2002.

Sawyer, T. (ed.). Corporal Punishment, *JOHPERD* 74:5, May/June 2003.

Sawyer, T. (ed.). Inclusion in Sport Activities: Disabilities and the ADA, *JOHPERD* 73:5, June 2002.

Sawyer, T. (ed.). Preventing Injuries, Deaths, and Liability Associated with Heat Illness, *JOHPERD* 74:7, September 2003.

Sawyer, T. (ed.). School Punishment and Physical Education, *JOHPERD* 74:2, February 2003.

Selective Web Sites

Explaination fo Legal Liability and Safety Issues: http://www.kin.sfasu.edu/finkenberg/kin511/liability.html

Legal Liability Guidelines for a School System: http://pe.usf.edu/projects/fctpa/county/pinells/pin-5.html

Legal Liability, Supervision, and Safety: http://cwabacon.presoned.com/bookbind/pubbooks/pangrazi_ab/chapter0/custom9/deluxe-content.html.

National Playground Institute: http://www.activeparks.org//education/safety.cfm

Playground Safety: http://www.uni.edu/playground/

Chapter

10

Fitness and Nutrition

After completing this chapter, the student should be able to:

1. List and describe each of the physiological and motor fitness components discussed in the chapter.
2. Describe ways that each fitness component can be evaluated.
3. Describe ways that each fitness component can be developed.
4. Describe some of the after-effects of maximum effort testing.
5. Describe an efficient means by which postural data can be obtained.
6. Describe the team approach to good postural development.
7. Describe ways good posture can be developed in children.
8. Define the terms in the nutrition section.
9. Measure the triceps skinfold accurately.
10. Describe the components and percentages of nutrients in a child's diet.
11. Indicate the role of exercise in a child's diet.
12. Describe the importance of liquids particularly as they relate to the cooling process.
13. Describe the essentials of an elementary nutrition curriculum.
14. Identify and describe three physical fitness assessment instruments.
15. Define the key terms listed below.

Key Terms

Body composition
Calisthenics
Duration
Flexibility
Frequency
Intensity

Motor fitness
Muscular endurance
Muscular strength
Overload
Physiological Fitness

Fitness and, in particular, children's fitness are growing concerns among physical educators. Over the past thirty years, there has been a significant decline in children's fitness. Of most concern has been the increase in body fat; children are growing bigger and fatter. Included in this declining fitness level is the increased awareness that a significant percentage of very young children already possess at least one cardiovascular risk factor. According to the American College of Sports Medicine, coronary artery disease risk factors include: high blood pressure, obesity, a sedentary life-style, high cholesterol, impaired fasting blood glucose, and cigarette smoking (ACSM, 2000). The long-term health implications of this continued decline in fitness is just beginning to be understood. Furthermore, there is concern for the health costs associated with poor fitness. Although the medical profession is unable to guarantee an increase in the quantity of life, being physically fit undoubtedly improved one's quality of life. As such, most people agree that there is a need to reverse this declining fitness trend among children.

Although a concern among physical educators, seldom does the person who can make the most difference in fitness, the classroom teacher, possess the knowledge or motivation to conduct a fitness program. Since most children seldom see a physical educator more than once a week, if at all, it is not possible to achieve health-related fitness goals during the time spent with the specialist. The responsibility, therefore, rests with the classroom teacher. The role of the physical educator is to provide the knowledge and motivation for a fitness program which can be conducted by the classroom teacher.

The purpose of this chapter is to provide the fitness knowledge as well as motivational ideas to conduct a health-related fitness program for elementary children. It also includes information about motor fitness, which is viewed as a valuable part of growth and development. Health-related fitness includes five components: (1) cardiovascular efficiency, which is how well the heart, lungs, and blood vessels provide oxygen and nutrients to the working muscles; (2) muscular strength, which is the muscle's ability to exert force; (3) muscular endurance, which is how often the muscle can repeat a muscular activity; (4) flexibility, which is the range of motion at a joint; and (5) body composition, which consist of determining the percent of the body mass which is due to fat and the percent of body mass which is due to lean tissue.

It is difficult to define fitness for everyone, but for children, there seems to be general agreement that fitness should focus on the five health-related (physiological) fitness components. Physical educators normally rely on national norms which have been developed by several groups. Although each group has its own norms, they vary so little as to be fairly interchangeable. The two most widely accepted sources of children's fitness are the *Presidents' Council on Physical Fitness and Sports* through its program titled, The President's Challenge *(2002)* and the *FITNESSGRAM,* a health-related physical fitness test developed by the Cooper Institute for Aerobics Research (American Fitness Alliance, 1999). The use of the National Children and Youth Fitness Study I and II are also gaining in popularity. This test battery is explained in more detail later in the chapter.

Fitness contributes to the quality of life, particularly among children. Being physically fit allows children to participate in activities with the peer group, and can help to keep off unwanted pounds. The social implications of being overweight or obese are well-documented, not only among adults but children as well. Although there is a trend toward overweight children being considered the norm, excess weight still is viewed by most as undesirable.

CHILDREN AND EXERCISE

The benefits of exercise have long been known. Improved bone and muscle growth, more efficient use of the body, cardiovascular improvement, a feeling of well-being, better acceptance by the peer group, improved looks, and a generally healthier body are all by-products of a well-planned physical fitness program. Exercise should begin as early in life as possible. Very young children can and should participate in vigorous play activities involving large muscle movement. Such exercise will result in a number of positive gains.

Growth

Growth is facilitated by exercise and retarded by sedentary life-styles. Vigorous exercise by children has caused no ill effects, although trauma such as that associated with contact sports may affect bone growth. Although exercise will not have a marked influence on the genetically-determined body size and somatotype (body proportions), it is necessary to reach the optimum level determined by heredity. As changing life-styles reduce an individual's exercise, the need for planned exercise programs increases. Children no longer must do field work, walk to school, or do vigorous daily chores. Current life-styles include riding everywhere, hours of television, and electronic gadgetry to ease life's "burdens." Lacking these natural exercise requirements, artificial programs such as jogging and calisthenics must become a daily part of one's life if optimum growth and development are to occur.

Strength

Muscles will grow if exercised and weaken if a sedentary life-style is pursued. Although large bulging muscles are not necessary for daily functioning, a minimal strength level is required to earn a living, to perform household chores, to respond in emergencies, and to perform motor tasks. It is well known that active children make strength gains as they grow.

Body Fat

Fat reduction through exercise has been found by a number of researchers. Although exercise is

Physiological	Motor
Cardiovascular efficiency	Speed
Flexibility	Power
Muscular strength	Agility
Muscular endurance	Balance
Body composition	Coordination
	Reaction time

Figure 10.1. Components of Fitness

a primary means of weight loss, it is complemented with proper nutrition. The combination of these two programs, exercise and proper nutrition, is considered the most efficient fat reduction approach.

Bone Growth

Most forms of exercise have a positive effect on bone growth. Vigorous exercise even for young children is beneficial.

Cardiovascular Efficiency

Appropriate endurance exercises at any age can significantly increase cardiovascular efficiency. These gains can be most dramatic at the elementary level when children participate in vigorous fitness programs.

PHYSIOLOGICAL FITNESS

CARDIOVASCULAR EFFICIENCY

Cardiovascular efficiency is the single most important fitness factor for all ages. This physiological fitness component is a specialized form of muscular endurance involving the heart, lungs, and blood vessels. Reasons for developing and maintaining an efficient cardiovascular system are:

1. The ability to resist fatigue is directly related to the system's ability to supply oxygen and nutrients and to remove waste products.
2. Developing cardiovascular endurance tends to lower resting heart rate which allows the heart more rest. While average heart rates range from seventy-two to seventy-eight beats per minute, it is not uncommon for conditioned individuals to possess resting heart rates as low as forty to forty-five beats per minute.
3. Many researchers believe cardiovascular training keeps the body's blood vessels free of fatty buildup which could eventually block the flow of blood to the heart.

Evaluating Cardiovascular Efficiency

Field tests utilized to measure cardiovascular efficiency in children generally take one of two forms. One is a timed run for distance. The object of this test is to determine how far a child can run in a specified amount of time. For elementary children, the time is nine minutes.

The other technique of measuring cardiovascular efficiency is a distance run for time. Here the object is to run a specified distance in the least amount of time. The distance for elementary children is one mile. (Norms of performance for the VCU fitness tests can be found in appendix A.)

Effects of Cardiovascular Testing

There are some possible negative after-effects which can occur following fitness assessments. While a few individuals may exhibit some of these symptoms following flexibility and/or strength assessments, these uncomfortable feelings are more frequently associated with cardiovascular evaluations.

1. *Discomfort:* Any prolonged stress will cause discomfort. If the child is aware of the changes which will take place, there will be less anxiety. Running or other cardiovascular activities seem to cause the most discomfort among children, and it is difficult, therefore, to motivate young children to maximum efforts. At first sign of pain, children (usually six to eight years of age) will tend to cease activity or significantly curtail efforts. Extrinsic motivators as well as stressing the test's importance do help.

2. *Nausea:* Highly-motivated children may experience nausea following maximal running tests. This is not unusual, but can be diminished by having children cool down (continue moving) after the test, and by avoiding testing immediately after eating. Morning testing is better than afternoon.

3. *Muscle Soreness:* Children will often experience short-term muscle soreness after a distance run test. The poorly-conditioned child, however, may have soreness for a day or two following the test. A preconditioning program of three to four weeks will greatly diminish the incidence of this residual soreness.

4. *Headache, Dizziness, and Fainting:* Some poorly-conditioned children who are highly motivated may experience headaches or dizziness, and some may faint, although this is unusual. First aid should be administered.

5. *Injury:* Muscle pulls and strains are not uncommon. Proper warm-up and preconditioning should precede testing.

6. *Loss of Sleep:* Interrupted sleep the night after a test is common and should not be a cause for concern.

The residual pain experienced by some children following maximum effort testing (distance running) can be upsetting to both parents and students. Parents have spent hours as well as money in emergency rooms fearing their child had some serious ailment only to learn that the pain was a result of running the day before. The teacher's understanding of the points just presented could have helped avoid this problem.

Developing Cardiovascular Efficiency

The criteria: frequency, intensity, and time (FIT) for developing cardiovascular efficiency are the same for both children and adults. The acronym, FIT + 50%, can be used to remember these criteria. The FIT is obvious, and the 50% suggests that at least 50% of the body's large muscles must be involved in the developmental activity in order for cardiovascular conditioning to take place.

Frequency is how many times a week one exercises. The recommendation is at least every other day, but many find a three times a week schedule works best for them. It is possible and not harmful to exercise daily as long as there are not two hard workout days in a row. In schools, a program such as Running for Life (appendix A) can be effectively used every other day to achieve cardiovascular conditioning.

Intensity. The aerobic exercise chosen must involve at least 50% of the body's large muscles, and raise the heart rate (intensity) to the "target" level.

Target heart rate is calculated by solving the following mathematical equation: Target HR = Desired HR Intensity [(220 - age) - Resting HR] + Resting HR. This formula is more accurate than the popular "rule of thumb" formula (target HR = 220 - age) since it takes into consideration differences in an individual's resting heart rate.

Compare the differences in target HR when the two formulas are used.

Case: A ten-year-old female who has a resting heart rate of eighty beats per minute desires to work out at a heart rate intensity of 60%.

Calculation of Target Heart Rate Using Rule of Thumb Formula: 220 - 10 = 210 (Predicted maximal HR) x .60 intensity = 126 Target heart rate (beats per minute).

Calculation of Target Heart Rate Which Takes into Consideration Resting Heart Rate:

.60 [(220 - 10) - 80] + 80

.60 [(210) - 80] + 80

.60 [130] + 80

78 + 80 = 158 Target heart rate (beats per minute).

Note the large difference in calculated target heart rate. The authors recommend that you use the longer but more accurate formula.

To increase aerobic capacity, a heart rate between 60-75% of the predicted maximum heart rate (220 - Age) is necessary. Although the 60% intensity heart-rate level is sufficient to improve the cardiovascular system, better results are achieved by moving to a 70 or 75% level as aerobic capacity is gradually improved. These higher percentages make for more efficient use of exercise time. Levels beyond 75% are for those who desire aerobic capacity beyond the health fitness level.

One nice thing about aerobic exercise is the ease with which the work load can be monitored. Since there is a direct relationship between heart rate and the amount of work done, all that is needed is a watch with a second hand or a digital watch. By periodically taking the pulse, the work load can be determined. It is difficult to calculate children's heart rates while participating in a running program, but it is usually safe to assume that the heart rate of a running child is high enough to bring about a conditioning effect.

The purpose of "intensity" is to condition the cardiovascular system by making the heart beat faster for short time periods in order to allow for more rest over the long haul. With conditioning, the heart becomes a more efficient pump and requires fewer beats to get the job done. By conditioning the heart, the resting heart rate (beats per minute) can be reduced ten to twenty or more beats per minute, thus saving thousands of beats per week.

Done properly, several activities meet the intensity criteria. These include running, lap swimming, stationary cycling, aerobic dance, aerobic calisthenics, and if done properly, even walking. The most logical ones for children are running, aerobic dance, and aerobic calisthenics.

Time. The exercise heart rate must be maintained for at least twenty minutes. With a five-minute warm-up to raise the heart rate gradually, twenty minutes at the target level, and a five to ten minute cool-down, the total exercise time should be around thirty to thirty-five minutes. Figure 10.2

Taking the pulse (left) at carotid artery and (right) at brachial artery.

is a presentation of the minimum workout time and intensity necessary to improve cardiovascular efficiency.

High intensity workouts lasting more than about forty minutes do not seem to produce any additional health benefits and often lead to overuse injuries. There is even evidence that those who go well beyond the thirty-minute fitness level may actually be adversely affecting their health.

Selected Cardiovascular Development Activities

There are a number of ways to develop the cardiovascular system. Remember, any activity which will elevate and maintain one's target heart rate for a minimal period of twenty minutes is an accepted activity.

Walking and/or running is one of the cheapest yet most effective means of developing the cardiovascular system. While it is not the purpose of this text to present a detailed description of correct running technique, a few precautions concerning running are warranted:

Running for Life (see the appendix)

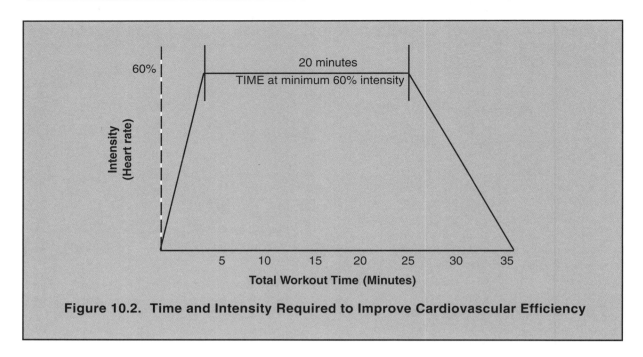

Figure 10.2. Time and Intensity Required to Improve Cardiovascular Efficiency

1. Exercise routines should be conducted on soft surfaces such as grass or a cushioned track. Running on pavement is to be avoided.
2. It is important to purchase a good pair of running shoes. These special shoes are designed to absorb much of the impact that otherwise would be transferred to ankles, knees, and hips.
3. Prior to jogging, take the time to walk the course to inspect for large rocks or potholes which may cause twisted ankles.

Fartlek training (speed play) is an exercise method which was first made popular by the Swedes. Moving at various speeds (walk, run, jog, sprint) on different surfaces (grass, soil, etc.) characterize this training method. This "play on speed" tends to excite most elementary school children. A portion of a Fartlek routine would go something like this:

Jog for 2 minutes

Run for 15 seconds

Jog for 30 seconds

Sprint for 5 seconds

Walk for 30 seconds

Jog for 1 minute

Jog backwards for 20 seconds

Run backwards for 15 seconds

Turn and sprint for 10 seconds

Walk for 30 seconds

Children will enjoy composing their own routines.

Circuit training requires the children to perform individual tasks at stations which are placed throughout the playground. The idea is to complete an assigned exercise at a given station, then quickly move on to another station. Progression can be determined by recording the number of stations completed in a given time period, usually fifteen to thirty minutes. While participating in the circuit, heart rate checks are encouraged to determine the intensity of the workout. A sample playground circuit is presented in figure 10.3.

Aerobic Dance is quickly becoming a popular form of cardiovascular training. Essentially, the activity requires children to perform various motor tasks (running, jumping, hopping, leaping, turning, etc.) to musical accompaniments. Music in 4/4 time (school fight songs, Star Wars, etc.) is an excellent accompaniment. While commercial records are available, children are urged to develop their own routines. A sample routine appears in figure 10.4.

Myths Associated with Cardiovascular Development

Myth: Young children who perform strenuous exercises will develop a dangerous condition known as "Athletic Heart" (an enlarged heart).

Fact: It is true that strenuous exercise will cause the heart to enlarge. The heart muscle, like skeletal muscle, will grow bigger and stronger when

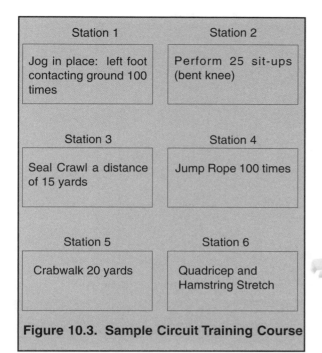

Figure 10.3. Sample Circuit Training Course

Station 1	Station 2
Jog in place: left foot contacting ground 100 times	Perform 25 sit-ups (bent knee)

Station 3	Station 4
Seal Crawl a distance of 15 yards	Jump Rope 100 times

Station 5	Station 6
Crabwalk 20 yards	Quadricep and Hamstring Stretch

#1: 16 beats
   Slide 4 steps to the right
   Jump forward, jump in place, jump back, jump in place
   Slide 4 steps o the left
   Jump forward, jump in place, jump back, jump in place

#2: Scissor jump with right foot forward
   Scissor jump with left foot forward
   Jumping jacks - do 2

#3: 16 beats
   Skip forward - 4 skips
   Jog back - 8 steps

#4: 16 beats
   Hopscotch - 4 times
   Hop on right foot - 4 times
   Hop on left foot - 4 times

#5: 16 beats
   Rocking horse kick - 4 times
   (Rocking horse kick: Rock forward on right foot, rock back on left, rock forward on right foot, kick left foot forward. This is one "rocking horse kick." The next rocking horse kick starts rock forward on left foot, back on right foot, forward on left foot, kick right foot forward.)

Figure 10.4. Sample Aerobic Dance Routine

overloaded. The misconception of exercise and an unhealthy heart is a result of doctors detecting that some individuals with large hearts are not healthy. It was later discovered, however, that this enlargement was caused by a diseased heart muscle. Enlargement of a healthy heart is a desired by-product of cardiovascular training.

Myth: Females should not participate in jogging programs because the pounding of the body can jar and damage the reproductive organs.

Fact: It was once believed that jogging could jar and damage the uterus. Recent evidence indicates, however, that the healthy uterus is suspended in a fluid environment and cannot be damaged by jogging.

Myth: Females should not participate in vigorous physical activity during menstruation.

Fact: No evidence exists which suggest that physical activity is harmful during menstruation. In fact, for some, menstrual cramps have been relieved through exercise.

FLEXIBILITY

Flexibility refers to the range of motion in a joint such as the shoulders and hips. The degree of flexibility you will be able to attain in a given joint is determined by the nature of the joint (bone structure) and the condition of the ligaments and muscles which surround the joint. Although the bony structure cannot be changed, the range can be increased through exercises which stretch the muscle fibers.

While flexibility has not been a major problem in normal children, it is fast becoming one. It is important, therefore, to stress this often-neglected component of physiological fitness. It appears that flexibility is important for the following reasons:

1. Strenuous demands are placed on the body when executing selected motor tasks. Being limber tends, therefore, to be one means of preventing muscle injury.

2. In order to exhibit "correct form" in movement tasks, flexibility is a must. Many believe the lack of flexibility is a major contributor to poor performance. For instance, a lack of shoulder flexibility can hinder one's throwing performance if joint stiffness will not permit an acceptable backswing of the arm.

3. Flexible individuals are able to conserve energy since their limberness allows them to perform muscular movements with minimal resistance to both tissue and joint.

Evaluating Flexibility

Flexibility is joint specific; flexibility in one or two joints is not a good indication of total body flexibility. For example, many individuals who possess a limber upper body may have a stiff lower body.

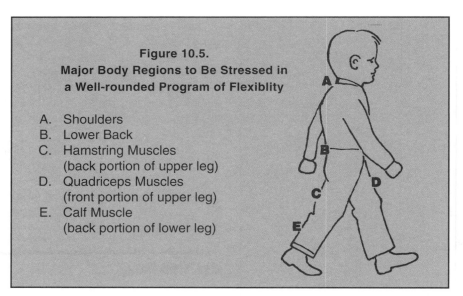

Figure 10.5.
Major Body Regions to Be Stressed in
a Well-rounded Program of Flexiblity

A. Shoulders
B. Lower Back
C. Hamstring Muscles
   (back portion of upper leg)
D. Quadriceps Muscles
   (front portion of upper leg)
E. Calf Muscle
   (back portion of lower leg)

The first step in a flexibility program is to determine which major body regions need work. Figure 10.5 depicts the major regions which should be subjected to flexibility evaluation. Following are simple activities which can be utilized to evaluate the degree of flexibility in each of the major body regions.

Shoulders: Have child lie face down on a mat with chin touching mat and arms reaching forward. While keeping the elbows and wrist straight and chin in contact with the mat, have child attempt to raise palms of hands as high off the mat as possible. Utilizing a yard stick, measure the distance between the mat and palms.

Lower Back: Child should be seated with knees slightly bent. Child attempts to touch nose to knee. If child cannot accomplish this task, a simple yard stick can be utilized to measure the distance between the child's chest and his knee.

Quadriceps: Have child lie on the stomach and bring one heel toward buttocks. The angle formed between the upper and lower leg should be approximately 130 degrees or, roughly speaking, the heel should be about one to two inches from the buttocks.

Hamstrings: Have the child lie on the back. While keeping the knees straight, have the child attempt to raise each leg, one at a time, keeping the other leg straight, and attempt to have the child's heel point straight at the ceiling (i.e., 90 degrees).

136

Calf Muscle: Child should be seated on floor with knees extended and locked. Child attempts to move the foot toward the shins until a 20-degree angle is achieved.

Test batteries such as the VCU Fitness Test also contain flexibility evaluation procedures (see appendix A).

Developing Flexibility

There are basically two types of flexibility development techniques, dynamic and static. While both are usually safe for children who are already fairly flexible, the static technique tends to produce less muscle soreness and is, therefore, recommended. The following are characteristics of these two techniques:

Dynamic. The common and possibly harmful flexibility development method is quick repetitions of the exercise, such as bouncing down to touch the toes. Those with poor flexibility, and particularly adults, may find the dynamic approach harmful to muscles. Rapid muscle stretching, which is common in dynamic flexibility exercises, can cause the activation of stretch receptors in the muscle. These receptors can trigger a reflex muscular contraction which, under the stretching condition, may cause injury.

Static. Unlike the forced bouncing movements of the dynamic method, the static method requires gradual easing into the stretch until a burning sensation (not pain) is felt in the exercised muscle. This position should be held from 30-60 seconds. During this period the burning sensation will ease thus allowing further stretching. Maximum benefit is achieved if the muscle being stretched is warmed up prior to being stretched. Therefore, you should engage in light physical work before beginning your stretching routine.

While standing with arms extended from the side, rotate arms in large circles, decreasing to smaller ones for thirty seconds. Repeat ten times.

Flexibility Exercises

The key to becoming flexible is persistence and patience. By faithfully performing the following exercises, flexibility will increase within four to six weeks. When time permits, best results are obtained when these exercises are performed twice daily.

Shoulder Stretch

While standing, rotate shoulders backwards attempting to touch both shoulder blades (scapulae) together. Repeat ten times.

While standing, bring arm across upper chest as far as possible with elbow locked. Use the other arm to assist in the stretch. Work both arms, one at a time. Repeat ten times for each arm.

While standing, bend elbows and attempt to reach as high as possible behind the back. Alternate arms and repeat ten times.

Quadriceps Stretch

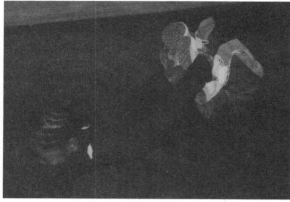

Lie on stomach and bend knees. Reach back and grasp ankles and pull toward buttocks. Repeat ten times.

Lower Back Stretch

While lying on back, raise right knee to chest, pull and hold. Opposite leg is kept straight. Alternate legs and repeat five times.

While seated on floor with knees bent, grab right ankle with left hand and slowly pull right leg up towards head. Repeat five times with each leg.

Hamstring Stretch

While lying on back with knees bent, press lower back downward, tilting pelvis. The object is to flatten the lower back area against the floor. Repeat twenty times holding each trial for six seconds.

While standing, bend at knees and grab toes. Slowly extend knees until a locked position is achieved. Repeat ten times.

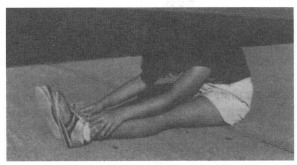

While sitting with legs extended and locked and toes pointing up, attempt to put nose first to right knee, then to left knee. Each stretch should be done slowly with locked knee position maintained at all times. Repeat five times.

The popular hurdler's stretch is to be avoided. It places too much stress on the inside portion of the knee joint. Instead, an alternative hamstring stretch is illustrated above.

Calf Stretch

Stand approximately one and a half feet from a wall. Lean forward, attempting to touch chest to wall while keeping the knees and back straight, and heels flat on floor. As flexibility is gained you gradually start by standing farther from the wall. Repeat fifteen times.

Attempt to walk on the heels while trying to point toes toward ceiling. Remember, keep the knees locked and straight while attempting the heel walk. Walk fifteen yards.

MUSCULAR STRENGTH

The amount of force which can be exerted by a muscle or muscle group for a brief period of time is referred to as muscular strength. Selected reasons outlining the importance of developing and maintaining muscular strength are presented below:

1. Physical educators agree that a minimal level of muscular strength and endurance is needed to perform all motor skills.
2. A strong muscle is able to absorb shock and is, therefore, capable of resisting injury.
3. Deficiencies in back and abdominal strength are a leading cause of poor posture and lower back pain.
4. Individuals possessing high degrees of strength are capable of performing motor tasks with greater ease and efficiency than weaker individuals.

MUSCULAR ENDURANCE

The ability to hold or perform repeated trials of a muscular contraction, which is an indication of the muscle's ability to perform work for an extended period of time, is referred to as muscular endurance.

Reasons for developing and maintaining muscular endurance follow:

1. Most sports activities require many repetitions of the same movements. For instance, in a tennis match one may hit as many as several hundred forehand ground strokes. Muscular endurance is needed to accomplish this feat.
2. A muscle which is easily fatigued is more likely to sustain injury.

Evaluating Muscular Strength and Endurance

The shoulder girdle and abdominals (stomach) are the body regions most often subjected to muscular strength and endurance evaluation during the elementary school years. Refer to the appendix for strength norms established by the VCU Fitness Test. Other evaluative techniques follow.

Evaluating Abdominal Strength and Endurance

The most frequently utilized activity to measure abdominal strength and endurance is the bent-knee sit-up. The child being tested lies on his/her back with knees bent so heels are eight to ten inches from the buttocks. With arms folded across the chest, child attempts to sit up so arms contact the upper thigh. Criterion norms of performance vary according to the source of validation.

Evaluating Shoulder Girdle Strength and Endurance

The likelihood of detecting deficiencies in shoulder girdle strength and endurance is great, for research suggests that American children are among the weakest in the world in this area of physical fitness. For girls over nine years of age, the flexed arm hang has been commonly employed to measure upper body strength and endurance. Only recently have norms been established for both boys and girls between six and nine years of age. Procedures for administering this test and accompanying norms can be found in appendix A.

Techniques for Developing Muscular Strength and Endurance

There are basically two types of exercise techniques which can be utilized to promote increases in muscular strength and endurance. The first, isotonic, requires the performer to place resistance against a moving muscle. The most frequently employed isotonic activities are lifting weights and calisthenics. While weight training is an effective method for improving muscular strength and endurance, the major disadvantages lie in the cost of equipment and of danger, both in terms of muscle injury as well as having weights fall on children. High resistance exercises (very heavy weights) are not recommended for the developing child. Calisthenics, however, are highly recommended and will be discussed later.

The other strength training technique is isometrics. Isometric means the length of the exercised muscle will remain the same throughout the contracting phase (*iso*, the same; *metric* length). To perform an isometric contraction, the child attempts to push, pull, or lift an immovable object, exerting as much muscular tension as possible and holding it for a period of five to eight seconds. To avoid muscle injury, tension should be gradually increased up to three to four seconds before attempting a maximum effect. *A word of caution: Breath holding is to be avoided.* The advantage of the isometric method is that it does not require a lot of space and equipment. Children can, for instance, perform these exercises while sitting at their desks. The major drawback associated with isometrics is that since the exercising muscle does not change in length, isometrics will only strengthen the muscle at one point. To insure strength improvement through a whole range of motion, each exercise should be performed at five to eight different angles.

Principles of Muscular Strength and Endurance Development

1. *Overload Principle:* Placing the muscle or muscle group under a work load greater than what it is normally accustomed to will increase muscular strength.
2. *Principle of Progressive Resistance:* Gradually increase the resistance applied to the exercised muscle. Too much too soon can cause injuries.
3. *Principle of Specificity:* Exercise tends to be task specific. For instance, if one trains for maximum muscular strength, significant gains in muscular endurance will not be accomplished. Muscular endurance is best acquired by performing many repetitions with a reduced amount of resistance, while the reverse holds true if the development of muscular strength is the goal.

Following these principles of strength development will increase muscular strength and endurance as well as muscle size (hypertrophy). Once training stops there will be a decrease in muscular strength accompanied by a decrease in muscle size (atrophy).

Selected Muscular Strength and Endurance Activities

The calisthenics and playground activities presented below utilize the isotonic technique for developing muscular strength and endurance. Selected isometric activities are also described.

Calisthenics are essentially isotonic exercises which are a way to develop strength and muscular endurance. Almost any calisthenics can be modified to increase or decrease the degree of difficulty. As a general rule, once a child can repeat a given exercise twenty times without a rest, he or she should move on to a more difficult exercise for the muscle group in question. Before moving on however, the child should be able to do the twenty repetitions correctly. Exercises performed incorrectly are of questionable value. The same calisthenics, when repeated many times, are valuable for developing muscular endurance. Anytime a muscular activity is repeated while in an overload situation, strength will be enhanced. Low resistance exercises repeated many times will have an effect on muscular endurance.

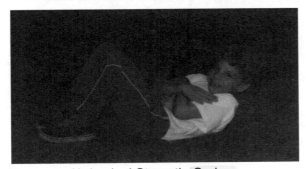

Purpose: Abdominal Strength: Curl-up
Equipment: None or use a mat
Task: Lie on back with arms resting across chest and knees bent so heels are about six to ten inches from buttocks. Perform a pelvic

tilt and while holding the pelvic tilt, attempt to raise the shoulder blades approximately three to four inches off the floor. To perform the pelvic tilt, simply rotate the pelvic structure upward to flatten the lower back against the floor.

Purpose: Arm and Shoulder Strength
Equipment: None
Task: Assume a push-up position. Slowly bend arms and attempt to touch chest to ground. Maintaining a straight back, return to starting position.

Variations:
  a. To make the task easier, the push-ups can be done from the hands and knees instead of hands and feet.
  b. To make the task more difficult, place hands about three inches apart.

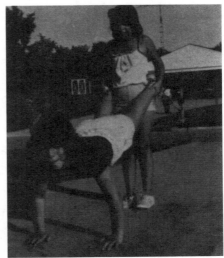

Purpose: Arm and Shoulder Strength
Equipment: None
Task: Assume a push-up position. Allow partner to grasp ankles and hold at partner's hip level. Now walk forward on hands, being careful not to over arch the back.

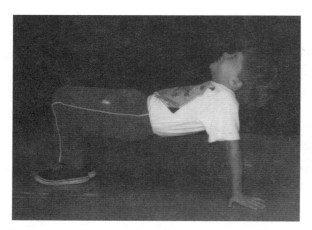

Purpose: Arm and Shoulder Strength
Equipment: None
Task: While sitting, pick buttocks off ground so that weight is supported on feet and hands. Maintaining this position walk forward (Crab Walk).
Variations:
  a. Walk backwards
  b. Walk sideways

Purpose: Arm and Shoulder Strength
Equipment: None
Task: Assume a push-up position. Walk forward on hands while grabbing feet (seal crawl).
Variations:
  a. To make the task more difficult, gradually spread the arms farther apart.

Purpose: Arm and Shoulder Strength
Equipment: Horizontal Bar
Task: Grasp bar with palms facing outward. With the aid of a partner, place chin above the bar. Without support, maintain this position as long as possible.
Variations:
  a. For weaker children who cannot maintain the chin above the bar position at least 10 seconds, allow partner to provide some support.

Playground Activities

Purpose: Arm and Shoulder Strength
Equipment: Horizontal Ladder
Task: Grasp bar with palms facing outward. Child attempts to reach other end of the ladder by alternately grasping each rung.
Variations:
  a. Grasp every other rung.
  b. For young child, a simple bar hang (no traveling) can be utilized.

Purpose: Arm and Shoulder Strength
Equipment: Horizontal Ladder
Task: Grasp bar with palms facing outward. Attempt to pull up until chin touches bar. Slowly return to starting position, and repeat.
Variations:
  a. Grasp bar with palms facing backwards.

Purpose: Arm, Shoulder, and Leg Strength
Equipment: Vertical Pole
Task: Attempt to climb pole utilizing a hand-over-hand motion. The legs are wrapped around pole to assist in the climb.

Isometrics

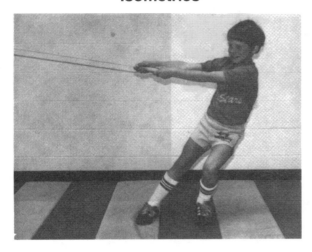

Purpose: Shoulder, Arm, and Leg Strength
Equipment: Jump Rope
Task: Tie rope around securely anchored pole. Attempt to pull the pole to the ground.

Purpose: Shoulder and Chest Strength
Equipment: None
Task: Place palms of hands together at chest level and push against one another.

Purpose: Shoulder, Arm, Wrist Strength
Equipment: Jump Rope
Task: Grasp both ends of the jump rope. While standing on the middle of the rope, attempt to pull yourself off the ground.

Purpose: Shoulder and Chest Strength
Equipment: Playground Ball
Task: Place palms of hands on each side of ball. Attempt to squash ball while holding ball at chest level.

Purpose: Leg Strength (Hamstrings)
Equipment: None
Task:	Lie on stomach with legs straight. Attempt to touch heels to buttocks while a partner supplies a downward resistance to the heels.

Purpose: Shoulder and Leg Strength
Equipment: Wall
Task: Place palms of hands against a wall. Attempt to push the wall down.

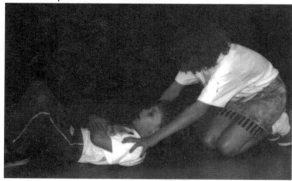

Purpose: Leg Strength (Quadriceps)
Equipment: Chairs or Table
Task: Assume a sitting position. Attempt to straighten one leg at a time while a partner applies downward resistance.

Purpose: Abdominal Strength
Equipment: None
Task: Lie on back with legs bent and arms folded across chest. While partner holds shoulders against floor, attempt to sit up.

Purpose: Leg Strength
Equipment: Playground Ball
Task: While standing, squeeze ball between knees.

Purpose: Back Strength
Equipment: None
Task: From a standing position, bend at the waist and attempt to touch toes. Attempt to once again stand erect while a partner applies downward resistance to your shoulders.

Myths Associated with Strength Development

Myth: Strength development in females is accompanied by bulging muscles.

Fact: Due to differences in sex hormones and other physiological factors between males and females, the likelihood of the average female developing bulging muscles is remote.

Myth: When one stops training for strength, the added muscle tissue accumulated during training will turn to fat.

Fact: It is important to realize that muscle and fat are two different types of tissue. As such, there is no possible way for these tissues to reverse roles.

BODY COMPOSITION: PERCENT OF BODY FAT

A major health problem facing today's society is the overweight and obese individual. A high percentage of weight problems can be found in children. Obese children tend to have a very high percent of body fat compared to their lean muscle mass. The importance of maintaining an acceptable fat-to-lean muscle mass ratio is outlined below.

1.   Overweight children tend to be excluded from many social groups. This is often due to their inability to perform motor skills as efficiently as their peers.
2.   When participating in physical activities, overweight children tend to be more prone to injury than children in the normal weight ranges.
3.   Excess adipose tissue (fat) is a leading cause of cardiovascular disease and other illnesses. For each pound of fat, one additional mile of blood vessels is required to supply nourishment, creating a heavier circulatory burden.

Changing the Body's Fat Content

Successful fat reduction is dependent primarily on exercise and proper nutrition. Calories are the energy source obtained through the diet which are used for body functions, including exercise. The balance between caloric intake and utilization determines body fat. Any calorie not burned is stored as fat. By combining exercise with sound nutritional habits, maintaining good body composition will become a life-style habit.

MOTOR FITNESS COMPONENTS

Power, agility, balance, coordination, reaction time, and speed are all motor fitness components. Since they play a major role in physical growth

Figure 10.6. Caloric Content of Fast Foods			
Restaurant	Food Item	Calories	Fat (grams)
Arby's	Junior Roast Beef	240	
	Super Roast Beef	750	
Burger King	Whopper	630	
	French Fries	220	
McDonald's*:	Hamburger	260	9.5
	Cheeseburger	310	13.8
	Quarter Pounder/cheese	520	29.3
	Big Mac	560	32.4
	Filet-O-Fish	440	26.1
	McLean Deluxe**	320	10.0
	McChicken	490	28.6
	Chicken McNuggets	270	15.4
	Large French Fries	400	21.6
	Apple Pie	260	14.8

*McDonald's Corporation (1990). Food analysis was performed by Hazleton Laboratories America, Inc., which is an independent international testing laboratory. Consumer brochure #9.

**McDonald's Corporation (1991). Consumer brochure McD 90-260.

The skinfold caliper may be used to determine percent of body fat.

and development, a physical education program should include extensive work on these fitness components. In addition, a minimal degree of competency in these fitness components has been found to foster both social and emotional development. This is because children are more readily accepted in the peer group if they can perform well physically. Unlike academic shortcomings, physical performance cannot be hidden. Clumsy children, therefore, are easily identified by peers and frequently ostracized. The implication of such exclusion should be obvious. A major physical education goal should be the identification of and help for clumsy individuals. This is not to say that every child should be a super athlete—only an efficiently functioning human being who can achieve success through movement.

The specificity of motor development precludes a lengthy discussion of motor fitness development. This is to say, for example, that speed in basketball will have little carry-over to speed in badminton or that an individual who possesses speed of hand may not possess speed of foot. Training programs, therefore, must be specifically designed for each motor fitness component. In an early childhood physical education program, a wide variety of motor development activities should be provided as a foundation for more specific training later. An early childhood motor development program should provide extensive eye-hand coordination, speed, power, reaction time, agility, and balance training.

Coordination

The ability to combine two or more body parts to produce a skilled movement is termed coordination. Coordination is developed primarily through use of objects such as balls, beanbags, scoops, etc. Children should be able to explore throwing, catching, kicking, and striking a wide variety of objects.

Speed

The ability to get from one place to another quickly, such as in sprint racing, is classified as speed. Although an individual's ultimate speed is determined by heredity, training can be used to realize potential. For the elementary child, running, and particularly short races requiring sprinting, will insure at least minimal speed development. The development of stronger legs and more flexible hips can also improve speed indirectly by increasing one's stride length.

Power

Power is a combination of speed and strength. An example would be the broad jump.

Reaction Time

The time required to react to a stimulus and make an appropriate muscular response is known as reaction time. The teacher should provide such stimuli in a situation requiring quick student response. Yarn balls can be thrown at any speed and at any body part without fear of injury. This is just one example of how students can respond quickly.

Agility

Agility is the ability to change total body direction quickly while maintaining balance. Obstacle courses and verbal commands can be used to develop agility. The obstacle course should be designed to require frequent changes in direction. Verbal commands can be used to get children moving quickly in different directions. When doing agility-type activities, a safe surface must be used. Blacktop should never be used for agility training. Indoor areas should be cleared of all dangerous objects, and children should be kept away from walls. The best agility training area is a large grassy area.

Balance

There are two types of balance: static and dynamic. Static balance would be required to do a handstand; walking a balance beam would be a dynamic balance activity. The balance development program should allow children to practice on many different types of apparatus, with eyes opened and closed.

MOTIVATING CHILDREN TO EXERCISE

To this point, information has been presented on methods of evaluating and developing each fitness component. Understanding training methods is only the first step in developing fitness. If children refuse to participate, fitness will not be improved. One of the primary roles of the teacher, therefore, is to keep the children motivated so they will not become exercise dropouts. Common deterrents to exercise tend to be discomfort during exercise performance and muscle soreness following exercise routines. Techniques to help alleviate these deterrents were presented earlier.

Another major factor accounting for exercise drop-outs is boredom. Children get tired of performing the same old calisthenics and exercises day after day. Just a little teacher creativity can change one's attitude toward exercise participation. The following motivational techniques have been successful:

1. **Music** played during the physical education period tends to take the children's mind off the discomfort which is sometimes associated with selected tasks. This probably, in part, accounts for the recent popularity in aerobic dance.
2. **Change exercise environment;** try to avoid conducting the class in the same location every day.
3. **A fitness report card** should be sent home after each testing period. This will allow both child and parents to keep abreast of fitness changes and will hopefully create intrinsic motivation.
4. **Fitness clubs** tend to challenge children to see who can accumulate the most miles ran in a given time period. Many schools even award T-shirts to individuals denoting their accomplishments such as "25-mile club," "50-mile club," etc.
5. **"Running for Life"** is a special fitness program which has proven successful as a motivator for exercise participation. Refer to appendix A for complete details about this program.

COMMONLY USED TEST BATTERIES

Since the 1950s fitness assessment has been incorporated within the public school physical education curriculum. Initially, motor fitness received the major emphasis. The first motor fitness assessment instrument developed by the American Association for Health, Physical Education, and Recreation (AAHPER) emphasized the measurement of agility, power, speed, strength, and cardiovascular endurance. However, now the emphasis in fitness has shifted toward what is termed, "health-related physical fitness." The main components of health-related fitness include: cardiovascular endurance, muscular strength, muscular endurance, body composition, and flexibility As addressed earlier in the chapter, the two most commonly used tests of health-related physical fitness are the test battery developed by the President's Council on Physical Fitness and Sports referred to as The President's Challenge, and the

second, and most widely used test battery of health-related physical fitness, is the FITNESSGRAM. Each of these two test batteries are described below.

The President's Challenge

The President's Challenge Youth Physical Fitness Program is sponsored by the President's Council on Physical Fitness and Sports (PCPFS). The program, designed for children 6-17 years old, allows participants to receive awards based on level of fitness. For instance, scoring above the 85th percentile on all five assessment items will lead to the Presidential Physical Fitness Award. Scoring above the 50th percentile will result in the National Physical Fitness Award. Awards are even granted to children who fall below the 50th percentile but who attempt all five assessment tests. The Presidential, National, and Participant awards are based mainly on normative data collected in 1985 for the PCPFS National School Population Fitness Survey. In 1998, they released a supplemental set of normative data. These data were used by the PCPFS with permission from the Amateur Athletic Union Physical Fitness Program and the Canada Fitness Award Program, Health Canada, Government of Canada. Items on the test include the following:

One-mile run/walk
    Optional 1/4 mile for 6-7 year olds
    Optional 1/2 mile for 8-9 year olds
Curl-ups
Shuttle run
Pull-ups
    Optional right angle push-up
    Optional flex-arm hang
V-sit reach
    Optional sit and reach

Regardless of the awards program selected, the PCPFS recommends the implementation of the assessment battery in conjunction with a physical fitness educational program. In other words, instructors should avoid administering a physical fitness test battery at the beginning and end of a school year. Instead, the assessment of physical fitness should be but one unit of instruction geared to the value of engaging in a long-term active lifestyle. To obtain a free copy of these guidelines, contact the President's Challenge, 501 N. Morton, Suite 104, Bloomington, IN 47404; (800) 258-8146; www.presidentschallange.org.

The FITNESSGRAM

Developed by the Cooper Institute for Aerobics Research, the FITNESSGRAM has rapidly become the most widely used instrument for the assessment of health-related physical fitness for youth and young adults (5-25 years of age). In fact, it is currently used at more than 6,000 schools around the country, and an estimated 10 million students will participate in the program [American Alliance of Health, Physical Education, Recreation, and Dance (AAHPERD), 1994]. Most recently, the state of California now requires its students in grades five, seven, and nine to participate in the FITNESSGRAM testing (American Fitness Alliance, 1999). This criterion-referenced instrument assesses aerobic capacity, body composition, muscular strength and endurance and flexibility. The FITNESSGRAM kit comes with a FITNESSGRAM Test Administration Manual (Cooper Institute for Aerobics Research, 1999), FITNESSGRAM 6.0 software (Cooper Institute for Aerobics Research, 2000), an online software version (Cooper Institute for Aerobics Research, 2003), and various auxiliary supplies, including plastic skinfold calipers. The FITNESSGRAM kit can be purchased from the American Fitness Alliance, a division of Human Kinetics publishers (800-747-4457 ext. 2407).

NCYFS - I

Another popular fitness assessment instrument gaining in acceptance is the outgrowth of a research study titled, "The National Children and Youth Fitness Study" (NCYFS). Specific fitness components measured include: (1) a one-mile run, (2) a timed, sixty-second, bent-knee sit-up test, (3) chin-ups, (4) a sit-and-reach test of flexibility, and (5) a test of body composition. Norms for these five test items were first established for children from ten through eighteen years of age. This entire test, including the norms are reported in the January 1985 edition of the *Journal of Physical Education, Recreation and Dance* (Ross, Dotson, Gilber, and Katz, 1985).

NCYFS - II

As an outgrowth of the first NCYFS, the Public Health Service, Office of Disease Prevention and Health Promotion, U.S. Department of Health and Human Services, commissioned in 1985 a second fitness study (NCYFS II). One purpose of this second study was to establish the first health-related fitness test norms for children ranging from six through nine years of age. A description of the second study complete with normative data was first reported to the public in the November/December 1987 edition of the *Journal of Physical Education, Recreation and Dance* (Ross, Pate, Delpy, Gold and Svilar, 1987). The test battery for the NCYFS II consisted of (1) a skinfold measure to predict percent body fat, (2) a sit-and-reach test to measure low back and hamstring flexibility, (3) a sixty-second, bent-knee sit-up test, and (4) a modified pull-up test.

One important aspect of the NCYFS II was the inclusion of a modified pull-up test. It was noted that in the first NCYFS as many as 30% of the ten to eleven year old boys and 60% of the girls between ten and eighteen years of age could not even do one pull-up. It is important to understand that the inability to do a pull-up does not imply the absence of upper body strength. Instead, it indicates that there is a major problem with the assessment instrument. As a result of this finding, researchers set out to develop a new pull-up type test which would allow all test participants to obtain a score.

The modified pull-up test used in the NCYFS II is administered using a specially constructed pull-up apparatus. The apparatus can be constructed for as little as fifteen dollars (Pate, Ross, Baumgartner, and Sparks, 1987). To perform the modified pull-up test the student lies on his or her back and then reaches upward to grab the pull-up bar so that the palms face outward. From this position, the child is instructed to make the body

Figure 10.7. The modified pull-up test

148

An example of good posture....

....and an example of poor posture.

straight so that only the heels come in contact with the ground. The child is then instructed to pull up until his or her neck comes in contact with an elastic band positioned seven to eight inches below the pull-up bar. Each time the neck comes in contact with the elastic band, a successful pull-up is counted as long as the hips and knees are extended throughout the attempt.

POSTURE

Posture refers to the alignment of the body segments. Posture is closely related to physiological fitness since strength and health are common to both. Two aspects of strength are important to posture. One is the imbalance between muscles causing unnatural spinal column curves while the other is a lack of strength necessary to maintain good posture. Fortunately, such muscular deviations, if discovered in time, can usually be corrected through exercise.

If these *functional* (correctable) problems are ignored or not identified, they can lead to *structural* abnormalities and physiological problems which adversely affect health. Structural problems can only be corrected through use of braces or surgery. Problems left unattended can sometimes cause severe crippling. Early diagnosis and treatment can usually prevent these problems.

Physiological problems are another possible outcome of possible deviations. Skeletal changes can cause pain as well as an unusual way of moving. Such movement changes can cause unequal

body part stress in a "domino theory" breakdown. Since the human animal's bony structure was never designed for upright movement (on two feet), even slight changes can create abnormal force on body parts. Internal organic problems have also been associated with postural deviations which cause nerve involvement.

Lower back pain, a leading reason given for visits to doctors, is often related to posture. Imbalance between the back muscles and abdominal muscles causes an increase in the anterior/posterior lower back curvature (lumbar region) known as lordosis. This accentuation causes lower back pain and in severe cases may have nerve involvement as a result of disc herniation (commonly incorrectly called a slipped disc).

There is no doubt about the importance of early identification and treatment of postural deviations. Such screening, if done systematically, can be efficient. Left undone, the consequences are far-reaching.

Screening

The teacher has a unique opportunity to evaluate which is usually not available to parents. By comparing numerous children, those with postural deviations are more likely to stand out. A properly prepared teacher should also have more postural knowledge than parents. Ideally, each preschool child should have been under a pediatrician's care as part of a comprehensive health program. Such care would include anthropometric examination and treatment of defects. In reality, only a small percentage of children (probably those who need it least) have good health care prior to entering school. The responsibility, therefore, falls on a qualified teacher to identify those needing further examination.

Systematic Observation

A screening device such as a checklist can be used to obtain information on children. This checklist can be used while children are in a guided movement activity. It is guided to allow for recording of information on each child. The arrangement can take the form of a circle or an obstacle course in which the children play follow the leader doing activities directed by the teacher. These activities should include walking, running, skipping, and other movement activities during which posture can be observed. No matter which arrangement is used, however, the teacher must be sure that each child is systematically observed. Movement activities are more valuable than static observation since children will be more natural, will have more fun, and will be developing movement competencies rather than standing in a line waiting to be tested. To insure naturalness, children should not be told the purpose of the activity. For those working with many children, a numbering arrangement can be used for more accurate identification of children.

Figure 10.8. Postural Checklist

Group Observation: This form is designed for use while systematically observing children during dynamic movement activities. Systematic observation can be accomplished by having children move in a circle while using the checklist as a guide. Any abnormal deviation should be recorded below the child's name.

NAME												
BODY PART												
Head												
Forward												
Shoulders												
Forward												
Uneven												
Rounded												
Back (back view)												
"S" curve (scoliosis)												
"C" curve (scoliosis)												
Back (side view)												
Lordosis												
Flat back												
Rounded												
Hips												
Uneven												
Legs												
Bowed												
Knock-kneed												
Feet												
Pigeon-toed												
Duck feet												
Weight on inside												
Weight on outside												

Observational Checklist

The checklist should be logically arranged to insure systematic observation. A sample checklist is shown in figure 10.8. As can be seen, the focus goes from head to feet. For ease of scoring, a child's number or name is recorded in the appropriate box.

Individual Testing

Certain deviations such as spinal cord lateral deviations (scoliosis) are most effectively identified during individual testing. There are basically two types of scoliosis, the S curve and C curve. The child, stripped from the waist up, is observed from the back while standing and also when bent ninety degrees at the waist. When viewing the child from the rear, one should look for uneven hips or shoulders as well as obvious spinal curvatures. When the child bends over, check for bumps or raised areas of the back which appear on only one side.

Team Approach

Diagnosis and correction should be a team approach. Diagnostic screening can be done by the classroom teacher or physical educator in conjunction with the school nurse. All suspected cases should be directed to a physician who can prescribe remedial work. Corrective exercises should be prescribed only by a medically qualified individual. By using a form such as that shown in figure 10.9, communication will be facilitated.

Exercises

Only those exercises designed for normal postural development should be given unless a physician has prescribed corrective exercises. Teachers are not qualified to make final postural diagnosis nor do most have the training to determine corrective measures. Exercises such as sit-ups, leg raises, back exercises, and general strength development exercises, however, should be given to all children to aid in normal development.

Strength

Overall posture is enhanced by a balanced strength development program. No one part of the body or body side should be neglected. Particular care must be given not to over strengthen one body part thus causing unnatural skeletal curves. Children will favor the dominant side of the body in movement activities. They must be encouraged to use both sides for even development.

Flexibility

Although most people do not think of children having flexibility problems, many do, particularly some special education children. This poor movement range can cause postural problems. Flexibility exercises for all children are important.

Figure 10.9. Medical Feedback Sheet for Children with Postural Problems

Name of Student:_____ Doctor's Name: _____ Date:_____

The above-named child has been diagnosed as having a postural deviation which:

_____ Restricts his activities as noted.

_____ Can be aided by the exercises listed below.

Restrictions:

Exercises:

YOUTH NUTRITION AND WEIGHT CONTROL

Few elementary physical education books deal with nutrition and weight control even though they may just be two of the most important factors to a child's fitness. Since space does not allow an extensive deliberation on the subject, this discussion must be considered an overview. The reader is encouraged to seek other sources on the subject.

Overweight and Obesity Defined

When is one overweight and when is one obese? Reliance on height/weight charts has been the primary way to determine overweightness or obesity. However, using height/weight charts is risky since they do not account for the percent of lean muscle mass to fat. The problem comes when there is excess fat.

The percentage of fat to lean muscle mass and bone, therefore, is a better way to ascertain the risk that weight has to health, and the most practical way to evaluate children's body composition is by measuring skinfolds. The most widely used measurement area for children is the back of the arm, the triceps. The *Physical Best Test* also includes the mid-calf measurement. The one site, triceps, measurement can be used for a general classification of children into thin, acceptable, and overweight. Those falling one standard deviation above the mean could be considered overweight, and those falling above the 95th percentile (using the VCU scale in appendix A) or three standard deviations above the mean would be considered obese.

Importance

The incidence of overweight and obese children is on the rise. In one study, a comparison was made between children in 1984 with those in school in 1960. The average skinfold measures were a significant three millimeters thicker in 1984. Although experts disagree on the percentages of overweight and obese children, all agree there is a problem and feel the incidence level is serious. The percentages of overweight/obese children are in the range of 20-35% of the population. Left unchecked, these percentages could become the national health crisis of the 21st Century.

Although the effects of adult weight problems are well documented, the long-term effects of childhood weight problems are not known. What is known, however, is the likelihood that children with weight problems which go unchecked have a ninety percent chance of becoming adults with weight problems. It would appear that habits developed in childhood are hard to break.

Another unknown is the psychological effects a weight problem may have on the child. Most children are very sensitive to their problem, and in a society that places much emphasis on the lean look, the problem is magnified. Children know when they are different, and when that difference is negative, the psychological implications on the development of a positive self-concept can be enormous.

Although excess weight is a considerable problem for both children and adults, another consideration is the food one ingests, whether it causes a weight problem or not. What are the long-term effects of highly fatty foods, red meat, simple sugars, dairy products, and foods high in cholesterol? The effects on adults are known, but what about consuming these foods from early childhood? It is not unusual to see babies, even in television advertising, being fed French fries and hamburgers at the local fast food stand. We have become a quick eat-and-go society. These fast foods are usually high in saturated fats, salt, sugar, and cholesterol.

Causes

There are various causes for overweight and obese children—some physical, some psychological, and nearly all preventable. The one cause most frequently given by the parents of an obese child is glandular. Although some cases of obesity are caused by hormonal imbalance, it is less then five percent.

Another reason for obesity is heredity. Recent findings suggest that parentage is an important consideration in some cases of obesity, but no reliable figures are available. It appears, however, that the percentage of cases related to heredity is small. This type of obesity, of course, is difficult to change.

Although obesity is more of a health hazard than just being overweight, the incidence is much higher and the exact health risks are not fully known. Contrary to popular belief, the overweight child does not consume substantially more calories than leaner peers; the difference seems to lie in the activity habits. The lean child is significantly more active than the overweight child and burns more calories.

Although obesity may have a number of psychological causes, only habits are within the scope of this book. A teacher must be extremely careful not to become involved in any form of psychological evaluation. Habits, however, are a combination of physical and psychological behavior and can be changed. The psychological nature of a habit is based on the notion that people do things not because of a need but because they have done something a particular way for a long period of time. Thus, some children who were trained using food as a reward will eat, not because they are hungry, but because of some ingrained psychological need. Many poor eating habits are a result of a reward system such as "You won't get any dessert unless you clean your plate." Unfortunately, schools are one of the biggest offenders in using food as a reward; it seems every PTA gives candy as a reward at such events as fairs and for fund raising schemes. Many teachers of special education children use food to modify behavior. The task is to convince people to change their habits.

The Curriculum

The curriculum information, of course, is determined by the children's ages. The newer elementary health books contain some useful information but are frequently under-used. Seldom do these books address the overweight or obese child. Since they are designed to cover the entire field of health, most do not contain sufficient nutritional information to assist teachers in helping children to make wise nutritional decisions. The following is an overview of nutrition for the teacher. No attempt is made to suggest an age level for which the information is appropriate. The best person to determine the material's suitability is the classroom or physical education teacher.

TERMINOLOGY

Knowledge of the following terms will help children understand nutritional information.

Calorie — A calorie is a measure of heat. It is the primary way foods are labeled to indicate how much potential weight a particular food will produce unless burned off. The basis for all diets is the number of calories consumed versus the number of calories burned off.

Carbohydrates — These are the *primary* energy source for all physical activity. They should comprise the majority of the diet, and are obtained through such foods as rice, pasta, breads, and fruits.

Fats — These are the *secondary* energy source and should be the next highest percentage of the diet. There are two types of fats, saturated or "bad" fats, and polyunsaturated or "good" fats. You can determine which is which since saturated fat such as butter is a solid at room temperature and will not dissolve in water. The bad, saturated fats are found most predominantly in four-legged animal meat such as cows. Bad fat is also found in dairy products, peanut butter, and some fish. Unsaturated fat is found in vegetable oil and poultry (chicken and turkey).

HDL and LDL — High density proteins (HDL) and low density proteins (LDL) designate good fats and bad fats, respectively. HDLs act as carriers to transport saturated fats to the liver where they are metabolized and stored for use as fuel. The LDLs act as an adhesive to stick saturated fat to arterial walls which gradually closes these important arteries and can lead to strokes and heart disease.

Proteins — These are the last source of energy and are used primarily as building materials in the bone and muscle tissue development. They are essential but comprise the smallest percentage of the diet. The various sources include fish, meats, nuts, poultry, and dairy products.

Vitamins — These are *enzymes which control bodily functions.* Since most are not stored in the body for any length of time, they must be continually resupplied. They are best obtained through the diet rather than through vitamin supplements which are expensive. Vitamins will be discussed at greater length later.

Minerals — These are *trace elements necessary for nerve impulses* and are sometimes referred to as electrolytes since they are responsible for the body's proper electrical functioning. Since the body is an electrical mechanism, they are extremely important. They include potassium, iron, magnesium, etc., and are obtained through the diet particularly from vegetables.

The Four Food Groups — These groups are: (1) Milk, (2) Proteins, (3) Fruits and Vegetables, and (4) Grain.

PROPER NUTRITION

The child's diet should consist of the following percentages: 60% carbohydrates, 25% fats, and 15% protein. The diet should include all four food groups, emphasizing such foods as rice, fish or fowl, skim milk, fruits, fiber, and whole grain breads. Things to avoid or take in small amounts are red meats, high fat foods such as fast food and fried food, whole milk, and simple sugars such as sugar-coated cereal, candy, and sugared sodas.

Other nutritional considerations include what to eat, when to eat it, and how much to eat. The most important meal is breakfast. It should consist primarily of carbohydrates found in such sources as cereals, breads, and fruits. Things to be avoided would be any kind of simple sugars, including anything containing honey—many foods promoted as "all natural" contain high levels of simple sugars. The amount to eat is determined by being sensitive to the number of calories consumed in the total day, always remembering that any calorie not used will be stored as fat. One way to lower caloric intake is to limit fatty foods such as fried food and red meat. Each gram of fat contains twice the number of calories as a gram of carbohydrate or protein.

The second largest meal should be lunch, and the smallest dinner. Again, the primary food for both should be complex carbohydrates such as rice, pasta, baked potato, fruit, and vegetables. The entree should never be primarily protein; the American diet, unfortunately, focuses primarily on a meat entree, particularly at dinner time. The 15% protein portion of the diet should come from fish or fowl. It should not, however, be fried.

Children should be encouraged to eat until they are full, to eat slowly, and should never be encouraged to clear their plate. Desserts, if they are served at all, should not be used to get children to eat everything on their plate. Hunger is satisfied when the stomach is full; when eating rapidly, many people do not allow for the hunger signal to subside and end up overeating.

Losing Weight

Weight is most effectively lost at one to three pounds a week, and is dependent primarily upon one's activity level. Rapid fat loss is not possible no matter what the diet books promise. Rapid weight losses experienced in low calorie diets is primarily water weight. It has also been found that rapid weight loss diets are extremely ineffective with less than four percent of those on them maintaining the weight loss for more than six months. Dieting can also be dangerous. No children, except those advised by a competent medical authority, should ever go on a diet.

OTHER IMPORTANT CONSIDERATIONS

Sugar

Simple sugars such as those found in sweets have varying effects on children. There is evidence that some children become *hyperactive* while others become *hypoactive.* Neither condition is desirable. Most sweets are known as empty calories because they have no nutritional value (no vitamins or minerals) and contain a lot of calories. Contrary to popular belief, candy just before an athletic activity is very detrimental to performance and should be avoided. In fact, simple sugars have no real nutritional value and cause numerous problems such as tooth decay and excess weight.

Honey, brown sugar, and refined sugar are all basically the same. Foods listed as "natural" because they are coated with honey are just as bad for children as anything covered with refined sugar.

Liquids

One of the most misunderstood and abused areas is liquid intake. Water intake is essential to kidney function, and at least four 8 ounce glasses of water should be consumed daily. There are many who still believe liquids, including water, should not be taken on a hot day because they will cause stomach cramps. Actually, cold water and lots of it should be taken on hot days, particularly when the humidity is high. Cold water will empty the stomach quickest and thus get into the system faster than warm water. Thirst is not a good indicator of need when the weather is hot and humid. Children, therefore, should be persuaded to drink plenty of cold water when exercising under adverse weather conditions.

The main problem under hot/humid conditions is the inability of the body to cool itself through the evaporation of sweat. The body produces sweat which must then be evaporated in order to keep the core temperature at a safe level. When the humidity is high there is no place for sweat to evaporate to and the core temperature rises which in turn produces more sweating. *Water losses in excess of 10% of the body weight can lead to a heat stroke.*

A heat stroke results when the body's temperature control fails. *This failure leads to a core temperature of 106 degrees or above and permanent brain cell damage.* The signs of an impending stroke are hot dry skin, sweating stops, slurred speech, uncoordinated movement, inability to think clearly, rapid but shallow heart rate, and eventual unconsciousness. First aid for a heat stroke victim is ingestion of cold water if conscious and rapid body cooling including immersion in ice if possible. One must be careful, however, not to lower the body temperature too low when using ice. Failure to act rapidly may lead to death. Drink, drink, drink while exercising.

Unfortunately, many adults still take *salt tablets* when they sweat a lot. These individuals then have their children do the same. In both cases the results can be a heat stroke. Salt tablets actually rob the body of precious fluid and accentuate the likelihood of a heat stroke. Salt tablets should not be taken under any circumstances.

Weight cannot be safely lost rapidly. The rapid weight loss some people experience on certain diets and during heavy exercise is water loss and, in most cases, is replaced within twenty-four to forty-eight hours after exercise. Rubber suits which promote sweating along with rubber devices placed on certain areas of the body which claim to reduce fat in these areas are a fraud and potentially very dangerous. In all cases, such devices promote water loss through sweating while eliminating the evaporation process necessary for cooling. Furthermore, spot reducing is not possible. During a diet, fat is lost from all areas of the body and exercising a certain area or isolating it under a sweating device will not cause more fat loss in that area.

Vitamins

Vitamins have become a multi-billion dollar industry in America which has lead to the most expensive urine in the world. Since most vitamins are not stored, any unnecessary amount is passed off through elimination. America's love for vitamin supplements has led to an unnecessary expense for most. Some have even taken it to the extreme by taking large quantities of potentially harmful vitamins. In particular, the fat soluble vitamins like A and E which, if taken in excess, could be harmful. Although there is a great deal of conflicting evidence, there is no definite evidence that excessive doses of any vitamin can be helpful in any situation. A vitamin supplement such as a daily multiple vitamin is not harmful, but in most cases is probably not helpful either.

Cholesterol

Cholesterol is absolutely necessary to proper bodily function, but in excess, it has been linked directly to heart disease and other cardiovascular diseases. It should be limited whenever possible and is found highest in red meats, dairy products and, in particular, eggs.

Recommendations

A government committee, The Select Committee on Nutrition and Human Performance, has made five recommendations:
1. Eat less saturated fat such as animal fat
2. Eat less cholesterol
3. Eat more complex carbohydrates such as rice, and fruits
4. Eat fewer simple sugars
5. Consume less salt

CHILDREN'S EXERCISE

The importance of exercise should be constantly emphasized to the children. The activity level of overweight and obese children is significantly less than their lean peers. Children should be active for at least six to eight hours a day; few children meet this goal. The role of the school personnel is to encourage, motivate, and provide information for leisure time activity. Special incentive programs such as the homebound fitness program in appendix A are designed to encourage activity at home. Maximum participation games which can be played in small groups at home should be taught in physical education. In school programs such as "Running For Life" (appendix A) should be done school wide. The main thing to do is get children active and away from the curse of the television.

Working With Parents

Probably the most difficult task for the teacher is to work with the overweight or obese child's parents. No parent likes to hear, even if they know it, that their child is negatively different from the other children and is going to be in a special program. It is therefore best to avoid special programs except in the most severe cases. It is these special programs, however, that can have the most dramatic results. The trick is to make the children feel special.

Each child should receive an individual contract and be on a behavior modification program as discussed in chapter 12. The children can be treated in a group under some catchy title which emphasizes positive health changes and rewards for staying on the program. Such a program is the ET program. ET stands for "Eat Right and Exercise Today" and is for overweight and obese children in the fourth grades in a local school system. The program personnel work with children, parents, administrators and teachers to bring about behavior changes in the children's exercise and eating habits. Since there would be little success without the entire family involved, the idea is to change the habits of all rather than just the child. The program is a combination of education, exercising, and counseling. It has been extremely successful.

Closing

Nutrition is a complex subject which has only been touched on here. There are a few absolutes, but a lot to learn beyond what could be covered here. Too many people are unaware of important nutritional facts such as water intake, proper foods, and ways to maintain body weight or lose it safely. Such ignorance can have far-reaching health implications for the individual and he health of the nation.

SUMMARY

Although all phases of physical education are important, fitness and nutrition are singled out in a separate chapter for emphasis. All aspects of physiological and motor fitness were covered. The focus, however, was on physiological and health-related fitness. Unlike motor fitness, everyone must possess a minimum level of efficiency in each component of health-related fitness. These components include cardiovascular efficiency, muscular strength and endurance, flexibility, and body composition. In both motor and physiological fitness, you were given a definition of the component, a way to test it, and various activities and/or programs to develop it. Since posture includes muscular strength, muscular endurance, flexibility, and to a certain extent, body composition, it was given a special section. The team approach to evaluation and treatment including the teacher, school nurse, parents, and medical doctor was discussed. The final section was nutrition for children, nutritional technology, the problem of overweight and obese children, evaluation techniques, and nutritional curriculum were all discussed.

REFERENCES AND SUGGESTED READINGS

ACSM. (2000). *ACSM's Guidelines for Exercise Testing and Prescription* (6th ed.). Philadelphia, PA: Lippincott Williams & Wilkins.

American Fitness Alliance. (1999). Teacher news: Three Fitness Education Leaders Join Forces to Encourage Healthy Habits by Young People. Author: Retrieved September 14, 2000, from the World Wide Web http://www.americanfitness.net/teacher-news.

Cooper Institute for Aerobics Research. (1999). FITNESSGRAM test administration manual. Dallas, TX. author.

Cooper Institute for Aerobics Research. (2000). FITNESSGRAM 6.0. Dallas, TX. author.

Cooper Institute for Aerobics Research. (2003). FITNESSGRAM/ACTIVITYGRAM 7.0. Dallas, TX.

Dotson, C. and J. Ross. Relationships Between Activity Patterns and Fitness, *JOPERD* 56:1, 1985, pp. 44-48.

Fox, K. and S. Biddle. The Use of Fitness Tests: Educational and Psychological Considerations, *JOPERD* 1988, pp. 47-53.

Pate, R. and J. Ross. Factors Associated with Health-Related Fitness, *JOPERD* 58:9, 1987, pp. 93-95.

Pate, R. et. al. The Modified Pull-up Test, *JOPERD* 58:9, 1987, pp. 71-73.

Payne, V.G. and L.D. Isaacs (2005). *Human Motor Development: A Lifespan Approach* (6th ed.). Boston, MA: McGraw-Hill.

President's Council on Physical Fitness and Sports. (2003). 2003-2004: The President's Challenge Physical Activity and Fitness Awards Program Packet. Washington, DC.

Ross, J. and R. Pate. A Summary of Findings, *JOPERD* 58:9, 1987, pp. 51-56.

Ross, J. et al. Are Kids Getting Appropriate Activity? *JOPERD* 56:1, 1985, pp. 40-43.

Ross, J. et. al. After Physical Education Physical Activity Outside of School Physical Education Programs, *JOPERD* 56:1, 1985, pp. 35-39.

Ross, J. et. al. Changes in the Body Composition of Children, *JOPERD* 58:9, pp. 74-77.

Ross, J. et. al. Home and Community in Children's Exercise Habits, *JOPERD* 58:9, 1987, pp. 85-92.

Ross, J. et. al. Maturation and Fitness Test Performance, *JOPERD* 56:1, 1985, pp. 25-30.

Ross, J. et. al. New Standards for Fitness, *JOPERD* 56:1, 1985, pp. 20-24.

Ross, J. et. al. What Are Kids Doing in School Physical Education? *JOPERD* 56:1, 1985, pp. 31-34.

Ross, J. et. al. What Is going On in the Elementary Physical Education Program? *JOPERD* 58:9, 1987, pp. 78-84.

Ross, J. et. al. New Health-Related Fitness Norms, *JOPERD* 58:9, 1987, pp. 66-70.

II. The Curriculum

11

Goals and Objectives

After completing this chapter, the student should be able to:

1. List an objective for each goal given in the chapter.
2. Give a general description of the curriculum for each of the age divisions.
3. Write a lesson plan for each of the age divisions.
4. Classify each of the instructional areas under its appropriate educational domain.
5. Define the key terms listed below.

―――――――――――――――――――――――――――――――――――― *Key Terms*

Affective domain	Objectives
Cognitive domain	Psychomotor domain
Goals	

Although each child's curriculum should be as individual as possible, it is not practical nor possible to establish an individualized curriculum within the confines of this text. It is necessary, therefore, to determine the most practical way to organize the curriculum information to help the teacher develop as individualized a curriculum as possible within his or her particular limitations. The following four age groups have been established based upon growth and development data: four to six years of age, six to eight, eight to ten, and ten to twelve years of age. Needless to say, when combining several growth and development years, there is going to be a wide variance in children's abilities within each age group.

Children, even of the same chronological age, differ significantly. Specifying goals and objectives for an age group, therefore, is difficult. When the age group spans two to three years, the task is further compounded. In specifying goals and objectives for an age group, it is assumed that the teacher must evaluate the children's ability and then individualize instruction so nearly all the children will achieve most of the goals and objectives prior to moving to a new age group division.

Even though they differ significantly, the age groups described in this section have common threads. The following are a few of these commonalities:

1. Movement is the basis for the curriculum, and all learning should be through movement.
2. All activities, teaching approaches, and discipline techniques should be evaluated based upon their effect on the child's attitudes with particular attention to developing a positive self-concept.
3. Health-related fitness should be an integral part of every child's curriculum.
4. Creative movement is not just for the younger children.
5. Structured and creative rhythmics should be offered to all elementary children.
6. Integrated activities should be offered whenever possible.
7. Cognitive information, particularly body image, directional terms, and fitness should be taught through movement.
8. A pupil-centered approach using open-ended questions should initially be used in most situations.
9. Safety rules and regulations must be established and strictly enforced.

Children of the same age may differ significantly in size.

GOALS AND OBJECTIVES FOR CHILDREN FOUR TO SIX YEARS OF AGE

The curriculum for four- to six-year-old children (normally preschool through kindergarten) should focus primarily on experiencing movement. The program should provide the opportunity for each child to *experience every way their body can move locomotorly and non-locomotorly, and every way their body can manipulate an object; this movement and manipulation should focus on the qualities of movement, force, time (speed), space (direction), and level.* Attempts at highly organized activities, including games, will meet with limited success. Although some simple games and structured rhythmics may work, the emphasis should be on developing a movement base and a positive self-concept.

The teacher must establish an appropriate environment which has all the children moving nearly all the time, analyze behavior constantly, and give appropriate individual help and encouragement to all the children. The motivational techniques, analysis, and individualized teaching can be exhausting. This, therefore, is not an easy age group to teach.

See chapter 8 for a basic competency unit for young children.

Outline

Following is an outline for the section on goals and objectives that follows. Each of the three domains is subdivided into developmental areas as indicated in the outline.

Psychomotor Domain
- Locomotor Movement
- Non-locomotor Movement
- Manipulative Ability
- Kinesthetic Awareness
- Balance
- Fitness
- Rhythmics
- Creativity
- Relaxation

Affective Domain
- Self-Concept
- Honesty
- Sharing
- Respect for Authority
- Patience
- Respect for Self and Others
- Leading and Following
- Positive Attitudes

Cognitive Domain
- Problem-Solving Ability
- Directional and Movement Terms
- Rules and Regulations
- Fitness, Health, and Safety Knowledge
- Body Image

PSYCHOMOTOR DOMAIN

Locomotor Movement

Goal: By age six, children will have developed all the locomotor movements.

Objectives: Before leaving kindergarten, most children should be able to do the following:
1. Run in a figure-eight pattern without falling.
2. Hop in place on either foot three times without losing balance.
3. Do a twenty-four inch standing broad jump.
4. Skip.
5. Slide.
6. Walk backward toe to heel.
7. Hop six inches forward on either foot without losing balance.

Goal: Children will improve the quality of their locomotor ability—force, speed, space, level, and direction.

Objectives:
1. Children will vary their force according to the music played—light moves for soft music and heavy moves for loud music.
2. When mimicking animals, children will apply appropriate force according to the animal they are imitating.
3. Children will respond correctly to varying rhythmic speeds by changing speed as the tempo changes.
4. Children will be able to demonstrate slow

motion action while mimicking sports activities.

5. By age five, a child should be able to walk briskly in a fifteen- by twenty-foot area with fifteen other children and not touch any-one.
6. Children should be able to demonstrate the ability to move at many levels, high and low, while traveling at different speeds and in various directions.
7. By age six, children should be able to do basic locomotor movements in any direc-tion forward, backward, or sideward.

Non-locomotor Movement

Goal: Children will be able to do all the non-locomotor movement which the body is capable of performing.

Objectives:
1. Children will be able to bend, stretch, twist, turn, shake, swing, and bounce all the body parts capable of such movements.
2. Children will show recognition of each non-locomotor movement term by demonstrat-ing appropriate body movement without any visual cues from the teacher.

Manipulative Ability

Goal: Children will be able to manipulate a variety of objects alone and with a partner.

Objectives:
1. With experience, the child, by age five and one-half, should be able to do the following
   a. Catch with one hand a 4" beanbag which has been thrown underhand.
   b. Kick an 8 1/2" rolling playground ball.
   c. Hit a rolling five-inch rubber ball with a 36" dowel.
   d. Run and kick a rolling 8 1/2" rubber ball.
   e. Catch with both hands a 2" rubber ball which has been thrown underhand.
2. Children will demonstrate the ability to manipulate objects using either the right or left side of their body.
3. Given an open area, a child should be able to keep a round balloon in the air almost indefinitely using both upper and lower body parts. Body parts should include hands, elbows, shoulders, head, knees, and feet.

Kinesthetic Awareness

Kinesthesia is a knowledge of the location of body parts in space. This awareness is dependent upon proprioception, which is sensory feedback from muscles. This section will focus on kinesthetic awareness and proprioceptive development.

Goal: Following training the child will im-prove kinesthetic awareness through proprioceptive development activities.

Objectives: Following instruction and practice, the child should be able to:
1. Without looking, be able to throw a bean-bag to a stationary partner one out of two times. The child can look to make a judgment but then must close his/her eyes or turn his/her back before throwing. The child should be successful at three differ-ent distances, using each hand, and be able to throw the beanbag at least three different ways.
2. Do a forward roll from a squatting position and end up in a sitting position.
3. Jump in the air, making at least a half turn, and land without losing balance.
4. With eyes closed, stand five seconds on one foot without losing balance.

Balance

Balance is one of the more important aspects of development since most locomotor movement depends on it.

Goal: Children will demonstrate static and dynamic balance with a variety of activities.

Objectives: Following exploration, the child should be able to:
1. Jump and make a half turn without falling.
2. Walk forward, backward, and sideward without falling off an eight-foot long bal-ance beam, four inches wide and seven inches off the ground.
3. Run a figure eight without falling down.
4. Stand on one foot for five seconds with eyes closed and not have to put the other foot down.
5. While standing on one foot, swing the other foot without losing balance.
6. Hop forward six inches on either foot and not lose balance.
7. Hop in place five times on either foot and not lose balance.

Fitness

The emphasis is on health-related fitness components rather than motor fitness components (see chapter 10).

Goal: Children will show improvement in all aspects of fitness each time a test is given.

Objectives:
1. To be able to jog continuously for a minimum of six minutes.
2. To be able to do five sit-ups, hands across chest while someone holds feet down and knees are bent.
3. To be able to do ten modified (knee) push-ups.
4. To be able to touch toes without bending knees while sitting on the floor (ground).
5. To be able to keep chin over a bar for a minimum of three seconds while doing a flexed arm hang.

Rhythmics

Rhythmic development should be a major component of early childhood education. Although many think of rhythms being only in music, many basic locomotor movements such as walking and running are examples of rhythmic activity.

Goal: Children will exhibit rhythmic development in a variety of movement activities, including dance.

Objectives:
1. Children will demonstrate rhythmic ability in basic locomotor movements by moving rhythmically to a tom-tom.
2. Children will keep time to music, using body parts or the entire body.
3. Children will recognize tempo changes, and make appropriate rhythmic adjustments with the body or body parts.
4. Children will keep time to music using lummi sticks.
5. Children will move creatively to different types of music.
6. Children will be able to do simple singing dances.

Creativity

Probably the most difficult developmental aspect to measure is creativity. Measurability, however, is not critical since there is general agreement

Children moving creatively to music.

on the importance of creativity and its need at all levels. Activities which aid the child's creative development should be a part of nearly every lesson.

Goal: Children will exhibit creativity in a variety of activities.

Objectives:
1. Each child will be able to create one original move to music if asked.
2. Children will move creatively to music.
3. Children will create original solutions to situations in a story play.
4. Five-year-olds will be able to create a lummi stick routine with three different moves.

Relaxation

In our pressure-filled world, many children have never experienced complete relaxation.

Goal: Children will exhibit relaxation in most activities.

Objective: A totally relaxed child who is lying down should be very supple with no tension, particularly in the arms. If a limb is dropped (only do on mat), it should drop freely to the mat with no resistance from muscles.

AFFECTIVE DOMAIN

Self-Concept

How a child feels about him/herself is termed self-concept.

Goal: Children will improve their self-concept.

Objective: Given an attitude questionnaire, nearly all the children will indicate a positive feeling about themselves.

Honesty

Goal: Children will exhibit honest behavior in most situations.

Objectives:
1. Children will admit to being caught in a tag game.
2. Children will admit guilt when they have done something wrong.

Sharing

Goal: To have children share materials when there are not enough for each of them.

Objective: Given a situation requiring sharing, children will voluntarily share with others.

Respect for Authority

Goal: Children will develop respect for those teachers who earn it.

Objectives:
1. No child will talk while the teacher is talking.
2. Children will stop, look, and listen on a prearranged signal.
3. Children will follow school and class rules.

Patience

Goal: Children will improve patience.

Objective: Children will wait their turn without complaining.

Respect for Self and Others

Goal: Children will develop self-respect and respect for others.

Objectives:
1. Children will not make fun of others who are different.
2. Children will not gang up on another child.
3. A child will accept an assigned partner without verbal or non-verbal complaint.
4. Children will not endanger themselves or others by violating safety rules.

5. Children will say "please" and "thank you" when dealing with peers or adults.
6. Children will give verbal encouragement to others during physical performance.

Leading/Following

Goal: Children will be good leaders and followers where appropriate.

Objectives:
1. Children will follow and do what the leader does during a game of "Follow the Leader."
2. Children will do what the teacher asks.
3. When called upon, children will be willing leaders in small group situations (eight to ten children).

Positive Attitudes

Goal: Children will develop positive attitudes toward health and physical education.

Objectives:
1. Children will give a high rating to physical education on an attitude questionnaire.
2. Children will willingly participate in all activities.
3. Children will indicate positive attitudes toward health practices, including fitness, by their response to statements on an attitude questionnaire.
4. Children will indicate a positive attitude toward the teacher and peers by their response to statements on an attitude questionnaire.

COGNITIVE DOMAIN

Many kindergarten activities provide opportunities to involve children cognitively. Flash cards with movement terms and letters, and problem-solving and creative activities all enhance cognitive knowledge and ability. One must not lose sight, however, of the main physical education objectives, which are primarily in the psychomotor domain.

Problem-Solving Ability

Goal: Children will improve problem-solving ability in a variety of situations.

Objective: Children will be able to solve movement problems at their own level in all psychomotor activities.

Directional and Movement Terms

Goal: Children will learn a number of directional and movement terms.

Objectives:

1. Children will demonstrate knowledge of the following directionality terms through pointing or appropriate movements: up, down, right, left, near, far, farther, nearer, over, under, on top of, beside, between, through, inside, next to, around, above, below, in front of, behind, upper, lower, and middle.
2. Children will demonstrate through movement an understanding of the following locomotor and non-locomotor terms: walk, run, hop, jump, leap, gallop, slide, skip, twist, turn, stretch, bend, shake, swing, and bounce.

Rules and Regulations

Goal: Children will be able to follow simple rules for class activities and games.

Objectives:

1. Children will be able to play and follow the rules of at least five games without assistance from the teacher.
2. If asked, children will be able to give at least three class rules.
3. If asked, children will be able to give at least two safety rules for tumbling and gymnastics.
4. If asked, children will be able to give the reason for a rule.

Fitness, Health, and Safety Knowledge

Goal: Children will learn fitness, health, and safety facts and concepts.

Objectives:

1. Children should be able to give at least two reasons for being physically fit.
2. Children should be able to give at least two reasons for doing each of the following: brushing teeth, keeping clean, exercising, wearing proper footwear for activity, following safety rules.
3. Children should be able to give at least one reason for each of the following safety rules: no pushing, no sliding on floor, staying inside boundaries, staying away from animals on the playground, stopping on a given signal, staying away from strangers, no horseplay during gymnastics and tumbling, and no running when in line.

BODY IMAGE

Body image is a knowledge of body parts.

Goals: Children will learn a number of body parts.

Objectives:

1. A four-year-old should be able to touch each of the following parts when asked: head, eyes, ears, nose, mouth, hands, fingers, knees, feet, back and front.
2. The five-year-old should be able to touch each of the following parts when asked: all those the four-year-old identified, plus shoulders, elbows, wrists, waist, neck, chin, and side.
3. Upon request, children will be able to move various parts mentioned in one and two above.
4. By age five, a child will be able to draw a self-portrait including each of the following parts: head, eyes, nose, mouth, arms, fingers and legs.

EXAMPLE LESSON PLANS FOR CHILDREN
FOUR TO SIX YEARS OF AGE

AGE LEVEL: 4

Outside or multipurpose room

Goals: To develop rhythmic ability and creativity. To learn class rules.

Objectives:

1. Children will move appropriately to the rhythm during activity II.
2. Children will respond appropriately to the class rules discussed, and if asked will be able to verbalize at least one of the class rules.

Activities:	*Formation*	*Time (minutes)*
I. Whistle Stop Status	I. Free	5-7

  1. Can you freeze like an animal?
  2. Can you pretend you are playing a sport?
  3. Can you freeze with a friend?

  Rules which will be emphasized during activity:
  1. The whistle only means stop.
  2. Stay inside the boundaries.
  3. Do not run into anyone else.
  4. No sliding on the floor or ground.

II. Moving to Music	II. Free	7-10

  1. Can you move just one body part to the music?
  2. How about two body parts? Three? Four?
  3. How many different body parts can you move to the music?
  4. Can you move about the room to the music?
  5. How does it make you feel? Show me.
  6. Can you move backward, sideward, high, low, turning, etc. to the music?
  The type and speed of the music must be changed frequently, and individual praise given to those showing unique creativity.

III. Ball Handling	III. One ball per child	5-7
	in a free formation	

  Using sponge balls, ask children:
  1. What can you do with this ball?
  2. Can you play with the ball and a friend?

Safety: If kicking the ball, watch where you kick your feet.

AGE LEVEL: 5

Outside or multipurpose room

Goal: To develop rhythmic ability and the quality of movement.

Objectives:

1. The students will move appropriately to the tom-tom which will be used to designate various qualities of movement, force, time, space, and level.
2. Students will move rhythmically to the tom-tom.

Activities:	*Formation*	*Time (minutes)*
I. Follow the Leader		
1. Teacher leads	*One line*	*1*
2. Children are leaders	4 or 5 lines	6

II. Moving to tom-tom   II. Free   15-18

   1. Ask children to demonstrate force on the loud drum beats with various body parts while moving rhythmically to the tom-tom. Encourage them to constantly change the body part used.

     a. On the loud beat, can you show force with a body part while moving to the tom-tom?

     b. Can you use different body parts each time I beat the drum loudly?

   2. Have the children move rhythmically in common space without touching anyone else. Constantly make the area smaller while increasing the rhythmic speed. Also change the direction (backward, sideward, forward) constantly reminding the children to watch where they are going. It is important to change the task frequently to keep the children's interest. Ask questions such as:

     a. Can you move funny?

     b. How else can you move?

     c. Can you change your direction to backward movement or sideward while still keeping in time with the beat.

III. Hokey Pokey Dance   III. Circle   5-8

   Emphasize basic body parts and right and left. "Put your right hand in. Put your right hand in and shake it all about."

Safety: Do not allow children to run into each other on purpose.

AGE LEVEL: 5

Multipurpose room

Goals: To evaluate the children. To have them learn what the whistle means.

Objectives:

   1. To evaluate the children's manipulative ability and interests.

   2. By the end of the class, the children will respond appropriately to the whistle.

Activities: *Formation*   *Time (minutes)*

I. Whistle Stop   I. Free   5-7

   Have students move randomly about room and blow whistle to have them stop. Try to fool them and blow the whistle when they are stopped to see how many move when the whistle is blown.

II. Manipulative Activities   II. Free   7-10

   Spread out many kinds of safe, manipulative objects.

    1. What can you do by yourself with these objects?

    2. What can you do with an object and a friend?

    3. Can you find a target to hit with your object?

III. Moving while balancing beanbag on various body parts.

Safety: Children must not throw objects at each other.

AGE LEVEL: 5

Outside or multipurpose room

Goal: To develop rhythmic ability.

Objective: Children will be able to keep the tom-tom rhythm with their body and the lummi sticks.

Activities: *Formation*   *Time(minutes)*

I. Can you: I. Free   5-7

   Walk like person, animal?

   Move as if you were made of stone, Jell-O, rubber?

   Move as if it was hot, cold, windy?

II. Moving to tom-tom using lummi sticks
    II. Two sticks per child   7-10
        in free formation

    1. Can you keep time with the tom-tom with your body and the sticks at the same time?
    2. What other direction can you move and keep the rhythm?
    3. How many ways can you move the sticks and still keep the rhythm?

III. Free play with manipulative objects
    III. Free   5

Safety: No hitting others with sticks or throwing them and no throwing objects at anyone.

AGE LEVEL: 5

Outside or multipurpose room
Goal: To evaluate and learn directional terms.
Objective: By the end of the class at least 80% of the children will show understanding of the terms covered by making appropriate movement using the hoops.

Activities:	Formation	Time (minutes)
I. Follow the leader	I. Free	3-5
II. Directional Terms Using Hoops	II. 1 per child in free formation	7-10

    Each child gets a hoop and the teacher asks them:
    1. Can you go around your hoop?
    2. In and out of your hoop?
    3. Face it and go around to the right?
    Other directional terms are: near, far, over, under, away from, near, between, up, down, next to, and beside.

III. Free play with hoops
    III. One per child   5
        in free formation

Safety: Do not throw hoops at each other.

GOALS AND OBJECTIVES FOR CHILDREN SIX TO EIGHT YEARS OF AGE

Many of the goals and objectives listed for the four- to six-year-olds are appropriate for children six to eight years of age. Although chronologically this age group is older, the six-year-olds may be developmentally similar to those in the four- to six-year-old age group. These older children, however, should progress rapidly, and by the end of second grade at least 80% of the children should be able to accomplish 80% of the objectives listed. The six-year-old children in this age group will continue to emphasize movement experiences. As these children mature, however, the movement base should be used to develop more specific skills such as throwing, catching, kicking, jumping, and landing.

Outline

Following is an outline for the section on goals and objectives that follows. Each of the three domains is subdivided into developmental areas as indicated on the outline.

Psychomotor Domain
    Quality of Movement
    Visual Discrimination and Manipulative Ability
    Kinesthetic Awareness
    Rhythmics
    Creativity
    Fitness
    Relaxation

Affective Domain
    Self-concept
    Honesty
    Sharing
    Respect for Authority
    Patience
    Respect for Self and Others

Leading and Following
Positive Attitudes

Cognitive Domain

Problem-Solving Ability
Creativity
Body Image
Rules and Regulations
Fitness, Health, and Safety Knowledge

PSYCHOMOTOR DOMAIN

Quality of Movement

The movement qualities are force, time, space, and level, all of which play a vital role in efficient movement.

Goal: The students will be able to demonstrate the qualities of movement, force, time, space, and level in a variety of situations.

Objectives:

1. Students will demonstrate force with body actions in response to loud and soft beats of a tom-tom.
2. The children's movements will be either slow, medium, or fast depending upon the rhythmic tempo.
3. Children will be able to move in a limited space with a number of children without bumping into one another.
4. Children will be able to bend, stretch, twist, turn, shake, bounce, rotate, and spin, demonstrating various forces and speeds appropriate (heavy to hard and slow to fast) to various stimuli (tom-tom, music, or chant).
5. Students will be able to do all the locomotor movements at both high, medium, and low levels and in all directions.
6. Children will demonstrate proper use of arms, legs, and head while running, walking, skipping, leaping, and galloping.

Manipulative Ability

Goal: The student will develop hand-eye coordination.

Objectives:

1. The child will be able to throw (stepping forward with the opposite foot) and catch a

Children six to eight years of age should be able to demonstrate hand-eye coordination.

6" beanbag four out of five times with a partner fifteen feet away.

2. Playing alone, the child will be able to throw and catch (using hands only) an 8 1/2" playground ball four out of five times when thrown above the head.
3. The child will be able to throw and catch a 7" sponge rubber ball with a partner and catch it four out of five times from a distance of ten feet.
4. The child will be able to throw and hit a 10" high target ten feet away with an 8 1/2" playground ball three out of four times.
5. The child will be able to bounce and catch an 8 1/2" playground ball four out of five times with a partner fifteen feet away.
6. The child will be able to dribble an 8 1/2" playground ball at least ten feet while walking forward, backward, or sideward.

Goal: The student will develop eye-foot coordination.

Objectives:

1. The child will be able to kick a stationary 8 1/2" playground ball twenty feet.
2. The child will be able to kick a stationary 8 1/2" playground ball and hit a bowling pin ten feet away one out of three times.

3. The child will be able to do long rope jumping, including getting in front door.
4. The child will be able to do single rope jumping, forward and backward four times in a row.
5. The child will be able to run forward for five steps while jumping a short rope.

Goal: The child will develop the non-dominant side of the body.

Objective: Students will be able to accomplish at least 60% of the hand-eye and foot-eye coordination activities using the non-dominant side of the body.

Kinesthetic Awareness

Kinesthesis is a knowledge of body parts in space, and is dependent upon sensory feedback from muscles (proprioception). This ability is important to movement quality, particularly in the areas of dance and gymnastics or any other activity which may place individuals in unusual positions.

Goals: The child will improve kinesthetic awareness through proprioceptive development activities.

Objectives:
1. Given a beanbag, the child will be able to throw it to a partner one out of two times without looking. The child can make a visual judgment prior to throwing, but must turn his/her back or close his/her eyes just before the actual throw. This should be accomplished using either hand in a variety of ways up to a distance of twenty feet.
2. The child should be able to jump in the air, make a three-quarter turn, and land on his/her feet without losing balance.

Rhythmics

Goal: Children will develop rhythmic ability.

Objectives:
1. Child will be able to walk, run, slide, gallop, hop, jump, and clap in rhythm.
2. Child will be able to keep time with music using lummi sticks.
3. Children will be able to recognize phrases in music by changing direction with each new phrase.
4. Child will be able to bounce a ball rhythmically to music.

5. Children will be able to do five simple folk dances without assistance from the teacher.
6. Child will be able to move appropriately to different rhythms; i.e., fast to fast and slow to slow.
7. Children will be able to move creatively to music.
8. Children will be able to demonstrate originality in movement to various musical selections.

Creativity

Goal: Children will exhibit creativity in a variety of activities.

Objectives:
1. Children will be able to design original activities as part of story plays.
2. Children will be able to create an original dance to music. This dance will include the following force, time, space, and level.
3. Children working in groups will be able to create original routines using lummi sticks.

Fitness

Goal: Children will improve on all physiological and motor fitness items each time the test is given.

Objectives:
1. While sitting, child will be able to touch his/her toes without bending the knees.
2. Child will be able to run a minimum of 450 meters in six minutes.
3. Child will be able to do a flexed-arm hang for a minimum of five seconds.
4. Child will be able to do a standing broad jump the distance of his/her height.
5. Child will be able to do ten push-ups.
6. Child will be able to do ten bent-knee sit-ups with someone holding his/her feet.
7. Child will be able to run, change direction on a given signal, and not fall down.
8. Child will be able to run thirty yards in eight seconds.
9. Child will be able to achieve at least 50th percentile on the school's fitness test.

Relaxation

Relaxation goals, objectives, and activities do not differ from those for four to six years of age.

AFFECTIVE DOMAIN

The goals, objectives, and developmental activities for six- and seven-year-old children differ only slightly from those four to six years of age.

Self Concept
Honesty
Sharing
Respect for Authority
Patience
Respect for Self and Others
Leading and Following
Positive Attitudes

COGNITIVE DOMAIN

Problem-Solving Ability

Goal: Children will develop some problem-solving ability.

Objective: During a problem-solving activity, each child will be able to think of one solution on his/her own for most of the problems presented.

Creativity

Goal: Children will develop creativity.

Objective: Given a creative movement situation, the child will be able to come up with one unique way of moving.

Body Image

Goal: The children will learn various body parts and how they move.

Objectives:
1. Children will be able to identify each of the following body parts by touching them if asked: wrist, waist, shoulders, elbows, ankles, cheeks, and forehead; plus all those identified by four- to six-year-olds.
2. Children will be able to keep time with music using various body parts.
3. A child will be able to draw a self-portrait and include each of the following: head, eyes, ears, nose, mouth, body, arms, fingers, legs, and feet.

Rules and Regulations

Goals: Children will learn new games and dances each year. Children will know the rules of the class.

Objectives:
1. If asked, at least 80% of the students will be able to give three class rules.
2. If asked, children will be able to give the reason for a rule.
3. Children will be able to play five new games and do five new dances a year from memory.

Fitness, Health, and Safety Knowledge

Goal: Children will gain safety, fitness, and health knowledge.

Objectives:
1. If asked, children will be able to give one reason for each safety rule established.
2. If asked, children should be able to give five class safety rules.
3. Children will be able to give one reason for each of the following: cleanliness, brushing the teeth after meals, cooling down slowly after a workout, being physically fit, running, and exercises.

Fitness: Children will exhibit knowledge of the following:
1. How to take pulse at wrist.
2. Why heart beats faster during exercise.
3. Exercises to develop fitness.
4. The necessity to cool down after an exercise bout.
5. Dangers of over-exercising in extreme heat.
6. The need for liquids during and after exercise which produces extensive sweating.

Safety: Children will exhibit knowledge of reasons for the following:
1. Proper footwear.
2. Following game rules.
3. Tagging without pushing.
4. No sliding on floor or grass.
5. Staying inside designated areas.
6. Wearing safety goggles over glasses.

Health: Children will exhibit knowledge of the following:
1. Proper diet.
2. Rest needs.
3. Exercise needs.
4. Cleanliness.

EXAMPLE LESSON PLANS FOR CHILDREN
SIX TO EIGHT YEARS OF AGE

AGE LEVEL: 6

Outside or multipurpose room

Goal: Develop rhythmic ability.

Objective: By the end of the class at least 80% of the children will be able to jump rope five times forward and backward without a miss.

Activities:	Formation	Time (Minutes)
I. Moving to tom-tom	I. Free	5
II. Jumping Rope	II. One per child	15-18
1. How many ways can you jump rope?		
2. Can you jump five times forward?		
3. Can you move around the room while jumping?		
4. Can you jump rope backward?		
III. Jump Rope Race	III. All race at once	5
Jump rope to line and back		

Safety: Do not hit others with ropes while jumping.

AGE LEVEL: 6

Outside or multipurpose room

Goal: To develop balance and manipulative ability.

Objective: By the end of the lesson, the child will be able to balance a 6" square beanbag on at least two different body parts and quickly move a distance of at least twenty-five feet without the beanbag falling off.

Activities:	Formation	Time (Minutes)
I. Human Vocabulary	I. Free	5-7
II. Beanbag Fun	II. One per child 15 in a free formation	
1. What can you do with your beanbag?		
2. Can you move around the room and play with your beanbag without bumping into anyone?		
3. Can you balance your beanbag on a body part and move? Another body part?		
4. Can you move backward while balancing it?		
5. Can you move quickly while balancing it?		
6. Can you throw and catch the beanbag by yourself? With a partner?		
III. Progressive Tag using 4" yarn balls	III. One ball per child	5-7

Safety: No throwing beanbags at each other.

AGE LEVEL: 6

Outside or multipurpose room

Goal: To develop manipulative ability.

Objective: By the end of the class, at least 80% of the children will be able to throw and catch the 7" sponge ball with a partner at least ten feet away at least five times in a row.

Activities:	Formation	Time (Minutes)
I. Seasons	I. Partners	5-7
II. Manipulative activities using sponge balls (one per child):	II. Free	15

1. What can you do with the sponge balls?
2. How many different ways can you throw and catch the ball?
3. Can you catch it without using your hands?
4. What body parts can you use to throw it?
5. Can you throw and catch with a friend?
6. How many different ways can you throw and catch with your friend?
7. How many times in a row can you catch it with each other?

III. Move Away	III. Partners	5-7

Children start close together and throw and catch the ball. With each successful catch, the child catching the ball moves back one step. If a child misses the ball, he/she must take two steps forward.

Safety: There is very little danger with sponge balls.

AGE LEVEL: 7

Hardtop or multipurpose room

Goal: To develop manipulative ability.

Objective: By the end of the class all the children will be able to dribble an 8 1/2" playground ball a distance of twenty-five feet without losing control of it.

Activities:	Formation	Time (Minutes)
I. If I were a _____, I would move like this. Things to fill in the line: train, plane, car, any animal, piece of dust, cloud, any person, etc.	I. Free	5-7
II. Dribbling	II. One ball per child in free formation	15-18

Using 8 1/2" playground balls, ask:
1. How many ways can you dribble the ball?
2. What are some different body parts you can use to dribble the ball?
3. What directions can you move while dribbling?
4. Can you skip, gallop, etc. and dribble?
5. Can you fancy dribble?
6. How fast can you dribble and move forward?
7. Can you dribble real low? Real high? Real slow?

III. Dribble Take Away	III. One ball per child free formation	5-7

Children dribble around area while attempting to knock the other children's ball away. As long as the child is dribbling the ball, the free hand may be used to knock someone else's ball away. A child losing his or her ball cannot touch anyone else's ball until his or her ball is retrieved. At the end, the children who lost control of the ball the least will be the winners.

Safety: No body contact during activity III.

AGE LEVEL: 7

Outside or multipurpose room

Goal: Develop manipulative ability

Objective: At least 80% of the students will be able to complete each of the tasks at the various stations.

Activities:	Formation	Time (Minutes)
I. Moving to Music	I. Circle	5-7
II. Manipulative Stations	II. 5 stations	20

Each station will have challenging tasks specified on paper and hung near the equipment. Use open-ended questions along with some specific tasks: Can you throw and catch the tennis ball with the scoop? What else can you do with the ball and scoop?

1. Scoops and tennis balls
2. Sponge balls
3. Groovy loops and plastic wands
4. Playground balls and targets
5. Hockey sticks and plastic balls

III. After having rotated through all the stations, the children will be allowed to go back to their favorite one.

Safety: No throwing balls at each other, and no kicking playground balls.

AGE LEVEL: 7

Outside

Goal: To develop foot-eye coordination.

Objective: Using soccer balls or 8 1/2" playground balls, the students will be able to dribble the ball a distance of twenty-five feet alternating feet without losing control.

Activities:	Formation	Time (Minutes)
I. Individual rope jumping	I. Free	5
Each child has a rope.		
II. Foot-eye coordination	II. Free	15-20

Each child will manipulate either a soccer ball (if available) or an 8 1/2" playground ball.

1. How many ways can you dribble the ball with your feet?
2. Can you dribble alternating feet?
3. Can you dribble backward? Sideward?
4. Can you dribble fast and stop the ball quickly when the whistle blows?
5. Can you dribble the ball in and out of the cones?

	Formation	Time (Minutes)
III. Dribble race	III. Line	3-5

All children line up side by side each with a ball. On go signal, they dribble to a line and back again. The winner is the first one who has control of his or her ball on the finish line.

Safety: No hard kicking during the race.

GOALS AND OBJECTIVES FOR CHILDREN EIGHT TO TEN YEARS OF AGE

Children eight to ten years old are in a transitional age group. They are ready to use the basic movement competencies and skills they have developed. These skills can be used, among other things, in lead-up activities to individual and team sports. The curriculum, however, must also include rhythmics, creativity, and fitness, to name but a few. As with the other age groups, at least 80% of the children should be able to accomplish 80% of the objectives. Accomplishing sports skill objectives, however, is not essential for everyone in every sport. Some children will be more success-ful in one sport than another, but all the children should have experience in all the activities offered.

This can be a particularly satisfying group to teach. The children tend to be enthusiastic, are willing to try most anything, and progress can be readily seen.

Outline

Following is an outline for the section on goals and objectives that follows. Each of the three domains is subdivided into developmental areas as indicated on the outline.

Psychomotor Domain
- Manipulative Ability
- Rhythmics
- Creativity
- Fitness
- Tumbling and Gymnastics
- Lead-up Games to Team and Individual Sports

Affective Domain
- Self-Concept
- Team Loyalty
- Self-Discipline
- Sportsmanship
- Self-respect and Respect for Others
- Sharing
- Respect for Authority
- Positive Attitudes
- Social Interaction

Cognitive Domain
- Rules and Regulations
- Body Image
- Movement Terms
- Physiological and Movement Concepts
- Safety Rules
- Health Knowledge

PSYCHOMOTOR DOMAIN

Manipulative Ability
Hand-Eye Coordination

Goal: The child will improve hand-eye coordination.

Objectives:
1. Child will demonstrate the correct throwing technique (left foot step when throwing with right hand and vice versa) and hit a three-foot diameter target fifteen feet away two out of three times. This is to be done both overhand and underhand.
2. Child will be able to bounce a tennis ball with a paddle racket ten times in a row on a smooth hard surface.
3. Child will be able to catch a beanbag thrown overhand from a distance of fifteen feet using a scoop made from a plastic bottle or plastic milk container.
4. Child will be able to dribble an 8 1/2" playground ball while walking in any direction.
5. Child will be able to hit a 7" sponge rubber ball into the air three times in a row using a paddle racket.

6. Child will be able to volley a 7" sponge rubber ball against a wall six times in a row.
7. Child will be able to catch two beanbags thrown simultaneously underhand from a distance of ten feet. Child must catch one in each hand.
8. Child will be able to throw a beanbag through a rolling bicycle tire from a distance of fifteen feet one out of three times.

Manipulative Ability
Foot-Eye Coordination

Goal: The child will show improvement in foot-eye coordination.

Objectives:
1. Child will be able to kick an 8 1/2" playground ball rolled at him/her on a smooth surface nine out of ten times.
2. Child will be able to punt an 8 1/2" playground ball forward two out of four times.
3. Using an individual rope, child will be able to jump rope forward or backward ten times in a row.
4. Using a long rope, child will be able to enter back door or front door and jump three times in a row.
5. Child will be able to run and kick a slowly rolling 8 1/2" playground ball and hit a goal area eight feet wide from a distance of fourteen feet, three out of four times.
6. Child will be able to run and hurdle three 1 1/2-foot-high hurdles placed ten feet apart.
7. Child will be able to dribble a soccer ball using feet only through a series of marker cones placed seven feet apart. Child must pass on alternating sides of cones and use each foot equally.

Rhythmics

Goal: Child will participate in creative rhythmic activities.

Objectives:
1. Children will work in pairs or small groups to design creative movements to both classical and modern music.
2. Child will design a unique rope jumping routine to music.
3. Children will demonstrate various moods and situations using their body while moving to various types of music.

(Moods—happy, sad, gay, afraid, mad; situations—crowded bus, lonely dark road, haunted house, in the snow, on ice.)

4. Children will be able to work together to create a unique lummi stick routine.

Goal: Children will continue developing rhythmic ability.

Objectives:

1. Child will be able to bounce an 8 1/2" playground ball in rhythm to various tempos.
2. Child will be able to keep time to music using the lummi sticks in a variety of ways either alone, with a partner, or in a group.
3. Child will be able to jump rope rhythmically.
4. Children will be able to work together rhythmically using the parachute.

Goal: Children will learn five new dances a year.

Objective: Without the teacher's assistance, children will be able to perform five new dances a year from memory.

Creativity

Goal: Children will continue to develop creativity.

Objectives:

1. Given various themes (day at the circus, going to the zoo) children will create unique miming activities alone, with a partner, or in a group.
2. Given various situations (cold day, swimming in cold water, flying a plane, floating on a cloud, sky diving) children will demonstrate creative mimicry.
3. Children will move creatively to poems.

Fitness

Goal: All children will show improvement on all test items from pre- to post-test.

Objectives:

1. Child will be able to broad jump five inches beyond his/her own height.
2. Child will be able to do a flexed-arm hang for a minimum of ten seconds.
3. Child will be able to do fifteen modified push-ups.
4. Child will be able to do a minimum of fifteen bent-knee sit-ups in sixty seconds.
5. Child will be able to climb a rope using hands and feet to one and one-half times his/her height.

6. In six minutes an eight-year-old child will be able to cover a minimum distance of 750 meters, and the nine-year-old will be able to go 800 meters or more in nine minutes.
7. On a level course a child will be able to run thirty yards in 6.0 seconds or less.
8. At least 80% of the children will have an acceptable amount of body fat.

Lead-Up Games to Team and Individual Sports

Goal: Children will successfully play at least five new lead-up games each year.

AFFECTIVE DOMAIN

The teacher must constantly observe students with the affective goals and objectives in mind. It is difficult to set up affective situations which will provide teachable moments, but any group of children in physical education will provide extemporaneous teaching opportunities in the affective domain. The teacher must be ready to handle such situations effectively.

Self-Concept

Goal: Children will improve their self-concept.

Objective: All children will indicate they feel better about themselves after having participated in physical education. This attitude will be measured using an anonymous questionnaire.

Team Loyalty

Goal: Children will begin developing team loyalty.

Objectives: Children will work together and not argue with each other while working toward a common goal.

Self-Discipline

Goal: Children will develop self-discipline.

Objectives:

1. Children will be able to organize and conduct competitive games without fighting or arguing and without the teacher's direction.
2. Children will voluntarily help those who need assistance.

3. Children will not fight during a game.
4. Arguments which do occur will be resolved within thirty seconds.

Sportsmanship

Goal: Children will develop good sportsmanship.

Objectives:
1. Children will not fight with members of the other team or argue with an official during a team game situation.
2. As spectators, children will not boo.
3. Children will congratulate the other team whether they win or lose.
4. Children will call fouls on themselves voluntarily during games.

Self-Respect and Respect for Others

Goal: Children will demonstrate self-respect.

Objectives:
1. Children will not take drugs or alcohol.
2. Children will voluntarily carry out a home fitness program.
3. Children will practice good health habits: cleanliness, rest, and diet.

Goal: Children will show respect for others.

Objectives:
1. Children will not call others names.
2. Children will not belittle others.
3. Children will not endanger others by violating safety rules.

Sharing

Goal: Children will demonstrate sharing.

Objective: Given a situation requiring sharing, children will voluntarily share with others.

Respect for Authority

Goal: Children will show respect for authority.

Objectives:
1. Children will listen when the teacher is talking.
2. Children will follow the teacher's directions.
3. Children and teacher will say "please" and "thank you."

Positive Attitudes

Goal: Children will develop positive attitudes toward fitness, health, and safety.

Objective: Children will follow all the safety rules established for the various activities.

Social Interaction

Goal: Children will effectively interact with others.

Objectives:
1. Children will accept an assigned partner without complaining.
2. Children will not call others derogatory names.

COGNITIVE DOMAIN
Rules and Regulations

Goal: Child will learn five new games and five new dances each year.

Objective: After appropriate instructions, children will be able to organize and play five new games and do five new dances a year.

Body Image

Goal: Children will learn various body parts.

Objectives:
1. If asked, children will be able to touch the following body parts: stomach, abdominal region, thighs, shins, calf, and hips.
2. If shown a flash card with the name of a body part, children will be able to identify the word and to touch the body part in question.

Movement Terms

Goal: Children will be able to recognize movement terms.

Objective: If shown flash cards with movement terms on them, children will be able to do the appropriate movements without verbal assistance from the teacher. These movement terms include: catch, throw, punt, kick, jump, leap, roll, backward, forward, and sideward.

PHYSIOLOGICAL AND MOVEMENT CONCEPTS

Integrated Planning

The sciences of movement and physiology should be an integral part of a physical education program. The information which follows should be learned by this age group.

Goal: Children will learn physiological and movement concepts.

Objective:
1. If asked, at least 80% of the children will be able to explain at least 80% of the following
   a. How to absorb shock when jumping from a height.
   b. How to strengthen a muscle.
   c. How to improve cardiovascular efficiency.
   d. The best way to lift heavy objects.
   e. The best way to push and pull an object.
   f. The value of exercise.
   g. The importance of good posture.
   h. How to lose or gain weight.
   i. The best way to throw and catch.

Safety Rules

Goal: Children will learn safety rules.

Objectives:
1. If asked, children will be able to recite at least 90% of the safety rules established for class.
2. If asked, children will be able to give the reason for any safety rule which has been established.

Health Knowledge

Goal: Children will improve their health knowledge.

Objectives:
1. If asked, children will be able to give the reasons for each of the following
   a. Being clean.
   b. Brushing their teeth.
   c. Being fit.
   d. Having the proper diet.
   e. Wearing proper clothing.

EXAMPLE LESSON PLANS FOR CHILDREN EIGHT TO TEN YEARS OF AGE

AGE LEVEL: 8

Outside or multipurpose room

Goal: Manipulative development and creativity development.

Objective: By the end of the class, each child or group of children will have created a target game.

Activities:	Formation	Time (Minutes)
I. Free play with variety of equipment: balls, hockey sticks, plastic containers, hoops, and ropes.	I. Free	5
II. Target activities Using the objects, the children make up their own target activity.	II. Free	10-12
III. Target game Working in groups of their choosing, children make up a target game which is different from any regular type of game they may have seen elsewhere, e.g., hockey.	III. Up to the students	10-12

Safety: All games must be safe and only sponge balls can be thrown or kicked anywhere. Children may not hit others with their equipment.

AGE LEVEL: 8

Outside or multipurpose room

Goal: To develop volleyball skills

Objective: By the end of the class, the children will be able to bounce a 7" sponge ball in the air seven times in a row using both hands in a legal volleyball hit.

Activities:	*Formation*	*Time (Minutes)*
I. Mimic legal volleyball hits	I. Free	5

Children imitate teacher's behavior as they do legal volleyball hits without a ball.

II. Ball manipulation	II. Free	15-20

Each child has a ball.
1. How many different body parts can you use to hit the ball into the air two times in a row?
2. Can you use just upper body parts?
3. Just your arms and hands?
4. How many times in a row can you do it?
5. Can you do it like (person's name) is doing it?
6. How about just doing it underhand?
7. Just overhand?
8. Can you do it seven times in a row?

III. Keep It Up	III.Groups of 5 or 6	5

Safety: Do not move far out of your space when trying to do the tasks in II.

AGE LEVEL: 9

Outside or multipurpose room

Goal: Learn fitness terms and exercises.

Objective: By the end of class, at least 80% of the class, if asked, will be able to name at least two exercises for developing each of the fitness areas covered at the stations.

Activities:	*Formation*	*Time (Minutes)*
I. Finding the pulse	I. Circle	5

Students are taught to take their carotid pulse. After finding their present heart rate, they jog in a circle and, after one minute, they take the pulse again. The speed of running is increased for one minute and they again find their heart rate. As the children are running, the teacher can talk about the direct relationship between workload (speed of running) and heart rate.

II. Fitness Stations	II. 5 stations	20

Prior to beginning the stations, the children should be told the lesson objective.

1. Cardiovascular: Tasks will include jumping rope, walking with hand weights, aerobic exercises, and jogging.
2. Upper body strength and endurance: Tasks include push-ups, pull-ups, modified pull-ups, and two person tug-of-war.
3. Abdominal strength and endurance: Tasks include sit-ups, crunchers, and leg lifts.
4. Body composition: Tasks include any muscular activity designed to burn calories.
5. Flexibility: Tasks include several back and leg flexibility tasks as well as shoulder flexibility.

Following the stations activities, the teacher should go around to children during the last activity and check the accomplishment of the objective. This questioning should be done quietly so as not to embarrass any child who does not know an answer.

III. Combatives	III. Partners	5-7

Safety: No rough play during combatives, and no horsing around at stations.

AGE LEVEL: 9

Gymnasium

Goal: Rhythmic and creative development.

Objective: By the end of the class, each group will be able to do a short routine to the music which meets the criteria established in class.

Activities:	Formation	Time (Minutes)
I. Exercises to music	I. Circle	5-7

Students take turns leading rhythmic exercises from the center of the circle.

II. Lummi Sticks	II. Free	10-12

Students follow teacher who does a variety of lummi stick activities, including getting up and moving around to the music. Children are then encouraged to do some of their own moves to the music.

III. Routine	III. Groups of no less than 3	10-12

Groups make up a routine which has five parts: an up move (all on their feet), a down move (sitting), a passing move when all the sticks must be passed simultaneously, a rhythm move when they must keep time with the sticks while also moving their body to the rhythm, and an ending move. Children are given just a couple of minutes to make up the routine and then they show it to the others, who keep time to the music with their sticks during the presentations.

Safety: No throwing the sticks or hitting anyone with the sticks.

GOALS AND OBJECTIVES FOR CHILDREN TEN TO TWELVE YEARS OF AGE

The curriculum for children ten to twelve years of age should include all aspects of development. Too often, the curriculum for these older children focuses primarily on sports while neglecting such areas as creativity, rhythmics, and dance. Although sports are a major curriculum emphasis, children want and need variety.

Outline

Following is an outline for the section on goals and objectives that follows. Each of the three domains is subdivided into developmental areas as indicated on the outline.

Psychomotor Domain

    Sports Skills

    Fitness

    Rhythmics

    Creativity

    Self-testing

Affective Domain

    Self-concept

    Sportsmanship

    Team Concept

    Interpersonal Relationships

    Leading and Following

    Safety

    Fitness

    Health

Cognitive Domain

    Rules and Regulations

    Body Image

    Fitness

    Health Knowledge

PSYCHOMOTOR DOMAIN

Sports Skills

Goal: Children will develop a variety of skills which can be used in various individual and team games and recreational activities.

SOFTBALL

Performance Objectives

Throwing:
1. Throw the ball underhanded a distance of twenty feet to another child.
2. While standing behind second base, throw the ball overhand to another child standing on first base.
3. Using an overhand throwing motion, throw the ball from home plate to second base.

Fielding:
1. Catch a softball thrown overhand from a distance of twenty feet three out of six times.
2. Catch a softball thrown twenty-five feet into the air three out of six times.
3. Catch a batted ground ball three out of six times.

Batting:
1. With a bat, hit three out of six softballs pitched in the strike zone.
2. With a bat, hit a self-tossed softball to another child standing ninety feet from home plate.

Base Running:
1. Run from home plate to first base in under four seconds.
2. Run from home plate to second base in under nine seconds.

SOCCER

Performance Objectives

Kicking and Dribbling:
1. Dribble a soccer ball alternating feet in and out of eight marker cones set ten feet apart within a twenty-second time limit without losing control of the ball.
2. Utilizing a four-foot running start, place-kick a stationary soccer ball a distance of twenty-five yards to a partner five out of seven times.
3. Kick a slowly rolling soccer ball into an eight-foot goal area thirty-five feet away three out of four times.
4. Punt the soccer ball a distance of forty yards three out of five times.

Passing:
1. Successfully (three out of five attempts) pass a soccer ball to a partner ten feet away so that the stationary partner does not have to take more than one step to foot trap the ball.

Learning sports skills is important to the ten- to twelve-year-old.

2. Successfully pass a soccer ball to a partner twenty feet away while both players are moving in the same direction. Note: The above directions should be accomplished while using all kicking techniques.

Trapping:
1. Successfully control a slowly kicked ball five out of eight times while utilizing the sole trap or foot trap.
2. Successfully body trap a soccer ball which has been thrown to you from a distance of fifteen feet.

Heading:
1. Head the soccer ball five out of eight times to a partner who has thrown the ball to you from a distance of fifteen feet.
2. Head the soccer ball three out of five times into an eight foot goal area while standing fifteen feet away.

Goalkeeping:
1. Successfully block (catch or knock away) a ball kicked from thirty feet away so as to keep it from entering the goal five out of eight times.

Throwing:

1. Using the proper two-handed throw-in technique, project the ball twenty feet to a teammate eight out of ten times.

FOOTBALL
Performance Objectives

Passing:

1. Successfully throw a spiral pass a distance of twenty yards using a junior football.
2. Successfully throw a spiral pass to a running partner ten yards away using a junior football.
3. Successfully throw a spiral pass through a suspended 15" tire from a distance of ten yards, two out of five times.

Pass Receiving and Catching:

1. Catch a junior sponge rubber football thrown from a distance of twenty yards three out of five times.
2. While running, catch a junior football thrown from a distance of ten yards three out of five times.
3. Catch a junior football which has been punted a distance of twenty yards three out of five times.
4. Catch a junior football which has been centered a distance of ten yards.

Kicking:

1. Kick a junior football off a tee a distance of twenty yards three out of five times.
2. Place-kick a junior football a distance of ten yards so that the ball passes between two marker cones positioned eight yards apart.
3. Punt a junior football a distance of twenty yards three out of five times.

Centering:

1. Correctly center the junior football to the team's quarterback who is standing directly under the center.
2. Center the junior football three out of four times to the quarterback who is standing four yards behind the center.
3. Center the junior football three out of four times to the punter who is standing eight yards behind the center.

FLOOR HOCKEY
Performance Objectives

Passing:

1. Pass the puck to a stationary partner who is standing fifteen feet away three out of five times.
2. Pass the puck twenty feet to a partner who is moving away from you three out of five times.
3. Successfully pass the hockey puck to a partner ten feet away while both are moving in the same direction.

Shooting:

1. Hit a hockey puck into a four foot goal area from a distance of twenty feet three out of four times.

Puck Control:

1. Dribble a hockey puck in and out of eight marker cones set ten feet apart in less than twenty seconds without losing control of the puck.

Fitness

Goal: By the end of the year each child will have improved their fitness level.

Objectives:

1. At least 50% of the children will score higher than the 50th percentile on the school's fitness test.
2. At least 20% of the children will score higher than the 80th percentile on the school's fitness test.
3. At least 90% of the children will improve their fitness level by at least 10% on the school's fitness test.

Rhythmics

Goal: Each child will learn a variety of dances and dance steps.

Objectives:

1. The child will be able to perform the following dance steps: polka, schottische, and bleking.
2. Without assistance the children will be able to do five new folk dances a year.
3. The children will demonstrate knowledge of the following dance terms by correctly executing them while doing a square dance: do-si-do, allemande, grand right and left, star, ladies' chain promenade, and swing.
4. The children will be able to perform two new square dances a year.

Goal: Children will demonstrate creative rhythmic ability.

Objectives:
1. The children will move creatively to various types of music—classical and modern.
2. The children working alone or in a small group will develop a creative dance routine to their own music incorporating all four of the movement qualities—force, time, space, and level—in their routine.
3. The children will develop original rhythmic routines alone or in small groups using each of the following pieces of equipment: jump ropes, lummi sticks, tinikling poles, wands, and streamers.

Creativity

Goal: Children will develop creative ability.

Objectives:
1. Children alone or in small groups will imitate machines which have moving parts.
2. Children will creatively act out various movement themes through pantomime such as: the circus, famous events, the city, sporting events, and weather.
3. Children will move creatively to various poems which include movement activities.

Self-testing

Goal: Children will learn a variety of self-testing activities each year.

Objective: Children will learn at least ten new activities a year for which they can test themselves.

AFFECTIVE DOMAIN

Objectives in the affective domain are specified in unit and yearly plans but not on lesson plans. Since attitudes are only changed over long periods, affective objectives would be inappropriate as short-term objectives such as those usually specified on lesson plans. Many of the objectives stated below are idealistic and will not be accomplished fully during a year or even in many years, but they serve as guides for teachers.

Self-Concept

Goal: Each child will improve his/her self-concept.

Objective: Given an anonymous questionnaire children will respond positively to questions regarding their self-concept as a result of physical education participation.

Sportsmanship

Goal: Children will improve their sportsmanship.

Objectives:
1. No child will physically fight with another child during a game situation.
2. Children will not boo for any reason.
3. Children will congratulate the other team, win or lose.
4. Children will call rule violations on themselves.

Team Concept

Goal: Children will learn how to work as a team toward a common goal.

Objectives:
1. All children, no matter what their ability, will be given an equal chance to play by the team captain.
2. Children will not openly ridicule members of their own team.
3. Children will verbally encourage members of their team no matter what the circumstances.

Interpersonal Relationships

Goal: Children will learn to get along with each other.

Objectives:
1. Children will not call each other derogatory names during physical education.
2. Children will show respect for the right of others by not violating safety rules which endanger others.
3. Children will accept partners of the opposite sex for rhythmic activities with sufficient ease so that the rhythmic activity can be successfully conducted.

Leading and Following

Goal: Children will learn to be both leaders and followers.

Objective: Children will be able to organize and conduct their own games with teacher supervision but not help.

183

Safety

Goal: Children will follow safety rules.

Objective: During all activities, children will not deliberately violate safety rules.

Fitness

Goal: Children will carry out a personal fitness program at home.

Objective: At least 70% of the children will carry on a home fitness program as evaluated by their response to fitness questions on an anonymous questionnaire.

Health

Goal: Children will have good health habits.

Objectives:

1. Given an anonymous questionnaire, children will respond positively to those questions dealing with good health habits.
2. Most children will show self-respect by not using dangerous drugs, including alcohol and cigarettes.

COGNITIVE DOMAIN

Rules and Regulations

Goal: Children will learn a variety of sport and game rules and regulations.

Objectives:

1. If asked, children will be able to organize and conduct at least five new games per year.
2. Without assistance, children should be able to organize and conduct at least fifteen different games.

Goal: Children will be able to do dances from memory.

Objective: Children should be able to do at least five new dances per year from memory and a total of fifteen different dances (old and new) in any year.

Body Image

Goal: Children will know a variety of body parts.

Objective: In addition to those learned in earlier years, children will be able to identify the following body parts by touching them or indicating their approximate location if they are internal organs: biceps, triceps, abdominal area, stomach, heart, forearm, sternum and clavicle.

Fitness

Goal: Children will learn fitness information which can apply to their daily lives.

Objective: If asked, at least 80% of the children will be able to indicate the meaning and importance of the following information.

Short-term Effects of Exercise:

1. When peak physical performance is desired, a warm-up which produces sweating is desirable. A warm-up is also necessary if the activity will require all-out muscular activity such as sprinting or broad jumping.
2. To facilitate recovery, a cool-down period should follow strenuous exercise.
3. One should continue to walk after vigorous running so leg muscles can massage the blood from the legs, thus avoiding blood pooling in the legs.
4. Fluids should be taken before, during, and following exercise as needed. During hot weather when large quantities of fluid are lost, an extra eight to sixteen ounces of water should be ingested even after thirst is quenched.
5. Suitable clothing, including proper foot-wear, should be worn during exercise. Rubber suits which hasten weight loss through sweating are extremely dangerous and could cause death under certain circumstances.
6. Judgment must be exercised regarding activity and climate—extreme heat or cold. Fluid loss during heat can lead to heat stroke or exhaustion, and frostbite can occur rapidly to exposed skin in cold weather.
7. Exercising when fatigued significantly increases the likelihood of injury.
8. No safe drug will improve fitness or increase skill performance.
9. Heart rate increases with exercise and will recover within two to three minutes following most exercise bouts.
10. A heart rate of 60% to 80% of the predicted maximum heart rate should be used for

cardiovascular training. For elementary children, this conditioning rate is about 160-170 beats per minute.

11. Muscle soreness will follow within twenty-four hours of an exercise bout which uses unconditioned muscles.

12. Vigorous exercise will produce the following conditions: sweat, increased respiration, decreased appetite, increased need for fluids, and increased body temperature.

Long-term Effects of Exercise:

1. A muscle will grow in size (hypertrophy) with use and decrease in size without use (atrophy).

2. Hormonal differences and body composition preclude the development of muscle definition on a female as compared with a male. Girls need not fear the development of bulging muscles as a result of exercise.

3. The cardiovascular system becomes more efficient with appropriate exercise (chapter 10). A decreased resting heart rate is one noticeable effect of a cardiovascular development program.

4. Weight can be controlled or reduced by combining good nutrition and exercise.

5. Strength and endurance training are activity specific; i.e., training in one activity will have minimal transfer to other activities.

6. Good posture is dependent upon muscle strength.

7. Fitness programs should progress gradually.

8. Fitness will (1) improve the ability to relax and (2) improve health.

Health Knowledge

There is a great deal of health knowledge which a fifth and sixth grader should know, some of which is possible to teach during physical education. Such subjects as the effects of smoking, and use of alcohol and drugs lend themselves to discussion as they relate to physical performance and fitness.

Goal: Children will learn health information as it relates to physical education.

Objective: Children will be able to answer at least 80% of the questions relating to alcohol, drugs, and smoking which were discussed in class. Evaluation can be a written test or oral questioning.

1. There is no *safe* drug which improves physical performance.

2. Alcohol has a detrimental effect on physical performance.

3. Long-term use of alcohol can lead to serious disease.

4. Alcohol is a depressant.

5. Smoking will decrease physical performance, particularly in the area of cardiovascular efficiency.

6. Smoking is related to cancer, emphysema, heart disease, and a number of other debilitating diseases.

EXAMPLE LESSON PLANS FOR CHILDREN TEN TO TWELVE YEAR OF AGE

AGE LEVEL: 10

Multipurpose room

Goal: To develop rhythmic ability.

Objective: By the end of the class each group will have developed a rhythmic routine to the musical selection using the equipment provided.

Activities:	Formation	Time (Minutes)
I. Partner rope jumping	I. Partner in a free formation	5-7
II. Small group rhythmic routines	II. 6-10 per group	15

Using a variety of equipment such as jump ropes, parachute, lummi sticks, wands, streamers, etc., each group will make up a routine to a short musical selection. They must begin and end with the music, and work effectively as a group.

III. Demonstrate Routines	III. Groups	5

Safety: No throwing equipment in II.

AGE LEVEL: 10

Multipurpose room

Goal: Rhythmic development.

Objective: By the end of the class, at least 80% of the children will be able to do the dance without assistance from the teacher.

Activities:	Formation	Time (Minutes)
I. Moving creatively to classical music	I. Free	5-7

Beginning with one body part, have children move to various classical selections. They progress until all children are moving about the room.

II. Dances without partners	II. Depends on situation	15

Select an appropriate dance and teach it to children. Children should be able to do the dance without teacher assistance within fifteen-minute time frame.

III. Chain Tag	III. Free	5-7

Safety: Children may duck under on activity III, but may not break through or try to jump over hands.

AGE LEVEL: 11

Outside or multipurpose room

Goal: To develop batting skills

Activities:	Formation	Time (Minutes)
I. Problem solving exercises	I. Free	5-7

Students are asked to demonstrate exercises in response to such questions as:
1. What is an exercise which will help develop arm strength?
2. What is an exercise which will help develop the heart and lungs?
3. Can you do a flexibility exercise?
   As the students do them, the teacher can select one child's exercise for the entire class to do. The child can be the leader. The teacher continues to give information about what each of the terms means.

II. Batting practice	II. Pairs	13

Children pair up with one plastic bat and several balls (if indoors, yarn balls). Children spread out in the area so as to insure no one will be hit by a bat or ball. If indoors, the batters should be against a wall and hit toward the center of the floor.

III. Must Swing Baseball	III. 12-person teams	7

Safety: Extreme care must be used to keep children spaced.

AGE LEVEL: 11

Outdoors or multipurpose room

Goal: To develop basketball skills

Objective: By the end of the class, at least 80% of the children will be able to do three different types of basketball passes using a junior size ball as discussed in class.

Activities:	Formation	Time (Minutes)
I. Free Dribbling	I. One ball per child	5-7
II. Passing using Guided Discovery	II. Pairs	15-18

    Each pair will have a junior size basketball or similar size ball.

    1. How many different ways can you pass the ball to your partner?

    2. How many ways with two hands? One hand? With one bounce?

    3. How many can do the pass like (name two individuals)?

       Continue to guide students toward a two-handed chest pass, one hand pass, and two and one-hand bounce passes.

III. Count six using any type pass	III. Teams of five	5-7

Safety: No body contact during game and no knocking ball out of person's hand.

REFERENCES AND SUGGESTED READINGS

Graham, G., S. Holt-Hale, and M. Parker. *Children Moving* (3rd ed.). Mountain View: Mayfield Publishing Co. 1998.

Kirchner, G. and G. Fishburne. *Physical Education for Elementary School Children* (9th ed.). Madison: W. C. Brown and Co. 1995.

Nichols, B. *Moving an Learning: The Elementary School Physical Education Experience* (3rd ed.). St. Louis: Mosby Publishing Co. 1994.

Pangrazi, R. and V. Dauer. *Dynamic Physical Education* (11th ed.). Boston: Allyn and Bacon. 1995.

Payne, V. and L. Isaacs. *Human Motor Development* (4th ed.). Mountain View: Mayfield Publishing Co. 1999.

Selective Web Sites

Lesson Plans: http://schools.eastnet.ecu.edu/pitt/ayden/physed8.htm

Omaha Public Schools: http://www.ops.org/pe/elem.html

PE Central: http://pe.cental.vt.edu/

PE Links 4U: http://www.pelinks4u.org/sections/elementary/elementary.htm

SPARK: http://www.acsm.org/

A great search engine: http://www.sparkpe.org/programElementaryPE.jsp?curricula=PhysEdK-2&program=ElementaryPE

12

Quality of Movement

After completing this chapter, the student should be able to:

1. Name and describe the four quality of movement factors.
2. Describe at least two activities which will help develop each of the four movement factors.
3. Develop four activities, one for each of the four movement factors.
4. Develop a thirty-minute lesson which will accomplish a quality of movement objective.
5. Define the key terms listed below.

Key Terms

Force
Level
Quality of movement

Space
Time

A primary purpose of the curriculum for children four to eight years of age is to provide activities which give children experience in every way the body can move using both locomotor and non-locomotor movement. The key elements in this process are the four qualities of movement, force, time, space, and level. *Force* deals with light or heavy movement and can be developed by having the children move like various animals, do creative activities, etc. *Time* means speed, and the teacher can use the tom-tom or music along with other creative activities to help children experience varying locomotor or non-locomotor speeds including very slow movement. *Space* includes both common and personal, and how effectively the child can move in each. With regard to safety, the more important space is common or shared space; children should be able to move even in confined space without bumping into others. They should also experience movement sideways and backwards. Children must also be given the chance to move at all *levels*.

Moving at all levels.

Although the average four-year-old possesses all the basic locomotor (walking, running, hopping, leaping, jumping) and non-locomotor abilities (bending, stretching, twisting, turning, rotating, pushing, pulling), few move very efficiently; and seldom have they experimented with varying their movements, i.e., walking backward or moving at various levels, speeds, and forces. During these early years, the children should also learn to associate the proper terms with the various movements (many adults do not know terminology, i.e., they often jump when they are told to hop).

QUALITY OF MOVEMENT ACTIVITIES

Nearly any movement could be labeled a quality of movement activity, but by focusing the child's attention on the four qualities of movement, an activity can be improved. Both games and developmental activities including rhythms (chapter 16) can be used to promote quality movement. It is the developmental activity, however, that is the best vehicle for improvement.

Developmental Activity

A developmental activity focuses on a specific objective, and has all the children moving all the time. Unlike a game, there are no winners or losers. Activities such as rhythmics, dance, story plays, and exploration are examples of developmental activities. Whenever possible, developmental activities should be used to develop the quality of movement.

Games

Although games should not be the first choice, they can promote quality movement. Games can be teacher or child developed, or an existing

Children need to explore the various levels of movement.

game's rules can be modified to include one or more of the four movement factors (force, time, space, and level). Many games in chapter 18 already include rules which will foster improved movement ability.

Rhythmics

One of the best ways to develop the quality of movement is through the use of creative and structured rhythmic activities. Moving to a tom-tom or to modern or classical music provides numerous opportunities for children to develop movement ability (see chapters 15 and 16).

Games such as Busy Bee have developmental value.

ACTIVITY ORGANIZATION

This chapter is organized into two age groups, four to six years of age and six to eight years of age. Although each activity has an age recommendation, most can be used with either age group. Games, however, are not recommended for the four- and five-year-old children. The following abbreviations are used in the presentation of the activities. Next to each name is whether it is an "activity" or "game."

N	=	Name of the activity
DA	=	Age of the student for which the activity is best suited (developmental age)
DV	=	The developmental value of the activity; i.e., fitness, manipulative ability, etc.
F	=	Formation
E	=	Any equipment needs
D	=	Description of the activity

FOUR TO SIX YEAR OLDS

N: Moving in Common Space to the Tom-Tom - Activity
DA: 4 to 6
DV: Quality of movement
F: Free
E: Tom-Tom (plastic container will work)
D: Children move rhythmically around the area to the beat of the tom-tom. The four qualities of movement should be emphasized by having the children move fast and slow, high and low, forward and backward, and heavy and light. As the activity progresses, the area should be made smaller, and an emphasis placed on moving without touching anyone else.

N: Body Dancing - Activity
DA: 4 to 6
DV: Quality of movement
F: Free
D: Children move body parts to music; they usually begin while children are sitting on the floor but can use a variety of bases of support, i.e., lying down on their front or back, on their knees, or standing. The teacher can say move one body part to the music and then add body parts until the whole body is moving to the music. The teacher could also ask them to do various movements such as bend and stretch a body part to the music and then add other body parts capable of that movement. Forward and backward movement can be requested. Specific body parts can be named or flash cards with body part names can be used. The music can be popular, classical, or any good moving music. The speed of the music should be varied throughout the activity. It is best to have short taped segments of about 15 seconds duration separated by a two to three

second pause to allow the teacher to give new instructions, "Move three body parts; move body parts backward; use only upper (lower) body parts; bend and stretch one body part."

N: The Rope - Activity
DA: 4 - 6
DV: Quality of movement
F: Free
E: Each child has a jump rope or length of cord
D: With their rope, each child makes a loop. They are then instructed to walk, run, hop, skip, or jump around their rope both forward and backward. Then going in and out of their rope in different ways, i.e., hop and jump forward and backward. Then ask the children to move in different ways among the ropes emphasizing the qualities of force, time, space, and level. This activity can also be done to different kinds of music.

N: My Aunt Left Town - Activity
DA: 4 to 6
DV: Quality of movement
F: Free
E: None
D: The teacher chants the phrase "My aunt left town," which is then repeated by the children. The teacher then says "She left like this," at which time the teacher does some movement. The children repeat the line as they also do the movement. The activity is then repeated, allowing a child to determine the movement which all the other children follow.

N: The Winds - Activity
DA: 4 to 6
DV: Quality of movement and creativity
F: Free
E: None
D: Have students move as if it is very windy. Vary the activity by presenting a variety of situations such as the child becoming a piece of dust or a leaf in the wind. The children can also be objects such as a weather vane, car, truck, clothes on a line, or

a boat on the water. Other ideas include being a bird, a ball, a balloon, or an airplane.

N: Abbracadabbra You - Activity
DA: 4 to 6
DV: Quality of movement and creativity
F: Free
E: A magic wand
D: The teacher waves the magic wand while saying "abbra ca dabbra you," followed by something the children are to be such as animals, people, things. The emphasis should be on presenting tasks which help to develop the quality of movement. An example would be "Abbracadabbra you are a big tiger stuck in the mud."

N: Happy Movement - Activity
DA: 4 to 6
DV: Quality of movement and rhythmic ability
F: Free
E: None
D: Using the rhyme "If you are happy and you know it," specify some movement which is done in rhythm to the song. Such things as swing your right arm or your left arm or right leg, hop up and down, etc. can be done. Large muscle movements should be specified and children should be encouraged to suggest new ways to move.

N: Funny Movement - Activity
DA: 4 to 6
DV: Quality of locomotor movement and creativity
F: Free
E: None or record player and record for moving to music
D: Children are given various movement problems which they solve in their own way. For example, "How can you move backward around the room without bumping into anyone?" The quality of locomotor movement, force, time, space, and level is emphasized: "Can you move like a big, heavy animal?" Music may be used to vary speed (time), force, or level.

N: Geometric Shapes - Activity
DA: 4 to 6
DV: Quality of movement
F: Free
E: Pieces of paper with geometric shapes drawn on them
D: Hold up a shape on a flash card and ask the children to move the shape using various locomotor skills such as running, walking, hopping, skipping, etc.; while also emphasizing the quality of movement by doing the skills at various speeds, different forces, in a variety of directions, and at many levels. Music can also be used in this activity. The name of the design, i.e., circle, square, triangle, etc., can also be written on the flash card.

N: Story Plays - Activity
DA: 4 to 6
DV: Quality of movement and cognitive knowledge
F: Free
E: None
D: Story plays can take many themes but the primary purpose is development of the quality of movement (force, time, space, and level) and creativity and problem solving. A secondary purpose is the integration of other subjects such as science, history, and social studies. The teacher's role is to set the theme and develop the story so as to provide considerable movement as the children create solutions and solve problems. Since children will tend to imitate rather than create, the teacher must be careful not to become involved in the movement portion of the story play. Themes include: science—trip to the moon, scuba diving in the ocean, trip to the jungle, spaceship to the planets, growing like a flower or tree; history—the pioneers, traveling west, the Civil War, Christopher Columbus' trip in 1492; social studies—a trip to the farm, being a fireman, a trip to the circus.

N: Five Ways to Get to Timbuktu - Activity
DA: 4 to 6
DV: Movement skills and creativity
F: Free
E: None
D: The teacher suggests a way, such as riding a horse, to get to Timbuktu. Children then imitate the movement. The children then suggest other ways they may get there. The teacher can suggest various barriers encountered along the way such as mountains, rivers, jungles, etc.; and seek suggestions from the children on how they will conquer the obstacles. The problems presented should suggest movements which will help develop the quality of the child's movement, i.e., vary the speed, direction, level, and force of the movement.

N: Leap the Brook - Activity
DA: 4 to 6
DV: Leaping and jumping
F: Free
E: Tape for the floor
D: A brook is taped on the floor. It is narrow at one end and gradually increases in size toward the other end. Children then attempt to leap the brook according to their ability. Depending upon class size, a couple of brooks can be made so all the children can be going at one time. You do not want children standing in line waiting for a turn. Do *not* use ropes to form the brook; children can easily land on the rope and fall on their back or hit their head on the floor.

SIX TO EIGHT YEAR OLDS

N: Story Plays - Activity
DA: 6 to 8
DV: Quality of Movement, and cognitive knowledge
F: Free
E: None
D: See 4 to 6 above

N: Three States of Matter - Activity
DA: 6 to 8
DV: Quality of movement and science knowledge
F: Free
E: None
D: Done similar to a story play. Children are asked to make a snow person; after some time, they are asked to pretend they are the snow person they made. They are then told this is a solid and the first state of matter. Then it begins to get hot and the snow person begins to melt and become the second state of matter, a liquid. After the students have melted to the floor, the heat increases and they slowly become the third state of matter, gas. As they move as gas about the room, tell them to begin forming a cloud by joining together. As it grows colder, they turn into snow flakes and the process begins again.

N: Wagon Wheels - Activity
DA: 6 to 8
DV: Agility
F: Circle of five to six children
E: None
D: The wagon wheel is created by the children making a circle by joining hands. They then roll around the gym by turning in a circle. They can roll against other wheels as long as there is no hard bumping.

N: Streamers - Activity
DA: 6 to 8
DV: Rhythmic development and creativity
F: Free
E: Streamers, record player, and music
D: Streamers can be made with plastic strips or crepe paper. They should be five to six feet long and have a handle of some sort. Children can have one or two streamers which they move in time to the music. The emphasis is on creative movement with the children moving about the room while also moving the streamers. For more creativity and variety, the music can be changed frequently or the children can be asked to do

special things, such as sitting while making the streamer move. Keeping the four qualities of movement in mind, children should be asked to move forward, backward, high, low, fast, slow, light, and heavy. They should also use both the left and right hand to move the streamer.

N: The Maze - Activity
DA: 6 to 8
DV: Spatial awareness and quality of movement
F: Large circle which is clearly marked with objects such as cones, ropes, or pieces of cloth.
E: Markers to define the circle.
D: On the go signal, children move as instructed through the center of the circle without touching anyone. The instructions should emphasize the four qualities of movement - slow, fast, turning, skipping, galloping, high, low, backward, sideward, in slow motion, and slow with eyes closed.

N: Frozen Bean Bag - Activity
DA: 6 to 8
DV: Balance, movement quality, and social interaction
F: Free
E: One beanbag per child and perhaps music
D: Children are asked to balance a beanbag on a specific body part such as the head, and then move about the room in various ways as specified by the teacher. The emphasis should be on the quality of locomotor movement (force, time, space, and level). If a child drops the beanbag, he/she is frozen until someone else places it back on the appropriate body part. The emphasis is on helping others. Music may also be used to guide movement.

N: Ringmaster - Activity
DA: 6 to 8
DV: Quality of movement and creativity
F: Free
E: None

D: The ringmaster cracks the imaginary whip and calls out an animal's name. All the children imitate that animal until a new name is called. If the ringmaster says "Come join the parade," all the children line up and begin the circus parade while imitating anything they might see at the circus. Instead of animals, the ringmaster may call acts such as the high wire act or the clowns which the children then imitate.

N: Bridges and Tunnels - Activity
DA: 6 to 8
DV: Creativity and quality of movement
F: Two groups scattered about the play area
E: None
D: As the groups move freely about the play area the teacher instructs one group to make either a bridge or tunnel. The other group then crosses (jumps over) the bridges or goes through the tunnels. The traveling group can go over or through a number of tunnels until the teacher calls for everyone to begin moving again. Both groups should be given equal opportunity to be the bridges and tunnels. Children should be encouraged to create various types of bridges and tunnels. The means of travel through the tunnels and over the bridges as well as all the movement during the activity should focus on quality of movement.

Bridges and Tunnels

N: Ships and Islands - Activity
DA: 6 to 8
DV: Cooperation and quality of movement

F: Free
E: Hoops
D: Scatter hoops around the play area. Have children do various locomotor movements around and between the hoops. When the teacher yells "shipwreck," children can go to any hoop. There can be any number of people in a hoop. The number of hoops is gradually reduced, requiring teamwork to get everyone inside the remaining hoops. The movement emphasis should be on quality of movement.

Ships and Islands

N: Spot - Game
DA: 6 - 8
DV: Quality of movement
F: Free
E: One beanbag per child less two
D: Beanbags are scattered about the area. The children move about the room as determined by the teacher. The quality of movement should be emphasized—force, time, space, and level—in determining the movement, i.e., walk backward, run heavy, slide, etc. As children move about the room, a signal is given at which time

each child tries to place one foot on a beanbag. There can be only one child per beanbag. Each child who is successful receives one point. After a given amount of time all those with points are declared good movers.

N: Pick Up Colors - Game
DA: 6 to 8
DV: Agility and quality of movement (common space)
F: Free
E: At least thirty pieces of paper (at least four different colors) and paper bags
D: Spread the paper over the play area. Each child is given a bag. When the color is called out, children race around picking up the appropriate colored paper and placing it in their bag. Then the next color is called out and so on until all the paper is picked up. Paper may be picked up in color order only. Children get one point for each piece of paper. Rules should be designed to make almost every child a winner.

N: Frogs - Game
DA: 6 to 8
DV: Movement ability and social interaction
F: Free
E: Hoops
D: The children are designated as frogs and the hoops as lily pads. One child is designated as the eagle which likes to eat frogs. Music is used to get children moving in various ways (quality of movement skills) among the lily pads. When the music stops, the children must hop on one leg to a lily pad without being tagged by the eagle. More than one frog can be on a lily pad. As the game continues, those tagged help the eagle and the number of lily pads is reduced. Eagles may not fly close to the lily pads and frogs are encouraged to see how far they can get away from the lily pads. Frogs are also encouraged to help each other stay on the lily pads. When only three or four frogs are left, they are declared the winners.

N: The Search - Game
DA: 6 to 8
DV: Locomotor movement and social interaction
F: Free
E: None
D: Children are given a piece of paper with a number from one to three. Children must keep their numbers secret. Children then move around the room using various qualities of movement (forward, backward, fast, slow, etc.) until a signal is given. Children then go to one person and tap that person on the shoulder the number of times indicated on their piece of paper. If the other child has the same number, they join hands and travel around the room together as the game begins again. Children may not talk to each other during the game. The next time the signal is given, the search continues, with couples using their free hand to tap others. The game continues until all those with the same number are joined together. The first group together is the winner.

N: Thread the Needle - Activity
DA: 6 to 8
DV: Agility and speed
F: Five to six children per group
E: Marker cones
D: One child is the leader and determines how the children will hook together: holding hands, hands on waist, hands on shoulders, etc.; and they begin moving as a group around the room. On the signal, "change," a new leader quickly takes over and the children hook together in a different way as they move. Emphasis should be placed on hooking together in unusual ways which still allow for the group to move together. Sufficient "changes" should be called to give every child a chance to be the leader.

N: Thread the Needle - Game
DA: 6 to 8
DV: Agility and speed
F: Five to six children per group

E: Marker cones

D: Each group lines up at a starting line. They are given instructions on how they are to join together, hands on waist, hands on shoulders, holding one hand, holding waist facing backward, etc. On the signal to go, each group traveling together goes around a marker cone and back. When the first person in the group crosses the finish line, that group is declared the winner as long as the group has stayed attached throughout the race. As soon as the last person gets across the finish line, the teacher calls out another way to hook together. The groups must get a new leader, hook together as specified, and go again. There is no "go" signal given; once the group is ready, it goes. The teacher should attempt to keep the movement almost continuous once the game begins. Various locomotor skills such as skipping and galloping can be used.

N: Newspaper Race - Game

DA: 6 to 8

DV: Agility and flexibility

Newspaper Race

F: Establish a starting line and a finish line

E: Newspapers

D: Each child is given one page of a newspaper which is then ripped in half. On a go signal, the child races to the finish line by using the paper as stepping stones, constantly stepping on the lead one while retrieving the back one and moving it to the front. The child who gets to the finish line first wins. Children are not allowed to slide the paper along the floor with their feet. A variation would be to have them move backward toward the finish line.

REFERENCES AND SUGGESTED READINGS

Graham, G., S. Holt-Hale, and M. Parker. *Children Moving* (3rd ed.). Mountain View: Mayfield Publishing Co. 1998.

Kirchner, G. and G. Fishburne. *Physical Education for Elementary School Children* (9th ed.). Madison: W. C. Brown and Co. 1995.

Nichols, B. *Moving an Learning: The Elementary School Physical Education Experience* (3rd ed.). St. Louis: Mosby Publishing Co. 1994.

Pangrazi, R. and V. Dauer. *Dynamic Physical Education* (11th ed.). Boston: Allyn and Bacon. 1995.

Selective Web Sites

Lesson Plans: http://schools.eastnet.ecu.edu/pitt/ayden/physed8.htm

Omaha Public Schools: http://www.ops.org/pe/elem.html

PE Central: http://pe.cental.vt.edu/

PE Links 4U: http://www.pelinks4u.org/sections/elementary/elementary.htm

SPARK: http://www.acsm.org/

A great search engine: http://www.sparkpe.org/programElementaryPE.jsp?curricula=PhysEdK-2&program=ElementaryPE

Chapter

13

Body Awareness

By the end of this chapter, the student should be able to:

1. Discuss how body awareness relates to self-concept.
2. Write a lesson plan which accomplishes a body awareness objective.
3. Design a body awareness activity.
4. Define the key terms listed below.

Key Terms

Body awareness
Self-concept

Body awareness is a knowledge of the body, its parts as well as how they function in a variety of movement situations. It includes such things as knowing right from left, the various body parts such as elbows, knees, wrists, etc., and the ability to do locomotor and non-locomotor movement efficiently. Body awareness also comes into play when movement tasks are done in unusual situations, such as when participating in gymnastics and diving. By being aware of their body, children can move more efficiently as well as being successful at many activities.

Body awareness is also important to the development of a positive self-concept. The child must first be aware of his or her body before the self-concept can be fully developed. If the awareness also means more efficient movement and success through activity, it should help the development of a positive self-concept.

Although all movement activities help a child become more aware of his or her body, certain activities seem better than others. This chapter contains only a sample of body awareness activities. The reader should also seek additional ideas from other activity chapters in this book.

As indicated in earlier chapters, a major physical education goal is to give every child the opportunity to experience every way the body can do locomotor and non-locomotor movement. Any body awareness activity, therefore, should provide

Tumbling is among the activities which enhance body awareness.

for maximum participation by everyone. They can be activities or games as long as everyone is participating all the time.

Although body awareness activities play a major role in the four to six and six to eight year old age groups, they are appropriate for all ages. Many of the activities cross over age levels and are successful with all elementary children. Each activity has a grade level recommendation; one should be cautious when presenting an activity to a younger age group when it is recommended for an older age group.

This chapter is organized into three age groups: four to six, six to eight, and eight to ten year old children. As indicated, however, some of the activities are appropriate for the ten to twelve year old age group.

KEY:

N = Name of the activity
DA = Age of the student for which the activity is best suited (developmental age)
DV = The developmental value of the activity; i.e., fitness, manipulative ability, etc.
F = Formation
E = Any equipment needs
D = Description of the activity
S = Safety

FOUR TO SIX YEAR OLDS

N: Hoopla - Activity
DA: 4 to 6
DV: Body awareness, directional terms, and creativity
F: Free
E: One hoop per person
D: Give the children a chance to play with their hoops any way they want. Then pose questions such as: "Can you make a bridge over your hoop? Can you go around your hoop? Can you put your hoop behind you?" Questions should emphasize directional and spatial terms, body parts, and creativity.

N: Carpet Squares - Activity
DA: 4 to 6
DV: Balance, eye-hand, eye-foot coordination
F: Free
E: Carpet squares
D: Using the carpet squares, allow each child to choose his or her own square and

explore with it. After exploring, have the children toss and catch the squares, balance on different body parts, spin on them with feet, knees, hands, bottom, and scoot on them.

N: Newspaper Concepts - Activity
DA: 4 to 6
DV: Body awareness, spatial concepts, and numbers
F: Scattered
E: One piece of paper per child
D: The piece of paper is on the floor (or ground) and the child is asked to move in association with the paper using various spatial concepts such as on, off, near, far, around, next to, away from, front, back, between, on top of, forward, backward, closer, farther, under, and over. Other tasks could include the concepts of right, left, upper, lower, and the numbers from one to ten. The concepts are presented in a questioning form such as: "Can you go around your piece of paper? or Can you face your piece of paper and go around it to the right? or Can you make a bridge over your paper?" At the end, the piece of paper can be balled up and used for manipulative activities including shooting into the basket to the end the activity.

Newspaper activities can be used for body awareness, spatial concepts, and manipulative activities.

N: Hokey Pokey - Activity
DA: 4 to 6
DV: Rhythmic development and knowledge of body parts
F: Circle
E: None
D: Children sing to tune of "Hokey Pokey" and do the action:

You put your right foot in,
You put your right foot out,
You put your right foot in and shake it all about.
You do the hokey pokey as you turn yourself about.
That's what it's all about.

The song continues with various body parts which can be determined by the children or the teacher.

Children learn body parts by doing the Hokey Pokey.

N: Body Parts - Activity
DA: 4 to 6
DV: Body awareness
F: Free
E: None
D: The teacher can either say or sing the following directions which the children follow:

Put your right hand in the air
Put your right hand on your nose
Put your left hand on your head
Now stretch and touch your toes
Put your right hand on your ear
Make your elbow touch your knee
Now pat your tummy three times
And smile so all can see

Body parts can be changed each time the verse is given.

N: Raggedy Ann - Activity
DA: 4 to 6
DV: Body awareness
F: Free
E: A Raggedy Ann doll
D: Children attempt to imitate the Raggedy Ann doll's movement created by the teacher. Relaxation and body awareness are emphasized. Although the primary

201

movements are non-locomotor, the teacher can also simulate locomotor movements which the children follow. The doll should be placed in various support positions such as on her back, stomach, etc., while moving the four limbs. Balance activities can also be encouraged.

N: Angels in the Snow - Activity
DA: 4 to 6
DV: Body awareness
F: Children lie on the floor or grass with lots of room between them
E: None
D: Children move body parts in response to the teacher's directions. When moving the arms, they stay on the floor and slide till they are above the head. The legs stay straight and the feet are slid across the floor until the legs cannot split any further. Directions should be: "Move the right arm, left arm, right leg, left leg, both arms, both legs, the right arm and right leg, the left arm and left leg, the right arm and left leg, the left arm and the right leg, and both arms and both legs."

Children respond to teacher directions in Angels in the Snow.

N: Traffic - Activity
DA: 4 to 6
DV: Body awareness
F: Free
E: One hoop per child
D: The child gets inside the hoop and holds it at waist level. The students then move around the play area pretending to be automobiles and the hoop is a steering wheel. The children are allowed to come close to each other but not touch. They begin by walking and then are allowed to run, skip, gallop, etc. This is also done in different directions, at various levels, and different speeds.

N: Shapes for All - Activity
DA: 4 to 6
DV: Body awareness, flexibility, and creativity
F: Free
E: Flash cards containing words, shapes, and pictures
D: Children are asked to use their bodies to interpret what they see on the flash card. Children hold a static pose until the flash card is changed.

N: Body Balance - Activity
DA: 5 to 8
DV: Balance
F: Free
E: None
D: Have children explore different ways to balance by asking questions such as: "Without doing a headstand or handstand, can you balance on two body parts? Two different body parts? One body part? Which is easier two body parts or one body part? How many different body parts can you balance on?"

N: Object Balance - Activity
DA: 5 to 8
DV: Body awareness
F: Partners
E: One balloon or beach ball for every two children
D: Two children try to hold the object between them in many different ways without using hands or arms. While balancing the object the children are encouraged to move in different ways around the area, forward, backward, high, low, fast and slow. Seven and eight year old children can do this activity in small groups.

N: Balance Beam - Activity
DA: 4 to 8
DV: Balance
F: One to two children per low beam
E: Eight foot long 2" x 4" boards are laid on the floor on the wide side to provide a four inch beam for the children.

D: Various tasks such as walking forward, backward, sideward, hopping on one foot, turns, jumps, etc. can be presented.

SIX TO EIGHT YEAR OLDS

N: Traffic Jam - Activity
DA: 6 to 8
DV: Eye-foot coordination, group cooperation
F: Anywhere along the designated line
E: Yarn or sponge balls, whistle, red and green rubber rings
D: Instructor sets up a system of city streets by chalking single lines on the pavement or by taping the gym floor. Include many intersections, curvy roads, and straight-aways. Also set red and green rings at several intersections designating which "drivers" are to stop and yield. To begin the activity, children find spots anywhere on the road (encourage children to spread out), and when a signal is given, the balls are gently and slowly kicked (to roll), along the lines. The children can travel anywhere within the city as long as they stay on the lines and observe the stop signs. At an intersection with a "red light," the child must stop his/her ball with the foot and wait for a clear road. The instructor can start and stop the traffic by blowing the whistle.

Use no balls; instead have children hop, jump, walk forward or backward, tip-toe, etc. A child can play the role of "policeman" by blowing the whistle or ticketing those drivers who fail to stop at stop lights.

N: Human Pretzel - Activity
DA: 6 to 8
DV: Body awareness
F: Free
E: None, although flash cards can be used to integrate the activity with language arts.
D: Children are told to pretend they are a pretzel and bend themselves in many ways using various body parts. They can be asked to touch their ear to their shoulder or cheek to shoulder, or nose to knee. Each time, two body parts are used. To integrate the activity with language arts, flash cards with the names of the body parts can be used.

N: The Tar Pit - Activity
DA: 6 to 8
DV: Body awareness, non-locomotor movement, flexibility and balance
F: Free
E: One hoop per child
D: Tell the children their feet are stuck in a tar pit inside their hoop and they cannot move. The teacher then asks the children to do non-locomotor movements such as bending, stretching, twisting and turning. The activities can be varied by suggesting that only one foot is stuck or having the hands stuck and moving only the feet.

N: Beanbag Balance - Activity
DA: 6 to 8
DV: Coordination, balance, agility
F: Standing in a small working space
E: Beanbags
D: Each child is given one beanbag. The teacher calls out different activities that the child is to perform with the beanbag.
1. Place beanbag on head and hop, turn around in a circle, slide two steps to the right, slide two steps to the left, bend your knees, sit down, stand up, etc.
(Note: Beanbag may be placed on other parts of the body.)
2. Pass beanbag to another
a) clap hands between passes
b) turn between passes
3. Place beanbag on foot, kick it up, and catch it with hands, etc.

N: Newspaper - Activity
DA: 6 to 8
DV: Body awareness, basic locomotor skills, balancing, eye-hand coordination
F: Free
E: Piece of newspaper for each child
D: Each child must have a space. The teacher gives different commands for the children to follow using their own newspaper. Examples: "Put one body part on the paper. Can you put two, three, or four body parts on the paper? Make yourself as small as possible on your paper. Can you go around your paper? Try another way to go around it." After the children have had several minutes to explore, tell them to put one hand behind their backs.

With the free hand crumble the newspaper into a ball. "Now, can you balance the ball on different body parts? Can you toss it lightly and catch it?" etc. Continue with these commands and then have the children clean up by tossing the ball at the target (trash can). Provide two trash cans to prevent waiting.

N: Put Hands - Activity
DA: 6 to 8
DV: Body awareness
F: Standing, seated, or scattered
E: None
D: A leader is chosen and stands in front of the class. He or she gives verbal directions trying to confuse the class by doing something else. For example, the child might say "Put your hands on top of your head." The leader might put his/her own hands on top of his/her shoulders. Children who make an error have a point scored against them. Lots of directions could be given to which the leader should make other movements. Examples: "Put your hands on shoulders (toes, head, chest, knees, elbows, etc.). Reach out to the side, front, back, high. Put your right hand (or left) above your shoulder, behind back."

N: Head, Shoulders, 1, 2, 3 - Activity
DA: 6 to 8
DV: Body image
F: Scattered
E: None
D: This activity can be spoken or sung. The children will be able to learn the words of the activity quickly and say them with the teacher.
Say "Head, Shoulders, Baby 1, 2, 3"
(Touch head, then shoulders, clap hands on 1, 2, 3)
   "Head, Shoulders, Baby 1, 2, 3
   Head, Shoulders
   Head, Shoulders
   Head, Shoulders, Baby 1, 2, 3"
Continue naming body parts in sequence until you name the toes. Then you may reverse and move up the body ("toes, ankles, Baby 1, 2, 3") or you may make up odd combinations such as "eyes, belly button, Baby 1, 2, 3."
You may vary the speed of this activity.

Working together to learn body parts.

N: Sticky Popcorn
DA: 6 to 8
DV: Body awareness
F: Begin in free position
E: Works well with music
D: Children begin sitting or lying on the floor pretending they are popcorn kernels. The music represents the heat. As the music grows louder, children begin to move as if being heated. Then children begin jumping around the room connecting onto others by touching them, i.e., shoulder to shoulder, back to back, etc. This continues until all the children are jumping together. The music volume is slowly turned down and children again return to the floor.

N: Balance Beaming
DA: 6 to 8
DV: Body awareness and balance
F: One child per beam
E: 4 or 5 eight-inch high balance beams in a station arrangement

D: Using a station arrangement, each child at the station has a balance beam upon which to walk. Children walk forward, backward, and sideward on the beam. They also attempt to get very low and walk forward and backward. Attempts to turn using a spin on one foot move is also encouraged. Jumping up slightly off the beam and landing while keeping balance is another stunt. Children can also balance on one foot in different ways.

EIGHT TO TEN YEAR OLDS

N: Body Dancing - Activity
DA: 8 to 10
DV: Body awareness, creativity, and rhythmic development
F: Free
E: Record player and music
D: Ask the children to use various body parts to dance to the music. They could start out with one body part and work up to many. This is good for any age group and is a particularly good way to get older children into creative rhythmic movement. The activity can begin with children sitting and then lying. Eventually, children can be on their feet using their whole body moving around the room to the music. Although modern music can be used, a better choice is classical music with its many tempo and force changes.

N: Obstacle Course - Activity
DA: 8 to 10
DV: Depends upon the course
F: Follow the leader
E: Depends on the obstacle course
D: Obstacle courses can take many forms and be of varying difficulty depending upon the age and ability of the children. The course can use playground equipment and/or small equipment such as ropes and hoops. In designing the course, it should be of sufficient size to allow children to spread out along the course so everyone can begin at the same time. Then everyone must follow the leader with the leader returning to the beginning when reaching the end. The path could be clearly marked and there should be no point where children must wait for a turn; it should provide for continuous movement.

N: Double Walk - Activity
DA: 8 to 10
DV: Cooperation
F: Partners
E: None
D: The first child stands on his/her partner's feet facing him/her. Partners grasp one another's upper arms. As the one child walks forward, the other shifts his/her weight from side to side in synchrony with the partner's movement. Partners can also stand back to back, elbows locked. One then tries to walk forward while the other must walk backward.

N: Spider Walk - Activity
DA: 8 to 10
DV: Body awareness and teamwork
F: Students in a straight line front to back
E: None
D: The first child takes a sitting position with his/her back against a wall. The next child gently sits on the first child's lap. Others continue to sit on the previous person's lap. Children then grasp the waist of the person in front of them. Walking is done by all children moving the same leg at the same time.

N: Standing Together - Activity
DA: 8 to 10
DV: Body awareness and teamwork
F: Students sitting back to back
E: None
D: Two children sitting back to back with their elbows linked together attempt to push against each other and stand up. Larger groups can be made by adding additional children. See how many children can simultaneously stand up by pushing against each other's back.

N: Caterpillar - Activity
DA: 8 to 10
DV: Body awareness and teamwork
F: Groups of 3
E: 2 eight-foot mats for each group
D: One child gets on his/her hands and knees; the next child gets in front and links his/her legs around the other child's head; finally, the third child gets in front of the other two and takes the same position as the second child. Once linked, the three try to move down the mat without coming apart.

N: Knots - Activity
DA: 8 to 10
DV: Body awareness and teamwork
F: Circle of about eight children
E: None
D: Each child in the circle joins his/her hands with others in the circle but not the person next to them or both hands to the same person. Once all hands are joined, children attempt to untangle their knot without letting go of any hand. The object is to end up in a circle; it does not matter which way a child is facing when the circle is completed.

N: Turtle - Activity
DA: 8 to 10
DV: Cooperation
F: Groups of about seven or eight
E: Large mats or blankets
D: A group of seven or eight children get on their hands and knees under the "turtle shell" (a mat) and try to move in one direction. At first the children may move in different directions, causing the mat to become unbalanced and fall off. Before long, it will become apparent to them that they must move together. The turtle can then move backwards, sidewards, etc. on cue. They can also try to manipulate an obstacle course.

In Turtle, children must move together.

N: Apparatus - Activity
DA: 8 to 10
DV: Body awareness and fitness
F: Divided among equipment
E: Various pieces of gymnastic equipment
D: Gymnastics—Apparatus
  1. Balance beam—8" high beam
     Jump up and touch heels.
     Jump and make a half turn.
     Pass another person without falling off.

Make a full spin on one foot.
Leap from one foot to the other.
Do a cartwheel off.
Do a round-off dismount.
  2. Vaulting
    (a) *Front vault*—front of the body passes over box. The right hand is placed on the near side of the box and the left is directly opposite on the far side. The feet stay together and the child lands facing sideways. The side of the body is next to the box. A lead-up is done by having children vaulting to a push-up position on box.
    (b) *Flank vault*—the side of the body passes over the box. Both hands are placed on the near side of the box and the feet are thrown out to one side or the other. The hand on the side where the feet must pass over is lifted and the weight is placed on one hand. The position is a side lean. The side of the body passes over the box, and the child ends up facing the same direction he/she was traveling with back to the box. A lead-up activity is to have the children vault to the top of the box in a side learning position.
    (c) *Squat vault*—the feet are squatted and passed between the hands which are placed in the middle of the box. Vaulter ends up facing away from the box.
  3. Rings
    (a) Inverted hang
    (b) Bird's nest
    (c) Skin the cat
  4. Ropes
    (a) *Climbing.* Children should not be allowed to climb the rope until they demonstrate the ability to descend correctly. Limitations should also be set for the height which they can climb. They should not be allowed to go higher than ten feet off the ground.
    (b) *Descending.* Children must be able to release from the climbing

position and assume the descending technique before being allowed to climb.

(c) *Two Ropes.* Two ropes closely spaced together can be used to do the same tricks as those listed under rings.

N: Tumbling - Activity
DA: 8 to 10
DV: Body awareness
F: On mats
E: Mats
D: Tumbling
1. Handstand with spotter.

Place hands shoulder-width apart with fingers straight ahead. Move shoulders over hands. Assume a push-up position with the rest of the body but draw one knee up under chest. Kick straight leg up to spotter while keeping head up with eyes looking straight down at mat. Slide other leg up beside the other.
2. Cartwheel

Lead-up—Place one hand on mat. Keep eyes on hand while jumping feet "around the corner." The second hand is placed down as the child jumps.

Learn the headstand prior to trying a handstand.

Lead-up—stand sideways and do full cartwheel with spotter.

Final—stand facing straight ahead. Kick as if going into a handstand but turn hand just before it touches mat and do a cartwheel.
3. Round-off

Must be able to do a cartwheel first. Trick begins as cartwheel but at vertical position, feet are brought together while lower part of body (feet, legs, and hips) makes a quarter turn. The feet are then snapped down and the individual ends up facing the directions from which he/she came.

N: Ring Around the Group - Activity or can be made into a game
DA: 8 to 12
DV: Body awareness and teamwork
F: Groups of three or four, or if multiple number of hoops are used, the groups could be larger.
E: One or more hoops depending upon the size of the group
D: Three children join hands with one hoop hanging from two joined hands. Children then attempt to see how quickly they can get the hoop around the circle while keeping their hands joined. Larger groups can be used as long as there are several hoops in the group. The idea is to keep everyone active. This can be made into a game by seeing what group can get the hoop around the quickest.

N: Stitcharu - Game
DA: 8 to 10
DV: Body awareness and teamwork
F: Relay formation with about three or four lines of six or seven children per line holding one hand to form a chain.
E: 30 hoops
D: Each line starts off with an equal number of hoops. On the go signal, the first hoop is maneuvered down the line. As soon as the first hoops moves to the second person, the first person picks up another hoop and starts it down the line. When the hoop gets to the end it is dropped to the ground. The first group to get all their hoops to the other end wins.

REFERENCES AND SUGGESTED READINGS

Graham, G., S. Holt-Hale, and M. Parker. *Children Moving* (3rd ed.). Mountain View: Mayfield Publishing Co. 1998.

Kirchner, G. and G. Fishburne. *Physical Education for Elementary School Children* (9th ed.). Madison: W. C. Brown and Co. 1995.

Nichols, B. *Moving an Learning: The Elementary School Physical Education Experience* (3rd ed.). St. Louis: Mosby Publishing Co. 1994.

Pangrazi, R. and V. Dauer. *Dynamic Physical Education* (11th ed.). Boston: Allyn and Bacon. 1995.

Selective Web Sites

Lesson Plans: http://schools.eastnet.ecu.edu/pitt/ayden/physed8.htm
Omaha Public Schools: http://www.ops.org/pe/elem.html
PE Central: http://pe.cental.vt.edu/
PE Links 4U: http://www.pelinks4u.org/sections/elementary/elementary.htm
SPARK: http://www.acsm.org/
A great search engine: http://www.sparkpe.org/programElementaryPE.jsp?curricula=PhysEdK-2&program=ElementaryPE

14

Manipulative Activities and Games

By the end of this chapter, the student should be able to:

1. Give five examples of manipulative activities.

2. Design a manipulative activity or game.

3. Develop a lesson plan with a manipulative objective.

4. Define the key terms listed below.

Key Terms

Manipulative ability
Manipulative equipment
Teaching style

Manipulative activities are those in which an object is controlled by some body part or parts. Although most people think manipulative is synonymous only with hand-eye and foot-eye coordination, the word implies much more. In dance and sports, various body parts are used to manipulate objects such as balls and hoops. During soccer, for example, the head and body are extensively used to both stop and propel the ball. In rhythmic gymnastics, nearly every body part is used to manipulate a ball, a hoop, and a ribbon.

THE WHY

Although physical education's purpose is not the development of athletes, many daily activities, including sports, require the manipulation of objects. In order to develop a well-rounded individual, therefore, manipulative ability should be developed. The purpose of manipulative activities varies according to the child's age and experience. A worthy objective for four- to eight-year-old children is to give the child the opportunity to experience every way his or her body can manipulate objects. This can be accomplished through exploration during creative activities, rhythmics, and problem-solving activities. For older children, eight to twelve years of age, sports skills can and should be developed.

Both the head and the body are used in soccer.

THE HOW

Initially, an indirect teaching approach using questions should be used. By asking questions such as "How many ways can you throw and catch the ball? or How many ways can you dribble the ball?," the teacher can observe the children's ability level, and guide the students accordingly. For many children this is all that is needed; through trial and error as well as imitation, many children will learn the basic skills of throwing, catching, kicking, and striking. Others may need a more direct approach including explanation/demonstration or manipulation. Even with those needing a more direct approach, the initial approach should have the children responding to problem-solving questions. The teacher can then determine where the children are developmentally, and go from there.

EQUIPMENT

The object to be manipulated is determined by ability and purpose. Large, soft objects are appropriate for the younger, less skilled children. If the purpose is to develop the ability to handle small objects, care must be taken to insure the object selected will not injure the child when missed. Beanbags, yarn balls, plastic balls, and low density sponge balls are safe equipment to use with four- to six-year-old children. As the children grow older—nine to twelve years of age—and the skill level increases, tennis balls, softballs, and other small equipment can be used according to the objective. When dribbling skills are desired, playground balls work well, but caution must be exercised; playground balls can cause injuries as well as damage glasses. Large playgrounds

A 16" playground ball can cause a ballance problem.

Sponge balls are safe.

For safety, use plastic bats and balls.

balls, 13" and larger, can knock over younger children and when carried, a 16" playground ball can raise the four to six year old's center of gravity causing instability.

Sponge Balls

The 7" to 10" low density sponge rubber ball (uncoated) is an extremely versatile object which eliminates problems associated with playground balls while still helping a child develop manipulative ability. It is lightweight; large enough to be caught successfully; can be safely hit, kicked, and thrown inside and out; and can even be used in a limited indoor space. Older children can use it to develop volleyball skills, and many balls can safely be used simultaneously to increase participation. The only drawback is the effect wind has on the ball. It works much better indoors but can be used outdoors on non-windy days.

The 7" to 10" high density sponge (uncoated) ball is very effective when teaching sport skills such as soccer, volleyball or basketball to older children.

Although it looks nearly identical to the low density ball, it is much better in windy situations and will bounce well off the floor or body parts.

Striking Instruments

Numerous sports require children to strike an object with another object, i.e., tennis, baseball, badminton, and hockey. Using such striking instruments requires extremely well-developed hand-eye coordination, and increases safety problems; striking objects can cause injuries. Most striking sports, therefore, should be reserved for eight- to twelve-year-old children, and then only under strict safety guidelines. Plastic baseball bats should be used during skill development and only during a controlled game should a regular bat be used. Only the batter may have a bat in hand; no one may warm-up with a bat while waiting his or her turn to bat. All other striking instruments should be lightweight or plastic. Children six to eight can use plastic hockey sticks during individual exploration activities, but should not use them for competitive games. When older children are using hockey sticks in a competitive situation, they should wear plastic eye guards.

ACTIVITY ORGANIZATION

This chapter is organized by age levels: four to six, six to eight, eight to ten, and ten to twelve, and is a mixture of developmental activities and games; the designation can be found immediately following the name of the activity or game. As the age recommendation indicates, many of the activities may be offered at more than one age level. The reader is also encouraged to modify activities and create new ones to help individualize instruction based upon a particular situation.

Each entry is designated as an activity or a game.

KEY:

N = Name of the activity or game

DA = Age of the student for which the activity is best suited (developmental age)

DV = The developmental value of the activity; i.e., fitness, manipulative ability, etc.

F = Formation

E = Any equipment needs

D = Description of the activity

S = Safety

FOUR TO SIX YEAR OLDS

N: Balloon Keep It Up - Activity

DA: 4 to 6

DV: Manipulative ability

F: Free

E: One balloon per child

D: A balloon is blown up for each child (children should not be allowed to blow up their own balloons). Children are then encouraged to see how many body parts they can use to keep the balloon in the air. They can also be encouraged to move around the room while keeping the balloon in the air and not bumping into anyone else.

Children of all ages enjoy Balloon Keep It Up.

N: Traffic Jam - Activity

DA: 4 to 6

DV: Manipulative ability

F: Anywhere along the designated course

E: Marker cones, ropes, containers, and one playground ball per child

D: A road course is designed on the blacktop or in the gym using marker cones, ropes, containers or chalk. The children then dribble the ball with their hand staying on the course. At intersections, they must stop or yield to others while maintaining control of their ball. The speed of travel can be designated by the child. No contact is allowed between children. The teacher can use colored cardboard to signal green light to go, red light to stop, or yellow light to slow the children down. If the children are good enough, an alternate activity is to use the same course but have the children dribble the ball with their feet.

N: Hoop Around - Activity

DA: 4 to 6

DV: Manipulative ability

F: Free

E: One hoop per child

D: Have children explore different ways to move their hoop. The activity can begin by asking, "How many ways can you make the hoop go around your body? Can you make the hoop go around while moving around the room? Forward, backward, sideward? How low can you be and make the hoop go around? What else can you do with your hoop?"

N: Hit the Bucket - Activity or Game

DA: 4 to 6

DV: Eye-hand coordination

F: Partners

E: Baskets (trash cans) and small rubber ball or yarn balls

D: As an activity, children try to throw their object into a bucket. They are encouraged to throw the object in different ways, i.e., one hand, the other hand, both hands, facing the target, back to the target, etc. They are also encouraged to try it from varying distances.

To make it a game, have one bucket for each set of partners and one ball for each student. Partners stand on opposite sides of the buckets and take turns tossing the ball into the basket. Students begin tossing the ball into the basket from a distance close to the basket and take a step back with each successful throw. Encourage children to use different ways to throw the object. When a child is successful, the other child must throw it the same way. Each time a child is successful, they get a point. After a given amount of time or when a certain number of points are scored, the child with the most points wins.

N: Ring Toss - Activity or Game
DA: 4 to 6
DV: Eye-hand coordination
F: Scattered
E: Deck tennis rings, stands
D: The child attempts to throw the ring on the target. Children should be encouraged to throw the object in different ways, i.e., one hand, the other hand, both hands, facing the target, back to the target, etc. They are also encouraged to try it from varying distances.

  As a game, two children compete with each other to see who can score the most points using various ways of throwing from various distances.

N: Tire or Hoop Targets - Activity or Game
DA: 4 to 6
DV: Eye-hand coordination
F: Partners
E: Yarn balls, rope, or cord fastened between two posts about shoulder high, several bike tires hung on the rope
D: Partners stand on opposite sides of hanging tires behind restraining lines five, ten, fifteen, and twenty feet from the tires. Practice tossing back and forth through tires from five-foot line. If successful, move on to the next line. "How many times can you get the ball through the tire at each line?"

N: Can You? - Activity
DA: 4 to 6
DV: Any
F: Free
E: See description
D: Although listed here as an activity, this is actually a teaching style. The style is determined by the type of question asked. If the question has a multitude of possible responses which allow each child to answer at his/her own ability level, the style is problem solving—i.e., "How many ways can you throw and catch the ball?" If a specific answer is required, it is command—i.e., "Can you throw and catch the ball with your right hand?" The problem-solving approach is preferred in most situations. The exception is when exploration could lead to injury—i.e., "How many ways can you tumble on the mat?" Nearly every activity, however, can use the questioning approach to teaching.

SIX TO EIGHT YEAR OLDS

N: Crumple and Toss - Game
DA: 6 to 8
DV: Hand-eye coordination
F: Two or more circles or squares with defined boundaries
E: Lots of newspapers
D: On the go signal, the children crumple a sheet of newspaper and attempt to shoot it into a box or trash can in the center of the area. If unsuccessful, the child retrieves the paper, returns to the line and tries again. If successful, the child gets another piece of paper and continues. After a given amount of time as determined by the teacher, those with a selected number of points are declared the winners. The game can then begin again using a different skill such as using the non-dominant hand, throwing underhand only, throwing with the back turned to the target, etc.

N: Ball Merriment - Activity
DA: 6 to 8
DV: Manipulative ability
F: Free
E: One playground ball per person
D: Each child explores how many different ways he or she can move their ball. The teacher challenges the children with questions such as "How many ways can you dribble the ball? How many different body parts can you use to dribble the ball? How many body parts can you make the ball go around? How many ways can you throw and catch the ball? How many ways can you move and dribble your ball? Can you be low and dribble the ball? Can you be on your feet and dribble the ball low?" These are just a few examples of questions to get children to explore every way they can manipulate the ball with and around their body as well as exploring various ways to move with the

ball. Children should be encouraged to move at various speeds, at different levels, use varying force, and move many ways through space. Children should also be encouraged to use the non-dominant side of their body while exploring. Kicking or punting the ball or other activities which might cause injuries to other children or damage to school property must be avoided.

N: Body Ball - Activity
DA: 6 to 8
DV: Manipulative ability
F: Free
E: One sponge ball per child
D: Using sponge balls only, children are encouraged to manipulate the ball using every possible body part with encouragement to kick the ball, throw it hard, hit it hard, and hit various targets. Unlike the playground ball activities which must be carefully controlled to avoid injuries, the sponge ball can be used safely in most any situation. Punting and kicking are even possible in fairly confined spaces, although one must be careful of flying feet. In selecting targets, children particularly like those which fall when hit or are otherwise self-testing type activities. A good example of a self-testing activity which children enjoy is shooting balls at a basketball hoop.

N: Human Bowling - Game
DA: 6 to 8
DV: Hand-eye coordination and agility
F: Two teams on opposite sides of the play area
E: One yarn ball per child
D: The indoor play area is divided by a line (tape). On the go signal, children must throw the yarn ball underhand in a bowling motion and roll them across the floor at the opposite team. Each time a child hits the feet of another child he/she gets one point. After a time, the children with the most points are declared the best bowlers.

N: Beanbag Horse - Game
DA: 6 to 8
DV: Manipulative skill
F: Pairs

E: One beanbag per child and a number of trash cans or boxes to serve as targets.
D: Targets such as boxes or trash cans are placed around the area. Pairs of children then play the basketball game of horse using the targets as baskets. Children must stay at least a certain distance away from the target as designated by a restraining line. One child then attempts a shot at the basket using any body part to propel the beanbag. If the beanbag goes into the target, the partner must exactly duplicate the shot. If unsuccessful, the partner receives an "h." The first child to receive the letters "h - o - r - s - e" loses the game.

N: Boccie Beanbag - Game
DA: 6 to 8
DV: Eye-hand coordination
F: Scattered in pairs
E: One sponge ball for each child and one beanbag for each pair
D: One member of each pair is to toss the beanbag out in front of them. They alternate who throws the beanbag and the distance thrown is the choice of the thrower. Then the two players simultaneously roll their ball to see which ball stops the closest to the beanbag. The child whose ball stops closest to the beanbag gets a point. The player at the game's end with the most points is the winner.

N: Bull's-Eye - Activity
DA: 6 to 8
DV: Eye-hand coordination
F: Free
E: Chalk drawn circles or Hula-Hoops, 2 bean bags per child
D: A circle twelve inches in diameter is drawn for each child or a Hula-Hoop can be used. Each child is given two beanbags and begins by standing about 5 feet away from the target. The child tosses the beanbags into the circle. With each successful toss, the child takes a step back and tries tossing from a distance farther away from the circle. Children are encouraged to toss the beanbag in different ways and with different body parts.

N: Moon Shot - Activity
DA: 6 to 8
DV: Hand-eye coordination
F: Circle around a target
E: Two beanbags per child
D: Basically the same as Bull's-Eye above, but children make their beanbag go into a trash can or similar object. If successful, they move out a predetermined distance for their next shot. Each time they hit the target, they move farther out. Some type of visual markers such as cones can be used to help students establish their distance from the target. They could also use one of the beanbags to mark their progress.

N: Object Race - Game
DA: 6 to 8
DV: Agility
F: Children lined up on long starting line
E: One beanbag per child
D: On the go signal, children race to a line on the opposite side of the play area where the beanbags have been spread out across the line. They pick up one and race back to the starting line. The first child back is the winner.

N: Racket Fun - Activity
DA: 6 to 8
DV: Hand-eye coordination
F: Free
E: Some type of racket such as a nylon hanger racket and a lightweight ball
D: Each child is given a racket and ball. The racket can be cheaply and easily made by taking a coat hanger and pulling it into the shape of an elongated diamond. An old nylon is then pulled tightly over it and secured at the handle to form a racket. A yarn ball or small sponge ball is then hit up and down or back and forth with a partner.

N: Small Fun - Activity
DA: 6 to 8
DV: Manipulative ability
F: Free
E: One or two objects per person. Objects can be any non-injurious small piece of equipment which will aid the development of manipulative ability. These objects include balloons, beanbags, yarn balls, plastic softballs, etc.

D: Each child manipulates one or two small objects either alone or with a partner. In selecting the object, it must be kept in mind that the hand-eye coordination of children is not well developed, and they may frequently miss the object. As long as they have more success than failure, and the object will not hurt them if missed, they should be encouraged to see how many ways they can manipulate the object. Small object manipulation should be done after children have had considerable experience with larger objects such as 8" sponge rubber balls.

Yarn balls may be used in small groups.

N: Scoop It - Activity
DA: 6 to 8
DV: Hand-eye coordination
F: Free
E: Scoops and balls
D: Each child is given a scoop and ball. The scoop can be made from a plastic container and balls can be small sponge balls or tennis balls. Children then throw and catch the balls alone or with a partner. Children can be motivated in several ways: seeing who can throw the ball the highest and catch it; seeing how many times partners can throw and catch the ball without a miss; or seeing how many ways they can move and still throw and catch the ball. Targets can also be introduced to increase motivation.

Handmade scoops may be used in Scoop It.

N: Throw and Go - Game
DA: 6 to 8
DV: Manipulative ability and running
F: Students standing on a straight line side by side
E: One ball per child
D: On the go signal, each child throws the ball straight ahead as far as possible. Each thrower then runs to retrieve any ball except the one he or she threw. The first player back to the starting line is the winner.

N: Cleaning Out the Backyard - Game
DA: 6 to 8
DV: Hand-eye and foot-eye coordination
F: Class is divided in half with each occupying half the play area. They are divided by a fence of marker cones which they may not cross during play.
E: One low density sponge rubber ball or yarn ball per child and marker cones
D: Each child begins with a sponge rubber ball or yarn ball (no substituting playground balls) which, on the go signal, is thrown over the fence into the other team's area. The object is to have more balls in the opposing team's area when the stop signal is given. Balls may be thrown, kicked, or hit in order to get them onto the other side of the fence. After a winner is determined, the teams switch sides quickly and play begins again.
S: Only low density sponge rubber balls or yarn balls can be used in this activity.

N: Partner Ball - Activity
DA: 6 to 8
DV: Manipulative ability
F: Partners freely scattered about the play area
E: A ball for each group—the type of ball depends on the age and purpose of the lesson
D: The children see how many ways they can throw and catch the ball with their partner. Any body part can be used. They can also be asked how many ways they can bounce the ball to a partner. Balls may vary in size with 8 1/2" playground balls for the young children to softball size balls for the older ones.

Sponge rubber balls are used in "Cleaning Out the Backyard."

N: Juggling - Activity
DA: 6 to 8
DV: Manipulative Ability
F: Free
E: Three scarves per child
D: Children begin by tossing and catching one scarf with each hand then alternating hands. Another scarf is added and children alternately catch two scarves in one hand and then the other hand. Eventually the third scarf is added. As an example, juggling begins by holding two scarves in the right hand and one in the left. One of the right hand scarves is thrown in to the air followed by the one in the left hand. As the one which was first tossed by the right hand is caught by the left hand, the second one in the right hand is tossed up. The empty right hand then catches the one which was tossed by the left. This motion of tossing the scarves into the air continues with an under, under motion. The child should be taught to keep their eyes on the highest scarf that is in the air.

N: Crab Soccer - Game
DA: 6 to 8
DV: Muscular strength
F: Class divided in half inside the gym or multipurpose room
E: Several 7" or 10" low density sponge rubber balls
D: Children assume the crab position which is sitting with hands behind their back. The objective is for a team to try and kick the ball over the end line behind the opposing team. The ball may be hit only with the feet or head. Play is continuous with several balls going at a time. Each time a ball is scored a member of the team which was scored upon must retrieve the ball and give it to the teacher who puts it back into play. When one team has scored five points, it is the winner and the game begins again. Players may go anywhere on the floor they wish after the game begins. All players, however, must be on their side of the field at the beginning of each game.
S: Children must keep both hands on the floor behind them when kicking the ball. They are not permitted to roll onto their back or side to attempt a kick. Squeez-

ing the ball between or under their feet and then attempting to advance it is not permitted. Only low density sponge rubber balls are allowed when playing with several balls at one time.

EIGHT TO TEN YEAR OLDS

N: Keep Away - Game
DA: 8 to 10
DV: Hand-eye coordination
F: Groups of three
E: One ball per group
D: Two children stand across from each other with one child between them. The object is for the center child to touch or intercept the ball as it is passed between the two players. If touched, the thrower takes the place of the person in the middle. The ball may be passed in any manner but may not go higher than the center person could reach. The center person must play aggressively by attempting to touch the ball while in the throwers' hands or just after it leaves their hands. The center person may not station him/herself near the receiver waiting for the ball to be thrown. Throwers must also stay in approximately the same place and not move to their left or right.

Keep away is an excellent activity for hand-eye coordination.

N: Beanbag Dribble - Activity
DA: 8 to 10
DV: Hand-eye coordination and dribbling skills
F: Partners
E: One playground ball or other type ball which can be dribbled plus one beanbag per child
D: Staying with their partner, children dribble around the area taking turns being the

leader. The leader determines how the ball is to be dribbled as well as what body part upon which the beanbag must be balanced. Then they throw and catch one beanbag while each dribbles his/her ball. Emphasis should be placed on practicing with both hands during the entire activity.

N: Creative Throw and Catch - Activity
DA: 8 to 10
DV: Manipulative ability
F: Partners
E: One object per pair
D: Children work as partners to see how many creative ways they can throw and catch an object such as a beanbag or ball. The person throwing establishes the manner in which the object must be thrown, and the receiver determines the catching style. The partner must duplicate what the other did. Encouragement is given by the teacher to attempt many various throwing and catching styles using numerous body parts. The partner only has to duplicate his/her partner's actions if the partner is successful. The throw must be accurate enough so the partner does not have to move more than one step to catch it.

N: Old Plug - Game
DA: 8 to 10
DV: Agility
F: Three children form a horse by grabbing each other's waist while one child stands in the front of the group and acts as the farmer. This activity can be played inside or out.
E: One beanbag for every group of four children
D: The purpose of the activity is for the farmer to hit the tail of the horse with the beanbag which is a "needle" for sick Old Plug. Old Plug may be sick but he is no dummy and he knows a needle when he sees one, so he tries to keep the farmer away from his tail which is the only place the farmer can put the needle. The needle, fortunately for the farmer, can be thrown. If it hits the "tail" anywhere but the head or arms, the tail becomes the new farmer and the farmer becomes the new head. The idea is to stay the head

Old Plug is a favorite game.

of the horse the longest. Winning and losing really cannot be determined accurately in this game, but that does not seem to bother the children who love this game.

S: This game must be demonstrated to avoid injuries. It is difficult for these younger children to grasp the concept of keeping the farmer in front of them. A demonstration usually does the trick. A favorite thing for the children to do, unfortunately, is move all over the play area which could cause the horses to collide. Students must therefore be cautioned to stay inside a predetermined area. Some horses will also begin backing up as soon as play begins thus ramming their tail into a wall or pole; obviously, this practice has to be discouraged at all costs.

N: Bounce Ball - Activity
DA: 8 to 10
DV: Hand-eye coordination
F: Free
E: One playground ball per child
D: Each child has a playground ball which is bounced according to the teacher's direction. Either a problem-solving approach ("How many ways can you dribble the ball?") can be used or a more directive approach ("Can you dribble around the room using your left hand?"). The teacher could also use ideas generated by the students: "Can you bounce the ball like Billy is doing?" Activities should be challenging, but there should be a variety of activities to give every child some success.

N: Hoop is Home - Game
DA: 8 to 10
DV: Hand-eye coordination and agility
F: Free with hoops
E: One ball per child and one hoop per child less one
D: On a signal, perhaps music playing, children dribble a ball with their hand around the play area among the hoops. When the music stops, each child dribbles to a hoop (home) and continues to dribble the ball while standing in the hoop. The one left without a hoop is "it." The "it" removes a hoop and the game continues until there are only a couple of hoops left. Those successfully getting one of these hoops is declared the best dribbler. Variations such as dribbling with the non-dominant hand, dribbling backward, and dribbling sideward should be included in the game to keep up the interest level.

N: Hot Potato - Game
DA: 8 to 10
DV: Hand-eye coordination
F: Partners
E: One beanbag or ball per couple
D: Children stand a reasonable distance apart to allow for proper throwing and catching. The teacher designates the way the object must be thrown and caught. When a signal is given or the music stops, the child holding the hot potato gets one point. After each stop, the way the object is thrown and caught is changed. At the end of the game, the partner with the least number of points is the winner.

Hot Potato

N: Poison Ball - Game
DA: 8 to 10
DV: Manipulative ability and lead up to volleyball
F: Two teams of eight to ten children
E: Ten to twelve 7"-10" high density sponge rubber balls
D: Each team begins with five to six sponge rubber balls. On the go signal, the balls are hit over the net using an underhand serve or a two-hand overhand set. Balls are returned using volleyball skills of two hand overhand or underhand hits. Any ball hitting the floor is returned using volleyball skills with the child throwing the ball up to him/herself and then hitting it over. On a stop signal, everyone stops, and the team with the least number of balls on their side of the court gets one point. No ball may be just thrown over or kicked under the net.

N: Progressive Tag - Game
DA: 8 to 10
DV: Hand-eye coordination and agility
F: Free formation with one person being it
E: Yarn balls or sponge rubber balls
D: One person is it and has a sponge ball. He/she attempts to hit anyone else who then becomes it until the game ends. The person who starts the game as "it" is no longer it after he/she hits the first person. If, however, he/she in turn is hit during the game he/she is also "it" until the game ends. When a person is hit by the ball, he/she is "it" and goes and gets a ball and hits others. The last person hit is the winner and begins the next game.
S: No one may be hit in the head with the ball. Players must be reminded to watch where they are going.

N: Manipulation - Activity
DA: 8 to 10
DV: Manipulative ability
F: Depends upon the activity
E: Various types of balls
D: The hand-eye and foot-eye coordination at eight to ten years of age is fairly well developed, but practice is needed in a variety of situations using various size balls and targets. Children should be capable of handling softball size balls (plastic ones are recommended). Targets

should be either moving or a good distance away (fifteen to twenty-five feet). For motivation, targets should fall when hit (pins, plastic containers, or old tennis ball cans).

Children like to be challenged at this age, and motivation is enhanced if low level competitive situations are established. Competition can be with self ("Can you throw the ball up, turn in a complete circle, and catch it?") or with others ("Who can knock over the most pins in two rolls?") Activities in which children can test their own ability also enhance motivation. These *self-testing* activities primarily focus on target activities (particularly targets that fall when hit), but can be activities such as: (1) the number of times the child can hit the ball in the air without a miss, (2) the number of catches made in a row, and (3) the distance the child can throw or kick a ball.

Many of the same questions used with six to eight year olds can be asked of this older group: "How many ways can you throw and catch the ball by yourself? How many ways can you throw and catch with a partner?" The difference is in the size of the ball and the skill level. Teachers must also be concerned with getting across the correct way to throw and catch.

N: Targets - Activity
DA: 8 to 10
DV: Manipulative ability
F: Depends upon activity
E: Various pieces of equipment
D: Throw various objects at targets; balls, beanbags, deck tennis rings, and/or hoops can be used. These should be self-testing activities meaning the child can determine success. Self-testing activities which work well are targets which fall down or make noise when hit; throwing the objects into a basketball hoop, barrel, or other container; looping the object over something such as having the hoop going onto a stick. Variety is achieved by challenging the children to be successful in different ways, i.e., vary the distance from the target; use different body parts to throw the object; do it while standing with one's back to the target; or try it with eyes closed.

Target activity

N: Catchup - Activity
DA: 8 to 10
DV: Manipulative Ability
F: Partners
E: Various kinds of balls
D: The activity begins by asking the children to show all the ways they can throw and catch the ball. Questions can be used such as: "How low can you be and catch it? Can you throw it up turn around and catch it?" As the children explore ways to throw and catch, the lesson can be moved toward catching only with the hands, and emphasis should then be made on catching with thumbs together for high throws and little fingers together for low ones. Children should be taught to let their body give with the throw. Catch different size balls thrown high and low. Catch while in a high position (as tall as possible) and at a low position (on knees). Catch while running, including over the shoulder (back to thrower). Use scoops to catch. Catch two beanbags (one in each hand) simultaneously.

N: Move Away - Activity
DA: 8 to 10
DV: Eye-hand coordination
F: Partners across from each other with line between
E: Plastic softballs or heavy yarn balls
D: Partners line up on either side of a common line for the entire class. Starting close together, they throw and catch the ball. Each time a child successfully catches a ball without moving both feet, he/she takes a step backward. If the ball is missed, the receiving child takes two steps toward his/her partner. The activity continues with each couple trying to get as far away from one another as possible.

N: Foot-eye Coordination - Activity
DA: 8 to 10
DV: Manipulative ability
F: Alone or with partner
E: Various size balls
D: (1) As in the case of hand-eye coordination, targets which fall when hit should be used. Bowling pins or plastic containers are best.
(2) Move ball right, left, forward, and backward as quickly as possible and still keep control.
(3) Kick rolling ball for distance.
(4) Stop rolling ball with feet.
(5) Stop bouncing ball with legs.
(6) Move ball around obstacle course—emphasize using both feet equally.
(7) Punting foam balls or playground balls; if there is sufficient room for safety, the playground balls can be used. Punting is a two step skill—dropping the ball and swinging the foot up to hit it before it reaches the ground. Many children have trouble coordinating the hands and feet and end up throwing the ball over their head or way into the air.
(8) Obstacle courses requiring leaping over hurdles.
(9) Jumping rope.

N: Tennis - Activity or Game
DA: 8 to 10
DV: Tennis ability
F: Depends upon activity
E: Depends upon activity
D: It the purpose is to keep hitting the ball with the partner in a non-competitive way, it is an activity. Once there is competition, it is a game. The following can either be activities or games:
One Wall Handball: Children play in pairs trying to hit a ball before it bounces more than once. The ball must hit inside a marked-off area of the wall and then bounce in a marked-off area of the floor.
Nylon Balloon Tennis: A nylon racket is used to hit a balloon back and forth over a low net. The balloon may not touch the floor.
Nylon Yarn Ball Tennis: A nylon racket is used to hit a yarn ball back and forth over a net. A yarn ball hitting the floor in a marked-off area is one point against the person allowing it to hit on his or her side of the floor.
Paddle Racket Tennis: A paddle racket is used to hit a 7 1/2" sponge rubber ball back and forth over a net. The ball may touch the floor but may not bounce more than once.
Four Square Tennis: A paddle racket is used to play "Four Square", usually with an 8 1/2" playground ball.
One Wall Tennis: This is played the same as "One Wall Handball," except a paddle racket is used instead of the hand.

N: Snowball - Game
DA: 8 to 10
DV: Manipulative ability
F: Two teams of equal number
E: One low density sponge rubber ball or yarn ball for every two students
D: Each team gets on opposite sides of a center line. On a go signal, balls are thrown at each other. If the ball is caught,

Using a modified racket for tennis.

it is immediately thrown at someone on the opposite side. If the ball strikes a player and is not caught, the player must immediately go to the side and do a designated exercise such as five push-ups or ten sit-ups prior to returning to the game. After a period of time, the team who had to do the least number of exercises is declared the winner.

S: Only low density balls or yarn balls can be used

N: Travel Catch - Game
DA: 8 to 10
DV: Hand-eye coordination, teamwork
F: Partners. Establish a starting line and a finish line.
E: One ball per group
D: On the go signal, one child runs a short distance toward the finish line which should be a good distance (50 - 100 yards) away. The other child cannot move until after he/she throws the ball which must be caught by the partner. If the ball is missed, both players must return to the starting line and begin again. If the ball is caught, the child with the ball may not move. The other child then runs past the child with the ball which is then thrown to him/her. The team progresses down the field until both are over the finish line; the first team to finish is the winner. For variety, use different size balls, or have students use the non-dominant hand to throw or just one hand to catch.

N: Soccer Ball - Game
DA: 8 to 10
DV: Agility and foot-eye coordination
F: Two teams on a soccer field — ten to twelve on a side
E: One high density sponge ball (no substituting other kinds of balls) per child
D: The balls are lined up at the center and the children are back by the goal area. On the go signal, children advance to the center of the field as quickly as possible and try to get as many balls into the opponent's goal as possible. If the children are older, and can understand offensive and defensive play, some children can stay back and play defense while others are on offense. Play contin-

ues until all the balls are in the goal or out of bounds. Balls which go over the sideline or end line are dead. After all the balls are off the field, the team with the most balls in the opponent's goal is the winner. No hands may be used by anyone and there is no goalie.

N: Soccer Dribble Fun - Activity
DA: 8 to 10
DV: Soccer skills
F: Free
E: One ball per child
D: Children dribble the ball around the play area responding to the leader's commands. Commands can be speed up, slow down, stop, go right or left, go backward or sideward, and use only one foot or the other.

Soccer dribbling

N: Balloon Football - Game
DA: 8 to 10
DV: Agility and teamwork
F: Equal teams on opposite sides of the play area.
E: One balloon per player with each team having its own color balloon.
D: The players begin with their balloon in their own end zone. The object is to get the balloon to the opponent's end zone. On the go signal, the players begin hitting their balloon toward the other team. The balloons must be kept above the head to make forward progress. When the teams meet in the middle, they must try to protect their balloons while knocking the other team's balloons to the floor. Any balloon touching the floor is dead

and may not be played. The team with the most number of balloons in the opponent's end zone after a given playing time is the winner.

N: Bombardment - Game
DA: 8 to 12
DV: Manipulative ability and aerobics
F: Two equal teams divided by marker cones which designate the center of the field. Targets are placed behind each team.
E: 7" or larger low density sponge rubber balls only, plastic containers for targets, and marker cones
D: The object is to obtain five points by knocking over the targets behind the opposing team. The balls may be kicked or thrown and may be stopped using any body part available. Players may not go over the field's center line. No one may play defense by standing in front of a target. Everyone must be trying to get a ball and then go to the center line and throw at the targets. A penalty point is awarded to the other team if a person is caught playing exclusively defense or if a player throws from the area near the targets. Four to five targets are on each side and as soon as a target is knocked down, it must be put back up by a player on that side of the field. A penalty point can be awarded if the team is slow at resetting the targets. As soon as five points are

scored, teams immediately switch sides and the game begins again without delay.
S: Only low density sponge balls can be used.

N: Count 6 - Game
DA: 8 to 10
DV: A lead-up game to basketball, hand-eye coordination, and agility
F: Class is divided into an even number of teams with about six on a team. A playing area should be marked off for each set of two teams. Teams should be identified with pinnies.
E: 7" sponge rubber ball
D: One team is given the ball. The objective of the game is to throw the ball between members of the same team without ever throwing it back to the person who threw it to you. A point is scored for each successful completion and when a team scores six consecutive points they win. The person with the ball may move only one pivot foot (basketball rules). Other players move around the play area trying to get open for a pass. The defense must play basketball rules and may not, therefore, touch members of the offensive team. If there is an unsuccessful pass, the ball automatically goes to the other team, and play continues uninterrupted. There is no fighting over a loose ball. The defense may intercept or knock

Bombardment is a game for developing manipulative ability.

down a pass which automatically gives them the ball and they become the offense. There is no stopping of play except for a foul with the non-fouling team getting the ball. If a foul is committed against the offensive team after they have scored some points, play is resumed with the offense keeping the points scored. Anytime the ball switches teams, the team must begin with zero as they attempt to score six consecutive points.

S: Fighting over a ball on the ground is not permitted. Any ball hitting the ground is dead, and, unless there was a foul, the ball goes over to the opposing team.

TEN TO TWELVE YEAR OLDS

N: Crazy Volleyball - Game
DA: 10 to 12
DV: Volleyball skills
F: Equal teams of about six to eight players on each side of a six-foot high volleyball net.
E: High density sponge rubber ball for each child
D: On the go signal, the balls are hit over the net using any legal volleyball skill. As balls come from the other side they may be returned using legal skills. Balls that hit the floor may be picked up and legally hit over. There are no boundaries, but balls must go over the net and no one may pass from one side of the court to the other. After a time determined by the teacher, a stop signal is given and those with the least number of balls on their side are the winners. Teams then switch sides and a new game begins.

N: Volleyball Bump - Activity
DA: 10 - 12
DV: Volleyball skill
F: Free and then free with a partner
E: One high density sponge ball per student
D: Children begin by exploring all the ways their body can bump the ball. Then they can be challenged to bump the ball with two arms while holding their hands together; while moving around the room forward, backward, sideward; while on their knees. They can be challenged to see how many times in a row they can bump it. In all cases, the ball must be bumped higher than their head. Then they can work with a partner.

N: Team Ball - Game
DA: 10 to 12
DV: Teamwork
F: Two equal teams, a home plate, and a first base about sixty feet away
E: A volleyball and two marker cones
D: A team member up to "bat" hits the volleyball into the field between the boundary lines. After hitting the ball, the hitter runs toward and around first base (a marker cone) while all other members of the team follow. If the entire team rounds first and makes it past home before the ball is successfully played by the fielders, they get one point. After every member up to bat gets a chance to hit the ball, teams switch places. In the field, a player must retrieve the hit ball and all other fielders must line up behind him/her. The ball is then passed between the feet and the last person picks it up and runs to the front of the line where the ball is held up and play stops.

N: Dribble Keep Away - Game
DA: 10 to 12
DV: Agility and hand-eye coordination
F: Partners
E: One basketball or playground ball per pair
D: One person tries to dribble the ball while keeping the other person from touching it. The non-dribbler gets one point every time he/she touches the ball. If the ball is taken away, the player gets five points. After a given amount of time, the players switch roles.

N: Basketball Catch - Activity
DA: 10 to 12
DV: Hand-eye coordination
F: Free
E: One 8 1/2" playground ball or basketball per child
D: Students stand in a side straddle position holding a ball between their legs with one hand in front and one behind. They then attempt to let go of the ball and switch hands without letting the ball hit the ground or touch any other part of their body.

N: Dribble Feel - Activity
DA: 10 to 12
DV: Dribble skill and kinesthetic awareness
F: Scattered
E: One ball per child
D: Children dribble the ball in various ways while staying in one place with their eyes closed. They can also be asked to use various body parts to do the dribbling such as the elbow or knee. They may open their eyes only to retrieve a loose ball. Particular emphasis should be placed on using the non-dominant side of the body.

N: No Net Tennis - Game
DA: 10 to 12
DV: Eye-hand coordination, agility, and tennis knowledge
F: Pairs on a tennis court, badminton court, or court drawn on the ground
E: Tennis racket or paddle, and rubber ball
D: The game is played by modified tennis rules on a tennis court, badminton court, or a court drawn on the ground with no net. A ball is good when it is hit beyond the service line but short of the end or base line. Any ball landing in the area between the two service lines is not good. Serving is done by bouncing and hitting the ball into the opposite court. The ball may be returned in any manner. Players are not allowed to go beyond their own service line to play a ball. Scoring can be done with either tennis or Ping-Pong rules. Sponge tennis balls can be used indoors on a badminton court.

N: Keep It Up - Game
DA: 10 to 12
DV: Volleyball skills
F: Groups of five
E: One ball per group
D: On the go signal, one person throws the ball into the air. The group then attempts to keep the ball in the air using volleyball skills. No person may strike the ball two times in a row, and if an illegal hit occurs, the group must stop. The group which keeps the ball up legally for the longest period receives one point. The game continues until a certain number of points are scored by one team.

Keep It Up uses volleyball skills to keep ball in the air.

N: Soccer Dribble Take Away - Game
DA: 10 to 12
DV: Soccer skills
F: Free
E: Soccer balls for all but five to eight children, depending upon the size of the group
D: On the go signal, those with a ball must dribble it continuously with their feet within a designated area (about one-fourth of a soccer field) while those without a ball try to take the ball away from those dribbling. If the tackler successfully gets between the dribbler and the ball, the tackler is the winner and the person who lost the ball may not try to get it back from that person but may go after anyone else dribbling a ball. The game goes for a period of time with those who lost the ball the least being declared the winners.

N: Ultimate Frisbee or Ultimate Football - Game
DA: 10 to 12
DV: Hand-eye coordination, agility, teamwork, and aerobics
F: Divide class into an even number of teams of about five or six to a side
E: Frisbee or sponge rubber football
D: One team gets the Frisbee or football beginning in the opposite end zone from the one in which they must score. The team advances by throwing the Frisbee or football to a teammate anywhere on the field. If the Frisbee (or football) is not caught or is intercepted, it immediately goes over to the other team from where it is retrieved. There is no fighting over the

Frisbee (or football) on the ground. The person with the Frisbee (football) may move only a pivot foot as in basketball. To score, the Frisbee (football) must be caught by someone with both feet inside the end zone. As soon as a score is made, the Frisbee (football) is dropped and the other team begins play in the opposite direction.

S: The area must be clear of obstacles. There is to be no contact between players.

REFERENCES AND SUGGESTED READINGS

Graham, G., S. Holt-Hale, and M. Parker. *Children Moving* (3rd ed.). Mountain View: Mayfield Publishing Co. 1998.

Kirchner, G. and G. Fishburne. *Physical Education for Elementary School Children* (9th ed.). Madison: W. C. Brown and Co. 1995.

Nichols, B. *Moving an Learning: The Elementary School Physical Education Experience* (3rd ed.). St. Louis: Mosby Publishing Co. 1994.

Pangrazi, R. and V. Dauer. *Dynamic Physical Education* (11th ed.). Boston: Allyn and Bacon. 1995.

Selective Web Sites

Lesson Plans: http://schools.eastnet.ecu.edu/pitt/ayden/physed8.htm
Omaha Public Schools: http://www.ops.org/pe/elem.html
PE Central: http://pe.cental.vt.edu/
PE Links 4U: http://www.pelinks4u.org/sections/elementary/elementary.htm
SPARK: http://www.acsm.org/
A great search engine: http://www.sparkpe.org/programElementaryPE.jsp?curricula=PhysEdK-2&program=ElementaryPE

Chapter 15

Creative Movement

By the end of this chapter, the student should be able to:

1. Describe how teaching styles are used to develop creativity.
2. Write at least five problem-solving questions which would help develop creativity.
3. Describe at least one creativity activity for each of the four age divisions.
4. Develop at least two creative activities for elementary children.
5. Define the key terms listed below.

Key Terms

Creativity

Free exploration

Guided exploration

Open-ended questions

Problem solving

All elementary age children should participate in creative movement. Although it should be more prevalent during the early development years, it should be included in each child's curriculum. By moving creatively, children learn how their body can move while also developing creative ability. Creative movement also can help a child feel good about him/herself.

This chapter's focus is primarily on creative movement activities. It represents, however, only a fraction of the possible activities. Chapter 16, *Rhythms*, also has many creative rhythmic movement activities which will also help develop creativity.

TEACHING APPROACH

Creative movement can only be achieved in an environment which encourages children to interact with it. There should be lots of room to move, and when equipment is available, children should be able to use it almost anyway they wish. The teacher's role is to encourage and guide but not direct student movement.

ACTIVITY ORGANIZATION

Each activity which follows includes an age range for which the activity should be successful. Although there is overlap, the chapter is basically organized by the four age levels: four to six, six to eight, eight to ten, and ten to twelve years of age. Although there are no games in this chapter, "Activity" appears beside each title to maintain consistency with the labeling process in other chapters.

Key:

N = Name of the activity
DA = Age of the student for which the activity is best suited (developmental age)
DV = The developmental value of the activity; i.e., fitness, manipulative ability, etc.
F = Formation
E = Any equipment needs
D = Description of the activity
S = Safety

FOUR TO SIX YEAR OLDS

A major portion of the curriculum for four- to six-year-old children should focus on creative movement. Not only do children enjoy these activities, they also help the child develop body awareness and self-concept. Creative activities give children a chance to explore their environment as well as learn how their body can move. Such nonthreatening, non-competitive, and individualized activities can also help a child feel good about him/herself.

N: My Aunt Left Town - Activity
DA: 4 to 6
DV: Creativity and quality of movement
F: Free
E: None
D: The teacher chants the phrase, "My aunt left town," which is then repeated by the children. The teacher then says, "She left like this" at which time the teacher does some movement. The children then repeat the line as they also do the movement. The activity is then repeated allowing a child to determine the movement which all the other children follow.

N: The Captain is Coming - Activity
DA: 4 to 6
DV: Reaction time and creativity
F: Free
E: None
D: The teacher calls out various commands in random order repeating them throughout the activity; the children react accordingly:
  1. "The Captain" students stand and salute
  2. "Jelly Fish" lay on back and wiggle
  3. "Starfish" spread limbs and move slowly
  4. "2, 3, 4, or 5 in a boat" students group accordingly and row the boat backward
  5. "Tidal wave" students get tossed around by wave

6. "Mopping the deck" simulate clearing the deck
7. "Blowfish" children use arms and face to appear like a blowfish
8. Other ideas include: crabs, octopus, jellyfish, shark, seahorse, climb the mast, lower the anchor, set the sails, and abandon ship.

N: Keep It Moving - Activity
DA: 4 to 6
DV: Creativity and body awareness
F: Free
E: None
D: This is a chant activity which is begun by the teacher and with increasingly more involvement by the children. The teacher chants, "Keep it moving, keep it moving, I've got _____, keep it (them) moving." In the blank space, the teacher can name a body part or parts which are moved; i.e., shake the hands, bend the elbow, bend the knees, etc. Eventually, the children should begin naming the body parts and suggesting ways to move them.

N: Ringmaster - Activity
DA: 4 to 6
DV: Quality of movement and creativity
F: Free
E: None
D: The ringmaster cracks the imaginary whip and calls out an animal's name. All the children imitate that animal until a new name is called. If the ringmaster says "Come join the parade," all the children line up and begin the circus parade while imitating anything they might see at the circus. Instead of animals, the ringmaster may call out acts such as the high wire act or the clowns which the children then imitate.

N: Happy Movement - Activity
DV: Quality of movement and rhythmic ability
F: Free
E: None
D: Using the rhyme "If you are happy and you know it," specify some movement which is done in rhythm to the song. Such things as swing your right arm or you left arm or right leg, hop up and down, etc. can be done. Large muscle move-

ments should be specified and children should be encouraged to suggest new ways to move.

N: Did You Ever See This? - Activity
DA: 4 to 6
DV: Creative movement
F: Free
E: None
D: Children move as they sing the verses to the tune of "Did You Ever See a Lassie?" The verses focus on animals, but could be machines or anything to which the children could move.
     Did you ever see a rabbit,
     A rabbit, a rabbit?
     Did you ever see a rabbit
     Go this way and that?
     Go this way and that way,
     Go this way and that way.
     Did you ever see a rabbit
     Go this way and that?
     Various children can be selected to determine the animal, but all children would be encouraged to do their own creative movement.

N: The Maze - Activity
DA: 4 to 6
DV: Spatial awareness and agility
F: Large circle
E: None
D: On the go signal, children move as quickly as possible through the center of the circle without touching anyone.

The Maze

N: Abbracadabbra, You - Activity
DA: 4 to 6

DV: Quality of movement and creativity
F: Free
E: A magic wand
D: The teacher waves the magic wand while saying "Abbracadabbra, you" followed by something the children are to be, such as animals, people, things, etc. The emphasis should be on presenting tasks which help to develop the quality of movement. An example would be, "Abbracadabbra, you are a big tiger stuck in the mud."

N: Days of the Week - Activity
DA: 4 to 6
DV: Rhythmics, movement skills, and learning days of the week
F: Free
E: None
D: Children move freely about the room singing "What shall we do on Monday?" After repeating the line three times, they answer, "We will all go _____ on Monday." The blank is filled in by the teacher or a child chosen by the teacher. The children then imitate what is suggested, i.e., skating, swimming, biking, etc., while saying the movement and the day. So if swimming is the suggested activity, the children imitate swimming while saying, "Swimming on Monday," repeating it four times or so before beginning again with Tuesday and so forth throughout the week.

N: Picture Pantomime - Activity
DA: 4 to 6
DV: Creative movement
F: Free
E: Flashcards
D: Mount pictures from magazines showing persons doing various movement activities. Hold up the pictures and ask students to move the way the picture shows them to move. The name of the movement could be placed below it to integrate the activity with language arts. After a while, abstract artwork pictures could be used to increase the creativity.

N: If I Was - Activity
DA: 4 to 6
DV: Creativity and quality of movement
F: Free

E: None
D: The teacher or, depending upon the age of the children, a child leader, says "If I was _____, I would move like this." In the blank, any number of things could be included:
1. A person such as a teacher, fireman, policeman, acrobat, clown, or an astronaut.
2. Various moods like happy, sad, lonely or mad.
3. Made of concrete, steel, rubber, or Jell-O.
4. In weather such as a snowstorm, wind, rain, tornado, or earthquake.
5. Playing a sport like tennis, golf, baseball, soccer, hockey, or football.

N: Aunt Mildred Went Shopping - Activity
DA: 4 to 6
DV: Creative movement
F: Free
E: None
D: The leader says "My Aunt Mildred went shopping today and guess what she bought?" Children answer: "What did she buy?" Leader, "She bought a ____." An object is named which the children then act out. After a while, the teacher can select a child to answer what she bought.

N: Animal Movement - Activity
DA: 4 to 6
DV: Fitness
F: Free
E: None
D: Children are asked to move like different animals such as:
1. *Inchworm* — from a push-up position, walk feet up to hands while keeping the knees straight and then walk out on hands to the push-up position.
2. *Bear* — with knees straight, bend over and touch the ground with the hands and then walk on all fours.
3. *Giraffe* — with arms straight, place hands together above the head and walk with legs stiff.
4. *Elephant* — walk bent over with one arm acting as the trunk and the other hand acting as the tail. Children can hook onto each other to form a circus parade.

Animal movements using flashcards.

5. *Seal* — in a push-up position, walk with the arms only while dragging the legs behind.
6. *Dragon* — two children kneel on all fours. The child in front puts his/her feet (shoes off) on the shoulders of the child in the rear. The children then coordinate their movement to move forward or backward and not have the feet fall off the shoulders.
7. *Snake* — children slither along the floor using knees and elbows.
8. *Crab* — in a sitting position, children use their feet and hands, which are on the floor behind them, to move.
9. *Frog* — children squat down with hands on the floor in front of them. Then using primarily the legs, the children jump off both feet like a frog.
10. *Gazelle* — children gallop about the floor and frequently leap through the air.
11. *Cheetah* — children run around the play area as fast as possible.

N: Shadows - Activity
DA: 4 to 6
DV: Body awareness and creativity
F: Partners
E: None

D: One child begins moving around the room doing various activities. The partner is the leader's shadow and attempts to do everything the leader does. After a period of time the two switch places.

N: Clouds and Nature - Activity
DA: 4 to 6
DV: Interpretative movement of body images and social development
F: Multiple (scattered, line and circle)
E: Drum, triangle
D: Teaching procedures:
  A. MOVEMENT INTRODUCTION
Arrange children in scattered formation and seated on the floor. The following questions and discussion period will provide the initial stimulus for later interpretative movements.
1. Think of coming to school on a nice warm day when the sky is filled with pretty white clouds. What do the clouds look like?
2. If you could touch a cloud, what do you think it would feel like?
3. If you were a big cloud what would you do on a nice warm day?
Possible responses from children:
1. Mashed potatoes, cotton candy or cotton balls.

2. Soft and fluffy like whipped cream, daddy's shaving cream.
3. Sleep, fly around and look at everyone, ride with the wind.

B. INTERPRETATIVE MOVEMENT
1. Let's all move about the room as if we were clouds in the sky.
2. To indicate light movements, can you run very lightly on the tips of your toes?
3. What else is soft and light and makes you feel like moving as you did?
4. Can you move your arms and your whole body very softly and lightly while I play the triangle? (Vary speed, but keep intensity very soft.)
5. Seated in scattered formation: We have talked about light and soft things and moved so we feel that way. What is very different from softness?
6. What can you think of that is just the opposite of soft, fluffy clouds?
7. Can you move around the room again but this time we will be heavy and hard? (Use drum or triangle for accompaniment.)

Possible responses from children:
1. Running, romping, moving on tiptoes or heavy pronounced steps.
2. Running lightly, swinging, or swaying.
3. Kitten, bunny, feathers.
4. Children may remain in same spot or may shift about the room with light expressive movements.
5. Stones, big and fat, heavy, rough.
6. Giants, elephants, sledge hammer.
7. Heavy pounding with feet, clenched fists, dragging arms to imitate elephant walk.

N: Funny Movement - Activity
DA: 4 to 6
DV: Quality of locomotor movement
F: Free
E: None or record player and record for moving to music
D: Children are given various movement problems which they solve in their own way; e.g., "How can you move backward around the room without bumping into anyone?" The quality of locomotor movement, force, time, space, and level, are emphasized; e.g., "Can you move like a big, heavy animal?" Music may be used to vary speed (time), force, or level.

N: The Winds - Activity
DA: 4 to 6
DV: Quality of movement and creativity
F: Free
E: None
D: Have students move as if it was very windy. Vary the activity by presenting a variety of situations such as the child becoming a piece of dust or leaf in the wind. They could also be objects such as a weather vane, car, truck, clothes on a line, or a boat on the water. Other ideas include being a bird, a ball, a balloon, or an airplane.

N: Story Plays - Activity
DA: 4 to 6
DV: Quality of movement, creativity and problem solving; integration with science, history or social studies
F: Free
E: None
D: Story plays can take many themes but the primary purpose is development of the quality of movement (force, time, space, and level) and creativity and problem solving. A secondary purpose is the integration of other subjects such as science and social studies. The teacher's role is to set the theme and develop the story so as to provide considerable movement as the children create solutions and solve problems. Since children will tend to imitate rather than create, the teacher must be careful not to become involved in the movement portion of the story play. Themes include: science—trip to the moon, scuba diving in the ocean, trip to the jungle, spaceship to the planets, growing like a flower or tree; history— the pioneers, traveling west, the Civil War, traveling to America in 1492; social studies—a trip to the farm, being a fireman, a trip to the circus.

SIX TO EIGHT YEAR OLDS

Many of the activities in the section for four- to six-year-olds are appropriate for use with this older age group. The individual nature and universal appeal of creative activities lend themselves to use across age levels. Children of all ages enjoy showing the teacher "their way" of solving the problem. Creative activities also provide the teacher numerous opportunities to praise individuals.

N: Streamers - Activity
DA: 6 to 8
DV: Rhythmic development
F: Free
E: Streamers, record player, and music
D: Streamers can be made with plastic strips or crepe paper. They should be five to six-feet long and have a handle of some sort. Children can have one or two streamers which they move in time to the music. The emphasis is on creative movement with the children moving about the room while also moving the streamers. For more creativity and variety, the music can be changed frequently or the children can be asked to do special things such as sitting while making the streamer move.

N: The Tar Pit - Activity
DA: 6 to 8
DV: Body awareness, non-locomotor movement, flexibility, and balance
F: Free
E: One hoop per child
D: Tell the child his/her feet are stuck in a tar pit inside the hoop and he/she cannot move. The teacher then asks the child to do non-locomotor movements such as bending, stretching, twisting, and turning. The activities can be varied by suggesting that only one foot is stuck or have the hands stuck and move only the feet.

N: Nature - Activity
DA: 6 to 8
DV: Flexibility and muscular endurance
F: Free
E: None, although soft music could be used
D: Children move freely about the room in response to the teacher's nature suggestions. Examples would be to move like a wave or rotate like the earth, move like a meandering stream, be rain or thunder, or grow like a flower or tree.

N: Rubber Person - Activity
DA: 6 to 8
DV: Flexibility
F: Free
E: None
D: Children are encouraged to explore every way they can stretch their body. Stretching should be done slowly. Every body part capable of being stretched should be explored. Slow music can be used to keep students moving slowly to avoid injuries.

N: Human Pretzel - Activity
DA: 6 to 8
DV: Body awareness
F: Free
E: None, although flash cards could be used to integrate the activity with language arts.
D: Children are told they are going to pretend they are a pretzel and will bend themselves in many ways using various body parts. They can then be asked to touch their ear to their shoulder or cheek to shoulder, or nose to knee. Each time, two body parts are used. To integrate the activity with language arts, flash cards with the names of the body parts can be used.

N: Bridges and Tunnels - Activity
DA: 6 to 8
DV: Creativity and quality of movement
F: Two groups scattered about the play area
E: None
D: As the groups move freely about the play area the teacher instructs one group to make either a bridge or tunnel. The other group then crosses (jumps over) the bridges or goes through the tunnels. The traveling groups can go over or through a number of tunnels until the teacher calls for everyone to begin moving again. Both groups should be given equal opportunity to be the bridges and tunnels. Children should be encouraged to create various types of bridges and tunnels.

Bridges and Tunnels

N: Symphony - Activity
DA: 6 to 8
DV: Rhythmic ability and creative movement. Can be an integrated activity if classical music is used.
F: Children face the conductor, spreading out so they can see the board.
E: Activity chart, record player, music and conductor's wand (stick)
D: As the music begins, the conductor (teacher) points to a movement listed on the board. The children then do that movement until the conductor changes it. Children may move freely about the room but must be attentive to the conductor. The movement should be done in time to the music. Movements can include galloping, skipping, walking, etc. The conductor should change the music and the activity with an emphasis on the quality of movement—force, time, space, and level. These four movement terms can be included on the board and used to direct the children's movements, i.e., skip backward, walk lightly, run heavy, etc.

N: Five Ways to Get to Timbuktu - Activity
DA: 6 to 8
DV: Movement skills and creativity
F: Free
E: None
D: The teacher suggests a way, such as riding a horse, to get to Timbuktu. Children then imitate the movement. The children then suggest other ways they may get there. The teacher can suggest various barriers encountered along the way such as mountains, rivers, jungles, etc., and seek suggestions from the children on how they will conquer the obstacles. The problems presented suggest movements which will help develop the quality of the child's movement, i.e., vary the speed, direction, level, and force of the movement.

N: Human Vocabulary - Activity
DA: 6 to 8
DV: Creative movement
F: Free
E: None
D: Working individually, children interpret vocabulary words through movement. Cat-egories and their subdivisions are:
Weather: rain, thunder, sun, snow, etc.
Occupations: doctor, dentist, teacher, policeman, fireman, etc.
Animals: elephant, snake, bear, tiger, deer, etc.
Food: popcorn, bacon, Jell-O, etc.
Sports: football, basketball, tennis, skiing, etc.

EIGHT TO TEN YEAR OLDS

Although creative activities often are reserved for younger children, all elementary age children enjoy and can benefit from creative movement. As can be seen with the suggested age groups for the activities in the previous age groups sections, many activities presented in the earlier years are appropriate for eight- to ten-year-old children.

N: Human Vocabulary - Activity
DA: 8 to 10
DV: Creative movement and social interaction
F: Free or in small groups
E: None
D: Children work alone or in small groups to interpret vocabulary words through movement. Suggested categories and some subdivisions are:
Body parts: but the body part mentioned may not be used to interpret the work, i.e., fingers to imitate "teeth."
Machinery: washing machine, toaster, copy machine, etc.
Tools: jackhammer, screwdriver, paintbrush, rake, etc.
Music: rock band, guitar, drums, conductor, parade, etc.
Emotions: fear, joy, frustration, love, anger, mad, etc.
Materials: wood, concrete, Velcro, metal, rubber, etc.

N: Creative Throw and Catch - Activity
DA: 8 to 10
DV: Manipulative ability
F: Partners
E: One object per pair
D: Children work in partners to see how many creative ways they can throw and catch an object such as a beanbag or ball. The person throwing establishes the manner in which the object must be

thrown and the receiver determines the catching style. The partner must duplicate what the other did. Encouragement is given by the teacher to attempt many various throwing and catching styles using numerous body parts. The partner only has to duplicate his/her partner's actions if the partner is successful. The throw must be accurate enough so the receiver does not have to move more than one step to catch it.

N: Make a Machine - Activity
DA: 8 to 10
DV: Creativity and social interaction
F: Groups of four or five
E: None
D: The object is create a machine which uses every member of the group. Each member must be a moving part of the machine. The teacher can try to guess what the machine is or other members of the class may guess, but it must be remembered that you want everyone participating in the creative aspect of the activity and not standing around for any length of time trying to guess what another group is doing.

Make a Machine

TEN TO TWELVE YEAR OLDS

The limited number of creative movement activities is not to suggest a lack of importance for these older children. Creative movement should still be included in the ten to twelve year old's curriculum. Many of those activities, however, focus on creative rhythmic routines and are included in chapter 16.

N: Human Vocabulary - Activity
DA: 10 to 12
DV: Creativity, problem solving, and group interaction
F: Small groups
E: None
D: Working in small groups, children interpret vocabulary words through movement. Categories and suggested subdivisions are:
Time: digital, analog, alarm clock, cuckoo, etc.
Colors: red, blue, green, etc.
Places: Hawaii, grocery store, movies, subway, sewer, etc.

N: Creativity - Activity
DA: 10 to 12
DV: Creativity
F: Free
E: None
D: Although the creative activities for ten- to twelve-year-old children are similar (if not identical) to those suggested for younger children, this older group hopefully will be more advanced in their movement activities. The ten- to twelve-year-old child should also be better able to work in small groups.
   1. A good way to get children moving creatively is to set themes for them to act out. These can be: (1) moving in a heavy snow, (2) moving on another planet, (3) being made of rubber, metal or plastic, (4) moving in different moods or like different people, (5) moving in slow motion while acting out sports activities, (6) moving to music and (7) moving to poems. Most creative rhythmic activities will be successful if presented properly. Children's inhibition is usually created by the teacher's inhibition.
   2. Gravity and planets can be studied with a trip to outer space, stopping at different planets. Children can act out how they would move and how they would react to the climate and surface.
   3. A good way to encourage creativity in upper elementary children is to ask them to create musical routines using equipment. A ball routine, for

example, could be done to modern or classical music, in which fast and slow portions of the music, accents, and phrases are highlighted by some change in the routine, i.e., bouncing ball hard on accent, switching the skill at the end of each phrase, moving slowly or quickly according to the tempo.

4. See creative rhythmics.
5. Many activities from the curriculum for eight- to ten-year-old children can be used with older children.

REFERENCES AND SUGGESTED READINGS

Graham, G., S. Holt-Hale, and M. Parker. *Children Moving* (3rd ed.). Mountain View: Mayfield Publishing Co. 1998.

Kirchner, G. and G. Fishburne. *Physical Education for Elementary School Children* (9th ed.). Madison: W. C. Brown and Co. 1995.

Nichols, B. *Moving an Learning: The Elementary School Physical Education Experience* (3rd ed.). St. Louis: Mosby Publishing Co. 1994.

Pangrazi, R. and V. Dauer. *Dynamic Physical Education* (11th ed.). Boston: Allyn and Bacon. 1995.

Selective Web Sites

Lesson Plans: http://schools.eastnet.ecu.edu/pitt/ayden/physed8.htm

Omaha Public Schools: http://www.ops.org/pe/elem.html

PE Central: http://pe.cental.vt.edu/

PE Links 4U: http://www.pelinks4u.org/sections/elementary/elementary.htm

SPARK: http://www.acsm.org/

A great search engine: http://www.sparkpe.org/programElementaryPE.jsp?curricula=PhysEdK-2&program=ElementaryPE

16

Rhythms

After completing this chapter, the student should be able to:

1. Describe at least two rhythmic activities for each of the four age groups included in the chapter.
2. Define the key terms listed below.

Key Terms

Creative rhythmic activity
Rhythmic activity
Structured rhythmic activity

Rhythmic activities can be done with or without rhythmic accompaniment. Most fundamental locomotor movements, for example, are rhythmic in nature. For purposes of this chapter, however, the emphasis will be on activities done to some rhythmic accompaniment. In most cases it will be recorded music, but a tom-tom, piano, or some other musical instrument could be used.

There are basically two types of rhythmic activities, creative and structured. In creative rhythmic activities, the children interpret the accompaniment in their own way using either locomotor or non-locomotor movement. In a structured rhythmic activity, the children do specific movement to the accompaniment; folk and square dances are examples of structured rhythmic activities.

The Chicken Dance is a structured rhythmic activity.

Rhythmic activities should be an integral part of the curriculum for every child. Although often reserved for younger children, there are numerous opportunities to have all elementary children participate in both creative and structured rhythmic activities. For the younger children, four to

eight years of age, the emphasis should be on developing the quality of movement through creative rhythmics. Some structured rhythmics are appropriate for this age level but they should be very limited.

Older children, eight to twelve years of age, can participate in both creative and structured rhythmic activities. Emphasis should be on having these older children create rhythmic routines using equipment such as jump ropes, lummi sticks, streamers, and/or a parachute. Activities such as tinikling and rhythmic gymnastics also offer opportunities to develop creative rhythmic ability. If introduced properly, upper elementary children, like their younger peers, will enjoy moving creatively to a variety of music. Structured rhythmics such as

The Bunny Hop.

Dances Without Partners, folk and square dance, and country dances are appropriate for older children. A particular problem when working with upper elementary children is partner dances. Dances requiring opposite sex partners should be introduced early—six to eight years of age—to minimize later problems. Partner activities are easier to conduct and are more successful with eight to ten year old children; partner activities, however, should be offered at all age groups.

Rhythmic Activities

The activities in this chapter represent only a few of the many possible rhythmic activities. Additional rhythmic activities can be found in chapters 15 and 17. The reader is also encouraged to create his or her own rhythmic activities.

Lummi Sticks.

ACTIVITY ORGANIZATION

The following rhythmic activities are organized into four age groups: four to six, six to eight, eight to ten, and ten to twelve years of age. The abbreviations are:

N = Name of the activity
DA = Age of the student for which the activity is best suited (developmental age)
DV = The developmental value of the activity; i.e., fitness, manipulative ability, etc.
F = Formation
E = Any equipment needs
D = Description of the activity
There are no games in this chapter, but to maintain consistency with other chapters, "Activity" is written next to the name of each activity in the chapter.

FOUR TO SIX YEAR OLDS

N: Keep It Moving - Activity
DA: 4 to 6
DV: Rhythmics, creativity and body awareness
F: Free
E: None
D: This is a chant activity which is begun by the teacher with increasing involvement by the children. The teacher chants: "Keep it moving, keep it moving, I've got _____, keep it (them) moving." In the blank space, the teacher can name a body part or parts which is (are) moved, i.e., shake the hands, bend the elbow, bend the knees, etc. Eventually, the children should begin naming the body parts and suggesting ways to move the parts.

N: Did You Ever See This? - Activity
DA: 4 to 6
DV: Rhythmics and creative movement
F: Free
E: None
D: Children move as they sing the verses to the tune of "Did You Ever See a Lassie?" The verses focus on animals, but could be machines or anything to which the children could move.
Did you ever see a rabbit,
A rabbit, a rabbit?
Did you ever see a rabbit
Go this way and that?
Go this way and that way,
Go this way and that way,
Did you ever see a rabbit
Go this way and that?
Various children can be selected to determine the animal, but all children should be encouraged to do their own creative movement.

Structured rhythmics, such as Dances Without Partners, are appropriate for older children.

N: Days of the Week - Activity
DA: 4 to 6
DV: Rhythmics, movement skills and learning days of the week
 F: Free
 E: None
 D: Children move freely about the room singing "What shall we do on Monday?" After repeating the line three times, they answer "We will all go _____ on Monday." The blank is filled in by the teacher or a child chosen by the teacher. The children then imitate what is suggested, i.e., skating, swimming, biking, etc., while saying the movement and the day. So if swimming was the suggested activity, the children would imitate swimming while saying, "Swimming on Monday," repeating it four times or so before beginning again with Tuesday and so forth throughout the week.

N: Rainy Day Rhythm - Activity
DA: 4 to 6
DV: Rhythmic development
 F: Free or circle
 E: None
 D: The activity starts with a rhyme, "I don't care if the rain comes down, rain comes down, I don't care if the rain comes down early in the morning." This is followed by verses which signify the action the children are to do as they sing, i.e., "I swing my arms as the rain comes down, rain comes down, I swing my arms as the rain comes down early in the morning." Other possible movement and words include: "move around, go up and down, jump up and down, skip around, creep around, turn around, gallop around, and/or stomp around."

N: Old McDonald Had a Body - Activity
DA: 4 to 6
DV: Body awareness and rhythmic development
 F: Free or in a circle
 E: None
 D: Children sing "Old McDonald had a body E-I-E-I-O, and on his body he had two arms, E-I-E-I-O. With a stretch, stretch here and a stretch, stretch there, and here a stretch, there a stretch, every-

where a stretch, stretch, Old McDonald had a body E-I-E-I-O." While singing and stretching, children can be standing in place or moving around the room forward/backward, high/low, or fast/slow. Other possible verses include: bend knees, bend elbows, stretch elbows, wiggle feet, twist hips, rotate wrists, rotate arms, rotate head, shrug shoulders, and twist trunk.

N: Making Stew - Activity
DA: 4 to 6
DV: Rhythmic development
 F: Free
 E: Variety of balls, beanbags, and other soft objects plus a parachute
 D: The parachute is laid on the floor and soft balls and objects are spread around the play area but not near walls. When the music begins, children move as instructed to pick one object for the stew pot. The movement to collect objects could be skipping, galloping, walking backward, turning, or running. When varying the movement, the four qualities of movement: force, time, space, and level should be considered. Children, therefore, could be told to move low/high, fast/slow, heavy/light, or forward/backward to get the objects. Once all the objects are on the chute, the children make stew by "boiling" it, move the chute to the music. As the music gets faster, the children make the chute move faster and faster trying to "pop" the ingredients off the chute. Once all the objects are off, the stew is finished.

N: Color Movement - Activity
DA: 4 to 6
DV: Rhythmic development and color recognition
 F: Free
 E: Many objects of different colors and music
 D: The colored objects are scattered about the play area; there should be about four or five objects for each color so children will not group around one object. Children do motor activities around the color chosen by the teacher. The movement activity and color should be changed

frequently. When deciding on the movement activity, quality of movement must be considered. Children should move high/low, fast/slow, heavy/light, and forward/backward. Music should be selected to help children to move appropriately.

N: Motor Square - Activity
DA: 4 to 6
DV: Rhythmic development and motor ability
F: Children stand on one of the four sides of a square marked by four chairs
E: Flash cards and music
D: When the music begins, children begin moving in the same direction around the square. When they get to the chair, they do the movement written on the card until they reach the next chair. During the activity, music can be played, and the cards can be changed frequently. Quality of movement should be considered when making the cards. Movements should be done high/low, fast/slow, heavy/light, and forward/backward.

N: Streamer Fun - Activity
DA: 4 to 8
DV: Rhythmics and creativity
F: Free
E: One or two streamers per child and a record player and music
D: Using one streamer made from paper or plastic (approximately four to five feet long including a handle), have the children move freely about the room to the music. The children also move the streamers creatively to the music. The children should be encouraged to make large sweeping moves with the streamers while twisting, turning, and moving their body. The older children could use two streamers.

SIX TO EIGHT YEAR OLDS

N: Body Dancing - Activity
DA: 6 to 8
DV: Body awareness, creativity, and rhythmic development
F: Free
E: Record player and music
D: Ask the children to use various body parts

to dance to the music. They could start out with one body part and work up to many. This is good for any age group and is a particularly good way to get older children into creative rhythmic movement. The activity can begin with children sitting and then lying. Eventually, children can be on their feet using their whole body moving around the room to the music. Although modern music could be used, a better choice would be classical music with its many tempo and force changes.

N: Dancing Scarves - Activity
DA: 6 to 8
DV: Rhythmic development and creativity
F: Free
E: Two scarves per child
D: Beginning with one scarf which should be about two feet long, each child moves the scarf and their body creatively to the music. The music tempo should be changed frequently and the children encouraged to move in different ways, high/low, forward/backward, while using each hand. Next the children use two scarves simultaneously including juggling them to the music.

N: Picturerama - Activity
DA: 6 to 8
DV: Rhythmic development and creativity
F: Free
E: Picture cards
D: Children begin moving around the room to music. When a picture card is held up, they are to move the way the picture makes them feel but keep time to the music. The music tempo should change frequently, and children should be asked to do their interpretive movement in different ways, high/low, forward/backward.

N: Musical Hoops - Activity
DA: 6 to 8
DV: Rhythmic ability and body awareness
F: Free
E: 8 to 10 hoops
D: This is similar to cooperative musical chairs except hoops are used. Children move according to the music which should be varied—fast/slow, heavy/

light—and when the music stops, children find a hoop and put at least one foot inside the hoop while striking a pose and freezing until the music begins again. More than one person can be inside a hoop. Each time the music begins, some hoops are removed. By the end, all the children must get at least one foot into the remaining hoops while striking a pose.

N: Number Statues - Activity
DA: 6 to 8
DV: Rhythmic development and body awareness
F: Free
E: Music
D: As the music begins, children begin moving appropriately to the speed of the music. They can be asked to gallop, skip, etc. as well as move high/low, heavy/light, or forward/backward. As they are moving, the teacher holds up a card with a number on it; children continue to move as instructed as they form groups according to the card number, i.e., #2, get a partner. When the music stops, the children form a statue. Add to the activity by holding up a card with a word on it which tells the children what kind of statue to make, i.e., baseball, car, house, dog, etc. When the music begins again, the children again move individually according to the music and the instructions.

N: Long Jump Ropes - Activity
DA: 6 to 12
DV: Coordination and rhythmic ability
F: Groups of three
E: 13' long jump ropes
D: Long jump roping is usually thought of as an activity for very young children, but children of all ages can enjoy long rope jumping with such complicated activities as double rope jumping reserved for eleven- and twelve-year-old children. Since two people are fairly inactive, however, long rope jumping should be done only until enough ability is acquired to do short rope jumping. The turners should move the rope primarily with the forearm while keeping their elbows at their side. Jumpers should stand in the center and face one of the turners. The following is

a progression of long rope jumping activities from easy to difficult:

1. Stand in the middle and jump the rope as it is rocked back and forth.
2. Jump while the rope makes complete turns.
3. Coming in the front door—the rope is coming toward the top of the child's head and down toward the feet.
4. Coming in the back door—the rope is coming up underneath child's chin.
5. There are a number of little rhythmic chants, such as reciting the alphabet, which can be done. Also, children can do such physical activities as turning, touching the ground, and skipping while jumping.
6. Short rope jumping while long rope jumping.
7. Simultaneously jumping two long ropes crossed at a 90-degree angle —this requires four turners
8. Double Dutch—jumping two ropes alternately turned by the same two turners.
9. There are some very complicated stunts which can be done while jumping either one or two long ropes at the same time, but their accomplishment goes beyond the normal physical education class.

N: Short Jump Ropes - Activity
DA: 6 to 8
DV: Rhythmic ability and coordination
F: Free
E: One rope per child
D: The first thing to do before beginning single rope jumping is be sure the child can long rope jump. The second thing is to be sure the rope is the correct length. To determine correct length, have the child stand on the rope with both feet fairly close together and then pull up on the ends; the ends should just touch under each arm pit. To turn the rope correctly, the arms should make very little movement with the wrists doing most of the work. The child should be taught to jump only high enough to let the rope pass under his/her feet; the knees should not be bent while jumping, and the movement should be done on the toes. Either a two

beat or single beat jump can be used. In the double beat, the child takes a jump between each actual jump of the rope. In single beat, a jump is only taken when the rope is about to go under the feet. There are literally hundreds of different rope tricks which can be done. The ones listed below are in order of difficulty from simple to complex. To add to the value of jumping rope, it should be done to music.

1. Front jumping
2. Back jumping
3. Jumping and doing various forward locomotor activities
4. Jumping and moving backward
5. Jumping forward and moving backward and vice versa
6. Cross in front
7. Cross in back while backward jumping
8. Go from front rope jumping to back rope jumping without stopping the rope and keeping it going in the same direction. Sound difficult? It isn't. While jumping forward, bring the two hands together at the side of the body while continuing to turn the rope forward. One arm should be across the body to keep the rope in the proper direction. The child then turns towards the hands and ends up facing the opposite direction. The opposite arm is now across the chest. The rope is now turning backward and the child needs to merely open the rope and begin jumping backward. This is an easy skill and an important one to development of routines.
9. Jumping with a partner - side by side, standing front to back, jumping in while one is turning, and the most difficult, standing back to back while turning the rope backward.
10. Double jump in which the rope goes under the feet twice on one jump
11. Rhythmic routines
12. There are numerous difficult single rope skills which could be mastered with considerable practice. Such skills, however, usually go beyond the scope of a physical education class.

N: Parachute Fun - Activity
DA: 6 to 8
DV: Rhythmic development and cooperation
F: Circle holding the chute
E: Parachute
D: The parachute's main value is rhythmic development with or without music. Children learn to cooperate as they must move rhythmically to accomplish the various stunts which follow. There are a number of records with parachute activities and rhythms.

The mushroom: Children pull up on the chute while taking one or two steps toward the center of the circle to form a giant mushroom. They then step back pulling the chute tight before doing it again. Children must move rhythmically to do this.

Waves: Children create waves either big or small by shaking the chute. This is done best to music.

A variety of activities may be performed with a parachute.

The clam: Children raise the chute like the mushroom but turn 180 degrees by releasing and then re-grabbing the chute so they have it over their heads. They then go down on one knee and snap the chute to the floor in front of them. If they have done it correctly, they will disappear under the chute.

The cloud: This stunt requires extreme cooperation and rhythmic ability. The children pull up on the chute as they would in the mushroom to a count of four. On the fourth count, everyone must release the chute at the same time. If it has been done correctly, the chute should continue up for a brief time and then peel off toward one side and come back down. If there is even a little wind, this cannot be done effectively outside.

The big roll: A 13 to 16" playground ball is rolled around the outside of the chute. This is done by raising and lowering portions of the chute at appropriate times.

The routine: The children develop a routine to music. This activity works best with eight to ten children in the group. Other children in the class could be simultaneously developing a routine to the same music using lummi sticks, ropes, or tinikling sticks.

A tinikling routine.

N: Symphony - Activity
DA: 6 to 8
DV: Rhythmic ability and creative movement. Can be an integrated activity if classical music is used.
F: Children face the conductor board, spreading out so all can see the board
E: Activity chart, record player, music and conductor's wand (stick)
D: As the music begins, the conductor (teacher) points to a movement listed on the board. The children then do that movement until the conductor changes it. Children may move freely about the room but must be attentive to the conductor. The movement should be done in time to the music. Movements can include galloping, skipping, walking, etc. The conductor should change the music and the activities with an emphasis on the quality of movement—force, time, space, and level. These four movement terms can be included on the board and used to direct the children's movement, i.e., skip backward, walk lightly, run heavily, etc.

N: If You're Happy - Activity
DA: 6 to 8
DV: Rhythmic ability
F: Circle or scattered
E: None
D: All players sing the song and follow the directions given:
1) If you're happy and you know it, clap your hands. [clap, clap] If you're happy and you know it, clap your hands. [clap, clap] If you're happy and you know it, then your face will surely show it. [smile] If you're happy and you know it, clap your hands. [clap, clap]
2) Stamp your feet
3) Nod your head
4) Do all three
Other directions may be used.

N: The Wheels on the Bus - Activity
DA: 6 to 8
DV: Rhythmic ability
F: Free
E: None
D: The leader will sing the song, showing the movements that go with verses.
The wheels on the Bus go round and round *(Body movement: arm circles)* all through the town.
The wipers on the Bus go swish, swish, swish *(Body movement: arm wave)* all through the town.
The driver on the Bus goes move on back, move on back *(Body movement: hitch hike)* all through the town.
The money on the Bus goes ching, ching, ching *(Body movement: fingers dropping money)* all through the town.
The people on the Bus go up and down *(Body movement: knee bend, sitting down and getting up)* all through the town.
The babies on the Bus go wah, wah, wah *(Body movement: face crying, hands up to eyes)* all through the town.
The mothers on the Bus go sh, sh, sh *(Body movement: finger up to mouth)* all through the town.

N: Moving to Cultural Music - Activity
DA: 6 to 8
DV: Rhythmic development and social studies

F: Free
E: None
D: This activity is coordinated with the study of other cultures and countries. Children move to classical music from a variety of countries associated with the classroom lesson. There movements can also be associated with things they have learned about the country, i.e., popular sports in that country, ethnic dances, etc.

EIGHT TO TEN YEAR OLDS

N: Lummi Sticks - Activity
DA: 8 to 10
DV: Rhythmic development and creativity
F: Free or in small groups
E: Lummi sticks
D: Children can create lummi stick routines. Lummi sticks can be used in a variety of ways.

   1. Children keep time to music by hitting sticks on floor, together or a combination of the two.
   2. Children can work in pairs to design ways to hit and pass sticks while keeping time to music.
   3. Small groups can be formed to create routines.
   4. Children can sit, kneel, be on their feet, or combine a number of positions.
   5. The best music to use is that which has a distinctive beat and phrases which are easy to detect. The teacher should practice with the records to check their suitability before using them with the children.

Working together in small groups, children can create lummi stick routines.

   6. At first, children can follow the teacher who goes through a variety of different moves.
   7. Children are then encouraged to create their own movements. "How many different ways can you pass the sticks with a partner (in a group) and still keep time with the music? How many different levels can you use in a routine? Can you keep time with your body and your sticks simultaneously?"

N: Ball Dribbling to Music - Activity
DA: 8 to 10
DV: Rhythmic and manipulative ability
F: Free
E: Each child has an 8 1/2" playground ball
D: Each child dribbles his/her ball to the music which should be changed frequently. They begin by dribbling in place high and low, and fast and slow according to the music. Then they begin moving around the room forward and backward while still using the other qualities of movement, high/low, fast/slow, and heavy/light.

N: Rope Jumping - Activity
DA: 8 to 10
DV: Rhythmic ability and creativity
F: Free or in small groups
E: Short jump ropes
D: *Rope jumping:* Rope should be long enough so that if a child stands on it with both feet, the arms could bend at less than 90-degrees. Jump rope forward and backward using double beat, then move to single beat (one jump for each rope turn).

Crossing rope in front: While jumping rope forward, arms are crossed until elbows touch and hands are on opposite sides. Child jumps through the crossed rope, uncrossing it as it goes up behind him/her.

Crossing rope in back: This is easier to do once learned, but is a harder skill for children to master. As the child is jumping rope backward, the hands and arms are crossed as in front crossing above. The crossing should be made as the rope is in front of the child. The tendency is to attempt to take the crossed arms overhead along with the rope which is impossible to do. Although this is not a necessary lifetime skill, it is a challenge to children that keeps them jumping—good for endurance development. It is also a good developer of coordination.

Front rope jumping to back rope jumping and vice versa without stopping the rope: "Can you go from front rope jumping to back rope jumping while continuing, and vice versa, without stopping the rope? Can you go from front rope jumping to back rope jumping while continuing to make continuous circles with the rope in the same direction?" This is another problem-solving challenge which helps children become more coordinated and is an important skill to learn if routines are to be created. There is a trick to this one. After jumping forward, the rope is held to the side with fists together in a sort of praying position. The child keeps the rope going, making full loops in the forward direction. The child then makes a 180-degree turn—turn forward the rope—and then again opens the rope and begins jumping backward.

Partner jumping: Pairs try to see how many different ways they can jump rope together using open rope—front to front, front to back, back to back, side to side facing the same or opposite directions, or one child jumps in while the other is turning a single rope.

N:	Cooperative Musical Chairs - Activity
DA:	8 to 10
DV:	Cooperation and rhythmic development
F:	Circle around chairs
E:	Music
D:	Played like regular musical chairs except no one is eliminated. As chairs are removed, children sit on each other's laps. Eventually a long chain of lap sitting is required when there are only a couple of chairs left.

In Cooperative Musical Chairs, no one is eliminated.

N:	Creative Rhythmics - Activity
DA:	8 to 10
DV:	Creativity and rhythmic development
F:	Free or in small groups
E:	Music
D:	Rhythmic activities should be a combination of structured (primarily dances) and unstructured (creative) with an emphasis on creative movement.

1. Work in pairs or small groups to create movement to classical or modern music.
2. Have children depict moods to suit various kinds of music. "How does this music make you feel? Can you move that way?" Moods can include: happy, sad, joyful, mad, afraid, gay, and unhappy.
3. Music can depict situations. "What could you be doing when this music

Partner Jumping.

is playing?" Situations could be: walking on a dark road, being in a haunted house, on a crowded street or bus, ice skating, or playing in a field.

    4. Children can all use other objects for rhythmic routines including: wands, balls, streamers, ropes, and a parachute.

N: Moving to Cultural Music - Activity
DA: 8 to 10
DV: Rhythmic development and social studies
F: Free
E: None
D: This activity is coordinated with the study of other cultures and countries. Children move to classical music from a variety of places associated with the classroom lesson. There movements can also be associated with things they have learned about the country, i.e., popular sports in that country, ethnic dances, etc.

N: Musical Manipulation - Activity
DA: 8 to 10
DV: Rhythmic development and manipulative ability
F: Free
E: About 20 rubber balls, 20 jump ropes, 20 beanbags, and 20 yarn balls
D: Children begin by manipulating one object to the music; they are then asked to manipulate two objects at a time; then two different ones; for those more adventuresome, they could try three objects at a time. After a period of individual activity, children select a partner and the two manipulate several objects simultaneously. Finally, the children form small groups (they determine the size) and see how many objects they can manipulate at a time. The music should be varied, and teacher should direct children to do their manipulation while moving around, forward, backward, high, low, fast, slow, heavy, and light. When with partners and in groups, the teacher should continue to challenge the students to move in different ways as indicated above.

TEN TO TWELVE YEAR OLDS

N: Rope Jumping - Activity
DA: 10 to 12
DV: Rhythmic ability and fitness
F: Free, partners, or in small groups
E: Long and short jump ropes
D: *Rope jumping:* Rope jumping is not only a self-testing activity, it also aids the development of coordination, rhythmic ability, and fitness. The skills described in the following list can be mastered by many ten- to twelve-year-olds.

    1. *Double jump:* In the double jump the rope passes under the feet twice in one jump. This skill requires a quick double turn of the rope while jumping higher than usual. Most children try to enter the double jump from a very fast single rope jumping speed. Only rope speed is necessary when the double jump is attempted. Some children will be able to master it from a single jump, returning to a single jump speed without losing control of the rope turn. Others will make it under the feet twice but lose their balance, causing them to stop jumping.

    2. *Routines to music:* Rope jumping routines combining a number of skills put to music are a valuable developmental activity.

    3. *Short rope jumping while long rope jumping:* Jumping a short rope while at the same time jumping a long rope requires body coordination and coordination of three people—the long rope turners and the short rope turner.

    4. *The long rope crisscross:* Two long ropes are turned simultaneously while crossed at a 90-degree angle. Children try to jump in after the ropes have begun moving.

    5. *Double Dutch and Irish:* To turn Double Dutch, two ropes are turned simultaneously by two turners holding one rope in each hand. In Double Dutch the turner's hands travel up toward the turner's chin and away from the body. Full arm circles are required. Double Irish is the same

as Double Dutch except the turner's 0hands begin moving down toward the feet and away from the body. The biggest difficulty initially with these two skills is getting the turners working properly. After the ropes are going, children try to jump in. Usually only a small percentage of children can do these double rope activities.

6. *Rope jumping:* Children attempt to do a dance while jumping rope.

N: The Grand March - Activity
DA: 10 to 12
DV: Rhythmic development
F: Two lines - one of boys and the other girls
E: None
D: This is a particularly good way to get the children into a boy/girl couple arrangement. When the music begins, the head two children come together so the boy is on the girl's left. Holding hands, they go between the two lines. The remaining children continue to form couples and follow the lead couple. As they near the end of the movement area, several patterns can be used. The couple can separate and go back into a line, or the first couple can go to the left and the next right followed by alternating left, right couples. One pattern which has been found to be successful is to have the couples alternate left and right and then when they come together again at the opposite end of the area, they form groups of four which they go down the center of the area, alternating left and right in fours. When they reach the top of the area a second time, they go back to two's again but this time they follow the lead couple forming a double circle of couples.

N: Hoops and Things - Activity
DA: 10 to 12
DV: Rhythmic development
F: Groups of four
E: A basketball for each person and one hoop per group
D: Each group develops a routine to music using all the balls and the hoop.

N: Folk and Square Dance - Activity
DA: 10 to 12
DV: Rhythmic ability

F: Depends upon the dance
E: Music
D: *Polka:* The polka can be developed from a two step which is relatively easy for children to learn. Have children form a single circle. When music starts all begin doing a slide (side gallop) counterclockwise while facing the center of the circle. On the teacher's command "change," the lead foot is changed by having the children face away from the center while still moving counterclockwise. The time between "changes" can gradually be shortened to the point the children are changing the lead foot every time, thus creating the two step. The sequence is step, together, step, turn. To create the polka step, ask the children to vigorously lift their knee as they change the lead foot. This lift will usually cause the hop required to change the two step to the polka.

The Schottische: The schottische step consists of three steps and a hop. The three steps are taken with the hop coming on the foot which leads on the third step. Beginning with the right foot, it would be step forward right, step forward left, step forward right and hop on right foot. The side schottische can be done either left or right. To the right, it would be step right on the right foot, close left foot to right, step sideward on the right foot and hop on the right foot.

Ladies Chain: The ladies chain is done between any two ladies by grasping right hands and going past each other extending their left to the opposite gent (boy). The gent takes the left hand and places his right hand on the girl's back making a half circle in place. These ladies have thus switched positions and partners. Frequently, they will chain back again right away.

Promenade: There are a variety of ways to promenade with the most popular one being the holding of both hands right to right and left to left in front of the couple. The boy is on the inside.

The Bleking: The bleking is sometimes referred to as the Mexican hat dance step. It is a quick alternating of the feet with the heel of the lead foot striking the floor in front of and slightly to the right or left of center of the body. The bleking is done in a series of three steps, right, left and right with a slight pause between series of threes.

Partners: The most difficult thing to do when teaching folk and square dancing to ten and eleven year olds is getting them into a partner arrangement. Although there is a whole series of *Dances Without Partners,* children will miss valuable rhythmic experiences if they never have partners. Most children enjoy partners of the opposite sex, but cannot acknowledge the fact because of peer pressure. No matter how hard one tries, children have to put on a show when pairing up. This normal behavior which is disruptive can be minimized by promising them a favorite activity for their cooperation. Such a tactic is justified because rhythmic activities requiring partners are valuable and children enjoy them even though they usually will not admit it.

A grand march can be used with the girls on one side of the floor and the boys on the other coming together at the top of the hall two at a time in a kind of follow the leader. The random selection minimizes the choosing process which can cause hurt feelings if someone is rejected.

Another method is to have the girls make a circle and then have the boys stand between two girls. The girl on the boy's right then becomes the boy's partner.

Folk Dances: There are a variety of folk dances ranging from simple to complex which can be taught to children. The children's past experience and ability dictate which to use. The best series for folk dances is *The World of Fun.* With dances for all ability levels and from numerous countries, this series will provide hours of fun. The *Dances Without Partners* series also provides a wide range of rhythmic experiences. Both of these series come with complete dance instructions. The *Dances Without Partners* records have verbal instructions.

Square Dancing: Square dancing is usually done in a four couple square with the head or number one couple being the

one with their backs to the music. Couple two is on their right, three is across from them and four is to their left. The lead couples are one and three, the side couples are two and four. The boy is on his partner's left side and the girl to the boy's left is the corner lady.

TERMS:

Do si do: The do si do is done either with the partner or corner lady and is executed by moving towards each other, arms folded across the chest. The two pass right shoulders, go back to back and then move backwards into place (can be done right or left).

Allemande: The allemande is done with the corner gent and lady taking left hands and making a half turn, moving past each other, returning to their original positions.

Grand Right and Left: The grand right and left is begun by facing one's partner joining right hands. The two pull past each other extending their left hand to the person coming toward them. This right, left, right continues until partners meet again, at which time they usually take hands and promenade back home. The grand right and left is almost always preceded by an allemande left which usually confuses children. Some prefer to teach the grand right and left in a large circle, but more success may be possible teaching it in the regular square. Most times only one or two persons are having difficulty, and they are easily identified and helped in the small groups. By creating a little competition among the squares, motivation and thus learning can be increased.

Star: The star is formed by four persons extending the same hand and grasping another's wrist to form a square. This can be done either right or left and the four usually circle in the direction they are facing.

Home Position: The home position is always where the boy began the dance. When partners are switched, they return to the boy's home position.

Calling: The caller is the person responsible for telling the dancers what to do. Some records have the callers on them, but these are not recommended during the early stages of learning. When mistakes are made, the record must be stopped and begun again. With the high noise level usually associated with early learning, the record caller is often difficult to hear. By using a microphone and calling one's own square dances, the teacher is able to control the pace. Those records with instructions on them are also difficult for children to understand. The teacher should teach the dance and rely on the record only for music.

N: Creative Rhythmics - Activity
DA: 10 to 12
DV: Creativity and rhythmic ability
F: Depends upon the activity
E: Depends upon the activity
D: Creative activities, and particularly creative rhythmics, are too frequently limited to younger children. The ten- and eleven-year-olds can gain valuable movement experiences while developing creative ability using rhythmics.

1. Modern dance to commercially available music or to music produced by the children can be successful with ten- and eleven-year-old. The movement qualities of force, time, space, and level can be used to establish guidelines to aid children in the development of original dance routines. Children can work together in pairs or small groups to develop dances.

2. For children unaccustomed to creative activities, familiar activities such as rope, lummi sticks, tinikling poles, wands, and streamers can be used to foster creative rhythmic routines. Rope, wand, and streamer routines can be done alone or in a group; lummi stick activities and tinikling are usually group activities. Establishing criteria for routines provides guidance during the early phases of creative development. Criteria for various activities could be as follows:

Ropes:
1. Jump both single beat and double beat.
2. Have both front rope jumping and back rope jumping.
3. Move around while jumping.

4. Use the rope in some other rhythmic way which does not require jumping.

Lummi sticks:
1. Do an activity while sitting or kneeling.
2. Do a move while on your feet and moving around.
3. Have one pass in which everyone's sticks are being passed at the same time.
4. Keep rhythm with your body as well as the sticks during one phase of the routine.

Tinikling:
1. Work with a partner who is doing a mirror image of your move.
2. Have a part in which partners are moving in opposite directions.
3. Have a part in which you follow each other through the sticks.

N: Tinikling or Bamboo Pole Dance - Activity
DA: 10 to 12
DV: Rhythmic development and creativity
F: Groups of three or four
E: One set of poles per group
D: Using either bamboo or plastic poles (six to eight feet long), two children (the clackers) in the group keep time to the music which can either be 3/4 or 4/4 music. When using 3/4 music, the children strike the poles two times on the floor about shoulder-width apart and one time together (about six to eight inches off the floor). In 4/4 time they hit the floor twice and together twice. For safety, they hold the sticks only with the ends of their fingers. Then if the sticks are stepped on, they will come out of the hands and not pinch the fingers between the pole and the floor, or cause the sticks to break. The dancers represent the long-legged Tickling Bird which the natives (the clackers) are trying to catch. The dancers move rhythmically through the sticks so as not to get their feet caught. There are a number of successful steps which can be used; success is determined by maintaining an in, in, out rhythm. When using 4/4 music, the number of possible steps is increased as the children move in, in, out, out. When using 3/4 music, the children must keep one foot above the sticks at all times or they will lose the rhythm. The children should be encouraged to create

their own routine, and two or more children can dance together using one set of sticks. Steps which can be used include straddling the sticks and jumping both feet into the sticks at the same time; and making a full turn as they go through the sticks by stepping into the sticks while turning. The full turn is easier when using 4/4 music. Another variation is to have two sets of sticks crossed at right angles, and having four dancers going in a circle; again, it is easier to use 4/4 music when using this cross stick arrangement.

REFERENCES AND SUGGESTED READINGS

Graham, G., S. Holt-Hale, and M. Parker. *Children Moving* (3rd ed.). Mountain View: Mayfield Publishing Co. 1998.

Kirchner, G. and G. Fishburne. *Physical Education for Elementary School Children* (9th ed.). Madison: W. C. Brown and Co. 1995.

Nichols, B. *Moving an Learning: The Elementary School Physical Education Experience* (3rd ed.). St. Louis: Mosby Publishing Co. 1994.

Pangrazi, R. and V. Dauer. *Dynamic Physical Education* (11th ed.). Boston: Allyn and Bacon. 1995.

Selective Web Sites

Lesson Plans: http://schools.eastnet.ecu.edu/pitt/ayden/physed8.htm
Omaha Public Schools: http://www.ops.org/pe/elem.html
PE Central: http://pe.cental.vt.edu/
PE Links 4U: http://www.pelinks4u.org/sections/elementary/elementary.htm
SPARK: http://www.acsm.org/
A great search engine: http://www.sparkpe.org/programElementaryPE.jsp?curricula=PhysEdK-2&program=ElementaryPE

Chapter 17

Integrated Activities and Games

After completing this chapter, the student should be able to:

1. Describe at least one example of an integrated activity for each of the following: language arts, science, social studies, and math.
2. Design an integrated activity for each of the areas in #1 above.
3. Define the key terms listed below.

Key Terms

Integrated activity
Integrated game

An integrated activity or game has as its primary purpose the accomplishment of some physical education objective, and a secondary purpose of teaching or reinforcement of some academic concept from an area such as language arts, math, science, or social studies. As in the case of a de-velopmental activity or game, the integrated game or activity must have all the children moving nearly all the time. Care must be taken in designing an integrated activity not to compromise the physical education objective by over-emphasizing the academic component.

EXAMPLES

The activities under each age group are only examples which can help the reader develop integrated activities and games for his/her particular situation. Some of the creative activities (chapter 15) and games (chapter 18) can be modified to make them integrated.

Integrated Activity: The Story Play

A story play is an example of an integrated activity. The primary purpose is to develop the child's quality of movement, and the secondary purpose is learning or reinforcing academic concepts in the areas of science or social studies. Using problem-solving questions, a teacher guides the children through the story; the problems presented in the questions should seek solutions which focus on the quality of movement, force, time, space, and level. Children are encouraged to be creative. Questions, for example, could be, "What would it be like to move inside your space craft (weightlessness)?" or "It is very smoky in the fire—How does the fireman have to move to get under the smoke (crawl on the floor)?" The story's theme, besides focusing on movement, has an academic component, i.e., children can take a trip into space, go into the jungle, swim underwater, pretend they are firemen, visit a farm or zoo, or reenact the pioneers trip west or the trip to the New World. As the children move, the teacher can help the children learn by totally involving them in the process, sight, sound, and body.

Integrated Game: Modification of Crows and Cranes

An example of an integrated game is a modification of Crows and Cranes. In regular Crows and Cranes, the class is divided in half with each group forming a straight line beside each other and facing the leader. A line drawn on the ground between them is helpful. One group is designated as the crows and the other the cranes. If the leader calls out "crows," the crows run to a safe base (a

Crows and Cranes is an example of an integrated game.

line only about five feet away) while the cranes chase and try to tag them. Any person tagging someone in the other line gets one point. If cranes are called, they run to their safe base which is in the opposite direction from the crows' base. Children do not know who will be called and either group can be called upon to run toward their base several times in a row.

To modify Crows and Cranes and make it integrated, one line is designated as vowels and the other consonants. If the word called out by the leader begins with a vowel, the vowel line runs to a safe base. If the word does not begin with a vowel, the consonants run to safe base. Another integrated variation has the children designated as odd and even. In this variation, math problems are used and the children respond according to whether the answer is odd or even.

In fact, the basic Crows and Cranes' rules can be applied to any academic information which can be dichotomized. If the answer is yes or no, odd or even, etc., the game can be played. A number of the possible variations (Past and Present Chase) are included in this chapter under the eight- to ten-year-old age groups.

Self-Designed Integrated Activities and Games

Probably the most meaningful integrated games and activities are self-designed. The physical educator can work with the classroom teacher who knows the concepts to be taught or re-enforced. On a regular basis, the teacher can write down those concepts which will be emphasized during a particular period. This could be done once a month or more frequently if possible. This interaction between the physical educator and classroom teacher should help develop rapport and make the education environment more meaningful.

AGE GROUP EXAMPLES

This chapter is organized by age levels: four to six, six to eight, eight to ten, and ten to twelve. The integrated subjects include language arts, math, science, social studies, and history. Some activities can be modified to be used within several age groupings.

Key to Abbreviations:

N = Name of the activity

DA = Age of the student for which the activity is best suited (developmental age)

DV = The developmental value of the activity; i.e., fitness, manipulative ability, etc.

F = Formation

E = Any equipment needs

D = Description of the activity

FOUR TO SIX YEAR OLDS

N: Hokey Pokey - Activity
DA: 4 to 6
DV: Rhythmic development, knowledge of body parts, and language arts
F: Circle
E: None
D: Children sing to tune of "Hokey Pokey" and do the action:

"You put your right foot in.
You put your right foot out.
You put your right foot in and shake it all about.
You do the hokey pokey as you turn yourself about.
That's what it's all about."
The song continues with various body parts which can be determined by the children or the teacher. Flash cards can be used to indicate the body parts.

N: Seasons - Activity
DA: 4 to 6
DV: Creative movement and knowledge of the seasons
F: Free
E: None
D: The leader calls a season of the year. The children then act out something associated with that season. Variety can be achieved by being more specific on the movement such as: "Show me a winter sport; a type of flower you would see in the spring; a tree that stays green in the winter; etc."

Body awareness.

N: Body Parts - Activity
DA: 4 to 6
DV: Body awareness and language arts
F: Free
E: None
D: The teacher can either say or sing the following directions which the children follow:
"Put your right hand in the air,
Put your right hand on your nose,
Put your left hand on your head,
Now stretch and touch your toes,
Put your right hand on your ear,
Make your elbow touch your knee,
Now pat your tummy three times,
And smile so all can see."
Body parts can be changed each time the verse is given and flash cards can be used to indicate the appropriate body parts to use.

N: Geometric Shapes - Activity
DA: 5
DV: Quality of locomotor ability
F: Free
E: Pieces of paper with geometric shapes drawn on them
D: Hold up a shape on a flash card and ask the children to move in the shape using various locomotor skills such as running, walking, hopping, skipping, etc., while also emphasizing the quality of movement by doing the skills at various

speeds, different forces, in a variety of directions, and at many levels. Music can also be used in this activity. The name of the design, i.e., circle, square, triangle, etc., can also be written on the flash card.

N: Dinosaur Days - Activity
DA: 5 to 6
DV: Creative movement and knowledge of dinosaurs
F: Free
E: None
D: This is basically a story play about dinosaurs which would follow a classroom discussion about them. The story could focus on how they move, what they eat, and how they protect themselves.

N: Human Vocabulary - Activity
DA: 5 to 8
DV: Creative movement and language arts
F: Free
E: None
D: Working individually, children interpret vocabulary words through movement. Categories and their subdivisions are:
Weather — rain, thunder, sun, snow, etc.
Occupations — doctor, dentist, teacher, policeman, fireman, etc.
Animals — elephant, snake, bear, tiger, deer, etc.
Food — popcorn, bacon, Jell-O, etc.
Sports — football, basketball, tennis, skiing, etc.

N: Rhyming Miming - Activity
DA: 5 to 8
DV: Creative movement and knowledge of rhyming words
F: Free
E: None
D: Children are given a word and are asked to show (mime) a word through movement which rhymes with the word given by the teacher. The teacher can they try to guess by calling out words he/she thinks certain children are acting out. The process can then be taken to couplets for the children to act out, i.e., "I like to eat all my ____." or "The big bee stung ____." The children must act out the line including the appropriate word for the blank.

N: Instruments - Activity
DA: 5 to 8
DV: Creative movement, knowledge of musical instruments and introduction to classical music
F: Free
E: Record player and classical music featuring solo instruments
D: Children are asked to either move to the solo instrument sound or to be the musical instrument they hear. In any case, children should move appropriately to the music, i.e., slow to slow music, lightly, heavily, or they could move low to quiet music and high to loud music. Music should be selected to vary the movement and cover all areas of quality of movement: force, time (speed), space, and level.

SIX TO EIGHT YEAR OLDS

N: Action Verbs - Activity
DA: 6 to 8
DV: Creative movement and knowledge of action verbs
F: Free
E: None
D: The teacher will say an action sentence, or it can be placed on an overhead, leaving out the action verb. The children will then act out an action verb to complete the sentence. There may be many appropriate actions, i.e., "Dan _____ the car." Words such as drove, washed, painted, wrecked, etc. are correct.

N: Opposites - Activity
DA: 6 to 8
DV: Movement quality and language arts
F: Free
E: Flash cards
D: Show children a series of flashcards and have them do the opposite movement from what is on the card. Possible cards include walk, run, stand up, lie down, walk forward, run backward, move slowly low, move fast high, etc. Changing the cards quickly can make the activity more enjoyable.

N: More and Most - Activity
DA: 6 to 8
DV: Movement quality and language arts
F: Free
E: None
D: A flash card is used to indicate a way to move such as slowly. Children then select a way to move slowly. The teacher then changes it to slower and finally slowest. Other combinations could be fast, faster, fastest; high, higher, highest; low, lower, lowest; and long, longer, longest.

N: Nouns and Verbs - Activity
DA: 6 to 8
DV: Creative movement and knowledge of nouns and verbs
F: Free
E: None
D: When the teacher calls out a noun, children drop to the floor; when a verb is called out, students will imitate the verb. After the students get the idea, one can be picked to be the leader.

N: Letters - Activity
DA: 6 to 8
DV: Creative movement and language arts
F: Free
E: Flash cards with letters on them
D: Children demonstrate a word through movement which begins with the letter on the card held by the teacher.

N: Moving Animals - Activity
DA: 6 to 8

DV: Movement quality and language arts
F: Free
E: None
D: The teacher holds up a picture of an animal with its name under it. Children then name the animal and move like the animal. The quality of movement is emphasized by presenting various animals such as those that move heavy or light, high or low, and fast or slow. Eventually, only the name is held up without the picture.

N: Rhyme Time - Activity
DA: 6 to 8
DV: Movement quality, creativity, and language arts
F: Free
E: Flash cards
D: The teacher holds up a flash card with a word on it. The children are then asked to show, through movement, a word that rhymes with the word on the flash card.

Flash cards are an excellent way to integrate language arts into the physical education curriculum.

N: Stations - Activity
DA: 6 to 8
DV: Depends upon station but written instructions can aid language arts development along with the physical
F: Stations spread out around area with about four to five children at a station.
E: Depends upon the station, but activities usually focus on fitness and manipulative skills
D: Written and/or recorded instructions are located at a series of (usually six to eight)

stations set up around the play area. A station may also include a picture along with the instructions to assist learning. Equipment should be available at every station sufficient to give each child his own piece of equipment. Children can either move from station to station (preferable) or complete a task prescribed in the instructions and then move on to the next station. Music can also be used to enhance the learning environment as the children play at the station.

N: The Snowman - Activity
DA: 6 to 8
DV: Creativity and science knowledge
F: Free
E: None
D: Begin the story by having the children pretend they are snowflakes falling. Then they can act as if they are walking through deep snow and then making a snowman. After the snowman is completed, they act out the part of the snowman melting when the sun comes out. Finally turning into water, they can pretend they are a brook. Emphasis can be placed on two of the three states of matter: solid and liquid.

N: The Weather - Activity
DA: 6 to 8
DV: Movement quality, creativity, and language arts/science
F: Free
E: Flash cards with weather terms on them
D: Flash cards are held up and children act out the terms. The terms should be associated with weather such as rain, wind, snow, storm, thunder, lightning, etc.

N: Metamorphosis - Activity
DA: 6 to 8
DV: Creative movement and metamorphosis of the Monarch butterfly
F: Free
E: None
D: This is a story play about the Monarch butterfly. The children move as if they were caterpillars crawling along and then up a weed branch where they shed their skin. They then eat and grow while winding a thread around and hang upside down. The wind blows them back and forth. They slowly work their way out of

the cocoon and unfold their wings. Finally, they fly away.

N: Animalrama - Activity
DA: 6 to 8
DV: Movement quality and science
F: Free
E: None
D: Various locations are selected such as the jungle, woods, desert, or backyard and children are asked what animals they might see in each location. They are then asked to move like the animals they name. The location can be changed frequently or one location can be selected and children can concentrate on a number of animals in that location.

N: Animals in Season - Activity
DA: 6 to 8
DV: Creative movement and science knowledge
F: Free
E: None
D: Ask children to show you through movement what animals do in the fall and then the winter, spring, and summer. Various animals could be squirrels, bears, birds, etc. Movements could include gathering food and storing it for winter, migrating south, hibernation, and playing during the summer.

N: Comparatives - Activity
DA: 6 to 8
DV: Creative movement, knowledge of comparatives
F: Free
E: None
D: Children use their bodies to show comparatives such as, "Can you make a thin shape? A thinner shape? The thinnest shape possible?" Other comparatives could be tall, taller, tallest; hot, hotter, hottest; fast, faster, fastest; short, shorter, shortest; slow, slower, slowest; etc.

EIGHT TO TEN YEAR OLDS

N: Human Vocabulary - Activity
DA: 8 to 10
DV: Creative movement, social interaction and language arts

F: Free or in small groups
E: None
D: Children work alone or in small groups to interpret vocabulary words through movement. Suggested categories and some subdivisions are:
Body parts — but the body part mentioned may not be used to interpret the word, i.e., use fingers to imitate "teeth"
Machinery — washing machine, toaster, copy machine, etc.
Tools — jack hammer, screwdriver, paintbrush, rake, etc.
Music — rock band, guitar, drums, conductor, parade, etc.
Emotions — fear, joy, frustration, love, anger, mad, etc.
Materials — wood, concrete, Velcro, metal, rubber, etc.

N: Nyms - Activity
DA: 8 to 10
DV: Reaction time, running, chasing, tagging, and language arts
F: Two equal groups standing side by side about four feet apart
E: None or flash cards could be used
D: One group is the Synonyms and the other the Antonyms. If the leader calls out a pair of antonyms, the Antonyms run to a safe base while being chased by the Synonyms. Anyone tagged joins the other team. If the words are synonyms, they run to a safe base while being chased. Flash cards with the nyms on them may be used.

N: Past and Present Chase - Activity
DA: 8 to 10
DV: Agility, past and present verb reinforcement
F: Two lines side by side; a safe base line is established beside each line about five to seven yards away
E: None
D: One group is designated as the Present and the other the Past. If the leader calls out a verb in the present tense, the Present team runs toward their safe base while the Past tries to take them. Anyone tagging a member of the other line gets one point. If the verb is in the past tense, the Past team runs and the Present tries to tag.

Any dichotomy (two possibilities only) can be used in this formation. Some other variations include: Farm Animals vs. Wild Animals; Land Animals vs. Marine Animals; Meat Eaters vs. Non-Meat Eaters; Flying vs. Non-Flying; Vowels vs. Consonants; Odd Answer vs. Even Answer; Living vs. Non-Living; etc.

TEN TO TWELVE YEAR OLDS

N: Human Vocabulary - Activity
DA: 10 to 12
DV: Language arts, problem solving, and group interaction
F: Small groups
E: None
D: Working in small groups, children interpret vocabulary words through movement. Categories and suggested subdivisions are:
Time—digital, analog, alarm clock, cuckoo, etc.
Colors—red, blue, green, etc.
Places—Hawaii, grocery store, movies, subway, sewer, etc.

N: Compass Exercises - Activity
DA: 10 to 12
DV: Fitness and knowledge of compass
F: Stations
E: Instructional cards at station
D: A large compass is drawn on the playground, and sequentially numbered cards with various exercises and instructions are widely placed about the play area.

Children begin at any station. Following the instructions, they do the exercises listed on the card and then try to find the next station according to the directions on the card, i.e., go fifty giant steps northwest. The children are instructed to find the cards in numeric sequence until they return to their original card. They are encouraged to use a natural compass such as the sun to help determine directions.

N: Stations - Activity
DA: 10 to 12
DV: Nearly any fitness area and language arts
F: Stations set up around the play area
E: Depends upon the lesson's purpose
D: Although stations can be used by any child who can read, they are very useful when working with this older age group. Written instructions are placed on cards which are distributed about the play area. Depending upon the task specified, appropriate equipment is included at each station. Instructions can be a task i.e., specific instructions on how to do something and/or problem-solving where the students try to solve various problems. This organizational method can be effective when there is limited equipment. If, for example, there are only two mats, the children can rotate to the mat station and complete specified tasks. This eliminates long lines waiting for a turn. The stations approach can also help reinforce knowledge of vocabulary words by integrating them into the instructions.

REFERENCES AND SUGGESTED READINGS

Davis, S. (Superintendent). *Standards of Learning Objectives. Department of Education*, State of VA, 1984.

Gabbard, C. Early Childhood Physical Education: The Essential Elements, *JOHPERD* 59:7, 1988, 99. 65-69.

Gabbard, C., et. al. *Physical Education for Children*. Engelwood Cliffs: Prentice-Hall, Inc., 1987.

Graham, G., S. Holt-Hale, and M. Parker. *Children Moving* (3rd ed.). Mountain View: Mayfield Publishing Co. 1998.

Hoffman, H., et. al. *Meaningful Movement for Children*. Englewood Cliffs: Prentice-Hall, Inc., 1987.

Kirchner, G. and G. Fishburne. *Physical Education for Elementary School Children* (9th ed.). Madison: W. C. Brown and Co. 1995.

Keogh, J. and D. Sugden. *Movement Skill Development*. New York: MacMillan Publishing Co., 1985.

Morris, G. and J. Stiehl. *Physical Education from Intent to Action*. Columbus: Charles E. Merrill Publishing Co., 1985.

Nichols, B. *Moving an Learning: The Elementary School Physical Education Experience* (3rd ed.). St. Louis: Mosby Publishing Co. 1994.

Pangrazi, R. and V. Dauer. *Dynamic Physical Education* (11th ed.). Boston: Allyn and Bacon. 1995.

Chapter

18

Games

After completing this chapter, the student should be able to:

1. Rate a game in each of the three domains using the scale, 0-5, described in the chapter.
2. Change a game to increase its value in any one of the three domains.
3. Design a developmental game.
4. Change a game using the method know as "games analysis."
5. Define the key terms listed below.

Key Terms

Developmental games
Educational domains

Low organizational games
New games

This chapter deals with low organizational games for children four to twelve years of age which should occupy no more than 10% of the curriculum for any age level. Although a game can be an effective way for children to learn, they require considerable instructional time. The competitive nature of games also can, if overused, be detrimental to the learning environment. This chapter describes the meaning of "low organizational games," as well as how to select games, rate them and change them. There is also a section on child-designed games. The final section has game descriptions, including charts which rate each game along with other helpful information.

LOW ORGANIZATIONAL GAMES

As the name implies, low organizational games normally require a brief explanation, minimal skills and have winners and losers. There are low organizational games for all ages and abilities. When selecting a physical education game, the children's age, ability, needs as well as the game's educational value must be considered.

This value is dependent upon several factors, including how children, as well as the teacher, are able to handle winning and losing. By definition, games are competitive and have winners and losers. To be most effective and fun, however, the competition should be kept to a minimum, particularly during the early elementary years, four to eight years of age. At all ages, winning and losing should be minimized and fun maximized. Game rules should be designed to make almost everyone a winner, particularly among younger children. As children get older, however, the win/lose factor becomes more important to them; but most older children, hopefully, will be able to handle winning and losing better than the younger children. Teachers can use winning and losing to help develop good sportsmanship which is so necessary in later athletic endeavors.

DEVELOPMENTAL GAMES

Another factor to consider when selecting a game is its developmental value. To be a developmental physical education game, it must make some contribution to the child's psychomotor growth and development. Another developmental factor is each child's participation time. For this book, a developmental game has all the children participating nearly all the time. There are literally thousands of games, but many games are primarily recreational with little psychomotor value. This is not to say that a recreational game is not fun or potentially valuable, only that the participation level is often so low that children may have little physical activity.

Brothers and Sisters is a developmental game.

QUESTIONABLE VALUE OF POPULAR GAMES

Many popular games such as Duck, Duck, Goose; Squirrels in Trees; and Red Rover; as well as circle games; elimination games; and relays afford very little physical activity. In fact, in some games such as Duck, Duck, Goose a child may never be chosen to participate physically. Elimination games tend to exclude the least skilled very quickly (those needing physical development the most) leaving them on the sidelines to watch their more skilled peers have all the fun. Most circle games and relays also have little active participation. If physical growth and development is the purpose, these low participation games should be avoided.

There are only two active people in Duck, Duck, Goose.

Circle games normally have little activity.

EDUCATIONAL DOMAINS AND GAMES

When playing a game, a primary concern should be how it relates to the three educational domains: psychomotor, affective, and cognitive. The psychomotor domain deals with the child's physical development in such areas as fitness and movement skills. The affective domain is concerned with attitudes such as self-concept and sportsmanship. The cognitive domain covers higher brain functions, including problem-solving and creativity as well as knowledge in such areas as body awareness and directionality.

NEW GAMES

Many educators concerned about the effects of competition and winning and losing often select New Games which is a trademark which often confuses people studying games. It must be emphasized that although the name includes "games," it is distinguished with a capital "G". Since there are no winners or losers, New Games are actually cooperative activities not games as defined in the dictionary. Those who advocate these "Games" point out that since everyone participates and has fun, everyone is winner. In New Games, everyone works cooperatively to accomplish a common goal.

Lap Sit is a New Game.

SELECTING A GAME

Game selection is normally determined by the children's developmental needs. If physical education is to be truly educational, the children's developmental needs should be assessed and then games are selected to help fulfill those needs. To be effective, all the children must be actively involved. Analyzing the game, therefore, is essential to determining the game's value.

1. Determine the child's needs.
2. Select a game which will help develop the child according to your evaluation.
3. Analyze the game to be sure it is developmental.
4. If necessary, change the game to make it better or more valuable according to the children's needs.

EVALUATING GAMES

In order to determine its value, a game must be evaluated. This evaluation should be based upon several factors such as the participation level, the amount of interaction, the intellectual level required, and the cognitive value are all factors which must be considered. Below is a game evaluation system.

Rating System

The rating system below uses a point scale from 0-5 with 5 designating the highest contribution. Each game will be rated in each of the three educational domains described earlier.

Psychomotor Domain. Games in which all the children are vigorously participating physically nearly all the time would receive a 5 psychomotor rating. Less vigorous games which have maximum participation would receive a 4. Where all the children eventually move but there are delays, the rating would be anywhere from 3 to 1. The range is determined by the amount of delay prior to moving. When all the children move after a delay, the game normally would get a 3 rating. Games requiring waiting for a turn such as relays or circle games, the rating would be 2 or 1. Games in which some children may never actively participate (most circle games) in the game or those in which children are systematically eliminated (Simon Says, Dodge Ball) would receive a psychomotor rating of 0.

Rating

5	Everyone is vigorously participating all the time.
4	Everyone is participating but not necessarily vigorously.
3, 2, or 1	Everyone eventually moves, but

there are delays between movement periods.

The number rating is determined by the amount of delay, i.e., relays are a good example of a game which would get a 2 or 1 rating.

0	Children are eliminated and/or some children might not get to play at all.

Affective Domain. Affective evaluation is determined by how much positive interaction there is among the children. The areas covered by the affective domain include attitudes such as self-concept, interpersonal relationships, respect for self and others, sportsmanship, sharing, patience, and respect for authority. Games which require physical contact between children and provide opportunities to develop positive attitudes would receive high ratings. Such games as Busy Bee, Brothers and Sisters, and some versions of Squirrels in Trees would, therefore, receive high affective evaluation.

Rating

5	The game requires interaction among all the children. Games which have children constantly changing partners, for example, would get a high rating.
4	The game requires having a partner.
3	The game requires some interaction. Tag games would be an example.
2	The game has a little interaction but is basically an individual game.
1	The game has almost no interaction.
0	Since all games have some interaction and are fun, a 0 rating is not given in the affective area.

Cognitive Domain. All games have rules, so they always get a minimum rating of 1 in this category. Games which make a contribution to the child's cognitive knowledge such as body parts, spatial terms, or fitness, health and safety; as well as knowledge in cognitive subjects such as science or language arts would get a rating of about 2 or 3 depending upon the degree of learning.

3   Games which make a significant contribution to knowledge in the cognitive area.

2   Games which make some contributions to cognitive knowledge.

1   Since all games have rules, this is the minimum rating. Low organizational games usually receive a cognitive rating of 1.

CHANGING GAMES

Many games may already be developmental, while others could be changed to make them better. The analysis mentioned above is the starting point. After analyzing the game, changes may increase its value.

Squirrels in Trees

The game appearing most frequently in elementary physical education texts is Squirrels in Trees. As described in most books, it is a good recreational game but a poor developmental one because only one-third of the children are active at any one time. Briefly, the game is usually described as follows:

Children are grouped in threes with two children holding hands to form a tree. The third child is the squirrel and gets "inside" the tree. There is at least one extra squirrel without a tree. When the leader says "change," all squirrels attempt to find a new tree including the one who did not have a tree. The child left out receives one point. During the game everyone gets to be a squirrel, and at the end those with the least points are declared the best squirrels.

In analyzing Squirrels and Trees, a low developmental rating of 2 or 1 would be given in the psychomotor area, since only one-third of the class is moving at any one time. Since interaction is required and there are frequent changes, it would receive a 3 in the affective area. The very simple rules would give it a 1 cognitive rating.

Changing Partners Version. To change Squirrels in Trees to increase its value, the number of children moving must be increased. One modification would be to have the trees do something, such as turning in a circle, when the change signal is given. However, a way to change its value in

Squirrels in Trees using hoops.

all areas is to have the trees change partners when the change signal is given. As soon as the teacher says "change," the trees separate and, holding arms (limbs) high in the air, begin chanting "tree, tree, tree," while quickly moving around to find another person to make a tree. The squirrels must wait until they see a completed tree to get inside. If the leader says "change" again, any tree left without a tree partner or a squirrel not inside a tree gets one point. This game can be played very successfully with six- and seven-year-old children. In this version, everyone is moving, there is a lot of interpersonal contact with many partners, and children must think a little more. This version would get a 4 psychomotor rating, a 5 affective rating and a 1 cognitive rating.

Using Hoops. Another Squirrels and Trees version is to give almost everyone a hoop which serves as the tree. On the leader's signal, everyone, including those without a hoop, tries to find a new hoop. Anyone not inside a hoop when the leader says "change" again gets one point. The signal can be "change" or the leader can call out a particular way to get to a new tree, such as hop, skip, jump, run backward, etc. This hoop version would receive a 4 or 5 psychomotor rating, a 2 affective rating and a 1 or 2 cognitive rating.

Old Mother Hen

Another game which has very low developmental value is Old Mother Hen. As written in most books, "Old Mother Hen" is inside a circle made by the class. With her are three chicks she must protect from being hit by a ball thrown by those making the circle. Having only one ball, the throwers have little activity and some children may never get into the center or handle the ball. The game, therefore, would receive a psychomotor rating of 0.

Modifying Old Mother Hen. A modification of Old Mother Hen is Old Plug the Horse. Children are divided into groups of four; three people make Old Plug by holding each other's waist. Old Plug thus has a head, body, and a tail. The fourth child is the farmer who is trying to give Old Plug a shot (beanbag). Old Plug does not want the shot and tries to keep the farmer in front of him at all times to protect his tail where he knows the shot must be placed. The farmer moves any way s/he likes to try to get behind the horse but may not touch the horse. If the farmer succeeds in hitting the tail's body (not the head or arms), s/he becomes the horse's new head and the tail becomes the new farmer. The game is continuous, with the winner being the person who remains as the head the longest. In this version, there is 100% participation, and all children develop agility. This game receives a psychomotor rating of 5, a 3 in the affective domain and a 1 in the cognitive domain.

Table 18.1. Squirrels in Trees — Original Version*

Players	Formations	Game Movements	Rules	Equipment
Entire Class	Group of 3. Two people hold hands to form a tree. Third person is a squirrel and stands inside of tree	Trees - Stationary Squirrels - Run	On signal, "Go," Squirrels run to get into a new tree.	None

Table 18.2. Squirrels In Trees — Changed Version*

Players	Formations	Game Movements	Rules	Equipment
Entire Class	Group of 3. Two people hold hands to form a tree. Third person is a squirrel and stands inside of tree.	Trees - Run to find new trees. Squirrels - Skip to new tree. While not in the process of changing, both trees and squirrels must jump in place.	On signal, "Go," trees must separate to find a new half tree. Once they are formed, squirrels can enter.	None

*See Chapter 8 for game description.

CHILD-DESIGNED GAMES

Whenever possible, the children should be given the opportunity to design and conduct their own games. This approach allows children to use their cognitive as well as affective skills. Cognitively, they attempt to design the game and then, working together, they play the games. Although this approach increases the cognitive and affective value of the activity, it will reduce its psychomotor value. The teacher must weigh the purpose of the activity, the time which will be devoted to it, and the children's needs. Although an excellent approach to games, the child-designed game may consume valuable movement time.

When appropriate, there are several ways to approach child-designed games. Each child can put a rule on a 3" x 5" card. Two or three cards can then be selected to begin the game. As the game progresses, additional cards are selected and the game modified to fit the new rules. Another approach is to begin with a known game and then have the children change it according to their wishes.

Old Plug the Horse is a modification of Old Mother Hen which has all children participating.

When using the child-design approach, one must be cautious to eliminate any dangerous situations the children may create. Many games children may use as a model to help design their game are extremely dangerous. A teacher must, therefore, be liability conscious.

GAME DESCRIPTIONS

Each of the four age level groups has a chart listing those games most appropriate for them. The chart also has the game's rating for each educational domain as well as a suggested teaching area. Some games are mentioned in more than one age group. This reflects the universal appeal of some games as well as their value across years.

Key:

P	=	Psychomotor Domain
A	=	Affective Domain
C	=	Cognitive Domain
G	=	Grass
MR	=	Multipurpose Room or Gym
HT	=	Hard top
Any	=	Any surface

GAMES FOR FOUR TO SIX YEAR OLDS

Very few games should be played during these years. Those which are used should minimize any emphasis on winning or losing while emphasizing fun. None of the games are suggested for four-year-old children, and even some five-year-old children could have problems with them.

NAME	Page #	P	A	C	G	MR	HT	ANY
Animal Movement	272	4	1	2				X
Brothers and Sisters	271	4	4	3	X	X		
Busy Bee	271	4	5	3	X	X		
Do This, Do That	271	4	1	2				X
Pick Up Colors	272	4	1	2	X	X		
Pick Up Trash	272	4	1	1	X	X		
Target Games	277	4	1	1				X
Where's a Partner	272	4	4	1	X	X		

GAMES FOR SIX TO EIGHT YEAR OLDS

Several of the games from the four- to six-year-old listing are included on this chart. This multiple listing reflects the universal appeal of certain games. Although the game is basically the same, each can be changed to account for the children's age. In Busy Bee, for example, the body parts which are emphasized should be different for each age level. Older children can often enjoy games designed for a younger age group. The same is not true when trying to go the other way; younger children may experience frustration when trying to play games designed for older children.

NAME	Page #	P	A	C	G	MR	HT	ANY
Brothers and Sisters	271	4	4	3	X	X		
Busy Bee	271	4	5	3	X	X		
Clean Out the Backyard	272	5	1	1	X	X		
Crows and Cranes	274	4	4	1	X	X		
Do This, Do That	271	4	1	2				X
Dribble Take Away	275	5	3	1	X		X	
Ghost Busters	274							
Hockey Fun	275							
Hoop Is Home	276	4	2	1		X	X	
In Stitches	273	4	3	1	X	X		
Jump the Shot	273	4	1	1	X	X		
Old Plug the Horse	274	5	3	1	X	X		
Over it Goes	271							
Pick Up Colors	272	4	1	2	X	X		
Pick Up Trash	272	4	1	1	X	X		
Progressive Tag	273	4	4	1	X	X		
Red Light, Green Light	273	4	2	1	X	X		
Scramble	280	4	2	1		X	X	
Simon Says	275	4	1	1				X
Spot	275	4	1	1	X	X		
Squirrels in Trees	274	4	5	1	X	X		
Target Games	277	4	1	1			X	
Tunnel Tag	275	4	2	1	X	X		
Where's a Partner	272	4	4	1	X	X		
Winds	273	4	4	1	X	X		

GAMES FOR EIGHT TO TEN YEAR OLDS

As with the previous age levels, many games cut across age levels. When games designed for younger children are used, they should be modified to reflect the children's ability and needs. A game should seldom be played identically across age levels.

NAME	Page #	P	A	C	G	MR	HT	ANY
Addition Tag	279	5	4	1	X	X		
Bombardment	277	4	2	1		X		
Catch the Dragon's Tail	278	5	3	1	X	X		
Combatives	276	5	3	1	X	X		
Crab Soccer	277	4	3	1		X		
Dribble Take Away	275	4	4	1		X	X	
Four Square	278	4	4	1			X	
Jump the Shot	273	4	2	1				X
Loop De Loop	276							
Monkey in the Middle	279	4	2	1				X
Newspaper Race	279	4	1	1				X
Old Plug the Horse	274	5	3	1	X	X		
Partner Pick Up	279	4	3	1	X	X		
Progressive Tag	273	5	2	1	X	X		
Protect Me Tag	278	5	3	1	X	X		
Sam Says	276	4	1	2				X
Scramble	280	4	4	2	X	X		
Spanish Leapfrog	279	4	2	1	X	X		
Target Games	277	4	1	2			X	
Travel Catch	280	4	2	1	X			
Wiggle Worm Race	279	5	4	1	X	X		

GAMES FOR TEN TO TWELVE YEAR OLDS

As can be seen, some of the ten- to twelve-year-old children's games receive low psychomotor ratings. This reflects this older group's changing developmental needs. Several games are designed to help develop teamwork and sportsmanship rather than physical skills.

NAME	Page #	P	A	C	G	MR	HT	ANY
Addition Tag	279	5	4	1	X	X		
All Tied Up	280							
Balloon Ball	283	4	2	1		X		
Balloon Bucket	283	4	2	1		X		
Beanbag Tug of War	281	5	3	1	X	X		
Bombardment	277	4	2	1		X		
Catch the Dragon's Tail	278	5	3	1	X	X		
Combatives	276	5	3	1	X	X		
Crab Soccer	277	4	3	1		X		
Crows and Cranes	274	4	2	2	X	X		'
Football Kick Across	281	3	3	1	X			
Four Square	278	4	3	1			X	
Frisbee Golf	282	4	1	1	X		X	
Frisbee Toss	283	4	1	1				X
Get Away	280	5	2	1	X	X		
Jump the Shot	273	4	2	1				X
Monkey in the Middle	279	4	2	1				X
Must Swing Baseball	281	2	3	1	X			
No Dribble Basketball	282	3	4	1		X	X	
Pillo Polo	282	4	4	1	X	X		
Plastic Hockey	281	4	4	1	X	X		
Progressive Tag	273	5	2	1	X	X		
Protect Me Tag	278	5	3	1	X	X		
Sam Says	276	4	1	2				X
Soccer Keep Away	283	4	4	1		X	X	
Spanish Leapfrog	279	4	2	1	X	X		
Squat Tug	280	5	2	1	X	X		
Target Games	277	4	1	2				X
The Dragon	280	5	3	1	X	X		
Two on Two Basketball	281	4	4	1		X	X	
Volleyball	282	3	4	2				X
Wall Ball	283	5	2	1		X		

GAME DESCRIPTIONS

Following is the code for the game descriptions:

N = Name
DA = The age for which the game is appropriate (developmental age)
DV = What the game will help develop (developmental value)
F = Formation
E = Equipment necessary
D = Description of activity
S = Safety

N: Busy Bee - Game
DA: 5 to 8
DV: Body image and social development
F: Free
E: None
D: Children move freely around the play area until the teacher calls out, "back to back or right knee to right knee" or some other body image concept. Upon hearing the instructions, children immediately find any person and take the position called for. There must be an uneven number of children at the beginning of the game. If there is an even number of children at the start, the teacher can join the game to make an uneven number. The person without a partner during the game is the Busy Bee and receives one point each time he or she is left without a partner. Those at the end of the game with the least number of points are the winners. Since the Busy Bee receives a lot of attention, some children will deliberately avoid getting a partner and thus ruin the game. The "point" idea will usually get the game moving well and a reminder about the rules to those trying to become the Busy Bee will usually suffice. The teacher can evaluate the child's knowledge of body parts, right and left, and the social interaction of the class during this game.

N: Over it Goes - Game
DA: 5 to 8
DV: Hand-eye coordination
F: Relay type lines of 8 to 10 in a line
E: At least one ball per person

D: The first person in the line takes a ball in both hands and passes it overhead to the second person, who then passes it overhead to the third person. As soon as the first person passes the first ball, s/he takes another ball and immediately begins passing it in the same fashion. Balls are passed down the line overhead until reaching the last person in line. As soon as the last person in line receives a ball, s/he runs to the front of the line and passes the ball overhead to the next person, and so on. A point is scored each time a child comes to the front of the line.

N: Brothers and Sisters - Game
DA: 5 to 8
DV: Body image and visual discrimination
F: Partners
E: None
D: Partners are in free formation around the play area. On the signal to go, children move away from their partners. Basic movements such as walking, running, etc. can be used. When the leader calls out, "back to back" or "right knee to right knee," partners must get back together solving the task established. The last two to come together get one point with a rule that any set getting more than three points has to sit out one turn. At the end, those with no points can be given special attention. Emphasis should be given to avoid collisions with others and a rule of no collisions could be added to the game to help develop better visual discriminations. This game, like Busy Bee, can be used to evaluate body image.

N: Do This, Do That - Game
DA: 5 to 8
DV: Fitness and auditory discrimination
F: Free
E: None
D: When the leader makes some physical move such as raising the arm and says, "Do this," everyone should do it. But if the action is followed by "Do that" anyone doing it receives a point. After a period of time, those with the fewest points are declared the best listeners. Exercise moves can be used in this game for fitness development.

N: Where's A Partner? - Game
DA: 5 to 8
DV: Locomotor movement, social interaction
F: Double circle—partners facing
E: None
D: Children are arranged in a double circle with partners facing. The inside circle has one more player than the outside. When the signal is given, the circles skip (or another locomotor movement) to the players' right. This means they are skipping in opposite directions. When the command "Halt" is given, the circles face each other to find partners. The player left without a partner is in the "mush pot" attempting to get a partner when the command "Halt" is given. The game can also be played using a record and record player. When the music stops, the players seek partners.

N: Pick Up Colors - Game
DA: 5
DV: Agility
F: Free
E: At least thirty colored balls (at least four different colors) and paper bags
D: Spread the balls over the play area. Each child is given a bag. When the color is called out, children race around picking up the appropriate colored balls and placing them in their bag. Then the next color is called out and so on until all the balls are picked up. Balls may be picked up in color order only. Children get one point for each ball. Rules should be designed to make almost every child a winner.

N: Pick Up Trash - Game
DA: 5
DV: Agility
F: Free
E: Scrap paper and paper shopping bags
D: Each child has a paper shopping bag and lots of scrap paper which they crumple up and scatter about the playing area. On the signal to go, the children run around the play area and pick up as much trash as possible. To eliminate a lot of time counting scraps of paper, each child who gets at least five pieces of paper gets a point. The paper is then scattered again and the game continues. The movement

Pick Up Trash

skill can be changed each time; i.e., skip, gallop, walk backward, hop, leap, etc.

N: Animal Movement - Game
DA: 5
DV: Fitness and science integration
F: Free
E: None
D: The leader begins doing an animal movement, such as flapping arms like a bird flying and says, "Birds fly." As long as the leader continues to name animals that fly, the children keep flapping their arms. As soon as the leader says something that does not fly, for example "Horses fly," the children must immediately stop flapping. Other possible movements include swimming, walking, hopping, and crawling. This is a good game to help children learn how various animals move.

N: Clean Out the Backyard - Game
DA: 6 to 8
DV: Throwing, catching, stopping ball with feet or hands, rolling ball
F: Class divided into two groups
E: Foam balls, one for each student, or as many as possible
D: Play area is divided into two courts, half of the class on each side. On signal, each person throws his/her ball across the center line. The object is to keep the balls in the opposite court. On signal all activity stops and balls are counted—the side with the least number of balls in its court wins.

Modifications:
   (1) Balls may be rolled instead of thrown, especially for kindergarten.
   (2) Balls may be stopped with feet, dribbled to the center line and kicked over the center line (without using hands).
 S: Only lightweight objects may be used such as low density sponge rubber balls or yarn balls. Beanbags, and playground balls should never be used.

 N: Progressive Tag - Game
DA: 6 to 12
DV: Hand-eye coordination and agility
 F: Free formation with one person being "it"
 E: Yarn balls or sponge rubber balls
 D: One person is "it" and has a sponge ball. He/she attempts to hit anyone else below the waist. The person can project him/herself by using his/her hands to block the throw. A person hit becomes "it" until the game ends. The person who starts the game as the "it" is no longer "it" after he/she hits the first person. If, however, he/she in turn is hit during the game, he/she is also "it" until the game ends. When a person is hit by the ball, he/she is "it" and goes and gets a ball and hits others. The last person hit is the winner and begins the next game.
 S: No one may be hit above the waist. Players must be reminded to watch where they are going.

 N: In Stitches - Game
DA: 6 to 10
DV: Agility and speed
 F: Five to six children per group lined up in a relay type fashion
 E: Two marker cones per group
 D: Each group lines up at a starting line facing a series of cones spaced out in front of them. They stitch together by joining one hand so they are all facing the same way. On the signal to go, each group runs across the area and around a marker cone and back. The group that has the lead person across the finish line first wins; the group, however, must stay stitched together the entire time. Once the winning group is determine the leader names a new way for the group to stitch together, i.e., hands on waist, hands on

shoulders, etc. The group must then have a new leader and get stitched together correctly. When ready, the group begins again; there is no start signal. Children can also do this using various locomotor movements such as skipping or galloping.

 N: Winds - Game
DA: 6 to 8
DV: Running, chasing, and fleeing
 F: Scattered
 E: Two blue ribbons and one yellow ribbon
 D: Two players are designated as the cold wind and marked with blue ribbons. Another child is termed the sun and marked with a yellow ribbon. The cold wind tries to freeze the children by tagging them. Tagged children must freeze in place. The sun may unfreeze a child by touching him/her and yelling "warm." After a given amount of time, those frozen the least number of times are declared the winners.

 N: Red Light, Green Light - Game
DA: 6 to 8
DV: Body awareness
 F: One straight line, children side by side, facing the leader on the other side of the play area
 E: None
 D: Leader calls out "green light," as he/she turns his/her back to the group, which begins moving toward the goal line. The leader counts to three or five depending upon the size of the area, and then turns to face the approaching group as he/she calls out "red light." Anyone caught moving after "red light" is called is sent back to the starting line to begin again. The game continues until one person crosses the goal line. This person becomes the new leader and the game starts again from the beginning. Children should call others by name which can aid the teacher and the children in learning names, particularly at the beginning of the year.

 N: Jump the Shot - Game
DA: 6 to 10
DV: Eye-foot coordination and fitness
 F: Circle of six or seven children with one child in the middle

E: Ten-foot-long ropes with beanbag tied to end

D: The center person turns a rope with a beanbag tied on the end in a circle. Children stay outside the arch of the beanbag until the rope is going (beanbag is kept close to floor), and then try to "jump in" as soon as possible. Anyone hit by the rope gets a point. Each person should take a turn in the center. At the end, those with the least number of points are the winners. To avoid dizziness, the center person should try to take the rope behind the back rather than turning in a circle. Older children should have no difficulty with the behind the back move.

N: Crows and Cranes - Game
DA: 6 to 12
DV: Auditory discrimination and agility
F: Two lines side by side, separated by about four feet
E: None
D: One group is the Crows and the other Cranes. If the leader calls out "Crows," the Crows run to a predetermined safe base (goal line) about five feet away while the Cranes chase and try to tag them. If "Cranes" is called, the Cranes run and the Crows chase. Anyone tagging a person in the other line gets a point. By adding confusing visual cues along with the verbal, the leader can increase the need to listen carefully; i.e., call Cranes, but point with the hand toward direction Crows would run. The leader can also call things like elephants or tigers to keep children on their toes.
S: Children may not hit or grab while tagging.

N: Ghost Busters - Game
DA: 6 to 8
DV: Agility
F: Children behind a starting line with one child in the middle of the play area
E: None
D: All the children begin by saying, "We are not afraid of any ghost," at which time they all try to reach the safe base (an open area on the other side of the play area) without being tagged by the person in the center. Those tagged must stay in the middle and help catch the others.

Once a child safely reaches the other side, they immediately repeat the "phrase" and attempt to go back to the other side. The last one caught is the winner.
S: Children must be reminded to watch where they are running and not try to watch the person chasing them.

N: Squirrels in Trees - Game
DA: 6 to 8
DV: Social interaction, agility, and movement competencies
F: Groups of threes
E: Hoops if playing variation
D: Two children make a tree by holding hands. The squirrel gets in the tree. There can be one or two squirrels without a tree. When the leader calls "change," everyone changes. A tree finds a new partner to make a tree (trees must seek out other trees, not pair up with a squirrel), and begins turning as soon as the tree is made. Squirrels must seek out a tree as soon as one is made. Any tree without a partner; or a squirrel without a tree when the next "change" signal is given, gets a point. At the end, those with the least number of points are declared the best squirrels. Everyone should get a chance to be a squirrel.

A good variation is to use hoops as trees. There must be one less hoop than children. On the "change" signal, children must switch hoops. Anyone not inside a hoop when the next "change" signal is given gets a point. The "change" signal can be a command on how the children are to move between hoops, i.e., "walk backward, skip, gallop, etc."

N: Old Plug the Horse - Game
DA: 6 to 10
DV: Agility, social interaction
F: Groups of four
E: Beanbags—one per group
D: Three persons make a horse, Old Plug. One person is the head, one the body, and another the tail; all of which are joined by holding onto each other's waist. Another person is the farmer who wants to give Old Plug a shot (with a beanbag) in the tail. The head tries to protect the

tail by keeping the farmer in front at all times. The farmer is allowed to do anything short of touching Old Plug to get to the tail and administer the shot (hit the tail with the beanbag). If the farmer is successful in hitting the tail or by causing the horse to come apart, he/she becomes the new head and the tail becomes the farmer. The idea is to be the head as long as possible. For safety, children must be instructed to stay in a designated area and not try to move, usually backward, all over the play area.

S: Children may not go anyway but in a circle. Often the horses head will force the horse to got backward. Children must be shown how to move only in a circle.

N: Simon Says—Body Image - Game
   Simon Says—Exercises - Game
DA: 6 to 8
DV: Body image and auditory discrimination or fitness
F: Free
E: None
D: One of the most versatile games, which is too frequently misused, is Simon Says. The game can be played in many ways depending on the objective. Basically, the children must do any command preceded by the phrase, "Simon Says...". Anyone doing the activity not preceded by the phrase is given one point. At the end, those with the least number of points are the winners. Asking the children to touch body parts can aid the development of body image. Exercises can be called for, as well as basic locomotor and non-locomotor moves. For purposes of evaluation, children can be asked to lie down and close their eyes as body parts are touched. This arrangement reduces the possibility of children watching each other and gives a truer picture of each child's knowledge of his/her body parts.

N: Dribble Take Away - Game
DA: 6 and older
DV: Hand-eye coordination and a lead-up to basketball or soccer (variation)
F: Free
E: One ball per child
D: Children begin dribbling their ball with one hand while at the same time trying to bat away another person's ball with their free hand. If a ball is knocked away, the child who lost the ball must retrieve it without touching anyone else's ball. As soon as the child begins dribbling again, s/he is back in the game. At the end, those who have lost their ball the least are declared the winners.
   A soccer variation is to have about 1/4 of the children without a ball. On the signal to go, the children dibble the ball with their feet around a predetermined area while those without a ball try to get a ball; if a person without a ball gets between one with a ball, then they get the ball. The child who lost the ball is not allowed to take it back from the person who took it, but can go after any other person with a ball.

S: Body contact is to be avoided. Rough play cannot be permitted

N: Tunnel Tag - Game
DA: 6 to 8
DV: Running, tagging
F: Free
E: None
D: Three people are "it." If a child is tagged, the tagger gets one point. Then the tagged child must get into a push-up position with the back arched up high to make a tunnel. The child is un-tagged when another child (not a tagger) goes under him/her. Every time a child un-tags a child he/she gets one point. After a period of time, the taggers are changed and the game continues. At an appropriate time as determined by the teacher, those with a certain number of points are declared the winners. The teacher should select a number of points so that everyone or almost everyone is a winner.

N: Spot - Game
DA: 6 to 8
DV: Quality of movement
F: Free
E: One beanbag per child less two
D: Beanbags are scattered about the area. There is one beanbag per child less two. The children move about the room as determined by the teacher. The quality of movement should be emphasized: force, time, space, and level in determining the

movement; i.e., walk backward, run heavy, slide, etc. As children move about the room, a signal is given at which time each child tries to place one foot on a beanbag. There can be only one child per beanbag. Each child who is successful receives one point. After a given amount of time all those with points are declared good movers.

N: Hoop is Home - Game
DA: 6 to 8
DV: Hand-eye coordination and agility
F: Free with hoops
E: One hoop per child less one
D: On a signal, perhaps music playing, children dribble a ball with their hand around the play area among the hoops. When the music stops, each child dribbles to a hoop (home) and continues to dribble the ball while standing in the hoop. The one left without a hoop is "it." The "it" removes a hoop and the game continues until there are only two hoops left. The child successfully getting one of these hoops is declared the best dribbler. Variations such as dribbling with the non-dominant hand, dribbling backward, and dribbling sideward should be included in the game to keep up the interest level.

N: Hockey Fun - Game
DA: 6 to 8
DV: Hand-eye coordination
F: All the children side by side behind a starting line
E: One hoop, a hockey stick, and ten tennis balls each
D: Children use the hockey stick to move one ball at a time from the starting line to their hoop on the other side of the play area. Once they maneuver their first ball into the hoop they go back and get the second and so on until all their balls are inside the hoop. The first child to get all balls in their hoop wins.
S: No hard swings with the stick will be permitted.

N: Loop De Loop - Game
DA: 8 to 10
DV: Body awareness and teamwork
F: Relay type lines of six to eight people
E: Thirty Hula-Hoops
D: The first person in each group picks up a Hula-Hoop and steps through it so it is on the joined arm/hand of the second person in line. Without letting go of hands, the second person steps through the Hula-Hoop and passes it to the third person. The first person in line immediately starts another hoop in the same manner as the first and continues passing hoops until they are gone. When a hoop reaches the end, it is dropped on the ground. The group must keep hands joined at all times. The first team to get all their hoops to the other end wins.

N: Sam Says - Game
DA: 8 to 12
DV: Fitness
F: Free
E: None
D: This game is identical to Simon Says, except for the cue which now is "Sam Says." This makes the game more difficult and more fun for older children. The activities presented by "Sam" should focus on fitness.

N: Combatives - Game
DA: 9 to 12
DV: Fitness
F: Partners of nearly equal size and ability
E: Wands for toe fencing and mats for leg wrestling
D: Combatives are usually one-on-one situations with pairs being of fairly equal size and ability. As the name implies, these are vigorous combative-type activities which children enjoy.
Crab Fight: Children get into a crab position and attempt to bump the other person until they sit down. The children are not allowed to kick with the feet or hit with the hands — they must bump or push the other person. This activity can also be done as a "free for all."
Chicken Fight: Children stand on one foot while holding the other foot behind them. Both hands must be held behind the back. Children then try to make the partner lose his/her balance and put both feet down. This activity should only be done in pairs of equal size and in a large cleared area.

Knee Tag: Children box with open hands attempting to hit the other person's knee. Each time a knee is hit, it counts as one point and the first one with five to seven points is the winner.

Pull Across: Two children join one hand across a line. The object is to pull the other person across the line.

Leg Wrestling: Two children lie on their backs with heads in opposite directions. They should be able to place their inside hands on the other person's shoulder. They both lift their inside leg and touch toes returning the leg to the floor. This toe touching is repeated a second time. On the third time up they lock knees and try to flip each other over backward. A mat should be used.

Indian Wrestling: Two children join their right hands while placing their right feet side by side, toes in opposite directions. By pulling or pushing with their hand and shoulder, they attempt to make the other person move his/her right foot. This activity can also be played where both feet must be stationary or from the left side.

S: Care must be taken to match children by size. This game can be very competitive and control is essential.

N: Crab Soccer - Game
DA: 8 to 12
DV: Eye-foot coordination and fitness
F: Two teams
E: Sponge balls
D: Players assume a crab position. A sponge rubber ball of approximately 7" to 10" is used. The ball is kicked until it crosses a goal line at one end of the play area (one goal line at each end). The team defending the goal line has one point scored against it each time the ball crosses its goal line. Children must move in a crab position and must have both hands in contact with the floor behind them when kicking the ball. Hands may not be used by anyone. Teams start on their half of the floor, but may travel to any part of the play area after ball has been put into play. Children with glasses must remove them or wear eyeglass protectors.

A 7" or larger sponge rubber ball is the safest ball to use for this activity. A variation of the game is to have three or four sponge rubber balls going at once. Each time one crosses the goal line, it is taken to the leader who immediately puts it back in play. The game is continuous and is stopped only for rule violations.

S: It is extremely important to insist that children keep both hands behind them on the floor when attempting to kick the ball. Also, this game should not be played outside.

N: Bombardment - Game
DA: 8 to 12
DV: Hand-eye coordination and agility
F: Two teams on opposite sides of the play area
E: Sponge balls and eight to ten plastic containers
D: A play area with a middle dividing line is marked off. About five markers are placed along each goal line at the ends of the area. The distance between the goal line and the center line should not be more than fifteen to twenty yards. The markers should be easy to knock over—plastic bottles will do. Each child is given a 7" playground ball, which is thrown at the targets. The teams may not cross the center line for any reason. The object of the game is to knock down as many targets as possible. A scorekeeper records hits. Play is continuous and ends after a set number of points have been scored. Targets knocked over must be immediately set up by team members on the side of area where the target was located. Players may use hands or feet to stop the ball. No "guarding" of the targets (standing closer than five feet) is allowed.

S: Only low density sponge rubber balls or yarn balls can be used in this game. Under no circumstances should beanbags or playground balls be used.

N: Target Games - Game
DA: All ages
DV: Hand-eye and foot-eye coordination
F: Varies—usually one person and one target
E: Varies with game

D: Children love target activities since they can immediately see results. They also love to knock things over which is often a part of target games. Children can use their hands or feet to propel the object—ball, beanbag, etc—toward the target.

Wastepaper Basket Toss: A good classroom activity requiring a couple of baskets or boxes and one beanbag, yarn ball, or sponge ball per child. Children stand behind a line and try to put beanbag in box.

Basketball Shot: Children of all ages enjoy trying to put a ball in the basket. Basketball goals should be eight feet high for elementary children and balls should be light enough for children to get them to the basket.

Bowling: Many objects can serve as pins—plastic bottles, plastic milk containers, or empty tennis ball cans. Children can keep score as they play.

N: Four Square - Game
DA: 8 to 12
DV: Agility and coordination
F: Four people per square
E: Playground ball (8") or volleyball
D: To begin the game, players stand in corners on numbers. Number 1 serves by bouncing the ball and hitting it underhand with the palm of hand. The ball may be hit into any of the other three squares. When serving, the ball may not hit any inside line but is considered good if it hits inside a square or on an outside line. A player in another square may play the ball only after it bounces in his/her square. He/she may play to any other square although the object is to get number 1 out so everyone else may move up. The object for Number 1 is to stay in that position as long as possible. He/she gets one point for each serve. After the serve, play continues until one player is unable to play the ball. That player must go to square 4 and everyone else moves up one square. Any ball hitting an inside line or the center circle is considered no good, and the player who hit the ball must go to position 4. Hits, except the serve, may be done in any way as long as ball is not caught and thrown. If a ball hits someone's square and begins traveling

toward another player, he/she must not touch it until it bounces a second time, thus giving the player in the square where it bounced a chance to play it. If the other player does touch it, he/she must move to square 4. Play can continue indefinitely or to a set number of points. The ball may not touch any part of the player except the hands.

N: Protect Me Tag - Game
DA: 8 to 12
DV: Teamwork, basic movement development
F: Groups of four—three form a circle
E: Beanbags
D: Three members of the group make a circle by holding hands. The fourth group member then attempts to tag a predetermined person on the circle using a beanbag. The other two circle members try to "protect" the third person by moving in a circle always keeping the person to be tagged away from the tagger. The beanbag must be thrown behind the protecting players. It may not be thrown between them (much too easy).

N: Catch the Dragon's Tail - Game
DA: 8 to 10
DV: Agility
F: Free
E: One jump rope per child
D: Each child tucks a jump rope into his or her waistband so that at least twelve inches drags on the ground. On the signal to go, each child tries to step on another child's tail while avoiding having his own tail stepped on. Once stepped on, the rope goes to the person stepping on it. If a person loses a tail, they are not out of the game. When they are successful at stepping on a tail, they must replace their lost tail and continue playing. A person may collect many tails, but may not hold onto extra tails unless they have one tucked into their waistband. The game continues until the teacher stops it. The one with the most ropes at the end is the winner.
S: Children cannot be permitted to grab someone or their tail while chasing them. They must get the tail by stepping on it.

N: Monkey in the Middle - Game
DA: 8 to 10
DV: Throwing and catching
F: Groups of threes
E: One ball per group
D: Two players stand across from each other at a distance dependent upon skill. One player stands between these two. The idea is for the person in the middle to intercept a pass between the other two.

N: Spanish Leapfrog - Game
DA: 8 to 10
DV: Agility and leg strength
F: A line of three children
E: Object such as a beanbag
D: The children get into a leapfrog formation with the first two bending forward with hands on knees or, if necessary, on all fours. The child at the end places the object on the back of the middle person. On the go signal, the back person must leapfrog the middle person while at the same time picking up the object. The object must then be placed on the back of the lead person as the child does a leapfrog of that person. The end person now repeats the action. This progression continues until the group reaches a goal line. The first group to cover the distance is the winner. If the object falls off, the group must return to the starting line and begin again.

N: Addition Tag - Game
DA: 8 to 10
DV: Teamwork and agility
F: Free with one person as the "it"
E: None
D: The "it" tags another who hooks on by holding the "it's" hand. These two then tag two others. As soon as there are four persons, they break into two sets of two and continue tagging. Every time there is a group of four, it is split into teams of two. The last person tagged is the winner. If a team's hands come apart, they may not tag anyone until they join back together.
S: Children must be cautioned to watch where they are going when being chased.

N: Partner Pick Up - Game
DA: 8 to 10
DV: Agility and teamwork
F: Partners in a straight line
E: One or more balls per child
D: Children stand back to back with a partner and hook elbows. Starting from a common line, partners move together toward another line where balls are lined up. Staying hooked, partners must figure out how to pick up a ball and return it to the starting line. In one variation, the winner could be the first couple back while in another, each couple could see how many successful trips they could make with the winner being the couple who retrieved the most balls. Any ball which is dropped while transporting it must be returned to the pick up area. The hands may not be used to pick up or transport the ball and only one ball per team may be transported at a time.

N: Wiggle Worm Race - Game
DA: 8 to 10
DV: Agility and teamwork
F: Equal lines of five to seven children
E: Marker cones
D: Each team lines up in relay formation on a starting line. They reach between their legs and grasp the hand of the person behind. On the go signal they advance to the turnaround point (marker cone) and back again without breaking the line. Any team which breaks at any time must go back and begin again. The first team to successfully run the course is the winner.

N: Newspaper Race - Game
DA: 8 to 10
DV: Agility and flexibility
F: Establish a starting line and a finish line
E: Newspapers
D: Each child is given one page of a newspaper which is then ripped in half. On a go signal, the child races to the finish line by using the paper as stepping stones, constantly stepping on the lead one while retrieving the back one and moving it to the front. The child who gets to the finish line first wins. Children are not allowed to slide the paper along the floor with their

feet. A variation would be to have them move backward toward the finish line.

N: Scramble - Game
DA: 5 to 10
DV: Social interaction, body image
F: Partners with one extra person
E: None
D: The teacher or perhaps the student without a partner calls out positions such as "head to head, right hand to right hand, back to back, elbows to elbows, etc." The partners must quickly take the positions until the leader calls out "scramble" at which time everyone must find a new partner and the "it" tries to get a partner. The one left without a partner gets a point and is the new "it." Those with the least number of points at the end are declared the winners.

N: Travel Catch - Game
DA: 8 to 10
DV: Hand-eye coordination, teamwork
F: Partners; establish a starting line and a finish line
E: One ball per group
D: On the go signal, one child runs a short distance toward the finish line which should be a good distance (50 - 100 yards) away. The other child cannot move until after he/she throws the ball which must be caught by the partner. If the ball is missed, both players must return to the starting line and begin again. If the ball is caught, the child with the ball may not move. The other child then runs past the child with the ball which is then thrown to him/her. The team progresses down the field until both are over the finish line; the first team to finish is the winner. For variety, use different size balls, the non-dominant hand to throw, or just one hand to catch.

N: All Tied Up - Game
DA: 10 to 12
DV: Teamwork
F: Teams of four or five
E: A jump rope for each team and numbered balls
D: All members of a team must hold onto a jump rope with both hands behind their back. They must then pick up a ball without using their hands or arms and hold the ball between two members of the team while transporting it to the finish line. They may not let go of the rope with either hand and may not use any part of their hands or arms to move the ball. While moving as a team with the ball, at least two team members must be touching the ball with a body part other than their hands or arms. The first team across the line wins.

N: The Dragon - Game
DA: 10 to 12
DV: Agility
F: Groups of three
E: None
D: Children are grouped in threes to form a line with each person holding onto the person in front. Groups are scattered freely about the room. On the go signal, each group tries to hook onto the tail of another group. The object is not to be the head group. After the last group hooks on, the head group gets one point and the game begins again with the original groups of three but with a new head for each group. The game should be repeated at least three times to give each child a chance to be the head.

N: Get Away - Game
DA: 10 to 12
DV: Agility
F: Partners scattered over a fairly large area
E: None
D: On the go signal, one partner tries to get away. The partner attempts to stay as close as possible. When the stop signal is given both players must stop immediately. If the chasing partner can reach out and touch the other, he/she wins. If not, the fleeing partner wins. For safety, the person running away must watch where he/she is going and must stay in a designated area to avoid collisions with others.

N: Squat Tug - Game
DA: 10 to 12
DV: Strength and balance
F: Partners
E: One rope per child

D: Opponents squat down holding a six-foot rope in each hand between them. The ropes are pulled taut. On a go signal, each person tries to make the other lose his/her balance by pulling on one or both ropes. The first person to touch the floor with a body part other than the feet is the loser. The children may not move their feet to maintain their balance.

S: Children must not be permitted to wrap the rope around their arm.

N: Beanbag Tug of War - Game
DA: 10 to 12
DV: Strength development
F: Pairs
E: One jump rope per pair and one bean-bag per child
D: Each child grabs the end of the rope. A beanbag is placed behind each child four to six feet away but the distance must be the same on each side. The object then is to pull the other player far enough to be able to pick up the beanbag. The best out of five or seven trials is declared the winner.

S: Children must not be permitted to wrap the rope around their arm.

N: Plastic Hockey - Game
DA: 10 to 12
DV: Fitness
F: Two teams
E: Hockey sticks, puck or ball, and eyeglass guards
D: Plastic ice hockey-type sticks can be used both indoors and out. Children love this very vigorous game, particularly in a large indoor area. The cheaper plastic sticks work well indoors, but are of little value on grass.
Area Hockey: Children are assigned areas which they cannot leave. Two or three players on each team are permitted to go anywhere in the area. This arrangement prevents all the children from gathering around the ball or puck, which can lead to an injury. Children must be instructed to keep the head of the sticks below their waist and must wear protective goggles over eyeglasses.

S: Children may not swing the stick above their waist.

N: Must Swing Baseball - Game
DA: 10 to 12
DV: Teamwork
F: Two teams
E: Bat and ball
D: Played like regular baseball except that the pitcher is a member of the team at bat. All pitches, therefore, are strikes no matter where they go. This arrangement eliminates both the need for an umpire as well as a long wait as the batter looks for the perfect pitch. No matter how many outs are made, everyone on the team gets one chance to bat and then the teams switch sides.

S: Only the person up to bat may have a bat in his/her hand.

N: Football Kick Across - Game
DA: 10 to 12
DV: Eye-foot coordination
F: Two players and one ball
E: Junior size football
D: Children are paired up with one football or round ball (soccer ball or playground ball) between them. Goal lines are established and each person tries to punt the ball in the air over the goal line. The first kick is made from the "forty yard line." If the ball is caught in the air, the catcher can take five giant steps toward his/her opponent's goal line before punting the ball. All other balls must be punted from where they are stopped. If there are only a few footballs, they should be traded off with other players using the round balls, so that everyone gets a chance to use the football (junior size football only).

N: Two-on-Two or Three-on-Three Basketball - Game
DA: 10 to 12
DV: Teamwork and coordination
F: Teams of two or three
E: Junior size basketballs and eight-foot baskets
D: Basketball is probably the most difficult game for elementary children to play so lead-up games must be used. By making the teams smaller than the usual five, children get more playing time. Even with small teams, however, rules must be greatly modified (see No Dribble Basketball). The equipment must also be

modified. Balls can be soccer size and the basket should be lowered to seven or eight feet. Children playing with regulation equipment and ten-foot baskets develop incorrect habits in order to have success in getting the ball in the basket. These habits are often hard to break later on. By modifying equipment and rules, children will have success and skills will carry over.

N: No Dribble Basketball - Game
DA: 10 to 12
DV: Teamwork
F: Two or three on a team
E: Junior size basketballs and eight-foot baskets
D: The ball may not be dribbled and can only be moved by passing off to teammates who can move freely when they do not have the ball. Emphasis can be placed on the walking rule during this game and what to do when you do not have the ball.

N: Volleyball - Game
DA: 10 to 12
DV: Teamwork and coordination
F: One team of six players on each side of the net
E: Volleyballs and six-foot-high net
D: It is very difficult for children, if not specially trained, to play a regulation game of volleyball. Modified games, however, are fun and use the same skills required for regular play.
   One Bounce Volleyball: the ball may bounce one time between each hit and any number of hits are allowed to get the ball back over the net.
   Three Hit Volleyball: same as "One Bounce" above, but the ball must be hit a minimum of three times before it can go back over the net.
   Multiple Hit Volleyball: one person may hit the ball more than once in a row.
   Other arrangements such as shortening the distance required for serving, lowering the net and banning the spike can all be added to any of the above games. The rules from the different games can also be combined to give the children success.

Frisbee Golf

N: Frisbee Golf - Game
DA: 10 to 12
DV: Hand-eye coordination
F: One Frisbee per person
E: Frisbees and hoops
D: A golf course is laid out using hoops (lying on the ground) and some kind of marker flags. Holes should be placed so as to avoid the possibility of children being hit by the Frisbee. Each throw counts as one point. The Frisbee must be completely inside the hoop to be successful. Children continue to throw from where the Frisbee stopped until they get it in the hoop. If the Frisbee is across the hoop, one additional point is added to the score. The person with the lowest score at the end is the winner. Distances between holes should vary and hazards should be included to increase the difficulty. A container can be placed in the hoop, and if knocked over on the initial throw, it counts as a hole in one. If not hit on the first throw, it is removed until the children complete the hole.
S: To avoid people being hit with Frisbees, the tee off area for the next hole should be well away from the previous hole.

N: Pillo Polo - Game
DA: 10 to 12
DV: Hand-eye coordination, fitness, and teamwork
F: Two teams

E: Pillo Polo set and eyeglass guards

D: This activity is similar to the polo played on horseback without the horse. The game comes with specific directions, although variations due to equipment and space are easy to design. The object of the game is to get the ball into a goal which should, like ice hockey, allow for play behind the goal. The reader is referred to the directions that come with the Pillo Polo set. It is a vigorous activity and fairly safe.

S: The pillo must be kept below the waist.

N: Soccer Keep Away - Game
DA: 10 to 12
DV: Kicking, eye-foot coordination
F: Triangle and one in center
E: Soccer ball
D: Three players form a triangle, each about thirty feet apart. One player stands in the middle. The players kick the ball to one another while the center person attempts to steal the pass or break it up. The ball is kicked in a clockwise fashion. If the center is successful, he/she changes places with the passer. Each child should get a turn in the middle eventually. This activity should be done outside for adequate space.

S: Passes must be made with the side of the foot and not kicked with the toe.

N: Balloon Ball - Game
DA: 10 to 12
DV: Eye-hand coordination
F: Two teams
E: Balloons
D: Divide the class into two teams. Half the players on each team have balloons. When the teacher starts the game, they try to bat their balloons to a goal behind the other team. Those without balloons will try to take them away from the other team by batting toward the other goal. Balloons must be kept in the air at all times and may not be grabbed.

N: Balloon Bucket - Game
DA: 10 to 12
DV: Hand-eye coordination
F: Partners
E: Balloons and hula hoops
D: One balloon is given to each pair. Hoops are spread around the floor. The students bat the balloon toward a hoop (no one partner can bat the balloon twice in a row). The hoop must then be picked up and the balloon batted through it. The object is to see how many hoops the team can get through in a given amount of time. A pair may not go through the same hoop twice, nor can they move the hoop around the room while batting the balloon through.

N: Frisbee Toss - Game
DA: 10 to 12
DV: Eye-hand coordination
F: Target stations
E: Frisbees and Hula-Hoops
D: Each student has two frisbees. He/she stands behind the restraining line ten feet away. One point is scored each time he/she tosses the Frisbee in the circle.

N: Wall Ball - Game
DA: 10 to 12
DV: Hand-eye coordination
F: Scattered around a wall
E: One ball per child
D: Children hit balls with their hands (emphasize using each hand) and make it hit the wall. They then must hit it before it bounces twice. This game can be played in pairs in which they must alternate hits. The opponent scores one point each time a child misses the ball.

REFERENCES AND SUGGESTED READINGS

Friedlander, R. and R. Lohmeyer. A place to start: games and sports tasks for young children, *JOHPERD* 59:7, pp. 7072, 1988.

Gabbard, C., t.al. *Physical Education for Children.* Englewood Cliffs: Prentice-Hall, Inc., 1987.

Graham, G., S. Holt-Hale, and M. Parker. *Children Moving* (3rd ed.). Mountain View: Mayfield Publishing Co. 1998.

Hoffman, H., et.al. *Meaningful Movement for Children.* Boston: Allyn and Bacon, Inc., 1981.

Kirchner, G. and G. Fishburne. *Physical Education for Elementary School Children* (9th ed.). Madison: W. C. Brown and Co. 1995.

Nichols, B. *Moving an Learning: The Elementary School Physical Education Experience* (3rd ed.). St. Louis: Mosby Publishing Co. 1994.

Pangrazi, R. and V. Dauer. *Dynamic Physical Education* (11th ed.). Boston: Allyn and Bacon. 1995.

Selective Web Sites

Lesson Plans: http://schools.eastnet.ecu.edu/pitt/ayden/physed8.htm

Omaha Public Schools: http://www.ops.org/pe/elem.html

PE Central: http://pe.cental.vt.edu/

PE Links 4U: http://www.pelinks4u.org/sections/elementary/elementary.htm

SPARK: http://www.acsm.org/

A great search engine: http://www.sparkpe.org/programElementaryPE.jsp?curricula=PhysEdK-2&program=ElementaryPE

Chapter
19
Fitness Activities and Games

After completing this chapter, the student should be able to:

1. Describe the criteria associated with a fitness activity.
2. Distinguish between physiological fitness and motor fitness.
3. Design a fitness activity for an elementary age group.
4. Design a lesson plan to accomplish a fitness objective.

━━━━━━━━━━━━━━━━━━━━━━━━━━━━ *Key Terms*

Fitness activity
Motor fitness
Physiological fitness

This chapter is a supplement to the activities included in chapter 10, and includes numerous fitness activities and games as well as a fitness program and field day activities which encourage fitness development. The reader should review chapter 10 for additional ideas and a better understanding of the terms discussed in this chapter.

Fitness Activities and Games

A fitness activity for purposes of this chapter is defined as an activity or game which helps develop some physiological or motor fitness component. The chapter activities have all the children participating nearly all the time. "Activity" or "Game" is written beside the name "N" of each to help the reader distinguish between the two.

Physiological Fitness and Motor Fitness

Although the distinction was made between physiological fitness and motor fitness, it is reviewed here to help the reader. *Physiological fitness* has five components which are important to one's health: cardiovascular efficiency, muscular strength, muscular endurance, flexibility, and body composition. Each of these is discussed in chapter 10. *Motor fitness* is not as important to one's physical health and deals with those areas important to sports participation: coordination, balance, agility, speed, and reaction time. Motor fitness was also covered in chapter 10.

ACTIVITIES AND GAMES ORGANIZATION

As in other chapters, the activities and games are organized into four age levels: four to six, six to eight, eight to ten, and ten to twelve years of age. Some activities, as indicated by the age group recommendations, can be conducted across age groups.

Following is the code for the activities and games descriptions:

N = Name
DA = The age for which the game is appropriate (developmental age)
DV = What the game will help develop (developmental value)
F = Formation
E = Equipment necessary
D = Description of activity
S = Safety

FOUR TO SIX YEARS OF AGE

N: Leap the Brook - Game
DA: 4 to 6
DV: Strength
F: Free
E: Tape for the floor

D: A brook is taped on the floor. It is narrow at one end and gradually increases in size toward the other end. Children then attempt to leap the brook according to their ability. Depending upon class size, a couple of brooks can be made so all the children can be going at one time. You do not want children standing in line waiting for a turn.
S: Do *not* use ropes to form the brook; children can easily land on the rope and fall on their back or hit their heads on the floor.

N: Flexibility Zoo - Activity
DA: 4 to 6
DV: Flexibility
F: Free
E: None
D: Tell the children that they are going to the zoo. In the zoo they will see animals that move in many different ways. First they meet a giraffe. He stands tall with straight legs. To get a drink of water, the giraffe must bend down slowly, keeping legs straight and reach his head (the child's hands) all the way to the ground. Next

they encounter a turtle. He lives in a tight little shell (the children lie on their stomachs and grasp their ankles with their hands). Around the corner is the monkey. He is being silly, sitting cross-legged and touching his ankle to his head (the children sit, hold their ankles with their hands, and pull the foot up to their heads). What is this lovely creature, standing so tall and spreading its wings? A swan. The children stretch their arms back at the shoulder. Soon they come to the reptile house. They see a snake. The children lie on the floor, hands over their heads and stretch out as long as a big snake. Now they see a crocodile, his mouth wide open. Seat the children on the floor, their legs spread as wide as the open crocodile mouth. Can the crocodile eat you? See if you fit in his mouth (the children slowly bend forward at the waist, stretching as close to the floor as possible).

N: Animal Movement - Activity
DA: 4 to 6
DV: Muscular strength and endurance
F: Free
E: None
D: Children are asked to move like different animals such as:

1. The *inch worm:* From a push-up position, walk feet up to hands while keeping the knees straight and then walk out on hands to the push up position.
2. The *bear:* With knees straight, bend over and touch the ground with the hands and then walk on all fours.
3. The *giraffe:* With arms straight, place hands together above the head, and walk with legs stiff.
4. The *elephant:* Walk bent over with one arm acting as the trunk and the other hand acting as the tail. Children can hook onto each other to form a circus parade
5. The *seal:* In a push-up position, walk with the arms while dragging the legs behind.
6. The *dragon:* Two children kneel on all fours; the child in front puts his/her feet (shoes off) on the shoulders of the child in the rear. The children

then coordinate their movement to move forward or backward and not have the feet fall off the shoulders.
7. The *snake:* Children slither along the floor using knees and elbows.
8. The *crab:* in a sitting position, children use their feet and hands, which are on the floor behind them, to move.
9. The *frog:* Children squat down with hands on the floor in front of them. Then using primarily the legs, the children jump off both feet like a frog.
10. The *gazelle:* Children gallop about the floor and frequently leap through the air.
11. The *cheetah:* Children run around the play area as fast as possible.

S: It is best to do these activities on mats.

N: Obstacle Course - Activity
DA: 4 to 6
DV: Depends upon the course—fitness
F: Follow the leader
E: Depends on the obstacle course
D: Obstacle courses can take many forms and be of varying difficulty depending upon the age and ability of the children. They can use playground equipment and/or small equipment such as ropes and hoops. In designing the course, it should be of sufficient size to allow children to spread out along the course so everyone can begin at the same time. Then everyone must follow the leader with the leader returning to the beginning when reaching the end. The path should be clearly marked, and there should be no point where children must wait for a turn. It should provide for continuous movement.

N: Long Jump Ropes - Activity
DA: 4 to 6
DV: Coordination and rhythmic ability
F: Groups of three
E: 13-foot long jump ropes
D: Long jump roping is usually thought of as an activity for very young children, but children of all ages can enjoy long rope jumping with such complicated activities as double rope jumping reserved for eleven- and twelve-year-olds. Since two people are fairly inactive, however, long

287

rope jumping should be done only until enough ability is acquired to do short rope jumping. The turners should move the rope primarily with the forearm while keeping their elbow at their side. Jumpers should stand in the center and face one of the turners. The following is a progression of long rope jumping activities from easy to difficult:

1. Stand in the middle and jump the rope as it is rocked back and forth.
2. Jump while the rope makes complete turns.
3. Coming in the front door: the rope is coming toward the top of the child's head and down toward the feet.
4. Coming in the back door: the rope is coming up underneath child's chin.
5. There are a number of little rhythmic chants such as reciting the alphabet which can be done. Also, children can do such physical activities as turning, touching the ground, and skipping while jumping.
6. Short rope jumping while long rope jumping.
7. Simultaneously jumping two long ropes crossed at a 90-degree angle—this requires four turners.
8. Double Dutch: jumping two ropes alternately turned by the same two turners.
9. There are some very complicated stunts which can be done while jumping either one or two long ropes at the same time, but their accomplishment goes beyond the normal physical education class.

SIX TO EIGHT YEARS OF AGE

N: Leapfrog - Activity
DA: 6 to 8
DV: Agility and strength
F: Pairs
E: None
D: One child gets on hands and knees and the other places his/her hands on the down person's back and jumps off both feet at the same time (leapfrogs) and ends up in front of the down person. He/

she then immediately goes onto all fours and the back child repeats the action.

N: Animal Exercises - Activity
DA: 6 to 8
DV: Strength and flexibility development
F: Free
E: None
D: Children are asked to imitate various animals as demonstrated:

Seal: Get into a push-up position and then walk on hands while dragging feet behind.

Inch worm: Start in a push-up position and walk feet up to hands and then walk out on hands while keeping feet still.

Elephant: Bend over and grab the ankles and walk.

Crab: Sit down on floor and put hands behind back. Walk on hands and feet while maintaining a sitting position.

Bear: Walk on all fours with knees slightly bent.

Snake: Slither along the floor on the belly.

Dragon: Two children get on hands and knees one in front of the other. The lead child puts his/her feet on the shoulders of the back person and they attempt to walk together, with the lead person only on the hands and the back person on hands and knees.

S: It is best to do these activities on a mat.

N: Quickies - Activity
DA: 6 to 8
DV: Physical fitness
F: Free
E: None
D: Children respond to quick commands given by the teacher. These commands focus on fitness activities and are given quickly to motivate students through a fun activity. Commands can be run in place, hit the deck (lie on the stomach), on your back, do two push-ups or sit-ups, slap your knees, turn around, jump and turn, or roll around.

N: Rubber Person - Activity
DA: 6 to 8
DV: Flexibility
F: Free
E: None

D: Children are encouraged to explore every way they can stretch their bodies. Stretching should be done slowly. Every body part capable of being stretched should be explored. Slow music can be used to keep students moving slowly to avoid injuries.

S: These flexibility activities must be proceeded by an aerobic activity which raises the core temperature sufficiently to produce sweating.

N: Nature - Activity
DA: 6 to 8
DV: Flexibility and muscular endurance
F: Free
E: None, although soft music could be used
D: Children move freely about the room in response to the teacher's nature suggestions. Examples would be to move like a wave or rotate like the earth, move like a meandering stream, be rain or thunder, or grow like a flower or tree.

S: These flexibility activities must be proceeded by an aerobic activity which raises the core temperature sufficiently to produce sweating.

N: Obstacle Fun - Activity
DA: 6 to 8
DV: Fitness—depends on course
F: Groups of four or five
E: Playground apparatus
D: One person serves as the leader and takes the children through an obstacle course using various playground equipment such as the horizontal bar, jungle gym, balance beam, tires, etc. Children are encouraged to help each other on more difficult activities such as chin-ups. The entire class is going at one time with each leader selecting a different route to take. Leaders are asked to keep moving continuously and not go to a place where there is another group. The emphasis is on continuous movement to promote cardiovascular development along with other aspects of fitness.

N: Wild Horse Roundup - Game
DA: 6 to 8
DV: Agility
F: Free
E: None

D: Four players are the cowboys and the rest are wild horses. They are moving freely about the play area using a locomotor skill determined by the teacher, i.e., skip, gallop, walk, run, etc. On a signal, the cowboys try to tag the horses. Any horse tagged becomes a cowboy and helps round up the rest of the horses. The last horse gets to choose the new cowboys.

S: Children must not be permitted to grab other children when tagging them.

N: Bumblebees - Game
DA: 6 to 8
DV: Agility
F: Two groups in a free formation
E: Pinnies for half the students
D: Half the students wear pinnies and are designated as the bees; the other half are the campers. The bees try to tag the campers who must freeze if tagged. The camper must count to ten out loud before continuing in the activity. After a given amount of time, the campers become the bees and the bees are the campers.

S: Children must not be permitted to grab other children when tagging them.

N: Racing - Game
DA: 6 to 8
DV: Cardiovascular efficiency
F: Free
E: Objects such as cones and hoops to set up various stations
D: Various racetrack-type stations are established for jeep racing, stock car races, and drag races. Children go from station to station and race against the course (obstacles) or each other (stock cars and drag races). A separate station designated as the refueling area can be established to give students a rest.

N: Newspaper Race - Game
DA: 6 to 8
DV: Agility and flexibility
F: Establish a starting line and a finish line
E: Newspapers
D: Each child is given one page of a newspaper which is then ripped in half. On a go signal, the child races to the finish line by using the paper as stepping stones, constantly stepping on the lead one while

retrieving the back one and moving it to the front. The child who gets to the finish line first wins. Children are not allowed to slide the paper along the floor with their feet. A variation would be to have them move backward toward the finish line.

N: Poison Tag - Game
DA: 6 to 8
DV: Strength, agility, and balance
F: Circle
E: None
D: Children are in a circle. They then try to tug others into a circle drawn on the floor or made with a large rope on the grass. Anyone pulled into the circle is poisoned and is "it." Everyone runs while being chased by anyone who has stepped into the circle. Anyone tagged is also poisoned and helps catch others. At the end, the last one caught is the winner.
S: Children must not be permitted to grab other children when tagging them.

N: Aerobic Exercises - Activity
DA: 6 to 8
DV: Cardiovascular efficiency
F: Stations or free
E: Depends upon activities selected
D: Children do exercises without stopping as they move from one exercise or station to the next. The exercises can be calisthenics requiring no equipment, or equipment such as jump ropes can be included at a station. When doing continuous calisthenics, one student can begin doing an exercise in the middle of a circle, and children continue to do the exercise until it is changed by that student or by another student who takes the center child's place. When using stations, children can move to a new station on a signal or can complete a specified task at the station and move on to the next. In either case, calisthenics or stations, music can be used to make the activities rhythmic.

N: Short Jump Ropes - Activity
DA: 6 to 8
DV: Rhythmic ability and cardiovascular efficiency
F: Free
E: One rope per child

D: The first thing to do before beginning single rope jumping is be sure the child can long rope jump. The second thing is to be sure the rope is the correct length. To determine correct length, have the child stand on the rope with both feet fairly close together and then pull up on the ends; the ends should just touch under each armpit. To turn the rope correctly, the arms should make very little movement with the wrists doing most of the work. The child should be taught to jump only high enough to let the rope pass under his/her feet; the knees should not be bent while jumping and the movement should be done on the toes. Either a two beat or single beat jump can be used. In the double beat, the child takes a jump between each actual jump of the rope. In single beat, a jump is only taken when the rope is about to go under the feet. There are literally hundreds of different rope tricks which can be done. The ones listed below are in order of difficulty from simple to complex. To add to the value of rope jumping, it should be done to music.
1. Front jumping
2. Back jumping
3. Jumping and doing various forward locomotor activities
4. Jumping and moving backward
5. Jumping forward and moving backward and vice versa
6. Cross in front
7. Cross in back, while backward jumping
8. Go from front rope jumping to back rope jumping without stopping the rope, and keep it going in the same direction. Sound difficult? It isn't. While jumping forward, bring the two hands together at the side of the body while continuing to turn the rope forward. One arm should be across the body to keep the rope in the proper direction. The child then turns towards his/her hands and ends up facing the opposite direction. The opposite arm is now across the chest. The rope is now turning backward and the child needs to merely open the rope and begin jumping backward. This is an easy

skill and an important one to development of routines.

9. Jumping with a partner
10. Double jump in which the rope goes under the feet twice on one jump.
11. Rhythmic routines
12. There are numerous difficult single rope skills which could be mastered with considerable practice. Such skills, however, usually go beyond the scope of a physical education class.

EIGHT TO TEN YEARS OF AGE

N: Travel Catch - Game
DA: 8 to 10
DV: Hand-eye coordination, teamwork
F: Partners. Establish a starting line and a finish line
E: One ball per group
D: On the go signal, one child runs a short distance toward the finish line which should be a good distance (50–100 yards) away. The other child cannot move until after he/she throws the ball which must be caught by the partner. If the ball is missed, both players must return to the starting line and begin again. If the ball is caught, the child with the ball may not move. The other child then runs past the child with the ball which is then thrown to him/her. The team progresses down the field until both are over the finish line; first team to finish is the winner. For variety, have the children use different size balls, the non-dominant hand to throw, or just one hand to catch.

N: Wiggle Worm Race - Game
DA: 8 to 10
DV: Agility and teamwork
F: Equal lines of five to seven children
E: Marker cones
D: Each team lines up in relay formation on a starting line. Children reach between their legs and grasp the hand of the person behind. On the go signal they advance to the turnaround point (marker cone) and back again without breaking the line. Any team which breaks at any time must go back and begin again. The first team to successfully run the course is the winner.

N: Partner Pick-Up - Game
DA: 8 to 10
DV: Agility and teamwork
F: Partners in a straight line
E: One or more balls per child
D: Children stand back to back with a partner and hook elbows. Starting from a common line, partners move together toward another line where balls are lined up. Staying hooked, partners must figure out how to pick up a ball and return it to the starting line. In one variation, the winner could be the first couple back while in another, each couple could see how many successful trips they could make, with the winner being the couple who retrieved the highest number of balls. Any ball which is dropped while transporting it must be returned to the pick up area. The hands may not be used to pick up or transport the balls and only one ball per team may be transported at a time.

N: Poison - Game
DA: 8 to 10
DV: Strength and agility
F: Circle of eight to ten players
E: None
D: A small circle is drawn on the floor or a hoop can be used and placed in the center. Children then try to tug or pull each other until one person steps into the circle or hoop. The person receives one point each time he/she steps inside the circle. The class is usually divided into two or three circles and participants can be changed around periodically to keep the interest. At the end, those with no points are the winners.

TEN TO TWELVE YEARS OF AGE

N: Squat Tug - Game
DA: 10 to 12
DV: Strength and balance
F: Partners
E: One rope per child
D: Opponents squat down holding a six-foot rope in each hand between them. The ropes are pulled taut. On a go signal, each person tries to make the other lose his/her balance by pulling on one or both ropes. The first person to touch the floor

with a body part other than the feet is the 0loser. The children may not move their feet to maintain their balance.

S: Children may not wrap the rope around their arm.

N: Pick-Up - Game
DA: 10 to 12
DV: Strength development
F: Pairs
E: One jump rope per pair and one bean-bag per child
D: Each child grabs the end of the rope. A beanbag is placed behind each child ap-proximately four to six feet away, but the distance must be the same on each side. The object then is to pull the other player far enough to be able to pick up the bean-bag. The best out of five or seven trials is declared the winner.

S: Children may not wrap the rope around their arm.

N: Olympic Runners - Activity
DA: 10 to 12
DV: Cardiovascular efficiency
F: Everyone goes around a "track"
E: None
D: Children run around a "track" which can be approximately 200 yards set up in an oval fashion. Each time the children pass the start/finish line they are given a stick to help them keep count. On subsequent days, the children are encouraged to go farther than they did the previous day. The emphasis is on improving oneself and not on meeting some standard. This activity should be done every other day and should never last more than thirty minutes.

N: Team Ball - Game
DA: 10 to 12
DV: Teamwork
F: Two equal teams, a home plate, and a first base about six feet away
E: A volleyball and two marker cones
D: A team member up to "bat" hits the vol-leyball into the field between the bound-ary lines. After hitting the ball, the hitter runs toward and around first base (a marker cone) while all other members of the team follow. If the entire team rounds first and makes it past home before the

ball is successfully played by the field-ers, they get one point. After every mem-ber up to bat gets a chance to hit the ball, teams switch places. In the field, a player must retrieve the hit ball and all other fielders must line up behind him/her. The ball is then passed over and under until the last person gets it and runs to the front of the line where the ball is held up and play stops.

N: Fitness Activities - Activity
DA: 10 to 12
DV: Fitness
F: Free
E: Depends upon activity
D: *Sit-ups:* only modified sit-ups should be used in which the children raise their trunk only 45 degrees from the floor.
Push-ups: The push-up is one of the better developmental exercises since it involves muscles in the arms, shoulders, chest, and abdominal region. It can be done using the knees or the toes as the fulcrum. The latter is more difficult.
Pull-ups: The biceps are developed through use of the pull-up. This can be done from a bar hang or can be modified by placing the heels on the floor and lean-ing the body back under a low bar and pulling the chest to the bar.
Running: To develop the cardiovas-cular system, running must elevate the heart rate to a sufficient level and main-tain that level for fifteen to eighteen min-utes (chapter 6). Such long runs are possible but not practical during physi-cal education class. Children should be taught to take their pulse, calculate the proper conditioning heart rate, and fol-low a fitness program featuring cardio-vascular development.
Rope Jumping: If done long enough, rope jumping can be a good cardiovas-cular activity. It is also good for develop-ing coordination and rhythmic ability.
Other good fitness activities: Gymnas-tics, Crab Soccer, Combatives.
S: Sit-ups should be done on a mat.

REFERENCES AND SUGGESTED READINGS

Graham, G., S. Holt-Hale, and M. Parker. *Children Moving* (3rd ed.). Mountain View: Mayfield Publishing Co. 1998.

Kirchner, G. and G. Fishburne. *Physical Education for Elementary School Children* (9th ed.). Madison: W. C. Brown and Co. 1995.

Nichols, B. *Moving an Learning: The Elementary School Physical Education Experience* (3rd ed.). St. Louis: Mosby Publishing Co. 1994.

Pangrazi, R. and V. Dauer. *Dynamic Physical Education* (11th ed.). Boston: Allyn and Bacon. 1995.

Selective Web Sites

Lesson Plans: http://schools.eastnet.ecu.edu/pitt/ayden/physed8.htm

Omaha Public Schools: http://www.ops.org/pe/elem.html

PE Central: http://pe.cental.vt.edu/

PE Links 4U: http://www.pelinks4u.org/sections/elementary/elementary.htm

SPARK: http://www.acsm.org/

A great search engine: http://www.sparkpe.org/programElementaryPE.jsp?curricula=PhysEdK-2&program=ElementaryPE

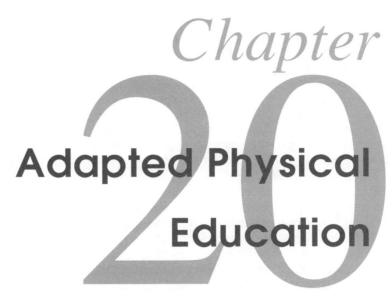

Chapter 20

Adapted Physical Education

By Marc Runac, Chesterfield County (Virginia) Public Schools

After completing this chapter, the student should be able to:

1. Define physical education as it relates to handicapped individuals.
2. List and explain each of the three components of Public Law 94-142.
3. List and explain the components of the IEP.
4. Design an IEP.
5. List and explain the components of a behavior modification program.
6. Define the key terms listed below.

_____ *Key Terms*

Behavior modification	Public Law 94-142
Fading	Shaping
Individualized education plan	Task analysis
Least restricted environment	Time-out
Prompting	

Most children, from the elite athlete to the uncoordinated child, have the basic need to engage in physical activities. In the past, children with special needs were denied physical education or were given non-participating roles such as scorers or equipment dispensers. The growth of humanism and instructional technologies beginning in the late '60s brought forth an era in which many individuals with special needs were identified and served through physical education programs. This chapter is an overview of physical education for special needs children.

Before proceeding, a definition of special needs children must be provided. A special needs child is defined for physical education purposes as an individual with psychomotor dysfunction that necessitates specialized instructional strategies. Our educational system traditionally has labeled children according to their intelligence quotients (IQs) or the degree of their impairment (e.g., total blindness and partially sighted). These classification systems have shortcomings in programming in adapted physical education. The physical educator must view children as individuals who possess different strengths and weaknesses.

Education is an ongoing process in which total growth and development proceeds in a predictable and organized fashion. The rate in which children progress along the developmental continuum, however, varies with each child. The educator, therefore, must employ an individualized approach to maximize the benefits derived from any program. Individualized instruction is achieved when a child's position on the developmental continuum is pinpointed and experiences are offered that enhance each child's future development. This approach underlies recent legislation and instructional technology related to education for special needs children.

PAST, PRESENT, AND FUTURE OF PHYSICAL EDUCATION FOR THOSE WITH SPECIAL NEEDS

Our American educational philosophy is based on each child's right to a free public education. Equal opportunity for all children was articulated through a statement issued from the Supreme Court in 1954. The statement reads:

Education is required in the performance of our most basic responsibilities. In these days, it is doubtful that any child may reasonably be expected to succeed in life if he is denied the opportunity of an education. Such an opportunity where the state has undertaken to provide it, is a right which must be made available to all on equal terms.

The principle later was supported specifically for special needs children in the court case of PARC, etc. vs. Commonwealth of Pennsylvania, et. al. The decrees stemming from this case mandated that a public and appropriate education should be provided to all special needs children.

The 1975 passage of Public Law 94-142, Education for All Handicapped Children Act, revealed a growing public concern for appropriate educational opportunities for special needs children. The major legislation provisions are: (1) a special needs child is entitled to an educational setting that is least restrictive or most normalized, and is designed to meet his or her needs; (2) education is provided at no cost to the parent; (3) the child, where appropriate, and his parents are involved in educational decisions; (4) the evaluation process is objective and non-discriminatory; and (5) clear management procedures are utilized in planning for a child's education program.

P.L. 94-142 specifically mentions physical education as a required curriculum area. Physical education is seen as an avenue which may lead to self-sufficiency in the community through the attainment of leisure and domestic skills. Physical education for special students is defined as:

(1) ...the development of:
(A) physiological and motor fitness, (B) fundamental motor skills and patterns, and (C) skills in aquatics, dance and individual and group games and sports (including intramural and lifetime sports).

(2) The term includes special physical education, adapted physical education, movement education, and motor development.

Due to funding, the future of adapted physical education is uncertain. As the federal government assumes more responsibility for public education, it has not provided adequate funds for the various mandated programs including P.L. 94-142. Despite the uncertainties, many positive movements are apt to continue: (1) the knowledge base derived from recent research in physical education for special needs children will stimulate additional research; (2) as the research knowledge base expands, instructional strategies and technologies will evolve that will allow for individualized instruction; and (3) the advancement in instructional technologies and a greater acceptance of special needs children will enable more special needs children to be mainstreamed with their normal peers.

Greater emphasis will be placed upon the multidisciplinary approach in formulating educational programs for special needs children. In multidisciplinary approaches, the child's total personality is examined, thus insuring a balanced program. Increasingly, more disciplines will be included in programs for special needs children. If the physical educator is to become a contributing member of a multidisciplinary staff, he or she must have a general understanding of all educational areas and be able to interact with other professional staff.

Decategorization of handicap labels was a trend in the later part of the 20th Century that will continue to grow in the 21st Century. Labeling often increases the stigma attached to possessing a handicap without providing additional information to the teacher. Furthermore, many educators believe that the factors underlying human development are common for all children and that children differ because they are at various positions on the developmental continuum. As a result, teaching models have evolved that develop generic teaching competencies in assessing, planning, teaching, and evaluating special needs children. According to these teaching models, the educator observes the child's behavior, diagnoses any problems, prescribes activities to alleviate the problems, implements the teaching plan, and evaluates the child's progress.

PUBLIC LAW 94-142

In drafting P.L. 94-142, Congress established guidelines and policies that required states to employ practices that insure equal educational opportunities for special needs students in a least restrictive environment. The Individualized Education Plan (IEP) is an integral part of P.L. 94-142 and provides the mechanism to assure that the states are meeting the law's provisions.

Individualized Educational Plan (IEP)

The IEP is formulated by a multidisciplinary staff consisting of a school representative, teacher, parents, and the child, if appropriate. Through staff meetings, the parents take part in decisions that will affect their child. Many potential problems between the parents and professional staff are alleviated if both parties are involved in the initial planning process. Additionally, rapport between the parent and teacher is frequently a direct result of the multidisciplinary meetings.

P.L. 94-142 requires that the following components, but not exclusive of others, be addressed in each child's IEP:

(1) *A statement of the present level of educational performance.* Assessment instruments must be valid and reliable, and measure content areas relevant to the child's needs, if sound educational decisions are to be made. The decision process may be further enhanced if two or more tests or observations are administered. A child's motor performance may be measured with a variety of assessment techniques, such as teacher observation, developmental scales, standardized fitness and motor tests, and teacher-made behavioral objectives.

(2) *A statement of annual goals and short-term instructional objectives.* Physical education goals are listed in the P.L. 94-142 definition of physical education. These goals are generic to all children, special needs or not. The physical educator must identify behavioral objectives that reflect specific goal areas that are essential to a child's well-being in his community. After each child is assessed on relevant objectives, the physical educator places those objectives in order of priority and establishes timeliness for their attainment.

(3) *A statement of the specific education services to be provided and the extent to*

which the child will participate in regular physical education. All special education and related services required to meet the child's needs should be described. Furthermore, the percentage of time that the child will receive instruction with his normal peers should be specified. If a child is unable to participate in a regular class, justification for alternate placement must be provided.

(4) *A statement of appropriate objective criteria and evaluation procedures and schedules for determining, on at least an annual basis, whether instructional objectives are being achieved.* A child's progress in the education program should be monitored periodically. P.L. 94-142 guidelines suggest evaluation should take place quarterly. The information obtained from these evaluations should be submitted to other multidisciplinary staff members because it forms the basis for subsequent educational decisions.

An Example IEP

In attempting to write an IEP both expediently and thoroughly, the teacher is often caught in a dilemma. The planning time afforded teachers for individual programming generally is limited. A partial solution to this dilemma is through use of a curriculum guide designed for local school district needs. By referring to the guide, the teacher is able to save valuable time that would have been wasted in replication and writing. For example, a teacher in many cases could refer to an instructional objective by number rather than formulating a new objective. The effectiveness of this process hinges on the comprehensiveness of the curriculum guide. The guide must address motor skills in a developmental connotation. That is, behavioral objectives should reflect performances at various points along the skill continuum. In cases when motor skills to be developed are unique to a child and are not included in the guide, the teacher must write his or her own behavioral objectives. See chapter 8 for information on writing behavioral objectives.

Figure 20.1 illustrates an example IEP. The required components of an IEP are addressed in the columns directly under the student information.

Goals appear in the first column. These goal areas which are common to all children include physical fitness, fundamental motor skills, sport skills, dance, and aquatics. In columns 2, 3, and 4, present and targeted performance levels are described in terms of behavioral objectives. Behavioral objectives can be obtained from a curriculum guide. If the teacher is referring to the curriculum guide, the design number that corresponds to the intended objective is listed. In the example IEP, objectives for the overhand throw and catch are indicated by their curriculum guide number. Timeliness for the initiation and termination of instruction for each objective is given in columns 5 and 6. The remaining columns are employed to describe the type of placement and support personnel needed to deliver physical education services. Total time or percent of time may be used to indicate the proportion of time spent in each placement.

LEAST RESTRICTIVE ENVIRONMENT

One of the most misunderstood aspects of P.L. 94-142 is "Least Restrictive Environment" which mandates that special needs children are placed in a setting that enhances their chances for optimal educational development. Many authorities believe that an integrative rather than a segregated approach is imperative to maximum development and that any type of segregation will further widen the gap in normalizing special needs children. The basis for their belief stems from the educational benefits derived from pupil interaction. This interaction, if planned appropriately, can result in a transfer of values and behaviors and a decrease in the stigma attached to possessing a handicap.

The law maintains that the placement must be least restrictive to the child, with placement decisions made from a continuum of alternatives. The placement may be a special class, a regular class with special help, a regular class, or a combination of the three. It can also be an institution. The IEP committee must determine the time the child should spend in each placement alternative. No matter what the setting, the school system in which the child officially resides must provide a free education, including the cost of a special school for the child. Whenever possible, however, a special needs child should be in a regular classroom.

Several factors need to be considered prior to making placement decisions. The teacher must first ascertain the child's physical, social, cognitive, and emotional performance levels. A child who deviates significantly from other class members often presents problems to others in the instructional setting. If individualized instruction is practiced, the

Figure 20.1
I CAN PHYSICAL EDUCATION IEP FORM

School District/School Demuke

Student Name or Number John Smith

Date Submitted 9/10/81

Date of Planning Meeting 9/29/81

Date(s) of Review (Listed when Scheduled)

Teachers Mr. Monk

Recommended Total Time in Physical Education 3 days/weeks 30 minutes/day

Current Placement Special Education

Program Goal Areas in Physical Education	Present level(s) of Performance	Annual Student Goals	Short Term Objectives	Time Required (min/day)	Duration Dates Begin	Duration Dates End	Regular Education Placement	Special Designed Instruction	Support Personnel Needed (See back)
Physical Fitness **Area 1**	A. Sit-ups - 5th %1 B. 9-min. run 25th %1	A. Sit-ups 20th %1 B. 9-min. run 25th %1	A. Increase 1 rep per week B. Dec. 2 sec. per week	10 min. a day	9/1/81	6/1/82	100%	0%	None
Fundamental Motor Skills **Area 2**	A. Overhand Throw (Obj. 1.1.2) B. Catch (Obj. 1.2.4)	A. O. Throw (Obj. 1.1.5) B. Catch (Obj. 1.2.6)	A. Obj. 1.1.3 1.1.4 1.1.5 B. Obj. 1.2.5 1.2.6	10 min. a day	4/3/82	5/26/82	50%	50%	None
Aquatics **Area 3**	The students will be able to swim 5 yard without stopping	The students will be able to swim 25 yards	The student will increase 5 yards a week	20 min./day 2 days/week	1/4/82	3/28/82	0%	100%	YMCA
Area 4									
Area 5									

heterogeneity effect of performance levels is greatly diminished. Problems associated with teaching physical education to a diversified group generally occur in game situations rather than in skill development oriented activities. Rules and strategies of games may be changed to include the children with lower performance levels. If the modifications make the games unrealistic or less challenging for other class members, however, the teacher has done a disservice to the class. Some teachers who are aware of difficulties in integrating special needs children in complex games often group children according to ability level during these activities. If this segregation becomes common, the teacher must reexamine the curriculum to insure that all children are being served.

Before the child is placed, the teacher must consider the possible effects the special needs child will have on other class members. Protection of optimal educational development should extend to all students. If the special needs child will have an adverse effect on other class members, separate programming may be warranted.

Teachers face three major stumbling blocks in their efforts to place children in the least restrictive environment. First, schools have failed to provide additional resources and staff necessary to integrate special needs children. This problem will persist as more resources are placed into the core subject areas at the expense of physical education. To compensate for the inadequate staff, the teacher must employ strategies such as individualized instruction, peer tutoring, squad leaders, and the utilization of older children to aid in physical education. Second, the needed instructional technology is not readily available to physical educators. The reader is referred to chapter 8 of this book and *Principles of Methods of Adapted Physical Education and Recreation* by David Auxter and Jean Pyfer for further reading related to strategies utilizing an individualized instructional approach. Third, many physical educators were inadequately trained to employ new instructional techniques for individualizing instruction. To compensate, many universities and state education departments offer courses and in-service training programs in physical education. One course or a workshop, however, is not sufficient to develop competencies necessary to implement a successful physical education program.

CHANGING BEHAVIOR

The teacher must arrange the classroom conditions to change a child's behavior. Certain actions, if done appropriately, will enhance learning. The teacher must first determine the cause of the behavior by observing the surrounding events that cause the behavior. Once the cause is identified, the conditions can be altered and the child's behavior changed.

1. *Task Analysis:* breaking down a skill into teachable units and proceeding to teach children the units that they do not possess. An example of task analysis is provided in figure 20.2.

2. *Shaping:* reinforcing a response that closely approximates or represents improvement toward a desired behavior. A teacher uses the shaping principle by developing a sequence of activities that gradually increase in difficulty and enable the child to move toward the desired goal. For example, a child could be rewarded for trapping a ball with the chest and arms before being required to catch a ball solely with his/her hands.

3. *Prompting:* assisting the child in performing a response with verbal, visual, or manipulative cues. Holding a child's hand while he/she is learning to walk up stairs is an example of a prompt.

4. *Fading:* withdrawing the prompts gradually as the child improves. The next step after physically assisting a child walking up stairs may be to provide a hand railing.

5. *Time-out:* isolating the child from classmates when he/she exhibits inappropriate behaviors. The teacher would require a child to sit out of a game if he/she misbehaves. The child should return to the activity after demonstrating appropriate behavior or indicating he/she will follow class rules.

6. *Knowledge of Results:* providing information concerning the child's performance. In most cases, this information should be

---

Figure 20.2. Task Analysis of a Kick

Objective: To kick a stationary 10" playground ball a distance of 20 feet, two out of three times, with a mature kicking skill.

PHASE		PHASE COMPONENTS
Preparation	a.	The approach involves one or more steps with the last step being a leap.
	b.	The swing leg is hyperextended at the hip and flexed at the knee.
	c.	The support leg is planted slightly to the side of the ball.
Force Production (execution)	d.	As the support leg contacts the ground, the shoulders are retracted and trunk is inclined backward.
	e.	The forward swing of the leg is initiated at the hip.
	f.	Prior to the ball contact, the speed of the thigh is diminished and the knee extends rapidly.
	g.	The arm and leg move in position.
Follow-through	h.	The leg continues its pendular motion.
	i.	The kicker lands by hopping on the support leg.

Kicking could be analyzed further by identifying prerequisite motor and cognitive skills. For example, dynamic lateral balance is needed to successfully perform kicking.

---

given concisely and immediately following a response. A child who is throwing well except the incorrect foot is placed forward, quickly should be told, "You are throwing well, but place your left foot forward before releasing the ball." The teacher may also demonstrate a correct throw or place footprints on the floor to aid the child's understanding of the throwing skill.

Behavior Modification

Children with special needs frequently require a different approach to control as compared with the normal child. Motor dysfunction, disfigurement, and/or lower mental capacity among special needs children are often misunderstood by their normal peers. These challenges and how people respond to them often lead to undesirable compensatory behavior by the special needs child in the form of disruptive behavior.

How disruptive behavior is handled depends on the child. Children of normal mental capacity who exhibit emotionally unacceptable behavior might possibly be dealt with using techniques discussed in chapter 5. Those with lower mental capacity as well as those with severe emotional problems seem to respond well to behavior modification.

By using behavior modification, the teacher seeks to eliminate the undesired behavior while at the same time seeking the behavior's cause; changing the behavior will not eliminate its cause. For this reason, behavior modification has been maligned by many. It must be emphasized, therefore, that modifying the behavior is only the beginning; the long-range goal is to find and cure the behavior's underlying cause.

The components of a behavior modification program are:
1. Identify the behavior to be eliminated.
2. Begin immediately to find the behavior's underlying cause.
3. Count the frequency of the behavior.
4. Establish a program objective including a time frame for accomplishment.
5. Design a program to bring about the desired change.
6. Assess the results.
7. Make appropriate changes.

Some key elements to remember in designing and conducting a behavior modification program are:
1. Focus on only one behavior at a time.
2. Award points for good behavior but never subtract points when the child falters.
3. Gradually increase the number of points required to obtain the reward.
4. Rewards can be anything positive which motivates the child. Activity time is highly recommended. Any form of candy is just as highly discouraged. Fruits can be used if the child does not have a weight problem. Whenever possible the reward should be getting something (positive reinforcement) rather than losing something (negative reinforcement). One emotionally disturbed and retarded girl who was also grossly obese responded only to threats of not being fed (which at times she was not).

5. Other negative reinforcers such as time-out
must also be handled carefully. Some parents have sued schools because their child was placed in special time-out areas.

One school actually placed children in locked wooden cabinets similar to upright coffins. Although the technique worked in changing behavior, such techniques are highly questionable.

Case Study

A large third grade boy was beating up his smaller peers. The frequency and severity were sufficient to call it a major behavior problem. The school personnel had an obligation to protect others from the child and, therefore, sought ways to change the disruptive child's behavior quickly. The objective was to eliminate all physical fights initiated by the child within three weeks. A committee was immediately established to seek the underlying cause for the fighting.

In consultation with the child, his love for basketball and physical activity in general was discovered, and this became the key to the problem. Initially, only a short period of time in which no fights occurred was sufficient to win extra activity time. The physical educator and classroom teacher worked out the cooperative program so the boy could join in any physical education class or could have supervised play in the gym. The good behavior time required for the reward was gradually lengthened. The behavior modification program combined with the committee's work were sufficient to meet the program's objective.

TEACHING TECHNIQUES FOR THOSE WITH REDUCED MENTAL CAPACITY

Certain teaching styles seem to be better than others when working with various handicapping conditions. Unlike the normal child, children with reduced mental capacity respond best to a command style approach (chapter 5). A firm but positive approach is recommended. Individual attention along with the command style is also required by many moderately retarded children. Lessons with these children will usually have fewer activities and less maximum participation as compared to those for the mildly affected and normal children. It is frequently difficult, therefore, to mainstream more than a few moderately retarded children into any one physical education class. The extent to which mainstreaming can take place is dependent upon the degree of attention required by any one child or group of children.

ACTIVITIES

Since each child's needs are different, it is difficult to cover every handicapping condition. The activities in this section cover a wide variety of handicapping conditions most frequently encountered by physical educators.

LACK OF STRENGTH

Certain principles should be applied in developing a strength program. They are:

Specificity: only muscles directly involved in a specific movement are strengthened.

Overload: gains in strength result from placing stress on the muscles.

Safety: excessive stress placed on the bones of pre-adolescents may retard bone growth or cause injury.

A strength program for elementary children should be designed to gradually develop moderate, rather than maximum, strength levels because the growth centers of pre-adolescents have not yet ossified. Injuries to these growth centers will often have a detrimental effect on the child's future development.

Strength Activities

Activity: Curl-up
Objective: To develop abdominal muscles
Formation: Scattered
Equipment: Mats
Procedure: The child lies supine with arms crossed in front of the chest and legs bent 90 degrees at the knees. The head and shoulders are lifted four to six inches off the floor while keeping the lower back on the floor. After the upper body is held in this up position for two seconds, the entire upper body is rotated at the waist to one side and then to the other side. Each position should be held for two seconds. The curl-up is effective because the abdominal muscles perform a majority of the work and undue stress to the lower back is avoided.

Activity: Downhill sit-ups
Objective: To develop abdominal muscles
Formation: Incline or slope of a hillside
Procedure: The downhill sit-up is appropriate for children who cannot perform one sit-up on a flat surface. The sit-up is performed as the child lies on a slope with the feet downhill and the head uphill. As the child performs more sit-ups, the slope should be decreased.

Activity: Roll weights
Objective: To develop wrist strength
Equipment: String, weight, tubing from wax paper roll
Procedure: A weight (sandbag) is attached to a paper tubing from a wax paper roll by a string (See figure 20.3). The ends of the roll are held with the hands and the weight is elevated to the tubing by rolling the wrists.

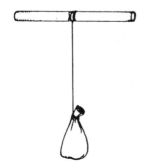

Figure 20.3

Activity: Inner tube activities
Objective: To develop strength (depends on the specific movement)
Formation: Scattered
Equipment: Inner tubes
Procedure: A discarded bike inner tube is used to provide resistance. The resistance can be altered by using inner tubes of various widths. Figure 20.4 illustrates the different tube exercises.

Place tube around feet straighten legs, pull toward chest.

Sit down, place tube around feet, spread legs apart laterally.

Step on tube, flex arm at elbow.

Place tube around hands above the head and pull outward.

Place tube around hands at chest level and pull outward.

Place tube around hands at chest level and pull as if pulling a bow in archery.

Place tube around head and arms, hold arms stable and move head at the neck.

Place tube around knees, pull knees outward.

 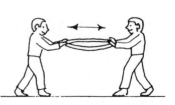

Lie prone and place tube around ankles and hands, extend legs at knees.

Place tube around the back and hands, extend arms at elbows.

Tug-of-War (May have to use more than one inner tube for safety)

Figure 20.4. Inner Tube Activities

Activity: Plastic milk carton pulley

Objective: To develop strength (depends on specific movement)

Formation: Scattered

Equipment: Rope, pulley, sand, plastic milk carton

Procedure: A rope is attached to a plastic milk carton loaded with sand. The weight is altered by the amount of sand in the milk carton. The rope is placed through a pulley anchored to a post or tree. Figure 20.5 illustrates different pulley exercises.

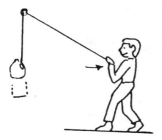

Face pulley, pull rope toward chest by flexing at the elbows.

Face away from pulley with arms upright, bring arms forward and downward.

Face away from pulley, hold arms straight and bring arms together in front of the body.

Stand with side facing pulley, bring arms in front and across the body.

Face pulley, bend downward at the waist.

Figure 20.5. Pully Exercises

BALANCE PROBLEMS

Balance is a key component in many skills. Children with poor balance often perform skills mechanically or inefficiently. Programs for these children should encompass all facets of balance: static, dynamic, and flight balances along the three body axes. The child should be required to maintain balance as he/she stands, walks, runs, jumps, and hops.

Balance Activities

Activity: Beam walking and standing

Objective: To develop static and dynamic balance

Formation: Lines or a balance beam for each child

Equipment: Boards of various widths

Procedure: Children stand or move forward or backward on a balance beam. Different locomotor skills should be used to cross the beam. The arms may be held outward or the hands may be placed on the hips as the children perform. The eyes may focus on the beam, up toward the ceiling, or closed. The width of the beam should be decreased gradually as the child's balancing ability improves.

Activity: Flight balance

Objective: To develop flight balance

Formation: Lines

Equipment: Spring board, mini-tramp (inner tube with canvas cover), mats

Procedure: The following movements are performed, while the child is airborne: (1) tuck, (2) pike, (3) V-sit, (4) straddle, (5) twist, (6) scissors, (7) touch various body parts, (8) side kick.

Activity: Balance stunts

Objective: To develop static balance

Formation: Scattered

Equipment: Mats

Procedure: The child performs the stunts depicted in figure 20.6.

Tripod   Frog Stand   Head Stand   Push-up

Stork Stand   Needle Scale   Single Squat Balance

Knee Scale   One Foot Scale   Two-point Balance

Figure 20.6. Balance Stunts

POOR BODY COORDINATION

Body coordination is the ability to integrate motor patterns of different body parts for a planned motor act. A clumsy child often has poor body coordination. A body coordination program should include activities that necessitate movements as the child assumes various positions.

Body Coordination Activities

Activity: Scooter
Objective: To develop ability to move the scooter in various positions
Formation: Scattered
Equipment: Scooters
Procedure: The child moves the scooter forward, backward, and sideward from various bases of support such as sitting, kneeling, or lying on his stomach. A maze or obstacle course should be added as the child can move on the scooter with efficiency.

Activity: Animal Walks
Objective: To develop the ability to move the body in various movements
Formation: Scattered
Equipment: Mats
Procedure: Where possible, the following activities should be performed forward, backward, and sideward: crab walk, inch worm, bear walk, monkey run, seal crawl, rabbit jump, hop, snake crawl

POOR BODY IMAGE

Some children have difficulty moving within the constraints of their space because they have a poorly developed body image which is an awareness of the body and the relationship between its parts. They frequently trip over or walk into objects in the course of a normal day. A well-developed body image is necessary to successfully perform many daily skills such as walking, eating, and playing. A body image program should consist of various locomotor movements through a variety of environmental spaces.

Body Image Activities

Activity: Hoop Jungle Gym

Objective: To develop the ability to perform various movements through a hoop jungle gym

Formation: Jungle gyms are scattered throughout the gym with children in lines or scattered.

Equipment: Hoop Jungle Gym—hoops are taped to each other so they are standing upright and form different shapes.

Procedure: Children form lines and play follow-the-leader through the hoop jungle gym. The leader should use various locomotor skills (walking, crawling, creeping, crab walking, inch worming, monkey running, jumping, and hopping) and directions (forward, backward, sideward, over, and through) when going through the hoop.

Activity: Hoop-scotch

Objective: To develop the ability to perform various locomotor skills through a hoop maze

Formation: Children in lines; hoops are placed flat on the floor in two rows next to each other (figure 20.7). Three different colors are alternated in serial order.

Figure 20.7. Hoop Formation

Procedure: Children form a line and play follow-the-leader through the hoop maze. Children can go down the maze in the following ways:
(1) walking or running with one foot per hoop
(2) jumping with one foot per hoop
(3) jumping with two feet per hoop
(4) hopping
(5) skipping

(6) bear walking or crawling
(7) jumping up with half twist
(8) activities 1-6 backward
(9) activities 1-8 stepping in only one color of hoops

POOR HAND-EYE COORDINATION

Children with poor hand-eye skills, such as catching, striking, and kicking, are at a distinct disadvantage in most activities. The physical educator must use a developmental approach to teach these skills. For example, trapping the ball should be taught before children attempt to catch a ball solely with the hands. Balloons enable children to track and react to a moving object more accurately due to the decreased speed. Children with cerebral palsy or loss of an upper limb may require prosthetic catching or striking devices.

Hand-eye Coordination Activities

Activity: Balloon activities

Objective: To develop hand-eye coordination

Formation: Scattered or in a circle, each child has a balloon

Equipment: Balloons

Procedure: Children perform the following activities:
(1) toss balloon up and trap it
(2) toss balloon up and catch it with the hands
(3) tap the balloon in the air ten times with your hands
(4) tap the balloon in the air with the: head; shoulder; knee; elbow; foot; two, three, four, etc. body parts
(5) toss balloon up and:
   a. clap your hands and catch it
   b. touch your head and catch it
   c. touch your shoulders and catch it
   d. touch your elbows and catch it
   e. touch your stomach and catch it
   f. touch your knees and catch it
   g. touch your ankle and catch it
   h. touch two, three, or four, etc. body parts and catch it
(6) with a partner:
   a. toss and trap balloon
   b. toss and catch balloon with hands
   c. tap the balloon back and forth
(7) with a partner, place the balloon between various body parts and move forward or backward:

a. between your partner's hip and yours

b. between your partner's shoulder and yours

c. between your partner's chest and yours

d. between your partner's head and yours

e. between your partner's back and yours

f. between your partner's knee and yours

g. between your partner's ankle and yours

Activity: Paper Plate Catching
Objective: To develop hand-eye or foot-eye coordination
Formation: Scattered with a partner
Equipment: Paper plates, paper fasteners, elastic cords, lightweight beanbags
Procedure: The paper plate catcher can be used with children who are missing hands or do not have use of the hands. Beanbags are passed between partners and caught by the paper plate catchers. The paper plate catcher (figure 20.8) is constructed by (a) cutting a slice to the center of the paper plate, (b) overlapping the edges, (c) attaching paper fasteners to secure the edges in that position, and (d) attaching another paper fastener and

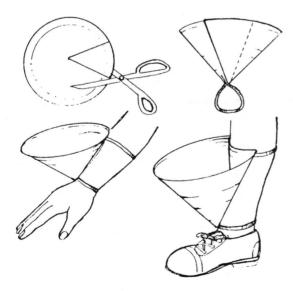

Figure 20.8. Paper Plate Catcher

a loop of elastic cord (6") to the plate's center. The catcher can be attached to the arms or legs.

Activity: Velcro catching mitt
Objective: To develop hand-eye coordination
Formation: Scattered individually or with a partner
Procedure: A ball with Velcro strips glued across its diameter is tossed in the air. A mitt shaped like a hand and constructed with two felt pieces sewn together is used to catch the ball. The ball sticks to the mitt upon contact.

Activity: Badminton striking
Objective: To develop striking skills
Formation: With a partner
Equipment: Badminton racket, shuttlecock, Velcro strips
Procedure: A badminton racket is attached to a child's arm with Velcro strips. The Velcro strips should be tightly secured to the racket to prevent rotation or propulsion of racket from arm.

VISUAL PROBLEMS

Children with visual problems often have difficulty understanding instructions because demonstration, a powerful teaching tool, is ineffective with these children. The teacher must utilize other instructional tools more effectively when introducing motor skills. Clear and concise verbal instruction, paired with kinesthetic prompts, enable the child to develop a mental picture of a skill. This mental picture then enables the child to reproduce the intended movements accurately and independently. Some children with visual problems benefit if they can feel dolls that the teacher is manipulating to perform the desired movements. This method allows a child to get an idea of the whole skill instead of segments of a skill. Scaled-down models of gyms, locker rooms, classrooms, and pools are also helpful because the child learns the environment as related rather than isolated parts.

Stimuli that elicit responses often have to be strengthened if the child with visual problems is to respond properly. Aural or stronger visual cues may be attached to balls, goals, and boundary lines. For example, a child could catch balls with bells or beepers inside or shoot balls at a basket with a sounder attached. Balls, goals, and boundary lines may also be painted bright colors—orange, yellow or red—so the child can discriminate the object from the background.

Activity: Line Goal Ball
Objective: To develop underhand roll and goal-keeping skills
Formation: Two teams; each team is spread out across their goal line. Space children so they cannot reach other teammates.
Equipment: Goal ball or ball (15" in diameter) with beeper/bells, and goal lines
Procedure: The game is played on a rectangular field with two goals located on opposite sides. Each team attempts to *roll* the ball across the opponents' goal while protecting their goal by intercepting the ball before it crosses the end line. All participants must keep the feet in a fixed position when goal tending and must always remain within a playing zone that extends one meter in front of the goal line. A sounder can be attached to the goals to provide directional cues. The referee must reposition any participant too close to another teammate. A penalty, one point added to opponent's score, results if: (1) a participant steps out of the playing zone, (2) a participant throws rather than rolls the ball, and (3) a participant touches a teammate or moves his/her feet while goal tending.

Activity: Toss Over (modified volleyball)
Objective: To develop throwing skills
Formation: Two teams, one team on each side of the net
Equipment: Audio sponge rubber ball, standards, and net placed at regulation volleyball height
Procedure: The rules are the same as volleyball except team members throw rather than volley an audio, brightly-colored ball over the net into opponent's court. The ball is permitted to hit the floor and roll before the receiving participant gathers the ball for play. Only one throw is allowed to cross the net. Bright colors or beepers should be added to the net to provide directional cues.

Activity: Guidewire or Tandem Running
Objective: To develop running skills and endurance
Formation: Child holding guidewire or paired with a sighted partner
Equipment: Wire or rope (minimum of 25 yards), 1" diameter metal ring and strap (optional)

Procedure: The rope or wire is suspended from a post or tree at waist height. Two rubber balls are attached to designate the end points so the child knows when to change directions. The child can use gloves or hold a strap and metal ring attached to the rope while running. A sighted person may also be used for running. The child with visual problems holds his/her sighted partner's arm slightly above the elbow and runs a half pace behind the partner.

HEARING PROBLEMS

The physical educator must arrange the gymnasium so children with hearing problems can utilize their vision or remaining hearing skills. Class demonstrations should be conducted so these children can easily observe the demonstrator. Directions should be given with the child directly facing the teacher. The use of signing may be required to communicate to a deaf child.

Most children with hearing problems can be integrated with hearing children with few adaptations to specialized activities. One activity designed for children with a little hearing is movements to rhythmic beats. The child may run, clap, skip, march, or beat a drum to various beats.

RESPIRATORY PROBLEMS

Children who suffer from asthma, bronchitis, and emphysema are included in this group. The child's physician should be consulted prior to planning a physical education program. The physical educator must be aware that some children with respiratory problems are sensitive to pollens; the gym should be as dust-free as possible. Gym floors and tumbling mats should be cleaned frequently, and dustless chalk should be used when writing on a chalkboard. The physical educator needs to be attentive to the child on days when the weather is changing, the humidity is high, or the child is required to perform strenuous activities. If they become thirsty during class, these children should be encouraged to drink water (not cold).

Activities for Individuals with Respiratory Problems

Activity: Ping-Pong Golf
Objective: To develop more efficient breathing patterns

Formation: Scattered

Equipment: Ping-Pong ball for each child, carpet with a hole 3" in diameter cut out of one end of the carpet

Procedure: The child attempts to blow the Ping-Pong ball into the hole. The child is assessed one stroke for each breath. The ball must come to a complete stop prior to the next breath. Sand traps and obstacles may be added to make the activity realistic.

Activity: Balloon Races

Objective: To develop more efficient breathing patterns

Formation: All children behind a starting line

Equipment: Balloons

Procedure: Children on all fours line up behind the starting line with a balloon. Upon a start signal, the children blow the balloons to the finish line. A maze may also be utilized in the races.

Activity: Bending breathing exercises

Objective: To develop more efficient breathing patterns

Formation: Scattered

Equipment: None

Procedure: The child assumes a standing position with feet shoulder-width apart. The child breathes out as he/she slowly bends at the waist to the right, left, or in front. All muscles are relaxed in the down position except the abdominal muscles should be contracted. The child inhales as he/she raises upward. The abdominal muscles are relaxed during the inhaling phase.

AMBULATORY PROBLEMS

Children who use crutches, braces, wheelchairs, or have difficulty moving due to inefficient locomotor skills need an accessible environment. These children should not be eliminated from activities because the setting is inaccessible. Ramps, easy-open doors, and wide doorways should be incorporated into the design of the gymnasium and outdoor facilities. The physical educator should consult with the child's physician to learn transfers needed to move the child and to discuss movements or activities that may be harmful to the child.

If available, an aquatics program should be provided to the child with poor ambulation. Many skills can be performed more easily in the water than on land because less weight is placed on the joints and less balance is required due to the body's buoyancy.

Activities for Individuals with Ambulatory Problems

Activity: Flexibility Exercises

Objective: To stretch muscles that are tight due to specific disabilities or confinement to a wheelchair, bed, or braces.

Formation: Scattered

Equipment: Mats

Procedure: Contractures occur if children confined to restricted positions or children who have cerebral palsy do not perform range of motion exercises daily. Tight muscles must be identified and moved throughout a wide range, actively or passively. Movements should be smooth and slow and the stretch should be held for five seconds. Flexibility develops gradually so excessive force should never be applied to a joint or muscle.

Activity: Ramp Bowling

Objective: To develop pushing and aiming skills

Formation: Children face bowling pins

Equipment: Commercial ramp or carpet roll (diameter larger than the bowling ball), bowling pins, and balls

Procedure: A commercial ramp or carpet roll is placed near child/wheelchair. The child aims the ramp in the direction of the bowling pins set on the floor. The bowling ball is lifted, placed on the ramp/roll and pushed down the ramp. A point is awarded for every pin knocked down.

Activity: Tabletop Tether Ball

Objective: To develop striking and hand-eye skills

Formation: Two children, one on each side of the tether pole

Equipment: Ball or balloon, dowel rod (36" length), string, and base (20" x 20")

Procedure: The activity is played on a tabletop tether ball model. Each player attempts to wind the ball/balloon around the pole by striking it in the opposite direction of his/her opponent. Paddles can be introduced after the children learn the game.

Activity: Alley Ping-Pong

Objective: To develop striking and hand-eye skills

Formation: Two children, one on each side of a Ping-Pong table

Equipment: Ping-Pong table, balls, and paddles (bihandle paddle)

Procedure: Ping-Pong rules apply to this activity except a wall two feet high is placed at the table's side to prevent the ball from leaving the table. The ball must cross over the net and land on opponent's side. A player is permitted one swing; the ball, however, may bounce more than once before it is hit. A point is awarded if after the ball strikes the table, it lands on the floor. A bihandle paddle should be used by children who have insufficient hand-eye skills or arm/shoulder strength to control a regulation paddle.

SUMMARY

This chapter was a presentation of P.L. 94-142 also known as the handicapped law. The major components of the law were discussed along with ideas on how to work with children with special needs. The three areas of emphasis were: (1) children should be placed in the least restrictive environment, (2) an IEP must be prepared for each special needs child, and (3) special needs children must be provided with a free and appropriate education. Specific areas covered were the IEP, a behavior change, and activities which will help develop children with various handicapping conditions.

REFERENCES AND SUGGESTED READINGS

Auxter, D., J. Pyfer, and C. Huettig. *Principles and Methods of Adapted Physical Education and Recreation* (9th ed.). Boston: McGraw Hill Co. 2001.

Payne, V. and L. Isaacs. *Human Motor Development: A Lifespan Approach,* (6th ed.). Boston: McGraw Hill, 2005.

Rizzo, T. Physical educators' attitudes associated with teaching individuals with disabilities, *The research consortium newsletter,* AAHPERD, Fall, 1994, pp 2 and 5.

Selective Web Sites

Adapted Physical Education: http://www.pecentral.org/adapted/adaptedmenu.html

Adapted PE (Palaestra): http://shcools.eastnet.ecu.edu/pitt/ayden/pesite10.htm

Palastra: http://www.palestra.com/

PE Link 4U: http://www.pelins4u.org/sections/adapted/adapted.htm

Sportime Adapted PE: http://www.sportime.com.adapted/index.jsp

Chapter

21

Basketball

After completing this chapter, the student should be able to:

1. Identify three common problems children frequently exhibit when dribbling a basketball.

2. Describe the basketball skill known as "pivoting."

3. Identify three common problems children frequently exhibit when attempting to pass a basketball.

4. Explain why the "baseball pass" is not recommended for elementary school age children.

5. Identify three common problems children frequently exhibit when shooting a basketball.

6. Identify three common problems children frequently exhibit when guarding an opponent.

7. Name and describe seven basketball drills, activities, or games.

8. Define the key terms listed below.

━━━━━━━━━━━━━━━━━━━━━━━━━━ *Key Terms*

Baseball pass	Free throw	Offensive skills
Bounce pass	Guarding	Pivoting
Chest pass	Jump shot	Set shot
Defensive skills	Lay-up	Two-hand overhead pass
Dribble		

Basketball, a true American game, was first played in Springfield, Massachusetts, in the year 1892. Its inventor, Dr. James Naismith, was attempting to develop a vigorous physical activity that could be played indoors during the very cold New England winters. Furthermore, it was his intention to develop an activity that would enable students to maintain an acceptable level of physical fitness between the football and baseball seasons.

The game of basketball has undergone many changes since its initial conception. Nevertheless, one aspect of the game, the height of the basketball goal, continues to resist change. Since the game's conception, the height of the basketball goal has remained at ten feet. For most elementary school age children, this goal height is not appropriate. Typically, when a young child attempts to project the basketball toward a goal which is too high, the youngster will more than likely use a less than desirable technique. For example, instead of exhibiting correct form, the child may use two hands to toss the ball underhanded or perhaps a two-handed over-the-shoulder shot.

The emphasis of an instructional skill theme unit involving elementary basketball should focus almost entirely on the development and refinement of the fundamental skills which make up the regulation sport activity. Said differently, very little time should be spent on playing the game of basketball; instead, the physical educator's major responsibility is to teach the skills of the game. This is best accomplished by modifying the height of the basketball goal and using a junior sized basketball or some other smaller ball. Children who desire to put their skills to test should be encouraged to participate in one of the many extracurricular basketball leagues offered in most communities.

BASKETBALL SKILLS

Basketball is made up of many fundamental motor skills. These in part include: catching, throwing, jumping, hopping, running, and even sliding (a gallop performed in a sideward direction). Not until the children have developed a reasonable amount of proficiency in these basic fundamental motor skills will they be capable of using these skills in a more specific sports context.

In the next section, we describe the basic skills of basketball which should be introduced to elementary school age children. These sport specific basketball skills include: dribbling, pivoting, passing, shooting, and guarding.

Dribbling

Dribbling, or repeatedly bouncing the basketball, is a skill which is used to advance the ball or maneuver about the court. This skill should be taught through the sensory modality of tactile perception. Simply put, the child should not have to look at the ball while dribbling. Thus the child's sense of vision will be free to look at the positioning of teammates and opponents.

Dribbling the basketball should be done with the fingers by pushing the ball toward the ground and keeping the ball in front of the body. Tell the students that dribbling is something like patting a dog on top of the head with your fingers; it is not like spanking the dog with the palm of the hand. One successful phrase which may help your students maintain fingertip control is to tell them to pretend that you have put mud over the entire ball. At the end of the class if you were to examine their hands, you should find dirty fingers but clean palms.

Children should learn to dribble the ball with either hand. In addition, they should learn how to protect the ball by dribbling low and by placing their body between the opponent and the ball. Junior basketballs, soccer balls, volleyballs, or playground balls can be used to practice the skill.

In dribbling, fingers are used to push the ball toward the ground.

Common Faults
1. Slapping or striking the ball with the palm of the hand.
2. Looking at the ball while dribbling.
3. Not keeping the ball in front of the body.
4. Occasionally contacting the ball with both hands (double dribbling).
5. Poor rhythmical coordination regarding ball-hand contact.

Teaching Suggestions

1. Draw a dog's face on the ball and encourage the children to pat the dog on the head using a gentle fingertip movement as opposed to a forceful striking movement.
2. Allow children to dribble balls of different inflation levels.
3. Allow children to dribble different size balls.
4. Children should first learn to dribble a ball while stationary before being allowed to dribble while moving.
5. Stress ball control.
6. Do not use a dribbling relay race in this unit of instruction. Such an activity is not conducive to emphasizing ball control.
7. To foster maximum participation, provide a ball to each student in the class.

Pivoting

Pivoting is a maneuver that allows you to move your body without attempting to advance the ball by dribbling. One of your feet, the pivot foot, must stay in contact with the ground at all times. This pivot foot is allowed to move about one central spot on the floor but cannot be moved off this critical point. Your other foot, however, can be freely moved, thus allowing you to keep your body between the ball and your opponent. Once again, be sure you do not drag the pivot foot or else you will have committed a violation called traveling (walking or moving the feet without dribbling).

Common Fault

1. Failing to keep the foot over one critical point—the pivot point.

Pivoting

Teaching Suggestion

1. Tell the students to pretend that their pivot foot has a stake driven through it, thus creating a pivot point.

Passing Skills

Chest Pass. Grasp the junior basketball with both hands so that the hands are on opposite sides of the ball. Spread the thumbs and pointing fingers so that the two hands form three sides of a box on the backside of the ball. With the ball close to the chest, quickly extend the arms and snap the wrist stepping in the direction of the pass.

The Chest Pass requires a speedy delivery of the ball.

Bounce Pass. When performing the bounce pass, the ball is held exactly like the chest pass. The difference lies in the manner in which the ball is delivered. The ball is pushed from the chest toward the ground with a light backspin. The ball should strike the ground about three-quarters the distance to the receiving player so that the ball will bounce up to his/her waist. A step should be taken by the passer while executing this skill.

The Bounce Pass is held like the Chest Pass, with lower ball delivery.

Two-Hand Overhead Pass. The junior basketball is held by placing both hands on opposite sides of the ball and the arms are held over the head.

The Two-Hand Overhead Pass is most useful when the player is closely guarded.

The pass is executed by slightly dropping the ball behind the head and then quickly extending the arms upward while at the same time snapping the wrist. This pass is most frequently used to pass the ball over the head of an opponent who is guarding you very closely. If possible a step should be taken in the direction of the pass.

Baseball Pass. While some authors suggest teaching the baseball pass to elementary school age children, it is not recommended here. Usually, when young children are allowed to use the baseball pass (throwing the ball with one hand like a baseball), the game will more than likely get out of control. This is because most children will start throwing the basketball the entire length of the court. At this level of play we believe that the emphasis should be on controlled and skilled behavior. Even on the rare occasion when the ball is thrown on target, the pass receiver is generally unable to handle the pass due to its velocity.

Common Faults

1. Telegraphing the direction of the pass.
2. Passing the ball too low so that it hits your teammate's foot.
3. Passing the ball too high in the air, allowing it to be picked-off by an opponent.
4. Failing to acquire enough speed on the passed ball, which is usually caused by failing to transfer the body's weight in the direction of the pass.
5. Simply failing to pass the ball to an open teammate. (Most children prefer to dribble the ball.)

Teaching Suggestions

1. Children need to understand that passing is a quicker and more effective way of moving the ball around the court (as opposed to dribbling).
2. Stress ball control and accuracy.
3. Use a smaller and lighter weight ball.

4. Do not allow the baseball pass.
5. Allow children to pass to a stationary teammate before attempting to pass to a teammate who is in motion.
6. Do not allow children to pass the ball behind their back.

Shooting Skills

Lay-up. The lay-up shot is a short shot taken under the basket. The shot is executed by taking off on the foot opposite from the hand which is shooting. In short, the shooting motion is actually a skip just before the ball is released. The ball should be aimed at the backboard just above and slightly to the near side of the basket's center. One hand should guide the ball while the other shoots it. A volleyball or soccer ball should be used with an eight-foot high (or less) basket during the initial stages of learning. A junior basketball can be substituted after success with the smaller ball.

After learning the lay-up in a stationary (near the basket) position, the child can dribble into the lay-up. This, however, is a highly coordinated activity which should be practiced slowly.

Arm-leg opposition is used when shooting the lay-up.

Set Shot. The set shot is usually taken with one hand while the other hand guides the ball. The body is turned slightly away from the shooting side while placing the shooting hand and arm closer to the basket. The foot on the same side of the shooting hand is in a forward stride position. The shot is done by bending both the arms and legs and then uncoiling them simultaneously with a follow-through of the shooting hand and arm toward the basket. A good arch (approximately 45 degrees) should be placed on the ball.

The set shot.

The jump shot.

Jump Shot. The jump shot is similar to the one-handed set shot with the primary difference between the two related to lower body mechanics. In performing the jump shot the shooter jumps straight upwards and does not project the ball toward the basket until he/she has reached the peak of the jump. This skill requires more coordination and strength than the set shot. Nonetheless, the jump shot is the bread and butter shot in basketball.

Free Throws. Any of the shots described above can be utilized to shoot free throws. One advantage of free throw shooting is the shooter does not need to rush. The shooter can take his/her time, bounce the ball a few times and, perhaps, even take a deep breath in order to relax before shooting.

Common Faults
1. Failing to follow through after the shot.
2. Failing to accomplish the appropriate arch on the shot (45 degrees in most cases).
3. Failing to use the backboard when shooting a lay-up.
4. Failing to use arm-leg opposition when shooting the lay-up.
5. Failing to correctly time the ball release when performing a jump shot.

Teaching Suggestions
1. Use a small lightweight ball. A ball which is too big or too heavy will cause an immature shooting form to be used. The teacher should stress the importance of correct shooting techniques.
2. Allow children to shoot at baskets of eight feet or less.
3. Children should learn to shoot while stationary before being allowed to shoot while moving.
4. Children should develop proficiency in shooting skills before a defensive player is introduced to the shooting situation.

Guarding

Guarding is a defensive skill used to keep an opponent from scoring a basket. When guarding an opponent you should bend the knees and keep the feet shoulder-width apart. This posture lowers your center of gravity, making it easier for you to quickly change directions. When moving with your opponent you should use a sliding motion, being careful that you do not cross your feet. If your opponent attempts a shot, hold your arms straight

Defensive stance used for guarding an opponent.

up into the air, being sure that you do not jump into your opponent or swing your arms downward in an attempt to block the shot.

Common Faults
1. Standing too erect.
2. Crossing the feet, thus failing to use a sliding movement to stay with your opponent.
3. Grabbing an opponent who is about to get by you.
4. Being too close to or too far away from the opponent.

Teaching Suggestions
1. Allow children to first guard a stationary object before requiring them to guard an opponent who is on the move. See the activity called "Pin Guard" described on page 317 in this chapter.
2. Use one-on-one situations when first introducing the skill of guarding an opponent.

BASIC BASKETBALL RULES AND OTHER CONSIDERATIONS
1. Each team consists of the following five players: two guards, two forwards, and a center.
2. The ball can be advanced by passing it to a teammate or by dribbling the ball down court.
3. A jump ball is held at center court to begin play at the start of the game.
4. A foul is called on any player who trips, kicks, pushes, holds, or charges into another player.
5. A player is guilty of a violation called traveling or walking if he/she advances the ball without dribbling it. When this violation is committed, the other team is awarded ball possession.
6. Whenever a basket is made (other than a free throw) the team making the basket is awarded two points.
7. A throw-in is used to put the ball back into play following all successful scoring attempts and whenever a ball goes out of bounds.
8. If a player is fouled while in the act of shooting he/she is awarded two free throws.

BASKETBALL ACTIVITIES AND GAMES

As mentioned previously, basketball is one of the most difficult games to teach elementary school age children and few are able to master even a good approximation of the regulation game. Therefore, the teacher should refrain from placing the children into regulation basketball games before they are capable of performing the basic skills. Children should be introduced to this difficult activity by taking part in basketball activities and other lead-up activities. Sample basketball activities and modified games are described below.

The following abbreviations are used in presenting the following activities:

N = Name of the activity or game
DA = Age of the student for which the activity is best suited (developmental age)
DV = The developmental value of the activity; i.e., fitness, manipulative ability, etc.
F = Formation
E = Any equipment needs
D = Description of the activity
V = Variation

N: Dribble Take Away - Game
DV: Dribbling without looking at the ball
F: Free formation in one-half of a basketball court
E: One ball for each participant
D: Each child is given a ball to dribble anywhere within the assigned playing area. While dribbling his/her ball, the child can attempt to knock someone else's ball away. A child who loses his/her own ball may not touch anyone else's until he/she retrieves it and begins dribbling again. At the end of a given time, those who have lost their balls the least number of times are declared the best dribblers.

V: Specify that the ball can only be dribbled with the non-dominant hand.

N: Three Player Weave - Activity
DV: Passing for the purpose of advancing the ball without dribbling
F: Groups of three standing side by side and approximately fifteen feet apart
E: One ball for each group of three participants
D: The three participants stand facing down court. The player in the middle starts the activity by passing the ball to one of the other two players, and then goes behind the player to whom the ball was passed while continuing to head down court. The individual receiving a pass heads toward the center position and passes the ball to the other player. This activity can be difficult at first and will require some practice. Having players draw out the movement patterns on paper can be of help in learning this important activity.
V: Specify the type of pass which must be used.

N: No Dribble Basketball - Game
DV: All fundamental basketball skills except dribbling
F: Same as regular basketball positions
E: Basketball goals and basketballs
D: This game is played just like regulation basketball with the exception that the ball cannot be dribbled. Thus the ball can only be advanced by passing off to teammates who can move freely when they do not have the ball. Emphasis can be placed on the walking rule during this game and what players should do when they do not have the ball.

N: One-on-One, Two-on-Two, or Three-on-Three - Game
DV: Most basketball skills
F: Each participant guards an opponent
E: Basketball goal and one basketball per group
D: This is just like regulation basketball except it is played with a limited number of participants.

N: Dribble Activities - Activity
DV: A series of activities to improve several aspects of dribbling

F: Free formation
E: One ball for each participant
D: 1. Dribble while kneeling
   2. Dribble circles around your body
   3. Dribble around one leg only
   4. Dribble the basketball as low to the ground as possible
   5. Dribble while sliding
   6. Dribble while skipping
   7. Dribble while jogging
   8. Dribble while running in a straight line
   9. Dribble while running in a circle
   10. Dribble while running in a zigzag manner
   11. Dribble while moving backwards
   12. Dribble with eyes closed (stationary dribble to be used)

N: Dribble Call Numbers - Activity
DV: Dribbling without looking at the basketball
F: Free in large open space
E: One basketball for each child
D: Each child has a basketball, and is scattered in a free formation facing the teacher. Children then dribble the basketball in different directions, forward, backward, sidewards right and left, in response to visual signals given by the teacher.

N: Keep Away - Game
DV: Passing and guarding
F: Three players per group
E: One basketball per group
D: Two of the three participants stand approximately twenty-five feet from one another and count the number of times they can successfully pass the basketball back and forth to one another within a specified time period. The third participant stands between the two passers and attempts to steal the pass.
V: The teacher should specify the type of pass to be used. Gradually increase the number of passers and the number of individuals attempting to steal the pass.

N: Pin Guard - Game
DV: Passing and guarding a stationary object
F: Groups of three
E: One ball and one plastic container per group

D: This activity is played like Monkey in the Middle except the middle person is trying to protect the plastic container from being hit. The two side players pass the ball quickly trying to eventually hit the target. Players should switch frequently.

V: The teacher should specify the type of pass to be used.

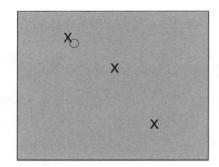

N: Twenty-One - Game

DV: Shooting a lay-up and passing to a teammate

F: Two teams each at their own basketball goal

E: Basketball and basketball goals

D: The two teams form a straight line at half-court and facing their respective basket. The first person in line dribbles the ball toward his or her goal and shoots a lay-up. Only one shooting attempt is allowed. This same individual gets the rebound, dribbles to within twenty feet of his or her team, and then passes the basketball to the next person in line. The first team to score twenty-one baskets is declared the winner.

V: 1. Specify shots other than a lay-up.
   2. Use more than one ball for each team.

N: Mirror - Activity

DV: Dribbling and guarding

F: Groups of two

E: One basketball for each participant

D: The two participants face one another. One of the two is selected as leader and dribbles the ball anywhere, in any legal way and at any speed within the assigned playing area. The other participant attempts to copy or mirror the actions of the leader.

V: Allow one child to dribble while the other child simply guards the dribbler. In other words, the follower does not have a basketball.

N: Shadow - Game

DV: Agility

F: Pairs

E: One ball per pair

D: One child dribbles the ball anywhere in the play area, and the other child tries to stay as close as possible. On a stop signal, both must stop. If the non-dribbling player can reach out and touch the dribbler, he or she receives one point. If not, the dribbler receives the point.

N: Speed Shooting - Activity

DV: Shooting and passing

F: Done as a basketball station. No more than two pairs of players per basket (eight-foot-high basket).

E: One junior basketball per pair

D: One of the pair stays outside a ten-foot restraining line and shoots the ball using a set shot or jump shot. The other partner rebounds and passes out to the partner. After ten tries, the two switch places. Scores can be the number made or the number made in a given time frame (emphasizing speed).

REFERENCES AND SUGGESTED READINGS

American Sport Education Program. *Coaching Youth Basketball* (2nd ed.). Champaign, IL: Human Kinetics, 1996.
Garchow, K. and A. Dickinson (Eds.). *Youth Basketball*. Dubuque, IA: Brown & Benchmark, 1992.
Krause, J.V., Meyer, D. and J. Meyer *Basketball Skills & Drills*. Champaign, IL: Human Kinetics. 1999.
Wooden, J. *Practical Modern Basketball*. Boston, MA: Allyn and Bacon, 1999.

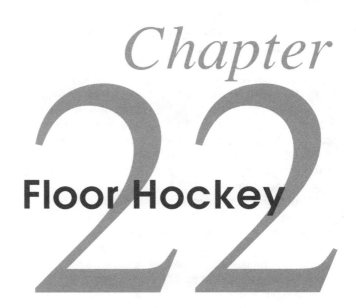

Chapter 22

Floor Hockey

After completing this chapter, the student should be able to:

1. List and describe two general stick handling principles.

2. List and describe two common faults that children experience when attempting to dribble the floor hockey puck.

3. List and describe two common faults that children experience when attempting to pass the floor hockey puck to a teammate.

4. List teaching suggestions which outline the progressive manner that one should follow when teaching children to pass the floor hockey puck.

5. List and describe two common faults that children experience when attempting to field a floor hockey puck.

6. List and describe two common faults that children experience when attempting to perform a drive shot.

7. Describe the correct procedure for conducting a face off.

8. List and describe the six team positions employed in floor hockey.

9. List and describe floor hockey rules relating to fouls, goalkeeping, and length of play.

10. List and describe seven different floor hockey drills, activities, or games.

11. Define the key terms listed below.

━━━━━━━━━━━━━━━━━━━━━━━━━━━━━ *Key Terms*

Blade
Dribbling
Drive shot
Face off

Fielding
Puck
Push pass
Tackling

Floor hockey is one of America's fastest growing elementary school sports. This exciting and fast-paced activity was originally played thousands of years ago by both the Greeks and the Egyptians. When first introduced, the activity was played outdoors and was referred to as field hockey. Initially the game was played by men, but when the game began to be played by Americans, it was considered predominantly a female activity. Recently, however, the introduction of floor hockey as a skill theme within the elementary school physical education curriculum has led to both male and female participation.

The emphasis of an instructional skill theme unit involving floor hockey should focus on the development and refinement of the fundamental skills which make up the activity. Various hitting implements can be used to speed up or slow down the pace of this exciting sport. For example, use a plastic whiffle ball if you desire to speed up the game's pace. If you desire to slow down the game's pace, then use a plastic hockey puck. The game's pace could be slowed down further by using light-weight bean bags. Because control and accuracy should be stressed at the beginning of the unit, start off with slower moving implements and proceed to faster moving implements. Not until reasonable competency in these basic fundamental skills is acquired, should children be allowed to engage in the regulation sport activity.

FLOOR HOCKEY SKILLS

In order to experience success in the sport of floor hockey it is necessary to demonstrate competency in the following basic floor hockey skills:

1. Stick Handling
2. Dribbling
3. Passing
4. Fielding
5. Tackling
6. Shooting
7. Facing Off

In the next section each of these basic floor hockey skills is described, pointing out common faults and offering teaching suggestions. The chapter ends with a description of several floor hockey activities and games. These movement experiences can be used to help children acquire and refine these basic skills.

Stick Handling

1. The suggested floor hockey stick is one produced by Cosom, a division of Schaper Manufacturing Company. Their floor hockey stick is made of plastic and is appropriately sized for elementary school children.
2. When holding the floor hockey stick, the hands should be placed on the shaft and separated eight to twelve inches. Right-handed players should keep the right hand in the lower position; left-handed players, the left hand.
3. The stick's blade (hitting portion of the floor hockey stick) should be carried low at all times.
4. Do not swing the floor hockey stick like a golf club. Strive for control and accuracy at all times.

Common Faults

1. Carrying the stick above waist level when running down field.
2. Swinging the stick above waist level when shooting.
3. Placing the hands too close together.

Separate the hands eight to twelve inches.

Teaching Suggestions

1. Place colored tape on the floor hockey stick to indicate the position of the hands.
2. Place a lightweight ribbon around the stick's shaft and the other end around the player's lower leg. This teaching aid is particularly helpful to use with those individuals who repeatedly swing the floor hockey stick too high. The ribbon is of such a length that it is impossible to swing the floor hockey stick above waist level. This teaching aid is best used in controlled drilling situations when the player is not being required to run at top speeds around the floor hockey playing area.

Dribbling

Dribbling is a skill which is used to advance the hockey puck (or ball). To dribble, the puck should be positioned to one side or the other and tapped lightly with either side of the stick's blade. Use short, rapid taps to keep the puck moving. Keep the puck within reaching distance to prevent opponents from taking it away.

Common Faults

1. Using the wrist instead of the shoulder to move the hockey stick.
2. Hitting the puck too hard.
3. Angling the stick's blade causing the puck to go over the top of the blade.

Teaching Suggestions

1. Swing the stick from the shoulder, not the wrist, when dribbling.
2. Keep the hockey puck within two to three feet of your body.
3. Keep the blade upright so that it forms a 90-degree angle with the ground.

Passing

The most frequently used pass in floor hockey is the "push pass." The push pass is used to get the puck to a teammate who is positioned a short distance from the passer. Execution of the push pass is very similar to dribbling and usually is a continuation of the dribbling motion. To perform, simply push the puck a little harder than that used when dribbling. Because this pass is truly nothing more than a "push," little backswing and little follow-through are required.

Common Faults

1. Hitting the puck too hard.
2. Taking too much of a backswing and follow-through.
3. Inaccurate pass.

Teaching Suggestions

1. Have students practice passing when both the passer and receiver are stationary.
2. After accomplishing #1, allow a moving passer to pass to a stationary receiver.
3. After accomplishing #2, allow a moving passer to pass to a moving receiver.
4. Not until all of the above steps have been accomplished would you introduce a defender.

Fielding

Fielding is the act of stopping an oncoming puck and is done by straightening the top arm to create a closed blade position. This closed blade position allows the puck to be trapped between the blade and the ground. Fielding a bouncing or an aerial puck is far more difficult. When the puck is not moving smoothly along the floor, the stick's blade must be raised up and used to knock the puck back down to the floor before control is maintained.

Close the blade when fielding the puck.

321

Common Faults

1. Failing to close the stick's blade.
2. Failing to keep the stick's blade in contact with the ground.
3. Incorrectly timing blade-puck contact when the puck is in the air.

Teaching Suggestions

1. Keep your eyes on the approaching puck and do not attempt to advance the puck until you first acquire control.
2. When fielding an aerial puck, pretend that you have a baseball glove over the stick's blade. This will help improve your ability to knock the puck back down to the ground.

Tackling

Tackling is the defensive player's means of taking away the puck from an opponent. To tackle, the defensive player should move in toward the approaching offensive player. As soon as the puck is dribbled and is out in front of the dribbler, the defender reaches in to knock the puck away.

Common Faults

1. Running into the offensive player.
2. Tripping the offensive player.
3. Taking a full swing at the puck.

Teaching Suggestions

1. Jab or poke at the puck with the stick's blade.
2. Time the tackle so that it occurs just after it has been struck by the offensive dribbler.

Shooting

Drive Shot. When shooting the puck, be sure to follow all of the general stick handling principles presented earlier. In addition, a "flicking" motion of the wrist can be added to increase speed. The most powerful and frequently used floor hockey shot is the "drive shot." The drive shot is done from a forward stride position with the puck to one side of the body. The stick is drawn back beside the body with one hand slightly higher than center and one on the top of the stick. The shot is executed with a drive motion forward while flicking the puck by quickly pulling the top hand back and pushing the bottom hand forward. The stick may not come higher than the waist on the follow-through.

The drive shot is generally used to score a goal.

Common Faults

1. Swinging the stick like a golf club.
2. Failing to contact the puck in front of the body. This problem is more pronounced when a moving player attempts to drive a moving puck. In other words, the player "over-runs" the puck.
3. Hitting the floor hockey ball or puck too high or too low.
4. Hooking the puck by hitting it too far on one side or the other.
5. Failing to acquire proper position with the puck to one side of the body.

Teaching Suggestions

1. Acquire control of the puck before attempting a drive shot.
2. Use a flicking motion of the wrist to provide power and maintain a low follow-through.

Facing Off

The face off is used to put the puck into play at the beginning of a game, after a goal is scored, and in special situations where two opposing players "tie-up" the puck. To face off, one player from each team stands on opposite sides of the puck with the left shoulder pointing to the goal in which he or she attempts to score. Each player touches his or her stick to the ground and then raises the stick off of the ground to touch each other's stick.

This procedure is repeated three times. Once the sticks have touched for the third time, each player attempts to get control of the puck or knock it to a teammate.

Common Faults

1. Not touching sticks the required number of times (three).
2. Using too much backswing following the third stick touch. This results in a slower "stick to puck" contact.

Teaching Suggestions

1. Jab or poke at the puck; do not take a backswing.
2. Anticipate the third stick touch and react quickly.

RULES FOR COSOM FLOOR HOCKEY

I. EQUIPMENT

Cosom has a variety of Hockey Sets to fit all age groups. Sticks are also available separately along with related items.

A. STICKS: Will be supplied for all games. Dowelling of wood up to one-half inch in diameter is allowed in the shaft to add strength, rigidity, and durability. One stick, for the sole use of the team's rover, shall be taped to look clearly different from the others. For shorter players, cut off sticks to eliminate need to choke up grip on handle.

B. GOALIE EQUIPMENT: The goalie may use a Cosom goalie stick if he or she wishes. It must conform to the same rules as the other sticks. Goalies may wear ordinary hockey shin pads and a stomach protector. *They may also use an ordinary ball glove, regular glove, or mitten on their catching hand. A regular player's hockey glove may be worn on the other hand.* The goalie must wear a face mask. Goalies who wear shin pads must tape the ridges with white or masking tape so that they won't mark the floor.

C. DRESS: There is a two minute penalty for delay of game while switching helmets. Each team needs some common identification. (Sweaters, scrimmage vests, same colored T-shirts, etc.) All players should wear gym clothes and running shoes.

D. Cosom #802 Kit and #800 Stick are approved

for play by Boys and Girls International Floor Hockey and Canadian Poly Hockey Association.

II. PLAYING AREA

A. Any area that is laid out for basketball, or any other smooth surface of comparable size, can be used. For elementary school children of grade 6 and under, it is recommended that the playing area not exceed 50 x 75 feet.

1. Center line is the mid-court line of a basketball floor.
2. Center circle is the basketball mid-court jump circle. Play always starts in this circle and resumes from this point after goals, roughing fouls, or misconduct fouls with the offended team given possession.
3. The goal shall not exceed 60 inches in width and 54 inches in height. The nets are to be placed with the net frames directly against the wall, or at the end of the court.
4. The goal box is a restraining line 5 feet from the front of the goal and 4 feet from each side of the goal. (Note: When gyms or other areas that do not have the proper lines are used, colored plastic tape may be used for lines, including goal box.)

III. THE TEAM

A. Each team consists of six (6) players.

1. One (1) GOALKEEPER who stops puck with hands, feet, or stick.
2. One (1) CENTER who is the ONLY player allowed to move full court and who leads offensive play. The CENTER has his stick striped with black tape. In Canadian Poly Hockey, the CENTER is often called the ROVER.
3. Two (2) DEFENSE men who cannot go past center line into offensive area and whose responsibility it is to keep the puck out of their defensive half of the floor.
4. Two (2) FORWARDS who work with Center on offensive plays and cannot go past center line into their defensive area.

IV. THE GAME

A. The game consists of three periods of eight minutes each, with a five-minute rest between periods. Goals are to be changed after each period.

B. A coin will be flipped for possession of the puck at the start of the game. Whichever team is behind in scoring at the end of the first and

323

second periods is given possession of the puck at the start of the following period. In case of a tie game at the start of a period, a coin will again be flipped for possession.

C. Play cannot start until whistle is blown. Penalty for starting before the whistle is loss of possession.

D. Players may not play the puck back into their goalie's crease. Penalty: Loss of possession. Play resumes at center circle.

E. Center (who must have one foot inside of center circle) starts play with a pass from circle. In cases where the center is out because of penalty, any other player on his or her team may start play, but must return to "on side" position immediately. There is no scoring from center circle unless puck is first touched by a defensive or offensive player. In starting play, shots directly on goal shall be returned to the defensive team with possession at center circle. All players must be outside the 10-foot restraining circle, with defensive players in an upright position.

F. When game is played in gyms where puck can go out of play in or under bleachers, etc., officials will carry extra pucks and will drop one into play area so that play is continuous. There are no time outs.

G. If a flying puck hits any object in playing area, such as backboard or basket, then drops outside goal area, it remains in play. However, if the first play after this happens results in a goal, such goal will not be counted. Play will be stopped and resumed at the center circle. However, when puck comes off hanging object and first shot after this does *not* result in a goal, play will continue. When spectators hit an out-of-bounds puck back into play to the advantage of one team or the other, play will be stopped and then resumed at center circle after a flip to see which team gets possession.

H. If the score is tied at the end of the third period, there shall be a five-minute rest period, followed by a "sudden death" period, or as many such periods as are needed to determine a winner. When such overtimes are played, teams shall change goals and flip for possession. However, for league play, it is recommended that no overtime periods be played. Instead, 2 points should be given for a win and 1 point for a tie, to be applied to point totals in league standings.

V. THE PLAY

A. The clock starts when puck is put in play from the center circle and is touched by a member of either team.

B. Play is continuous and clock will stop only when whistle is blown.

C. When any player accumulates 5 fouls for roughing and/or misconduct, he or she is out for the duration of the game. A bench penalty does not count in this total.

D. Free substitution is allowed. A player entering the game as a substitute should use the stick of the player being replaced. Change of goalies can only take place when the clock is stopped.

E. Change of positions between guards and forwards can only be made when puck is dead and clock is stopped.

F. Officials may stop play for injuries or extenuating circumstances.

VI. SCORING

A. A goal is scored any time the puck touches or crosses the goal line or is above the goal line.

B. Under no circumstances will a goal be counted on a foul, or with offensive players in the crease (goal box).

C. On shots where the puck is deflected off a player or equipment into the goal, the goal counts, but a puck deliberately kicked or hit by hand into goal does not count.

D. Goal *will not* count when puck hits off front frame of goal and ricochets out.

E. In cases where goalie has kicked the net or his net is not sitting squarely on goal line, goal will count if puck goes into the net, regardless of position of net, or if puck touches goal line, regardless of position of the net.

VII. GOALKEEPING

A. The goalkeeper may use either hands or stick to clear puck away from goal.

B. It is a misconduct foul if a puck thrown by the goalie crosses the center line when it ricochets off the sideboards.

C. Clearing the puck with the stick directly across the center line is a misconduct. (Clearing off the sideboards is legal if puck first hits sideboard on goalie side of center line.)

D. At no time is goalie exempt from penalty for roughing, slashing, high sticking, or leaving his feet when he goes outside the goal box to play the puck.

E. All rules pertaining to the goalie clearing the puck are in effect whether he is in or outside the goal box. Exception: When a team is behind or the score is tied in the last minute of the game, and the goalie is obviously being pulled to add offensive strength to his team. When a goalie has been pulled in the last minute of play, any defensive player can play the puck out of the crease, and the three-second count is waived.

F. The goalie has only three seconds to play the puck from the crease, once he has full and controlled possession. Penalty: Loss of possession. Play resumes at center circle.

G. It is a misconduct when the goalie throws the puck out of play.

H. Shots directly on goal or directly above the goal that go out of play shall be returned to the goalie to be put back in play. Exception: When shots are deflected, the puck will be put back in the normal procedure.

VIII. FOULS

A. Roughing Fouls
1. Slashing—when an opponent is hit with the stick and, in the judgement of the official, the player slashing has no chance to hit the puck (playing through an opposing player).
2. Contact with an opposing player with the stick above the shoulder.
3. Contact with the goalie while in the goal box (crease).
4. Pushing.
5. Blocking with the body.
6. Tripping or hooking with the stick.

B. Bench Penalty
1. Unsportsmanlike conduct by anyone on the bench.
2. Excessive delay of game. Note: 2-minute penalties for both 1 and 2. Team must play shorthanded. Position optional.

C. Misconduct
1. Entering into play either coming from or going to the bench during substitution by deliberately hitting or kicking the puck.
2. Any time play is deliberately stopped by holding, laying, or placing foot on puck to delay game.
3. Players may not deliberately leave feet (slide) to block puck. Will be called on both offense and defense.

4. Falling down - no foul unless player plays puck while lying on floor. Then a foul will be called.
5. Guards and forwards over the center line— position of feet is determining factor.
6. Offensive and defensive players with the exception of the goalie, cannot be in goal box or play puck from goal box area (crease) with their sticks. A penalty should not be called if a player accidentally steps in goal box while play is away from goal, unless contact with goalie is made. When a goalie has been pulled in the last minute of play, any defensive player can play the puck out of the crease and the three-second count is waived.
7. DELAY OF GAME - when an individual player controls puck against board by tapping puck back and forth within a three or four foot area, this is not delay of game. If an opponent attempts to get the puck away and player in control is using his body to block the opponent, a foul will be called on player controlling puck. Players may not play the puck back into their goalie's crease. Penalty: Loss of possession. Play resumes at center circle. In all circumstances when it is an advantage to a team to keep possession of the puck - killing of penalty time or keeping possession when they are leading in the last few minutes of a game, neither a defensive or offensive player will be allowed to stick handle along the boards, so an opposing player has no chance to gain possession. When this situation arises, the official will give the opposing team possession at center. This interpretation and rule is not intended to discourage stick handling, nor does it take the place of using your body to play the opponent.
8. Player other than goalie catching or closing hand on puck. Hitting the puck with hand is allowed, but a puck played with the hand to a member of the same team will have a penalty called - loss of possession. Play will resume at center circle.
9. Deliberately hooking, grabbing or kicking the stick out of an opponent's hand.
10. Swinging the stick above the shoulders during play. Note: The *carrying* of the stick above the shoulder shall be ignored. High sticking at start of play from center circle is no foul, but team will lose possession. Note: Stick crossing above front line of goal box, but not touching either goalie or floor; no foul.

IX. ADMINISTRATION OF FOULS

1. A player who is charged with a roughing foul or misconduct must sit out two minutes. Team must play shorthanded during this time.
    a. If a goal is scored by opposition before two-minute penalty time has elapsed, player or players out on foul may return to floor, providing foul is not the fifth one on any player. If it is the fifth foul, substitute may be sent in.
    b. Roughing or misconduct against goalie. Goalie may remain in the game but team must play shorthanded. Position optional.
2. Any player charged with five fouls (combination roughing and misconduct) must be removed for duration of game. It is the responsibility of the team manager to know the number of fouls on each of his team members and he must remove such members from the game as soon as fouls reach this total.
3. The official scorer, as well as the officials on the floor has the authority to call a bench penalty for unsportsmanlike conduct on coaches or players.
4. When a bench penalty is paired with a misconduct or roughing foul, the team must play two men short for two minutes, or until a goal is scored by the opposition.
5. Fighting or deliberately fouling another player calls for automatic ejection from the game plus a two-minute penalty. Team must play shorthanded the full two minutes, regardless of the number of goals scored against them.

FLOOR HOCKEY ACTIVITIES

AND GAMES

The following abbreviations are used in the presentation of activities which follow:

N = Name of the activity
DV = The developmental value of the activity; i.e., fitness, manipulative ability, etc.
F = Formation
E = Any equipment needs
D = Description of the activity
V = Variation

N: Obstacle Dribble - Activity
DV: Hand-eye coordination
F: One child per set of marker cones
E: One hockey stick and one plastic ball per child plus about eight marker cones per child
D: Done best at a station, each child dribbles through a series of marker cones. This can be set up like a race but should not be a relay race.

8 feet

N: Area Floor Hockey - Game
DV: All hockey skills
F: Two teams positioned as illustrated in the accompanying diagram
E: Playing area, puck, goals, and floor hockey sticks for all participants
D: Similar to regular hockey but children are assigned areas which they cannot leave. Two or three players on each team are permitted to go anywhere in the area that they are assigned. This arrangement prevents all the children from gathering around the hockey puck at one time which could lead to an injury.

O		
XO XO	XO XO	XO XO
XO XO	XO XO	XO XO
XO XO	XO XO	XO XO
XO XO	XO XO	XO XO
XO XO	XO XO	XO XO
X		

Area Floor Hockey

N: Alley Floor Hockey - Game
DV: All hockey skills
 F: Two teams positioned as illustrated in the accompanying diagram
 E: Playing area, puck, goals, and floor hockey sticks for all participants
 D: Similar to "Area Floor Hockey" but instead of players being assigned to a limited area, they are assigned to a lane or alley. Players can move anywhere within their assigned alley but cannot move to a new alley or reach across their alley to acquire the floor hockey puck. Because players in the middle alley get the most shots on goal, the teacher should periodically allow children to rotate to different alleys.

N: Zone Floor Hockey - Game
DV: All floor hockey skills
 F: Two teams positioned as illustrated in the accompanying diagram
 E: Floor hockey sticks for all participants, goals, and floor hockey puck
 D: Similar to both "Alley Floor Hockey" and "Area Floor Hockey" except for the positioning of the players (see the illustration).

N: Pinball Floor Hockey - Game
DV: Shooting accuracy and fielding
 F: Two teams each positioned on one-half of the playing area and facing one another
 E: Floor hockey pucks, plastic bowling pins, and floor hockey sticks for all participants.
 D: The class is divided in half and placed at opposite ends of the playing area. A series of bowling pins or empty milk cartons are placed at mid-field in a ten-yard safety zone. Each pin or carton is placed one yard apart. The object of the game is to see which team can hit the most targets with the hockey puck. Players are not allowed to shoot at the targets if standing in the safety zone. The only time a player is allowed in the safety zone is to retrieve a hockey puck.

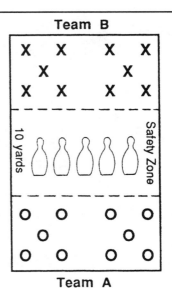

327

REFERENCES AND SUGGESTED READINGS

Daccord, B. *Hockey Goaltending.* Champaign, IL: Human Kinetics, 1998.

Gwozdecky, G. and V. Stenlund *Hockey Drills for Passing & Receiving.* Champaign, IL: Human Kinetics, 1999.

Smith, M.A. *The Hockey Coach's Manual: A Guide to Drills, Skills, Tactics and Conditioning.* Willowdale, Ont.: Firefly Books, 1997.

Chapter 23

Football

After completing this chapter, the student should be able to:

1. Identify three common faults that children frequently experience in passing a football.

2. Identify three common faults that children frequently experience when punting a football.

3. Identify three common faults that children frequently experience when place-kicking a football.

4. Identify three common faults that children frequently experience when centering a football to the quarterback or to the punter.

5. Describe the "shot gun" formation.

6. Describe the difference between "touch football" and "flag football."

7. List and describe the rules of touch and flag football.

8. Describe seven drills, activities, or games designed to practice movement skills associated with football.

9. Define the key terms listed below.

Key Terms

Centering	Line of scrimmage	Punting
End zone	Off sides	Safety
Flag football	Pass interference	Touchdown
Forward pass	Place kicking	Touch football
Lateral pass		

Even though football is one of America's leading spectator sports, its inclusion in the elementary physical education curriculum is questioned by many. Those who question its value think of football as a rough and tumble activity. In addition, they perceive this activity to be an inappropriate one for young girls. Fortunately, these need not be concerns. The key to overcoming the above-mentioned concerns lies in the teacher's ability to appropriately modify the activity. Instructional emphasis should not be on playing competitive games. Instead, emphasis should be placed on learning and refining the many basic fundamental motor skills associated with football—throwing, catching, running, kicking, and guarding an opponent; just to name a few. In fact, football provides an opportunity for children to manipulate balls which are oblong instead of round—a totally new experience for many children.

The teacher may desire to spend a brief period of time playing the game after the basic skills have been acquired. However, no tackling and no blocking should be allowed. Instead, the teacher should have the children play either "touch football" or "flag football." Briefly, in touch football the ball carrier is considered down when touched by an opponent. Often it is difficult to determine whether the ball carrier was touched or not. This problem can be overcome by playing "flag football." In "flag football" each player wears flags (strips of cloth, old towels, or you can purchase special flag football belts to be worn by the participants) which hang at waist level on each side of the body. When an opponent pulls one of the flags off of the ball carrier, the play is stopped.

Once again, remember the instructional emphasis should be on the acquisition and refinement of motor skills which make up the game of football. In the remainder of this chapter, these football-related skills are described and common faults frequently experienced by young children are pointed out. In addition, teaching suggestions are offered as well as selected activities and games which children can use to improve motor performance.

PASSING SKILLS

Forward Pass

The forward pass needs to be mastered because it is the most potent offensive weapon in the game of football. To execute a forward pass, lightly grasp the ball so that the fingers are spread out and come in contact with the football's laces. The thumb should be wrapped around the top portion of the ball. The non-throwing hand is used to grasp the opposite side of the football and serves as a safeguard to insure that the ball is not accidentally dropped.

In throwing the forward pass, both hands bring the ball up and over the throwing shoulder. While

Running with the football

Passing the football

stepping in the direction of the intended pass, the throwing arm is brought forward in an overhand motion.

Lateral Pass

The lateral pass is actually an underhanded toss that is used when you desire to get the football to a teammate who is positioned behind you. The lateral pass cannot be used to advance the ball to a teammate whose position is in front of you.

The lateral is an underhand pass which must be passed backwards.

Common Faults
1. Failure to grasp the football with both hands.
2. Failing to step in the direction of the pass.
3. Failing to follow through once the ball has been released.

Teaching Suggestions
1. Lead the pass receiver so that the ball and receiver arrive at a designated spot at the same time.
2. Do not telegraph the pass by visually following only one receiver.
3. The quarterback should have in mind a secondary receiver, just in case the primary receiver is covered by an opponent.

PASS RECEIVING SKILLS

Pass receiving or the ability to catch a projectile is initially a difficult task for young children to master. Not only does this task require a great deal of eye-hand coordination, but, the task is made

more difficult because of the shape of the ball. Most children's catching experiences have involved the use of a round ball. The football, however, is an oblong object and no doubt more difficult to bring under control. Therefore, until sufficient eye-hand coordination is developed, a hard rubber football should not be used. The pointed end of a misjudged ball can injure the child. Instead, a sponge rubber football is recommended during initial experiences.

Catching High Passes

Whenever the pass is thrown at chest level or above, the hands should be positioned close together with thumbs pointed at one another. As soon as the ball is brought under control with the hands, the ball should be brought into the body.

When catching a high pass, the thumbs come together.

When catching a low pass, the little fingers come together.

Catching Low Passes

Whenever the pass is thrown at waist level or below, the hands should be positioned close together with little fingers nearly touching one another. As soon as the ball is brought under control with the hands, the ball should be brought into the body.

331

Catching Over-the-Shoulder Passes

When the pass receiver is moving away from the pass, it is sometimes necessary to catch the football over the shoulder while running down field. The over-the-shoulder catch is best accomplished by placing the little fingers together. This difficult skill requires a lot of concentration and practice.

Catching an over-the-shoulder pass.

Common Faults

1. Failure to watch the ball all the way into the hands.
2. Making initial ball contact with the body instead of with the hands.
3. Keeping arms too rigid and failing to "give" with the catch.
4. Hands spread too wide apart, allowing the ball to slip through.

Teaching Suggestions

1. Keep your eyes on the ball and not the pass defender.
2. Do not attempt to advance the football up field until you have caught the ball with both hands and then brought it into the body.
3. When the football contacts the hands, pretend that your elbows are shock absorbers. In other words, "give" with the catch.

KICKING SKILLS

When the foot is used to strike the football, the skill is referred to as kicking. Kicking can take various forms. More specifically, the football can be punted or it can be kicked off a kicking tee. Which type of kick is used depends upon the situation. For example, a kicking tee is used when the football is place-kicked. Place-kicking occurs at the beginning of each half and after each score. In contrast, the football is generally punted on fourth down when a team has very little chance to advance the ball far enough to get a first down. Techniques used to both punt and place-kick the football are described next.

Punting

Punting is a two-part skill: the ball drop and the contact between the foot and the ball. Both must be executed correctly for any success. The ball should be dropped flat so that it will bounce straight up if allowed to strike the ground. If either end is tilted it will result in a poor kick. The point of the ball farthest from the kicker should point in slightly. The normal procedure is to take one or two steps and drop the ball as the kicking foot is behind the body. The lead (non-kicking foot) is planted and the other foot is swung forward and upward to contact the ball when it is about at waist level or just slightly below waist level. While we use the term "drop" the ball, in actuality the ball drops only a couple of inches before being struck by the kicking foot. The kicking foot then drives up and through the ball making contact with the top of the foot's instep and toward the outside portion of the foot. The toe should be pointed and the leg straight when the ball is struck.

In punting, the football is kicked out of the air as it leaves the hands.

Common Faults

1. Dropping the ball too soon.
2. Contacting the ball too far below waist level.
3. Kicking the ball with the toe instead of the instep.
4. Taking too many forward steps before punting the football.

Teaching Suggestions

1. Hold the ball out over the kicking foot and let the foot come to the ball.
2. Keep your eyes on the ball until it is well on its way down field.
3. Receive the centered ball while stepping forward onto the non-kicking foot. As soon as the centered ball is caught, the kicking foot is prepared to start its forward swing into the ball.
4. Follow through with the kicking leg so that the non-kicking leg comes up off of the ground.

Place kicking

Place kicking is not quite as difficult as punting. Unlike punting, which requires the performer to kick a football that is airborne, place kicking the ball rests on the ground. It is either held on the ground by a teammate when one attempts to kick a field goal or it rests on a kicking tee which is employed during kick-offs.

Soccer Style Place kicking. The soccer style kick is executed with the instep (shoelaces) of the foot. The toe should be pointed down and slightly to the outside edge of the ball. The ball is generally approached from an angle when this style of kicking is employed. This style of kicking is gaining favor among high caliber performers.

Traditional Place kicking. The regular place kick involves approaching from directly behind the ball and swinging the foot primarily from the knee joint with the ankle locked at a 90° angle to the leg. As the mature kicker approaches the ball, the last step prior to ball-foot contact is actually a leap onto the "plant foot." The ball should be struck just below the middle with the toes, and the "plant foot" should be placed approximately one foot behind the ball and slightly to the ball's left (for a right footed kicker).

Common Faults

1. Contacting the ball above its midpoint.
2. Failing to approach the ball from an angle when using the soccer style place kick.
3. Taking the eyes off the ball before football contact.
4. Failing to take a "leap" step onto the "plant" foot just prior to football contact.
5. Placing the "plant" foot either too close or too far away from the football.

Teaching Suggestions

1. Draw lines on the ground to remind the child of the correct angle of approach that should be taken to the football.
2. Use some type of ground markings to indicate the proper placement of the "plant" foot.
3. Place brightly colored tape on the football to indicate where the football should be struck with the foot.
4. Place brightly colored tape on the kicker's shoe to indicate the part of the foot which should strike the football.
5. When the football is placed on the kicking tee, it is helpful if the football leans slightly backward toward the kicker.

CENTERING SKILLS

Centering is the skill used to put the ball into play. Depending upon the situation, the ball is centered either to the quarterback or to the punter.

Centering to the Quarterback (Traditional)

When the football is centered to the quarterback the skill is executed with one hand. The center should take a position slightly behind the ball with legs spread a little more than shoulder-width apart. The center then bends at the waist and flexes the knees while grasping the football with the dominant hand. The opposite hand is placed on the ground to help maintain balance. When centering, the ball is turned sideward and brought backwards and placed in the quarterback's hands which are positioned under the center's buttocks.

In placekicking, the football is kicked off a kicking tee.

Centering to the Quarterback (Shotgun)

Sometimes it is to the quarterback's advantage to receive the football from the center when being positioned several feet behind the center. When the ball is delivered in this manner the quarterback is said to be in a "shotgun" formation. The shotgun formation is particularly useful in cases where the quarterback needs sufficient time to find a pass receiver. The "shotgun" formation is the most frequently employed formation used in touch or flag football.

Centering to the Punter

Centering the football to the punter is significantly more difficult than either of the two situations described earlier. This is because the football must be accurately delivered to the punter who is generally positioned about ten to fifteen yards behind the center. To accomplish this task, the center assumes a position very similar to that described above with one exception. Instead of placing one hand on the ball, both hands grasp the football. The dominant hand propels the football while the other hand acts as a guide. This very difficult skill requires much practice.

Centering to the punter

Common Faults

1. Leaning too far forward, placing too much of the body's weight onto the ball.
2. Not being in a balanced position.

3. Centering the ball either too high or too low to the quarterback (shot gun) or punter.

Teaching Suggestions

1. After the football is centered, the center should be able to maintain balance by moving forward and upwards.
2. Set up a teaching station and require the children to center the football toward a target such as a trash can or a 2' x 2' box.
3. Set up a teaching station and require the children to center the football through a suspended Hula-Hoop.

BASIC TOUCH AND FLAG FOOTBALL RULES

1. The playing field should be approximately twenty-five yards wide and fifty yards long. The end zones should be ten yards deep.
2. To start the game, a coin is flipped to determine which team will kick off and which team will receive the kick off.
3. The receiving team receives four downs (plays) to either score a touchdown or obtain another first down.
4. According to teacher directive, a first down can take any one of the following forms:
   a. Complete three forward passes in four downs.
   b. Advance the ball downfield a total of ten yards or more within four downs.
   c. Place lines on the playing field every ten to fifteen yards. Whenever the offensive team advances the ball across one of the lines, a first down is awarded.
5. No blocking is allowed.
6. No tackling is allowed.
7. When the ball carrier is downed (touched or loses his or her flag), the ball is spotted at that point and that is called the "line of scrimmage."
8. If the ball carrier is downed near a sideline, the ball will be moved inward to a point approximately ten yards from the sideline.
9. If a pass is intercepted and recovered by the defensive team, the defensive team may advance the ball until the ball carrier is downed.
10. For reasons of safety, the offensive team can at any time call for a "free punt." This means that the offensive team tells the defensive

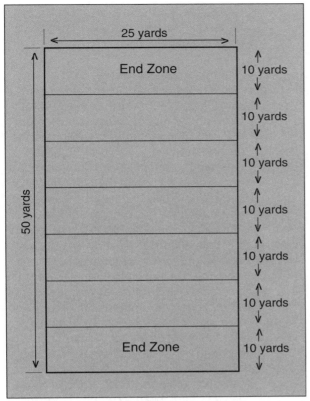

Illustration of a marked off football field for flag or touch football.

25 yards

End Zone

10 yards

10 yards

10 yards

10 yards

10 yards

10 yards

End Zone

10 yards

50 yards

team that they will punt the football and, as such, no one is allowed to rush the punter. The purpose of this rule is to protect the punter. If the punter were to be tagged (pushed) when in the act of kicking the football, he or she could be shoved to the ground because of having one foot in the air as the ball is being kicked.

11. If a defensive player runs into or shoves the offensive pass receiver before the ball arrives, the defensive player is guilty of pass interference. The penalty would be an automatic first down and the ball would be spotted at the point of the infraction.

12. The defensive team is not allowed to cross the line of scrimmage until the ball is centered. To do so will result in a penalty call "off sides." Off sides carries a penalty of five yards and the down is repeated.

13. The length of the game should be two eight-minute halves.

14. Scoring:
   a. Six points are awarded to the team scoring a touchdown.

b. One point is scored if the team scoring the touchdown can put the ball back in the end zone with one additional play with the ball being spotted three yards out from the goal line.

c. Two points are awarded to the team scoring a safety. A safety occurs when the offensive team is downed in their own end zone.

FOOTBALL ACTIVITIES AND GAMES

The following abbreviations are used in the presentation of activities:

N = Name of the activity
DV = The developmental value of the activity; i.e., fitness, manipulative ability, etc.
F = Formation
E = Any equipment needs
D = Description of the activity
V = Variation

N: Target Pass - Activity
DV: Throwing ability
F: Straight line
E: One ball and one hoop per child
D: Usually best as a station arrangement, each child has a football which they use to attempt to hit the target which is a hoop suspended from a fence. Each time the ball hits inside the target, the child takes a step backward. The idea is to see how far away the child can get from the target.

N: Intercept - Game
DV: Passing accuracy, pass receiving and guarding an opponent
F: Two teams with approximately eight to ten on a team.
E: Six to eight sponge rubber footballs
D: Two teams are positioned on each side of a neutral zone (size of the zone can vary based on skill level). Each team is further divided in half with each half being positioned on each side of the neutral zone. The object of this activity is for Team A (the X's) to pass the football across the neutral zone to a teammate positioned on the other side of the neutral zone. Team B members (the O's) attempt to intercept the pass. To keep score, each successfully completed pass across the neutral zone counts as one point.

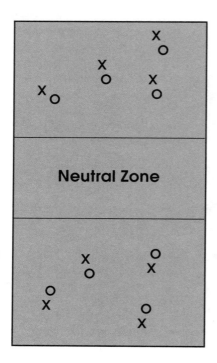

Neutral Zone

N: Centering - Activity
DV: Centering ability
F: Partners with one ball per pair
E: One football per pair
D: Starting five feet away from each other, children begin alternating centering to partner. With each successful center, partners take one step away from each other to see how far apart they can get and still center the ball to each other. A center is successful if the receiving partner catches the ball without moving.

N: Keep Away - Game
DV: Passing and catching, plus agility
F: Groups of three
E: One sponge rubber football per group
D: One child is between the other two who attempt to throw the ball back and forth without the middle child touching the ball. The ball may not be thrown higher than the middle child can reach. Throwing children are encouraged to lateral the ball underhand as well as throwing regular passes. If the center child touches the ball, the child who threw it takes his or her place. If the center child cannot touch the ball, someone should take that child's

place after a reasonable time period. All three children should have a chance to be in the middle.

N: Ultimate Football - Game
DV: Football skills
F: Two teams of no more than five to a team
E: One sponge rubber football or junior football and marker cones to designate the playing area.
D: One team attempts to advance the ball from one end zone to the other by passing the ball. The ball may be passed in any direction, but the passer may not move more than one step after receiving the ball. All other players can go anywhere they want in order to get open and have the ball thrown to them. If a pass is incomplete, it automatically goes to the other team who immediately begin advancing the ball in the opposite direction. The ball may be intercepted or knocked down; in either case, there is no fighting over the ball. Once the ball is caught, the defender may not touch the ball in the passer's hand but may guard the thrower. Points are scored when the ball is caught by a player who has both feet in the end zone. As soon as a score is made, the person drops the ball and the other team continues the game by picking up the ball and attempting to advance it down the field toward the other end zone. No contact between players is allowed.

N: Punting - Activity
DV: Foot-eye coordination
F: Straight line with lots of room between children
E: One ball and one hoop per child
D: Usually best as a station, children attempt to punt their football and have it land as close to their hoop as possible. They can start fairly close to the hoop and then back up with each successful hit of the target. There must be plenty of room between children, and the arrangement must guarantee that children will not be hit by someone else's ball

N: Punt Across - Game
DV: Punting and catching
F: Pairs

E: Junior size footballs

D: The children are paired up with one football between them. Goal lines are established and each person tries to punt the ball in the air over the goal line. The first kick is made from the forty-yard line. If the ball is caught in the air, the catcher can take five giant steps toward the opponent's goal line before punting the ball. All other balls must be punted from where they are stopped. A point is scored each time an uncaught ball is punted over the goal line (rollers do not count).

V: Pass Across — the ball is passed instead of kicked

REFERENCES AND SUGGESTED READINGS

American Sport Education Program. *Coaching Youth Football* (2nd ed.). Champaign, IL: Human Kinetics, 1997.

Cvengros, J. *Youth Football.* Dubuque, IA: Brown & Benchmark, 1992.

Winder, S.R. *Teaching Kids Football.* Bristol, CT: ESPN Home Video, 1986.

Chapter

24

Soccer

After completing this chapter, the student should be able to:

1. List and describe the common faults and teaching suggestions for two soccer kicking skills.

2. List and describe the common faults and teaching suggestions for one soccer passing skill.

3. List and describe the common faults and teaching suggestions for two soccer trapping skills.

4. List and describe the common faults and teaching suggestions for heading the soccer ball.

5. List and describe the common faults and teaching suggestions for tackling the soccer ball.

6. List and describe the basic soccer rules.

7. Describe ten soccer drills and lead-up activities.

8. Define the key terms listed below.

━━ *Key Terms*

Dribbling	Inside foot kick	Tackling
Heading	Instep kick	Throw-in
Heel kick	Punt	Trapping

Soccer is one of America's fastest growing youth sport activities. Once considered a fall sport, this fast-moving activity is rapidly becoming a year-round activity in many parts of the country. This extended seasonal playing time is made possible by youth organizations, which now offer indoor soccer during the winter months.

Soccer appeals to children for many reasons. First, children are movement-oriented and generally enjoy vigorous physical activity. Unlike many sport activities which are less than action-packed and require one to stand around to await a turn, soccer is truly a maximum participation activity. In other words, the young participants seldom find themselves stationary. Thus an added benefit of soccer participation is the potential development of the physiological fitness component, cardiovascular endurance. Soccer is also appealing because it appears to be a relatively safe activity. Although the American Academy of Pediatrics has classified soccer as a contact sport, a survey of the literature suggests that it is nevertheless a safe activity with most injuries being minor scrapes and bruises (Payne & Isaacs, 2002).

An additional advantage of including soccer as a unit of instruction is that little equipment is needed in order to implement a quality program. Other than an outdoor grassy playing field, all that is needed are soccer balls which, by the way, are now produced in varying sizes to accommodate for differences in children's skill level. If you intend to teach an indoor soccer unit, it is suggested that you also purchase foam rubber balls. These balls tend to be safer since they move at a slower rate of speed, are easier to control in the confined indoor space, and if a person is struck, will not likely cause injury.

Soccer is truly a large muscle activity which should be a part of every elementary school physical education program.

SOCCER SKILLS

Soccer is composed of the following basic skills:
1. Kicking
2. Dribbling
3. Passing
4. Trapping
5. Heading
6. Tackling
7. Throwing (as used in the throw-in)

In the next section each of these basic skills is described.

KICKING SKILLS

Kicking is a fundamental motor skill in which various parts of the foot are used to give impetus to a ball. Regardless of the type of soccer kick employed, several general kicking principles should be observed:
1. Maintain good balance on your supporting leg.
2. Learn to kick equally well with both the right and left leg.
3. Do not attempt to over-kick (kill) the soccer ball.
4. Whenever possible, a step in the direction of the intended kick will result in a more powerful kick.

Instep Kick

The most frequently used kicking skill is the instep kick. The skill is executed by approaching the stationary or rolling ball from an angle. The non-kicking leg is planted beside the ball while the kicking leg swings through the ball making contact with the top of the foot. Players should be encouraged not to kick the ball with the tip of the toes but instead contact should be made along the shoelaces.

Instep kick

Common Faults
1. Not contacting the ball on the instep portion (shoelaces) of the foot.
2. Planting the support leg either too far behind or too far ahead of the ball.
3. Kicked ball lacks speed.

Teaching Suggestions
1. Place colored tape on the shoe to serve as a reminder regarding ball-foot contact point.

2. Place tape on floor to illustrate appropriate ball approach and plant position of support leg.

3. After the ball is kicked, the kicking leg should follow through toward the intended target. When a powerful kick is intended, the follow-through will cause the child's support leg to rise up on the toes or, in some cases, even come off of the ground.

Inside Foot Kick

The inside foot kick is accomplished by turning the toe of the kicking foot outward and striking the soccer ball on or slightly ahead of the arch of the foot. The sole of the foot is maintained parallel to the ground. Once ball-foot contact has been made, the kicking leg is allowed to swing freely to a natural stopping position. This kick is most often used to pass the ball to a teammate.

Inside foot kick

Common Faults

1. Striking the ball too far ahead of the arch, which results in the ball rolling over the top of the foot.
2. The moving ball is not contacted in the ideal striking zone. Ideally the foot should contact the ball when it is slightly ahead of the support leg.

Teaching Suggestions

1. Place colored tape on shoe to indicate correct striking portion of foot.
2. Have child point toe of kicking foot toward a target located ninety degrees from ball-foot contact point.

Heel Kick

While the heel kick is not a very powerful kick, it is frequently used to pass the soccer ball a short distance to a teammate whose position is behind yours. Simply step in front of the ball and, while moving the kicking leg forward, point the toes upward. When swinging the leg backwards, the player can flex and then extend the hip to generate more force if needed.

Heel kick

Punting

Punting is a two-part skill: the ball drop and the contact between the foot and the ball. While taking a step onto the supporting leg the performer must time the release of the dropped ball such that the kicking leg will make contact with the airborne ball at approximately thigh level and at the very instant the flexed knee is straightened. Once contact between foot and ball is achieved the kicking leg should not be voluntarily stopped but instead should be allowed to follow through as high into the air as individual flexibility will allow. This special form of kicking is frequently used by goalkeepers. (Remember the goalkeeper is the only individual allowed to use the hands.)

Punting

Common Faults
1. Failing to contact ball on instep of foot.
2. Tossing ball into the air instead of properly dropping ball to meet foot.
3. Failing to meet dropped ball in proper hitting zone.
4. Failing to use a proper follow-through.
5. Failing to extend ankle so that toes point outward. Failing to extend ankle will result in the ball striking the toes and being projected back over one's head instead of being projected down field.
6. Failing to take a step onto the support leg prior to kicking.

Teaching Suggestions
1. Ball should be held with straight arms out over kicking foot.
2. Keep visual contact with the dropped ball.
3. Place colored tape on foot's instep to serve as a reminder as to where ball should contact the foot.

DRIBBLING

Dribbling is a skill in which an individual uses the feet to control and maneuver the ball. This ball manipulation is accomplished by tapping the ball with either the inside or outside of the foot. A good dribbler should be able to use both feet equally well and should be able to keep the ball close in order to avoid the ball being stolen by an opponent.

Dribbling

Common Faults
1. Always looking only at the ball instead of teammates' field position.
2. Dribbling the ball too forcefully so that it gets too far ahead of the dribbler's body.
3. Attempting to dribble for too long a period of time. It is better to advance the ball by passing to teammates.
4. Kicking the ball with the toes.

Teaching Suggestions
1. Both feet should be used when dribbling.
2. Children should learn how to change the pace and direction of their dribble.
3. Tell children to "tap" the ball instead of "kick" the ball. This change in terminology emphasizes less forceful striking.

PASSING

Passing is an essential soccer skill and is the ability to successfully kick the soccer ball to one's teammate. Thus any of the kicking skills described above could be used to project the ball to a teammate. Without doubt, passing is a more effective means of advancing and maneuvering the ball than is dribbling. As such, much emphasis should be placed on the development of this skill. Furthermore, passing is critical to the development of teamwork.

Common Faults
1. Kicking the ball too hard to a teammate.
2. Kicking the ball too high, making it difficult for a teammate to handle.
3. Failing to accurately kick the ball to a teammate.

Teaching Suggestions
1. If possible, keep the pass low to the ground; it is easier for a teammate to trap and control.
2. Practice passing the ball to a teammate who is moving down field.

TRAPPING

Trapping is a soccer term which refers to one's ability to bring a moving ball under control. Because soccer rules prohibit the use of the hands and arms for gaining control of the ball, players must use other body parts to stop and control the soccer ball. At the elementary level of play there are three basic trapping techniques each of which is described below.

Sole Trap

The sole trap is used primarily to gain control of a rolling ball. Simply position yourself in front of the ball while extending the trapping foot and pointing the toes upward. The ball is trapped between the sole of the foot and the ground. Do not attempt to stomp on the top of the ball but instead let the ball come to your foot.

Sole trap

Foot Trap

After positioning yourself in front of the oncoming ball, the toes of the trapping foot are turned outward allowing the ball to contact the inside of the foot. In order to keep the ball from rebounding off of the foot you should "give" with the ball in order to absorb some of its momentum. The foot trap can also be performed by turning the toes inward thus making the ball contact the outside portion of the trapping foot.

Foot trap

Body Trap

Balls which are not rolling smoothly along the ground are usually brought under control by employing a body trap. The high bouncing or aerial ball is allowed to contact the chest, stomach, or thigh. So as not to injure yourself you should "give" with the ball to reduce its impact with the body. The trap should result in the ball being deflected downward, thus allowing you to gain control of the ball with the feet.

Body trap

Common Trapping Faults

1. Failing to watch the ball.
2. Failing to "give" with the trap in order to absorb the impact of the ball.

Teaching Suggestions

1. Keep your eyes on the ball.
2. Put your body in front of the ball.
3. "Give" when the ball contacts your body.
4. Attempt to get the ball onto the ground as quickly as possible.

HEADING

Heading refers to a specialized skill in which the head is used to redirect the path of an oncoming soccer ball. This skill is most useful when an approaching ball is too high in the air to be trapped. As the ball approaches, the student should be positioned in line with the oncoming ball. Legs should be spread into a front-back straddle position, knees slightly bent, hips forward, and weight on the back foot. The upper body is brought forward and the knees are straightened as the ball contacts the head at the hairline.

Heading

Common Faults

1. Closing the eyes before ball-head contact.
2. Letting the ball contact the top of the head.
3. Lowering the chin to the chest causing the head to miss the ball.
4. Failing to move the upper body into the approaching ball.

Teaching Suggestions

1. Use a lightweight foam rubber ball when first introducing this skill.
2. Students should first learn to head from a stationary position.
3. Allow students to practice heading a self-tossed ball before allowing a partner to toss the ball.

TACKLING

Tackling refers to the use of the feet to steal the soccer ball away from an opponent. The authors recommend that elementary school children learn two tackling techniques—the straight tackle and the hook tackle. The straight tackle is performed by approaching the dribbler straight on. As your tackling foot reaches forward to contact the on-coming ball, it is important to also shift your body weight forward as well. The hook tackle is performed essentially the same way as the straight tackle with one exception. As you approach the dribbler straight on, quickly move your body to one side or the other as you reach in, attempting to hook the ball and draw it away from the dribbler.

Tackling

Common Faults

1. Leaning backwards instead of leaning into the dribbler.

2. Running out of control into the dribbler.
3. Failing to correctly time the reaching in of the tackling leg.

Teaching Suggestions

1. Bending the knee of the support leg can result in a longer reaching movement of the tackling leg.
2. Keep the tackling leg and ankle stiff as the foot contacts the ball.

THROW-IN

The throw-in is used to put the ball back into play once it has gone out of bounds over one of the sidelines. To execute the throw-in, you must bring the ball back behind the head. The arms are then brought upward and forward to project the ball. The ball must be thrown in the direction you are facing. The throw-in must also be performed with two hands while keeping both feet on the ground. The feet can be placed shoulder-width apart or in a front-back straddle position.

Throw-in at start

Throw-in at finish

Common Faults

1. Propelling the ball with only one hand.
2. Failing to keep both feet on the ground.

Teaching Suggestions

1. Encourage the students to put the ball into play within five seconds.
2. Encourage teammates to maneuver away from their opponents and come to the thrown-in ball. In other words, go to the ball; don't let the ball come to you.

BASIC SOCCER RULES

The objective of any soccer team is to direct the soccer ball into your opponent's goal by contacting the ball with body parts other than the hands and arms.

1. In regulation soccer each of the two teams is composed of eleven players—more specifically, one goalkeeper, two fullbacks, three halfbacks, and five forwards. The goalkeeper and fullbacks are primarily defenders while the forwards are primarily offensive players. The halfbacks play a major role in both offense and defense.

2. Both teams must remain positioned in their half of the playing field until the center forward of the offensive team kicks the soccer ball from the center circle to a teammate. Once the ball has rolled its full circumference and is touched by a teammate, then players are allowed to cross the center line.

3. Only the goalkeeper can utilize his or her hands to control a ball in play.

4. Balls kicked out of play, over the goal line of the opponent, are placed into play by the goalkeeper who can use a throw-in, kick, or punt.

5. If the defending team causes the soccer ball to cross their goal line, the opponents must put the ball back into play with a corner kick.

6. When a serious foul, such as tripping or kicking, is committed in the penalty area of the playing field; the opponent is awarded a penalty kick. In a penalty kick, the soccer ball is placed on the penalty mark (twelve yards in front of goal) and only the goalkeeper may defend the goal. All other players must remain outside of the penalty area until the kick is completed.

7. If a penalty is committed outside of the penalty area, the opponent is awarded a free kick from a spot on the field where the foul took place. Opponents must be at least ten yards away from the ball until it is kicked.

8. One point is awarded for a goal. Following a goal the ball is returned to the center circle, and the opposing team is allowed to kick off.

SOCCER ACTIVITIES AND GAMES

The following abbreviations are used in the presentation of activities:

N = Name of the activity
DV = The developmental value of the activity; i.e., fitness, manipulative ability, etc.
F = Formation
E = Any equipment needs
D = Description of the activity
V = Variation

N: Obstacle Dribble - Activity
DV: Hand-eye coordination
F: One child per set of marker cones
E: One soccer ball per child plus about eight marker cones per child
D: Done best at a station, each child dribbles through a series of marker cones. This can be set up like a race but should not be a relay race.

N: Dribble Take Away - Game
DV: Soccer skills
F: Free
E: Every child except about four have a soccer ball
D: Children must dribble the ball continuously anywhere within a designated area. The four children without a soccer ball attempt to take one away from anyone dribbling the ball. If the attacking player gets between the attacked player and that player's ball, it is the attacking player's ball and there are no takebacks. The new child without a ball may go after anyone else to try and get a ball. No one may stop dribbling at any time.

N: Soccer Monkey in the Middle - Game
DV: Passing and trapping
F: Circle of three players and one person (soccer monkey) in the middle of the circle
E: Soccer ball
D: Circle players attempt to pass the soccer ball to one another while the Soccer Monkey in the middle attempts to intercept the pass. Circle players must make a pass within three seconds after receiving a pass. Circle players must also

use a trap to gain control of a passed ball. The Soccer Monkey is not allowed to tackle.

N: One on One - Game
DV: Foot-eye coordination, including dribbling and tackling
F: Partners
E: One soccer ball and two marker cones per couple
D: Place the two marker cones about ten feet apart. One partner stands between the two cones while the other partner tries to dribble the ball between the cones without losing it to the other person.

N: Side to Side Passing Activity - Activity
DV: Passing to a moving teammate
F: Two children per group
E: Soccer ball and three marker cones per group
D: Player #1 and #2 stand facing one another from a distance of approximately ten yards. Player #2 runs toward one of the marker cones while player #1 attempts to time his/her kick of the soccer ball so that ball and player #2 arrive at cone at the same time. Player #2 returns ball to player #1 and then sprints toward other cone as activity continues back and forth.
V: Vary the distance between the marker cones.

N: Keep Away - Game
DV: Soccer skills and agility
F: Three children form a triangle and another child in the center
E: One ball per group
D: The goal is to have three children pass the ball and prevent the person in the center of the triangle from touching it. If the center person touches the ball, the person responsible for allowing it to be touched (kicker or receiver) must then go to the center.

N: Through the Zone Soccer - Game
DV: Dribbling, tackling, and goal shooting
F: One dribbler, two defenders, and one goalkeeper
E: Soccer ball and marker cones used to outline a play area consisting of two- to ten-yard zones and a soccer goal.

D: The object of this activity is for the offensive player to dribble the soccer ball through each of the two established playing zones and attempt to shoot the ball into the goal. Each of the two defenders attempts to tackle the ball when the dribbler enters their zone. One point is awarded for each zone the dribbler successfully passes and one point for each goal scored.
V: Alter the number of soccer zones.
Alter the length and width of each soccer zone.

N: Goal Heading Activity - Activity
DV: Goalkeeping and goal shooting using the head
F: Three children per activity group
E: Soccer goal and soccer ball
D: Player #1 tosses a high ball in front of the goal. Player #2 runs under the ball and attempts to head the ball past the goalkeeper and into the goal. The goalkeeper is not allowed to come out past the goal line.
V: Corner kick the ball high in the air instead of using a hand toss.

N: Alley Soccer - Game
DV: Basic soccer skills
F: Playing field is divided into three to five alleys which run the length of the entire playing field. One or two players from each team are assigned to an alley.
E: Soccer ball
D: The alley players can run the length of the playing field but cannot leave their alley. All other players are placed on the two endlines and serve as goalkeepers. The object of the game is to kick the soccer ball below waist level across your opponent's endline. All goalkeepers are allowed to stop the ball with their hands. Players change positions after each score.
V: Use more than one ball in play.
For large classes, also use sideline players.
Vary the number of alleys.
Use a traditional soccer goal instead of the entire endline.
Do away with the alleys so active players can go anywhere on the field.
Instead of alleys which run the length of

the field, divide the field into sections which run the width of the field (i.e., Sectional Soccer).

N: The Goalie - Activity
DV: Hand-eye coordination and goalie skills
F: Partners
E: One high-density sponge ball and two marker cones
D: One child is the goalie and stands between two marker cones placed about 20 feet apart. The goalie faces away from the person either kicking or throwing the ball. The person in charge of the ball says "go" at which time the ball is kicked or thrown and the goalie is allowed to turn around. The object is to keep the ball from going between the goals. The ball must be kicked or thrown below the head level of the goalie. The distance between the ball and the goalie varies according to the ability of the goalie.
V: The goalie can be made to lie on his/her back with the head closest to the ball.
If the ball is rolled on the ground, a regular soccer ball can be used.

N: Hit The Container - Activity
DV: Soccer skills
F: Station arrangement
E: One high-density sponge ball per child and several plastic containers
D: This is a station idea that requires about five people per station. The children stand behind a restraining line at least 20 feet from the targets. Several plastic containers serve as targets. The idea is to see how many different ways you can kick the ball and knock down the targets, i.e., either foot, inside and outside of the foot, instep kick with either foot, etc. Children are also encouraged to see how far away they can get and still hit the targets.

N: Score - Activity
DV: Soccer skills
F: Station arrangement
E: One low-density sponge ball (no substitutes) per child and a soccer goal
D: Using low-density sponge balls only, a station is established in which about five children simultaneously try to kick the ball into the goal while one child, acting as

goalie, tries to stop the ball from reaching the goal. Children can only make attempts from outside a restraining line determined by the ability level of the class and wind conditions (low-density sponge balls are easily affected by the wind). Because many balls are coming simultaneously at the goalie, only low-density sponge balls may be used.

N: Swarm Ball - Game
DV: Foot-eye coordination - game
F: Two teams of about six children each
E: One high-density sponge ball and two small soccer goals
D: This is a game designed for young children six to eight years of age. It is played like a regular soccer game, but there is no emphasis on playing positions. All the children are encouraged to go after the ball and kick it toward and into the opponent's goal. One child is the goalie. After each goal, the goalie position is changed. The field should be small to allow for many shots on goal. The idea is to encourage lots of activity as well as dribbling and tackling.

N: Head Volleyball - Activity
DV: Heading and juggling
F: Two equal teams each in free formation in their assigned court area.
E: Tennis net or rope, soccer ball or an appropriate lightweight ball.
D: Similar to volleyball except each team must head the ball into their opponent's court. The ball is allowed to bounce one time between headers. The children are allowed to juggle the ball in order to position it so it can be headed. The game is started by a throw-in across the net from the back of the court. Like volleyball, only the serving team can score a point. The first team to score eleven points wins the contest.

N: Circle Dribble - Activity
DV: Soccer skills
F: A large circle of marker cones
E: One marker cone and one ball per child
D: A large circle is made and each child stands by a marker cone with a ball. On the signal "go," all the children begin dribbling around the circle in the same

direction. They must follow commands given such as, "weave in and out of the marker cones," "change the direction you are dribbling," "dribble backward around the circle," "dribble through the center of the circle and don't let your ball hit anyone else's." Children may be encouraged to go quickly or slow down, and to always maintain control of their ball.

N: Soccer Race - Game
DV: Dribbling skills

F: Straight line of children each with a ball
E: One ball and one marker cone per child
D: Children stand on one long line with their marker cone directly in front of them about 20 yards away. On the "go" signal, all children dribble their ball around their marker cone and back. The first person back to the original line with one foot on top of their ball is the winner. The distance from the line to the marker cones may vary according to the age and ability of the students.

REFERENCES AND SUGGESTED READINGS

American Sport Education Program. *Coaching Youth Soccer* (2nd ed.). Champaign, IL: Human Kinetics, 1995.

Brown, E.W. *Youth Soccer: A Complete handbook.* Dubuque, IA: Brown & Benchmark, 1992.

Buxton, T. *Soccer Skills for Young Players.* Buffalo, NY: Firefly Books, 2000.

Payne, V. G. and L. Isaacs. *Human Motor Development: A Lifespan Approach* (6th ed.). Boston, MA: McGraw Hill, 2005.

Rosenthal, G. *Soccer Skills and Drills.* New York: Simon & Schuster, 1994.

Wein, H. *Developing Youth Soccer Players.* Champaign, IL: Human Kinetics, 2001.

Chapter 25
Softball

After completing this chapter, the student should be able to:

1. List and describe the four components which make up the skill of hitting.
2. List and describe two common faults that young children experience when attempting to field a ground ball.
3. List and describe two common faults that young children experience when attempting to catch a fly ball.
4. List and describe the three ways a softball is generally thrown.
5. Draw an illustration of a softball field and draw the runner's path from home plate to second base.
6. Describe three rule modifications which have been proven effective to use with young children.
7. Name and describe five softball related activities and games.
8. Define the key terms listed below.

━━━━━━━━━━━━━━━━━━━━━━━━━━━━━━━━━ *Key Terms*

Bunting
Choking-up
Closed stance
Fielding

Grip
Open stance
Ready position
Stride

Without any doubt, softball is the number one participation sport in American society. Perhaps one reason softball is so popular is because there appears to be an organized league of play for all interested individuals. Each summer millions of Americans, both young and old, participate in leagues from Bobby Sox to Seniors. Furthermore, softball can be played as either a fast-pitch or slow-pitch game. Because successful participation in softball demands a great deal of eye-hand coordination, the slow-pitch version is recommended for elementary school age children.

Softball, when compared to many other team sports, can be a relatively slow-moving game. Because of the game's slow-moving nature, little time should be spent actually playing regulation softball. Instead, most of the class time should be spent on developing and refining the skills which make up the game. A great deal of fun can be introduced to skill practice by using game analysis to modify regulation softball. Selected fun activities and games are described at the end of the chapter.

Choking up

SOFTBALL SKILLS

If one is to excel in the sport of softball then it is necessary to demonstrate competency in the following basic skills:
1. Hitting
2. Throwing
3. Fielding
4. Base running

Each of these basic softball skills is described in the following section.

HITTING

Hitting is a fundamental motor skill in which a bat is used to strike a ball. Hitting can be a difficult skill to learn and requires a great deal of attention and visual coordination. When teaching this skill to young performers, the teacher should address each of the following components which make up the skill of hitting: (1) grip, (2) stance, (3) swing, and (4) follow-through.

Grip

The term grip refers to the manner in which one holds the striking implement—the bat. In general, the bat should be held with both hands with the batter's dominant hand on top of the non-dominant

hand. In other words, when a right-hander bats, the right hand rests on top of the left hand. In addition, the hands can be placed at the bottom of the bat or several inches up from the bottom. This latter example is referred to as "choking up." Choking up makes the bat feel lighter and easier to control while holding the bat at its end increases the batter's power to hit the ball a greater distance.

Stance

Stance is the term used to describe how the batter is positioned in relationship to the pitched ball. The batter should stand facing home plate with the shoulder facing the pitcher. The feet should be shoulder-width apart and knees slightly flexed. The batter is said to be in a "closed stance" when the forward foot is slightly closer to home plate than the rear foot. When the forward foot is slightly further from

Closed stance

Open stance

home plate than the rear foot the batter is said to be using an "open stance." Regardless of the stance used, most of the body's weight should be placed on the rear foot and the bat should be positioned behind the batter. More importantly, the elbows should be held away from the body.

Stride

As the pitched ball approaches, body weight should be transferred from the rear foot to the foot closest to the pitcher. This weight transfer occurs as the batter steps toward the approaching ball.

Swing

While keeping the shoulders level throughout the swing, the batter should attempt to open up the hips (the hips are open when the batter's stomach faces the pitcher) and make contact with the approaching ball. At bat-ball contact the arms should be fully extended.

Follow-through

A natural extension of the swing is the follow-through. After bat-ball contact is made, the batter should be encouraged to continue the swing until the bat comes to a natural stop. For purposes of safety, the teacher must emphasize the importance of keeping both hands on the bat. At no time should a child be allowed to throw the bat after making contact with the ball.

Common Faults

1. Placing the hands either too high or too low on the bat.
2. Grasping the bat with hands several inches apart.
3. Laying the bat on the shoulder and resting elbows against the body.
4. Using a stance which is too "open."
5. Swinging the bat either downward or upward (a level swing is desirable).
6. Failing to watch the approaching ball all the way to bat-ball contact.
7. Standing too erect.
8. Failing to step forward toward the pitched ball.
9. Swinging too late at the pitched ball.
10. Failing to follow through after bat-ball contact.

Teaching Suggestions

1. Draw footprints on the ground to show the child how to stand in the batter's box.
2. Batting attempts should first be taken from a batting tee.
3. Allow children the opportunity to bat using different size balls and bats.
4. Teacher should stress proper footwork, proper weight transfer and a controlled swing to direct ball flight.

Bunting

Bunting is a variation of batting in which the batter attempts to make bat-ball contact with as little power as possible. Stand in the batter's box as if you intend to take a full swing at the ball. As soon as the ball is released from the pitcher's hand, pivot on your front foot and bring the back foot up. At the same time, slide the top hand down the bat so the thumb rests on the top of the bat's trademark and the first one or two fingers below the trademark. Be careful that you do not wrap the fingers around the bat or else they may get hit by the ball. Keeping the bat level, allow the bat to make contact with the pitched ball. Let the arms give with the hit and direct the ball down either the first or third baseline.

In the photos above, the proper batting stance is shown on the left; while bunting, a batting maneuver, is demonstrated on the right.

THROWING

The softball is generally thrown in one of three ways: overhand, sidearm, or underhand. The overhand throw is used when it is necessary to throw the ball a long distance and also when there is a need to throw the ball at a high rate of speed. In contrast, the underhand throw is used when there is a need to throw the ball softly and for a short distance. The underhand throw is also used in softball to pitch to the batter. Infielders frequently use a sidearm throw after fielding a ground ball. As should be evident, the type of throw one should employ is determined by the specific task that one is attempting to accomplish. At the elementary school level of play the underhand and overhand throwing patterns are the most frequently used.

Overhand Throwing

Stand with your body sideward to the throwing target. Hold the softball so that the first two or three fingers are on top of the ball and placed across the ball's largest seams. Place the thumb and little finger on each side of the ball. With your weight mostly on your back foot bring the throwing arm downward, backward, and then upward cocking the ball behind the head at ear level. While stepping forward, uncoil the upper body and hips and then quickly snap the arm and wrist forward. Follow through after releasing the ball.

Overhand

Underhand Pitching

Stand with your body facing home plate. Grasp the ball so that the fingers are underneath. While stepping with the opposite leg, extend the pitching arm forward then downward and backward similar to the movement path of a swing. Quickly bring the arm forward, releasing the ball approximately eight inches in front of your thigh. Let the

Underhand

pitching arm continue upward after the release to complete the follow through.

FIELDING

Fielding, or catching a ball which has been hit by the batter, is an important defensive skill. This defensive skill can take one of two forms, namely, fielding ground balls or fly balls.

Ground Balls

When fielding a ground ball which has been hit to an infielder you should stand with your feet shoulder-width apart, knees flexed, eyes up, and both hands hanging loosely approximately three inches off the ground. Move forward to meet the ball, paying particular attention to keeping the hands near the ground and your body in front of the ball. Use your throwing hand to secure the ball in your glove or catching hand.

Common Faults
1. Failing to get the body directly into the ball's flight path.
2. Failing to keep the body and hands close to the ground.
3. Bending too far forward at the waist instead of at the knees, thus losing balance.

Fly Balls

As soon as the fly ball is hit in your direction, quickly move to position yourself under the ball. Both the gloved hand and free hand should be placed at face level or above awaiting the arrival of the ball. Use the free hand to assist in the catch to insure that the ball does not pop out of your glove. If runners are on base and there is a possibility that the runner may tag-up and attempt to advance a base, then the outfielder must be prepared to make a quick throw toward the infield.

In order to facilitate a quicker throw when catching the fly ball, the outfielder should position his or her dominant leg forward (i.e., right-handed thrower has right leg forward). In this position, as soon as the ball is caught the outfielder will only need to take one step forward onto the non-dominant leg.

Common Faults

1. Failing to get lined up under the ball.
2. Holding the arms too rigid and failing to "give" with the catch.
3. Failing to use the throwing hand to trap the ball in the glove.

Stay down on ground balls.

Proper positioning for catching a fly ball.

BASE RUNNING

One softball skill which is frequently overlooked is the skill of base running. This skill can be broken down into three important aspects: (1) running to first base, (2) making the turn at first base, and (3) running between the bases.

Running to First Base

As soon as you hit the ball, drop the bat and run as fast as possible down the baseline being careful to stay in foul territory. If your ball was hit to an infielder, run as fast as possible down the baseline and do not turn your head to watch the fielder throw the ball. Try to time your stride so

that you touch the front edge of the base and continue your run into foul territory.

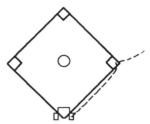

Run all the way through first base and veer into foul territory.

Making the Turn at First Base

If your hit has gone into the outfield you may be able to run further than first base. If this is the case, you should, while running to first base, look up to see where the ball is and then make a decision as to whether you will attempt to reach second base or not. Once you have decided to attempt to reach second base, you should veer to the right of the first base bag making it possible to cut across the inside of the base. This technique will keep you from making a wide loop, thus shortening your running distance.

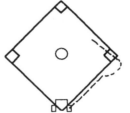

Making the turn at first base.

Running Between the Bases

In softball you are not allowed to leave the base until the pitched ball is hit by a teammate. While waiting for your teammate to hit the ball you should face the base you will be running to, being sure to keep one foot on the base. Turning your head to look at your teammate will insure a faster start.

Correct position for base running.

BASIC SOFTBALL RULES AND OTHER CONSIDERATIONS

The following account describes the basic rules of softball and suggested modifications which can be employed when the game is played by young children.

1. In slow pitch softball a team is made up of ten players: three basemen, a shortstop, a catcher, a pitcher and four outfielders. Whenever there are more than twenty children in a class, modifications should be made so that all can participate.
2. The batting team is allowed three outs. Quite frequently it is difficult to keep track of the batting order and this can result in some children losing their turn at bat. This problem can be overcome by allowing all players to bat once before sides are changed.
3. Players are not allowed to steal bases.
4. Base runners are not allowed to leave the base until the pitched ball has been hit by the batter.
5. To insure safety, players are not allowed to slide into a base.
6. Any player who throws the bat while hitting is automatically out. If bat throwing becomes a problem, require the batter to carry the bat with him/her to first base where it can be placed in a designated area outside of the base path, or simply mark off an area close to the batter's box into which the bat must be placed before the runner is allowed to run to first base.
7. In slow pitch softball the pitcher must deliver the ball to the batter with an arc of six to twelve feet above the ground.

SOFTBALL ACTIVITIES AND GAMES

The following abbreviations are used in the presentation of activities:

N = Name of the activity
DV = The developmental value of the activity; i.e., fitness, manipulative ability, etc.
F = Formation
E = Any equipment needs
D = Description of the activity
V = Variation

N: Plastic Bat and Ball - Activity
DV: Softball skills with an emphasis on hitting
F: Groups of three outside and two inside
E: One plastic bat for each group and one plastic ball if outside or two or more yarn balls (size of softballs) if inside
D: Groups of threes spread around an outside area. One person pitches, one bats, and one fields. They rotate after a certain number of hits or swings. If inside, all the batters get against the wall around the room. Pitchers get in the middle of the room and pitch yarn balls to them. Many yarn balls are necessary to be successful inside.

N: Pick-up - Activity
DV: Stresses lateral movement while fielding grounders
F: Groups of two in a random formation
E: Softball
D: Two players stand facing one another approximately ten feet apart. The players roll the ball back and forth to each other alternating the roll to both the right and left sides. Each player must maintain a good fielding position at all times.
V: Each couple uses two softballs instead of one. Roll the first ball approximately five feet to your partner's right. As soon as your partner catches the first ball and tosses it back to you, immediately roll the second ball but this time roll it approximately five feet to your partner's left. Keep your partner moving back and forth. Once your partner gets tired, it's your turn to do the scrambling.

N: Base Race - Game
DV: Base running
F: Groups of two
E: Bases
D: Two participants stand on home plate. On the signal "go" one player runs around the bases in the traditional direction while the other player runs the bases in the opposite direction. The first player to

return to home plate is declared the winner. Special care must be taken to insure that players do not run into one another when arriving at a particular base at the same time. To help avoid collisions at home plate, the teacher may desire to establish two different finishing points in the area of home plate instead of using only the one home plate.

N: Ball Flick Activity - Activity
DV: Development of throwing skills by emphasizing a flicking wrist action
F: Groups of two
E: Ball and gloves
D: Players position themselves approximately ten to fifteen feet from one another. The elbow of the throwing arm is held in front of the body and placed in the player's glove. The player now attempts to use a flicking wrist motion to project the ball to his/her partner. No other body movements are allowed.
V: Instead of standing, have both players perform the above described activity from both knees or from just one knee.

N: Throw and Run - Game
DV: Throwing, fielding and base running
F: Regular softball positions
E: Softball and bases
D: Similar to a regulation softball game but instead of batting the ball into play, the pitcher tosses the ball underhanded to the batter who catches the ball and then throws the ball out into the field instead of hitting it with a bat.

N: Must Swing Softball - Game
DV: All softball skills
F: Regulation softball positions
E: Softball, bat, and bases
D: Played like regular softball, except the pitcher is a member of the team at bat. All pitches, therefore, are strikes no matter where they are thrown. This arrangement eliminates both the need for an umpire as well as a long wait since the batter is not looking for the perfect pitch. Each batter gets three chances to hit the ball into fair territory. After three attempts including foul balls, the batter is out. After everyone gets a chance to

bat including the pitcher, the teams switch sides. If there is an odd number of players, the team with the one less player designates one of its players who gets to bat twice.

N: Basket-Baseball - Game
DV: Hitting, base running, throwing, and catching
F: Regular softball positions
E: Softball, bases, and basketball goal
D: After the batter hits the softball, he must run all the way around the bases while the fielders attempt to catch the batted ball and then throw it to a teammate who stands under a basketball goal. The appointed individual standing under the basketball goal must now toss the softball through the goal before the runner crosses home plate. If this task is accomplished then the batter is out, if not, a run is scored.

N: Around the Horn - Game
DV: Hitting, throwing, catching, and base running
F: Regular softball positions
E: Softball, bases, and gloves
D: After the batter hits the softball the fielding team attempts to throw the ball to first base, then to second base, then to third base, and finally to home plate. The batter is out if the defensive team can throw the ball around the horn before the batter can run all the way around the bases. In other words, the batter is safe if he can touch home plate before the ball reaches home plate.
V: Vary the number of throws which must be made to different individuals before the ball is allowed to be thrown to home plate. In this variation, the number of throws is specified, but no specific order of throw is mandated.

REFERENCES AND SUGGESTED READINGS

American Coaching Effectiveness Program. *Rookie Coaches Softball Guide.* Champaign, IL: Leisure Press, 1992

American Sport Education Program. *Coaching Youth Softball* (2nd ed.). Champaign, IL: Human Kinetics, 1996.

Elliott, J. and Ewing, M. *Youth Softball: A Complete Handbook.* Dubuque, IA: Brown & Benchmark, 1992.

Ledeboer, S. *A Basic Guide to Softball.* Torrance, CA: Griffin Publication Group, 1998.

Potter, D. and G. Brockmeyer *Softball: Steps to Success* (2nd ed.). Champaign, IL: Human Kinetics, 1999.

Rikli, R. *Softball Skills Test manual.* Reston VA: American Alliance for Health, Physical Education, Recreation, and Dance, 1991.

Chapter 26

Track & Field

After completing this chapter, the student should be able to:

1. Identify the most common sprint distances for third through sixth grade.
2. Describe the difference between straight relay and medley relay.
3. Describe the differences in the starting stances used in sprinting and in distance running.
4. Describe the differences in the manner in which the hands and arms are used in sprinting and distance running.
5. Describe the appropriate hand position when making a blind baton pass.
6. List and describe two common faults and two teaching suggestions regarding the running long jump.
7. Explain the three elements that make up the triple jump.
8. Name and describe three different high jump styles.
9. Describe the correct shotput approach.
10. Define the key terms listed below.

Key Terms

Baton passing	Medley	Shotput
Distance running	Relays	Softball throw
Fosbury Flop	Roll style	Sprints
High jump	Scissor style	Triple jump
Long jump	Scratch	

Track and field are exciting activities enjoyed by most elementary school age children. Most children can identify with track and field because of the association made between these events and the Olympic games. Basically, track and field events can be used to help children further refine the fundamental movement patterns of running, jumping, and throwing.

RUNNING EVENTS

Sprints

One of the most exciting track events is the short sprint, the ability to run from point A to point B in the least possible time. Many factors can influence running speed, and running form is perhaps the most important. When sprinting, children should be taught to use their arms, legs, and body properly. The arms should drive straight ahead while keeping a ninety-degree angle at the elbow joint. The legs should reach out on each stride with a high leg lift behind the body (the heel should nearly hit the buttocks). The feet should be pointed straight ahead and the child should run on his or her toes. The head should be held evenly, neither leaning forward or backward. All motions such as shaking the head, which do not assist in moving forward, should be minimized or eliminated. In an attempt to avoid injury, sprinting activities should be preceded by warm-up activities including leg stretching and slow jogging.

Common Faults

1. Not running in a straight path.
2. Slowing down before crossing the finish line.
3. Allowing the arms to pump across the body's midline causing upper body rotation.

Teaching Suggestions

1. One technique that the teacher can use to help children overcome their tendency to slow down before crossing the finish line is to establish a false finish line. To set up this situation, the teacher simply stands ten yards past the true finishing point but stops timing the event as soon as the sprinter crosses the true finish line. The children, thinking that the teacher is standing on the actual finish line, will be running full speed when crossing the true finish line.
2. Vary the distance of the sprints depending on age and developmental level. Common sprinting distances are as follows: Grade 3—30 to 40 yards; Grade 4—40 to 60 yards; Grade 5—50 to 75 yards and Grade 6—50 to 100 yards.
3. Teach the sprint starting position when running short distances at top speed.

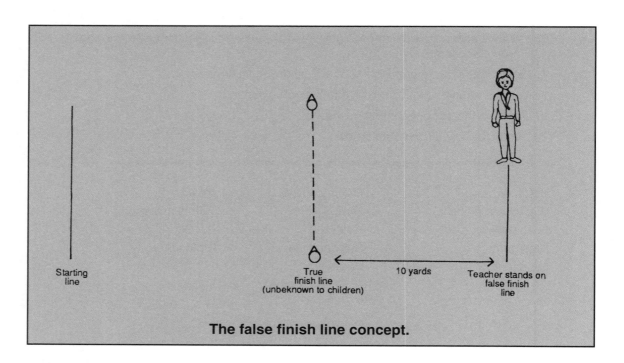

The false finish line concept.

Starting line

True finish line (unbeknown to children)

10 yards

Teacher stands on false finish line

The sprint starting position.

Running Distances

Children should be taught the differences between sprints and distance runs. The differences in body motion and pace are two factors which children must learn. In distance running, the arms are carried so hands are near the waist. Rather than driving straight ahead as in the sprint, the arms should be held in a very relaxed fashion. The hands should be loose. The feet should hit either flat or on the heels rather than on the toes. The head should be level and still with the jaw relaxed. The pace must be determined by the distance to be covered and will also vary because of individual differences in level of cardiovascular fitness.

Common Faults
1. Running at too fast a pace.
2. Carrying the arms and hands too high. This creates too much tension in the shoulders.

Teaching Suggestions
1. To help establish a comfortable pace, allow children to run for time, not distance. For example, children should select a pace which can be maintained for a period of so many minutes. This mind set is helpful because the children soon realize that no matter how fast they run, time does not go by any faster.
2. Once the children are capable of continuous jogging for a period of fifteen minutes,

then allow them to attempt to improve upon distance performance.
3. Children should realize that a standing starting position is most frequently used in distance running events.

The standing start is used in distance running events.

Relays

Relays are a form of team competition where each individual on the team must run a predetermined distance in a predetermined order. Common relay distances include the 4 by 100, 4 by 400, and the 4 by 800. The first number identifies the number of individuals running on each team. In the examples above, there would be four individuals on each team. The second number identifies the distance that each runner is to run. In the examples stated above the distance would be either 100 yards, 400 yards, or 800 yards. Sometimes it may be desirable to have members of each team run varying distances instead of all runners running the same distance. Whenever runners are assigned different distances to run, the relay is called a "medley relay." When running relays, a baton must be passed or exchanged with teammates. This baton pass can take one of several forms and is described in more detail later in the chapter.

Common Faults
1. Not passing the baton to a teammate within the baton passing area. This baton

passing area usually measures between ten and twenty yards.

2. In a shuttle relay, crossing the restraining line before receiving the baton.

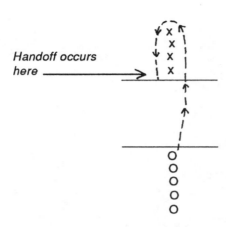

Handoff occurs here

Baton Passing

Visual Baton Pass. Baton passing for relays should first be taught using visual passes. The approaching child places the baton with the right hand. The receiving child stands sideways extending the left hand back toward the approaching runner. The lead runner should begin moving before the other child arrives so the pass is made on the run. The palm of the hand should be facing the approaching runner and the fingers pointing downward. The thumb of the receiving hand should be toward the body.

Blind Baton Pass. The technique here is the same as the visual pass, except the receiving individual extends the left hand backward and does not look at the baton as it is placed into his or her hand by the individual giving up the baton.

Common Faults

1. Lead runner runs faster than the passer who is unable to catch up in order to make the pass.
2. Baton passer fails to position the baton correctly into the hand of the receiver.
3. Baton receiver incorrectly positions receiving hand.

Teaching Suggestions

1. First practice baton passing in slow motion.

2. Tell passer to place the baton in the "V" formed by the thumb and index finger of the receiver's hand.

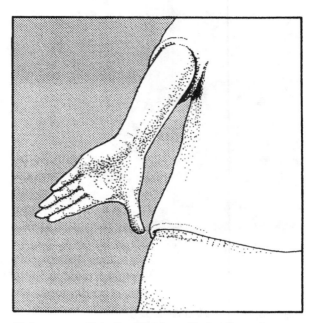

Baton pass. Note the thumb and index finger form a "V".

JUMPING EVENTS

Standing Long Jump

The standing long jump should be used to develop leg power. The child should place the toes as close to the restraining line as possible with feet shoulder-width apart. The child should be encouraged to swing the arms and bend the knees in order to establish a rhythm. At the moment of takeoff the legs and ankles are extended and the arms are thrown forward. During the landing phase the feet are brought under the body. Care should be taken to insure that the legs are not extended too far forward or else the jumper will land on the buttocks. The child's jumping score is the distance from the front of the restraining line to the point where the body touches closest to the restraining line. Therefore, the jumper should fall forward, not backward.

Common Faults

1. Not using the arms to provide forward momentum.

2. Taking a forward shuffle step across the restraining line before jumping.
3. Landing with feet too far forward resulting in the child falling backwards toward the restraining line.
4. Jumping too high instead of upwards and outwards.

Teaching Suggestions
1. Use the arms to swing forward to increase jumping distance.
2. Fall forward, not backwards.
3. The best angle of takeoff is forty-five degrees.

Running Long Jump

The child takes a running start and attempts to propel his or her body into the air with a one foot takeoff. For the jump to be valid, the takeoff must occur behind the restraining line. If the foot crosses the restraining line before the takeoff, a violation called a "scratch" is committed and that attempt is not scored. This event should not be attempted unless there is a soft pit for landing.

Common Faults
1. Taking off either too soon or too late in reference to the restraining line or takeoff board.
2. Running too slow on the approach.
3. Slowing down too much just prior to takeoff. Children will usually do this in an attempt to avoid "scratching."

Teaching Suggestions
1. In order to help the children find the proper approach distance, allow them to approximate the distance by performing the event backwards. In other words, start at the restraining line and count the number of steps to the children's starting area on the approach.

Triple Jump

The triple jump is a hop followed by a step and then a jump. In other words, the child leaves the ground with one foot, lands on the same foot, takes one giant step, then floats through the air to finally land on both feet. This skill requires a lot of practice to learn the sequence. All three must be done consecutively without any stopping between phases. After the sequence has been mas-

tered, the child should be allowed to attempt the event from a running start.

Common Faults
1. Attempting to cover too much distance on the initial hop.
2. Performing the three jumps out of sequence.
3. Stopping between each of the three jumps.
4. Not acquiring enough speed on the running approach.
5. Failing to take off behind the restraining line (scratching).

Teaching Suggestions
1. To help children who have a tendency to over-jump during the first phase, the teacher can place a series of marks on the jumping surface to guide the child. For instance, if a child was attempting to jump twenty-three feet, the following guide might be used: Hop—eight feet, Step—six feet, Jump—nine feet.
2. Children should first master, at a slow rate of speed, the three intra-task skills of the hop, step, and jump before being allowed to take a running approach.

High Jumping

High jumping involves propelling one's body over a suspended bar. Most frequently, one of three techniques can be employed to accomplish this task. These three techniques include the scissor style, the roll style, or the Fosbury Flop.

Scissor Style. In the scissor style of high jumping, the child runs at a thirty-degree angle to the bar and kicks the foot closest to the bar up first. Once airborne, the trail foot (or propelling foot) is brought upward. The child goes over the bar in a sitting position with legs doing a scissor motion.

Roll Style. The roll is done by approaching the bar at a moderate speed on a fourty-five-degree angle. The heel nearest the bar is planted while the other leg kicks up to provide lift. The child then rolls over the bar with the belly nearest the bar.

Fosbury Flop. In this style of jumping the child who approaches the bar from the right would take off on the left foot. As the body becomes airborne, the body is rotated slightly so that one's back is to the bar. Once the upper body is over the bar, it is thrust backward as it heads toward the landing mat. The landing occurs on the upper back.

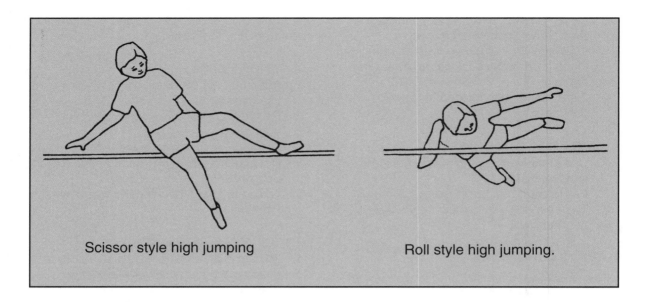

Scissor style high jumping

Roll style high jumping.

Caution: While children may enjoy learning this style of high jumping, the authors do not recommend its inclusion in the elementary physical education program. The potential for injury, such as landing on the head and neck, is too great.

Common Faults
1. Approaching the bar straight on.
2. Approaching the bar too slowly.
3. Jumping forward into the bar instead of jumping upwards over the bar.

Teaching Suggestions
1. Approach the bar from an angle.
2. Jump upwards instead of outwards when arriving at the bar.

THROWING EVENTS

The two most common throwing events introduced to elementary school age children are the softball throw for distance and the shotput. Each of these two events is described below.

Softball Throw for Distance

In this event the child is instructed to use an overhand throwing pattern to throw the softball as far as possible. The child is allowed a running approach toward a restraining line, behind which the softball must be released. Once the softball is released, the child is allowed to follow through across the restraining line with the entire body. For best results, the child should release the softball at a 45 degree angle.

Common Faults
1. Not running fast enough on the approach.
2. Throwing the ball too far off to one side or another.
3. Using a sidearm throwing pattern.

Teaching Suggestions
1. Release the softball at a fourty-five-degree angle.
2. For greater distance, throw the softball straight ahead instead of on an angle to the right or left.

Shotput

While the shotput is classified as a throwing event, in reality it is not. This is because the shot must be "put," not thrown. To put the shot, the shot should be held in one hand mainly with the three middle fingers. The thumb and the little finger should rest on the side of the shot. To position the shot, the child needs to bend at the elbow and place the shot on the side of the neck. Once this ideal position is acquired, the child should be instructed to stand with his or her back to the direction of intended projection. To increase the distance of the put, the child takes a short hop on the right foot (right-handed shotputter) and as the left foot comes in contact with the ground, the upper body is rotated into the direction of the put. As the body rotates, the propelling arm is quickly

Preparing to put the shot.

straightened and the wrist and fingers are snapped in the direction of the release. Elementary school age children can generally handle shots weighing between four and eight pounds.

Common Faults
1. Throwing the shot.
2. Scratching following the release of the shotput.

Teaching Suggestions
1. Allow children to first learn to shotput a lightweight softball before using a weighted shotput.
2. Allow children to first learn the proper technique, within the 7' 2" diameter shotputting circle, without using a shotput.

REFERENCES AND SUGGESTED READINGS

Carr, G. *Fundamentals of Track and Field.* Champaign, IL: Human Kinetics, 1999.

Rogers, J. *USA Track & Field Coaching Manual / USA Track & Field.* Champaign, IL: Human Kinetics, 2000.

Wallace, E. *Track & Field Coach's Survival Guide: Practical Techniques and materials for Building an Effective program and Success in Every Event.* Englewood Cliffs, NJ: Parker Publishing Company, 1998.

Chapter

Volleyball

After completing this chapter, the student should be able to:

1. List and describe four categories of volleyball skills.
2. List and describe two common faults that children experience when attempting to serve a volleyball.
3. List and describe two common faults that children experience when attempting to execute a forarm pass.
4. List and describe two common faults that children experience when attempting to execute a spike.
5. List and describe two common faults that children experience when attempting to execute a block.
6. Describe and illustrate two useful teaching modifications regarding net configuration.
7. List and describe the basic rules of volleyball.
8. Draw a volleyball court and indicate position names and locations.
9. Name and describe five volleyball drills, activities, or games.
10. Define the key terms listed below.

Key Terms

Blocking
Forearm pass
Overhand serve
Overhead set
Rally

Rotation
Side out
Spiking
Underhand serve

Volleyball was first played at a Holyoke, Massachusetts YMCA in 1895. Since its introduction by William Morgan, the sport has continued to gain in popularity. Perhaps one reason why volleyball has been so well accepted is because it appeals to individuals at all levels of play.

The emphasis of an instructional skill theme unit involving elementary volleyball should focus almost entirely on the development and refinement of the fundamental skills which make up the regulation sport activity. In short, volleyball is predominantly a striking activity. These striking skills are best acquired by modifying the height of the net, using a smaller than regulation size court, and using different types of balls other than regulation-size volleyballs.

VOLLEYBALL SKILLS

If one is to excel in the sport of volleyball, then it is necessary to demonstrate competency in the following basic volleyball skills:
1. Serving
    Underhand Serve
    Overhand Serve
2. Volleying
    Overhead Set
    Forearm Pass (bumping)
3. Spiking
4. Blocking

In the next section, each of these basic volleyball skills is described, pointing out common faults and offering teaching suggestions. The chapter ends with a description of several volleyball activities and games. These movement experiences can be used to help children acquire and refine these basic skills.

The underhand serve is recommended for beginners.

SERVING

Acquiring a good offensive serve is important because it is the first shot of every point. To start the point, the ball can be put into play in one of two ways: an underhand serve or an overhand serve.

Underhand Serve

Elementary school children can experience a great deal of success when putting the ball into play by using an underhand serve. This skill is executed by hitting the ball out of one hand with the heel of the other hand. The child should step forward with the opposite foot and keep the fingers of the hitting hand curled up. The ball should not be tossed into the air, but instead, hit out of the supporting hand. Some children will prefer to use a "hammer fist" striking technique when executing an underhand serve, instead of the heel strike technique described above. With the "ham-

mer fist" striking technique the child simply closes the entire hand to make a fist. The fist is then rotated so the knuckles face toward a side wall and the thumb and pointing finger will provide the striking surface. Serves should be attempted from about fifteen feet, over a six-foot high net.

Common Faults
1. Looking up too soon before making ball-hand contact.
2. Not striking the ball in the middle of its underside.
3. Tossing the ball into the air instead of striking it out of the hand.
4. Bending the elbow.
5. Taking too little backswing and thus not having enough power to hit the ball across the net.

Teaching Suggestions
1. Keep your eyes on the ball and do not look up until one second after the ball has been struck.
2. Pretend that your arm is in a splint in order to keep the elbow straight during the service motion.

3. Tell students to pretend that a net is not present. Then have them aim the serve to a spot, somewhere in their opponent's court.

Overhand Serve

Most elementary school children will experience a great deal of difficulty when first attempting to learn the overhand serve. This skill requires greater strength, timing, and coordination. The first step in executing the skill revolves around a correct ball toss. This ball toss should be approximately two to three feet in the air and slightly in front of the server's striking side. The server should be positioned so the feet are in a straddle position and the trunk is turned so the left shoulder faces the net (for a right-handed server). As the volleyball is tossed into the air, the striking hand (heel of the palm) is brought back behind the head at ear level as if you were going to throw a ball. While shifting the body weight forward, the arm extends and makes contact with the ball.

Common Faults

1. Not turning the trunk so that one's shoulder faces the net.
2. Inaccurate ball toss.
3. Not following through toward the target.

The overhead set or pass is a skill which takes lots of practice to master.

4. Backswing of hitting hand is inadequate.
5. Improper weight shift.
6. Striking the volleyball too much toward its top.

Teaching Suggestions

1. The volleyball net has been referred to as a psychological barrier. As such, children should first be allowed to learn the correct stroke technique by hitting the ball toward a wall instead of over a net.
2. Do not practice any volleyball striking skill for too long a period of time. Repeated striking of the ball against the child's bare skin will sometimes create a sore spot.
3. When first learning a new striking skill, let the child use a lighter weight ball to help reduce the stinging which frequently accompanies striking a regulation volleyball.

VOLLEYING

The volleyball is generally passed to a teammate or volleyed across the net in one of two ways: the overhead pass or set, and the forearm pass.

Overhead Pass

The overhead pass is used whenever an approaching volleyball is at chest level or higher. The body should be positioned so that the ball descends toward the forehead or body's upper midline. The hands are placed at eye level with fingers spread apart and the thumb very close to the index finger. When looking up, the ball can be seen through the "window" formed by the thumb and fingers. Ball contact should occur with the thumb and fingers as the body and arms are extended toward the approaching volleyball.

Common Faults

1. Not lining the ball up with the body's midline. In other words, being out of position.
2. Not extending the arms and snapping the wrist at ball-hand contact.
3. Contacting the volleyball with the palm instead of the fingers and thumb.
4. Contacting the volleyball too low causing it to go forward instead of upwards.
5. Striking the volleyball with one hand instead of two hands.

Teaching Suggestions
1. Look through the "window" formed by the thumb and index finger to help line up the body with the approaching volleyball.
2. Extend the knees, arms, and wrist in order to apply greater force to the volleyball.
3. Have children pretend that they are going to dribble the volleyball off of the ceiling. This emphasizes the need to strike the ball upwards instead of outward.

Forearm Pass (Bump)

The forearm pass, commonly referred to as the bump, is used for balls that are hit too low to set with an overhead set. Furthermore, most service returns employ the forearm pass. To acquire the proper bumping grip, instruct the students to open both hands and have the palms face the ceiling. Now lay one hand across the other so that they form an X. Slowly roll the thumb of each hand over toward the middle until the thumbs come together. The upper aspect of the forearm and flattened surface formed by the thumbs becomes the appropriate hitting surface. Because the bump is used to return low balls, it is important to get down by bending the knees to lower the entire body. As you get ready to strike the volleyball, the knees are to be extended as you shift your weight upward into the volleyball. Be sure to keep the elbows straight and follow through in the direction of the hit.

Common Faults
1. Not getting in line with approaching volleyball.
2. Bending too much at the waist instead of at the knees to get down to a low ball.
3. Not keeping the elbows close together.
4. Bending the elbows when striking the volleyball.

Teaching Suggestions
1. Contact the volleyball at the junction of the thumbs and forearm.
2. Get under the volleyball by bending at the knees.
3. Contact the volleyball when it is between the knees and waist.
4. Extend upwards into the volleyball as contact is made.

Make sure students use both arms when executing a forearm pass.

SPIKING

Spiking is an offensive skill where the ball is contacted above net level and driven sharply downward into the opponent's court. Generally, a teammate sets the ball up very close to the net and, as mentioned, above net level. The spiker takes a running start, jumps straight up, and slams the ball downward using a motion similar to the overhand serve. Care must be taken that the spiker does not touch the net with either the body or the striking arm.

Common Faults
1. Not jumping high enough over the net.
2. Jumping outward into the net instead of jumping straight upwards.
3. Striking the ball on its underside instead of getting on top of the ball.

Teaching Suggestions
1. Lower the net when first introducing this offensive skill.
2. Start the upward jump just as the volleyball begins to move downward.

Instructional Suggestions for All Volleyball Striking Skills
1. Let children first practice striking the volleyball against a wall.

2. After wall practice, let children practice by keeping the ball in the air, hitting only to themselves.

3. After mastering self-hitting, allow the children to hit the volleyball back and forth to a partner, then proceed to hitting in small groups. No net is used at this time.

4. When first introducing a new skill, allow children to let the ball bounce between hits. This will give them more time to get into the correct striking position.

BLOCKING

The ability to block an opponent's shot will, in part, depend upon the height and jumping ability of the defensive player. The block is accomplished by jumping straight up, attempting to place both hands above the net and in line with the intended offensive shot. The defensive player must, however, remember that he or she is not allowed to touch the net.

Common Faults

1. Failing to appropriately time the jump.
2. Not placing the hands close together.
3. Jumping into the net instead of straight up.
4. Following through and striking the net with the hands.

Teaching Suggestions

1. When first introducing this skill, lower the net.
2. Do not follow through. Let the ball bounce off of the block.

USEFUL VOLLEYBALL TEACHING MODIFICATIONS

Children have slow reaction and movement times. This, coupled with their short leg lengths, make covering the court a very difficult task. To help overcome these innate problems, the teacher can use projectiles which move slower than a regulation volleyball. For instance, balloons, beach balls, Nerf balls, and other balls will all move slower than the regulation volleyball. You will find that when children use these slower moving balls, the techniques they use will resemble a more mature style. Simply put, they will not be rushed; they will have more time to strike the ball correctly.

Throughout this section on volleyball, it is suggested that the instructor use a lowered net when teaching volleyball skills to elementary school children. From time to time, however, various net configurations can be employed as a change of pace. The net arrangements below can be useful, especially when some children have difficulty projecting the ball over a regulation (or a six-foot or seven-foot) net.

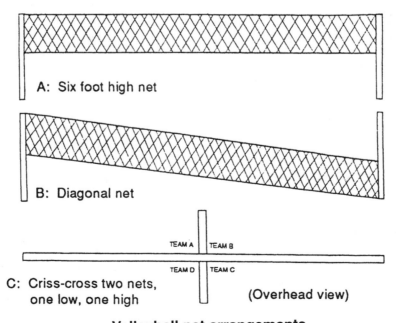

A: Six foot high net

B: Diagonal net

C: Criss-cross two nets, one low, one high

TEAM A | TEAM B
TEAM D | TEAM C

(Overhead view)

Volleyball net arrangements

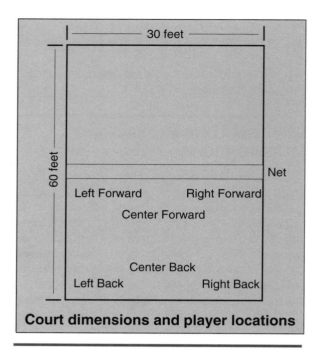

Court dimensions and player locations

BASIC VOLLEYBALL RULES

Listed below are some of the most general rules associated with the sport of volleyball. Teachers are, however, encouraged to modify the rules of the game in order to account for individual differences in level of skill. Useful modifications include: lowering the net, changing the size of the court, using balls other than volleyballs, allowing the ball to bounce between hits, and altering the number of players on a team.

1. There are six players on a team. Three are positioned on the front row, close to the net, and three are positioned on the rear row.
2. Each point is started by a serve which is performed by the "right back" who must stand behind the baseline to put the volleyball in play.
3. Unlike tennis, the volleyball server is allowed only one serve.
4. If the receiving team fails to legally return the serve, then the serving team is awarded one point. Only the serving team can score a point.
5. A player may not hit the volleyball more than one time in succession.
6. Each team must return the volleyball to their opponents within three hits.
7. If the serving team fails to win the rally, the opponents receive "side out." Side out means that their team receives the right to serve, but is not awarded a point for winning the rally.
8. Players on the "rally winning" side rotate one position clockwise whenever a side out occurs.
9. A rally is stopped whenever a player touches the net.
10. A rally is stopped whenever the volleyball strikes the floor.
11. A game is won whenever a team scores fifteen points and is ahead by at least two points.
12. A match is won by the first team to win two out of three games.
13. Players change sides of the net after every game.

VOLLEYBALL ACTIVITIES AND GAMES

The following abbreviations are used in the presentation of activities:

N = Name of the activity
DV = The developmental value of the activity; i.e., fitness, manipulative ability, etc.
F = Formation
E = Any equipment needs
D = Description of the activity
V = Variation

N: Keep It Up - Activity
DV: Setting
F: Individual or with a partner
E: One volleyball per individual or group of about five individuals
D: An individual attempts to set the volleyball repeatedly to himself or herself and attempts to keep the ball in the air as long as possible.
V: Work with a partner
Work in small groups
The teacher can specify different striking skills to be used.

N: Volleywall - Game
DV: All striking skills
F: One team is assigned a spot in front of a wall
E: Volleyball and a wall to hit the volleyball against
D: This game is played like volleyball, but instead of using a net, a team plays against a wall. Since the wall will always return the ball, children are allowed more

N: One Bounce Volleyball - Game
DV: All volleyball skills
F: Two teams of approximately six per team
E: Volleyball and volleyball net
D: This game is similar to regulation volleyball, with one exception—the ball may bounce one time between each hit and any number of hits are allowed to get the ball back over the net.

N: Bump, Pass, Spike - Activity
DV: Volleyball skills
F: Station - Group of three
E: One volleyball and one six-foot net
D: This is best done in a station with groups of three working together. One person tosses the ball up and then uses a volleyball bump pass to the second person who uses an overhand set pass to the third person who spikes the ball over the net. Children rotate a position after every spike.

N: Three Hit Volleyball - Game
DV: Fosters teamwork
F: Two teams of approximately six per team
E: Volleyball and volleyball net
D: Frequently, children will attempt to return the volleyball as soon as the ball comes to them. This lack of teamwork is not desirable. To encourage teamwork, play three hit volleyball. The game is similar to one bounce volleyball but the ball must be hit a minimum of three times before it can go back over the net.

N: Sponge Ball Volleyball - Game
DV: Volleyball skills
F: Two teams of six to nine players on a sit

E: About ten high-density sponge rubber balls
D: Each team begins with five balls which they simultaneously hit over the net. The goal is to prevent any ball from touching the floor by catching or hitting it back over the net. Balls that are caught must be hit with a bump or a set type hit (no spiking is allowed). Any ball that touches the floor must remain there until one side has five balls on the floor. The other team wins that round, and teams switch sides of the court. Balls that go under the net or out of bounds on the opposite side of the net count against the team that hit the ball.

N: Multiple Hit Volleyball - Game
DV: All volleyball striking skills
F: Two teams of approximately six per team
E: Volleyball and volleyball net
D: In regulation volleyball it is a violation to strike the ball more than once without it being touched by another player. In multiple hit volleyball this rule is not enforced. Simply put, one person may hit the ball more than once in succession.

N: Shower Serve - Game
DV: Serving
F: The class is divided in half, each spread out across one of the two volleyball court baselines.
E: Fifteen to twenty sponge rubber balls
D: On the signal "go," players from both sides serve the volleyballs to their opponent's half of the court. After a set amount of time the teacher will blow a whistle to stop play. The purpose of this activity is to have the least number of volleyballs in your team's possession when time expires.

REFERENCES AND SUGGESTED READINGS

American Coaching Effectiveness Program. *Rookie Coaches Volleyball Guide.* Champaign, IL: Human Kinetics, 1993.
American Sport Education Program. *Coaching Youth Volleyball* (2nd ed.). Champaign, IL: Human Kinetics, 1997.
Asher, K. *Coaching Volleyball.* Indianapolis, IN: Masters Press, 1997.
Bertucci, B. *Volleyball Drill Book: Individual Skills.* Indianapolis, IN: Masters Press, 1992.
Viera, R. and B. Ferguson *Teaching Volleyball: Steps to Success.* Champaign, IL: Leisure Press, 1989.

III. Other Considerations

Chapter

Competition

28

After completing this chapter, the student should be able to:

1. Describe the role of competition in the elementary physical education curriculum.
2. Describe the extent to which youth sport injuries may be detrimental to the growth and development process.
3. Describe problems associated with utilizing age-group records to motivate young children.
4. Discuss dietary concerns of the young athlete and associated problems.
5. Describe the key role of youth sports as a contributor to physical fitness.
6. Define the key terms listed below.

Key Terms

Athlete's diet
Competition
Epiphyseal
Physiological effects

Competition is an inherent part of American life. This fact is frequently used to justify high levels of competition among children's groups such as Little League. Like any other aspect of growth and development, however, competition must be introduced gradually. There are those who advocate no competition among children in early childhood. Children will, however, create their own competitive situations. Any attempt to eliminate competition will probably be futile; control and amount are the keys to introducing competition.

COMPETITION IN SCHOOL

Teachers should be aware of the need to introduce competition gradually. Activities in early childhood should stress competition with self-testing activities and reward coming internally when each person has done his/her best. Open competition among children in the academic area can lead to frustration and discouragement among the poorly skilled or slow learner. Such practices as posting grades, displaying progress charts with children's names, and ridiculing certain children should be eliminated. Any technique which could embarrass a child should not be used.

COMPETITION IN PHYSICAL EDUCATION

Unlike classroom work, a child's physical performance is hard to hide. The early childhood curriculum, therefore, should consist primarily of activities which focus on individual physical development and non-competitive group interaction. Highly competitive activities have no place in the curriculum for young children. Low-key competitive activities, such as simple games and relays, can be played with a minimum of emphasis on winning and losing.

After third grade, children will have been exposed to considerable competition both in and out of school. They are ready, therefore, to participate in more highly competitive sports activities. This is not to suggest extremely high levels of competition, only more intensive levels than in early childhood. Lead-up games to team sports and individual sports, therefore, can be included in the physical education curriculum.

The standing long jump is an excellent self-testing activity.

COMPETITION IN ATHLETICS

The number of young athletes participating in organized youth sports continues to accelerate. In a recent survey, researchers estimate that the number of youth sport participants now exceeds thirty-nine million. This means that a majority of the children in any elementary school classroom are participating in an organized youth sports program. Table 28.1 presents the specific categories of youth sports and the estimated number of participants in each category.

Controversy has surrounded competition, particularly with the advent of highly competitive athletics for elementary children. In early years, teams were directed by poorly qualified people, there were few meaningful rules to protect the children, and coaches emphasized winning over the joy of playing. Despite some changes for the better, there are still some disturbing trends. One trend is toward earlier involvement. Just a few years ago, growth and development specialists shuddered at the fact that children as young as five or six years of age were participating in team activities such as "T" baseball. Today, a four-year-old holds an age group record for running a marathon in six hours and three seconds — a distance of over twenty-six miles. In fact, there have been attempts to conduct an "Infant Olympics." Thus, in the near future, there may be national and international records for creeping and crawling.

Table 28.1 Estimated Percent of Youth Enrolled in Specific Categories of Youth Sports°

Category of Activity	Percent of All Eligible Enrollees[a]	Approximate N of Participants
Agency-Sponsored Sports (i.e., Little League Baseball, Pop Warner Football)	45	22,000,000
Club Sports (i.e., pay for services, as in gymnastics, ice skating, swimming)	5	2,368,700
Recreational Sport Programs (i.e., everyone plays—sponsored by recreational departments)	30	14,512,200
Intramural Sports (middle, junior, senior high schools)	10	451,000
Interscholastic Sports (middle, junior, senior high schools)	12[b] 40[c]	1,741,200 5,776,820 6,195,247[d]

°Total population of eligible participants in the 5–17 year age category in 1995 was estimated to be 48,374,000 by the National Center for Education Statistics, U.S. Department of Education, 1989.

(a) Total does not equal 100 percent because of multiple-category by some athletes.

(b) Percent of total population age 5–17 years.

(c) Percent of total high-school–age population (14,510,000).

(d) Total number of interscholastic participants based on 1996–1997 National Federation of State High School Associations Survey.

SOURCE: President's Council on Physical Fitness and Sports (1997).

Like it or not, competition for young children is no longer an issue—it is a fact. Since competition is here to stay, schools need to focus their efforts toward educating parents, coaches, and even the young children about competition. Reviewing the literature makes one aware of the many concerns regarding competition for preadolescent children. Presented below are a selected group of frequently asked questions regarding competition. An understanding of these physiological and psychological concerns will hopefully lead to better supervised competitive youth programs.

Question: Why do children participate in youth sports?

Answer: Often cited reasons for children's participation in youth sports include the following:

to improve skills, to have fun, to be with friends, to be part of a team, to experience excitement, to receive awards, to win, and to become more physically fit. Of these reasons, "to have fun" appears to be the most important. In fact, in a study conducted by the Athletic Footwear Association, not only did the children rate "having fun" as the most important reason for participating in sport, but they rated "winning" as the least important reason.

Question: Why do children drop-out of sport activities?

Answer: Like the previous question, children drop out of sport for many reasons. Some of these reasons include the following: a loss of interest, not having fun, took too much time,

377

Simple games provide low-key competition.

illustrates how this unpleasant state is evoked (See figure 28.1).

The four stages are situation, appraisal, emotional response, and consequences. First, the stress process is evoked whenever a person is placed in a demanding situation, and the person views the outcome of the situation as being important. Second, the person appraises the situation in an attempt to determine if he or she can meet its demands. A young boy may become threatened and feel anxious before the start of an athletic contest, because he wants to perform well but is not sure that he has the motor skills necessary for success. Third, whenever a person is threatened, emotional responses become evident. According to Passer, these emotional responses are made up of not only physiological components but also cognitive-attentional components. For instance, the boy may become so preoccupied with worrying about the outcome of performance that he does not pay attention to important task-related cues that are necessary for successful performance. Passer's fourth and final stage, consequences, examines the possible outcomes of competitive stress. As mentioned previously, when sport participation loses its appeal, children will frequently either withdraw from the disliked activity to pursue a more enjoyable activity or, in some cases, withdraw permanently from sports.

coach was a poor teacher, was tired of the activity, coach played favorites, sport was boring, and there was an overemphasis on winning. When these same children were asked what changes they would like to see in the sport activity that they had just dropped, they responded by saying: make practices more fun, have the coaches better understand the players, and allow players more playing time.

Question: What is competitive stress?

Answer: Stress is generally viewed as an unpleasant emotional state. M. W. Passer has developed a four-stage model that precisely

Question: How stressful are youth sports?

Answer: Proponents of youth sport programs do not argue with the fact that excessive stress is not beneficial. However, they do argue that youth sport participation is by no means the only stressful situation young people encounter in

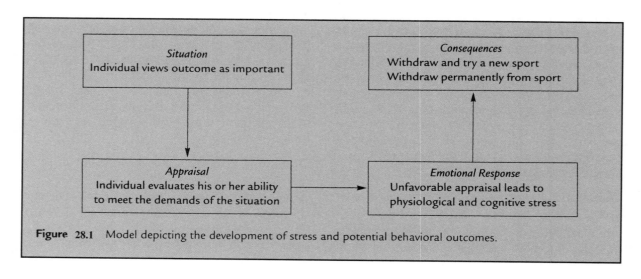

Situation Individual views outcome as important	*Consequences* Withdraw and try a new sport Withdraw permanently from sport
Appraisal Individual evaluates his or her ability to meet the demands of the situation	*Emotional Response* Unfavorable appraisal leads to physiological and cognitive stress

Figure 28.1 Model depicting the development of stress and potential behavioral outcomes.

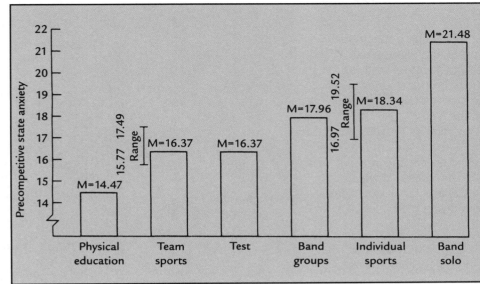

Figure 28.2 Children's precompetitive state anxiety in 11 sport and nonsport activities. The pre-competitive state anxiety scale ranges from 10 to 30. "Team sports" include football, hockey, baseball, and basketball, while "in-dividual sports" include swimming, gymnastics, and wrestling.

SOURCE: Adapted from Simon and Martens (1979).

their lives. The proponents' view is best supported by a study conducted by Simon and Martens. These two researchers examined the level of pre-competitive state anxiety among 468 boys who took part in various youth sport programs and 281 boys who competed in other achievement-oriented activities; including a softball game played in a physical education class, a general school test, group competition with a band, and a band solo competition. As illustrated in figure 28.2, the researchers found the greatest amount of precompetitive state anxiety among the band solo contestants. Furthermore, among the 11 sport and nonsport activities examined in the study, state anxiety was greatest in the individual activities. In fact, on average, participating in team sports was no more stressful than taking a paper and pencil test.

Question: To what extent are sport-related injuries detrimental to the growth and development of young participants?

Answer: The physiological effects of athletic participation have been fairly well-documented. On the positive side, any vigorous physical activity, except extremely long distance running, is physically beneficial. There is some evidence to indicate that long distance running by children can adversely affect long bone growth.

Some negative physiological effects may occur as a result of contact sports and other activities which stress certain areas, such as the elbow and shoulder. Damage can occur to the epiphyseal (growth portion) ends of the long bones as a result of trauma. Trauma can occur from a severe blow in a contact sport or, more subtly, by constant irritation, the common cause of "Little League elbow" or shoulder. Increased interest in tennis has also created "tennis elbow," which is medically the same condition as Little League elbow. Both problems are created by irritation of the elbow joint while throwing curves in baseball or putting spin on the tennis ball. While traumatic injuries to the growth portion of the bone (epiphyseal) may have some long-term effects on the growth and development of some children, recent research evidence indicates that such injuries are infrequent. One doctor notes that about half of all athletic fractures he sees involves injury to the growth portion of the bone. He also notes, however, that about half of all free play fractures involved the epiphyseal. Furthermore, 98 percent of the epiphyseal injuries were uneventful. Similar findings have been reported by other researchers.

Question: What can be done to reduce the number of youth sport injuries?

Answer: Researchers have concluded that many youth sport injuries are avoidable. Selected guidelines for avoiding youth sport injuries follow:

1. Use quality constructed and proper fitting protective gear.
2. Match teams for competition on the basis of physical fitness, skill level, and physical maturation (biological age)—not chronological age only.
3. Children should not be forced into sport participation. Children who don't want to be

involved in a sport are at high risk for injury.

4. Young participants should be encouraged to play different sports and experience different positions within a given activity. This practice tends to reduce injuries which may be a result of overstressing a particular movement pattern.

5. Pay close attention to signs of physical fatigue. Many injuries occur late in a game or practice session when the children are tired. Unfortunately, the image conveyed by some coaches, "be tough," keeps many young athletes from telling the coach of their fatigue.

Question: At what age should children be allowed to participate in competitive sports?

Answer: Authorities generally agree that young children are capable of learning and practicing sport skills around six years of age. The emphasis at this time should, however, be on self-improvement, not success in regard to "outdoing" an opponent. Involvement in true competitive sports can be safely introduced at about eight years of age. Unfortunately, the trend in the United States is toward earlier competitive sports involve. Nowadays, children as young as three years of age are being introduced to competitive sports.

Question: Should the juvenile athlete be given special nutritional considerations?

Answer: The nutritional requirements of the young athlete are essentially the same as for any other active youngster. For the most part, an individual's appetite is an indicator of caloric needs. Thus, parents should provide well-balanced meals, being sure that portions are served from each of the four basic food groups. It appears that problems arise when parents alter children's diets in an attempt to give their child an additional competitive edge. For instance, many youth sports leagues are organized according to "weight classes"—not age. Some parents have been known to place their children on diets, even periods of fasting, so their child will be able to compete in a lower weight class. Such practices are to be avoided. Dietary supplements have also been a source of nutritional problems. It appears that some parents are not aware that certain vitamins when taken in large dosages are toxic. Dr. Nathan Smith, a well-known pediatrician, has recently

A what age should children begin learning sport skills? How young is too young?

reported five cases of Vitamin A poisoning. In one case, parents of a young tennis player who had experienced Vitamin A poisoning, repeatedly kept putting their child back on the vitamin. Vitamin supplements are not necessary when the young athlete is eating balanced meals.

Question: When young children are placed in training programs at an early age and become successful at their sport, will this competitive edge carry over into the high school and college years?

Answer: Not necessarily. Researchers who conducted the Medford, Oregon Boys Growth Study found that many individuals who were competitively successful during the elementary and junior high school years were later surpassed by the skilled abilities of their peers in the adolescent years. While children who mature early may have a competitive edge during the elementary years, they are often smaller and weaker than their late-maturing peers during the adolescent years.

Question: What is "psychological burnout?"

Answer: When young children are required to adhere to strict training schedules, year after year, many tend to lose interest in their sport activity. Many young swimmers, for instance, train two hours before school and several hours after school throughout the year. Allowing children to participate in many different positions in a given sport is one method of reducing psychological burnout.

Question: What steps can be taken in order to reduce competitive stress?

Answer: One way to reduce stress is to change some aspect of the game which will make the child more successful. For example, T-baseball allows the child to hit a stationary baseball instead of a moving baseball. The result is more success at hitting the baseball. Other changes in various sports which can lead to greater performance success is lower hoops in basketball, wider goals in soccer, lower nets in volleyball, just to name a few. In short, when children experience a fair amount of success, they will develop more self-confidence about their ability to meet the demands of the activity.

A second way to instill self-confidence and thus reduce stress is by spending more time on skill training. Coaches should spend more time on how to handle specific game situation so that when the situation arises within the context of a real game, the child will have confidence that he/she can successfully execute the necessary movement skill needed to handle the situation. Basically, skill practice helps the child develop an attitude of, "I can do it."

To further reduce competitive stress, the outcome of the contest (winning or losing) should be placed into perspective. There should not be too much emphasis on winning the game. For children, winning needs to be defined as "doing ones best" instead of outperforming an opponent."

Lastly, self-imposed competitive stress can be reduced by helping each child set realistic goals. Realistic goals are those that motivate the young child to do his or her personal best and to recognize self-limitations. For example, left to a child, the child may set a goal of hitting 50 home runs during the baseball season. Instead, with the help of the coach or teacher the child can be guided to set more realistic goals which will ensure success and therefore the reduction of self-imposed competitive stress.

Question: Does participation in a contact or otherwise aggressive sport make children more aggressive in other phases of their life?

Answer: Researchers have not been able to distinguish whether an individual selects a particular sport because of his/her personality or whether one's personality is created by the sport.

Question: At what age should "age group records" be kept as a means of motivating children to push themselves to reach higher goals?

Answer: It has been suggested that age group records should not be kept until the child is capable of abstract thinking—generally around eleven or twelve years of age. At this age, the youngster is more capable of intrinsic motivation. Prior to this age, the danger lies with the psychologically immature child who may push him/herself beyond his/her capabilities just to obtain adult approval.

Question: Will participation in youth sport programs improve physical fitness?

Answer: Yes and no. It appears that participation in youth sports programs is accompanied by improvements in motor fitness. The effect, however, on health-related fitness is questionable. Recent evidence indicates that the most popular youth sport activities, such as baseball and football, are primarily motor fitness oriented. Many believe that children would be better off selecting activities which would significantly elevate their heart rate high enough to obtain a training effect (see chapter 10). Youth programs in soccer, track, and swimming tend to emphasize health-related fitness.

Children are not going to obtain optimal personality development from youth sports participation until adult organizers stop trying to turn children's play into work. Thus it becomes the job of the professional community to educate their coaches concerning the physiological and psychological needs of the young participants. Positive steps toward accomplishing these goals are now being taken in states such as New York and Michigan, where specific "Volunteer Coaches Training Clinics" have been developed. In the near future, several states will also require all volunteer coaches to be certified by the state's Athletic Commission.

Question: How can I stay more current on youth sport issues.

Answer: Table 28.2 presents seven organizations dedicated to the advancement of knowledge in youth sports. Note that we have provided organizational web site addresses for each of these organizations.

Table 28.2 Organizations Dedicated to the Advancement of Knowlede Through Coaching Certification

American Sport Education Program
Box 5076
Champlaign, IL 61820
(800) 747-5698
www.asep.com

Coaching Association of Canada
141 Laurier Ave. West
Suite 300
Ottawa, Ontario K1P 5J3
(613) 235-5000
www.coach.ca

National Alliance for Youth Sports
2050 Vista Parkway
West Palm Beach, FL 33411
(800) 729-2057
www.nays.org

National Association for Sports and
Physical Education
1900 Association Drive
Reston, VA 20191
(800) 213-7193
www.aahperd.org/naspe

National Federation of State High School Associations
11724 N.W. Plaza Circle
Kansas City, MO 64153
(816) 464-5400
www.nfshsa.org

North American Youth Sport Institute
A Division of Paradox Group, Ltd.
4985 Oak Garden Drive
Kernersville, NC 27284-9520
(800) 767-4916
www.naysi.com

Youth Sports Institute—Michigan State University
213 IM Sports Circle Building
East Lansing, MI 48824-1049
(517) 353-6689
http://ed-web3.educ.msu.edu/ysi

SUMMARY

This was a brief chapter dealing with competition. The emphasis at the elementary level should be competition with self. Competition, like any developmental component, should be introduced gradually over the years. Athletic competition should be reserved for middle school and high school. The competition in the elementary school should be in physical education upper division classes or during intramural sports for fourth and fifth graders. Where there is athletic competition for elementary age children, it should be for the older students and contact sports should not be played. Soccer is the only competitive sport highly recommended for elementary children. The young athlete does not require any additional dietary considerations and should not be placed under any great stress to win.

REFERENCES AND SUGGESTED READINGS

American Academy of Pediatrics. Medical concerns in the female athlete. *Pediatrics,* 106, 610-613, 2000.

Athletic Footwear Association. *American youth and sports participation.* North Palm Beach, FLL Athletic Footwear Association, 1990.

Ewing, M.E., V.D. Seefeldt, and T.P. Brown, Role of organized sports in the education and health of American children and youth. In A.Poinsett (Ed.), *The Role of Sports in Youth Development.* Meeting convened by the Carnegie Corporation of New York, New York, NY, March, 1996.

Jeziorski, R.M. *The Importance of School Sports in American Education and Socialization.* Lanham, MD: University Press of America, 1994.

Maron, B.J., M.S.M. Link, P.J. Wang, et al. Clinical profile of commotio cardis: An underappreciated cause of sudden death in the young during sports and other activities. *Journal of Cardiovascular Electrophysiology,* 10, 114-120, 1999.

Micheli, L.J. Overuse injuries: The new scourge of kids sports. Retrieved September 12, 2000, from the World Wide Web http://sportsparents.com/medical/overuse.html.

Payne, V.G. and L.D. Isaacs. *Human Motor Development: A Lifespan Approach* (6th ed.). Boston, MA: McGraw-Hill, 2005.

Passer, M.W. Psychological stress in; youth sports. In R.A. Magill, M.J. Ash, and F.L. Smoll (Eds.), *Children in sport.* Champaign, IL: Human Kinetics.

President's Council on Physical Fitness and Sports. Youth sports in America: An overview. P*resident's Council on Physical Fitness and Sports Research Digest,* ser. 2, no. 11, 1997.

Simon, J., and R. Martens, Children's anxiety in sport and nonsport evaluative activities. *Journal of Sport Psychology,* 1, 160-169, 1979.

Chapter

29 Free and Inexpensive Equipment

After completing this chapter, the student should be able to:

1. Cite three ways to equip the program.
2. Give the names of at least three inexpensive or free pieces of equipment which are not included in the chapter.
3. Design and make a homemade piece of equipment.
4. Define the key terms listed below.

―――――――――――――――――――――――――― *Key Terms*

Homemade equipment
Junk day

EQUIPMENT

Physical education budgets rarely are sufficient to meet children's equipment needs. Administrative knowledge and attitudes are frequently reflected in their commitment toward physical education. Even where there are sympathetic principals, budgetary constraints have created problems in all curriculum areas. To minimize the limitations created by fiscal problems, one must seek alternatives to school purchased equipment and supplies. These alternatives include using homemade equipment and supplies, having a junk day, getting parents involved, seeking funds from the Parent Teacher Association, and/or having senior high industrial arts classes make elementary physical education equipment.

Junk Day

A carefully-organized junk day can bring in a number of useful items from students' homes. A list of items which might be considered useless at home but useful at school could be prepared and sent home with the children. Such items as old tennis rackets, badminton rackets, used milk containers, and cloth for beanbags might be included on the list. Care must be exercised to guarantee that children do not bring valuable items from home to please the teacher. By analyzing needs and specifying items as well as requiring parental permission to bring such items, the junk day can be very successful.

Parental Help

Parents frequently volunteer their services to schools and are seeking opportunities to aid children and teachers. These willing parents can be asked to make beanbags, streamers, yarn balls and other easily constructed supplies. Funds for materials can often be obtained from the P.T.A.

Industrial Arts

An industrial arts class or students at the vocational technical center can be asked to build the larger pieces of equipment—a vaulting box, or materials for a creative playground. Such equipment can be as good, if not better, than commercially produced materials and can be constructed inexpensively.

Value

Seeking alternative resources for equipment and supplies takes a little more teacher time and

A vaulting box made by an industrial arts class.

effort, but seeing the rapid growth and development of children when each child has a piece of equipment makes it worthwhile. Maximum participation can become a reality with a little knowledge and minimal effort.

There are some distinct values that evolve within the school setting from the use of homemade equipment. They are as follows:

1. Students who have input into their learning are more motivated to participate in activities.
2. Cooperation and communication channels are enhanced between parents and P.T.A.s, high schools, elementary schools, and the community.
3. The opportunity for innovation through creative efforts does a great deal to promote student and parent interest in the program.

When one is making or designing homemade equipment that will be for use in the classroom, one must consider a variety of factors. These factors listed below have become increasingly important in light of legal suits that have appeared on the educational scene today for a variety of reasons:

1. Above all—*be sure it's safe!*
2. To insure safety, make certain that it's sturdy, use nontoxic paint, and keep the equipment clean.
3. Have a regular maintenance system and do not hesitate to discard a piece of equipment when it can no longer be used safely.

A big advantage of using homemade equipment over commercially made equipment is that it often permits the teacher to satisfy the special need of each and every child to a higher degree. Equipment should be designed with the idea in mind that regardless of the skill level of a child, he or she can find a place for entry into the activity without experiencing any problems. Then the equipment or any activity can truly meet the needs of every child, regardless of where the child is on the spectrum of development. Entry level according to ability requires extra planning and work, but homemade equipment can assist greatly in making this concept a reality.

EQUIPMENT DESCRIPTIONS

The following is just a sampling of the free and inexpensive equipment possible. The reader is encouraged to explore how items normally discarded might be used to help equip a physical education program.

Item(s): Coat hanger racket
Materials: Metal coat hanger and nylon stockings
Directions: Pull the coat hanger into a diamond shape and squeeze hook together. Cover with an old stocking, and tape at the end to form a handle.
Use: Use as a racket with yarn balls or newspaper balls.

Item(s): Scoops
Materials: Plastic containers which have handles (bleach, milk, etc.)
Directions: Cut the containers to form a scoop being sure to protect against any sharp or jagged edges. It may be necessary to put tape on the cut portion of the item.
Uses: Use to catch and throw yarn balls, paper balls, or beanbags.

Item(s): Tom-Tom
Materials: Containers with handles on them
Directions: Several items can be used for making tom-toms, including bleach bottles, large plastic milk containers, and an antifreeze container (this seems to work best).
Uses: To provide rhythm for activities. They can also be used by the children as a rhythm instrument while they are moving.

Item(s): Tires
Materials: Tires, large and small, from a variety of vehicles
Directions: Care must be taken to eliminate the possibility of water accumulating in the tire. Holes must be drilled to insure drainage.

Uses: Tires can be placed upright in the ground to provide hurdles; they can be used lying flat for agility activities; and they can be put together to produce a variety of climbing equipment.

Item(s): Tug-of-war tubes
Materials: Old bicycle inner tubes
Directions: None
Uses: Use as tug-of-war between two to four individuals.

Item(s): Yarn balls
Materials: 6" square pieces of cardboard and yarn
Directions: Wrap yarn around the cardboard numerous times. Then pull off and tie in the middle to create a bundle. Clip the ends of the bundle with scissors. Create numerous bundles and then tie them all together to create a ball.
Uses: For manipulative activities including use with nylon rackets and scoops.

Item(s): Foam balls
Materials: Various size pieces of foam
Directions: Cut off edges to make them as ball-like as possible.
Uses: For manipulative activities

Item(s): Beanbags
Materials: 6" square pieces of sturdy cloth
Directions: Using two pieces of cloth with the backsides together, sew three sides together. Fold inside out and fill three-quarters full with navy beans, plastic beads or some other safe material. Be careful when filling with something like birdseed. Food attracts rodents when beanbags are stored.
Uses: Manipulative activities

Item(s): Wands
Materials: Old broom or mop handles
Directions: Cut handles in about 36" lengths
Uses: Can be used for rhythmic activities or for balancing on various body parts.

Item(s): Balance beam
Materials: 2" x 4" x 8' pieces of wood or 4" x 4" x 8' or longer
Directions: Sand all sharp edges. Secure one 2 x 4 on top of another 2 x 4. The bottom one should be on its 2" side while the top one is placed so the children can walk on the 4" side. The 4 x 4s can be used as is but should be elevated by bolting legs onto the beam. Beams

385

Equipment such as wands (left) and balance beams may be made inexpensively.

should not be higher than eight to ten inches off the ground.
Uses: For balancing activities

Item(s): Hoops
Materials: Old garden hose and wooden dowels
Directions: Cut lengths of garden hoses; place ends around a 3" long piece of dowel, drive short tacks in each side and tape ends together.
Uses: Use for hoops which are placed on the ground. The hoops can be used for directional activities as well as for markers.

Item(s): Rings
Materials: Old garden hose and wooden dowels
Directions: Cut hose into short pieces depending upon how large you want the rings to be. Then cut a piece of dowel about two to three inches long. Use small tacks to secure the dowel inside the hose and tape area.
Uses: Manipulative activities

Item(s): Newspaper rectangles
Materials: Newspapers
Directions: Rip newspaper into one page rectangles.
Uses: Can be used for directional activities. Can also be used for agility and balance activities by having each child move around play area as quickly as possible using two pieces of paper. Children place one piece in front and step on it and then pick up other piece. Children may not touch the floor. This can be done as a race.

Item(s): Paper balls
Materials: Large pieces of paper, including newspaper, and tape
Directions: Crunch paper into a ball and secure with tape.
Uses: Any manipulative activity

Item(s): Jump Ropes
Materials: Number 8 or Number 10 sash cord
Directions: Cut rope in appropriate length (9' for short and 13' for long) and then tie or tape ends. If using a plastic sash cord, the ends can be burned to keep the rope from unraveling.
Uses: Rhythmic activities, cardiovascular conditioning, and coordination

Item(s): Tennis ball
Materials: Old tennis balls—most players throw them away after about three sets.
Directions: None
Uses: Manipulative activities

Item(s): Targets
Materials: Nearly any plastic container; plastic tennis ball containers work well
Directions: None
Uses: Use for self-testing, target activities

Item(s): Boundary Markers
Materials: Any plastic container with a handle and a large base
Directions: Place a small amount of water or stones in container to give it weight
Uses: To mark off play area. Containers can be stored or carried by placing a rope through the handle.

Item(s): Bicycle tires
Materials: Old bicycle tires
Directions: None
Uses: Use as targets or tug of war

Item(s): Weights
Materials: Plastic containers with handles, sash cord, and any other items necessary for the task
Directions: Place sand in containers to make them a certain weight but not in excess of ten pounds.
Uses: Set up a weight lifting station for the handicapped (see chapter 20).

Chapter

30

Cognitive Learning through Movement

After completing this chapter, the student should be able to:

1. Define the term "Cognitive Learning Through Movement."

2. Differentiate between Cognitive Learning Through Movement and Integrated Physical education by citing three similarities and at least three differences.

3. List and describe the three reasons movement is a positive medium for teaching or reinforcing cognitive information.

4. Describe from memory at least two chapter activities for each of the subject areas discussed.

5. Determine if an activity meets the criteria for a cognitive activity.

6. For each subject discussed in the chapter, design one original activity which meets the criteria established in the chapter.

7. Define the key terms listed below.

Key Terms

Cognitive learning through movement
Feedback
Integrated physical education

Knowledge of results
Motivation
Proprioception

Cognitive Learning Through Movement (CLTM) is the process by which movement is used to teach or reinforce academic concepts in such areas as language arts, science, and mathematics. Movement as a learning medium has long been recognized. Leading learning theorist, Piaget, for example, has emphasized the relationship between moving and intellectual development. He found that children learn not by sitting but by interacting with their environment. Much of an infant's first learning is of and through movement. Movement and learning, however, should not be reserved for infants only.

When children enter most elementary schools, there is usually less emphasis on movement as a learning medium. The current public school philosophy does not seem to value movement; children are expected to learn while sitting quietly and listening to the teacher. Verbal learning, however, involves almost complete abstract symbolic manipulation, and a young child's ability to interpret such symbols is questionable.

Although CLTM is a valuable tool for the classroom teacher, it must not be confused with or take the place of a comprehensive physical education program. Even many physical educators have been using CLTM activities and games during physical education. Seldom do these activities or games meet the movement criteria appropriate for a physical education activity or game. Since cognitive development is the goal of CLTM activities and games, the emphasis is cognition not movement. Physical education is no more important then the core subject areas but it not less important either. CLTM activities and games should be reserved for that time designed for the subject being emphasized whether it be language arts, math, science, or social studies.

Why It Works

There are three reasons why Cognitive Learning Through Movement works: motivation, proprioception, and knowledge of results. Although most people understand motivation and knowledge of results, proprioception or sensory feedback from the muscles is not usually familiar. It is, however, a key element; if this method is going to work, the child must be totally involved in the learning; sight, sound, and body.

Motivation

It is motivating, it involves whole body learning, and it provides immediate feedback. Children like to move, so they are more motivated to participate in movement activities as compared with passive learning so typical of the academic classroom. The activities are often low level competitive games which children also find motivating. Whether a game or just creative movement, however, children respond favorably to movement.

Proprioception

Besides motivation, movement involves the entire body in learning, and involves proprioception or sensory feedback from the muscles. So frequently, only the eyes and/or ears are the learning medium, but movement involves nearly all the senses. Proprioception seems to be a primary factor which makes this approach work. Those teaching foreign language, for example, have recognized the value of living the language; they encourage students to live in the country where the language is spoken. Whole body involvement is far superior to a classroom environment where only the eyes and ears are stimulated.

Knowledge of Results

The third factor, knowledge of results, is associated primarily with games. These games are designed to have every child thinking of the answer to the problem presented. The correct answer then is revealed prior to moving on to the next problem. This total cognitive involvement with corresponding feedback is nearly identical to the linear programming process advocated by Skinner.

COGNITIVE LEARNING THROUGH MOVEMENT ACTIVITIES AND GAMES

The activities which best reflect the three factors associated with movement and cognitive development have been given the name "Cognitive Learning Through Movement" activities. Although several activities which appear in this chapter are similar to those in other sections of the book, the objective is different. The primary purpose is the teaching of or reinforcement of an academic concept. These activities, therefore, should not be done during time allotted to physical education. Although many may help develop a child's movement ability, they are clearly not intended for this purpose. Since the process requires all the children to be thinking and not necessarily moving, there may be considerable non-movement time.

CLTM activities should not be confused with *Integrated Physical Education* activities. They differ most notably in their objective. In the former, it is cognitive development, while integrated activities are designed to fulfill a physical education objective. In the CLTM activity, everyone must be thinking of the answers 100% of the time and there must be some movement by everyone some of the time. The integrated activity, on the other hand, has everyone moving all the time.

It is important to note that CLTM activities should be conducted during time set aside for the subject area in question, and should *not be done during physical education time.* They are presented as an aid to the classroom teacher as an alternative to more traditional teaching. Since they also involve some movement, they may also help the child develop physically even though that is not their intent.

Activity Code:

 N = Name of activity
DA = Developmental age—age group for which activity is appropriate
DV = Developmental value—what aspect of the child will be affected
 F = Formation
 E = Equipment
 D = Description of activity
 S = Safety

Language Arts

 N: Speedy Spelling - Game
DA: 6 and up
DV: Spelling
 F: Two or more teams of ten to twelve (can be smaller)
 E: Two sets of letters appropriate to the words to be asked
 D: Prior to the class, the teacher prepares identical sets of letters (number of sets is determined by the number of teams) which contain all the letters necessary to spell the vocabulary words to be presented. Each team is given a set which is then divided equally among the players. Children should have at least two letters each but may have as many as four. The children get behind a restraining line equal distance from the area where the word is to be spelled out. When the teacher says the word, all the children must think of how to spell it to see if they have one of the required letters. If they do, they run to the spelling area and place their letter down along with their teammates to correctly spell the word. It there is any question about the word, i.e., a homonym, the teacher can use the word in a sentence to help the students. The first team to have the word spelled correctly wins one point.
 S: There should be sufficient space between the two team's spelling area to avoid collisions.

Speedy Spelling

 N: Speedy Antonyms - Game
DA: 7 and older
DV: Learning antonyms
 F: Same as Speedy Spelling above
 E: Same as Speedy Spelling above
 D: This is nearly identical to Speedy Spelling except the emphasis is on antonyms. The teacher develops a list of antonyms and then prepares the cards. The teacher calls out a word, and the students must think of an opposite to that word and spell it.
 S: There should be sufficient space between the two team's spelling area to avoid collisions.

 N: Speedy Homonym - Game
DA: 7 and older
DV: Learning homonyms
 F: Same as Speedy Spelling
 E: Same as Speedy Spelling
 D: Same as Speedy Antonym except the teacher says a homonym and then uses it in a sentence; the children must think of a word which sounds the same as the word in question but is spelled differently.

The first team to spell this different word gets one point.

S: There should be sufficient space between the two team's spelling area to avoid collisions.

N: Body Spelling - Activity
DA: 6 to 8
DV: Spelling
F: Small groups of three or four depending upon the number of letters in the words to be asked
E: None
D: Teacher calls out a three- or four-letter word and students must make the appropriate alphabetical shapes with their bodies in order to spell the word.

Body Spelling

N: Match the Opposite - Game
DA: 6 to 8
DV: Learning Antonyms
F: Free
E: Cards with antonyms
D: The teacher makes a set of cards with antonyms which are then worn around each child's neck (one word per child); the children then move freely about the room and on a signal must find the person wearing the opposite of their word. Each group that finds their opposite before the stop signal is given gets one point. Children then quickly switch their card with someone else but not the person they just found and the game begins again.

N: Verbs in Motion - Game
DA: 6 to 8
DV: Learning verbs
F: Free

E: None
D: Teacher calls out various words. When the teacher calls out a verb, the children immediately begin acting out the verb. When any other word is called out, the children must remain frozen.

N: Human Punctuation - Game
DA: 6 to 8
DV: Learning punctuation
F: Free
E: None
D: The teacher reads sentences to students or they can be written on the board or shown on an overhead projector. When reading the sentence, the teacher can ask the children to form the end punctuation for the sentence, i.e., period, question mark, etc., with their bodies. When on the board or overhead, a number can be placed where punctuation must go; and the teacher could ask what belongs at the number "2" position. Again the children use their bodies to form the appropriate punctuation.

N: Moving to Read - Activity
DA: 4 to 8
DV: Learning to read
F: Free
E: None
D: Children listen to a story read by the teacher or from a commercially produced record. The story should have considerable movement activities built in. After listening to the story, children do creative movement based upon the story. Then the children again listen to the story, but this time they follow along using a script with the exact same words being read or played by the teacher.

N: Crows and Cranes Vowels - Game
DA: 8 to 10
DV: Language arts
F: Two teams side by side
E: None
D: Team members stand one behind the other and opposite the opposing team. One team is designated as the vowels and the other the consonants. If the word called out begins with a vowel, the vowel team runs about five feet towards its safe

base and the consonants chase and vice versa. Anyone tagging a member of the other team gets one point. The people with the most points are declared the winners.

S: There can be no grabbing or hitting while tagging.

Crows and Cranes Vowels

N: Verb Charades - Activity
DA: 8 to 10
DV: Learning verbs and creativity
F: Partners
E: 3" X 5" cards with action verbs on them
D: One of the partners selects an action verb from the box. S/he then acts out the verb while the partner tries to guess it. Once guessed, the partners switch roles. They continue to take turns acting out the word until the teacher stops the activity.

N: Action Blanks - Game
DA: 8 to 9
DV: Learning action verbs
F: Free
E: Flash cards with sentences on them
D: Using flash cards with sentences which are missing the action verb are shown to the children who then act out a verb which will complete the sentence, i.e., Dan _____ the car. Choices include drove, started, dented, painted, washed, etc.

N: Make a Sentence - Game
DA: 8 to 11

DV: Language arts
F: Free
E: Cards with various words representing different parts of speech
D: Each child is given a card with one of the parts of speech (noun, adjective, verb, adverb) on it. On the "Go" signal, children begin moving around the room trying to find other children whose words will help them form a sentence. As soon as a group completes a sentence, they form a line with their words in front of them. Each child in a sentence group gets one point. Additional words are then given out and the game begins again.

N: Parts of Speech Scramble - Game
DA: 8 to 9
DV: Language arts
F: Free
E: Carpet squares or large pieces of paper or cardboard
D: Carpet squares or large pieces of paper or cardboard have one of the parts of speech written on them (noun, verb, adjective, or adverb). Children move to music freely about the room. When the music stops, the teacher calls out a word and uses it in a sentence. The children then quickly move to the square which contains the name of the correct part of speech. Those that go to the correct square (there can be more than one person to a square) get one point. At the end, those with the most points win.

N: Correct, Incorrect Tag - Game
DA: 8 to 9
DV: Language arts
F: Two teams standing side by side
E: None, although flash cards could be used effectively
D: Two teams line up side by side in a Crows and Cranes arrangement. One team is designated as "Correct" and the other "Incorrect." The teacher then spells a word or holds a word up on a flash card. If the word is correctly spelled, the "Correct" group runs to a safe base and the other group chases and tries to tag them. Anyone tagged must go to the other team. If the word is incorrectly spelled, the "Incorrect" group runs.

N: Synonym Circle - Game
DA: 8 to 9
DV: Language arts
F: Double circle
E: Cards with synonyms on them
D: The inner circle has one set of words and the outer circle has a synonym for the inner circle words. When the music begins, the circles go in opposite directions. When it stops, children quickly match words. The last group to squat down gets one point. The cards are scrambled and redistributed or there can be additional cards distributed.

N: Noun or Verb? - Game
DA: 6 to 7
DV: Movement and being able to distinguish between nouns and verbs
F: Free
E: None
D: The teacher says a word which is either a noun or a verb. If a verb, the student does the action; if a noun, they say, "fooler." Words can also be put on flashcards to improve its cognitive value.

N: Nouns and Verbs - Game
DA: 8 to 9
DV: Language arts
F: Two teams side by side
E: None
D: Two teams line up in a Crows and Cranes arrangement each with a safe base area beside them. The teams are designated as "Nouns" and "Verbs." If the word called out by the teacher is a noun, the Noun group runs and is chased by the verbs. Anyone tagged must join the other team. If the word is a verb, the Verbs run. A variation would be to use flashcards instead of saying the word.

N: Sentence Scramble - Game
DA: 8 to 9
DV: Language arts
F: Teams of six to seven
E: Words and punctuation marks on pieces of paper.
D: Each child has a word and a punctuation sign. The teacher says, "Make a question, or make an exclamation, or a sentence." The children work to get their sentence correct including the punctua-

tion and then rush to a designated spot and place their sentence down. The first team to have the sentence correct wins.

N: Human Concepts - Game
DA: 5 to 6
DV: Learning concepts
F: Children are divided into groups of three
E: Flash cards with concepts on them
D: The teacher holds up the flash cards with such concepts as: over, under, through, on top of, behind, in front of, down, below, around, between, and through. Children then demonstrate the concept in their group. Each successful group gets a point.

N: Compound Partner - Game
DA: 8 to 9
DV: Compound words
F: Free
E: Flash cards of compound words
D: Each child receives a flash card with a part of a compound word on it. On a signal, children move around to find someone to make a compound word with their flashcards. When two people find a correct match, they link elbows and go to a predetermined area. The last group to get together or those who cannot make the compound word receive a point. The cards are then scrambled and distributed again. Those with the least points at the end are the winners.

N: Syl-la-ble Run - Game
DA: 9 to 11
DV: Language Arts
F: Two lines side by side
E: None
D: Two teams line up in a Crows and Cranes formation. Each has a safe base area beside them marked by a line. A word is said by the teacher. Children must figure out how many syllables it contains. If it is odd, one team runs to their safe base while the other tries to tag them, and, if even, the other team runs. Anyone tagged must switch teams. At the end of the game, the team with the most players and anyone not tagged during the game are the winners.

N: Look, Listen, and Run - Game
DA: 6 to 7
DV: Language arts
F: Single line side by side
E: Letters on flash cards
D: The children stand side by side on a line facing the teacher who is a distance away on a finish line. The teacher holds up a letter and says a word which may or may not begin with that letter. If it does, the children run toward the finish line and the first to cross is the winner and the game begins again. Any child who begins running when they are not suppose to must take one giant step backward from their starting point. There must be room behind the starting line, therefore, for those children who must take a couple of giant steps backward.

N: Puzzled Words - Game
DA: 9 to 11
DV: Language arts
F: Groups of five to eight players
E: Pieces of paper
D: Letters are placed on pieces of paper which are given to each group. The groups must then unscramble the letters to form a word which uses all the letters. They then must act out the word. The first group to assemble and act out the word is the winner.

N: Math Match Up - Game
DA: 6 to 8
DV: Mathematics
F: Free
E: A piece of paper with a number on it for each child
D: The teacher gives each child a piece of paper with any number on it from 0-10 and then holds up a number (0-10). For example, the teacher puts the number 6 on the board. When he/she says "Math Match Up," the children must go around the room and find another number that will make an equation that will equal the number on the board. Example: Johnny has a 4 so he will look for the number that can be added to his 4 to make a 6. Or he might look for a number that it can be subtracted from that will make a 6. All those who get the answer correct get a point.

N: Make a Sentence - Game
DA: 10 to 12
DV: To reinforce parts of speech, making complete sentences correctly
F: Free
E: Cards with certain words (parts of speech) written on them
D: Each child is given a card with one of the parts of speech (such as noun, adjective, verb, adverb) on it. The children spread out in the room. When the teacher gives the signal, the children move about in the room trying to find other children with whom they can join together and form a sentence. For example, a child with the word *girls* joins with *pretty, watch,* and *television,* and *quietly* to form the sentence: "Pretty girls watch television quietly."
As soon as a group of children make a sentence, they form a line so the teacher can read their sentence. The first ones to form a complete sentence get a point. You could also award points to those forming unusual or good sentences that might make use of several adjectives and nouns or verbs, etc.

N: Exploration with Ropes - Activity
DA: 6 to 8
DV: Locomotor skills, balancing, knowledge of body parts, language arts
F: Scattered

Exploration with Ropes

395

E: One rope for each child (or two)

D: Have children make the letter V with their rope. Some questions the teacher can ask: Can you start at the vertex of the V and jump down the rope? Can you leap over the skinny part? Over the wide part? Make an O with your rope. Can you make a bridge over the O? Can you hop around the outside? Jump in sideways? Jump out backwards? Can you make a B? Can you balance on one body part in each section of the B? Can you put your elbow in the B and your ankle outside the B? etc.

Continue with whatever letters are being studied, or numbers being studied. Some second graders are using cursive letters and could form letters for that.

N: Compound Partners - Activity

DA: 8 to 10

DV: Locomotor movement, social interaction

F: Scattered

E: Cards with words that will make compound words, record, record player

D: Each child will be given a card with a word on it. Play music as children move around the room to find a partner that will make a compound word. When everyone has a partner each must read the new word. Collect cards and repeat by having the children move in different ways as they look for a new partner by skipping, galloping, sliding, crawling, and hopping. When the music stops, the children must find a partner as quickly as possible.

Use word cards such as dog, house, light, bulb, light, house, milk, man, news, paper, sun, flower, pine, cone, bed, room, bath, room, waste, basket, lamp, shade, sun, shine, etc.

N: Parts of Speech Game - Game

DA: 10 to 12

DV: Integration of language arts (parts of speech) with physical education

F: Free

E: Carpet square with labels (various parts of speech); Hula-Hoops may be used, flash cards

D: This activity reinforces parts of speech lesson. Each carpet square has a part of speech label (noun, verb, adjective, adverb). These squares are scattered around on the floor. The children are moving freely around the floor. The teacher holds up a flash card with a word on it. Students go to the carpet square that is the correct part of speech. The teacher then turns the flash card over and reveals the correct part of speech.

Example: The teacher holds up a card that says "antelope." Students move in the specified way (walk, run, etc.) to a carpet square. The teacher turns over the flash card and it says "Noun." Then a discussion of why it is a noun can take place.

N: True and False Tag - Game

DA: 8 to 12

DV: Running, spelling

F: Two teams

E: None

D: The class is divided into two teams (one false, one true). The teacher spells a word (spelling words) either correctly or incorrectly. If spelled correctly the true team runs to their goal and the false team chases them. If spelled incorrectly the false team runs to their goal and the true team chases them. If you are tagged you become a member of that team.

Movements can be changed. This could also be played as a review of a social studies or science unit. You could also check reading comprehension with this activity.

N: Paren-Vayan (Stop-Go) - Game

DA: 8 to 10

DV: Learn simple Spanish commands, movement

F: Single line facing leader

E: None

D: Leader calls out simple Spanish action words that have been discussed in class. Using a "red light, green light" format, the leader calls out the instruction. The teacher says "Paren" (stop) when the children are to stop. Game continues until one person reaches the leader. If a child does not respond with the correct action, he/she goes back to the starting line.

Examples: corran — run
anden — walk
salten — jump

brinquen — skip
gateen — crawl

Note: In a school with some Spanish speaking population even a few words are helpful for English speaking teachers and pupils.

N: Think Fast - Game
DA: 8 to 10
DV: Reinforcement of different types of sentences and punctuation
F: Four teams
E: Four stacks of cards containing either a word or a punctuation mark
D: Each person on each team will receive a couple of cards. The cards will contain either a word or a punctuation mark. The teacher will then say, "Make a question (or sentence, or command, etc.)." Each team must put its cards together to form a question and the correct punctuation at the end. Then they rush to a designated area, and line up with their cards in the correct order. The first team to accomplish this is the winner of that round.

N: Prove It - Game
DA: 10 to 12
DV: Motor skills, reinforcement of parts of speech
F: One line or circle
E: Cards, name boxes (parts of speech written on them)
D: Each child is given four cards with the name *Noun, Verb, Adjective,* and *Adverb* written on them. The teacher tells the children how to approach the box, then uses a sentence and names a word in the sentence. The students must decide which part of speach the word is, go to the box as directed, and place the card in it.

Example: Children, I would like for you to hop to the name box with your card when you have made your decision and place the card in the correct box. Return back to your line. After the answer is given, go back to the box and get a card.

My sentence is: Look at her big smile. My word is *smile.*

If the children understand the way the word is used, they must "Prove It" by immediately hopping with their card to

the Noun Box. Be sure to explain (teacher or student) why the word *was* a noun.

The game may continue by using different motor skills such as: jumping, skipping, creeping, galloping, etc. Make it exciting with lots of fun!

N: Word Line-Up - Game
DA: 6 to 8
DV: To reinforce long and short vowels in sounding and blending of words. Simple one-syllable words may be used to introduce the activity and later increasing to more difficult words.
F: Free
E: Ten cards (5" x 8") with long and short vowel picture-associations and forty-two cards (5" x 8") with small consonant letters. Two large cards with the words, *BEFORE* and *AFTER.*
D: The major objective of this activity is to reinforce medial vowel recognition using the sounding and blending of letters. You may distribute special-picture cards for the long and short vowel sounds (faster recognition with picture association). Each child is given two letters. To begin, the vowel sound is announced: "short i." That "person-card" comes to the predetermined location where he/she stands in the middle of two cards labeled: *BEFORE* and *AFTER.* Everyone thinks of a word that has the "short i" sound in the middle. The consonants place themselves accordingly. The *BEFORE* person names the word and the *AFTER* person spells the word. The children work together locating partners to assist in the spellings. The difficulty may be increased by having more than one vowel up front. The children would need to determine which of these vowels they should use in the spelling of their word.

N: Alphabet Scramble - Game
DA: 6 to 8
DV: Reinforcement activity for short vowel sounds
F: Large circle
E: None
D: Children are assigned a short vowel sound (A, E, I, O, U). At least two children must have the same sound. The caller stands in the center and must think

of a word with a short vowel sound. When the children hear the word, they must determine if their vowel sound is heard in the word. The children whose vowel sound is used in the word must change places. The caller tries to get into one of their places before they complete the change. If he/she does, the child without a place is the new caller. Caller gets two tries and then a new caller is chosen. Encourage the caller to use different vowel sounds. Variations can include using long vowel sounds, beginning consonants, etc.

Mathematics

N: Speedy Math - Game
DA: 8 and older
DV: Mathematics
F: Teams—two or more; teams should only be about seven to ten on a side
E: Cards with numbers and mathematical signs
D: This is similar to Speedy Spelling, but the card sets contain numbers and signs such as minus, plus, and equals. Depending upon the grade level, other signs such as less than and more than could be used. Each person has two numbers and a few people also have the signs along with their number. There are several versions which are presented from easy to more complex.

Equation: The left side of the equation, i.e., 5 + 3 is given. Students then must run to a predetermined area and place down 5 + 3 = 8.

Answer: In this version, the answer is given. Using either the plus sign or the minus sign but not both, the team must then determine the appropriate numbers to place on the left side to balance the equation.

Plus and Minus: A number is given and both the left and right side of the equation must equal that number. One side of the equation uses the plus sign and the other the minus sign.

Double Trouble: The answer is given, but this time the left side of the equation must contain both the plus and minus sign.

Speedy Math

DA: 8 and older
DV: Mathematics
F: Equal teams—about seven to a side
E: Plastic container with a handle
D: Each child on a team is assigned a number consecutively until everyone has one. The other team has corresponding numbers. A mathematics equation is called out and the child with the answer (one from each team) attempts to carry the container back to his/her team without being tagged by the other player. If successful, his/her team gets two points, but if tagged, the other team receives one point. The container may not be kicked, hit, or thrown. When both children arrive at the container simultaneously, they will have to maneuver, fake, and rely on quickness to get the container. If one just goes out and grabs the container, he/she will almost always be tagged unless the player from the other side is unable to solve the equation or is just asleep. Should neither player attempt to grab it after some brief maneuvering, the leader can call another equation and there will be four players out there. No body contact is allowed except to tag.

Grab the Club Math

N: Call Ball Math - Game
DA: 8 to 10
DV: Mathematics
F: Circle of about twelve children
E: 8 1/2-inch playground ball
D: Children number off consecutively until everyone in the circle has a number. One child is selected to go to the middle of the circle to start the game. This child calls out a math equation and tosses the ball in the air. If the child with the same number as the answer is able to catch the ball before it bounces more than once, he/she gets to be the new leader. If not the original child continues the game. Be sure to insist that the entire equation be said before the ball is thrown straight into the air.

N: Spud - Game
DA: 8 and older
DV: Mathematics
F: Circle of ten to twelve
E: 8 1/2 inch playground ball
D: Same organization as Call Ball, except when the child goes in to catch the ball, the rest of the children run as far away as possible being sure to stay inside the boundaries. If the ball is caught before it bounces more than once, the child calls another equation and throws the ball in the air again. This continues until the designated catcher cannot retrieve the ball before it bounces twice. When the child does get it, he/she yells "SPUD" at which time everyone must freeze. The child then is allowed to roll the ball at anyone, and any child hit gets an "S". If the child misses, he/she gets the "S". The child receiving the letter continues the game. Anyone who gets SPUD would be out of the game. The teacher, however, must be sure to end the game before anyone is eliminated. Those with the fewest letters are declared the winners.

N: Crows and Cranes Math - Game
DA: 8 and older
DV: Mathematics
F: Two teams side by side, separated by about four feet
E: None

D: Team members stand one behind the other and opposite the other team. One team is designated as odd and the other the even. Math equations are then stated, and if the answer is odd, the odd team runs about ten feet towards its safe base and the evens chase. Anyone tagged by the evens becomes an even and joins their side. If the answer is even, they run toward their base and the odds chase. After a period of time the team with the most players and all those not tagged are declared the winners.

N: Twister Math - Game
DA: A series of discs with numbers drawn on a sheet as shown in the diagram below.
DV: Mathematics
F: Three or four children per sheet
E: Sheets
D: The leader calls out something like "right hand 2 minus 1" or "left foot 2 plus 1". Children must solve the problem and place the proper part on the correct number. This is a balance activity with each person trying to cause the others to lose their balance and fall. No pushing, shoving, or bumping is allowed. Children merely try to get into a favorable position by getting numbers close to them and forcing others to make long unbalanced stretches to other numbers. Only one person can be on any one disc at a time. Each time a person falls or cannot complete the move or makes an incorrect response, he/she gets a point. After a period of time, the one with the least points is the winner.

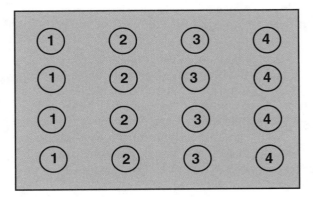

N: Stew Pot Math - Game
DA: 8 and older
DV: Mathematics
F: Two equal teams of about eight to ten across from each other. One child is in the stew pot between them.
E: Cards with numbers and equations
D: Children line up in two lines facing each other about fifteen to twenty feet apart. Each person has a number on the floor in front of him/her. One child stands between the two lines. The leader holds up two equations—one for each line. The child who has the solution to the problem in front of him must change places with the child in the other line without being tagged by the person in the middle. If tagged he/she must go in the center and the tagger takes his/her place on the line. The center person can also solve the problem and tag the person before he/she gets a chance to move.

N: Human Math - Game
DA: 8 and older
DV: Mathematics
F: Teams of eight to ten
E: None
D: Each team stands shoulder to shoulder behind a restraining line. An answer line is drawn about five feet in front of each team. The leader calls out a math problem. The object of the game is for each team to move to their answer line and be the first to display the answer by the number of children standing. All others must squat down.

N: Human Math Groups - Game
DA: 6 to 8
DV: Mathematics
F: Free
E: Flash cards with numbers
D: Children move freely about the room using various locomotor movements as dictated by the leader. The leader then holds up a card on which a number is written. Students must then holds hands and sit in a group corresponding to the flashed number. The teacher then can talk about how many groups are formed based upon the number and the remainder (children not able to get enough to form the number).

N: Multiplication Scrabble - Game
DA: 8 and older
DV: Mathematics
F: Free
E: One tennis ball per child
D: Each child has a tennis ball with an equation on it. On the leader's signal, they throw it as far as possible beyond a minimum distance marker. They then run and retrieve any ball they can get and try to think of the answer to the equation. They then run with the ball to a series of flashcards spread over a fairly large area (this will avoid congestion). Finding the flashcard with the solution on it, the child holds it up along with the ball. The first five players to get the correct answer get one point.

N: Human Equation - Game
DA: 8 and older
DV: Mathematics
F: Equal size teams of eight to ten
E: None
D: Teams stand behind a starting line. An answer is called out, and each team must run to a predetermined area and make the equation, including the answer with their bodies. Variations such as those for Speed Math described earlier can also be used.

Human Equation

N: Number Toss - Game
DA: 8 and older
DV: Mathematics
F: Partners
E: One beanbag per person and sheets with numbers on them
D: Children compete in pairs. Both throw their beanbag at the same time onto the sheet. They must then quickly go to a series of face down flash cards with equations on them which correspond to the various numbers on the sheet. The first one to find the correct solution wins one point. Cards are mixed up and spread out face down after each point.

N: Human Numbers - Game
DA: 5 and older
DV: Mathematics
F: Free or in small groups depending upon age
E: None
D: When the leader calls out a number, the children form the number with their bodies. For older children, Roman numerals can be used.

N: Metric Merriment - Game
DA: 8 and older
DV: Mathematics
F: Partners
E: Metric yard sticks or regular yard sticks
D: One child does an athletic event such as the long jump, hop, step and jump, or standing broad jump and the partner marks the distance. Both then measure the distance and convert from metric to inches or vice versa. Then the other child takes a turn as the jumper.

N: Math Match Up - Game
DA: 6 to 7
DV: Mathematics
F: Free
E: Cards with numbers
D: Every child has a card with a number 1 - 9 on it. The teacher writes a number on the board. The children must move around and find one other child whose number can be used in a mathematical equation to match the number on the board. If the number on the board is 8 then 6 and 2 (addition) could be together,

or 9 and 1 (subtraction), 4 and 2 (multiplication), etc. Each child in a correct twosome gets a point.

N: Products and Factors - Game
DA: 8 to 9
DV: Mathematics
F: Teams of eight to ten facing each other
E: Cards with numbers on them
D: Each child receives a card with a number from 0 - 9 on it. The teacher then calls two factors such as 3 and 7. The children with the correct card (2 and 1) move quickly to a predetermined area and place the numbers down. First team to get the answer down correctly is the winner. The teacher can also call out a product such as 18 and the children must place down two correct factors such as 3 and 6 or 2 and 9.

N: Paper Plate Math - Game
DA: 6 to 9
DV: Mathematics
F: Free
E: Paper plates with numbers on them
D: Each child receives a paper plate with a number on it. The same number will appear on two plates. Children place the plates on the floor in a free formation. The leader tells the children to move (i.e., walk backward, run heavy, etc.) around the plates. On the stop signal, children quickly stand beside a plate. The leader calls out a math problem, the solution will appear on two of the plates. The first child to squat down next to the correct answer is the next leader.

N: Hoop Group - Activity
DA: 5 to 6
DV: Mathematics
F: Free
E: Hoops, number determined by size of class
D: Hoops are randomly placed around the play area. Children move to music among the hoops. The teacher will then hold up a number no larger than six. As soon as the music stops, children quickly group themselves according to the size of the number inside the hoops. Both feet must be inside the hoop. Those left

over are designated as the remainder. The teacher can then discuss groupings and remainders.

N: Shapes - Activity
DA: 5
DV: Learning geometric shapes
F: Free
E: Cut-out shapes, one per child
D: Each child is given a geometric shape, circle, square, triangle, or rectangle. A hoop is placed in each corner of the play area and is designated as one of the four shapes by placing that shape in the middle of the hoop. Children then begin to move around the play area using a locomotor movement specified by the teacher. The teacher then calls out something which is represented by the shape the children have been given, i.e., a polka dot, a roof top, the sun, etc. Children who have the shape go to the appropriate corner using the designated locomotor skill and drop their shape in the hoop. The teacher checks for correctness. The children then pick up their shapes and go again. Shapes can be exchanged during the activity. There are no winners or losers in this activity.

N: Body Math - Activity
DA: 8 to 9
DV: Mathematics
F: Groups-size determined by the math problems to be presented
E: None
D: A math problem is called out by the teacher. Each group must form the problem including the answer using their bodies. The first one to complete the problem correctly is the winner. The teacher may give the problem such as 5 + 7 and the children would have to form the 5, the plus sign, the 7, the equals sign, followed by the answer; or the answer could be given, and the children could create the other side of the equation.

N: The Multiples - Game
DA: 8 to 9
DV: Mathematics
F: Two lines standing side by side
E: None

D: Children stand in a Crows and Cranes formation with two teams standing side by side, each has a safe base area marked by a line beside them. Each group is given a number, i.e., one group could be seven and the other five. The teacher then calls out a number which may or may not be a multiple of 7 or 5. If it is, the group which is the multiple must run to their safe base while the other group chases and tries to tag them. If tagged, the player must switch teams. Anyone who runs when the number is not a multiple of either number must switch teams. The assigned numbers can be changed during the game and the numbers given should be based upon the ability of the students.

N: Make a Number - Activity
DA: 5
DV: Forming number sets
F: Free
E: Numbers on flash cards
D: The teacher holds up a number which the children call out. Then they run to form a set of the number with other children by joining hands, feet, legs, arms, or any body part with others. If there are any extra children they are called the remainder.

N: Math Cake Walk - Activity
DA: 8 to 10
DV: Reinforce simple math facts
F: Circle
E: Paper plates, record player, and record
D: Prepare two sets of paper plates. In each set the plates are numbered 0 - 10 in large, bold numerals. If there are more than twenty-two students, prepare a third set of numbered plates. Place the plates randomly (not in numerical order) around a circle. Each child stands to the outside of a plate and the teacher starts the music. When the music plays, the children move (skip, walk, run, jump, etc.) around the circle. When the music stops, the children stand next to a numbered plate. The leader reads an equation to the class, two children will be next to plates with the right answer. The first child with the correct plate to sit down will get to be the leader next.

Plates can be lettered, and words read. Children sit if the word starts with their letter.

N: Products and Factors - Activity
DA: 8 to 10
DV: Movement and mathematics
F: Two teams on lines (six feet apart) facing each other
E: Flash cards, carpet squares (2)
D: Divide class into two teams. Place a carpet square for each team in center of game area. Teacher makes *two sets* of flash cards (red, blue) and gives one or more cards to each player (red for one team, blue for the other). Each card has one digit (from 0 to 9). The teacher calls two factors. (Example: 7 and 3). Children think of the product (21) and those holding cards 2 and 1 (correct response) run to the carpet square and place their answer. The team with the first correct answer scores one point. (Winners-first team to get five points).

The teacher may call a product and children respond with two factors (There may be more than one correct answer).
Example: Product = 18
Factors = 6, 3; 2, 9
First correct response gets one point for team.

N: Hoop Groups - Activity
DA: 5 to 8
DV: To be able to recognize and form groups for 1, 2, 3, or 4
F: Free
E: Hula-Hoops, record player, 1-2-3-4 signs, record
D: Randomly place Hula-Hoops around play area. The number of hoops will depend on your class size remembering that the maximum number of children that will beariybd a hoop will be four and the minimum will be one. Children will walk around the area while music is playing. The teacher will hold up a number sign. When the music is stopped, children will walk quickly to a hoop and using only one foot will form a group or set of that number. If number 3 is being held up, three children will each have a single foot in the hoop forming a set of three. They will be able to immediately tell if they are cor-

rect by observing the others, listening to teacher's praise for being correct, or help from their classmates to get into a correct group. On numbers where there will be a "leftover" child, that child can be a "helper" by holding up a number sign or stopping and starting the music. The helpers will then join the game again on the next turn.

Modifications may be added as children become involved with higher numbers by adding more cards.

N: Dribble Math - Activity
DA: 6 to 8
DV: Math ability
F: Free
E: Each child has a ball that bounces
D: A flash card is held up with an equation on it. The child must then dribble the ball the correct number of times to equal the correct answer.

Science

N: Simon Says Globe - Game
DA: 9 and older
DV: World Geography
F: Free
E: Have a large globe handy
D: Each child envisions him/herself as a globe of the world. Playing by the rules of Simon Says, children are asked to touch the equator (the waist), the North Pole (top of the head), and North America (the chest). With these reference points established, ask children to touch other spots. Children who touch parts when Simon does not say to do so get one point or those who touch the wrong spot get one point. Those with the least points are the winners. Children can work in pairs to keep track of each other's points.

N: Weather Vane - Game
DA: 8 and older
DV: Compass direction
F: Free
E: None
D: After children are oriented to the basic compass directions, the leader calls out various directions, i.e., North, South, etc. Children must then jump (using both feet simultaneously) and turn in the appropri-

ate direction. Anyone caught turning the wrong direction gets a point. For older children directions such as Northeast, South, Southwest, etc., could be called out.

N: Solar System - Activity
DA: 6 to 8
DV: Learning the solar system
F: Groups of nine
E: One playground ball for each group
D: Using the ball as the sun, the students take the position of the nine known planets (if there are extra children, two children can be one planet) and orbit around the sun. Children should turn on their orbit as they revolve around the sun. Variations could be to have more in a group and take the position of moons around certain planets such as the Earth or Jupiter. Other things which could be emphasized would be the elliptical nature of most orbits.

N: Muscle Show - Activity
DA: 10 to 12
DV: Knowledge of the body
F: Free
E: Flash cards with names of muscles

D: When the flash card with a muscle name on it is shown, the class must do a movement using that muscle.

N: Electric Shock - Game
DA: 7 and older
DV: Knowledge of electricity
F: Two equal teams holding hands and connected by a leader
E: None
D: The leader holds one hand of the end child on each team. Team members also are holding hands. The leader simultaneously squeezes both hands to start the electricity flowing. The squeeze is then passed on until it reaches the end. When the end child receives the electricity, he/she quickly raises his/her hand. The first team to get the hand raised gets a point. The leader can fake a signal by saying, "Here it comes." If the team raises their hand on a fake signal, it counts two points against them. The teacher can emphasize such things as broken circuits and short circuits when signals get confused.

N: States - Activity
DA: 8 to 10
DV: Social Studies: Geography

Electric Shock

F: Two teams facing each other

E: None

D: One team decides on a state. They advance toward the other saying, "We are a state as you will see; Guess which one then catch me." The children then act out some activity which will help the other team identify the state. The other team tries to guess which state. If someone calls out the state, the team which has been doing the acting runs back toward their safe base while the other team chases and tries to tag them. Anyone tagged must switch teams. The other team then does the acting. Children can all act out some prearranged activity or each child can think up their own idea (the latter is more creative).

N: Animal Environment - Game

DA: 8 to 10

DV: Science: Knowledge of water and land animals

F: Two teams side by side

E: None

D: Children are on two teams standing side by side each with a safe base marked with a line beside them. The children are designated as land or water. The teacher calls out an animal. If the animal lives on land, the land people run and the water people chase and try to tag them. Anyone tagged must switch teams. If the animal lives in the water, the water team runs and the land people chase.

N: Trades - Game

DA: 6 to 8

DV: Creativity, learning about jobs in the community, chasing, and tagging

F: Class divided in half

E: None

D: One-half the class decides in secret what trade (occupation) they would like to imitate. All players must imitate the same occupation. After deciding, they walk in a line side by side across the play area saying, "Here we come." The other half of the class they are walking toward asks, "Where from?" While still advancing forward, the first group responds, "New York" (or the children's home town). The other group then asks, "What is your trade?", which is answered by

"Lemonade." By this time the moving group should be within about five or six feet of the other group, which says finally, "Show us." With that, each person begins imitating (no sound) the trade. Children from the other group raise their hands and, when called upon, guess. If they guess the correct occupation the imitation group turns and runs toward safe base while being chased by the other group. Anyone caught joins the chasing group, which then gets the chance to do the imitating. The game continues for a set period of time with winners being the biggest group and those not tagged at all during the game.

N: Explorers - Game

DA: 6 to 8

DV: Creativity, social interaction, learning about different modes of transportation

F: Free

E: None

D: Briefly discuss different ways to travel on land, in water, and in air. Have children be explorers and choose a way to travel. When the teacher gives the signal, children move around at random imitating their mode of transportation. The teacher calls out, "Explorers unite." Children then move to form small circles of three explorers—one for land, one for water, and one for air. Explorers left over have one point. Those with the least number of points are winners.

N: Famous People - Activity

DA: 9 to 12

DV: Creativity, social interaction, and knowledge of famous people

F: Free

E: Paper, markers, and clip type clothes pins

D: Children secretly write the name of a famous person on a piece of paper. The name can be drawn from the child's own experience, or the teacher can have a theme, or even make the names up rather than having the children do it. After the papers are ready, each child pins one of them on another child without letting that child see the name. Children then pair up and one tries to help the other guess the name on his/her back by using movement only, no sounds. As the children guess his/her name correctly, he/she attempts to help their partner guess. When both have guessed their names, they go to other couples and help them. At times there may be many people in front of one child trying to help through creative movement.If a child is having particular difficulty, he/she can ask yes and no questions of the persons doing the imitations.

Appendices

Appendix A
Evaluating Fitness

The V.C.U. Fitness Test

For Whom: Children six to twelve years of age.

Norms: Norms are available for most test items, although more norms are needed for younger children. The test items are just as useful without such norms, however, since norms can be determined from data at individual schools or within a school system.

Ease: The test items are easy to administer and data is simple to interpret.

Validity: Each item has a validity of .90 or above unless otherwise specified.

Reliability: Reliabilities of .90 or above unless otherwise specified.

Objectivity: All test have an objectivity of .90 or above.

Time: The entire test should not take more than one hour to administer.

Flexed arm hang

Test Item 1: Flexed Arm Hang

Component: Upper body strength and endurance.

Equipments: Stopwatch and a horizontal metal or wooden bar approximately 1 1/2 inches in diameter placed high enough for a student to maintain the flexed arm hang position with the chin over the bar and the legs fully extended.

Procedure: Child is lifted to the flexed arm position. As soon as the support is removed, a stopwatch is started. The amount of time the child can maintain his or her chin over the bar is recorded. As soon as the chin drops below the bar, or touches the bar, the watch is stopped.

Scoring: The number of seconds the child held his or her chin over the bar is recorded.

Norms: Flexed Arm Hang (Girls 10-12)

		(In Seconds)	
Age—	10	11	12
Rating			
Excellent	31	35	30
Good	18	17	15
Average	10	10	8
Poor	6	5	5

Flexed Arm Hang (Girls & Boys 6-9)

		(In Seconds)		
Age—	6	7	8	9
Rating				
Excellent	30	45	55	60
Good	20	24	30	40
Average	9	12	13	14
Poor	2	5	7	7

Flexed arm hang indoors using parallel bars

Test Item 2: Sit-Ups

Component: Abdominal strength.

Equipment: A stopwatch and mats for testing indoors (Mats not needed if grass is available for outside testing).

Procedure: Children should be paired with one holding the other's feet. The child being tested lies on his back with knees

Sit-ups

Ready to run

bent so heels are six to eight inches from the buttocks. Arms are folded across the chest opposite hand to shoulder. The holder applies pressure to the other child's feet only. When the go signal is given, the child sits up, keeping the arms across the chest at all times.

Scoring: One point is given for each sit-up completed during a 60-second time period. A child in the up position when time is called gets credits for a completed sit-up.

Norms: Sixty-Second Sit-up Test - Boys

Age Rating	5	6	7	8	9	10	11
Excellent	30	35	40	45	48	50	51
Good	23	25	32	37	38	40	42
Average	18	20	25	30	32	34	37
Poor	11	15	20	25	27	29	31

Norms: Sixty-Second Sit-up Test - Girls

Rating	5	6	7	8	9	10	11
Excellent	28	35	40	43	44	47	50
Good	25	28	30	35	37	39	40
Average	20	22	25	30	31	32	35
Poor	12	15	20	22	23	25	28

Test Item 3: Timed Runs

Component: Cardiovascular efficiency

Equipment: a 100-meter tape, a stopwatch, numbered pinnies (about 10 with numbers on both sides), and ten clip-type clothespins.

Procedures for a mile run: if the mile run is selected, children are paired with one child running first and the other counting laps and listening for the finish time. For this test it is best to mark off a quarter mile oval or some distance which will allow for the start and finish to be at the same place. Space restrictions may necessitate making a tenth of a mile oval and have the children go around ten times. The more times they have to go around, however, the more chance there is for error when children are counting the laps. To avoid this problem you can use the numbered pinnies and check sheet to record each person's laps.

Procedures: a 100-meter tape is placed on the grass in an oval resembling a one-forth mile track (it should be oval to reduce the sharpness of the turns). Each child is assigned a numbered pinnie and a numbered clip-type clothespin corresponding to the pinnie number. The clothespin can be clipped to the pinnie during the run. A form such as the one in figure A-1 is used for recording. Ten students can be tested simultaneously by one tester who records the number of times each child crosses the start/finish line. Children ages six to nine run as far as they can in six minutes, while children ages ten to twelve run for nine minutes. At the end of the time, a whistle is blown and the children stop immediately and clip their clothespin on the tape. This is followed by a cool down period consisting of walking. An alternative test procedure is to pair the children with one recording laps, while the other runs (this works only with 4-6 graders). Older children (fifth or sixth graders) can test the younger children using this pairing system.

Scoring: scores are recorded to the nearest meter with a total determined by multiplying the number of laps by 100 and adding the nearest meter to where the child's pin was placed (remember, it has the same number as the pinnie) to get the total, i.e., Jimmy (#10) crossed the start/finish line 17 times giving him a score of 1700 meters; his pin was clipped closest to 27 meters, so his total run was 1727 meters.

Norms: Mile Run - Boys

Age Rating	5	6	7	8	9	10	11
Excellent	900	905	800	755	715	655	650
Good	1130	1055	935	915	835	810	800
Average	1345	1230	1125	1100	955	920	905
Poor	1605	1510	1400	1330	1200	1105	1130

Norms: Mile Run - Girls

Age Rating	5	6	7	8	9	10	11
Excellent	945	915	850	845	715	800	745
Good	1310	1125	1055	1035	1000	930	915
Average	1510	1350	1230	1200	1115	1105	1025
Poor	1800	1525	1430	1415	1320	1255	1210

Norms: Nine Minute Run - Boys

Age Rating	5	6	7	8	9	10	11
Excellent	1750	1740	2020	2200	2175	2250	2300
Good	1320	1470	1685	1810	1840	1910	1925
Average	1170	1280	1440	1600	1660	1700	1725
Poor	990	1100	1250	1380	1450	1490	1550

Norms: Nine Minute Run - Girls

Age Rating	5	6	7	8	9	10	11
Excellent	1550	1700	1900	1850	2050	2070	2100
Good	1300	1450	1550	1560	1650	1660	1725
Average	1140	1210	1350	1360	1425	1460	1480
Poor	950	1020	1200	1225	1250	1260	1350

Figure A-1
Scoring Sheet for Timed Distance Run

Test Item 4: Skinfold Measurement

Component: Body Composition as determined by percent of body fat.

Equipment: A skinfold caliper (an excellent and inexpensive, $10, plastic caliper is available from Ross Laboratories in Columbus, Ohio).

Procedure: This is a one site measurement test using the skinfold at the back of the arm (tricep area). Locate a point midway between the elbow and shoulder joints. Using the thumb and first finger of the left hand, gather all the skin on the back of the arm making sure the muscle is not included. With a little practice, it is obvious when the muscle is eliminated from the process. Keeping the fingers in place until the testing is complete, place the caliper on the middle of the skinfold immediately below the pinching fingers. Read the number of millimeters of skinfold from the instrument. Important - do not remove the pinching fingers until after the reading has been made.

Scoring: Results are recorded in millimeters.

Norms: See Figure A-2 and A-3.

Figure A-2
Tricep Skinfold of Children by Sex and Age

Sex and age	Mean	Standard Deviation	Percentile						
			5th	10th	25th	50th	75th	90th	95th
			In Millimeters						
Boys, 6-11 yrs	9.4	4.28	5.0	5.5	7.0	8.0	11.0	15.0	18.0
6 years	8.1	2.79	5.0	5.0	6.0	8.0	9.0	12.0	13.0
7 years	8.4	3.17	4.5	5.0	6.0	8.0	9.5	12.0	14.0
8 years	9.0	3.77	4.5	5.0	6.5	8.0	11.0	13.5	17.0
9 years	10.0	4.96	5.0	6.0	7.0	8.5	12.0	16.0	20.0
10 years	10.1	4.43	5.0	6.0	7.0	9.0	12.0	16.0	20.0
11 years	11.0	5.32	5.0	6.0	7.0	9.5	14.0	19.0	22.0
Girls, 6-11 yrs	11.5	4.61	6.0	7.0	8.0	10.0	14.0	18.0	21.0
6 years	9.7	3.39	5.5	6.0	7.0	9.0	11.0	14.0	16.0
7 years	10.4	3.61	6.0	6.5	8.0	10.0	12.0	16.0	17.0
8 years	11.4	4.43	6.0	6.5	8.0	10.5	13.5	18.0	20.0
9 years	12.3	4.84	6.0	7.0	9.0	11.0	14.5	19.0	22.0
10 years	12.6	5.12	6.0	7.0	9.0	12.0	15.0	20.0	23.0
11 years	12.6	5.19	6.0	7.0	9.0	12.0	15.0	20.0	23.0

Figure A-3
Skinfold Measures for Obesity*

Age	Tricep Skinfold Thickness Indicating Obesity (In Millimeters)	
	Males	_Females_
5	12	14
6	12	15
7	13	16
8	14	17
9	15	18
10	16	20
11	17	21
12	18	22

*Caucasian Americans

Reference: _Health Related Fitness Manual._ Reston. AAHPERD

Tricep Skinfold of Children by Race, Sex, and Age

Race, Sex, and Age	Mean	Standard Deviation	Percentile						
			5th	10th	25th	50th	75th	90th	95th
			In Millimeters						
WHITE Boys, 6-11 yrs.	9.8	4.33	5.0	6.0	7.0	8.5	11.0	15.5	19.0
6 years	8.3	2.82	5.0	6.0	6.5	8.0	9.5	12.0	13.0
7 years	8.7	3.20	5.0	6.0	7.0	8.0	10.0	12.0	14.5
8 years	9.3	3.80	5.0	6.0	7.0	8.0	11.0	14.0	17.0
9 years	10.4	5.06	5.0	6.0	7.0	9.0	12.0	17.0	21.0
10 years	10.5	4.41	5.5	6.0	7.5	9.5	13.0	16.0	20.0
11 years	11.5	5.32	5.5	6.0	8.0	10.0	14.0	19.0	22.0
Girls, 6-11 yrs.	11.8	4.55	6.0	7.0	8.5	11.0	14.0	18.0	21.0
6 years	10.0	3.39	6.0	6.5	8.0	10.0	11.0	14.0	16.0
7 years	10.8	3.47	6.5	7.0	8.0	10.0	12.5	16.0	18.0
8 years	11.7	4.34	6.0	7.0	9.0	11.0	14.0	18.0	20.0
9 years	12.7	4.83	7.0	8.0	9.0	11.5	15.0	20.0	22.5
10 years	13.0	5.08	6.0	7.0	9.0	12.0	16.0	20.0	23.0
11 years	12.9	5.07	7.0	7.5	9.0	12.0	16.0	20.1	22.0
BLACK Boys, 6-11 yrs.	7.2	3.13	4.0	4.0	5.0	6.5	8.0	11.0	13.0
6 years	7.0	2.25	4.0	5.0	5.5	7.0	8.0	10.0	11.0
7 years	6.4	2.14	4.0	4.0	5.0	6.0	7.0	9.0	10.0
8 years	7.1	2.98	4.0	4.0	5.0	6.5	8.0	12.0	13.0
9 years	7.2	2.99	4.0	4.0	5.0	6.5	8.0	11.0	14.0
10 years	7.6	3.49	4.0	4.0	5.5	7.0	9.0	11.0	13.0
11 years	8.1	4.32	4.0	4.0	6.0	7.0	9.0	12.0	18.0
Girls, 6-11 yrs.	9.5	4.50	5.0	5.5	6.5	8.0	11.0	15.0	20.0
6 years	7.9	2.84	5.0	5.0	6.0	7.0	9.0	11.0	14.0
7 years	8.3	3.68	5.0	5.0	6.0	7.0	9.0	12.0	16.0
8 years	9.6	4.59	5.0	5.0	6.5	8.0	11.0	14.0	20.0
9 years	10.2	4.45	5.0	6.0	7.0	9.0	12.5	15.5	19.0
10 years	10.3	4.74	5.0	6.0	7.0	9.0	12.0	20.0	20.2
11 years	10.9	5.58	4.0	6.0	7.0	10.0	12.0	20.0	25.0

Test Item 5: Sit and Reach Test

Component: Flexibility of back and hamstring muscles.

Equipment: Millimeter measuring stick and tape.

Procedures: Millimeter measuring stick is taped to the floor and the child sits so the 23 cm mark on the stick is even with the heels. The child then bends forward and touches the stick as far down toward or beyond his or her feet as possible. The child's score is recorded to the closest centimeter that he or she was able to reach and hold for one second.

Norms: Sit and Reach Test (in centimeters) - Boys

Age Rating	5	6	7	8	9	10	11
Excellent	32	35	34	34	33	33	34
Good	29	29	28	29	29	28	29
Average	25	26	25	25	25	25	25
Poor	22	22	22	22	22	20	21

Norms: Sit and Reach (in centimeters) - Girls

Age Rating	5	6	7	8	9	10	11
Excellent	34	34	34	36	35	35	37
Good	30	30	31	31	31	32	34
Average	27	27	27	28	28	28	29
Poor	23	23	24	23	23	24	24

Sit and Reach Test

Figure A-4
Physical Fitness Report Card

Text Explanations: The physical fitness test components included here are those directly related to the health of your child. Most fitness tests emphasize motor fitness components such as speed, agility, power, etc., which have little relationship to a child's well being. The data from this test should aid you in evaluating our child's health needs. A brief explanation of the test items follows:

1. Running. The child tries to see how far he or she can run in a given time, six minutes for grades 1-3 and nine minutes for grades 4-6. The test is used to estimate cardiovascular efficiency which is considered to be the most important fitness component.

2. Sit-ups. This test is used to measure abdominal strength and endurance. The child lies on his or her back with the knees bent and hands behind the head. The number of sit-ups which can be completed in 60 seconds is recorded.

3. Percentage of Body Fat. This test is used to estimate the child's percentage of body fat. Since excess fat is considered a health hazard, maintenance of a low percentage is desirable. The estimate is made by measuring the skinfold at the back of the arm.

4. Bar Hang. This test is used to measure upper body strength and endurance. The child is lifted into a flexed arm position (pull-up) with the chin over a horizontal bar. Upon being released, the child tries to keep the chin over the bar as long as possible. The time is recorded in seconds.

5. Sit and Reach Test. This test is used to determine the flexibility of the back and hamstring (back of the leg) muscles. The child is asked to sit on the floor and reach as far as possible toward or beyond his feet if possible. Scores are recorded in centimeters.

Score interpretation: Three pieces of information are recorded on the following pages: (1) your child's raw score, (2) the percentile rank of that score, and (3) a classification of your child based on his or her performance.

The percentile rank is based on your child's score compared with other children his or her age at (name of school) or with national norms. National norms are available for percentage of body fat, bar hang for girls ten years of age and older, the nine-minute run for boys and girls, and sit-ups for boys and girls ten years of age and above. All other percentiles are comparison of (name of school) children only. A percentile rank of 63, for example, means your child scored better than 62 percent of the children taking the test.

The four-point classification system is: 1 = Excellent, 2 = Good, 3 = Average, 4 = Needs Improvement. The rating are for information only, not as a means of grading students.

The main concern is to see improvement, so fall and spring scores will be color-coded and placed on the same chart for easy comparison. Fall scores will be in blue and spring in red. The test will be given at the beginning and end of the school year.

Test Data

Fall Test Date _____ (Blue)   Spring Test Date _____ (Red)

Percentiles

| | Abdominal Strength | % of Body Fat | Upper Body Strength | Cardiovascular Efficiency | Flexibility |

|||||||

Percentiles chart from 0 to 100, columns: Abdominal Strength, % of Body Fat, Upper Body Strength, Cardiovascular Efficiency, Flexibility

	Sit-ups (Abdominal Str.)		*Percent of Body Fat*	
	Fall	Spring	Fall	Spring
Your child's score				
Percentile rank				
Classification				

	Bar Hang (Upper Body Str.)		*Running (Cardiovascular Eff.)*	
	Fall	Spring	Fall	Spring
Your child's score				
Percentile rank				
Classification				

	Flexibility	
	Fall	Spring
Your child's score		
Percentile rank		
Classification		

Appendix B
Evaluation Insturments for the Affective Domain

Figure B-1
Attitude Questionaire for Kindergarten and First Grade

Instructions

Have the children place an X on the face which best reflects their feelings regarding the various statements. The three faces on the answer sheet should be randomly placed for each question. The question mark face should be X'ed if a child does not understand the question.

Most children follow using the numbers to the left of each of the faces, but familiar objects may be used (book, tree, spoon) in place of numbers for non-readers.

Practice: Check childrens answers to be sure they understand.

______a. When I get ice cream, I am .....

______b. When I hurt myself, I am .....

Questions

______1. When I know we are going to physical education, I am .....

______2. When (teacher's name) is not in school, I am .....

______3. When we dance, I am .....

______4. When we tumble, I am .....

______5. When we have to play wth partners, I am .....

______6. When (teacher's name) gets mad, I am .....

______7. When I have to sit out of an activity, I am .....

Kindergarten Questionnaire Answer Sheet

Key

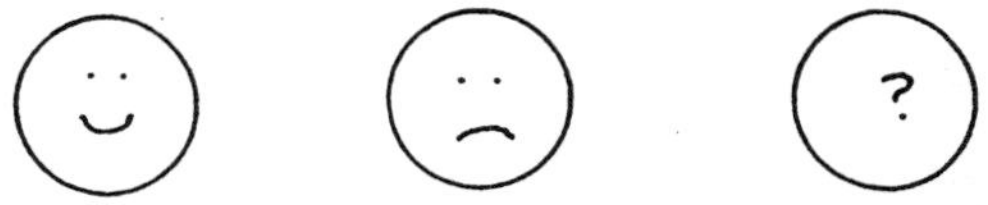

Happy Sad Do not understand

Practice

a.
b.

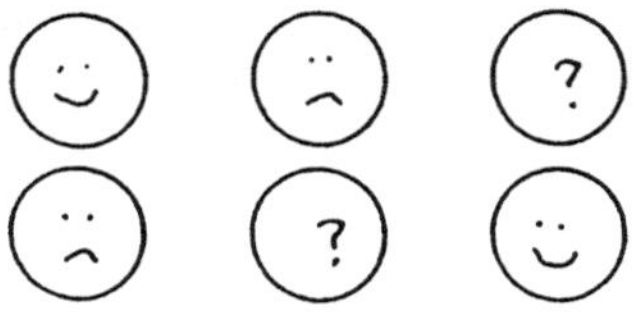

Statements

1.
2.
3.
4.
5.
6.
7.

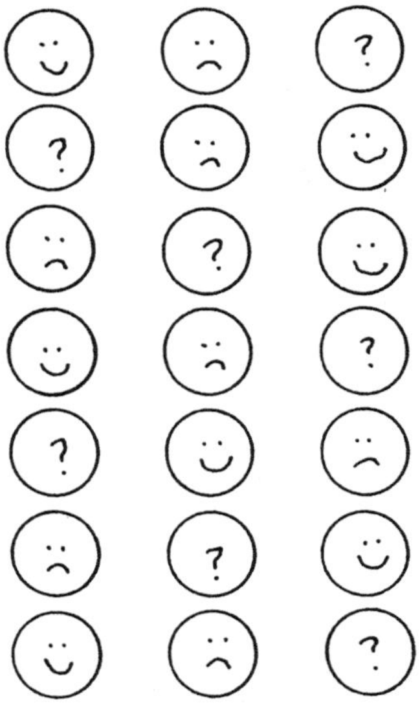

Figure B-2
Attitude Questionnaire for Seven- to Nine-Year-Old Children

This questionnaire will help me design a better physical education program for you. Please, do not put your name on the questionnarie.

Section One

Instructions. Look at the scale below and and place the number corresponding to the word or phrase which best indicates your feelings about the statement. Place the number on the line to the left of each statement.

Scale

1. Agree
2. Disagree
0. No not understant statement

Examples:

_____ a. Ice cream tastes good.
_____ b. I like to fall down and hurt my knees.

Statements

_____ 1. Physical education is fun.
_____ 2. (Teacher's name) likes me.
_____ 3. I do not like physical education.
_____ 4. I like to dance in physical education.
_____ 5. (Teacher's name) makes me feel good.
_____ 6. I like to do things with a partner,

_____ 7. (Teacher's name) praises me when I do well.
_____ 8. I do not like tumbling and gymnastics.
_____ 9. (Teacher's name) gets mad too easily.
_____ 10. I do exercises at home.
_____ 11. I like (teacher's name).

Section Two

1. My favorite activity is _____

2. My least favorite activity is _____

3. The game I like to play the most is _____

Figure B-3
Attitude Questionnaire for Ten- and Eleven-Year-Old Children

This questionnaire will help me design a better physical education program for you. Please, do not put your name on the questionnarie.

Section One

Instructions. Look at the scale below and and place the number corresponding to the word or phrase which best indicates your feelings about the statement. Place the number on the line to the left of each statement.

Scale
1. Strongly agree
2. Agree
3. Disagree
4. Strongly disagree
0. No not understant statement

Examples:

_____ a. Ice cream tastes good.

_____ b. I would like to fall and break my leg

Statements

_____ 1. Physical education is an important part of the curric ulum.

_____ 2. (Teacher's name) likes me.

_____ 3. We do too many exercises in physical education.

_____ 4. I do a lot of physial fitness activities at home.

_____ 5. I enjoy working in groups during physical education.

_____ 6. I like to dance in physical education.

_____ 7. (Teacher's name) yells too much.

_____ 8. (Teacher's name) has embarrassed me in class.

_____ 9, Physical education should be voluntary.

_____ 10. (Teacher's name) does not give me much attention in class.

_____ 11. I do not learn much in physical education.

_____ 12. (Teacher's name) praises me in physical education.

_____ 13. Playing on a team is fun.

_____ 14. (Teacher's name) is fair with everyone.

Section Two

Give a one (1) to the activity you like the most, a two (2) to your next favorite activity, and so on until you have given a number to each activity

_____ Football

_____ Dance

_____ Track & Field

_____ Softball

_____ Small group activities

_____ Tennis

_____ Basketball

_____ Fitness Activities

_____ Hockey

_____ Volleyball

_____ Rhythmics

_____ Gymnastics

_____ Tumbling

Section Three

Respond to the following question in the space provided or use the back of your paper.

1. What do you like most about (teacher's name)?

2. What could (teacher's name) do to be a better teacher?

3. What would be a way to improve the physical education program?

419

Appendix C
Running for Life: Integrating Fitness with the Classroom

Running For Life is a fitness program that combines exercise with topics like geography, language arts, and history, and is easily integrated into school curricula that emphasize these programs. It is particularly suited to the flexible schedule of most elementary school programs. In addition to its fitness and academic value, *Running for Life* is easy to organize and administer. Although the program is coordinated by one individual, daily team activities are led by the classroom teachers. It can be undertaken by a single classroom, a combination of classrooms, or an entire student body, with any combination of grade levels. Once organized, the program may be implemented at anytime during the year but is possibly most enjoyable in the spring and toward the end of the academic year, perhaps culminating in a field day. At this time, children are eager to be outside and may have more stamina than during winter months.

Running for Life begins with the selection of an academic theme that features geography together with relevant cultures and history, if appropriate. Once a theme is selected, a large map depicting the geographical area involved and the route to be "followed" by students is posted in a conspicuous, centrally-located area of the school. Next, the number of teams is determined (for ease of administration, a maximum of four teams is recommended) each is identified by name. For example, if the United States is selected as the geographic area for study, a large map of the U.S. is posted and teams might be designated Red, White, and Blue. A broader study of the world would feature a world map and teams might be named for continents or oceans. Each participating classroom is divided equally by the number of teams selected and names of team members are recorded on the *Running For Life* recording sheet.

The exercise featured in *Running for Life* is running, measured in laps, which is translated into distance along the route previously determined and depicted on the school's large, posted map. Team laps are counted weekly and each team's progress is marked along the route using Pins and color-coded chart tape. As students move toward the final destination, classrooms study the geography, people, culture, and history they might encounter along the way. To maintain interest and momentum ,the program should not exceed eight weeks.

Nuts and Bolts

Exercise. Once *Running for Life* is organized, classrooms begin by running three times a week (Mondays, Wednesdays, and Fridays) around an oval track of approximately 200 meters (can be shorter for younger children). The number of laps completed by each student is confirmed by handing runners a lollipop stick or tongue depressor each time they pass the start/finish line. These are counted by the classroom teacher at the end of each exercise session and recorded on the *Running for Life* worksheet. Each Friday, worksheets are submitted to the program administrator (usually the physical educator) who calculates the number of laps completed by each team, converts them to distance "traveled" along the previously identified course, and marks each team's progress on the posted map using pins and colored chart tape.

In order to determine the desired weekly location of each team, the *Running for Life* program coordinator divides the total trip distance by eight (the maximum number of weeks recommended) and places the week's leading team at that point. Second-, third-, and fourth-place teams are placed at locations along the marked route ,reflecting their weekly performance in relation to the leading team. Although the weekly location may be somewhat arbitrary, it is important for illustrating team performance and ensuring successful completion of the course. Let us say, for example, that the Red Team ran a total of 350 laps in week one, while the White Team ran 300 laps and the Blue Team ran 250 laps. The Red Team's pin would be placed at the desired point for the end of week one with pins fore the White Team and Blue Team showing their corresponding positions. Laps completed during the second week (and so on through week eight) are added to the previous week's total, and pins (and chart tape) are adjusted weekly.

Classroom Learning. As they "travel" along the route established and marked on the school map, classrooms may examine the topography, weather, people, and history of the areas through which they travel. Students may be encouraged to use the internet to discover and present information they learn along the way, and possibly to meet e-mail correspondents with whom they can discuss their journey. Any attempt by students to visit web sites or establish e-mail communications, of course, must be strictly monitored by a supervising adult. Teachers may also provide photographs and personal descriptions of places they have visited.

Suggested Geographic arrangements

Running for Life: Around the World. Here, each classroom is divided into four teams, each named for one of the seven continents. The "trip" begins in home state, and must include travel through each of the continents. In determining the route, teachers can be consulted as to places they wanted their class to visit. All teams, of course, must travel the same route. Other considerations about places to visit include current events as well as historic areas. The children travel around the world, returning to their point of origin.

Running for Life: A Capital Idea! The Red, White, and Blue teams begin in their state capital, and travel in a circular route passing through every capital of the U.S.

Running for Life: Discovering (name of state here). Children travel throughout their state, usually in a circular route, stopping at historically significant locations as well as significant geographic areas while covering the entire state.

Running for Life: Exploring (city/town/county name here). This program presents the opportunity for students to learn about the history surrounding them in their hometown. Teams representing North, South, East, and West study the geography and history of their city/town/county.

A Suggested Historical Arrangement

Running for Life: The Lewis and Clark Expedition. Teams representing names associated with the Lewis and Clark expedition follow the historic route in search of the Northwest passage while mapping the Louisiana Purchase.

Running for Life: The Lewis and Clark Expedition
Teacher_____ Date _____

Lewis	Monday	Wednesday	Friday	Individual Total	
					TeamTotal

Clark	Monday	Wednesday	Friday	Individual Total	
					Team Total

Sacagwea	Monday	Wednesday	Friday	Individual Total	
					Team Total

422

Appendix D
Resources

AAHPERD Publications   Physical Best
P.O. Box 704   Education Program
Waldorf, MD 20604 PB 89
http://www.aahperd.org/

Educational Activities, Inc.   Records
Freeport, NY 11520
http://www.edact.com/

Flaghouse   Equipment
150 N. MacQuestern Parkway
Mt. Vernon, NY 10550-9989
http://www.flaghouse.com/

Kimbo Records   Records
Box 246
Deal, NJ 00723

Snitz Manufacturing   Equipment
2096 S. ChurchStreet
East Troy, WI 53120

Sportime   Equipment
2905 E. Amwiler Road
Atlanta, GA 30360
http://www.sportime.com/

Things from Bell   Equipment
230 Mechanic Street
P.O. Box 206
Princeton, WI 54968

Wolverine Sports   Equipment
745 State Circle
Box 1941
Ann Arbor, MN 48106
http://www.wolverinesports.com/

World of Fun Series   Records
Melody House Publishing Co.
819 N.W. 92nd Street
Oklahoma City, OK 73114

U.S. Games, Inc.   Equipment
Box 117028
Melbourne, FL 32936

Laboratories

CONTENTS

LABORATORY 1.1

Accomplishing Physical Education Goals

Purpose: To develop a list of activities designed to help accomplish physical education goals.

Size of Group: Three or four

1. Each group selects a domain from Figure 1.2 being sure that all three domains are covered.
2. Using activities from this text or from their memory, each group lists at least two activities for each subdivision under the domain selected. These activities, when conducted, should help develop the area in question.
3. The class then comes together to develop a master list for each subdivision. This master list should include the page number from this text or, if it is not in the text, a short description of the activity.

DOMAIN _____

    Activity 1 _____

    Activity 2 _____

MASTER LIST

Domain	Activities
Psychomotor	_____
	_____
	_____
	_____
Affective	_____
	_____
	_____
	_____
Cognitive	_____
	_____
	_____
	_____

LABORATORY 1.2

Developing a Child's Self-Concept

Purpose: To determine teacher behaviors which foster or hinder the development of a child's positive self-concept.

Size of Group: Three or four

1. Each group develops a list of positive and negative teacher behaviors which influence a child's self-concept.

2. Each group then shares its list, and a master list is developed.

Positive Teacher Behavior	Negative Teacher Behavior

LABORATORY 2.1

Age Group Characteristics

Purpose: To better understand the growth and development characteristics of children.

Size of Group: Alone

1. Observe a child in a play setting, and write a report detailing the behaviors you observed which fit those described in this text.

2. In your report, have a separate section covering other behaviors you feel may be typical of this age group.

Time and date of observation _____

Place of observation _____

Age of child _____

Activity observed _____

Behaviors observed _____

_____

_____

_____

_____

_____

_____

_____

_____

_____

_____

_____

_____

_____

_____

_____

_____

_____

_____

_____

_____

_____

LABORATORY 2.2

Characteristics and Their Implications

Purpose: To determine how a characteristic influences teaching and/or learning.

Size of Group: Alone

1. Select one of the four age groups from the chapter.

2. Give one implication beyond that which is in the text for these characteristics listed.

3. During class discussion, a master list of implications can be developed.

Age group selected_____

Characteristic_____

   Implication

_____

_____

_____

Characteristic_____

   Implication

_____

_____

_____

Characteristic_____

   Implication

_____

_____

_____

Name _____ Section _____ Date _____

LABORATORY 3.1

Practice and Its Influence on Learning

Purpose: To demonstrate the effect of practice on learning a motor task.

Size of Group: Alone

1. Hold two tennis balls in your dominant hand. Attempt to juggle them, keeping one ball in the air at all times. Place your other hand behind your back. Practice five minutes a day for five days. Record the number of catches each time you try it (each trial). To score, count the number of balls which you are able to catch without missing; record that number as the number of successful catches for trial number 1. Then perform trial number 2, etc. After five trials your scores may be as follows: 0-2-1-3-4. Record your scores on the table provided.

2. Following each day's practice, take about five minutes to record your feelings regarding your performance. Use the space below labeled "Comments."

Day 1

Trial	Score	Trial	Score	Trial	Score
1		11		21	
2		12		22	
3		13		23	
4		14		24	
5		15		25	
6		16		26	
7		17		27	
8		18		28	
9		19		29	
10		20		30	

Comments: _____

_____

_____

_____

Day 2

Trial	Score	Trial	Score	Trial	Score
1		11		21	
2		12		22	
3		13		23	
4		14		24	
5		15		25	
6		16		26	
7		17		27	
8		18		28	
9		19		29	
10		20		30	

Comments: _____

_____

_____

_____

_____

_____

_____

_____

_____

_____

Day 3

Trial	Score	Trial	Score	Trial	Score
1		11		21	
2		12		22	
3		13		23	
4		14		24	
5		15		25	
6		16		26	
7		17		27	
8		18		28	
9		19		29	
10		20		30	

Comments: _____
_____
_____
_____
_____
_____
_____
_____
_____
_____
_____

Day 4

Trial	Score	Trial	Score	Trial	Score
1		11		21	
2		12		22	
3		13		23	
4		14		24	
5		15		25	
6		16		26	
7		17		27	
8		18		28	
9		19		29	
10		20		30	

Comments:_____

_____

_____

_____

_____

_____

_____

_____

_____

_____

_____

_____

Day 5

Trial	Score	Trial	Score	Trial	Score
1		11		21	
2		12		22	
3		13		23	
4		14		24	
5		15		25	
6		16		26	
7		17		27	
8		18		28	
9		19		29	
10		20		30	

Comments: _____
_____
_____
_____
_____
_____
_____
_____
_____
_____
_____

Name_____ Section_____ Date_____

LABORATORY 3.2
Body Type and Performance

Purpose: To determine how body type will influence motor performance.

Size of Group: Alone

1. While observing an elementary physical education class, locate a representative member from each of the three body types: endomorph, ectomorph, and mesomorph.

2. Watch each member while he/she performs identical tasks.

3. Discuss differences in their motor performance as a possible function of body type.

Date of observation_____

Place of observation_____

Activity observed_____

Endomorph_____

_____

_____

_____

_____

Ectomorph_____

_____

_____

_____

_____

Mesomorph_____

_____

_____

_____

_____

LABORATORY 3.3

Gender Differences in Motor Performance

Purpose: To determine the differences between male and female motor performance.

Size of Group: Alone

1. Observe an elementary age male and female who are approximately the same age, size, and weight while they perform various movement tasks.

2. Contrast the differences in their performances, and indicate possible factors which might account for these differences.

Date of observation _____

Place of observation _____

Activity observed _____

Male _____

_____

_____

_____

_____

_____

_____

_____

_____

Female _____

_____

_____

_____

_____

_____

_____

_____

_____

LABORATORY 4.1

Using the Mental Measurements Yearbook

Purpose: To become acquainted with the Mental Measurements Yearbook

Size of Group: Alone

1. Go to your college or university's library and obtain a copy of the Mental Measurements Yearbook.

2. Look through the book and identify ten assessment instruments which could be employed in a physical education class.

3. Report in detail on one of the ten identified assessment instruments. Your report should include the following information:
   a. Name of assessment instrument.
   b. Name of author and publisher.
   c. State what the instrument purports to measure.
   d. Identify the appropriate age range for individuals taking the assessment.
   e. Report test reliability and objectivity coefficients.
   f. How was the instrument validated?
   g. Can the test be administered to groups? If so, what size?
   h. How long does it take to administer the instrument?
   i. Does the assessment instrument contain norm-referenced data?

LABORATORY 4.2

A Survey of Assessment Instruments

Purpose: To identify the most frequently used type of assessment instruments employed by elementary physical educators in your local school districts. Also, to determine what physical educators are doing with the assessment results.

Size of Group: Five per group.

1. Each individual in the group should identify five elementary physical education teachers that they will make arrangements to interview.

2. The interview can be done in person or over the telephone.

3. In your interview ask the following questions:

    a. Ask for the names of the assessment instruments that the physical educator administers to the students during the school year. Be sure to ask what age children are administered each of these instruments.

    b. For what purpose was the instrument administered (i.e., screening, program content, student progress, program evaluation or classification)?

    c. Ask why those particular instruments were selected.

    d. Ask whether or not the results of the student's performance are reflected in the child's physical education grade.

    e. Ask what is done with the assessment results.

    f. Ask whether or not the results are shared with the parents.

4. Once all data have been collected, write a summary report of your findings.

LABORATORY 5.1

What is a Good Teacher?

Purpose: To generate a list of objective teaching behaviors.

Size of Group: Three or four

1. Each group generates a list of all the terms which they believe characterize a good teacher.

2. They then must try to identify two measurable teacher behaviors which indicate the teacher possesses the characteristic.

3. Bringing everyone back together, generate a master list of measurable teacher behaviors.

Characteristic   **Measurable Behaviors**

1. _____   _____

    _____

2. _____   _____

    _____

3. _____   _____

    _____

4. _____   _____

    _____

5. _____   _____

    _____

6. _____   _____

    _____

7. _____   _____

    _____

8. _____   _____

    _____

9. _____   _____

    _____

10. _____   _____

    _____

LABORATORY 5.2

Principles of Learning

Purpose: To recognize the application of principles of learning in a teaching/learning situation.

Size of Group: Alone

1. Observe a teaching/learning situation, preferably at the elementary level.

2. Using the chapter's principles of learning, check those principles which are observed and indicate the teacher behavior or situation which indicated the principle was being applied.

Teaching/learning situation observed:_____

_____

Principle observed:_____
Teacher behavior:_____

_____

_____

Principle observed:_____
Teacher behavior:_____

_____

_____

Principle observed:_____
Teacher behavior:_____

_____

_____

Principle observed:_____
Teacher behavior:_____

_____

_____

Principle observed:_____
Teacher behavior:_____

_____

_____

LABORATORY 5.3

Objective Evaluation

Purpose: To do an objective evaluation of a teaching/learning environment.

Size of Group: Three

1. Observe a teaching/learning situation at the elementary level.

2. Each member of the group is to focus on a different aspect of the lesson: praise/criticism, student activity level, and number of type of questions asked.

3. Using the information from the chapter, do the analysis as follows:

   a. Praise/criticism: Count the number of each.

   b. Student activity level: Randomly select a child to observe. Every time the child is doing purposeful movement doing what he/she is supposed to be doing, start a cumulative stopwatch; when the child is not moving (such as when the teacher is talking or he/she is misbehaving or not doing what is expected), stop the watch. At the end you should have the total time the child was in class by appropriately recording the beginning and ending of class, and the total time the child was engaged in purposeful movement.

   c. Question analysis: Count and classify the questions asked by the teacher.

   d. Write a report regarding what you observed based upon the data collected. Try not to be subjective in your evaluation.

4. After analyzing the data, indicate the style of teaching which was used (refer to the styles in the chapter).

LABORATORY 6.1

Control and Discipline

Purpose: To learn behaviors important to control and discipline.

Size of Group: Alone

1. Observe a teaching/learning situation at the elementary level and record control factors you can observe as well as discipline techniques used.

2. Discuss your observation as it relates to the information in the chapter.

Date of observation _____

Place of observation _____

Activity observed _____

Situation _____

_____

_____

    Action taken _____

_____

_____

_____

Situation _____

_____

_____

    Action taken _____

_____

_____

_____

Situation _____

_____

    Action taken _____

_____

_____

_____

LABORATORY 6.2
Behavior Modification

Purpose: To learn how to design a behavior modification program.

Size of Group: Alone

1. Using a condition which requires a behavior modification program, design a program to correct the condition.

2. If possible, design it for a real life situation with which you are familiar.

Behavior_____

_____

_____

Progress

    Goals _____

    _____

    _____

    Objective_____

    _____

    _____

    Progress_____

    _____

    _____

    _____

    _____

    _____

    _____

    _____

LABORATORY 7.1
Bulletin Board

Purpose: To learn how to make a bulletin board.

Size of Group: Alone

1. Get a posterboard approximately 3' x 2 1/2'.

2. Make a bulletin board following the criteria established in the chapter which promotes some aspect of elementary physical education. It should focus on fitness or movement.

LABORATORY 7.2

Analysis of a Playground

Purpose: To focus attention on playground safety.

Size of Group: Alone

1. Go to an elementary school playground which has equipment.
2. Draw a diagram of the area including the equipment placement.
3. Analyze each piece of equipment using the criteria in the chapter.

Place observed _____

Diagram

Analysis:

LABORATORY 7.3

Designing a Playground

Purpose: To develop a developmental playground.

Size of Group: Alone

1. Design a playground which has at least five pieces of playground equipment.

2. Justify the equipment selected as well as its placement.

Draw playground here:

LABORATORY 8.1

Behavioral Objective Test

Purpose: To learn the criteria for writing a behavioral objective.

Size of Group: Alone

1. Complete the following programmed test on behavioral objectives.

A Programmed Test on Writing Behavioral Objectives

1. A BEHAVIORAL objective describes: (choose one)

   a. What the instructor does in teaching the student.
   b. What the student does to learn something.
   c. What behavior the student exhibits as a result of the learning experience.

   Answer___

2. The correct answer is c. Behavioral objectives describe behavior. Label each of the following objectives as behavioral (B) or non-behavioral (N).

   a. Teach the student to do a forward roll.
   b. Learn to write behavioral objectives.
   c. Write objectives in behavioral form.
   d. Differentiate between behavioral and non-behavioral objectives.

   Answer___

3. "a" is non-behavioral since it focuses on what the teacher is doing — not student behavior. "b" moves the focus to the student, but describes the learning experience — not the outcome. "c" and "d" describe outcomes — things the student can do as a result of the learning experience — so they are behavioral.

4. Behavioral objectives are like blueprints for instruction. A builder's blueprint specifies:

   a. The shape and dimensions for the final structure.
   b. Procedures required to build the structure.

   Answer___

5. The first answer is correct. The blueprint is similar to the curriculum.

6. Curriculum design begins with:

   a. The student's prior knowledge.
   b. The entering behavior of the student.
   c. The instructor's experience of what a student knows at this grade level.

   Answer___

7. "a" and "b" mean the same thing, and are correct. "c" is subject to error, however qualified the instructor. The entering behavior is best determined by:

   a. Pretest.
   b. Personal knowledge of the student.
   c. The student's performance on standardized tests.
   d. The student's performance record from previous classes.

   Answer___

8. Since we want specific information, the pretest is best, but obviously all sources of information are helpful. Incidentally, should:

    a. The pretest be administered separately, or
    b. It be incorporated into the learning experience?

    Answer____

9. Either is appropriate, and can be left to the discretion of the teacher.

10. Let's write a behavioral objective. You are shooting an arrow at the target. Your object is to____the bull's-eye. Check your answer. Are you describing what the teacher does? Or how you learn? Or the outcome?

11. Hit the bull's-eye or (some similar action word) specifies the objective. The action or performance must be observable and measurable. Check objectives in the following list which meet the criterion.

    a. Understand physiology.
    b. Know about rhythmics.
    c. Compute federal tax using form 1040.
    d. Like gymnastics.

    Answer____

12. All, except "c," are too vague to be "Observable and measurable." Objectives such as "a" would be improved by a more specific action like "interpret or communicate." Change the action word in the following to something more specific:

    a. Know basketball rules._____
    b. Understand zone defense._____
    c. Like sports stories._____
    d. Appreciate gymnastics (limit yourself to one minute on this one!). _____

13. Perhaps many action words suggest themselves. We could write or recognize basketball rules; construct or play zone defense; read or write sports stories. The fourth objective needs to be broken down into many specific behaviors. A specific action or performance is a good start. In some objectives, the thing acted upon is also vague. To know about birds raises many questions. How do birds fly? What species? Bird migration? Behavioral objectives must be SPECIFIC, and we may need to write a number of objectives to specify the outcome. Rewrite the objective "draw pictures" to make it more specific.

14. Be your own judge on this last one. You may have said "draw boxes" or "sketch trees." Sometimes specification assumes 100 percent performance.
For example:

    a. (Safely) land an airplane, or
    b. (Correctly) add whole numbers less than ten.

    In other instances, we should specify level or performance, such as:

    c. Spell 100 words with not more than five errors, or
    d. Run 100 meters in less than 15 seconds.

    Add a "level of performance" specification to the following:

    e. Throw a ball_____
    f. Translate five sentences into sign language _____

15. "Level of performance" tells us how well the student will perform. It might include time, distance, direction, quantity, number and kind of errors, and so on. So far we have described:

    a. Outcome (what does the student do).
    b. Level of performance (how well), to what we must add:
    c. Conditions (under which performance is demonstrated).

Underline the phrase describing the conditions for each of the following behavioral objectives. For example:

Run 100 meters in less than 20 seconds, <u>carrying a ten pound sack of flour.</u>

a. Using a junior basketball and an eight foot basket, the student will make 3 out of 5 baskets from less than 15 feet.
b. Run a cross country course in 15 minutes or less.
c. Answer at least 15 out of 20 questions on a test of basketball rules without using a book.

O.K., see if our answers agree:

a. <u>Using a junior basketball and an eight foot basket.</u>
b. <u>a cross-country course</u>
c. <u>without using a book</u>

16. For each of the following objectives, identify:

1. Outcome
2. Level of performance.
3. Conditions under which performance is demonstrated.

a. ( ) Using the task force approach
   ( ) To identify five major problems
   ( ) In the area of curriculum
b. ( ) To increase cost/effectiveness
   ( ) By a factor of two
   ( ) Utilizing educational technology
c. ( ) In thirty minutes or less
   ( ) Analyze (and express) the causes
   ( ) In outline form

Now check your answers:

a. 3 - 1 - 2
b. 1 - 2 - 3
c. 3 - 1 - 2

17. Arrange the following learning behaviors as a learning hierarchy starting with 1 for the most general behavior:

( ) Solve chemical equations
( ) Write the names of chemical compounds in symbol form
( ) Analyze an unknown chemical compound containing only group 1 metals

Answer: 2,1,3. While analysis is the most complex of the three behaviors, it represents a higher level on the learning hierarchy (taxonomy).

LABORATORY 8.2
Writing Behavioral Objectives

Purpose: To learn to write a behavioral objective for each of the three educational domains.

Size of Group: Alone

1. Write one elementary physical education behavioral objective for each of the three educational domains which meets the criteria established in this chapter.

2. Be sure to indicate the domain when writing the objective.

Objective   *Domain*

_____   _____

_____

_____

_____

_____

_____

_____

Objective   *Domain*

_____   _____

_____

_____

_____

_____

_____

_____

Objective   *Domain*

_____   _____

_____

_____

_____

_____

_____

_____

Name _____ Section _____ Date _____

LABORATORY 8.3

Constructing a Year Plan

Purpose: To learn how to construct a year plan.

Size of Group: Alone

1. For each grade level (K-6) list the units of instruction and the percent of time you would spend on each unit.

2. Given that you will meet with each class a total of thirty-six times during the school year, calculate how many class meetings you will devote to each unit of instruction.

3. Construct a year plan grid and completely fill in this grid.

Grade Level: K

Unit of Instruction	% Time	No. Class Meetings	Unit of Instruction	% Time	No. Class Meetings

See back of this page for year plan grid.

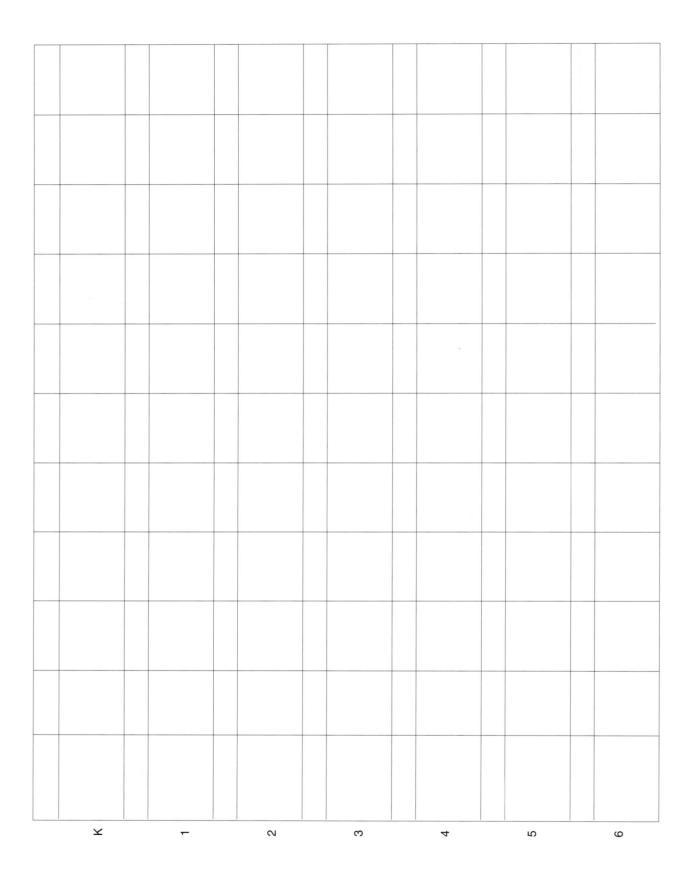

K 1 2 3 4 5 6

456

LABORATORY 8.3, continued

Grade Level: 1

Unit of Instruction	% Time	No. Class Meetings	Unit of Instruction	% Time	No. Class Meetings

See back of this page for year plan grid.

K   1   2   3   4   5   6

LABORATORY 8.3, continued

Grade Level: 2

Unit of Instruction	% Time	No. Class Meetings	Unit of Instruction	% Time	No. Class Meetings
_____	_____	_____	_____	_____	_____
_____	_____	_____	_____	_____	_____
_____	_____	_____	_____	_____	_____
_____	_____	_____	_____	_____	_____
_____	_____	_____	_____	_____	_____
_____	_____	_____	_____	_____	_____
_____	_____	_____	_____	_____	_____
_____	_____	_____	_____	_____	_____

See back of this page for year plan grid.

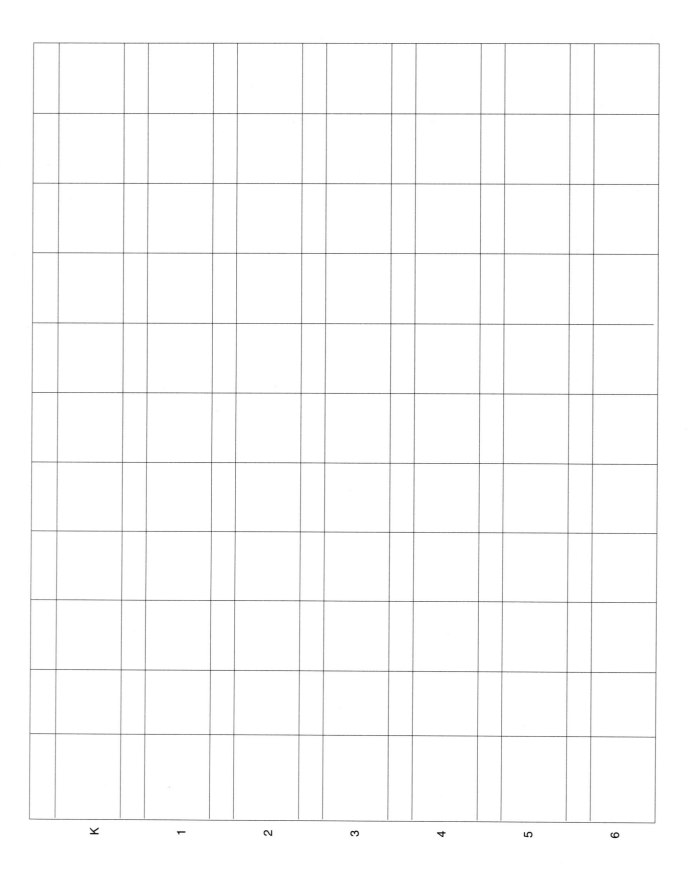

K 1 2 3 4 5 6

460

LABORATORY 8.3, continued

Grade Level: 3

Unit of Instruction	% Time	No. Class Meetings	Unit of Instruction	% Time	No. Class Meetings
_____	_____	_____	_____	_____	_____
_____	_____	_____	_____	_____	_____
_____	_____	_____	_____	_____	_____
_____	_____	_____	_____	_____	_____
_____	_____	_____	_____	_____	_____
_____	_____	_____	_____	_____	_____
_____	_____	_____	_____	_____	_____
_____	_____	_____	_____	_____	_____

See back of this page for year plan grid.

K

1

2

3

4

5

6

462

LABORATORY 8.3, continued

Grade Level: 4

Unit of Instruction	% Time	No. Class Meetings	Unit of Instruction	% Time	No. Class Meetings

See back of this page for year plan grid.

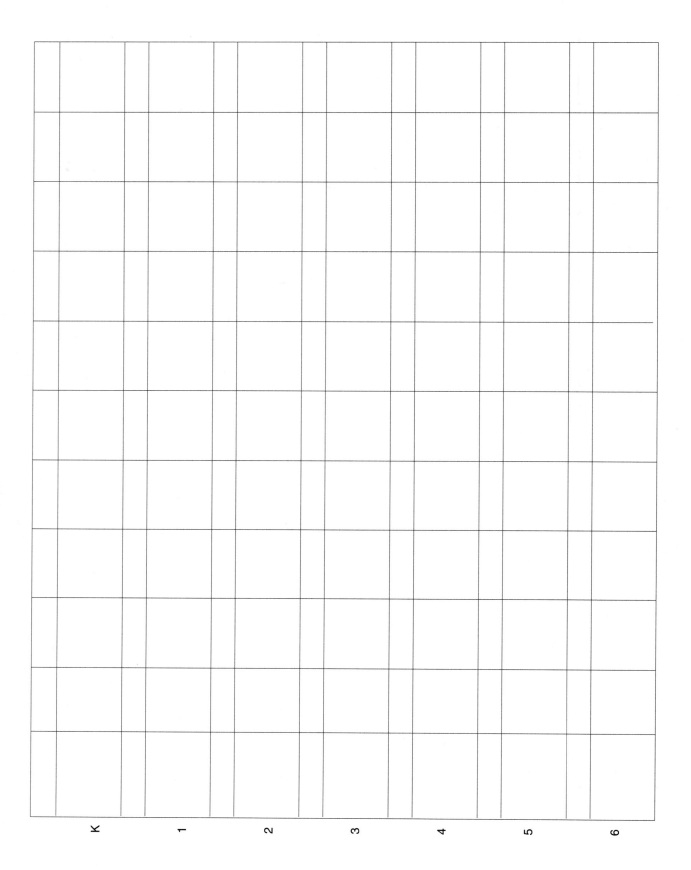

K

1

2

3

4

5

6

464

LABORATORY 8.3, continued

Grade Level: 5

Unit of Instruction	% Time	No. Class Meetings	Unit of Instruction	% Time	No. Class Meetings
_____	_____	_____	_____	_____	_____
_____	_____	_____	_____	_____	_____
_____	_____	_____	_____	_____	_____
_____	_____	_____	_____	_____	_____
_____	_____	_____	_____	_____	_____
_____	_____	_____	_____	_____	_____
_____	_____	_____	_____	_____	_____
_____	_____	_____	_____	_____	_____

See back of this page for year plan grid.

K

1

2

3

4

5

6

466

LABORATORY 8.3, continued

Grade Level: 6

Unit of Instruction	% Time	No. Class Meetings	Unit of Instruction	% Time	No. Class Meetings
_____	_____	_____	_____	_____	_____
_____	_____	_____	_____	_____	_____
_____	_____	_____	_____	_____	_____
_____	_____	_____	_____	_____	_____
_____	_____	_____	_____	_____	_____
_____	_____	_____	_____	_____	_____
_____	_____	_____	_____	_____	_____
_____	_____	_____	_____	_____	_____

See back of this page for year plan grid.

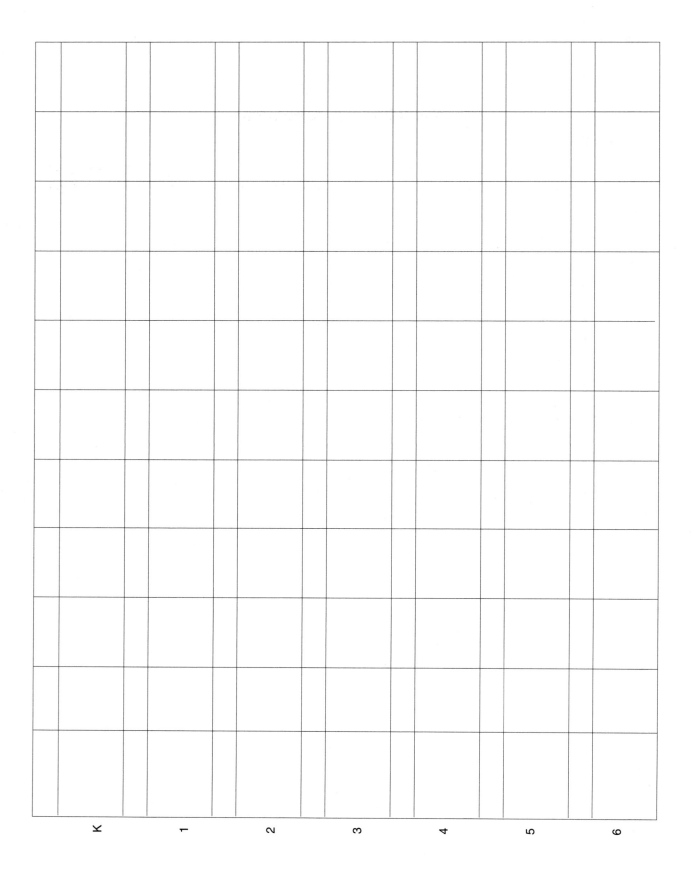

K

1

2

3

4

5

6

LABORATORY 8.4
Unit Planning

Purpose: To learn how to write a unit plan.

Size of Group: Alone

1. Select one elementary physical education skill theme.

2. Design a unit plan being sure to include all the parts as indicated in the Chapter.

3. Attach your completed unit plan to the back of this sheet.

Skill theme selected_____

LABORATORY 8.5

Lesson Planning

Purpose: To learn how to write a lesson plan.

Size of Group: Alone

1. Design a thirty-minute elementary physical education lesson plan for an age group of your choice.

2. Be sure to include all the parts of the lesson plan, and assume there will be three activities during the lesson.

3. Include a series of problem-solving questions for the middle activity.

Name _____ Section _____ Date _____

LABORATORY 9.1
Identifying Potential Hazards (Indoor Facilities)

Purpose: To demonstrate the ability to recognize potential hazards and offer appropriate suggestions on how to correct the potential hazards observed in an indoor physical education facility.

Size of Group: Alone

1. Make a tour of an indoor physical education facility and note potential hazards which exist.

2. How would you correct the potential hazards that you found during your tour of an indoor physical education facility?

Facility Toured: _____

Hazards   *Correction*

_____   _____

_____   _____

_____   _____

_____   _____

_____   _____

_____   _____

_____   _____

_____   _____

_____   _____

_____   _____

_____   _____

_____   _____

_____   _____

_____   _____

_____   _____

_____   _____

_____   _____

_____   _____

LABORATORY 9.2
Identifying Potential Hazards (Outdoor Facilities)

Purpose: To demonstrate the ability to recognize potential hazards and offer appropriate suggestions on how to correct the potential hazards observed in a tour of an outdoor physical education facility.

Size of Group: Alone

1. Make a tour of a local playgound. Note any potential hazards which exist.

2. How would you correct the potential hazards that you found during your tour of a local playground.

Playground Hazards   *Correction*

_____   _____

_____   _____

_____   _____

_____   _____

_____   _____

_____   _____

_____   _____

_____   _____

_____   _____

_____   _____

_____   _____

_____   _____

_____   _____

_____   _____

_____   _____

_____   _____

_____   _____

_____   _____

LABORATORY 10.1
Exercise Heart Rate

Purpose: To determine various exercise heart rates.

Size of Group: Alone

1. Take the resting heart rate by lying down for at least five minutes, and then using the fingers of one hand and the radial pulse of the opposite wrist, count the number of heart beats for one minute. Since the thumb has its own pulse, be sure to use the fingers and not the thumb to do the counting.

2. Repeat #1 above. If the count differs by more than two beats, take it again and use the average.

3. Write down the formula, .6 [(220 - Age) - RHR] + RHR

4. Put your age in where it says "age," and put the figure you obtained from #2 above in the two places where "RHR" appears. RHR stands for "resting heart rate."

5. Do the calculations to determine your 60% exercise heart rate. An example for a twenty year old with a resting heart rate of 70 beats per minute is given below:

   .6 [(220 - 20) - 70] + 70

   .6 [(200) - 70] + 70

   .6 (130) + 70

   78.0 + 70 = 148

   The 148 is the 60% exercise heart rate for a twenty year old with a resting heart rate of seventy beats per minute. This is the minimum heart rate which must be achieved in order to improve cardiovascular efficiency. Some feel that exercising at the 70% and 80% levels make more efficient use of the exercise time.

6. Calculate your 60%, 70% and 80% exercise heart rate levels.

Resting HR = _____

60% level = _____

70% level = _____

80% level = _____

LABORATORY 10.2

Resting Heart Rate

Purpose: To see reduction in resting heart rate during a fitness program.

Size of Group: Alone

1. Using the figure below, plot your resting heart rate over a period of 10-14 weeks.

2. Once a week take the resting heart rate by lying down for at least five minutes, and then using the fingers of one hand and the radial pulse of the opposite wrist, count the number of heart beats for one minute. Since the thumb has its own pulse, be sure to use the fingers and not the thumb to do the counting.

3. Place the resting heart rate determined in #2 above on the figure below.

4. If you are on a cardiovascular exercise program, you should begin to see a reduction in your resting heart rate within a few weeks.

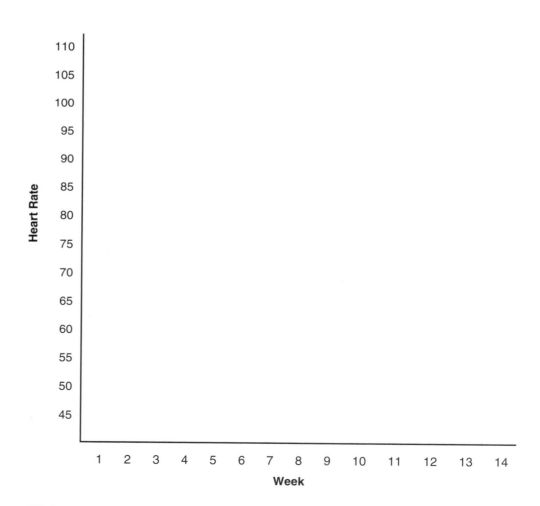

Name _____ Section _____ Date _____

LABORATORY 10.3

Posture Evaluation

Purpose: To become a more critical evaluator of posture.

Size of Group: Two to three

1. Working with others and using the figure below, evaluate each other's posture.
2. Do it while the person is standing still and then walking.
3. Record your results on the chart.
4. Look for uneven shoulders or hips (scoliosis).
5. Have the individual bend at the waist and place hands on the knees. Check for uneven humps (scoliosis) on the back around the shoulder blade area.

NAME															
BODY PART															
Head															
Forward															
Shoulders															
Forward															
Uneven															
Rounded															
Back (back view)															
"S" curve (scoliosis)															
"C" curve (scoliosis)															
Back (side view)															
Lordosis															
Flat back															
Rounded															
Hips															
Uneven															
Legs															
Bowed															
Knock-kneed															
Feet															
Pigeon-toed															
Duck feet															
Weight on inside															
Weight on outside															

LABORATORY 11.1
Age Group Lesson Plans

Purpose: To learn how to write lesson plans for various age groups.

Size of Groups: Alone

1. Write one lesson plan for each of the four age groups.

2. Be sure to refer back to Chapter 8 for information on lesson plans.

3. Your lesson plan must be different from those that appear in the text.

Age group 4-6 years:_____
_____
_____
_____

Age group 6-8 years:_____
_____
_____
_____

Age group 8-10 years: _____
_____
_____
_____

Age group 10-12 years: _____
_____
_____
_____

LABORATORY 12.1

Movement Competency Lesson

Purpose: To develop a lesson plan which will aid the development of movement competency.

Size of Group: Alone

1. Select an age from the age group four to six years of age.

2. Design a thirty-minute physical education lesson plan which will aid the development of movement competency. Follow the criteria for lesson planning in Chapter 8.

LABORATORY 13.1

Body Awareness Lesson

Purpose: To develop a lesson plan which will aid the development of body awareness.

Size of Group: Alone

1. Select an age from the age group four to six years of age.

2. Design a thirty-minute physical education lesson plan which will aid the development of body awareness. Follow the criteria for lesson planning in Chapter 8.

LABORATORY 14.1

Manipulative Lesson

Purpose: To develop a lesson plan which will aid the development of manipulative ability.

Size of Group: Alone

1. Select an age from the age group eight to ten years of age.

2. Design a thirty-minute physical education lesson plan which will aid the development of body awareness. Follow the lesson plan format in Chapter 8.

Name _____ Section _____ Date _____

LABORATORY 15.1
Creative Lesson

Purpose: To develop a lesson plan which will aid the development of creativity.

Size of Group: Alone

1. Select an age from the age group ten to twelve years of age.

2. Design a thirty-minute physical education lesson plan which will aid the development of creativity. Follow the lesson plan format in Chapter 8.

LABORATORY 16.1

Rhythmic Routine

Purpose: To learn how to design a rhythmic activity for upper elementary children.

Size of Group: Determined by the activity chosen but no less than three.

1. Select a piece of equipment — parachute, lummi sticks, tinikling, jump rope, or streamers.

2. Working with other class members design a rhythmic routine to the music selected by the instructor.

3. The routine should include a variety of moves, depending upon the equipment selected, but should have a definite ending move.

4. After designing and practicing the routine (eight to ten minutes), demonstrate the routine to the other members of the class.

LABORATORY 17.1

Integrated Activity

Purpose: To develop an integrated activity.

Size of Group: Three

1. Using the criteria from the Chapter, the group will develop an integrated activity in one of the following areas: language arts, math, social studies, or science.

2. One person will serve as the spokesperson and present the activity to the class. Whenever possible, the class should actually do the activity.

LABORATORY 17.2

Integrated Lesson

Purpose: To develop a lesson plan which will include at least one integrated physical education activity.

Size of Group: Alone

1. Select an age from the age group six to eight years.

2. Design a thirty-minute physical education lesson plan which includes an integrated physical education activity and which follows the lesson plan format in Chapter 8.

LABORATORY 18.1

Game Analysis

Purpose: To analyze a game using the criteria from the chapter.

Size of Group: Alone

1. Select a game from an outside source.

2. Write a brief description of the game including the reference, author, title, date, and page.

3. Analyze the game in each of the three areas, psychomotor, affective, and cognitive using the 0-5 scales discussed in the chapter.

4. Justify each point value given with a sentence or two.

LABORATORY 18.2

Changing Games

Purpose: To change games to increase their value in a particular domain.

Size of Group: Alone

1. Select a game from this book or another. If from another source, please include the reference, author, title, date, and page. Most of the games in this book are already good developmental games and may be more difficult to change than ones from an outside source.

2. If from another source, please include a brief description of the original activity.

3. While maintaining the general rules of the game, modify it to increase its value in another domain. For example, if it is strong in psychomotor but weak in affective, change it to increase its affective value.

LABORATORY 18.3

Games

Purpose: To develop a lesson plan which will include one game at the end of the class.

Size of Group: Alone

1. Select an age from the age group eight to ten years of age.

2. Design a thirty-minute physical education lesson plan which has a game as the ending activity. Follow the lesson plan format in Chapter 8.

LABORATORY 19.1

Fitness

Purpose: To develop a lesson plan focusing on fitness development.

Size of Group: Alone

1. Select any elementary age group.

2. Design a thirty-minute physical education lesson which focuses on fitness development. Follow the lesson plan format in Chapter 8.

LABORATORY 20.1

Designing the IEP

Purpose: To develop an IEP.

Size of Group: Alone

1. Using the following data, write an IEP.
    Name of student: John Doe
    Age: 10
    Condition: Educable mentally retarded
    Goal: Health fitness development
    Time: One year
    Frequency: Three, thirty-minute classes per week for thirty-six weeks
    Present status: Weak in all five fitness components (see Chapter 10)

2. You are to write annual goals, short-term objectives, time requirements, duration dates, placements, and support personnel for each objective.

3. Be sure to follow the format as well as include all the data from the IEP example in the chapter.

LABORATORY 20.2

Adapting Activities

Purpose: To learn ways to adapt activities to various handicapping conditions.

Size of Group: Alone

1. Describe two different ways to adapt a throwing and catching activity for each of the following handicapping conditions:

   Visual impairment
   Wheelchair bound
   Spastic cerebral palsy

2. Using the same conditions, give one way to adapt a rhythmic activity for each condition.

Name _____ Section _____ Date _____

LABORATORY 28.1

Participation Level in Youth Sports

Purpose: To determine the amount of participation time a child receives during various youth sporting activities.

Size of Group: Alone

1. Observe a youth sport competition and observe the following:
   A. Did all the children get to play?
   B. While playing how active were the children in general?
   C. Were some children more active than others? Which positions?
   D. How many children were injured?

2. Write a report, and give your impressions both pro and con of what you observed.

3. Indicate in your report how the activity or rules might have been changed to improve the sport.

LABORATORY 28.2

The Coach's Views

Purpose: To gather information from the viewpoint of a youth sport coach.

Size of Group: Alone

1. Interview the coach of both the winning and losing teams. Compare the two coaches' viewpoints about the game. The following questions are examples of questions which might be asked:
   A. Do you have a systematic approach to determine how much playing time each child receives?
   B. How do you prepare the children for the game?
   C. As a volunteer coach, what are your goals for coaching?
   D. What intrinsic rewards do you get from coaching?

2. Write a report based upon the data from both coaches. Compare the differences or similarities between them.

Name _____ Section _____ Date _____

LABORATORY 28.3

Parental Behavior at Youth Sports Contests

Purpose: To determine parental behavior during a competitive youth sport activity.

Size of Group: Alone

1. Attend a youth sports' competition and observe parental behavior. The following should be observed:

   A. What were the comments made which could be heard by others? How many positive? Negative?

   B. Did anyone make any negative physical moves toward or contact with the coach? Umpire/referee? A child?

2. Write a report based upon the data from above, and give your impressions both pro and con.

LABORATORY 29.1

Homemade Equipment

Purpose: To develop a piece of homemade equipment.

Size of Group: Alone

1. Design a homemade piece of equipment from some item which you might normally discard.

2. Describe three different ways the equipment could be used in a developmental situation.

Name of equipment: _____

Equipment uses:

A. _____

_____

_____

B. _____

_____

_____

C. _____

_____

_____

LABORATORY 30.1

COGNITIVE LEARNING THROUGH MOVEMENT ACTIVITY

Purpose: To learn how to develop a Cognitive Learning Through Movement Activity.

Size of Group: Three or four

1. Design a Cognitive Learning Through Movement Activity for one of the following subject areas: language arts, math, science, or social studies.

2. One person from the group presents. Have the class participate in the activity.

Cognitive learning activity description:

_____

_____

_____

_____

_____

_____

_____

_____

_____

_____

_____

_____

_____

_____

_____

_____

_____

_____

_____

Index

Activities and Games